D0906636

Wiley Blackwell Bible Commentaries

Susan Gillingham

WILEY Blackwell

Psalms Through the Centuries
A Reception History Commentary on Psalms 73–151
Volume Three

Registered Offices
John Wiley & Sons, Inc., 111 River Street, Hoboken, NJ 07030, USA
John Wiley & Sons Ltd, The Atrium, Southern Gate, Chichester, West Sussex, PO19 8SQ, UK

Editorial Office
9600 Garsington Road, Oxford, OX4 2DQ, UK

For details of our global editorial offices, customer services, and more information about Wiley products visit us at www.wiley.com.

Wiley also publishes its books in a variety of electronic formats and by print-on-demand. Some content that appears in standard print versions of this book may not be available in other formats.

A catalogue record for this book is available from the Library of Congress

Hardback ISBN: 9781119542254; ePub ISBN: 9781119542261; ePDF ISBN: 9781119542230; oBook ISBN: 9781119542285

Cover images: © Life of William Blake (1880), Volume 2, Job illustrations by Cygnis insignis is licensed under CC BY-SAA
Cover design by Wiley

Set in 10/12.5pt MinionPro by Integra Software Services Pvt. Ltd, Pondicherry, India
Printed and bound by CPI Group (UK) Ltd, Croydon, CR0 4YY

C093489_240522

For my three grandchildren

Sophia and Noah Boutayeb
and
Ayaan Gillingham-Ahmed,

the next generation.

תִּכָּתֶב זֹאת לְדֹור אַחֲרֹון וְעַם נִבְרָא יְהַלֶּל־יָהּ

يُكْتَبُ هَذَا لِلْجَيْلِ الآتِي الَّذِي سَيُخْلَقُ فَيُسَبِّحُ الرَّبَّ

Let this be recorded for a generation to come,
so that a people yet unborn may praise the Lord.
(Ps. 102:18)

Contents

Illustrations

Figures

Book Three (Psalms 73–89)

Book Four (Psalms 90–106)

Book Five (Psalms 107–151)

Plates

Preface

It was almost twenty-five years ago when my initial conversations with Christopher Rowland and John Sawyer resulted in a contract to produce a volume on the Psalms in the Blackwell Bible Commentary Series. It took two years of research to recognise the size of a project which was to examine the Jewish and Christian reception history of the Book of Psalms over two and a half millennia. The first step required setting up a data base, both digitally and in hard copy, which would organise the vast amount of material into time periods and types of reception. Even with the support of several short-term research assistants, and two sabbaticals, I was not able to start writing what would become Volume One until 2004. Very soon I realised that this publication could not be an actual commentary: it was a distinctive cultural history of the Psalter, referring to selected psalms as examples of different types of reception.

Before submitting that manuscript I had to seek permission to extend this work to a second volume which would then become the commentary. Hence the title *Psalms through the Centuries: Volume One* for the 2008 publication. It then became clear that I could not write any commentary until I had created another data base, psalm by psalm, adapting the earlier prototype. There was no other Psalms Commentary like it to use as a model, so the preparation time, even given two more sabbaticals and several effective research assistants, took far longer than anticipated. The contract for the entire commentary (Volume Two), was mainly achieved through the mediation of the then Old Testament editors of the Wiley Blackwell Bible Commentary Series, John Sawyer (Newcastle) and David Gunn (Fort Worth), but it was ultimately dependent upon the extraordinary support of the then Publisher for Religion, Rebecca Harkin.

Using the general chronological and geographical framework established in Volume One, the commentary required a particular format for each psalm. I start by assessing each psalm as part of the process of compilation of the Psalter as a whole, for this represents the earliest stage of its reception in Hebrew; I then look at corresponding evidence from the Dead Sea Scrolls; this leads on to examining reception through translation, especially the Greek and Latin versions, which witness to both Jewish and Christian reception; I then turn to the Christian commentary tradition in the New Testament, Church Fathers, and Medieval and Reformation Commentators, and similarly the Jewish commentary tradition in the *Midrash Tehillim*, the *Mishnah*, the *Targums*, and Medieval Commentators. After this I assess non-verbal reception, especially the vast number of illustrated Psalters from the ninth-century onwards, both in the West and the East, at this point mainly Christian. This is followed by an evaluation of musical reception history, particularly from the fifteenth-century onwards, and thence to an assessment of poetic imitations of the psalms and their use in literature and film. At the final stage I explore the different sorts of discourse which develops from the seventeenth-century onwards—political, ethical, historical, and social.

Although I began writing up this commentary in 2011, I decided at the same time to undertake a more experimental work on just two psalms, looking at their reception history as comprehensively as possible. *A Journey of Two Psalms: The Reception of Psalms 1 and 2 in Jewish and Christian Tradition* was published by Oxford University Press in 2013. Its length was 140,000 words, and even allowing 70,000 words for each psalm, it was thirty-five times as much as I could allow for each of the 150 psalms in this present project. So for this Wiley-Blackwell commentary I tried to be as selective as possible, but by the time I had reached Psalm 89 the length was well over the limit originally agreed, and by 2015 it became clear that the commentary needed to be extended to a third volume. Understandably, these were difficult negotiations, and again I was extremely grateful to John Sawyer, David Gunn, Christopher Rowland, and Rebecca Harkin (in her new role as Publisher for Humanities) for being so persistent on my behalf. Volume Two was published in 2018, actually finishing at Psalm 72 to achieve the required word count: Psalm 89 would have been a more natural place, coming at the end of Book Three, but this was not a time to argue for niceties.[1]

As I gained speed from experience, Volume Three has taken only three years to write. The format is as for Volume Two, except that here I often approach more contentious psalms thematically, selecting two or three key issues arising from their reception, integrating these themes into the template outlined above. This third volume has been supported by two younger editors representing the Wiley Blackwell Commentary Series, Andrew Mein (St. Andrews) and Lena-Sofia Tiemeyer (Örebro). Their different skills have vastly improved this present manuscript: Lena has given it meticulous attention to detail and Andrew has brought to it many linguistic, musical and historical insights. I am equally grateful to Catriona King, now Director of the Global Publishing Team at John Wiley & Sons, and also to Juliet Booker, who did so much to promote the publication of Volume Two and prepare the way for Volume Three. Hannah Lee has taken important initiatives in the editorial management of this volume, and to my great relief both the copy-editor for Volume Two (Carolyn Holleyman) and the indexer for that volume (Caroline Jones) agreed to use their skills in this present volume as well.

Over this twenty-five year period it is difficult to single out the legacy of particular research assistants on this third volume. John Ritzema (London) and Natasha O'Hear (St. Andrews) deserve special mention, but Holly Morse (Manchester) undoubtedly stands out: she worked on the data base for both Volumes One and Two, and her contribution in matters of art history has been invaluable for Volume Three as well. Danny Crowther (Oxford) has also done sterling work, complementing Holly in his text-critical skills and in his passion for early Jewish reception. He has honed the data-base, making it more easy to access, managed the bibliographical resources, prepared many of the resources psalm by psalm, and has read through the text more times than I can remember. Lucinda Armstrong, undergraduate at Worcester and now a doctoral student, stepped in at the last minute to undertake some final proof-reading. I am grateful she did. Finally, I am also indebted to Eleanor Vivian, another undergraduate student turned graduate, now researching at Birmingham University, for her eagle eye for detail and her work on tedious end-projects such as the Glossary, list of Abbreviations, and the

---

[1] John Sawyer sadly died in January 2022, so never saw the final publication of Volume Three, despite his ongoing investment in it. I owe him a good deal.

final Bibliography. It is now becoming a cliché, but it is nevertheless sincere: the mistakes that remain are solely my responsibility.

Volume Three was begun in employment and completed in retirement. In 2018 Worcester College and the Faculty of Theology and Religion together granted me one essential, final sabbatical. I owe a huge debt to Peter Groves for having taken on administrative and tutorial responsibilities in my absence: Peter's insights at the academic level have provided a vital support throughout the entire project. I am also grateful for the use of the Bartlett Sisters' Theology Fund, supported mainly by alumni from Worcester College, for this has paid for much of my research assistance. Various College Officers and Fellows at Worcester played a major part in launching this third volume: for all their practical support in so many ways my thanks extend to Afifi Al-Akiti, Mark Bainbridge, Coleen Day, Scott Scullion, Elizabeth Smith, Emma Standhaft, Carmy Strzelecki, and Phillipa Tarver.

Post retirement I have been dependent for ongoing funding from the trustees of the St. Luke's College Foundation, Exeter. David Benzie and his trustees provided for the costs of the permissions and the production of images, and then also for payment of the indexing and other research assistance costs. Their continual support throughout this entire project has been vital.

Academic colleagues in the Faculty of Theology and Religion here at Oxford have provided much specialist advice. Above all I have valued the support of John Barton—mentor, colleague, and friend of over forty years. Other Faculty members who have also given this project their support in different ways include Hywel Clifford, John Day, John Goldingay, John Jarick, Justin Jones, Laura Quick, Frances Roach, Deborah Rooke, Katherine Southwood, and Jenn Strawbridge. Outside my Faculty Matthew Cheung-Salisbury has been a continuous source of encouragement: his unfailing patience has vastly improved my account of the musical and liturgical reception of different psalms. Outside Oxford, Nicolas Bell, Librarian of Trinity College, Cambridge, has offered me invaluable advice about various illustrated Psalters: the *Eadwine Psalter* appears many times in this volume and has been used in two of the Plates.

Two Oxford-based research centres have continued to provide new incentives. The Centre for the Reception History of the Bible has broadened my horizons of what reception is and does, and I am grateful to Chris Joynes, its director, for the opportunity to speak there and to learn from other projects. The Psalms Network which works under the auspices of The Oxford Research Centre in the Humanities ('TORCH') has been a major inspiration, not least through working with my co-founders, Francis Leneghan and Helen Appleton, whose expertise in Medieval English Literature as it impinges on the Book of Psalms has taught me much. Together we have produced a wide variety of events concerned with all aspects of the reception of psalmody, some of which have been incorporated here. Other TORCH members who deserve mention are Elizabeth Solopova (Oxford) who helped with my research on illuminated Psalters, and Beatrice Groves (Oxford) who has been a conversation partner on the psalms in Early Modern literature. Other members have freely allowed their own work to be used in this book: Roger Wagner (Oxford) and Michael Jessing (Peebles) have produced some of the artwork; David Mitchell (Brussels) has produced musical scores intuiting ancient psalmody; Alexander Massey (Oxford) has made invaluable contributions on Jewish psalmody; and Edward Clarke (Oxford) has offered several of his poems. Howard Goodall's memorable performance and explanation of his own psalm compositions through the auspices of TORCH made me work on the relevant psalms in a new way, and Andy Mackay (Roxy music), also associated with TORCH, prompted me to study the reception history of other psalms in a different context, namely for his performance '3 Psalms' at Southbank.

My membership of two societies has also been invaluable in this long-term project. The Society for Old Testament Study, for which I served as President from 2018 to 2019, has been an important resource in bringing together colleagues with distinctive sorts of expertise; they include James Aitken (Cambridge), Margaret Barker (Borrowash), Richard Briggs (Durham), David Clines (Sheffield), Katharine Dell (Cambridge), Graham Davies (Cambridge), David Firth (Bristol), Bill Goodman (Sheffield), Charlotte Hempel (Birmingham), Alastair Hunter (Glasgow), Philip Johnston (Cambridge), Paul Joyce (London), Shioban Dowling-Long (Cork), Heather McKay (Edge Hill), Jonathan Magonet (London), Sean Maher (Carlow), James Patrick (Oxford), Cat Quine (Nottingham), David Reimer (Edinburgh), David Shepherd (Dublin), Rebecca Watson (Market Harborough), Jenni Williams (Oxford), Hugh Williamson (Oxford) and Paul Winchester (Oxford). The Psalms Section of the Society for Biblical Literature has also been an ongoing resource: I am grateful for the support of Karl Jacobson (Minneapolis), Rolf Jacobson (Minnesota), Chris Jones (Jefferson City), Joel LeMon (Atlanta), and Brent Strawn (Durham, NC), and most especially Melody Knowles (Alexandria).

The legacies of †Erich Zenger, †Klaus Seybold, †Peter Flint, and †Frank-Lothar Hossfeld have been considerable, as my footnotes amply testify. Between the publication of Volume Two and Volume Three I have participated in various psalms projects globally, some *in memoriam* of these extraordinary colleagues, and hearing and giving papers and producing articles have offered me further insights in writing up the commentary. Colleagues who have been especially important include Johannes Bremer (Bochum), Alma Brodersen (Bern), Susan Docherty (Birmingham), Christian Frevel (Bochum), Erhard Gerstenberger (Marburg), Friedhelm Hartenstein (München), Bernd Janowski (Tübingen), Corinna Körting (Hamburg), Beate Kowalski (Dortmund), Dominik Markl (Rome), Nancy Rahn (Bern), Jonathan Schnocks (Münster), Till Steiner (Jerusalem), Åke Viberg (Stockholm), Beat Weber (Liestal), David Willgren (Örebro), and Alexandra Grund-Wittenberg (Marburg). My greatest debt, however, is to Hermann Spieckermann (Göttingen) for his insights, friendship, good humour, and continuous support. Collaborative work with American colleagues especially through the Society of Biblical Literature has also been important over these years, especially with Debra Band (Washington DC), Bill Bellinger (Baylor), Joseph Blenkinsopp (Notre Dame), William Brown (Columbia), Walter Brueggemann (Decatur), Dennis Tucker (Baylor), Clinton McCann (Saint Louis), Jamie McClung (Georgia), and Nancy deClaissé-Walford (Atlanta). I have been associated with Pro-Psalms, Faculty of Theology and Religion, University of Pretoria SA for nearly fifteen years, when I first became a research associate, and I acknowledge the continuing support of Dirk Human, Alphonso Groenewald, and Philip Botha. Finally, in giving named papers for Stefan Attard (Malta), and Giovanni Barbiero (Rome) I have gained invaluable insights from their advice and friendship.

Retirement meant a slight shift from academic community to church, not least because of my ordination to the Permanent Diaconate in 2018. Reception history is very much about performance as well as a written script, and the congregation at St. Barnabas' Church have received, especially through Zoom during Lockdown, more papers on the Psalms than they probably would have chosen, but their support through conversations in the church and pub has been immeasurable. I am enormously grateful to Fr. Christopher Woods, who has trained me as a Deacon whilst understanding that I needed much time and space for academic work. In these latter stages he has been an exceptionally supportive colleague and friend. At the Diocesan level, +Steven, Bishop of Oxford, also the holder of a doctorate in the psalms, has been a seminal influence in challenging me to view the reception history of psalmody in a contemporary setting, especially during Lockdown. The community of Benedictines at Mucknell Abbey has been an important reminder of psalmody and the *Opus Dei*. I have also given several papers on the psalms before and during the Covid-19 pandemic at Exeter Cathedral, where I am Canon Theologian, and equally significant have been conversations with +Robert, Bishop of Exeter, Jonathan and Pamela Greener, Christopher Palmer, Morwenna Ludlow, and Clare Bryden.

Family members have grown old since the inception of this project. Volume One was dedicated to my long-suffering husband, Dick Smethurst, and I am as grateful now as then for his unfailing practical love and patient support. Volume Two was dedicated to my daughters, Abbie and Esther, who in their earlier years earned money to travel by working on the ever-expanding data base, and up to the present day their loving encouragement has kept me going. It seems appropriate to maintain family interests, and so in a work about reception through the centuries I am dedicating Volume Three to the next generation—to my three lovely grandchildren, Sophia and Noah Boutayeb, and Ayaan Gillingham-Ahmed.

Abbreviations

1. *All English citations are taken from the New Revised Standard Version and the enumeration of psalms and psalm verses follows that version unless otherwise stated. An Appendix is given on pp. 454–458 which indicates the different numbering of the psalms and psalm verses in the Hebrew, Greek and Latin versions respectively, and where these versions are cited directly in the text this enumeration is also given.*
2. *A Glossary of Terms is found on pp. 459–472. Each word or phrase explained in the Glossary is indicated with an asterisk (*) the first time it occurs in the commentary for each individual psalm.*
3. *All websites were checked during January 2022 and were fully accessible up to that time.*

ABC	Anchor Bible Commentary
ACCS	*Ancient Christian Commentary on Scripture*
ACTP	Ambrose: *Commentary on Twelve Psalms*
ACW	Ancient Christian Writers
AIL	Ancient Israel and its Literature
ALW	*Archiv für Liturgiewissenschaft*
AnSac	*Analecta sacra et classica spicilegio solesmensi.*
AOAT	Alter Orient und Altes Testament
ATANT	Abhandlungen zur Theologie des Alten und Neuen Testaments
BASOR	*Bulletin of the American Schools of Oriental Research*
BBB	Bonner biblische Beiträge
BETL	Bibliotheca Ephemeridum Theologicarum Lovaninensium
BHT	Beiträge zur historischen Theologie
Bib	*Biblica*
BTT	Bible de tous les temps
BThSt	Biblisch-theologische Studien
BZ	*Biblische Zeitschrift*
BZAW	Beihefte zur Zeitschrift fur die alttestamentliche Wissenschaft
CBQ	*Catholic Biblical Quarterly*
CCL	Corpus Christianorum Series Latina (Turnhout, Belgium: Brepols. 1953–)
CTJ	*Calvin Theological Journal*
CurTM	*Currents in Theology and Mission*
EETS	Early English Texts Society
EJL	Early Judaism and its Literature
Est Bib	*Estudios bíblicos*
EV	English Version
Exp	*Expositor*
ExpTim	*Expository Times*
FAT	Forschungen zum Alten Testament
FC	Fathers of the Church: A New Translation (Catholic University of America Press, Washington, DC: 45 volumes)
FRLANT	Forschungen zur Religion und Literatur des Alten und Neuen Testaments
HBTh	*Horizons in Biblical Theology*
HeyJ	*Heythrop Journal*
HKAT	Handkommentar zum Alten Testament
HSS	Harvard Semitic Monographs
HTR	*Harvard Theological Review*
HTS	*Harvard Theological Studies*
HUCA	*Hebrew Union College Annual*
JANES	*Journal of the Ancient Near Eastern Society*
JBL	*Journal of Biblical Literature*

JHS	*Journal of Hebrew Scriptures*
JQR	*Jewish Quarterly Review*
JSNTSup	Journal for the Study of the New Testament Supplement Series
JSOT	*Journal for the Study of the Old Testament*
JSOTSup	Journal for the Study of the Old Testament Supplement Series
JTS	*Journal of Theological Studies*
KAT	Kommentar zum Alten Testament
KHAT	Konkordanz zum Hebräischen Alten Testaements
LCC	The Library of Christian Classics (Philadelphia: Westminster Press, 1953–1966; 26 vols.)
LHBOTS	The Library of Hebrew Bible/Old Testament Studies
LNTS	Library of New Testament Studies
MusicLett	*Music and Letters*
NCB	New Century Bible Commentary
NICOT	New International Commentary on the Old Testament
NPNF	A Select Library of the Nicene and Post-Nicene Fathers of the Church (eds. P. Schaff *et al.*, Buffalo: The Christian Literature Company, 1886. 14 vols.
NTS	*New Testament Studies*
NRSV	*New Revised Standard Version*
OBO	Orbis biblicus et orientalis
OECS	Oxford Early Christian Studies
OrChrAn	Orientalia Christiana Analecta
OTE	*Old Testament Essays.* (The Old Testament Society of Southern Africa [OTSSA])
OtSt	*Oudtestamentische Studiën*
PG	*Patrologiae cursus completus. Series Graeca.* Ed. J.-P. Migne. Paris: Migne, 1857–1886. 166 vols.
PIBA	*The Proceedings of the Irish Biblical Association*
PL	*Patrologiae cursus completus. Series Latina.* Ed. J.-P. Migne. Paris: Migne, 1844–1864. 221 vols.
POG	*The Proof of the Gospel.* Eusebius. 2 vols. Trans. W. J. Ferrar. London: SPCK, 1920.
RB	*Revue Biblique*
RES	*The Review of English Studies*
RevQ	*Revue de Qumran*
SBB	Stuttgarter biblische Beiträge
SBLDS	Society of Biblical Literature Dissertation Series
SBLMS	Society of Biblical Literature Monograph Series
SBLSCS	Society of Biblical Literature Septuagint and Cognate Studies
SJT	*Scottish Journal of Theology*
SNT	Schriften des Neuen Testaments

StBibLit	Studies in Biblical Literature
STDJ	Studies on the Texts of the Desert of Judah
STSA	Studi e testo di storia antica
StPat	*Studia Patristica*
StTh	*Studia Theologica*
SymS	SBL Symposium Series
TGUOS	*Transactions of the Glasgow University Oriental Society*
TNTC	Tyndale New Testament Commentaries
ThLZ	*Theologische Literaturzeitung*
TS	*Theological Studies*
TU	Texte und Untersuchungen zur Geschichte der altchristlichen Literatur
UCOP	University of Cambridge Oriental Publications
VT	*Vetus Testamentum*
VTSup	Supplements to Vetus Testamentum
WBC	Word Biblical Commentary
WGRW	*Writings from the Greco-Roman World*. Ed. R. F. Hock. Atlanta: Society of Biblical Literature, 2001-.
WSA	*Works of St. Augustine: A Translation for the Twenty-First Century*. Ed. J. E. Rotelle. Hyde Park, NY: New City Press, 1995–
WTJ	*Westminster Theological Journal*
WUNT	Wissenschaftliche Untersuchungen zum Neuen Testament
YJS	Yale Judaica Series
ZAW	*Zeitschrift für die alttestamentliche Wissenschaft*
ZThK	*Zeitschrift für Theologie und Kirche*

Abbreviations of Greek and Latin Works

Justin Martyr	*1 Apol.*	*First Apology*
	Dial.	*Dialogue with Trypho*
Augustine of Hippo	*Enarrat. Ps.*	*Enarrationes in Psalmos/ Expositions on the Psalms*
	Civ.	*The City of God*
	Conf.	*Confessions*
Origen	*Sel. Ps.*	*Selection from the Psalms*
Cassiodorus	*Exp. Ps.*	*Expositio psalmorum/ Explanation of the Psalms*
Theodoret	*Com. Ps.*	*Commentary on the Psalms*
Eusebius	*Com. Ps.*	*Commentary on the Psalms*

Basil	*Hom. Ps.*	*Homilies on the Psalms*
Jerome	*Tract. Ps.*	*Tractus in Psalmos*
Ambrose	*Exp in Ps*	*Explanations of Psalms*
Athanasius	*Interp. Ps.*	*Interpretation of the Psalms*

Abbreviations of Talmudic and Mishnaic Works

Avot.	*Pirkei Avot*
Ber.	*b.Berakhot*
Sop.	*Sopherim*
Ros Has.	*b.Rosh HaShanah*
Sanh.	*b.Sanhedrin*

BOOK THREE: PSALMS 73–89

Remembering, Human and Divine

Book Three is a selection of seventeen psalms, mainly communal in tone, whose shared themes include the destruction of the temple, the dispersion of the people and the humiliation of the king. Two early crises seem to have given rise to the composition and preservation of these psalms: the defeat of the northern kingdom by Assyria (722–21 BCE), and the defeat of the southern kingdom of Judah by Babylon (597–96 and 587–86 BCE). As for their reception history, most of these psalms have been interpreted further in the light of other later crises, such as the desecration of the Temple under Antiochus Epiphanes in c. 167 BCE, the fall of Jerusalem under Titus in 70 CE, the fall of Rome in 410 CE, the fate of Jerusalem during the Crusades in 1099 CE and 1187 CE, and, later, the fate of Constantinople in 1204 CE and 1453 CE. The earliest Assyrian and Babylonian crises nevertheless left an indelible mark on these psalms: often these two invasions merge together, sometimes reflecting in part a northern Israelite experience,[1] and sometimes in part a southern Judean one.[2] The theme of exile dominates this entire collection—a theme which is developed further in the seventeen psalms of Book Four. But whereas some answers are offered in Book Four, here in Book Three, the questions about

---

[1] For example, the references to 'Joseph' (77:15; 78:67; 80:1; 81:5), to 'Ephraim' (78:67; 80:2) and to the 'God of Jacob' (75:9; 76:6; 81:1,14).
[2] Psalms 74 and 79 seem to lament the destruction of Jerusalem; whilst Psalms 75–76 and 82 speak of God's presence in Zion.

Psalms Through the Centuries: A Reception History Commentary on Psalms 73–151, Volume Three, First Edition. Susan Gillingham.
© 2022 John Wiley & Sons Ltd. Published 2022 by John Wiley & Sons Ltd.

theodicy, almost always from the point of view of the entire people, are more prominent.[3] Here the psalmists wrestle with the problems of injustice, both human and divine, alongside the importance (and problem) of memory in recalling the past, asking whether God has forgotten them because they had forgotten God.[4]

Again the process of compilation constitutes the first stage of reception. In this case, the compilers seem to have arranged Book Three as a series of questions. 'Has God forgotten to be gracious?', and 'How Long, O Lord?', and 'Will you be angry for ever?' emerge frequently in these psalms (see for example 77:7–9; 79:5; 80:4; 82:2; 89:46), and whenever a partial answer is given, it is overtaken by further questions in a following psalm. Two main collections are discernible here seen in the headings 'A Psalm of Asaph' (73–83) and 'A Psalm of the Sons of Korah' (84, 85 and 87). Those with less clear headings (86, 88 and 89) may have other *Korahite associations; this would explain why they have been included into these collections. The *Asaphite collection has two sub-groups of five psalms (73–77 and 79–83), with Psalm 78, a more didactic psalm, playing a pivotal role at the heart of the whole collection, reflecting on the importance of remembering God's covenant, first with Moses and then with David. The Korahite collection comprises six psalms (counting in Psalms 86, 88 and 89 here). Psalm 89, at the very end of Book Three, might be compared to Psalm 78: it also takes up the theme of remembering, but the focus here is only on God's covenant with David, and (unlike Psalm 78) it ends with a cry of desolation because God seems to have forgotten (89:38–51) rather than remembered (78:67–72).[5] The following analysis will start with the placing of individual psalms into coherent collections, noting that this work by the compilers marks the first stage in the process of reception.

---

[3] See deClaissé-Walford 1997: 79–80; Cole 2000: 9–14, 231–5.

[4] See Pavan 2014: 127–8 and 183–84.

[5] See Pavan 2014: 127–8 (on Psalms 73–83) and 183–4 (on Psalms 84–89); also 185–270 (on Psalms 78 and 89 being pivotal psalms).

Psalms 73–83: The Asaphite Collection: 'How Long, O Lord?'

Looking at the first part of Book Three, it seems that the editors carefully combined the end of the so-called 'Davidic Psalter' (Psalms 51–72) in Book Two with the beginning of Book Three. Psalm 72 (Book Two) reflects positively on the importance of justice whilst 73 (Book Three) considers the consequences of injustice in the world. Both 73:3 and 72:3 contrast the 'prosperity' (*shalom*) of the faithful people and the wicked; and 73:6, 72:14, 73:8 and 72:4 speak of the effects of 'violence' (*ḥamas*) and 'oppression' (*'osheq*) on the poor.

The entire *Asaphite collection (Psalms 73–83), set in the heart of the entire Psalter, is possibly the oldest part of it. As we have noted, it has many references to the northern kingdom (and so some of it must precede 721–22 BCE when the kingdom fell), and its nationalistic and militarist focus, reminiscent of the prophetic voice in this period, suggests some psalms were composed before the exile. It is a coherent collection, set in two parts (73–77, 78–83) to which Psalm 50 also belongs: as noted in Volume Two, the Second Davidic Psalter (51–72) is enclosed by Asaphite psalms (50, 73–83).[6]

[6] See Gillingham 2018: 256.

Psalms Through the Centuries: A Reception History Commentary on Psalms 73–151, Volume Three, First Edition. Susan Gillingham.
© 2022 John Wiley & Sons Ltd. Published 2022 by John Wiley & Sons Ltd.

Psalms 73–77: 'Has God Forgotten to be Gracious?'

Psalms 73–77, the first *Asaphite sub-group, is a collection with several internal correspondences. For example, Psalms 73 and 74 each reflect on the absence of God, from a context of violence and blasphemy. 73 is a psalm of instruction; 74 is a communal lament. 75 and 76 are set as two divine responses to these questions, affirming that God's presence is still in Zion. 77 is an individual lament.[7] The theme of 'violence' (*hamas*) in 73:6 is continued in 74:20; 73:23 speaks of being held by God's 'right hand' (*yad-yemini*) whilst 74:11 asks why God has withdrawn his 'hand' (*yad*); 73:17 refers to God in his sanctuary (*miqdeshe-'el*, or 'the sanctuaries of God') and 74:7 also refers to the sanctuary (*miqdashekha*, or 'your sanctuary') which has been set on fire. Other shared themes in the entire collection are of a common experience of God's anger (Pss. 74:1; 75:8; and 76:7); an affirmation of God's Name (Pss. 74:10, 18, 21; 75:1; and 76:1); and pleas to God to judge fairly (Pss. 74:22; 75:2, 7; 76:8–9). Other inter-psalm connections include the term 'God of Jacob' in 75:9 and 76:6, the centrality of Zion in 74:2 and 76:2, and the pleas to God not to forget (*'al-tishkaḥ, or* 'do not forget!') in Pss. 74:23 and 77:9.

---

[7] This order of instruction/communal lament/divine response/individual lament is mirrored in Psalms 78–83, as will be seen shortly.

Psalms Through the Centuries: A Reception History Commentary on Psalms 73–151, Volume Three, First Edition. Susan Gillingham.
© 2022 John Wiley & Sons Ltd. Published 2022 by John Wiley & Sons Ltd.

Psalm 73: A Didactic Psalm about the Impious

Psalm 73 stands not only at the beginning of Book Three but close to the centre of the Psalter. It is both protest and affirmation: it questions the rewards for obedient faith expressed in Psalm 1 (see 73:2–14) yet it ultimately affirms the vision of Psalm 150 where God is praised (see 73:23–26).[8] It contains three strophes (vv. 1–12; 13–17; and 18–28), each starting with 'truly, indeed' ('ak). Verses 1–17 reflect on the problems and possibilities of the injustice in the world, whilst verses 18–28 address God: here there is an unusual 'vision' of God and some rare reflections about life beyond death. In terms of its reception history, it stands somewhat apart from the other psalms in the *Asaphite collection because of its more personal nature and its consideration of *universal* themes of justice.

The first issue in its reception is one of translation in the first verse: is God good 'to Israel' or 'to the upright'? Some manuscripts divide these words differently in Hebrew, and because the vowels were a later addition it is possible to insert different vowels or break the line in a different place—both of which change the meaning.[9] 'God is good to Israel, to the pure in heart' (*tob leyisra'el elohim: lebarei lebab*), which the Greek translation also follows, gives the psalm a more national tenor; 'God is good to the upright, Elohim to the pure in heart' (*tob leyasar 'el: elohim lebarei lebab*) suggests more individual concerns. Given that all the other Asaphite psalms have more communal interests, 'to Israel' is probably preferable; but the psalm is undoubtedly more personal than the others, and this small issue of translation can change the emphasis and so the reception of the psalm.

The first part of verse 4 presents another problem: the Hebrew reads literally 'for they have no torment in their death', although the NRSV reads 'For they have no pain' (with no reference to death). The Greek however translates 'torment' as *ananeusis*, a feminine noun found nowhere else in the *Septuagint, probably from the verb 'to refuse, reject' and a loose translation of the Greek would be, literally, 'There is no refusal for their death', that is 'For they refuse death'. The *Vulgate* reads this a little differently: '*non est respectus morti eorum*' which could mean, simply, 'they have no care about their death'.[10] This could however be translated (in the light of the interest in death in verses 23–24) as 'the wicked will not return from death' which alters the meaning altogether.[11]

---

[8] Brueggemann 1991: 81–88.
[9] For a clear overview of this problem, see Tate 1990: 228.
[10] Bons 2008: 139.
[11] Schaper 1995: 70.

Another example is an additional phrase in the Greek at the end of the psalm (not brought out in the NRSV) which gives the psalm a more national bias: the final phrase reads 'to tell of all your works *in the gates of the daughter Sion*'.[12]

Targum reads verse 1 as being about 'Israel', and the mockery and pride of the 'wicked' in verses 2–9 relate to the Gentiles who threaten the entire people. Verse 10 is amended to read '*Therefore he is returning for the sake of the people of the Lord, and they shall strike them with hammers and cause many tears to run down*'. Verses 18–20 are also about the Gentiles: '*...as a dream from a drunken man who awakens, O Lord, at the day of the great judgement when they awake from their graves, with anger you will despise their image*'.[13] Here a personal reading has been absorbed into a communal one.

There is no evidence of this psalm in the New Testament. Later Christian commentary is not very creative with it, although, unlike Jewish readings, the psalm is usually seen in more personal terms in its view of the good life in the face of death. According to *Ambrose, it is about 'growth in moral perfection': it is important to rejoice in chastisement, knowing that future consolation will come, for the peace of sinners is deceptive.[14] Ambrose also 'Christianises' the psalm by reading the reference to God holding the psalmist's 'right hand' (verse 23), as meaning our holding of Christ's right hand, so that we possess Christ alone in heaven.[15] *Augustine is mainly interested in the moral impact of this psalm: he compares verses 15–20 (describing the fate of the wicked) with the parable of Abraham and Lazarus in Luke 16:20–31.[16] A more explicitly Christian reading is attributed to *Bede, who, following *Cassiodorus, sees Psalm 73 as an expansion of Psalm 72: the hymns of David have failed (72:20) and the temporal rule of Jesse has now been fulfilled in one from the stem of Jesse, Christ himself (Isa. 11:1; Matt. 1:5–16); hence Psalm 73 is about that Son who conquers sin and oppression.[17] A reading associated with *Aquinas could not be more different from *Targum*: now the ungodly are the Jews, of whom Christ speaks in verses 18–19: '...Those who brought to nothing the image of God in their earthly city, shall have their image brought to nothing in his city'.[18]

Typical anti-Jewish readings are also found in Byzantine Psalters. For example, the *Khludov Psalter* (fol. 70v) illustrates verse 9 ('they set their mouths

---

[12] Pietersma 2000: 70–71.

[13] Stec 2004: 143–44.

[14] See 'Prayer of Job and David' 3.2.3 and 3.3.5 in *FC* 65:369–74, in *ACCS* VIII: 101–03.

[15] See 'Prayer of Job and David' 3.10.27–28 in *FC* 65:385–7, in *ACCS* VIII: 109–10.

[16] See Sermon 15A.2 cited in *WSA* 3:1:332, in *ACCS* VIII: 108.

[17] Neale and Littledale 1874–79: 2/466–67.

[18] Neale and Littledale 1874–79: 2/479.

against heaven') with Jewish *iconoclasts: the inscription reads 'the ones who are heretics and speak against God.'[19]

*Carolingian Psalters are less polemical and more practical in their illustrations. For example, the *Utrecht Psalter* (fol. 41v) is a narrative about the victory of the righteous over the wicked. At the top right the psalmist is sitting on a hillock, and below him is a mare and colt (a literal translation of the Hebrew 'beasts' in verse 22, to which the psalmist compares himself). The 'sanctuary' of verse 17 is behind him, next to a walled city with a gate (noting the Greek and Latin additions about 'Zion' at the end of verse 28). At the top left we see the wicked, reading from scrolls (verse 9), and in the bottom right is another group trampling on the poor and a different group gorging at a table full of food. The hand of God comes out from heaven to grasp the psalmist's right hand (verse 23) and above a group of angels is another wingless angel holding a whip (suggested by the Latin '*flagellabuntur*' and '*flagellatus*' of verses 5 and 14), who is driving a large number of the wicked into a fiery pit of Hell (verse 27).[20] The *Stuttgart Psalter* (fol. 85r) depicts the psalmist sitting with a mare and colt (like *Utrecht*, following verse 22), thus illustrating in a single image a more Christian reading of the psalm, where Jesus enters Jerusalem on these animals in Matt. 21:2–7.[21]

A more overtly Christian reading is found in the twelfth-century *St Albans Psalter*. In the illuminated initial 'Q' (for *Quam bonus Israel* in verse 1), the psalmist, stripped to the waist, turns, terrified, to look up at God in heaven: this also illustrates the hope for survival beyond death in verses 22–26, verses which were used by the Prioress, Christina of Markyate (to whom the Psalter was dedicated), after she had given her final vows.[22]

Turning to examples from poetry, an intriguingly personal use is by George *Herbert in *The Temple*. 'The Collar' follows the same theme on the unjust success of the wicked in the first part of Psalm 73, although Herbert's start of the poem (lines 3–9) is even more angry and intense than the psalm itself.[23] This is partly due to the fact that Herbert's speaker is not outside the sanctuary (i.e. unable to find an answer until he goes to it, as in Ps. 73:17) but actually within it, 'at board' (i.e. at the altar) all along: 'He struck the board, and cry'd, No More/I will abroad!' (lines 1–2). Although the speaker is tempted to affirm

[19] Corrigan 1992: 14; also fig. 17.
[20] See https://psalter.library.uu.nl/page/90.
[21] See https://bit.ly/31O0u5N.
[22] See https://www.albani-psalter.de/stalbanspsalter/english/commentary/page213.shtml.
[23] https://www.ccel.org/h/herbert/temple/Collar.html.

and share in the prosperity of the wicked, there is eventually some epiphany and resolution:

> But as I rav'd and grew more fierce and wilde
>   at every word
> Me thoughts I heard one calling, 'Child!'
>   And I reply'd, 'My Lord.'
>
> (Lines 33–36.)[24]

Another personal literary appropriation of this psalm, also reflecting on the problem of injustice and the plight of the righteous and the wicked, with an explicit Christian focus, is found in John *Bunyan's *Pilgrim's Progress*: as Christian sinks in the mire, despairing that he will die for his sins, Hopeful responds by citing Ps. 73:4–5: 'the troubles and distresses that you go through in these waters are no sign that God hath forsaken you; but are sent to try you...'[25]

The last part of the psalm, with its references to the life beyond, has provided the most explicit Christian readings. This is found especially in both metrical psalmody and hymnody. Charles *Wesley, for example, on his death bed, reflecting on verse 25 ('Whom have I in heaven but you?...) dictated the following hymn to his wife: 'Jesus, my only hope thou art, Strength of failing flesh and heart: O could I catch a smile from thee, and drop into eternity!'[26]

The ending of the psalm, with its suggestion of the afterlife, has inspired several musical arrangements. Heinrich *Schütz arranged verses 25–26, using a double chorus, as the second of three motets (1636): this was commissioned by Prince Heinrich von Reuss, to be used at his funeral.[27] Dietrich *Buxtehude (c. 1668) composed 'Herr, wenn Ich nur Dich habe' on the same verses, as a plaintive solo with strings. The Hungarian composer Franz Liszt's '*Mihi autem adhaerre*' (1868) is another example, composed for the Mass of St. Francis, based on verse 28 of this psalm.

The other prominent theme of the psalm, namely its vision of the wicked oppressors who are finally destroyed by God, is found in Lauryn *Hill's track 'The Final Hour', on her 1998 solo album 'The Miseducation of Lauryn Hill':

---

[24] See also Kinnamon 1981: 21–23.

[25] From *Pilgrim's Progress*, Tenth Stage. See http://www.ccel.org/ccel/bunyan/pilgrim.iv.x.html.

[26] Prothero 1903: 305. See http://www.hymnary.org/text/in_age_and_feebleness_extreme.

[27] See Dowling Long and Sawyer 2015: 162.

> You can get the money
> You can get the power
> But keep your eyes on the Final Hour…
> And I remain calm reading the 73rd Psalm
> Cause with all that's going on I got the world in my palm.[28]

Much of this reception has been specifically Christian; there is little use of the psalm in Jewish music or art, and not much evidence of it in Jewish or Christian liturgy, despite its twin themes of injustice and life beyond death. But since the Second World War there have been several post-Holocaust reflections on the psalm, of which Martin *Buber's 'Why do the Wicked Prosper?' is particularly pertinent. Given that the wicked clearly do not 'fall' in this life, as the psalmist hoped, Buber considers that the problem for the suppliant and for those using the psalm today is as much psychological as theological: he protests that God is not absent, even if we perceive him to be so. Buber's interpretation of the whole of Psalm 73 has influenced several later post-war Jewish writings.[29] From this the psalm might also be applied to the history of white privilege and black oppression, where verse 17 ('until I went to the sanctuary of God') has a real force.[30]

It is nevertheless surprising to find that a psalm with such a clear theme of justice and injustice, with so many universal implications, has not produced a richer history of reception.

Psalm 74: A Communal Lament about Ongoing Exile

Psalm 74, like Psalm 78, is entitled 'A *Maskil* of Asaph' and each has an instructional element. Each looks back to the past as a means of facing the future, but whilst Psalm 78 is more positive, Psalm 74 does this by way of lament, using mythical traditions, with Babylonian and Canaanite associations, concerning God's battle with the chaotic sea (the '*Chaoskampf*'). It falls into three strophes: verses 1–11, beginning and ending with the question 'why?'; verses 12–17, which is a hymn on God's kingship; and verses 18–23, which form a series of imperatives, echoing verses 2–3. We have already

---

[28] The lyrics are at http://genius.com/894873; for the performance see https://www.youtube.com/watch?v=xEnKURp0hlc.

[29] See Buber 1953: 39–41, cited in Levine 1984: 217. See also Magonet 1994: 164–78.

[30] Dombkowski Hopkins 2016: 235.

noted its links with its neighbouring psalms, pointing to the probability that its inclusion here was deliberate.[31]

Although the setting is most probably the Babylonian attack in 587/6 BCE, later Jewish reception applies the theme of grief for a city torn apart with strife to new situations. One obvious period is when Antiochus Epiphanes took over the Temple, burnt swine's flesh on the altar and erected a statue to Zeus in c. 167 BCE. The *Targum's* addition to verse 22 ('remember the dishonour of your people by the foolish king all the day') seems to be an implicit reference to this Gentile king.[32] Another period of strife was the destruction of Jerusalem in 70 CE: later Jewish commentators on this psalm refer explicitly to Titus' acts of desecration (lying with a prostitute on a Torah scroll, slashing the curtains of the Temple) as if the psalm were a prophetic witness to this period.[33] Other Jewish comments on verse 1 ('O God, why do you cast us off forever?') interpret the psalm in the light of the experience of ongoing exile, still under 'Rome', but now symbolised, even after Alaric's sack of Rome in 410 CE, as all hostile Gentile powers: 'The first (Babylonian) exile was limited to seventy years; but this second (Roman) Exile still continues, with no end in sight.'[34]

The Christian reception also has examples of using the psalm as part of an expression of grief over a lost homeland. Such a literal appropriation is found, for example, in the Huguenots' use of it, when in the seventeenth-century, under Louis XIV, they were driven out of their homes, and entered Geneva singing this psalm.[35] In the twentieth-century we read of a comment pencilled by *Bonhoeffer in his Bible against verses 8–11 ('...they burned all the meeting places of God in the land...'). He simply wrote 9.11.38—the date of *Kristallnacht* and the start of the pogroms, so in this case we see a Christian empathy with the Jewish cause: Bonhoeffer's identification with the Jews, even though it took him to his death, is well known.[36]

Christian reception in the earlier commentary tradition has, however, usually read the psalm allegorically. *Athanasius viewed the psalm as about Christ's incarnation and crucifixion; *Augustine developed this and explained the phrase 'Yet God my King is of old, working salvation in the earth' (verse 12) as a reference to the pre-existent Christ who achieved such salvation 'in the midst of the earth' through the womb of a Virgin, by his

---

[31] See pp. 2–3.
[32] See Feuer 2004: 925.
[33] See Feuer 2004: 925–26.
[34] Taken from *Sforno, cited in, Feuer 2004: 926.
[35] Prothero 1903: 217–18.
[36] Miller 1994: 281.

incarnation.[37] *Cassiodorus read 'God my King' in the same verse also as a reference to Christ, and verse 13 ('you divided the sea by your might' as not only an allusion to the crossing of the Red Sea but also a prefiguring of Jesus' Baptism, when the water was purified by 'breaking the power of the heads of the dragons' (unclean spirits), also in verse 13.[38]

The *Utrecht Psalter* (fol. 42r) connects verse 12 with the incarnation. Here we see an image of the birth of Christ, and two midwives are bathing the Christ Child in the presence of Mary and Joseph; at the bottom of the image the sea is writhing with serpents.[39] The same interpretation is captured more clearly in the related *Eadwine Psalter* (fol. 128v), as seen in PLATE 1.

An example of an image of baptism is found in the historiated initial letter for Psalm 74 in the *St Albans Psalter*. The image is of a haloed Christ, with a hammer, slaying a dragon held by a figure personifying the waters.[40]

Visual exegesis in the Byzantine tradition, with its propensity for anti-Jewish polemic, focusses neither on the incarnation nor on Jesus' baptism but on the cross. Both the *Khludov* and *Pantokrator Psalters* (fol. 82v and fol. 98r respectively) use this image.[41] The illustration next to verse 12 depicts Jerusalem at the centre of the cosmos (referring back to verse 2: 'Remember Mount Zion, where you came to dwell') but the image is also of Christ on the cross outside the city, with Mary and John on the right, and a figure (apparently a Jew) stabbing with a spear at the cross. This is a statement against both Judaism, which denied the passion of Christ, and Islam, denying Christ actually died on the cross. The reference in verse 9 ('we do not see our emblems,') is read as the refusal to see the cross, specifically the 'emblem' of the Greek letter *Tau*, as pertaining to Christ. A similar image is also found in the *Theodore Psalter* (fol. 96r).[42]

These different illustrations also reveal the use of the psalm in various forms of Christian liturgy: at Christmas in the western churches, at Easter in the eastern churches, and at Epiphany in both traditions when the Baptism of Christ was commemorated.

An interesting musical association of this psalm with Christmas is found in J. S. *Bach's 'Gott ist mein König', composed in 1708 for an annual church

---

[37] *City of God* 17.4: CG 722–23, in *ACCS* VIII:116.

[38] *Expositions of the Psalms* 73:13, *ACW* 52:218 and *ACCS* VIII:117.

[39] See https://psalter.library.uu.nl/page/91.

[40] See https://www.albani-psalter.de/stalbanspsalter/english/commentary/page216.shtml. The *Khludov, Pantokrator* and *Barberini Psalters* also illustrate verse 13 through the context of Jesus' baptism. See Corrigan 1992: 91.

[41] See Corrigan 1992: fig. 87 for *Pantokrator* (p. 290) and fig. 88 for *Khludov* (p. 291).

[42] See http://www.bl.uk/manuscripts/Viewer.aspx?ref=add_ms_19352_f096r.

service in Mühlhausen. Parts I and IV were based on Psalm 74, verses 12 and 16: God in Christ has been born as a King, working salvation from of old.

Poetic reception has responded especially to the grief expressed in this psalm. Mary *Sidney, for example, compares the destruction of the Temple (verses 4–7) with the destruction of a forest, thus circumventing the difficult Hebrew in these verses and maintaining a sense of urgency through her use of rhyme and rhythm:[43]

> As men with axe on arm
> To some thick forest swarm,
> To lop the trees which stately stand:
> They to thy temple flock,
> And spoiling, cut and knock
> The curious works of carving hand.

A late twentieth-century Jewish perspective which takes up the same theme of grief and bereavement is Laurance *Wieder's 'Why always angry, O God?': here we see many connections with the post-Holocaust reflections by *Buber on Psalm 73 previously.[44]

> Why always angry, God? Why smoke against us and inhale
> Sacrifices? Zion's rubble. Temple hacked
> To splinters, they burn children with their teachers...
>
> You taught us, now deliver us
> From those who worship templed darkness. Look,
> We blush for you, your name,
> Though we are poor, and weak, and strangers roar.

It does seem as if the integrity of the psalm as a whole is best understood when it is attuned to the perspective of the Jewish people. As a recent Jewish commentator observes, it is as if 'Asaph' asks throughout this psalm why God has abandoned his people for eternity; when the Holy One responds that they have abandoned him (Hos. 8:2), the people reply that the Holy One's reputation will be imperilled if he does not save them. The Shepherd of Israel comes to protect, not to destroy (verse 1).[45]

---

[43] See Hamlin *et al.* 2009: 139–40; also Rathmell 1963: xxii, who notes similar forestry imagery was used by Mary Sidney in Psalm 92.
[44] Wieder 1995: 110–11.
[45] Feuer 2004: 925–26.

Psalm 75: God's Abode is in Zion (i)

Psalm 75 contains an additional title 'Do not destroy', showing a link made by the editors with 'Do not forget' in the last verse of Psalm 74. Psalm 75 has several associations with 1 Sam. 2:1–10, the Song of Hannah (which also refers to insolent talk, to the arrogant horn, to the world on pillars, and to God casting down and lifting up) although the direction of borrowing is difficult to ascertain. The psalm can be divided up into the following strophes: verse 1 is a hymn, verses 2–5 appear to be a divine oracle, verses 6–8 are a prophetic-like judgement speech by the psalmist, verse 9 is another hymn, and verse 10 suggests another oracle where God speaks through the psalmist.[46] These prophetic elements have played an important part in the psalm's reception history, as also have three vivid metaphors: the world being shaken on its pillars (verse 3), the cup of foaming wine (verse 8) and the horns of the wicked (verses 4, 5 and 10). The second of these has been particularly potent in Christian interpretation, as will be seen below.

The only pertinent addition in the *Septuagint which changes the tenor of the psalm is the reference to the 'boastful' in verse 4, who are now the 'violators of the law', reflecting the debates about the authority of the Torah in later Judaism. *Targum* makes other changes: verse 1 (Heb. v. 2) is expanded to read, somewhat typically, 'the *Shekinah* of your name' and the references to 'east and west' in verse 6 are expanded to include 'the north, the place of wilderness' and 'the south, the place of the mountains'. These changes suggest a greater sense of God's transcendence and hence power over the entire cosmos. The most significant addition is in *Midrash Tehillim*: the reference to the 'horns' in verse 10 (Heb. v. 11) is seen to allude to the 'ten horns' in Jewish tradition (of Abraham, Isaac, Moses, Samuel, Aaron, the Sanhedrin, Heman the Levite, Jerusalem, the King Messiah, and David the King to come). This is seen as a messianic reference to the coming king (also using Hannah's Song in 1 Sam. 2:10), soon to become the light of the world (Ps. 132:17).[47]

As was seen in Psalm 75, the main tenor in Jewish commentary tradition is to read this psalm from the viewpoint of a community still in exile: hence, according to *Rashi and *Kimḥi, for example, 'the righteous' in verse 10 (Heb. v. 11) are Israel, the people of God.[48] The 'cup of foaming wine' (verse 8 (Heb. v. 9)) is the

---

[46] That is, if the verb 'cut off' is to be read as first not third person. We may note some correspondences with Psalm 82 which also contains two divine speeches.

[47] See Braude 1959: 2/11–12.

[48] See Feuer 2004: 945.

one which Israel has been compelled to drink from first (Isa. 51:17) but when the exile is at an end Israel's enemies will then be forced to drink it.[49] Not surprisingly the psalm is one of those recited throughout the day the week before *Rosh HaShanah.

In Christian reception this 'cup' had a very different connotation. *Cassiodorus focusses on the reference in verse 8 to the wine being 'well mixed', and notes that the Jews had the 'unmixed wine' of the old covenant, whilst the Christians possessed the 'mixed wine' of the old and new covenants; this is actually an attack on the *Manicheans, whom Cassiodorus saw as having only the 'unmixed wine' of the New Testament, in their rejection of much of the Old, and so as guilty of false religion as the Jews.[50] This interpretation does not seem to fit the context of judgement on the wicked in the rest of the verse; hence a different reading might be to read verses 8 and 9 together, so that the Cup is of the Passion of Christ; verse 8 is thus about judgement on the Jews and verses 9–10 are a reference to Christ's kingdom, achieved through his drinking the cup to its dregs.[51] This association of the 'cup' with the passion of Christ has resulted in this psalm being frequently used on Maundy Thursday. As with Psalm 74, Christian reception of this psalm is more optimistic than Jewish reception. *Augustine, for example, saw verse 3 ('it is I who keep the pillars [of the earth] steady') as Christ speaking about the victory of his judgement in the light of Rev. 20:12.[52]

Although there are few arrangements of this psalm in music, J. S. *Bach's triumphant 'Wir danken Dir, Gott' is based on the hymns of praise in verses 1 and 9: composed in 1731, on the election of councillors in Leipzig, it is therefore a celebratory piece, with an orchestral sinfonia, motet-like chorus, and ends with 'Now Praise My Soul the Lord' accompanied by trumpets.[53] Similarly the seventeenth-century Dutch composer Henry Du Mont's *'Confitebimur tibi Deus'* is taken from verse 1; the same verse is the focus of the eighteenth-century Dorset composer Joseph Stephenson, in his 'To Thee, O God, we render praise': each is a Christian reading (although Stephenson actually became a Unitarian) and each emphasises the psalm's more positive aspects. The same mood is captured

---

[49] See Feuer 2004: 943–44.
[50] See *Expositions of the Psalms* 74.9 in *ACW* 52:229, *ACCS* VIII: 120.
[51] See Neale and Littledale 1874–79: 2/508, citing *Thomasius on *Aquinas.
[52] See Neale and Littledale 1874–79: 2/510. See also *Expositions on the Psalms 74 (75).4* in *PL* 36. 948–49 on the way Augustine reads this Psalm as 'Christ our Head' speaking for us, and 'Christ our Body' speaking with us.
[53] Dowling Long and Sawyer 2015: 269.

in the more strident metrical psalm by *Tate and Brady, which praises God as the great disposer:

> His hand holds forth a dreadful cup,
>> With purple wine 'tis crowned;
> The deadly mixture, which his wrath
>> Deals out to nations round.
>
> Of this his saints may sometime taste;
>> But wicked men shall squeeze
> The bitter dregs, and be condemn'd,
>> To drink the very lees.[54]

This sort of vindictive emphasis contributed to the political use of this psalm in England and America in the seventeenth and eighteenth centuries: Isaac *Watts transformed Tate and Brady's words to contemporise the psalm for the court of George I, so it was subtitled 'Power and Government belong to God alone: to be applied to the Glorious Revolution by King William, or the Happy Succession of George I to the Throne'. Watts' *Psalms of David Imitated* was popular in New England: hence by 1787 John *Mycall had revised the title so it read *Applied to the Glorious Revolution in America, July 4th, 1776*.[55] Conversely, in *Lamentation over Boston*, ascribed to William *Billings (1778), parts of this psalm—now a protest hymn against the horrors of the aftermath of the American Revolution—were used alongside Psalm 137.

One of the most vivid interpretations of this psalm is in the *Utrecht Psalter* (fol. 43r), which depicts the earth on its columns, fast dissolving (verse 3) whilst on a solid part the wicked are trampling on the just. In the heavens is a haloed Christ, with his angels, pouring out wine from one cup to another (verse 8). In the top right the psalmist, with a group of 'the just', holds a stag's head, and with a rod is attacking the antlers of another stag held by the wicked ('all the horns of the wicked are cut off': verse 10).[56]

By contrast, the illuminated initial C to verse 1 in the *St Albans Psalter* (*Confitebimur tibi Deus*) depicts the psalmist rejoicing in the fate of the just, whilst God looks down from heaven with three of the faithful who have been saved: this hints at verse 7, 'putting down one and lifting up another.'[57]

A final image is from Moshe *Berger. The image has a deep blue background on three sides, with a turquoise semi-circular wreath-shape set against it; a

[54] See http://www.cgmusic.org/workshop/newver/psalm_75.htm.

[55] Gillingham 2008: 161–62.

[56] See https://psalter.library.uu.nl/page/93.

[57] See https://www.albani-psalter.de/stalbanspsalter/english/commentary/page218.shtml.

bright white light emerges from the fourth side and in the centre is an emblem, in purple and red, of David. Berger comments that David still praises God's faithfulness, for even when he sent the seed of Jacob into exile, he remained Israel's God and protector.[58]

So the psalm as a whole is an example of the very different, irreconcilable interpretations given by Jewish and Christian interpreters, although each speak about God's judgement on their enemies.

Psalm 76: God's Abode is in Zion (ii)

Psalm 76 has some correspondences with Psalms 46 and 48.[59] Its mood is more positive: here the God of Zion can redeem his people. However, the more prophetic elements in Psalm 76, and its references to the terror of God's judgement, make it closer to the more negative tenor of Psalm 75. If one reads 'Salem' in verse 2 as a reference to a northern sanctuary, then verses 1–3 of the psalm might pertain to the Assyrian crisis; these verses would then have been 'received' in the South sometime after Sennacherib's siege of the city in 701. This is certainly the way this was understood in the *Septuagint: an addition to the title reads 'A Song against [in view of] Assyria', whilst verses 1–3, the most likely verses from this period, are presented in the past tense. Later Jewish tradition tended to read the psalm as influenced by the Assyrian crisis.

This is a difficult psalm to organise into strophes. Verses 1–3 might be seen as one unit; verses 4–6 suggest another, perhaps from an ancient hymn; verses 7–9 suggest another, marked at the end by *selah;* and verses 10–12 could be another, later, addition. So this is another composite psalm also with several problems in translation.[60]

Much of the psalm's reception history relates to the violent imagery in the psalm. *Targum* tries to temper the harsh tone by adding to verse 4 (Eng. v. 3) that God's *Shekinah* dwelt with his people when they did his will, and the reading of verse 11 (Eng. v. 10) is 'When you are angry with your people, you will have compassion on them, and they shall praise your name; and you will gird yourself with the residue that remains to you of the heat of your anger with which you raged, to destroy the nations'.[61] *Kimḥi reads the psalm as about the last battle against Gog and Magog, bringing in the end of the exile and establishing God's

---

[58] See http://themuseumofpsalms.com/product/psalm-75/.

[59] See the discussions on Pss. 46 and 48 in Gillingham 2018: 276–84 and 288–92.

[60] See Tate 1990: 262–63 which focusses especially on verses 4 and verse 11.

[61] See Stec 2004: 148–49.

world rule. The eleventh-century *Talmudic scholar, Hai Gaon, is more specific: this war would be waged during the month of Tishri, at the time of Tabernacles and hence the psalm is to be the 'Song for the Day', that day, according to the Talmudic tractate *Sopherim* (19:2), being the first of *Sukkot.[62] Because of the addition of 'Assyria' to the title in Greek, as well as the reference to the deposition of the nations in verse 13 (Eng. v. 12), Hezekiah is discussed as a potential Messiah; however, being too proud in his own might, and refusing to sing songs, the honour was returned to David.[63] The shared concern in all these writings is with the eventual release of the Jews from exile and the coming of God's kingdom.

A Christian reading again moves in a different direction. *Ambrose is amongst the first to read the psalm as about the epiphany of God through Christ, causing the earth to tremble. By interpreting 'Zion' in verse 2 as the Christian church, a Christian narrative is possible which begins with Christ's 'dwelling place' in Zion: this begins in the tomb of Joseph of Arimathea (verse 2), and ends with the earthquake announcing his resurrection (verses 8–9).[64] So a *Gloria* to this psalm runs 'Glory be to the Father, known in carnal Jewry; glory be to the Son, known in spiritual Jewry.'[65] *Cassiodorus connects the 'terror of judgement' in verses 8–9 with the saving 'all the oppressed of the earth': this is exemplified in Jesus Christ, who when he judges the earth will save the meek.[66] These readings explain the use of the psalm as an offertory for Easter Sunday, as seen in the *Terra tremuit et quievit* settings of verses 8–9. *Handel took up this celebratory theme in his use of verse 6 (alongside Ps 89) in the seventh of his *Chandos Hymns* (1718–19), 'Why so full of grief, O my soul?' which finishes with a joyful chorus celebrating God's saving justice.[67]

The celebration of the faithful over the wicked is vividly portrayed in the *Eadwine Psalter* (fol. 132r) in its reinterpretation of the *Utrecht Psalter* in colour. The *Christ-Logos sits on a globe in the heavens, surrounded by six angels, and just below it is a fortification which appears to be the tabernacle (verse 2) where the righteous are praising God (verse 11); also taken from this verse is a man outside the walls, with his hand to his mouth, making his vow. The Christ-figure is also in the middle of the scene, subduing the wicked (verse 3). Below him three men on horseback appear to be in some sort of stupor (verses 5–6). This is an allegory of Christ's defence of the church.[68]

---

[62] Feuer 2004: 947–48.

[63] See Feuer 2004: 948, referring also to *Midrash on Song* 4:19.

[64] Neale and Littledale: 2/517.

[65] See Neale and Littledale 1874–79: 2/526.

[66] *Expositions on the Psalms* 75:9–10; ACW 52:235–6; in ACCS VIII:122–23.

[67] Dowling Long and Sawyer 2015: 44.

[68] See https://bit.ly/3rUKjuV.

Jewish art occasionally represents the celebratory tone of the psalm: this focusses on God's defence of his people in Zion. The *Parma Psalter* (fol. 105A) has an image of a human figure with an eagle's head, playing a stringed instrument. Four other instruments, most unusually, are also represented in the spaces above the psalm and below the initial word. Together they illustrate part of the heading of the psalm in Hebrew: 'with stringed instruments'.[69]

A different mood of majesty and serenity is captured by Mary *Sidney, who chose a hexameter metre to suggest a royal and heroic theme; the lack of structure in the Hebrew is now turned into five stanzas of a-b-a-b-c-c. The last stanza, based on verses 10–12, reads:[70]

> Then let your vows be paid, your off'rings offerèd
> Unto the Lord, O you of his protection:
> Unto the fearful let your gifts be profferèd
> Who loppeth princes' thoughts, prunes their affection.
> And so himself most terrible doth verify,
> In terrifying kings, the earth doth terrify.

John Endicott was a fierce Puritan who sailed to the New World in 1628 and co-founded the New English Company in Massachusetts. In 1629 the Indian name of that first English settlement was changed from Naumkeag to 'Salem'. Tradition has it that this was an intentional allusion to 'Salem' in Ps. 76:2 ('His abode has been established in Salem'): this was the New Jerusalem, in line with Puritan political theology.

Christian reception succeeded in reading positively all four psalms of this *Asaphite collection; but this is the first psalm in the collection which Jewish reception also viewed in a more optimistic way. So even though this psalm has been interpreted very differently throughout Jewish and Christian tradition, both concur that God will have victory over the forces of evil.

Psalm 77: An Individual Lament about Ongoing Exile

Psalm 77 again suggests earlier northern elements: verse 15, with the reference to Jacob and Joseph, is the best example. However, the final cause for the lament is more likely to be the Babylonian exile rather than the Assyrian crisis: its use of cosmic and mythological traditions to describe the crossing of the Sea has correspondences with Psalm 74.[71] Like the two previous psalms, there are a few

---

[69] See Metzger 1996: 84.
[70] Hamlin *et al.* 2009: 144–45.
[71] See pp. 9–10; also Prothero 1903: 230 and Kselman 1983: 51–8.

complexities of translation: for example, *ketib/qere'* occurs three times, and the tenses and moods of the verbs are hard to follow. Two long strophes might be suggested: a lament in verse 1–12, with the theme of 'remembering' in verses 3, 6 and 11; and a hymn anticipating God's victory in verses 13–20, which moves from the world of myth to a Jewish view of their history.

The *Septuagint translates verse 1 (and indeed most of verses 1–6) in the past tense, thus, like Ps. 76:1–3, making it clear that this is a prayer from the past which the psalmist is now reconsidering. Jewish reception again emphasises the long sojourn of exile up to the present time, thus linking together all the psalms in this first collection of Book Three. *Rashi, for example, interprets the reference to 'night' in verse 2 (Heb. v. 3) as an allusion to the exile, as in Ps. 74:16.[72] Much is made of verses 18–21 (Eng. vv. 17–20) at the end of the psalm, reading this as an incitement to the people to purify themselves (as did Moses and Aaron) if God is to perform the same wonders again.[73]

The Christian response in both the eastern and western traditions is more positive, focussing on the hymn rather than the lament. *Eusebius, for example, reads 'When the waters saw you… they were afraid' in verse 16 as a reference to Jesus' baptism.[74] *Ambrose uses the same verse to argue that 'turning back' of the waters is an allegory for the church, which, gathered together like the waters, has to learn how to fear and obey.[75] A similar interpretation is found in *Ephrem the Syrian's commentary, who sees verse 16 as fulfilled in Mark 14:25 and 32, where both the waters and the disciples testify to the Deity of Christ.[76] *Thomasius, again citing *Aquinas, follows *Augustine in taking a broader reading of the hymn and its prologue: both verses 11–12 and the hymn itself (verses 13–20) are the voice of Christ to the Father, who alone works great miracles.[77] Verses 18–19 are read as the 'chariot of Christ', making its way through the chaotic seas.[78]

There is, however, one interesting example of the use of this lament in literature. The focus of the lament is a reproach to God for preventing the psalmist sleeping (verses 2, 4) because of the lack of answered prayer (7–10). A re-reading of this complaint is offered by Shakespeare in his Sonnet 61, which is not so much a prayer to God as the poet's jealous reflections about his friend's love which he fears is not as strong as his love is for him. So the initial lines address

[72] Gruber 2004: 514.
[73] Feuer 2004: 955.
[74] See *Commentary on the Psalms*, in *PG* 23 1857:896.
[75] *Six Days of Creation* 3.1.2 in *CF* 42:67–68. See *ACCS* VIII:128.
[76] *Commentary on Tatian's Diatessaron* 12.9 in *ECTD* 194. See *ACCS* VIII:129.
[77] Neale and Littledale 1874–79: 2/527.
[78] Neale and Littledale 1874–79: 2/539.

the friend (referred to later as 'my love'), not God, but use the language of Ps. 77:1–10:[79]

> Is it thy will thy image should keep open
> My heavy eyelids to the weary night?
> Dost thou desire my slumbers should be broken,
> While shadows like to thee do mock my sight?

Shakespeare's attribution of the lack of sleep to his friend's absent love, rather than to the absence of God, was in part influenced by the annotations made to this psalm in the *Genevan Psalter*, which also places the blame on the psalmist's distress more than on any failure by God.[80]

> Is it thy spirit that thou send'st from thee
> So far from home into my deeds to pry,
> To find out shames and idle hours in me,
> The scope and tenure of thy jealousy?
> O no, thy love, though much, is not so great:
> It is my love that keeps mine eyes awake,
> Mine own true love that doth my rest defeat,
> To play the watchman ever for thy sake.
> > For thee watch I, whilst thou dost wake elsewhere,
> > From me far off, with others all too near.

This is perhaps the most radical re-working of the psalm in its reception history. Although there are specific allusions to this psalm in Christian art and music, they usually focus on the hymn rather the lament. One of the few musical examples is Henry *Purcell's 'Thy Way, O God, is Holy', based on verses 13–18, which is sung by alto and bass against a short *SATB chorus of hallelujahs.

More positive (and Christianised) representations are found in Byzantine psalters. For example, the *Khludov Psalter (fol. 75v) and the *Bristol Psalter (fol. 124v) depict Christ, cross-*nimbed, before the personification of two rivers (illustrating verses 16–20): this is not the parting of the Red Sea, but rather Christ's baptism in the river Jordan, as seen in the hand of God and the dove of the Spirit descending from heaven. The *Theodore Psalter has a similar theme: Christ's baptism is represented on the first folio next to the hymn, and

---

[79] See http://www.shakespeares-sonnets.com/sonnet/61.
[80] See Groves 2007: 120–21.

the second folio is of a full frontispiece, illustrating verses 19–20, with Christ enthroned between the rivers, with sheep, and Moses and Aaron.[81] A similar but contemporary reading, also echoing that of Ephrem above, is found in Roger *Wagner's woodcut accompanying these verse of the psalm: he illustrates verses 18–20 with Christ as a lone figure walking on the crest of a wave, against a dark sky filled with lightening forks; the terrified disciples in their pitching boat form the foreground (Figure 1).[82]

The difference between Christian and Jewish readings is exemplified in Marc *Chagall's hand etching of verses 19–21 (Eng. vv. 18–20) which is about the experience of Israel not the Church: the interpretive text is Exodus 15 not the Gospel of Mark. The seas are represented, and the pathway through the sea suggests a drowning figure, but the tambourine of Miriam (Exod. 15:20–21) in the foreground intimates that this is, ultimately, a hopeful victory song.[83] This compares with *Berger's equally positive depiction of verse 16 of the psalm: Hebrew letters emerge and unfold from the changing colours of deep red, yellow and white. Of this image Berger writes: 'My heart meditates and my spirit searches

Your path		בַּיָּם
Is in the sea		דַּרְכֶּךָ
Your road		וּשְׁבִילְךָ
Is in		בְּמַיִם
The great waters		רַבִּים
Your footsteps		וְעִקְּבוֹתֶיךָ
Are unknown		לֹא נֹדָעוּ׃

You guided your people
Like a flock
By the hand of
Moses and Aaron

FIGURE 1 *Jesus Walking on the Water in a Storm.*
Source: Wagner, R. 2020. *The Book of Praises. Translations from the Psalms.* Norwich: Canterbury Press.

[81] See http://www.bl.uk/manuscripts/Viewer.aspx?ref=add_ms_19352_f099r; also http://www.bl.uk/manuscripts/Viewer.aspx?ref=add_ms_19352_f099v.
[82] Wagner 2020 (no page numbers). Reprinted here with the artist's permission.
[83] See https://bit.ly/3mzXhNO.

the ancient days of history for a solution to the problem of exile. For, since the fall of Adam, all nations are in exile. Only concerning the Jews is exile evident. But, says David, I find comfort in the study of God's past wonders.'[84]

Hence although the interpretations of the psalm are again vastly different, both Jewish and Christian reception usually agree that the psalm can be read with hope, but do so by focussing mainly on the hymnic elements at the end of it.

[84] See http://www.biblical-art.com/artwork.asp?id_artwork=15206&showmode=Full.

Psalms 78–83: 'Will You be Angry Forever?'

Psalms 78 and 79–83 together form the second *Asaphite sub-group, and like Psalms 73–77 they suggest a similar structure and a number of internal correspondences. As for structure, Psalm 78 is a psalm of instruction, like 73; 79–80 are both laments concerning the destruction of Jerusalem, like 74; 81–82 ask questions about injustice and the permanency of God's abode in Zion, like 75–76; and 83 is an individual lament, like 77. So this repetitive arrangement uses the two themes of the judgement of God and yet confidence in God's presence in Zion—themes which were prevalent in the eighth and seventh-century prophets. Even the first and last psalms of the entire twelve-psalm Asaphite collection echo it as well (see 50:2–3 and 83:17–18, where 'God Most High' is a familiar name for God in relation to Jerusalem).[85] Furthermore, Psalm 78, with its overall theme of the memory of God appealing to the memory of the people, plays a critical part at the heart of the Asaphite psalms, just as Psalm 89, with its similar theme of divine and human remembering and forgetting, plays a critical part at the conclusion to the *Korahite collection. So in this intricately formed collection, the first stage of reception, namely the placing of certain psalms within a particular group of psalms, is clearly evident.

Each psalm in this latter collection is also linked to its neighbour by specific themes and vocabulary. Examples include the shepherding imagery at the end of Psalm 77 and the end of Psalm 78; the concern with David and the Temple at the end of Psalm 78 and the beginning of Psalm 79; the shepherding image, again, at the end of Psalm 79 and the beginning of Psalm 80, with the plaintive cry in each, 'Why?' (79:10 and 80:13); the Israel/Joseph references in 81:5,6 echoing

---

[85] See Gillingham 2005: 324–26.

Psalms Through the Centuries: A Reception History Commentary on Psalms 73–151, Volume Three,
First Edition. Susan Gillingham.
© 2022 John Wiley & Sons Ltd. Published 2022 by John Wiley & Sons Ltd.

80:2; and the shared concern about gods and mortals in Psalms 82:6 and 83:19 which is also a challenge as to who is the 'true god', where in 82:6 the deities fall down as dead and in 83:10–11 the nations fall down, defeated. Yet again, this first stage of reception through compilation does not seem to be accidental.

Psalm 78: A Didactic Psalm about God's Judgement on His People

It would also appear that Psalm 78 has been intentionally placed next to Psalm 77. Just as Psalm 77 ended with Moses and Aaron leading the people 'like a flock' (verse 29), Psalm 78 ends with David as the shepherd of his people (verse 71). Psalm 77:1 begins by asking God to hear; 78:1 asks by asking the people to do so. And just as Ps. 77:5 and 11 (Hebrew verses 6 and 12) reflect on God's mighty deeds 'of old' (*mi-qedem*) so in 78:2 the psalmist will speak of them too (also using *qedem*). The story in Psalm 78:11 is about the same mighty 'acts' (*pele'*) as God's 'work' as in 77:12, using the same Hebrew word with a different ending (*pile'eka*). Similarly we read again of the mighty waters (77:16, 19; 78:13, 16, 20), of God's 'redeeming' his people (77:15 and 78:35) who are addressed again as Jacob (78:5, 21, 31, 71 and 77:15), and who in Ps. 78:52 are led 'like a flock' (*ka'eder*), as in 77:20 (*ca-ṣo'n*).

Despite these connections, Psalm 78 is clearly different: it is not a lament, nor even an epic poem; it is closer to the speeches of Moses in Deuteronomy, except it is expressed more obviously in poetry, and the key focus of its seven strophes (ending at verses 9, 17, 32, 40, 56, 65) is the importance of 'remembering' and learning lessons from the past (verses 8, 39). Pavan argues that Psalm 78 is the only *Asaphite psalm with a consistent focus on 'remembering' and this explains its central position not only within the eleven psalms forming the Asaphite collection, but also within Book Three as a whole.[86] The order of 'remembering' is not chronological: it starts with the arrival in Canaan (verses 9–39), then returns to the plagues (verses 42–51: here only seven, rather than ten), then moves forward to the wilderness wanderings (verses 52–55) and finishes with the time of the judges (verses 56–66). Unlike any of the previous psalms in Book Three, it is interested in David (verses 67–72). From this psalm onwards Book Three moves towards an increasing concern for David and Zion.

Jewish reception tends to view the psalm in its entirety, whilst Christian reception prefers to isolate separate verses. As with most of the Asaphite psalms,

---

[86] Pavan 2014: 337.

Jewish reception is more reflective and pessimistic. The whole psalm is seen as a 'parable'—as a story about the Law.[87] The theme of exile is assumed and this is read in the light of the giving of the laws, and Israel's failure to keep them, although the ending proclaims positively that only David and his seed are the true Torah rulers of Israel.[88] Some Jewish commentators note some positive elements in the psalm: the men of the wilderness, despite their transgressions, are still seen as 'giants of faith', and the miracles testify to the Merciful God, who, even without evening sacrifice (verse 38) can still forgive iniquity.[89]

Christian readings tend to view the psalm in the light of the Jews' rejection of Christ, although the church is exhorted to learn from these lessons as well.[90] For example, in the New Testament, 1 Cor. 10:8 uses the historical reflections in the psalm (using here verse 18) to exhort the early Christians to repentance. 1 *Clement 15 also uses Psalm 78 (amongst its several citations) about the church's need 'to be joined to those who are 'peaceful, and not to those who pretend to wish for it'; *Justin Martyr makes the same appeal in his *Dial.* 27.4; 48.2; 80.4; and 140.2. The psalm is thus used in part as practical instruction and in part as allegory. The citation of verses 24–25 in the 'bread discourse' in John 6:31—partly using the same Exodus typology—encouraged commentators such as *Augustine to comment: 'Let us turn back to the one who performed these miracles. He himself is the bread that came down from heaven… for people to eat the bread of angels, the Lord of angels became a human being… if he had not become this, we would not have his flesh…'[91]

But above all, it is the reference to the didactic and even parabolic nature of the psalm in verses 1–2 (heightened by the Greek translation of the Hebrew word *mashal* in verse 2 as *parabolais*) which gave Christians the license to allegorise. (This has been the case with all of Psalms 73–77; it is simply made more explicit here.) Matt. 13:35 cites Ps. 78:2 to illustrate the theory of parables; from this, the early fathers also had much to say on these two verses. *Clement of Alexandria, for example, uses these verses as key texts in *Miscellanies* 5.25.1 where the references to 'parable' and 'dark sayings of old' are seen as a witness to Jesus, the eternal word, the Logos, who is eternally present in the psalms and able to unlock for us enigmatic truths.[92] (This is a different but related view of the expanded heading to the psalm provided in the *Targum*: 'The insight of the Holy Spirit, by the hands of Asaph'.) *Eusebius reads the psalm in a

---

[87] *Rashi in Feuer 2004: 968.

[88] See Hirsch in Feuer 2004: 967.

[89] Feuer 2004: 968.

[90] For example, *Luther's *First Lectures* 2:44 (cited in Goldingay 2007: 516).

[91] Sermon 130:2, *WSA* 4:311, in *ACCS* VIII:133.

[92] Carleton Paget 1996: 491; also Gillingham 2008: 28.

similar *prosopological way as Augustine: the psalmist begins by speaking in the name of Christ; and Christ ends it by speaking in the name of the Church. So Ps. 78:1–2 is 'the voice of the prophet' (i.e. Asaph) through whom Christ is speaking. In all these readings the 'hidden things' in the psalm are brought to light through the person of Christ. The dividing of the sea in verse 14 is now a reference to the bringing of 'spiritual Israel' (the church) through the waters of baptism; the cloud in verse 14 speaks of the incarnation of Christ, and the fire, to that latter day of judgement; the smitten rock in verse 16 is Jesus Christ crucified, out of whose side flowed living water. The manna in verses 24–25 speaks of Christ descending from heaven to give us the food of angels; the water turned to blood in verse 44 is a reference to the new covenant; and the 'enemy's hand' in verse 61 refers to Judas and Pilate.[93] In some cases this led commentators such as *Luther to accuse the Jews of trusting too much in the 'temporality' of their Law (using Ps. 78:5, 'He has established a decree in Jacob…') rather than seeing the eternal covenant made manifest in Christ.[94]

Nevertheless the use of this psalm for penitential worship, in both faiths, is clear. In Jewish tradition, in the weekday evening service according to the rite of the ninth-century Babylonian liturgist Amram Gaon, verse 38 is used after Ps. 22:10 and the *Kaddish, to be followed again by Ps. 20:10. Preceded by Psalm 134, this develops the theme of repentance and the mercy of God.[95] The psalm as a whole is read in Christian tradition as an exhortation for repentance, and is part of the *Commination service, concerned with the judgement of God, in the *BCP.

Perhaps the most intriguing reading is of verse 69, which in the NRSV reads: 'He built his sanctuary like the high heavens'. The Hebrew for 'high heavens' (*ramim*) is unclear; the noun, here in the plural, could come from the word for ox, and indeed the *Targum* paraphrases this verse 'And he built his sanctuary like the horn of a wild ox, established like the earth, which he set in order for ever and ever'. The *Septuagint prefers to read 'like wild oxen' as 'like unicorns' (*hōs monokerōtōn*, i.e. mythical creatures 'with one horn'), as indicating an invincible animal which was nevertheless under God's power. This was perpetuated through the Latin translation ('*et aedificavit sicut* unicornium *sanctificium suum*'), and although this was a strange comparison, it encouraged a distinctively Christian reading. The 'sanctuary' was the Virgin Mary; the unicorn was Christ, who 'took sanctuary' in her womb.[96] So in these verses at

---

[93] See Neale and Littledale 1874–79: 2/542–53. See also Howell 1987: 192.

[94] See Preuss 1969: 204–5, citing the *Dictata*. This could not be more different from the image to Psalm 78 in the *Parma Psalter* (fol. 107v), to be discussed shortly.

[95] See Elbogen 1993: 85–86.

[96] See comments on the translation 'unicorn' in Psalm 22; Gillingham 2018: 137–38.

the end of Psalm 78, which speak of God's choice of David, it is Christ, the son of David, the 'unicorn' from the sanctuary of Mary, who is really being spoken of—all highlighting the parabolic nature of this psalm.

Allegorical exegesis provided a rich tradition of visual exegesis in illuminated manuscripts, and again centred on individual verses rather than on the psalm as a whole. For example, the *Theodore Psalter* (fol. 100r), alongside verse 1, shows Asaph on a throne, teaching, but the figure of a beardless Christ stands behind, offering inspiration; in the *Bristol Psalter* (fol. 125v) and *Barberini Psalter* (fol. 103r) it is Christ himself who is teaching. *Carolingian Psalters are the first to develop the motif of the unicorn. The *Stuttgart Psalter* (fol. 108v) depicts an image of a unicorn at the end of the psalm: a hand from heaven points down to the animal, and David is blessing it: this is represented in PLATE 2.

A different image is in the *Utrecht Psalter* (fol. 45r) where the hand of God points down to a figure (possibly Moses) reading from the law to a crowd of people. Behind him (and three other figures) is a youthful David, crowned, with sheep at his feet; and behind David is a unicorn.[97]

The Byzantine *Pantokrator Psalter* (fol. 109v) also ends the psalm with a motif inspired by the Latin translation of 'unicorn', where here the Virgin is actually suckling the animal. The psalm is actually given a Christian focus from beginning to end. At the beginning in *Pantokrator* it is Christ, not Moses, who is preaching to the Jews about their disobedience (fol. 102v), and verses 24–25 (on the manna from heaven) depict Christ addressing the Jews (fol. 105r), with an inscription from John 6.[98] Verse 65 ('Then the Lord awoke as from sleep') has an image in both *Pantokrator* (fol. 109r) and *Khludov* (fol. 78v) of Christ outside the tomb; *Khludov* adds an image of David facing Christ as if he is prophesying his resurrection.[99] *Khludov* (fol. 79r) has other interesting illustrations for verses 67–70: of a church on a high mountain, inscribed with 'Holy Sion' with the Virgin and Child in a courtyard below;[100] at the foot of the mountain is inscribed 'David anointed by Samuel', as if the motif of Christ coming from Zion has been prophesied by David himself (using Rom. 11:26 as an interpretative text).[101] The fourteenth-century Byzantine *Kiev Psalter*, by contrast, has David, at the foot of the mountain, pointing towards the summit at the shining icon of Mary and Jesus.[102]

---

[97] http://psalter.library.uu.nl/page?p=96&res=1&x=0&y=0.
[98] See Corrigan 1992: figs. 59 and 32 respectively. The *Khludov Psalter* (fol. 76v) has a similar image; see fig. 62 in Corrigan 1992.
[99] See Corrigan 1992: fig. 66.
[100] See Corrigan 1992: fig. 70.
[101] See Corrigan 1992: 52 on Christ from Zion as part of the *Adversus Judaeos* literature.
[102] Gillingham 2008: 101.

The Jewish *Parma Psalter* (fol. 107v) by contrast emphasises the didactic nature of this psalm, and the possibility of the obedience of the Jews in learning from the past: a figure in a light red garment raises an open book in his right hand and extends his left to an assembly of eight figures; they look intently at the book which has the first two words of the ten commandments, illustrating verses 1 and 5 and the Jewish message of the psalm overall.[103]

Because of its rich interpretation, despite its salutary and serious contents, and on account of its long narrative form, Psalm 78 became a challenging psalm for experimentation in English in the sixteenth-century. Mary *Sidney, for example, casts this in *ottava rima*: a form of Italian origin, connected with heroic poetry, with eight-line stanzas using ten or eleven syllables, rhyming *a-b-a-b-a-b-c-c*; this was the form the Elizabethan poet Michael Drayton used in *The Barons' Warres* on account of its 'majesty, perfection and solidity'.[104] Sidney's account of verse 1–3 (a short example of the twenty-seven stanzas in all) runs as follows:[105]

> A grave discourse to utter I intend
> The age of time I purpose to renew
> You, O my charge, to what I teach attend;
> Hear what I speak, and what you hear ensue.
> The things our fathers did to us commend,
> The same are they I recommend to you,
> Which though but heard we know most true to be:
> We heard, but heard, of who themselves did see…

This psalm has inspired surprisingly little Church music, most of which uses the beginning of the psalm rather than the end. For example, both Giovanni *Gabrieli and Heinrich *Schütz composed pieces, with a Latin setting, nearly half a century after Mary Sidney, of the first three verses of this psalm. Gabrieli's 'Attendite popule meus' was performed at St. Mark's, Venice; Schütz's 'Attendite popule meus legem', was probably performed in his church in Dresden. Whether the speaker is assumed to be Christ or Moses is not made explicit. *Handel's arrangement is different because, using Charles Jennens' libretto, it is for the concert hall rather than the church. His 'Israel in Egypt' was performed in 1739, and the texts are Psalms 105, 106 and 78 rather than anything from Exodus. Psalm 78:12–13 is used in Part I, as part of the 'Plagues in Egypt', thus

---

[103] See Metzger 1996: 84.
[104] See Rathmell 1963: xviii.
[105] This translation is from; Hamlin *et al.* 2009: 148.

illustrating that the message of the psalm is essentially about the importance of remembering God's mercy for his people.[106]

The theme of God's overall mercy is also brought out in Arthur *Wragg's more contemporary stark black and white image of Ps. 78:38: 'But he, being full of compassion, forgave their iniquity and destroyed them not' (Figure 2). Wragg, greatly influenced by the Great Depression, sketched the psalms with graphic social comment. Here we see the horrors of the suffering of humanity, and violent deaths throughout time. Yet memory prevails: to the right and left of these interwoven images are two palms: each bears the stigmata.[107]

The reception of this psalm testifies in both faith traditions to the importance of remembering, followed by penitence and trust in God's mercy, with each tradition recognising the 'parabolic' nature of the psalm. Christian readings, through verbal and visual exegesis, have been more allusive, whilst nevertheless emphasising the motif of human failure in this psalm.

FIGURE 2   *'But he, being full of compassion, forgave their iniquity and destroyed them not'*. (Ps. 78:38).

Source: Wragg, A. 1934: *The Psalms for Modern Life*. New York: Claude Kendall.

---

[106] See Stern 2011: 93.

[107] Wragg 1934: no page numbers.

Psalm 79: A Communal Lament about Ongoing Exile (i)

Psalm 79 marks an abrupt contrast with Psalm 78, in that whereas 78 ends with the hope that God has chosen David and Zion, this psalm begins with the Temple and city having been destroyed. But the placing of these two psalms is not accidental. The references to the gift of food in 78:24–29 now contrast with the people being like food to be consumed by their enemies (79:2). The blood-like rivers in 78:44 are now a reminder of the spilt blood of God's people (79:3). From having been fed exceedingly (*me'od*) well in the desert (78:29) the people are now brought exceedingly (*me'od*) low (79:8). Even if these correspondences are coincidences, the general contrast is deliberate: the great miracles described in Psalm 78 are now replaced with groans from the people and taunts from the enemies (79:11–12). And yet the psalm ends, as in Psalms 78 and 77, with knowing that the people are still God's flock (78:71 and 79:13).

Psalm 79 continues this second group of *Asaphite psalms (78–83), with the military and nationalist details and the same spirit of questioning having resonances with the first group (73–77). It is possible to discern three strophes in the lament form of Psalm 79: verses 1–4 describe the oppression by enemy nations; verses 5–9 question God in prayer, using the familiar phrase 'How Long?'; and verses 10–13, addressing God with imperative pleas, imagine the overturning of the nations. Thus there is some movement in the psalm towards hope for a change of fortune. One of the problems is that the psalm has a large store of formulaic language, so that, for example, in trying to account for the obvious correspondences between verse 4 and 44:14, between verse 5 and 89:46, and between verse 11 and Ps. 102:20, it is difficult to know which text has used the other, or indeed if each is from a common liturgical and formulaic source.

One clear example of later reception history is the use of verses 2–3 in 1 Macc. 7:16–17, which describes the treacherous slaughter of Jewish scribes by the Seleucid governor, Bacchides: the writer sees this as 'in accordance with the word which was written…' and then cites a paraphrase of 79:2–3. This is the image against verse 2 in the *Bristol Psalter* (fol. 132v) which depicts Antiochus IV, crowned and seated, whilst the Maccabean faithful are being cast to the beasts. A similar image is found in the *Theodore Psalter* (fol. 106v).[108] Similarly at *Qumran, 4QTanh 1 lines 3–4, Ps. 79:1–3 is cited, suggesting its relevance to the fate of a sectarian non-Temple community as well.[109] Baruch 3 and 4 also alludes to verses 1–3 and 8–13, applying the psalm to a later crisis of the people,

---

[108] See Schnocks 2012: 155. For the image in the *Theodore Psalter* see http://www.bl.uk/manuscripts/Viewer.aspx?ref=add_ms_19352_f106v.

[109] Flint 1997: 220.

probably under Antiochus V Eupator.[110] The painful memory expressed in the psalm is used to relate to the continual experience of exile throughout Jewish history: this is brought out by *Kimḥi, who stresses the use of the word 'forever' in verse 5. Asking questions as to why such a horrific description of distress could possibly merit the title 'song', or '*mizmor*', Kimḥi answers that only the Temple was destroyed, not the people as a whole.[111]

Not surprisingly the Jewish liturgical use of this psalm places it with 137 and both are used at the end of the day on the 9th of *Av*, to commemorate the destruction of the first and second temples (*Sop.* 18:3); they are recited at the Wailing Wall on the 9th of *Av* to the present day.

Christian reception also emphasises the lament mood of the psalm, as it did for Psalm 74, to express horror at injustice during times of persecution. This was actually a psalm much loved by *Augustine, as he had been considering verse 8 ('Do not remember the iniquities of our ancestors…') just before be heard the mystical voice 'Take up and read' which precipitated his conversion a year later, as in *Confessions* 8.12. Augustine interpreted verses 1–4 in the light of Matt. 10:28: 'Do not fear those who kill the body but cannot kill the soul'. When writing at the time of the sack of Rome in 410 CE, Augustine makes direct reference to the psalm: unburied bodies will still be redeemed by God.[112] *Jerome also referred to this psalm in his Homilies, using verse 1 to refer to the same attack on Rome (*Letter* 127.12).[113] By contrast, *Bede and *Aquinas focus more generally on the burden of sin and the expressions of human suffering found in the psalm, affirming that it is Christ who will nevertheless avenge the blood of Christian martyrs.[114] An unusual Christian reading is found in Bede's *Abbreviated Psalter*, probably influenced by Jerome's reading of verse 9 ('Help us, O God of our salvation…'). Bede interpreted the word 'salvation' as explicitly referring to Jesus, so he translates verses 8–9 explicitly as: 'Help *us O God our Jesus*, on account of the glory of your name'.[115]

Christian sufferers have clearly embraced this psalm. Pope Innocent III (1161–1216) had verse 1 inserted into the Eucharistic liturgy to describe the shame and horror felt by Christians when the 'Holy Land' was occupied by the Muslims. It was used (in the form of Clément *Marot's metrical version) by the persecuted *Huguenots in the sixteenth-century: when taken out to the scaffold in 1546 this was the psalm they chanted.[116] It also expressed the experiences of

[110] Steck 1994: 367–78.
[111] Feuer 2004: 1004.
[112] See *City of God* 1.12 in *CG* 21–22, from *ACCS* VIII:136.
[113] *Letter* 127.12, cited in Howell 1987: 192.
[114] Neale and Littledale 1874–79: 2/581.
[115] Bede in Browne 2002: 57.
[116] Prothero 1903: 191–92. Also Reid 1971: 46.

Roman Catholics in the seventeenth-century: for example, in 1608, when the Catholic mystic Luisa de Carvajal witnessed the execution of so many believers near London Bridge, she wrote 'We can hardly go out to walk without seeing the heads and limbs of our dear and holy ones stuck up on the gates that divide the streets, and the birds of the air perching on them; which makes me think of the verse in the Psalms "The dead bodies of thy servants have been given to be meat unto the fowls of the air" (Ps. 79:2)'.[117] More recently, verses 1–3 were used to describe the sufferings incurred by the Armenians during their holocaust under the Ottomans in 1915.[118]

Out of the experiences of religious persecution in sixteenth- and seventeenth-century England, *Byrd was motivated to write a motet based on Ps. 79:9, *Emendemus in Melius* ('Let us Amend for the Better') using a five voice setting, which was published in 1575. This became associated with *Matins in the Roman Rite either for the first Sunday in Lent, or Ash Wednesday: set in bipartite form, its focus was on both the sins of the people and the mercy of God.[119] *Purcell wrote a similar arrangement of verses 4, 7–8, and 13 ('O remember not our old sins'); so too did *Tallis, on verses 7–9 and 13, alongside Ps. 100:3 ('Remember not, O Lord God'). Samuel Sebastian *Wesley produced an arrangement from *Coverdale's version, using just verse 8, entitled 'Lord how long wilt thou be angry?'.

This joint Jewish and Christian experience is cleverly captured by the eighteenth-century poet Christopher *Smart, who moves between one tradition and the other and typifies the key theme in the psalm's reception.[120]

> From afar, O God, the nations
> > Thy possessions storm and weep,
> Churches now are desolations,
> > And Jerusalem an heap...
>
> Human blood, like wasted water,
> > Round about the wall is shed,
> And such universal slaughter
> > Leaves no burial for the dead.
>
> Us of God's own circumcision,
> > All our adversaries brand;
> Scorned we are, the trite derision
> > Even for outcasts of the land...

---

[117] Prothero 1903: 192–93.
[118] See Thomson 1997: 289–90, here citing the prayers of one of the Armenian martyrs, Elise.
[119] Dowling Long and Sawyer 2015: 76.
[120] Wieder 1995: 116–7.

Even more than Psalm 74, with which it is closely related, this is a psalm with universal significance through shared experiences of communal suffering.

Psalm 80: A Communal Lament about Ongoing Exile (ii)

Psalm 80 has an additional superscription in the Greek: 'for the Assyrian' links this psalm with Psalm 76, which has a similar title. Here the focus is more on exile than explicitly on Zion. Psalm 80 reveals other northern associations, with its specific references to the 'Shepherd of Israel, you who lead Joseph like a flock' in verse 1 and the references to Joseph, Manasseh and Ephraim in verse 2. The southern *and* northern elements suggest a complex period of early reception. Its threefold refrain (verses 3, 7, 19) and the division of the psalm into four parts (1–3, 4–7, 8–13, 14–19) give further evidence of this process: the refrain itself ('let thy face shine') would suggest a plea for restoration to the presence of God in the Temple, showing its ultimate southern provenance.

It seems clear that the editors intended Psalms 79 and 80 to be read alongside each other. The shepherding imagery at the end of 79 is taken up at the start of 80. The cry 'how long?' begins the second part of each psalm (79:5 and 80:4) and the question 'why?' (79:10 and 80:12) also lies at the heart of each. The request for God to 'return' (in each case, using the root of the verb *sh-w-b*) is used in 79:12 and 80:4, 8 and 15 (Eng. 3, 7 and 14). The last reference almost seems to ask *God* to repent—of his anger.

Verses 14–15, with their imagery of the destroyed vineyard, have been used in *2 Baruch 36–40* and also in one of the *Qumran scrolls (1QH[a], line xvi) to describe those communities' sense of a broken past.[121] The Jewish view of a continued and extended exile is thus applied to this psalm from an early period. *Targum* extends the threefold refrain 'Restore us, O God...' to 'God, return *us from our exile.*' The nineteenth-century psalms commentator Samson Raphael *Hirsch argues that the psalm refers to three exiles—Assyrian, Babylonian and Roman—and he sees them each alluded to in verses 2–4, 5–8 and 9–20 (Eng. vv. 1–4, 4–7 and 8–19). This is in part taken from *Rashi, who argues that the three parts of the psalm suggest Babylonian, Greek and Roman subjugation, with the 'Roman exile' as the ongoing present experience.[122] A contentious verse within this hope for restoration is verse 15 (Heb. v.16), which is difficult to translate. *Targum* expands the verse to read it with a Messianic emphasis: '...[have regard for this vine], and the shoot

---

[121] See Streett 2014: 163–70.
[122] Feuer 2004: 103. On Rashi, see Gruber 2004: 532.

that your right hand has planted, *and the anointed king who you strengthened for yourself.* This would suggest the final section is to be read as a prayer for the coming of the Messiah to end the exile: the use of this psalm on the second day of the Passover week offers some evidence of this. This view is strengthened when noting two other possible 'Messianic' references in verse 17 (Heb. v. 18) to, first, 'the man of our right hand' (also found in psalms which refer to the king, such as 18:35 and 20:6) and, second, to 'the son of man whom thou hast made strong for thyself'. So in Jewish tradition Psalm 80, like 79, is a psalm about exile which is given a messianic orientation.

Despite the more empathetic reception of Psalm 79, Christians have tended to interpret Psalm 80 from a more specifically Christian perspective, focussing again on one or two verses rather than the psalm as a whole. The shepherding and vineyard imagery (verses 1 and 8–13) are metaphors most open to allegory, using New Testament texts such as John 10:7–18 (on Jesus as the Good Shepherd) and 15:1–7 (on Jesus as the True Vine). *Augustine, for example, takes up the idea of the church being the new vineyard planted by Christ, and notes this fits with the title of the psalm in Greek, which he translates into Latin as 'for the things that shall be changed'.[123] Like *Targum*, *Jerome reads verse 17 ('… the one at your right hand, the one you made strong for yourself') as a reference to the Messiah; but here it is Jesus Christ.[124] A similar view is expressed by *Eusebius, who interprets 'Give ear, O Shepherd of Israel' as Christ, King of the Jews, leading Joseph, his Church.[125] So in the refrain in verse 7 the address to 'God of Hosts' implies Christ, in his resurrected power, and verses 8–11, on the vine, are about the eternal history of the church, emerging from darkness into light, spreading from the eastern to western sea (verse 11). Hence the references to the 'man of our right hand' and to the 'son of man', following Jerome, are to Christ, sitting at the right hand of God.[126] *Cassiodorus adds a comment on the three refrains: the triple repetition denotes the mystery of the Trinity, or the Mystery of the Birth, Passion and Advent; according to *Bede, this 'sums up all Christian prayer'.[127] *Thomasius, citing *Aquinas, combines this with another *motif* of Christian interest, namely the reference to God enthroned 'upon the cherubim' in verse 1, and reflects on how Christ, sitting on the cherubim, protects the vineyard which is the church.[128] A similar emphasis is found in

---

[123] See 'In Answer to the Jews' 6.7, in *FC* 27:399–40, from *ACCS* VIII: 141.
[124] See Shereshevsky 1971: 81.
[125] See Carleton Paget 1996: 536.
[126] See Neale and Littledale 1874–79: 2/606. It is interesting to see that more inclusive translations, including the NRSV, avoid this reading: 'But let your hand be upon *the one at your right hand, the one* whom you made strong for yourself.' (italics mine).
[127] See *ibid.*, 2/610.
[128] *Ibid.*, 2/592.

Isaac *Watts' version of this psalm; its melody, taken from the *Genevan Psalter*, was the same as an Easter *plainchant hymn, '*Victimae pascali laudes*'):

> …Lord, when This vine in Canaan grew,
> Thou wast its strength and glory too;
> Attacked in vain by all its foes,
> Till the fair Branch of Promise rose:
>
> Fair Branch, ordained of old to shoot
> From David's stock, from Jacob's root;
> Himself a noble vine, and we
> The lesser branches of the tree.
>
> 'Tis thy own Son; and he shall stand
> Girt with thy strength at thy right hand;
> Thy first-born Son, adorned and blest
> With power and grace above the rest.

A contemporary liturgical application of this reading is in the use of this psalm in 'Christingle' services (part of an Advent liturgy used in many churches, and designed for children, using oranges and candles to symbolise light overcoming the darkness in the world). Verse 1 is quoted within the prayers for children in danger, followed by the refrain 'O God, bring us home;/show us the light of your face/and we shall be safe'. This is followed by verse 17, with the same refrain, and verse 18, with the refrain again.[129]

John *Milton also composed an imitation of the psalm in his collection of Psalms 80–88 (1648), but for literary rather than liturgical purposes. It is paraphrased into one long stanza, and its theme is the relentless pursuit of justice, through reminding God of what he has done for his people in the past. Milton offers nothing specifically Christian until the penultimate verse of the psalm (the last in the following selected citation), which is probably the result of his use of Jerome's Latin version:[130]

> …A vine from Egypt thou has brought,
> Thy free love made it thine,
> And drovest out nations proud and haut
> To plant this lovely Vine.
>
> Thou didst prepare for it a place
> And root it deep and fast
> That it began to grow apace
> And fill'd the land at last…

[129] Pickett 2002: 60.
[130] See Wieder 1995: 117–19; also Baldwin 1919: 459–60.

> But now it is consum'd with fire
> And cut with Axes down,
> They perish at thy dreadful ire,
> At thy rebuke and frown.
>
> Upon the man of thy right hand
> Let thy good hand be laid,
> Upon the son of man, whom thou
> Strong for thyself has made...

Jewish composers who set this psalm to music evoked a longing for the end of exile. The best known is Salamone *Rossi's version of verses 4, 8 and 20 (English 3, 8 and 19) in Hebrew, entitled '*Elohim Hashivenu*' from the repeated refrain ('Restore us, O Lord'). This is an extraordinary piece, in three parts, based on the three refrains, with each part intensifying its plea for restoration by continuous use of bass and soprano parts, ending (as the highest hope) with the highest note throughout, top E.[131] A more recent example is A. Hovhanes' *Roeh Yisrael*: 'Give ear, O Shepherd of Israel, thou that leadest Joseph like a flock'.[132]

Another composition suggesting Jewish influence is Felix *Mendelssohn's '*Qui regis Israel*', which was composed in 1833 for the church in Dusseldorf as part of the liturgy of *Vespers: it is the third of a four-part choral setting called '*Adspice domine*' (from Ps. 119:132, with which the setting starts), sung by a male choir with cello and double bass. Its Trinitarian 'Gloria' gives it a Christian interpretation, but Mendelssohn typically followed the Jewish mood of the psalm, with its yearning for restoration.

Within art, a most symbolic illuminated initial Q to this psalm ('*Qui regis Israhel intende*) is found in the *St Albans Psalter.[133] In the upper medallion Christ is flanked by two turtle-doves, a reminder of the ancient Jewish offering for sins of omission and commission; Christ is pouring tears of repentance (see verse 5) into a small vessel held by a tonsured monk in the lower part of the medallion; the monk has a sparrow on his head, a symbol of penitence. The trees on each side of the monk symbolise both the vineyard (verses 8–11) and perhaps also a reminder of the expulsion from Eden. The beasts and the dragon attacking the monk depict the 'boar from the forest' in verse 13.

Two contemporary illustrations show how it is possible for different Jewish and Christian readings to inform each other in interpreting this psalm. Moshe *Berger's image is of a central figure set in red flames, crying, in Hebrew calligraphy, to the heavens which are depicted as azure strands of Hebrew letters; this is the king (suggesting here some messianic connotations) berating God

---

[131] Gillingham 2008: 166.

[132] Gorali 1993: 267.

[133] See https://www.abdn.ac.uk/stalbanspsalter/english/commentary/page233.shtml.

to take care of his creation, his city and his people.[134] The Northumbrian artist Michael *Jessing, meanwhile, brings an environmental reading into the psalm. Jessing centres on the motif of the vine, both as a gift of creation which has been taken away and as a symbol of longing of humanity to find again the creative and spiritual dimension of life, and return to God. The vine covers the page and the figures reach out to connect to it (Figure 3).[135]

FIGURE 3   *Michael Jessing, Ps. 80:8–9. The Vine with Human Figures.*
Source: http://www.psalms-mixastudio.com/psalms-69-84.php.

[134] See https://www.abdn.ac.uk/stalbanspsalter/english/commentary/page233.shtmlhttp:// themuseumofpsalms.com/product/psalm-80/ Contrasts with the very negative portrayal of Shechem in Gen. 34, again, post-Exilic focus.nifested in the odd sister-wife stor.
[135] See http://www.psalms-mixastudio.com/psalms-69-84.php.

Thus whether in commentary, poetry, liturgy or art, Psalm 80 serves each faith tradition as a psalm of suffering to be received in similar but nevertheless distinctive ways.

Psalm 81: God's Abode is in Zion (i)

Psalm 81 is one of the most obviously liturgical psalms in Book Three. Its movement is from praise (verses 1–5a) to admonition (verses 5b–16), the latter including two divine speeches (verses 6–10 and 11–16) where God speaks as if through a prophet, but in this case through the psalmist. This makes the overall genre of the psalm as hard to define as was Psalm 78. It has less of the accusatory tone of other *Asaphite psalms: in much of the psalm God speaks to Israel rather than Israel to God. Nevertheless, the editors seem to have included this alongside Psalm 80 with reason: each has strong ties to 'Joseph' (80:1–2; 81:5–6); each uses the Exodus traditions (80:9; 81:9–10); and each sees its authority as a 'warning' or 'testimony' ('*edut*)—in the title to Psalm 80 and in 81:5).[136]

The psalm has played a prominent part in Jewish liturgy, and much of the reason for this hinges around verses 2–3, which refer to the music (timbrel, sweet lyre, harp and trumpet) and the occasion ('the new moon. the full moon') of the act of worship. A common view is that this was for *Sukkot, the vintage festival also known as Tabernacles or Booths; the use of '*Gittit*' in the title, whose meaning can be 'winepress', could strengthen this further: the word *Gittit* is cited in instructions for the festival of Tabernacles in the *Talmud (*b.Sukka* 55a).[137] The *Septuagint also translates '*Gittit*' in this way, although this might be to give the psalm a more eschatological focus, implying that God will come to 'harvest' his people not only at the turn of the year but at the end of time. There is some evidence at *Qumran that the beginning of this psalm was used to accompany the blowing of the *shofar* in their Sabbath liturgy (*Damascus Document XI–XII*). *Targum also reads the psalm in a liturgical way: verse 4 (Eng. v. 3) reads 'Blow the trumpet in the month of Tishri, in the month when our feasts are concealed'.[138] (This refers to the uniqueness of the festival as it takes place at the beginning of the month, when the moon is still 'concealed': all other festivals take place in the middle of the month at the full moon.) The *Talmud* also connects this psalm, several times, with the autumnal New Year: *Ros Has.* 8a/8b speaks of the blowing of the *shofar* at the New Year (as in verse 4) to

[136] For other possible examples see Cole 2000: 96–101.
[137] Some would see that the Exodus references link this psalm instead to Passover, but there is no reason to exclude the Exodus tradition from the Feast of Sukkot.
[138] Stec 2004: 158–59.

be a 'statute and ordinance'. *Sop.* 19.2 also refers to this New Year festival when apples and honey are to be consumed in anticipation of 'a sweet new year'.[139] As the psalm makes clear in its later references to the Exodus, the festival is not only agricultural, but it also has a historical focus: the idea that bondage in Egypt ceased on the day of the New Year is connected with the blowing of the *shofar* to proclaim the hope for release from servitude.

The psalm has been adapted for other liturgical settings as well. Although the title is lacking in the *Septuagint, in *Mishnah Tamid* 7.4, Psalm 81 is the 'song for the fifth day of the week', i.e. Thursday.[140] As to why Psalm 81 is suitable for the 'fifth day', the (somewhat convoluted) argument is that this was the day when God created the birds and the fish, and just as these need to be sustained by God, so the people need to trust God for their sustenance as well, learning lessons from God's provision during the wilderness wanderings (verses 5–7).[141] The Exodus allusions and the different liturgical contexts give occasion for further reflections on the continuation of the Jewish exile: more than any other psalm in Book Three, this is a prayer for 'release from Egypt' which has not yet come about.[142]

Early Christian commentators emphasise instead the Christological relevance of particular verses, rather than the meaning of the psalm as a whole, often allowing one phrase to produce a small treatise. A typical example is *Cassiodorus, whose interest in music and liturgy provided an extensive discourse inspired by the reference to 'blowing the trumpet' in verse 3. Cassiodorus first offers an exposition about the discipline of music in the ordering of the world, and its unleashing of great forces. He then outlines its importance: first, this is through harmonics, rhythmics and metrics; secondly, through musical instruments (percussion, strings and wind); thirdly, in creating the six harmonies; and fourthly, in ordering the fifteen tones.[143] Psalm 81 has somehow disappeared from view.

*Theodoret of Cyrus attends more practically to the admonitions in verses 8, 13–16, interpreting these as references to heretics in the Christian community of his day (such as *Arians and *Nestorians) who would be judged by their false teaching.[144] *Bede, by contrast, focusses on the *Vulgate title of the psalm which, following *Mishnah Tamid*, also assigns it to the fifth day of creation: the references to the sea evokes a discourse on the waters of baptism, and the regeneration Christ offers to his church.[145]

---

[139] See Willems 1990: 412–13.
[140] Trudinger 2004: 121–35.
[141] Feuer 2004: 1025–26.
[142] Feuer 2004: 1029.
[143] See 'Expositions of the Psalms' on 80:4, in *ACW* 52:294–95; see *ACCS* VIII: 143.
[144] See 'Commentary on the Psalms' on 81:8, in *FC* 102:54–55. See *ACCS* VIII: 144.
[145] Neale and Littledale 1874–79: 3/1.

Some illustrations in Christian manuscripts have also been influenced by liturgical traditions. The popular liturgical Psalter called the *Psalterium Feriale* had eight liturgical divisions, and Psalm 81 (in the Latin, Psalm 80) was at the beginning of the sixth of these divisions, often resulting in a larger illuminated initial or illustration next to the first letter of the first word ('E' for Exultate) in other Psalters. An amusing example is in Bodleian MS. Canon. Liturg. 151, fol. 146v, an Italian secular Psalter with *antiphons, possibly from Naples, dating from the latter part of the fourteenth-century. The somewhat rotund psalmist, dressed in red, is playing his viola (or lyre) to God, who is lying in a cloud looking down and blessing him as he plays. Three or four nude figures (perhaps souls?) also listen to the psalmist with outstretched arms. The image is reproduced as PLATE 3.[146]

Other illuminated manuscripts either develop musical allusions or use visual allegories. For example, the *Stuttgart Psalter* (fol. 97v) and *Utrecht Psalter* (fol. 48r) offer images of horns, harps and bells. Similarly the fifteenth-century *Isabella Breviary* (fol. 155v) has an image of David and his musicians, reading (or singing?) from the Law, with the Temple in the background.[147] An early Jewish illumination does the same: the *Parma Psalter* (fol. 116A), humorously depicts a hybrid with a long body, a dog's hind legs and a horse's head, beating a kettledrum with a drumstick whilst with his left hand he is playing a small pipe, illustrating verses 2–3.[148] Irwin *Davis provides a similar but contemporary musical and liturgical image of Ps. 81:3, for *Rosh Hashanah. His illustration is of Jerusalem, painted against a dark star-filled sky; the crescent moon is shining, and at its first appearance the watcher is blowing the *shofar* to awaken the Jews from their spiritual slumber and begin the period of self-examination that ends on *Yom Kippur.*[149]

Allegorical readings are more evident in Byzantine Psalters. The *Khludov Psalter* (fol. 82r) for example, illustrates verse 16 with an image of Moses striking the rock, upon which Christ sits, with water coming out: the inscription reads 'Moses striking the water from the rock, and the rock is Christ' (1 Cor. 10:2–5).[150] The *Theodore Psalter* (fol. 110r) has a similar image, with the addition of Deut. 32:13.[151] This is also found in the *Pantokrator* (fol. 114r), *Bristol* (fol. 137v) and *Barberini* (fol. 142r) Psalters.

---

[146] See also E. Solopova 2013a: 475–79 (fig. 82).

[147] This is now in the British Library (*MS. 18851*).

[148] See Metzger 1996: 85. Contrasts with the very negative portrayal of Shechem in Gen. 34, again, post-Exilic focus in the odd sister-wife story.

[149] See https://dwellingintheword.wordpress.com/2016/12/15/1989–psalm-81/.

[150] See Corrigan 1992: fig. 93, also p. 91.

[151] For *Theodore*, see http://www.bl.uk/manuscripts/Viewer.aspx?ref=add_ms_19352_f110r.

It is inevitable that a psalm with such a liturgical history should have a large repertoire of musical arrangements. J. Braun's recent 'Take up a Psalm, Take up a Drum, the Tuneful Psaltery and Harp, Take up a Harp for the New Moon, Blow the Horn to Herald our Solemn Feast Day' is a Jewish example set as a canon in two verses.[152] Another recent Jewish arrangement of verses 13–17 (Eng. vv. 12–16) is Max Stern's *'Ha'azinu'*, a cantata for contrabass and orchestra on the theme of Moses' Farewell to the children of Israel: these verses, alongside Deut. 32:29, are used in Part 1 Scene 6, as part of a Hasidic wedding song symbolising the love between God and his people.[153]

There are also many Christian arrangements. *Byrd's 'Sing Joyfully'—probably his last surviving anthem—was composed to be performed at the christening of Mary, daughter of James I, in 1605 (with the play on the Hebrew name 'Jacob', in verse 1, and the Greek derivation, 'James'): the piece has a dance-like quality, ending with a trumpet fanfare.[154] Da *Palestrina arranged these verses in Latin ('Exultate Deo') for St. Peter's Rome in the late sixteenth-century. *Mozart, when aged 16, arranged the whole of this psalm as a motet ('Exultate Jubilate', or 'Rejoice, Be Glad') which was in three movements, for soprano and orchestra (1773). Verses 1–4 were adapted by William *Walton in his 'Belshazzar's Feast', first performed in 1931: they are used in Part 3, as a song of praise by the exiles, and again a dance-like rhythm is used.[155] *Howells also wrote a choral setting for this psalm, also titled 'Exultate Deo', in 1977. More recently still, James *MacMillan's *Blow the Trumpet in the New Moon* had its world première in June 2017 at the Royal Festival Hall: this is a dramatic setting of the first four verses of Psalm 81, taken from the Geneva Bible. It offers a celebratory fanfare for trumpets and trombones, with the choir singing modern Polish music alongside the more typical Celtic folk-derived *melismas: the unexpected 'limping rhythm' (long-short-two longs) adds dance-like energy to the hymnic summons to worship at the start of this psalm.

In conclusion, overall—and unusually in these Asaphite psalms—one of the most important aspects of the reception history of Psalm 81, in both Jewish and Christian traditions, is liturgical and musical, bringing to life elements of hope, even in earlier Jewish reception.

---

[152] Gorali 1993: 274. On the use of Braun's work in Jerusalem, see http://or-nah.com/info.html?pid=22.

[153] Stern 2011: 137–44.

[154] Dowling Long and Sawyer 2015: 221.

[155] Dowling Long and Sawyer 2015: 30.

Psalm 82: God's Abode is in Zion (ii)

Despite its more hopeful beginning, Psalm 81 ends with God's complaint against his people. In the light of this, this is a second complaint by God (here we would assume that God is speaking against the gods of other peoples in verses 2–4 and 6–7); or it is a complaint by the people to God, contrasting with Psalm 81 and here assuming that the psalmist is speaking throughout verses 2–8, charging God in several ways about issues of injustice. It is difficult to know which reading fits best: it is possible to see as many as four speakers in this psalm (vv. 2, 3–4, 5–6, 7) and the use of a prophetic oracle is much less clear than in Psalm 81. Whatever the interpretation, it is clear that verse 8 ('Rise up, O God, judge the earth...') is an address by the psalmist to God: much depends on whether we see this as an affirmation of the justice of God, or an accusation that God is hidden and doing little about injustice. In either case, in the context of verse 1, where God takes his place in the heavenly council, this is a psalm which both challenges and affirms monotheism.

The link with Pss. 79:5 and 80:4 is clear in the theme of 'How Long?' in verse 2. The interaction between human and divine speech—wherever the boundaries are—has resonances with Psalm 81, and Psalm 82 also anticipates Psalm 83 in its imagined downfall of the wicked: here the wicked seem to be deities (although as we shall see below, this has been much debated), whilst in Psalm 83 they are the enemies of the people (noting the deliberate connection made in the *Septuagint, which for 82:7 and 83:11 uses the same Greek word for 'prince': the Hebrew uses two different words). It is the mythical background of this psalm which is most contentious. The myth of a heavenly council, the myth that gods have lands, and the myth of one god rising to prominence are all evident in this one psalm; it may well originate from an early period when the attraction of Canaanite religion was seductive. Later Jewish and Christian reception was thus faced with how to read these traces of polytheism in the psalm.

The *Septuagint, surprisingly, preserves the mythical connotations. For example, it reads the reference to the gods in verse 1b as an 'assembly of gods', whilst other Greek versions refer to an 'assembly of the mighty'. *Qumran, meanwhile, uses the term 'the holy ones of God': verses 1–2 are found in *11QMelch2*, lines 10–11, which combines Lev. 25:9, 13, Deut. 15:2, Isa. 52:7, 61:1–3 and Dan. 9:25 along with Ps. 7:7–9 to describe in eschatological terms the redemption to be brought about by the heavenly Melchizedek: in the 'year of grace' he will execute judgement over these mysterious 'holy ones of God', who are perhaps by that time angelic beings.[156]

Interestingly, the New Testament also does not explicitly deny the mythical and polytheistic associations of this psalm. John 10:34 cites Ps. 82:6 (here calling the Book of Psalms 'your Law') and the implication seems to be that those who reject Jesus as God will be judged, *by angelic deities*, as blasphemers and thus strangers to God. In the light of the Qumran reading, which in effect understands the 'sons of God' as angelic judges, acting as God's agents, it might be that the Johannine use of this psalm might be a way of demonstrating that Jesus is the supreme Divine Judge.

The Church Fathers, influenced by the use of this psalm in John 10, had much to say about its contribution to the doctrine of what later became known as the 'deification' of humanity (encapsulated in his *De Incarnatione* by the fourth-century theologian, *Athanasius of Alexandria: 'God became man so that we might become God'). For example, the second-century Apologist (or defended of the faith) *Justin Martyr, in *Dial.* 124, discusses whether Christians are 'sons of God' and cites this psalm in full; without criticising its polytheistic stance he reads this as about the disobedience of all humankind, and the judgement on all things, earthly and heavenly, thus negating the (later) idea of 'deification'. It would appear that Justin used two Greek texts, only one of which was the *Septuagint. So here he reads verses 6–7 as 'You are gods... you shall die like a man' as a reference to humanity losing its godlike status through Adam in Eden.[157] *Irenaeus cites this psalm over sixty times, and his view of verse 1 is that the threefold use of the word 'God' refers to the Father and the Son and Holy Spirit, whilst in verse 6 the phrase 'gods' is addressed to humanity: hence 'you are gods' applies to humankind as a whole and illustrates a Pauline view of humanity being *adopted* as divine sons (rather than the Johannine notion of being *begotten* as children of God).[158] *Clement of Alexandria, one of the first theologians to express more explicitly the idea of deification (and in this influenced by Hellenistic and Platonic ideas, for example in *Stromata* I v. 155.2), uses Ps. 82:6 ('you are gods') as an example of humanity losing, in Adam, the gift of immortality to regain it in Christ. Hence Clement reads verses 6 and 7 as an account of the whole of salvation history, from Adam to Christ.[159] By contrast, *Tertullian, in *Marc.* (Book II Ch. XIX and Book I Ch. VII), cites Ps. 82:1 and 6–7, also against the background of John 10:34, and sees that it refers not to

---

[156] Although several other psalms in Book III are actually found amongst the Qumran scrolls, this is a rare example of a *pesher* reading of a psalm.

[157] See Skarsaune 1996: 447–48 and Russell 2011.

[158] See Mosser 2005: 46, 41.

[159] See Mosser 2005: 57–59.

humanity but to *other beings* who are to be judged as 'non gods'. Only later, for example in *Cyril of Jerusalem's *Catechetical Lectures*, is there a re-reading that 'you are gods' refers to mere human beings whom only the divine Judge can appraise.[160] *Cassiodorus, asserting that the Godhead as Trinity is the only 'God of gods', also read the references to the judgement of the gods as about judgement on humans: here too there is no indication of their deification.[161]

Jewish tradition is of course neither interested in deification nor in the effects of any Trinitarian doctrine; so, arriving at the same issue by a different route, and eradicating all polytheistic references, it reads this psalm as about human rebellion and judgement by God. This might explain the title in the *Targum: 'A Psalm by Asaph. As for God, his *Shekinah dwells in the assembly of the righteous who are mighty in the Law; he judges among the judges of truth.' So for verses 6–7 Targum reads: 'You are like angels ... in truth as humans you will die'.[162] Here we are not dealing with gods who will die like men, nor with men who will die like the gods; they are, quite simply, ordinary men. This reading dominated rabbinic tradition: the psalm is a general condemnation of all who falsify God's law.[163] *Rashi makes this clear: he reads verse 1 not about a divine assembly but about a judicial body—i.e. about Israel's law courts over which God works through human judges.[164]

This controversial psalm has nevertheless been assigned in the *Mishnah Tamid* 7.4 as 'The Song of the Day as the Third Day of the Week'. Like Psalm 81 before it, this heading is omitted in the *Septuagint, which assigns only five psalms (in the NRSV, Psalms 24; 48; 94; 93 and 102) to different days of the week.[165] The third day of creation was when God, separating the waters from the land (Gen. 1:9), covered the earth with his wisdom; it was also when the earth brought forth vegetation: *Pirkei Avot* 1:18 notes that the word for vegetation, *deshe'*, could be an acronym for the Hebrew words *din* (justice), *shalom* (peace) and *emet* (truth), thus fitting with the theme of judgement in this psalm. So as well as indicating God's role in creation it also is about God standing in the congregation of the mighty, to judge all human corruption.[166]

It is extraordinary that a psalm with so much drama, both human and divine speeches, and so many possibilities for liturgical responses, should present such little evidence of later musical engagement: perhaps the theological issues

---

[160] See *Procatachesis* 6 in *LCC* 4:68–69, from *ACCS* VIII:146.
[161] See Cassiodorus, *Expositions of the Psalms* 49.1 in *ACW* 51 480, from *ACCS* VIII:146.
[162] Stec 2004: 160.
[163] Feuer 2004: 1035.
[164] Gruber 2004: 544.
[165] Trudinger 2004: 14–18, 87–108.
[166] See Tur-Sinai 1950: 274.

FIGURE 4 Interpretation of singing of Psalm 82 in its earliest setting.

referred to above hindered such creativity. The contemporary musicologist David Mitchell's reconstruction of the psalm in its earliest setting is an original exception.[167] The proposed score, offered in Figure 4, is imagined as part of a temple performance, sung by a chorus and an *Asaphite precentor, usually half verse by half verse. The first two verses are an introduction. The term *selah at the end of verse 2 Mitchell reads not as a pause, but as a derivation from the verb 'lift up': he argues that the use of *selah* is therefore to bring in the trumpets and cymbals to announce the theme of the justice of God in the following section. For emphasis, verse 3 is envisaged as sung entirely by the precentor and verse 4 entirely by the choir. The rest of the psalm is an exchange, again in half verses, between the two parts; the finale is in verse 8 ('Rise up!') which allows the cantor's voice to rise from the tonic to the fifth, accompanied, possibly, by the *shofar*—with all its associations of military advance, fitting well the subject matter of the verse (O God, judge the earth!'). The performance of the entire psalm reaches a resolution by closing on the tonic, ending (in the Hebrew) with the word 'nations'. It is of course impossible to know precisely what the psalm sounded like in its original performative setting, but Mitchell has given us fresh insights on the possibilities of Hebrew cantillation, as his score makes clear.

The references to God taking his place 'in the midst of the gods' (verse 1) and God's address 'you are gods' (verse 6) have received several different interpretations in art. The image in the *Stuttgart Psalter* (fol. 98v) is simply of Christ judging the people; that in the *Utrecht Psalter* (fol. 49v) is of the Christ Logos (with six angels) judging groups of men from his place in the heavens: on the left are the poor and needy, walking into the safety of a cave (although their bearing crosses might indicate they are martyrs, 'children of the Most High' who will die [verse 6]). To the right is another group and the angels are hurling down idols from pedestals: these are the 'gods' whom God has been addressing in verse 1 and who will fall like princes (verse 7).[168]

Another motif found in other Psalters is the depiction of the *Harrowing of Hell: the *Khludov Psalter* (fol. 82v) offers this. The *Pantokrator Psalter* (fol. 114v) uses the psalm for anti-Jewish polemic: it presents an image of the Jews threatening to stone Christ, taken from John 10:33–34 (the text is above the scene). The wickedness of the Jews is portrayed in their menacing and hunched stance.[169]

---

[167] See Mitchell's reconstruction of Psalm 24 in Gillingham 2018: 160. What follows is part of an email correspondence with the composer, dating from September 2016.

[168] See http://psalter.library.uu.nl/page?p=103&res=1&x=0&y=0.

[169] Corrigan 1992:47, also fig. 56.

By total contrast, and as a contemporary Jewish example, this psalm was the third of five used by Martin *Buber to address the apparent eclipse of God after the Holocaust and the attendant challenge to Jewish faith.[170] Psalm 82 is a psalm of 'startling cruelty', revealing God as a hidden ruler allowing injustice to reign on earth. The only resolution is in the last verse, where the psalmist cries to God to judge all the earth (including all inferior gods). 'The cry... becomes our own cry, which bursts forth from our hearts and rises to our lips in a time of God's hiddenness'.[171]

This is a mysterious psalm which has elicited a wide range of theological responses, particularly about God's relation to humanity and humanity's relation to God and to heavenly (angelic?) beings. It is not surprising that it has had such a different reception in Christian and Jewish tradition. The only reading which brings the two traditions together is again one which sees the psalm as essentially about God's protection of the weak and poor, and about his ultimate judgement on evil.

Psalm 83: An Individual Lament about Ongoing Exile

Psalm 83 looks at the injustice in the world from the viewpoint of the scheming of the nations, and is similar to Psalm 82, which looked at injustice from the perspective of a heavenly council. Just as Ps. 82:7–8 is about the deposition of the gods and their nations, Ps. 83:18 is also about the defeat of foreign nations; both end similarly, that Israel's God, the 'Most High' (82:6 and 83:18) is God of all nations. So, again, we may note the first stage of reception in the placing of similar psalms alongside one another.

This psalm falls into two strophes: verses 1–8, which list nine nations who allegedly join together in a 'covenant' against Israel, and verses 9–18, which describe their being scattered throughout the world because of it. The psalm ends, unusually, with naming God as 'Adonai', thus anticipating this frequent use of this name in the *Korahite psalms which follow. (In the *Asaphite collection the usual name for God is Elohim.) This psalm is an interesting conclusion to this collection: after all the trauma of defeat and destruction, it envisages all nations coming to acknowledge God's power. *Targum* makes this point clearer by naming the king of Assyria as Sennacherib in verse 9 (Eng. v. 8). Hence the alliance of nine nations in verses 6–12 includes a tenth—namely Assyria, a

---

[170] See Levine 1984: 214–17, citing Buber 1952.
[171] Buber 1952: 60–61.

horrific symbol of hostility—a nation which has been referred to in the reception of several psalms in this collection.

Psalm 83 is used at Passover along with Psalm 135 (*Sop.* 18.2).[172] This is appropriate in its claims about God's protection of Israel in the past, and about all nations acknowledging the 'Most High' in the future.

In the *Septuagint the translation of verse 3 reads that the enemies no longer conspire against God's 'protected ones' (the noun in Hebrew comes from the verb ṣ-p-n, 'to shelter' or 'hide') but against God's 'holy ones' (*kata tōn hagiōn sou*). An allusion to the Temple is made more explicit in changing the Hebrew phrase 'Let us take the pastures of God for our own possession' to 'Let us take the holy place of God (*to hagiastērion tou theou*) for our own possession'.[173] The attack on the Jerusalem Temple by Antiochus Epiphanes in the second-century BCE may well have a more sacral emphasis in later tradition.

The names of the enemies (verses 5–12) have had an interesting reception in Christian tradition. *Jerome applies these names to schismatics in the church: these are now those 'in the churches of Christ (who) read of the tents of Edom, and the Ishmaelites, and so on, with all other names'.[174] Similarly *Theodoret of Cyrus refers to the enemies as priests, deacons, and leaders of the church, all who are tainted with heresy.[175] The argument of *Aquinas, by contrast, is that the enemies are those outside the church: these are the Jews and all other persecutors of the church.[176] A sermon on Psalm 83 by *Erasmus (1533) understands the nine 'enemies' in the psalm to have even broader scope: his 'On Restoring the Unity of the Church' has specific references to the Turkish threat and the effects of the Reformation.[177]

Images in art have two main themes. The *Utrecht Psalter* (fol. 48v) and the related *Eadwine Psalter* (fol. 147r) depict military scenes of God's victory over pagan forces. By contrast, images in eastern Psalters tend to portray spiritual scenes of martyrdom set alongside images of the crucifixion: this is evident in the *Khludov Psalter* (fol.83r), the *Pantokrator Psalter* (fol. 115v), the *Barberini Psalter* (fol. 143v), the *Bristol Psalter* (fol. 139r), *Theodore Psalter* (fol. 111r and 111v), and the *Hamilton Psalter* (fol. 159r).[178] One of the reasons for these latter images may be the use of the psalm, from the eighth-century

---

[172] See Willems 1990: 412.

[173] Pietersma 2000: 83.

[174] See Howell 1987: 187–88.

[175] *Ecclesiastical History* 2:19; *NPNF* 2/3:85–86, from *ACCS* VIII:150.

[176] Neale and Littledale 1874–79: 3/22.

[177] Aldridge 1996: xviii. This is taken from *Collected Works of Erasmus. Expositions of the Psalms Volume 63*.

[178] For the image in *Theodore*, see http://www.bl.uk/manuscripts/Viewer.aspx?ref=add_ms_19352_fl11r which is of the saints of the church being killed by barbarians.

onwards, in Good Friday liturgies and in burial liturgies such as the Office of the Dead.[179] So whilst one tradition rejoices in military victory for the faithful, the other laments the departed.

The political resonance of this psalm was a key motif in metrical psalmody in the seventeenth-century. The version by *Sternhold and Hopkins was apparently sung by Cromwell before the Battle of Marston Moor in 1644, when an allied army of Parliamentary and Scottish troops led by Sir Thomas Fairfax and the Earl of Manchester inflicted a heavy defeat on the Royalists. Cromwell wrote about the outcome that 'God made them as stubble to our swords…', an allusion to Ps. 83:13.[180] It is easy to see how the Sternhold and Hopkins version could be applied to seventeenth-century politics:

> Make Them Now and Their Lords Appear
> like Zeb and Oreb then;
> As Zebu and Zalmana were,
> the kings of Midian;
>
> 12. Who said, let us throughout this land,
> in all the coasts abroad,
> Possess and take into our hand
> the fair houses of God…
>
> 17. And let them daily more and more
> to shame and slander fall,
> And in rebuke and obloquy
> confound and sink them all;
>
> 18. That they may know and understand
> thou art the God most high
> And that thou dost with mighty hand
> the world rule constantly.

The references to the scheming of the nations and then to their ultimate defeat has enabled this psalm to be used in many different political, social and ecclesial contexts, by Jews and Christians alike. The enemies may be identified in different ways both within and between the two traditions, but the final appeal to God's 'world rule' is a constant in each.

---

[179] Gillingham 2008: 55.
[180] See http://www.cgmusic.org/workshop/oldver/psalm_83.htm. A much later Scottish rendering of this psalm by the nineteenth century poet Hately Waddell is found in Wieder 1995: 122.

Psalms 84–89: The Korahite Collection: 'Will God Remember Zion?'

Psalms 84–88: 'Restore us Again, O Lord!'

If the *Asaphite psalms lament God's absence in Zion, the *Korahite psalms as a whole long for a deeper experience of God's presence there. The editors seem to have intentionally placed these collections side by side. So Psalm 84, heading up this second Korahite collection, and coming after the Asaphite psalms, seems to have an intentional setting. There are some specific links contrasting Psalm 84, despite its yearning for the Temple, with Psalm 83. The tents (*ʾoholim*) of the enemies in 83:6 are now the tents (*ʾoholim*) of wickedness, more generally, in 84:10, which the psalmist rejects; the 'faces' of the enemy in 83:16 are replaced by the 'face' of God's anointed in 84:9, using the same Hebrew word in each case.

The role of the editors—again, suggesting the first stages of reception history—is also evident in the similarities between this and the collection of other Korahite psalms in Psalms 42–49. As was discussed in the commentary for Psalms 42–29, there is a corresponding format of personal lament about the Temple (42–43/84); communal lament about the loss of land (44/85); psalms associated with David (45/86); Zion and Kingship Hymns (46–48/87); and a final lament on innocent suffering (49/88). Psalm 89, being a complex composition, stands outside this sequence. The shared language includes expressions such as 'the living God'; 'your dwellings'; 'the house of God'; 'the city of God'; 'holy mountain'; 'Jacob'.[181] This suggests that each Korahite collection was

---

[181] See Gillingham 2018: 256–8; also Gillingham 2008 213–24, 2005: 322–24 on the linguistic and generic correspondences between the two collections of Psalms 42–49 and 84–89.

Psalms Through the Centuries: A Reception History Commentary on Psalms 73-151, Volume Three, First Edition. Susan Gillingham.
© 2022 John Wiley & Sons Ltd. Published 2022 by John Wiley & Sons Ltd.

intended by the editors to introduce and close Books Two and Three, although the fact that Psalms 43–49 predominantly use the name Elohim for God and Psalms 84–89 usually call God Yahweh suggests that they came originally from different provenances.

Psalm 84: Longing for the Temple

Psalm 84 has several liturgical associations. For example, in all three strophes (1–4, 5–7, 8–12) the term 'Lord of Hosts', reminiscent of the prophet Isaiah's vision of God in the Temple in Isaiah 6, occurs (verses 1, 3, 8 and 12). The motif of 'blessed' at the end of the first strophe (verse 4), the beginning of the second (verse 5) and the end of the third (verse 12) also suggests liturgical influence. It is unclear whether the suppliant is literally entering the Temple, or whether, like its counterpart, in the first *Korahite collection, Psalms 42–43, the psalm has been composed far from it, using liturgical language in memory of the Temple; this would continue the theme of ongoing exile which is throughout Book Three. *Kimḥi, for example, sees Psalm 84 as about David fleeing from Saul to live in Philistia, where he longed to be in the sanctuary of God (at this stage, not the Jerusalem Temple, as yet unbuilt), and so argues that the early setting corresponds with the present Jewish experience of Diaspora without a Temple. According to Kimḥi this makes sense of the reference to the homing instincts of the birds in the sanctuary (verse 3).[182]

Verse 3 is a one of the three most debated verses in the reception of this psalm. Whereas the 'home' and 'nest' are, in Jewish reception, an allusion to the Temple, in Christian reception they refer to the church—according to *Jerome, a place of rest for the body and soul, inaugurated through Christ.[183] Another issue is whether verse 3 is about a future (eternal) rest or an imminent (this-worldly) one. Many Jews read the verse in the latter way. *Rashi, for example, understands the 'sparrow' as a metaphor for the congregation of Israel, still not having found a home.[184] He also reads 'the tents of wickedness' in verse 11 (Eng. v. 10) in the light of Ps. 83:6 ('the tents of Edom'). Reading Edom/Esau as European Christendom, Rashi thus argues that this psalm is about Jerusalem as the proper home of the Jews alone.[185] However, not surprisingly, a Christian reading, using Heb. 13:14 as an example, reads verses 3 and 4 as not only about the

---

[182] Feuer 2004: 1051.
[183] *Homilies on the Psalms* 16, FC 48:121, from *ACCS* VIII:151–52.
[184] Gruber 2004: 549 and 551.
[185] Gruber 2004: 550 and 552.

church but about the Christian's pilgrimage towards a heavenly sanctuary. *Calvin, for example, notes how the blessings of pilgrimage (verses 4 and 5) are also interspersed with great hardships through the 'Valley of Baca' (verse 6), yet the final verse of the psalm ends with a final blessing and confident prayer.[186]

A second disputed verse is 84:6. Here both the *Septuagint and *Vulgate* translate 'Baca' metaphorically as a 'valley of tears', taken from the Hebrew *b-k-h*, 'to weep'. It could however refer literally to a pilgrimage to the Temple through a Valley called Baca. *Targum*, meanwhile, identifies *baka'* with the bitter-tasting balsam shrub grown in the valley of the same name (see 2 Sam. 5:23–24), and so views it as a reference to *Gehenna and the bitter experience of being transported from a near-death experience back to life. 'The wicked who pass through the valleys of Gehenna weep tears; they make it as a spring.'[187]

Verse 9 ('look on the face of your anointed') also has an interesting reception history. *Aquinas (of whom it is said verse 10 inspired his choice to become a *Dominican friar) read this as the voice of Christ in the psalm, praying to the Father on behalf of the Church, and advises this psalm be read alongside the Gospel of Matthew.[188] *Rashi, in order to counter a Christian reading, inserts 'David' before the 'anointed one', thus giving the verse a historical focus.[189]

It is not surprising that this psalm has played a prominent role in Jewish liturgy. It is often used at Jewish weddings and indeed opens the marriage service of the Reform Synagogues of Great Britain.[190] Its theme of yearning for the Temple also gives it a place in the *Siddurim*: verse 5 is often cited after the *Pesuke de-Zimra* and the Torah reading and before Psalm 145 in the *Ashkenazi morning service, and in the Sephardic tradition the psalm opens the afternoon service.[191]

The psalm also plays a prominent liturgical part in different Christian traditions, mainly by reading the 'dwelling place' (verse 1) and the 'house of my God' (verse 10) as the church. The hymn 'Jerusalem the Golden!/The glory of the elect!/O dear and future vision/that eager hearts expect…', written by the twelfth-century Benedictine monk, *Bernard of Cluny, may have been influenced by this psalm, along with Psalms 48 and 87.[192] It was traditionally sung in its entirety at *Matins during the Feast of Corpus Christi, and verse 1 is a communion *antiphon in Lenten services in the western churches. '*Rorate Caeli Desuper*' ('Drop Down Ye Heavens From Above'), a Plainsong version known also as '

---

[186] See http://www.sacred-texts.com/chr/calvin/cc10/cc10018.htm.

[187] Stec 2004: 162. *Midrash Tehillim* 84:3 also identifies Baca as Gehenna.

[188] Neale and Littledale 1874–79: 3/36, citing *Thomasius.

[189] Gruber 2004: 550–1.

[190] Magonet 1994: 5.

[191] Elbogen 1993: 85.

[192] Neale and Littledale 1874–79: 3/39.

Advent Prose', expressing longing for the Messiah (as in Ps. 84:9) combines texts from Isaiah 45 with parts of this psalm; the arrangements for this liturgy by *Byrd and da *Palestrina are perhaps the best known. Byrd also arranged a setting of this psalm in English, in his 1588 *Psalms, Sonnets and Songs of Gladness and Pietie*.*Schütz also used this psalm in his *Psalms of David*, to be sung with *SATB and *basso seguente*.[193] Other choral settings to this psalm abound, including *Lyte's 'Pleasant are thy courts above'; *Weelkes', *Parry's and *Vaughan Williams' different arrangements of *Coverdale's 'O How Amiable are thy Dwellings' from the *BCP*; and *Howells' 'One Thing Have I Desired', all of which capture the spirit of this psalm in English.

Other than choral settings, several arrangements of this psalm might be cited. An unusual musical arrangement—partly because *Brahms was not an orthodox believer—his 'Wie lieblich sind deine Wohnungen' (from Ps. 84:1–2 and 4) which was used in his *German Requiem*, possibly composed following the death of his mother and first performed at Leipzig in 1869. The psalm is the fourth of seven movements, used as a 'Beatitude' (taken from one of psalm's blessing formulae in verse 4), and this corresponds with the first and last movements, which are also Beatitudes. The arrangement of Psalm 84 sets a more joyful and earthy tone, imitating a Viennese Waltz, and contrasts with the other movements which reflect more on death.[194] *Rutter also used Psalm 84 in his *Psalmfest* (1993).[195] A more poignant arrangement is by Howard *Goodall: *How Lovely are Your Dwellings/Quam Dilecta* is sung by an all-female choir accompanied by a string quartet, capturing the nostalgic yearning for the presence of God, using the traditional Latin text in modern vein.[196]

A Christianised appropriation of this psalm is also common in metrical psalmody: for example, Isaac *Watts composed four versions of this psalm, including the following which focusses not so much on 'the church', as on Christ himself:[197]

> The sparrow builds herself a nest,
> And suffers no remove:
> O make me, like the sparrows, blest
> To dwell but where I love.
>
> To sit one day beneath thine eye,
> And hear thy gracious voice,
> Exceeds a whole eternity
> Employ'd in carnal joys.

[193] Dowling Long and Sawyer 2015: 191.

[194] See Stern 2013: 135–43; also Dowling Long and Sawyer 2015: 90; also Gillingham 2008: 223–24.

[195] See Dowling Long and Sawyer 2015: 276 and 173; also Gillingham 2008: 298–300.

[196] See https://www.youtube.com/watch?v=xffzgZvM8Zk.

[197] See http://www.ccel.org/ccel/watts/psalmshymns.Ps.176.html.

> Lord, at thy threshold I would wait
> While Jesus is within,
> Rather than fill a throne of state,
> Or live in tents of sin.

The liturgical prominence of Psalm 84 also resulted in several seventeenth-century imitations in English poetry, but without any obvious Christian overlay. Three very different paraphrases must suffice. The first is by George *Sandys, who experimented with the idea of 'longing for God' (84:2) by using a trochaic (stressed, then unstressed) metre, creating 7 syllables to one line, and a rhyme for every couplet, thus creating an unevenness of expression:[198]

> Lord for thee I daily crie;
> In thy absence hourely die.
> Sparrowes there their young ones reare;
> And the Summers Harbinger
> By thy Alter builds her nest,
> Where they take their envi'd rest.
> O my King! O thou most High!
> Arbiter of Victorie!
> Happie men! Who spend their Dayes;
> In thy Court, there sing thy Praise!

This could not be more different from his near contemporary Samuel Woodford's version, which interprets same idea of longing for God so that, like the rest of his paraphrased psalms, it suggests a Pindaric ode, with its repeated three lines formula. Like Sandys, this was a personal contribution and unsuitable for liturgical use (as stated in his dedication to the Bishop of Winchester). The introductory verse, setting the psalm against a military background, creates a somewhat different focus from Sandys' version:[199]

> Triumphant General of the Sacred Host,
> Whom all the strength of Heav'n and earth obey,
> Who hast a Thundering Legion in each Coast,
> And Mighty Armies lifted, and in pay;
> How fearfull art Thou in their head above,
> Yet in Thy Temple, Lord: how full of Love?

---

[198] From *Paraphrase upon the Psalms and Hymns dispersed throughout the Old and New Testaments* (1636). See Hamlin 2004a: 68.

[199] On the poets of the sixteenth century who experimented in psalmody, see Gillingham 2008: 168–80. This extract is from *Paraphrase upon the Psalms of David* (1667). See Hamlin 2004a: 108.

> So lovely is Thy Temple, and so fair,
> So like Thy self, that with desire I faint;
> My heart and flesh cry out to see Thee there,
> And could bear any thing but this restraint;
> My Soul dost on its old Remembrance feed,
> And new desires by my long absence breed.

A final example is by *Milton, who unusually chose a common metre (8–6-8–6) but combines this with his love of enjambment; the form and content suggest a private and personal tone:[200]

> How lovely are thy dwellings fair!
>   O Lord of Hoasts, how dear
> The pleasant Tabernacles are!
>   Where thou do'st dwell so near.
>
> My Soul doth long and almost die
>   The Courts O Lord to see;
> My heart and flesh aloud do crie,
>   O living God, for thee.
>
> There ev'n the Sparrow freed from wrong
>   Hath found a house of rest,
> The Swallow there, to lay her young
>   Hath built her brooding nest...

Artistic representation has also been very much influenced by the liturgical prominence of this psalm. One of the most interesting occurrences is in synagogue architecture. In the thirteenth-century synagogue of Cordoba the walls are covered with Mudéjar stuccowork and psalm quotations, originally written in beige on a blue background, in square Hebrew characters. Ps. 84:1–3 dominates the south wall, and Pss. 13:5–6 and 26:8 follow it. Similarly the fourteenth-century synagogue, El Tránsito, in Toledo, also using Mudéjar stuccowork with fruits, flowers and geometric designs, has walls which teem with verses from the psalms, but only Psalm 84 and 100 are in complete form, dominating the east wall. In each case this fits so well with the Jewish interpretation that the psalm is about longing for the Temple in exile.[201] A similar interpretation is found in the *Parma Psalter* (fol. 119v) which shows a human figure set between the first word and the rest of the line, pointing to the buildings in the margin: these are

---

[200] From *Shorter Poems* (1648). See Hamlin 2004a: 75–6.
[201] Gillingham 2008: 108–110.

of palaces with slender towers (the one on the right enclosed by a wall) and doors with golden arches, illustrating verses 1, 2 and 4: see PLATE 4.[202]

Other representations take up two prominent tropes. One is of the sparrow and turtle dove (or swallow) in verse 3. For example the *St Albans Psalter* depicts in the capital Q ('*Quam dilecta tabernacula…*') two trees with birds nesting in their branches; in the two nests at the top a larger bird feeds and a smaller one watches, whilst at the bottom two parent birds are feeding their young.[203] A second repeated image is 'the valley of tears' (verse 6). A painting on this theme by Gustave Doré (1882–1883) is at the Musée d'Art Moderne et Contemporain, Strasbourg. This 'Valley of Tears' depicts the suffering and sorrow of Christ, carrying his cross, with a play of darkness and light.[204]

To conclude, it is undoubtedly the liturgical use of this psalm (whether composed for worship or in memory of it) which has influenced the vast number of responses, especially in music, poetry and art. So despite the different views by Jews and Christians about the identity of 'the house of God', it is a psalm which has been appropriated, without much acrimony, by both traditions alike.

Psalm 85: Praying for National Deliverance

Psalm 85 does not mention the Temple, but like Psalm 84 its experience of dissonance is the same, and the prayer to God to 'listen' and 'look' in 84:8–9 is also found in 85:8–9. So too the reference to the glory of God (*kabod*) in 84:11 is found again in 85:9, and the motif of God 'giving his favour' in 84:11 is found in 85:12 As noted in the introduction to this *Korahite collection, its theme of communal loss gives it a clear correspondence with Psalm 44 in the first Korahite group.

Like Psalm 84, there is no reference to the Temple having been destroyed, as in some of the *Asaphite psalms. The two strophes (1–7 and 8–13) form a prayer and an expression of confidence in God's answer, with the play on the literal and metaphorical use of the word *shub* ('return' or 'restore') in verses 1, 4 and 6. Given the prominence of penitential liturgy after the exile, it is quite possible that the psalm was also used as a prayer of repentance.

Whilst *ibn Ezra reads this psalm as a Jewish prayer for redemption after the Babylonian exile, *Rashi somewhat predictably reads it as a prayer for redemp-

---

[202] See Metzger 1996: 86.

[203] See http://www.abdn.ac.uk/stalbanspsalter/english/commentary/page240.shtml.

[204] See https://www.art-prints-on-demand.com/a/dore-gustave/the-valley-of-tears.html.

tion during the Jews' continuing exile.[205] The Christian approach, however, is to read the prayers for restoration in a spiritual, not literal way: *Bede, for example, in his abbreviated Psalter, reads verse 5 as 'Turn us, *God our Jesus*, and relax your anger against us'.[206] Furthermore, the emphasis on 'return' is now also about praying for the Jews' conversion to Christ.[207]

One important verse in Christian exegesis is 85:11 ('Faithfulness will spring up from the ground, and righteousness will look down from the sky'). By the time of *Augustine this was seen as a prophecy about the Virgin Mary and the Incarnation. Augustine writes:

> Truth hath sprung out of the earth: Christ is born of a woman. The Son of God hath come forth of the flesh. What is truth? The Son of God. What is the earth? Flesh…But the Truth which sprang out of the earth was before the earth, and by It the heaven and the earth were made: but in order that righteousness might look down from heaven, that is, in order that men might be justified by Divine grace, Truth was born of the Virgin Mary…[208]

This in turn influenced the developing liturgical use of this psalm: it was used in Christmas Day liturgies in ancient Roman Rites, and is still a psalm for Christmas Day as prescribed in the *BCP.

Another important verse is 85:10. This reads: 'Steadfast love and faithfulness will meet; righteousness and peace will kiss each other'. This verse is used in Langland's allegory of the Four Daughters of God In *Piers Plowman*, Passus XVIII.[209] Psalm 85:2 ('You forgave the iniquity of your people') is used first, as it witnesses to the possibility of the forgiveness of sins. The setting is an evocative description of the passion and death of Christ. 'Will the Dreamer' then observes the dispute between (the female personifications of) Mercy, Peace, Truth and Righteousness, 'the four daughters of God', whose four qualities come from 85:10. Truth and Mercy are in Hell: Mercy ('steadfast love') suggests that the patriarchs and prophets can be redeemed from Hell, but Truth ('faithfulness') insists that no one could be released from 'that inferno'. Peace arrives to agree with Mercy, whilst Justice ('righteousness') takes up Truth's point: all those condemned to eternal punishment cannot be saved. Righteousness and Truth read the Bible literally, without compassion, resembling the old covenant, whilst Mercy and Peace read the Bible more figuratively and imaginatively. The crucifixion, however, supports the former view: it brought about forgiveness of

---

[205] Feuer 2004: 1062.
[206] Bede in Browne 2002: 60.
[207] Neale and Littledale 1874–79: 3/53.
[208] See https://carm.org/augustine-on-psalms-85-88.
[209] See Kuczynski 1995: 196–201; also Thomas *et al.* 1997: 30–31.

sins and release from death for all who have the humility to respond to it. Christ finally appears at the end of Passus XVIII and cites a verse from Ps. 51:4: true penitence reaps its rewards.

The use of Ps. 85:10 to describe the 'Four Daughters of God' was not original to Langland; it was developed from a much earlier *Jewish* tradition of four virtues by the throne of God, inspired by the visions of Isaiah 6 and Ezekiel 1 and the tradition of the four angels (Michael, Gabriel, Raphael and Uriel) for example in 1 Enoch 9 and 10.[210] This motif was taken up in the Middle Ages by Christian thinkers such as the Cistercian Abbot Bernard of Clairvaux and *Hugh of St Victor. An eleventh-century church vestment preserved in the Diözesanmuseum at Bamberg has the most unusual representations of 85:10 on its shoulder pieces: here the two pairs are cited alongside the two lists of six of the twelve tribes of Israel.[211] Several later medieval miniatures develop this motif: one, from the fifteenth-century *Missel de Paris*, from the school of Jean Fouquet, is of the Trinity, surrounded by three angels, and below them, personifications of Mercy and Truth and Righteousness embracing Peace.[212] The 'Four Daughters' are also found in a fifteenth-century morality play, *The Castle of Perseverance* (where Mercy is in white, Justice red, Truth 'sad green', and Peace, black) which centres around the hero Humanum Genus, representing all humankind, eventually being admitted to heaven.[213]

Images of this verse are also often found in thirteen and fourteenth-century hand-produced Books of Hours, usually in the Annunciation section, alongside verse 11, now clearly read as about the Virgin Mary and the Incarnation. There are many representations of verses 10–11 in art; William *Blake's is probably the best known. The title of his painting (completed in 1803) is 'Mercy and Truth are met together, Righteousness and Peace have kissed each other'. There are in fact only two figures embracing, under God the Father and his twelve angels of light: these are of an adult Christ and Mary. This image is represented here as PLATE 5.

This interpretation of verse 11 ('faithfulness will spring up from the ground') also accounts for the frequent use of the figure of the Virgin Mary in illustrations of this psalm. The *Stuttgart Psalter* (fol. 100v) has two images: the upper one recalls the Visitation (verse 4, with its 'restoration' theme) and the lower one is of Mary and Elizabeth in embrace (illustrating verses 10 and 11, but outside the tradition of the 'four daughters').[214] An image in the *Theodore Psal-

---

[210] See Thomas et al. 1997: 30, citing L. Ginzburg, *Legends of the Jews*, 6.82.

[211] See https://bit.ly/3wzYUzn.

[212] This is kept at the Bibliotheque Mazarine, Paris, with the Bridgeman Images (*MS 412*).

[213] See Thomas *et al.* 1997: 31 for other examples of this trope in Middle English and Renaissance literature. See also; Murphy 1992: 290.

[214] See https://bit.ly/3uz3BYm.

ter (fol. 113v, alongside verse 11) depicts the Virgin Mary embracing Elizabeth in front of a building with a cross and two basilicas; on the roof the young Christ blesses the young John the Baptist. The text is Luke 1:39–56.[215] Similar images are found in the *Khludov Psalter* (fol. 85r), the *Pantokrator Psalter* (fol. 118v), and the *Barberini Psalter* (fol. 146v).

Some Psalters develop the motif of forgiveness of sins found in the psalm; using verse 2 ('You pardoned all their sin'). This is also found in the *Khludov Psalter* (fol. 84v), the *Pantokrator Psalter* (fol. 118r) and the *Barberini Psalter* (fol. 145v).

Few Jewish illustrations of this psalm are to be found. One contemporary image, adopted by UNESCO in its work on justice and peace, is by the French artist *Benn, created in 1964, which is again of verse 10: 'Righteousness and peace kiss each other'. A light blue background highlights a white dove, symbolising peace, flying downwards, and a bluebird, symbolising righteousness, flying upwards. They touch each other, beak to beak: a red line runs across the page but another double red loop over it ostensibly links the two birds together.[216]

Although the psalm is not rich in reception in Jewish tradition, it offers a rich literary and visual reception in Christian tradition. This is mainly because of the popular appeal of just two verses (10–11). Unusually, one focus is on the women 'hidden' in this psalm: Mary, Elizabeth and the 'Four Daughters of God'.

Psalm 86: In Memory of David

Psalm 86 has a unique title amongst the *Korahite Psalms, as 'A Prayer of David'. It is the most personal in Book Three, and is a good example of a later Davidic 'imitation'. But again the placing does not seem to be totally accidental: there are some associations with Psalm 85, not least in the theme of God's steadfast love (85:10; here verses 5, 13 and 15) and the combination of 'love and faithfulness' (*ḥesed ve'emet*) which are found in Pss. 85:10 and 86:15. Similarly the themes of 'fear' and 'glory' occur together in 85:9 and 86:11–12.

Psalm 86 in this Second Korahite collection corresponds to the royal Psalm 45 in the first: both focus on the king. Throughout the three strophes (verses 1–7, 8–13, 14–17) we find several motifs from other psalms. Examples include its cluster of imperatives ('cry'; 'hear'; 'save'; 'protect'); its references to 'your servant' (verses 2, 4, 16); and its expression 'poor and needy' (verse 1). One

[215] For the *Theodore Psalter*, see http://www.bl.uk/manuscripts/Viewer.aspx?ref=add_ms_19352_f113v.
[216] See Benn 1970: Psalm 85:11 (no page numbers).

seminal example is the adaptation, in verses 5 and 15, of an ancient creedal formula found in Exod. 34:6 ('. the Lord. merciful and gracious... slow to anger...')
and used in other biblical texts (for example, Ps 103:8, 145:8, Neh. 9:17, Joel
2:13 and Jonah 4:2). This rich intertextuality raises questions about which text
'received' from another.[217] Another issue of reception history is that, given the
end of Psalm 72 clearly states that the prayers of David had ended, why did the
editors include another Davidic psalm here, and indeed elsewhere in Books
Four and Five of the Psalter? It would seem that the ongoing interest in David as the paradigmatic psalmist lived on beyond Books One and Two, even if
those books contain by far the most psalms ascribed to David.

In *Targum* the personal elements seem to confirm a Davidic authorship: the
heading is now 'A Prayer that David Prayed' and the last verse (17), anticipating David's vindication, reads: 'Perform for me a sign of good: *in the time when
Solomon my son brings the Ark into the house of sanctuary, let the gates be opened
on my account*; and let those who hate me see that you have pardoned me...'[218]
*Rashi, unsurprisingly, sees the psalm again as a reference to exile: 'all day long'
in verse 3 is read as 'all day during the exile' (here following *Midrash Tehillim*).[219]
*Kimḥi interprets verse 9 as referring to the future, not the past: the reference to
the incoming of all nations concerns the age of the Messiah, rather than referring to David.[220] Finally, the creedal formula in verse 15 ('But you, O Lord, are a
God merciful and gracious, slow to anger and abounding in steadfast love and
faithfulness') is used to express seven of the Thirteen Attributes of God's mercy.

The Christian use of the psalm is very different. The emphasis is on the
importance of prayer. *Augustine, for example, speaks of the importance of
the heart's becoming 'fixed', and God bearing our failings when we 'lift up our
soul' to him (verse 4).[221] According to *Bede, Christ is the one who is praying;
in the tradition of *Aquinas, the voice in the psalm is that of Christ, but it is
also a prophecy about Christ, but it can also be used as a prayer addressed to
Christ.[222] *Erasmus' sermon on this psalm refers both to a mystical sense, seeing the psalm in the light of Christ, and also to a tropological sense, viewing the
psalm in the life of the Church. Ignoring any philological issues which might
arise from the Hebrew, Erasmus' emphasis is essentially on what we learn about
knowing God, and fighting off evil in the world.[223] Viewing the psalm in the

---

[217] For other comments on this creed see p. 138 (Psalm 103) and pp. 405–6 (Psalm 145).

[218] See Stec 2004: 164.

[219] Gruber 2004: 556–57.

[220] Feuer 2004: 1076.

[221] Augustine *Expositions on the Psalms* 85.7; CCSL 39, 1181–82.

[222] Neale and Littledale 1874–79: 3/65.

[223] See Rademaker 1988: 192–3.

light of Christ is not new: it is evident as early as the New Testament, for in Rev. 15:4, parts of Ps 86:9–12 are used to illustrate the victory of faith, where all nations bow to Christ as Messiah.

This idea is also taken up in artistic representation: the theme of the right attitude in prayer is apparent in many images. The illustration alongside verse 9 in the *Khludov Psalter* (fol. 85v) and the *Pantokrator Psalter* (fol. 119v) depicts five ethnic groups, discerned by facial features and dress, bowing before Christ (one in the foreground being of Arab descent). In its context this is another interesting example of visual polemic against Muslims as well as Jews.[224] Another example is the illustration in *Khludov* (fol. 86r) and *Theodore* (fol. 115r) alongside verse 17 ('Show me a sign of your favour').[225] The 'sign' of God's favour is depicted as the cross, with an icon of Christ at its intersection: the inscription reads, provocatively in the *iconoclastic context of that Psalter, 'the sign of the cross'.[226]

The *Stuttgart Psalter* (fol. 101r) also focusses on the psalmist in prayer: he is looking up to God, and the hand from heaven is seen to be extended as an open palm.[227] The same idea of the psalmist praying as one 'poor in spirit' is found in the *Utrecht Psalter* (fol. 50r): the psalmist points with one hand to a poor and needy old man (verses 1–2) standing beside a tree, and with other to the cross-*nimbed Christ who bows his ear to listen. Behind the psalmist is a crowd—those who 'bow down before the Lord' (verse 9) and resist the worship of the idols set on a pedestal (verse 8). The wicked await their fate among death and the demons, in a pit set in the side of a hill (verse 13).[228]

One interesting musical example of this psalm is from *Mendelssohn's *Elijah* (composed for the Birmingham Festival in 1846). Part 1, which concerns Elijah's earlier years of ministry during the famine, has a recitative after the raising of the widow's son (Movement 8) which combines 1 Kgs. 17:9 and, later, verse 21 with verses from psalms, especially 86:15–16 and 88:11.[229] The emphasis here is on God's 'steadfast love and faithfulness' to his servants who are poor and in need (verse 1).

Other musical arrangements have a more obvious liturgical context. They include arrangements by J. S. *Bach, for the churches in Leipzig, and by *Purcell, for the court of Charles II. de *Monte arranged several pieces from this psalm, in Latin: 'Deduc me Domine in via tua' was based on verse 11 and 16–17,

[224] Corrigan 1992: 98, fig. 95 and fig. 96.
[225] For the *Theodore Psalter*, see http://www.bl.uk/manuscripts/Viewer.aspx?ref=add_ms_19352_f115r.
[226] Corrigan 1992: 72, fig. 86.
[227] Bessette 2005: 245–46.
[228] See http://psalter.library.uu.nl/page?p=106&res=1&x=0&y=0.
[229] Stern 2011: 264; also Dowling Long and Sawyer 2015: 75.

with Ps. 88:2; '*In die tribulationis*' was based on verses 7–10; and '*Miserere mei Domini*', was from verses 3–5. Samuel Sebastian *Wesley also composed a piece, in English, taken from *Coverdale, on verses 5 and 9–10. *Herbert's 'Teach me my God and King' (taken from *The Temple* [1633], there entitled 'The Elexir'), which became a well-known hymn, was probably influenced by Ps. 86:11. This could not be more different from the rather grandiose interpretation by the late nineteenth and early twentieth-century English composer Gustav Holst; this arrangement probably dates from his time as organist at Thaxted parish church (from 1916 to 1925): 'Bow down Thine ear, O Lord' uses the first part of the psalm, adapting the melody by L. Bourgeois in the *Genevan Psalter*, with verse 1 sung as tenor solo, verse 6 soprano, verse 2 tenor solo, and finally verses 2–3 by soprano, alto and tenor.[230]

Hence this is a psalm used in similar ways despite the different expressions of faith: despite its title, David is not at the centre of much interpretation. The theme shared in both Jewish and Christian reception is the importance of prayer.

Psalm 87: God is King in Zion

Psalm 87 relates to Ps 86:9 in that it amplifies the eschatological idea of all nations acknowledging the rule of God. This psalm is however more specific. Here Zion is described as a mother (verse 5) who gives birth not only to the people of Israel but, seemingly, to other peoples as well (verse 6). This *Korahite psalm, which is very different from the earlier *Asaphite psalms which view the nations in such a negative light, has generated a vast amount of interpretation over the centuries. It raises questions as to whether these 'peoples' are the Jews in the Diaspora, who will always be citizens of Zion; or perhaps proselytes in the Diaspora, thus explaining the references to Rahab and Babylon in verse 4; or perhaps a prophecy to be fulfilled by (Gentile) Christians, who are heirs to this hope. Its interests in Zion, and in God as King there, link it to Psalms 46–48 in the first Korahite collection.

The fact that the text of this psalm is badly damaged does not help. It may have been reconstructed on the basis of the other Zion hymns such as 46 and 48. For example, the reference to 'holy mountain' in verse 1 echoes Ps. 48:1; 'city of God' in verse 3 is the same as in 46:4 and 48:1,8; 2,9; 'he founded it' in verse 5 resembles 48:8; and 'my springs are in you' in verse 7 echoes 46:4.[231] It

---

[230] Gorali 1993: 278.
[231] See Zenger 1994: 188.

is possible to discern a concentric pattern in the structure, whereby verses 1 and 7 cite 'songs' of Zion, verses 2 and 6 focus on God's relationship with Zion, whilst verses 4–6, between the two words *selah, suggest some interlude. The *Septuagint makes some interesting changes: verse 5 starts directly with 'Mother Zion (*mētēr Ziōn*), which explicitly elevates the city over other nations, and verse 7 amends the Hebrew word for 'springs' to read 'dwellings' (*pantōn hē katoikia en soi*: this requires the change of one Hebrew letter, the omission of another and the addition of the definite article). This now emphasises the physical hope for Jerusalem-as-mother that is expressed here. This more explicit maternal imagery influenced Christian interpretations, as we shall see.

Targum omits such maternal implications. The 'gates of Zion' in verse 2 become 'the gates of the houses of study that are fixed in Zion', a particular reference to specific places for the study of the Law in the Diaspora. The end of verse 4 ('This one was born there') has a particular Davidic/Messianic reading in that *Targum* reads it as '*this king was anointed there*'.[232] Verse 5 ('This one and that one were born in it/her') now reads '*King David and Solomon his son were anointed there*'.[233] Later Jewish interpretation, represented by *Rashi, tends to look forward rather than back: making it clear that this is a promise that all exiles will be escorted home, Rashi argues that those coming to Zion from outside are only assimilated or converted Jews. This could be about proselytes, but it is not about the Gentiles.[234]

In the light of the destruction of the Temple in 70 CE, Christians often read the psalm in a less physical way, understanding 'Zion' to mean 'the presence of God'. This is clearly the case in texts such as Heb. 12:22–23, and although the psalm is not explicitly used in the New Testament, later writers read it in this light. The most obvious is *Augustine, for whom 87:3 ('Glorious things are spoken of you, O city of God') is the citation which opens his great work, *The City of God*. Seen in the light of the destruction of Rome in 410 CE, rather than the devastation of Jerusalem over three hundred years earlier, the sense of an enduring city, where the presence of God eternally dwelt, was paramount in Augustine's thinking.[235] *Jerome, meanwhile, sees the psalm (with its references to Rahab and Babylon in verse 4) as about the calling of the Gentiles: there is very little in common between Jerome's sermon and the views noted earlier by Rashi.[236]

---

[232] This is not uniformly the case with all of the *Targums*, but is in the version used by Stec (2004): 165.
[233] Stec 2004: 165.
[234] Gruber 2004: 560–61.
[235] Augustine, *City of God* 1.1, at http://www.ccel.org/ccel/schaff/npnf102.iv.ii.i.html. See also *ExpositionsonthePsalms*, 87, at http://www.ccel.org/ccel/schaff/npnf108.ii.*SEPTUAGINTXVII.html.
[236] See *Homilies on the Psalms* 18, taken from *FC* 48:137–8. See *ACCS* VIII:158.

An interesting link with the previous psalm is the reading of Zion in these verses as a reference to the Virgin Mary. An allegorical reading of verse 5 ('this one and that one will be born in her') is seen as referring to the Virgin birth, so that Mary becomes a type of Zion: in this reading the 'streams of water' in the Hebrew of verse 7 refer both to Jesus' birth and to Jesus as the 'living water' in John 4. This theme, found in two adjacent psalms, is developed in Christian art, as we shall see.

This 'birthing imagery' in verse 5 also resulted in Psalm 87 becoming a 'baptism psalm', due mainly to its themes of entry into the church, the mission to the Gentiles, and the water imagery in verse 7. This liturgical use also influenced the composition of several hymns. One is 'Jerusalem the Golden', based on Psalm 48 as well as 84 and 87, by *Bernard of Cluny in about 1145.[237] Another interesting use of 87:3 is found in a work by the eighteenth-century hymn-writer, John *Newton: his hymn, 'Glorious Things of Thee are Spoken' is used along with other texts such as Ps. 46:4 and Isa. 4:5–6 to speak of a spiritual understanding of the city at a time when nationalistic concerns needed to be addressed. Newton's version was published in *Olney Hymns* in 1779, and later it was used to the tune of *Haydn's version of the Austrian imperial anthem, which in turn was based on a Croatian folk song. The same tune (known as 'Austria') was later used for the German national anthem. Hence just as *Luther's adaptation of Psalm 46 was used in different ways to address sixteenth-century concerns about the church and state, so too Newton's reading of Psalm 87 served similar eighteenth-century concerns; these were reinforced by the later adaption of the text to the same tune to serve German nationalistic interests.[238] Psalm 87 can undoubtedly be read in very different theological and political ways.

The composer and musician David Mitchell offers a reconstruction of the Jewish liturgical and musical setting of this psalm from a time when these national concerns would have been more focussed on Jerusalem and its Temple.[239] As we have seen previously, Mitchell uses the Hebrew diacritical marks to create a musical score, and this psalm is pertinent because it again offers several responsorial elements (for example, the citations about Zion in verses 4, 5, 6 and 7).[240] In addition, the two occurrences of *selah* after verses 3 and 6 also allow for some dramatic musical interludes, perhaps with trumpets and cymbals, as with Psalm 82. Unlike Psalm 82, which is a typical Asaphite psalm in its

---

[237] See Gillingham 2018: 291 on Psalm 48 and Bernard of Cluny; also Psalm 84, p. 52.

[238] See Watson 2002: 216–18; also Dowling Long and Sawyer 2015: 92; Gillingham 2018: 280–83.

[239] What follows is part of an email correspondence with the composer, dating from September 2016. See also the composer's website: www.brightmorningstar.org.

[240] For other such reconstructions, see Mitchell's musical reading of Psalms 24 (Gillingham 2018: 160) and Psalm 82, p. 45.

sense of judgement, Psalm 87, as a Korahite psalm, has a clear festal mood, and is an ideal psalm for a reconstruction of Hebrew cantillation and performance. Whilst admitting that the stresses in the Hebrew do not inform us on this matter, Mitchell sets the psalm in triple time, arguing that either duple or triple time fits the rhythm well, thus bringing to life the psalm's cheerful overall tone. The chorus and the (Korahite) cantor/precentor sing responsorially, in half verses, throughout. Mitchell's creative adaption of the score in Figure 5 shows how the two halves of each verse are marked by mid-verse divisions indicated by an *atnah*, represented as an inverted v: such a pause suggests a possible precursor to Christian psalmody sung as *plainchant. The score also reveals how the different notes (for example at the beginning of verse 4) have been extended for dramatic effect.

The liturgical and musical use of the psalm was influenced by its different dramatic forms and its changing moods, and these provided ideal material for the interpretation of this psalm in art, where there are three dominant motifs. The most unusual of these is the so-called 'Christianisation of Zion'—a theme which was encouraged by Church Fathers such as *Athanasius, whereby Zion is not only the Christian Church, or a type of the Virgin Mary, but Christ Himself. Hence in the *Khludov Psalter* (fol.86v) David is represented as a prophet, standing before a Christian basilica set on high ground, with an image of the Virgin and Child on the walls. The inscription reads: 'David prophesises' (i.e., about the Incarnation). A second motif, as was seen in Ps. 86:11, is of the Virgin Mary. This is illustrated in the *Pantokrator Psalter* (fol. 121r) where the inscription reads: 'Holy Theotokos' [or, God-bearer]—referring of course not to Zion, but to Mary. Other images of Mary as 'Mother Zion' are found in the *Barberini Psalter* (fol. 149r) and *Theodore Psalter* (fol. 115v).[241] Perhaps one of the most telling images is in a twelfth-century manuscript by Jacobus (*Biblioteca Vaticana, gr.1162*) which has a series of scenes where the Virgin Mary is questioned by Joseph: in one (fol. 170r) Mary is sitting, making her defence in silence, with an open book inscribed (in Greek) with Ps. 87:3.[242] A third common motif is to read Zion in the psalm as the Christian Church. The *St Albans Psalter* illustrates the upper 'F' of the first word of the psalm ('Fundamenta eius in montibus sanctis') with a bishop and five clerics consecrating a church.[243]

Of course, the alternative Jewish depiction in art is to read Zion literally, as the city of Jerusalem. Moshe *Berger's image is of the 'gates of Zion' (verse 2) which are depicted abstractly, shining in blue and white with red, symbolising

---

[241] See Corrigan 1992: 98; also fig. 99 for *Khludov* and fig. 100 for *Pantokrator*.
[242] See http://digi.vatlib.it/view/MSS_Vat.gr.1162; see fol. 170r.
[243] See https://www.abdn.ac.uk/stalbanspsalter/english/commentary/page245.shtml.

Psalm 87

FIGURE 5   *Interpretation of singing of Psalm 87 in its earliest setting.*

Reproduced with the kind permission of David Mitchell, Director of Music in Holy Trinity Pro-Cathedral, Brussels; website https://brightmorningstar.org/wp-content/uploads/2020/06/Ps-087.pdf

a portal to heaven through which the prayers of the people ascend to God and the blessing of God descend to the people.[244]

The feminine imagery in this psalm has attracted some distinctive observations by Denise Dombkowski Hopkins. Noting that 'Mother Zion' stands at the heart of this psalm, she remarks that, unusually in the female personification of Jerusalem, which is often of a woman raped and devastated,[245] the female metaphor is here given dignity. She is a place of refuge and pilgrimage, providing a peaceful and universal vision instead of that of aggression as a result of the 'wounds of war'. This psalm today thus offers a female voice for those who, like the other voices in the psalm, often feel outside the community of faith—by reasons of colour, race, and gender, for example—and allows them a voice of their own.[246]

The key theme in the reception of this psalm, shared by both traditions, is Zion, whether interpreted literally or allegorically. A key difference is how one reads the female imagery and the inclusion of the outsiders into 'Mother Zion'.

Psalm 88: A Psalm of Complaint and Instruction

Psalm 88, the darkest psalm in the Psalter, has one of the most extensive and detailed superscriptions, and appears to have gone through many stages before it was placed at this point in Book Three. The final part of the title ('A *Maskil* of Heman the Ezrahite') suggests, as with Ethan the Ezrahite in Psalm 89, some *Korahite associations (see for example 1 Chron. 6:18, 15:17, 19) and this is perhaps why it was included in this collection.[247] Another heading, '*al maḥalat le'annot*, may suggest some accompaniment to the flutes (Psalm 53 has a similar heading), which were used for lamentation (Jer. 48:36), and certainly 'lament' is a feature of this bleak psalm. The editors possibly placed it here to highlight its differences, rather than similarities, with Psalm 87: God who loves Zion (87:2) and is known by his people (87:4) is neither loved nor known by this suppliant (88:11–12); and the waters which represented life in 87:7 signify drowning and death in 88:5. If Psalm 87 was about faith in God's promises, Psalm 88 expresses outrage at broken trust. It has some correspondences with Psalm 49, the final lament in the first Korahite collection, although it is much bleaker than that

---

[244] See http://www.biblical-art.com/artwork.asp?id_artwork=15116&showmode=Full.

[245] For example, Ezekiel 16, Ezekiel 23 and Lamentations 5.

[246] Dombkowski Hopkins 2016: 347–54.

[247] For a further explanation of this proposal, see Gillingham 2014: 201–13.

psalm. It can be divided into three strophes (verses 1–7, 8–12 and 13–18); the first is discernible by *selah* (although the second occurrence of this term is in verse 10, in the heart of the middle strophe and the second *diapsalma* is absent from the LXX recension). Rhetorical questions dominate, bringing this depressing lament close to the complaints of Jeremiah and Job.

There are several difficulties of translation here, with alternative readings supplied both in the Hebrew and in the Greek and Latin translations, for example in verses 2, 4, 5, 8, 15 and 16.[248] None of the emendations vastly change the thrust of the psalm. The *Septuagint perhaps uses more metaphors of shades and darkness (for example in verse 6–7), and in verse 10 where the reference to dead spirits or 'shades' (*rofe'im*) is changed to 'physicians' (*iatroi*), taking away the more polytheistic element, now indicating it is the doctors who might restore the dead. *Targum also takes out the mythical implications of this verse: 'Is it possible that you will work wonders for the dead, or that the bodies that have dissolved in dust shall rise to give praise before you?'. But in terms of translation there is little else which has affected the reception of this psalm.

Later commentaries reveal the differences between Jewish and Christian approaches to Psalm 88. In Jewish tradition the psalmist is personified as a 'lonely Jew' who represents Israel in exile, whose complaint is based on a false accusation that the Jews do not believe their 'home' is the Torah which is still with them.[249] *Rashi reads verses 5, 9 and 10 (Eng. 4, 8 and 9) as 'concerning the congregation of Israel' and sees the psalm as a lament of the Jewish community overcome by Gentile oppression.[250]

In Christian tradition, by contrast, the psalm was read as a prediction of the passion and resurrection of Christ, or, more precisely, as a psalm spoken by Christ to the Father when on the cross (in which reading, the abandonment by friends in verse 18 corresponds with Jesus' betrayal by his disciples). *Cyril of Jerusalem speaks of Christ as the one who was in the pit (verse 4), without friends (verse 8) and the one who can indeed work wonders amongst the dead (verse 10).[251] *Ambrose's observation that verse 4 ('I am like those who have no help') is a prediction of the prayer of Mary at the foot of the cross is also typical of this type of interpretation.[252] *Augustine reads the psalm as a prayer by Christ in his humanity, taking upon himself the burden of our frailty, and so praying on our behalf to the Father.[253] *Chrysostom also reads the psalm as a prediction of the passion of Christ, who was put in the lowest of places, death

---

[248] See Tate 1990: 393–98.

[249] Feuer 2004: 1089.

[250] See Gruber 2004: 563–67.

[251] *Catechetical Lectures* 14.8 in *FC* 64:36–37, from *ACCS* VIII: 159.

[252] *Letters*, 59 in *FC* 26:362, from *ACCS* VIII:159.

[253] See *Expositions on the Psalms* 87.3 CCSL 39.1209.

itself (verse 6).[254] *Cassiodorus, following Augustine, writes of how the psalm shows us how Christ was filled with evils (not his own) which burdened his soul in his prayer for us.[255]

Such Christian reception resulted in the psalm having a central place in funeral services; the origins go back at least to Chrysostom. It was also used in the offices of *Lauds and *Prime, with their focus on our temporal nature as darkness turns to dawn. This is also an Easter psalm: the *BCP prescribes its use for Good Friday (along with Psalms 22, 40, 54 and 69), and it is frequently used on Easter Saturday, where verses such as 88:14 ('Why do you cast me off?') have echoes of Psalm 22:1, a key psalm in the Gospels which is seen to predict the suffering and death of Christ. The use of this psalm at Eastertide goes back to the ancient Roman Rite.[256]

The association of this psalm with death in general as well as with the death of Christ has resulted in a number of choral arrangements and hymns. Philippe de *Monte's arrangement of verses 15–19 is a late Renaissance example; another is by the nineteenth-century composer John *Whittier: 'Immortal Love, for ever full' is a more positive reading of Ps. 88:11 (presuming an answer 'yes' to the question about God's love extending beyond the grave). We have already noted its appearance in *Mendelssohn's *Elijah*, at the point when the widow's son is raised from the dead.[257] A more recent example is its use in the night vigil in *Tavener's 'Veil of the Temple', which plays on the shades of light and darkness in the psalm through the medium of Orthodox Liturgy, using an intricate formation of ascending pitches.[258]

The sheer bleakness of this psalm intrigued sixteenth and seventeenth-century poets who frequently created their own imitations of it. These are profoundly personal appropriations; they could not be more different from the more communal Jewish readings. The Earl of Surrey, imprisoned in the Tower in 1546, before his execution in 1547, composed his own version of Psalm 88, and his letter to Sir Anthony Denny reveals how this brings out the 'particular grief of a particular person'.[259] Mary *Sidney's dramatised version of this psalm, punctuated with questions, hesitations and anxieties, gives the psalm

---

[254] *Demonstration against the Pagans* 4.12 in *FC* 73:207, from *ACCS* VIII:160.

[255] *Explanation of the Psalms* 87.4 CCSL 98, 795.

[256] Neale and Littledale 1874–79: 3/91.

[257] See comments on Psalm 86, p. 61.

[258] See http://johntavener.com/inspiration/the-veils/the-veil-of-the-temple/; also Dowling Long and Sawyer 2015: 75; Howard 1997.

[259] See Zim 2011: 104.

a conversational feel and a sense of urgency. This is seen, for example, in this extract from verses 10–12:[260]

> Alas, my Lord, will then be tyme,
>   When men are dead,
>   Thy truth to spread?
> Shall they, whome death hath slaine,
> To praise thee live againe,
> And from their lowly lodgings clime?
>
> Shall buried mouthes thy mercies tell?
>   Dust and decay
>   Thy truth display?
> And shall thy workes of mark
> Shine in the dreadfull dark?
> Thy Justice where oblivions dwell? (Lines 43–54.)

One of the earliest identifications of Psalm 88 with Christ's passion in art is a Gospel Book Miniature, *Codex Purpureus Rossanensis*, held in the Biblioteca Arcivescovado, Rossano, dating around 500 CE. The full page prefatory is of Christ, bearded and cross-*nimbed, in Gethsemane, addressing three sleeping apostles. Below are two images of David, crowned, with two prophets associated with the Assyrian crisis, Jonah and Nahum; one figure of David holds an inscribed roll with the words of Ps. 109:4 and the other, Ps. 88:2 ('let my prayer come before you …').[261]

The *Theodore Psalter* (fol. 116r) illustrates verse 4 ('I am counted as those who go down to the Pit') with an image of Christ being placed in the tomb by Joseph of Arimathea and Nicodemus (John 19:38–42). An angel reaches down; Mary and two women close by are grieving.[262] *Khludov* (fol. 87r), *Pantokrator* (fol. 122r), *Bristol* (fol. 415r) and *Barberini* (fol. 149v) have similar images. The illustration to verse 7 ('…You overwhelm me with all your waves') in the *Theodore Psalter* (fol. 117v) is of Christ in a sailing boat, in a storm, with two figures in red personifying the wind and sea. 'Wind' has a hand to her mouth, indicating she has been silenced.[263] The text is Mark 4:36–41 and the illustrations are also found in *Khludov* (fol. 151v), *Bristol* (fol. 147r) and *Barberini Psalters* (fol. 151v). Here the psalm has been turned into an expression of hope.

---

[260] See Rathmell 1963: xviii; also Fisken 1985: 171.
[261] See http://www.artesacrarossano.it/eng/details_works.php?IDo=39.
[262] See http://www.bl.uk/manuscripts/Viewer.aspx?ref=add_ms_19352_f116r.
[263] See http://www.bl.uk/manuscripts/Viewer.aspx?ref=add_ms_19352_f117v.

The *Stuttgart Psalter* (fol. 102v), by contrast, reads this in the light of western commentators: Christ is the actual speaker of the psalm. The title given is '*vox Christi ad patrem*'. Christ is alone on the cross except for the presence of a demon, yet he still stretches out his hands in this prayer.[264]

By contrast, the *St Albans Psalter* encloses the illuminated letter 'D' ('*Domine Deus salutis meae die*') with an image of the psalmist drowning beneath the waves, surrounded by four fish. This is a very different illustration of verses 4–7, and it is of the psalmist praying to Christ: 'I spread out my hands to you' (verse 9). Christ, flanked by two other figures, leans over to listen. Though a different reading, this psalm somehow still evokes hope.

There are many contemporary interpretations of this psalm, not least in the light of the atrocities of World War II. One example is of the appropriation of verses 6–9, with its metaphorical description of being cast 'in the depths of the Pit, in the regions dark and deep.' During the Holocaust years those who hid in makeshift bunkers and cellars called them '*bor taḥtiyyot*' ('the pit of the depths') making literal what was once figurative in this psalm.[265]

This is one of the few psalms whose reception really wrestles with unanswered personal questions about the character of God: in Christian tradition, the questions are about the extent to which God in Christ suffers with and for his people, and in Jewish tradition, the questions are about his justice and power to 'restore' his people.

---

[264] See Bessette 2005: 319–22; for the image, see https://bit.ly/2R7yzIM.
[265] See Levine 1984: 204.

Psalm 89: Remembering the Covenant with David

This composite psalm is linked to 88 by virtue of it being another '*maskil*' of Ezrahite (and hence perhaps also from *Korahite) origins, although it stands somewhat apart from the rest of the Korahite collection. The beginning of Ps. 89 is a stark contrast to 88. For example, whereas 88:11 questions God's steadfast love and faithfulness, 89:2 affirms it; similarly, God's 'wonders' which are questioned in 88:10 are affirmed in 89:5. The editors have probably set these psalms side by side because at the end of the psalm, its questions about man and death (89:48) mirror those in 88:4–5 (although as we shall see, the end of Psalm 89 might also be seen in a more positive light). Each psalm speaks of God's rejection (89:38; see 88:14) and of his hiding (89:46; see 88:14). But Psalm 89 is very different as it is a composite psalm, brought together from at least three parts: it first rejoices in the Davidic covenant (verses 1–4) and in the kingship of God (verses 5–18); it then confidently proclaims, in detail, the making of the Davidic covenant (verses 19–37) in a recital of history, using 2 Sam. 7:8–17, which has several affinities with Psalm 78. *Selah* occurs at verses 4, 37 and 45, marking off two of these four divisions. The psalm ends with a lament because the king has been defeated and the covenant seems to have been forgotten (verses 38–51).

Given that most of the psalms in Book Three have focussed on the Moses and Exodus tradition (the end of Psalm 78 and the heading to Psalm 86 being exceptions), the introduction of David within the psalm is a surprise, not least because the extended focus is more on the king himself and not on the

Psalms Through the Centuries: A Reception History Commentary on Psalms 73–151, Volume Three, First Edition. Susan Gillingham.

Zion/Temple traditions which were prominent in earlier psalms. Given that the introduction and praise of David is effectively used as a means of protesting to God at the end of the psalm because of the demise of the monarchy, it is clear that the overall impact of the psalm is not to express confidence in the Davidic covenant, but perplexity in its having been broken. Nevertheless, much depends on how we interpret verse 47 ('How long, O Lord? Will you hide yourself for ever?') and verse 50 ('Lord, where is your steadfast love of old?') which might be seen, in line with the pleas for God to 'remember' which have resonated throughout Book Three, as intended to move God to act favourably on his people once again rather than as an accusation that God has completely forgotten his people. If one can read the ending of this psalm in a somewhat more hopeful light this actually places the tenor of the psalm closer to Psalm 78; as we noted, this psalm too has an equally interesting place in the heart of the *Asaphite psalms.[266] A more hopeful ending also places the end of Book Three closer to Psalm 73 at the beginning of it, with its similar questions about God's justice, but with its more positive ending.[267] Recent scholarship has mainly emphasised the pessimistic ending to Psalm 89, arguing that Book Three ends without hope and can only be made sense of in the light of Psalm 90 ('A Psalm of Moses') at the beginning of Book Four. If we see Psalm 89 as still reflecting hope rather than accusation, there is more continuity between Books Three and Four, a point we shall return to in looking at Psalm 90.[268] This is a point developed by Adam Hensley in his book on covenant relationships in the Psalter, and it is quite convincing.[269]

Early Jewish reception of Psalm 89 nevertheless contrasts more starkly the two parts of Psalm 89: on the positive side of the covenant made with David (verses 1–4; 5–18; 19–37), and on the negative aspects of that covenant having been broken (verses 38–51). The *Septuagint makes some interesting changes to the prominence of the king, often applying to the whole people what was once intended to refer to the king. For example, in verse 40 (Eng. v. 39) the Hebrew speaks of the king's 'crown' (*nezer*) being profaned; the Greek text, interested in the fate of Jerusalem, reads this as 'the holy sanctuary' (*hagiasma*) which has been defiled.

Psalm 89, with its focus on the rise and fall of the monarchy, is found in two of the *Qumran scrolls. Verses 20–22, 26, 23 (*sic*), 27–28 and 31—all on the positive aspect of the Davidic covenant—are found in 4QPs^x (4Q236), one of the oldest scrolls. Verses 44–48, 50–53, meanwhile are found in 4QPs^e—the

---

[266] See pp. 24–5 (on Psalm 78).
[267] See p. 5 (on Psalm 73).
[268] See pp. 82–3 (on Psalm 90).
[269] Hensley 2018.

part of the psalm which laments the end of David's house.[270] This suggests that the two parts of the psalm may once have had a separate reception history.

Targum traces the history of this psalm back beyond David to Abraham (who in Jewish tradition is often seen as the composer of the psalm). Of its title, we read 'Good insight, which was spoken by Abraham who came from the east'. This translates 'Ezrahite' as 'from the east' and 'Ethan' as 'he came'. One other feature in *Targum* is the reinterpretation of mythological details: for example, the 'heavenly beings' in verse 7 (Eng. v. 6) are now 'angels'; the reference in verse 11 (Eng. v. 10) to God crushing Rahab, the mythological dragon, is now also a reference to 'Pharaoh, the wicked one'. The most telling reference, because it has an eye not only on the end of the monarchy after the Babylonian exile but on the end of the Temple itself, is verse 45 (Eng. v. 44). Rather like the Greek transformation of verse 40 (Eng. v. 39), 89:45 (Eng. v. 44) now reads: 'You have caused the priests who sprinkle upon the altar and cleanse his people to cease…' This is a bitter tale of exile, from Abraham to David, and from David to the loss of the Temple in the present day.

This reading was common in later Jewish writings. *Rashi actually reads the reference to the 'anointed one' in verse 51 as pertaining to 'King Messiah', a future figure whom God will raise up to end the present exile. This is quite different from his concern to read the 'anointed one' historically, as David, in Ps. 84:10 (Eng. v. 9) and Ps. 2:2, in refutation of the Christian beliefs about Christ the Messiah. Here, in the light of what is read as the failure of the Davidic covenant, a reference to David himself as the 'anointed one' would be impossible.[271] *Kimḥi also sees the lament in verses 38 onwards as a prayer for the coming of the Messiah, to renew the covenant with Abraham and David.[272]

This psalm was used to speak of Jesus as the 'anointed one' as early as New Testament times; he becomes the means of God continuing to 'remember' the covenant made with David. In Peter's first speech in Acts 2:25–36, Ps. 89:4–5 is one of four psalms to be used to show that Jesus is even greater than David, for he alone has risen from the dead. In Paul's speech in Acts 13:17–41, Ps. 89:20 is adapted, along with Pss. 2:7 and 16:10, to argue that Jesus is the Messiah.

This Messianic reading persists throughout the Church Fathers to reformation writers. *Augustine, for example, reads 89:3 as about the 'new' covenant with the '*son of* David'. Thus the first part applies to Christ, not to David, and of special importance is verse 26: 'He shall cry to me, "Thou art my Father…"'.[273] The final part of Psalm 89—the lament—is thus, like Psalm 88, read as a prophecy predicting Christ's suffering.[274] (Verse 38 is a difficult verse, for it speaks of

---

[270] Flint 1997: 64.

[271] Gruber 2004: 568–74, especially p. 571 and note 43 on p. 574.

[272] Feuer 2004: 1119.

[273] Neale and Littledale 1874–79: 3/112. See also *City of God* 17.12 in *CG* 740–41 from *ACCS* VIII:164.

[274] *Bede, in Neale and Liitledale 1874–79: 3/107.

God's wrath against his servant; here—ironically, this is seen to apply to David, not to Christ.) *Evagrius, writing on verse 6 ('Who in the skies can be compared to the Lord?'), presumes the answer is Christ, and that this refers to Christ's unique nature, as Creator and Redeemer, with unique knowledge of both the Father and creation.[275]

The different readings of this psalm by *Luther and *Calvin provide good examples of their distinctive modes of exegesis: Calvin reads verse 27 ('I will make him the firstborn.') as a reference to *David*, who is a *type* of Christ, i.e. preparing the way for the Messiah.[276] Luther, in the *Dictata*, reads Psalm 89 as a whole as about 'the perpetuity and stability of the reign of David'—i.e. assuming this means the spiritual reign of Christ.[277] Hence verse 29 ('I will establish his line forever') Luther sees as an unfulfilled promise if this was about the literal David: but the promises have been fulfilled, in Christ and his Church.[278]

In Jewish liturgy, the ceremony of the Blessing on the Moon's Reappearance (*Birkat Levanah*), praising God for sustaining the world through its seasons, has implicitly been linked to verse 38 (Eng. v. 37) of this psalm: 'It (i.e. the Davidic covenant) will be established *like the moon* forever'. From this link between the moon and the Davidic dynasty, the Blessing on the Moon's Reappearance has also linked to the coming of the Messiah at the time of the new moon.[279] A near parallel is found in Christian liturgy: because the first part of this psalm speaks of the descendants of the king and the promise of a covenant 'forever', it has been used as early as the *Roman Rite for the liturgy for Christmas Day, celebrating the arrival of the 'Messiah'. The latter part of the psalm (verses 38–51), on the sufferings of the king, is associated with Easter.[280] Many hymnic versions of this psalm focus on one part or another. For example, the *Genevan Psalter* (1562) takes up the more positive aspects of the psalm; a recent version is found in the *Anglo-Genevan Psalter* of the Canadian Reformed Church.[281] Isaac *Watts wrote at least seven metrical versions of this psalm, taken from verses 1–6; 7–14; 15–18; 19–37; 38–41; and 42–52. Of the two on 42–52, one has intriguing correspondences with Watts' 'O God our Help in Ages Past', from Psalm 90.[282] A more recent Methodist version, of verses 1–4,

---

[275] See Dysinger 2005: 163–64.

[276] See Russell 1968: 39–40.

[277] See Preuss 1969: 201, citing *WA* 4.37.2: '*De stabilitate et perpetuitate regni David spiritualis, id est Christi*'.

[278] See Preuss 1969: 201, citing WA 4.37.15–19.

[279] Donin 1980: 276–77.

[280] Neale and Littledale 1874–79: 3/107.

[281] See http://www.genevanpsalter.com/attachments/GenPs089_vocal_homoph_BoP84.MP3. The version is by Jacobus Kloppers (1985).

[282] On 89:42–52 'A Funeral Psalm', see http://www.ccel.org/ccel/watts/psalmshymns.Ps.188.html.

19–37 (again, the positive parts), is 'O Lord Your Love is Constant', arranged by Don Saliers.[283]

Musical performances for a concert audience are also mostly from verses in the first part of the psalm. *Handel, for example, used verses 13–14 in his 'Let Thy Hand be Strengthened', a coronation anthem (1727) for mixed chorus and orchestra, which was sung as George I was presented to the people, ending with a triumphant alleluia.[284] Handel's composition 'My Song shall be Alway' (1717–1718) is also taken from selections of the first part of this psalm, using a chorus for verse 5, tenor for verse 6, soprano, tenor and bass for verse 9, bass for verse 11, chorus for verse 14, cantor for verse 15, and a final triumphant chorus for verse 17.[285] Other choral settings include da *Palestrina's settings of verse 25 and of verses 12, 15 in Latin, and *Purcell's arrangement of verses 1, 5–10 and 14–15 in English.

Its use in liturgy, as well as its narrative about the promises and broken promises to the king, have resulted in a number of poetic imitations.[286] The eighteenth-century writer Christopher *Smart has a work attributed to him called *A Song to David*, which is about the relationship between David and Christ; it is a lengthy poem in imitation of Psalm 89. Each verse is a four-line stanza, set in 6–8–6–8 with the rhyme a-b-a-b; unlike Mary *Sidney's version, this loses some of the composite complex nature of the psalm, yet at the same time creates a simple directness in its account of God's dealing with his people: the Christian overlay is only implicit. Verses 34–37, on the promises to David and his descendants, read:[287]

> But yet I will not wholly take
>   My kindness from his seed;
> Nor void that blessed promise make
>   To which my truth agreed.
>
> I will for my own glory care
>   Nor change the word I past;
> Once by my holiness I swore
>   That David's house should last.
>
> The line of his descent shall run
>   With deathless heroes crowned;
> Before my presence, as the sun,
>   His throne shall be renowned.

---

[283] See http://www.hymnary.org/text/o_lord_your_love_is_constant.
[284] Dowling Long and Sawyer 2015: 145.
[285] Gorali 1993: 246–48, with score.
[286] See Wieder 1995: 129–34.
[287] Wieder 1995: 129–34, here 132–3.

Illuminated psalters usually 'Christianise' this psalm. Byzantine examples, such as *Theodore* (fol. 118r), use verse 12 ('Tabor and Hermon joyously praise your name') as an inspiration for an image of Jesus' transfiguration.[288] This is also taken up in *Khludov* (fol. 88v), *Bristol* (fol. 147v), and *Barberini* (fol. 152r). *Carolingian psalters record different Christian episodes. The *Utrecht Psalter*, for example, has two images of Christ which conform to the two parts of the psalm. One is set in heaven, in a globe-*mandorla, and the other on earth, depicted by a scene of his crucifixion. To the left of the crucifixion is a nude David, anointed by an angel: kings are seen bearing gifts (the seas are represented at the bottom of the image) illustrating verse 25 ('I will set his hand on the sea') and verse 27 ('I will make him... the highest of the kings of the earth').[289] By contrast, one of the images in the *Stuttgart Psalter* (fol. 103v) focusses on verse 5 ('your faithfulness... in the assembly of the holy ones') and has a scene of Christ in glory (not his transfiguration) with Saint Peter, Saint Paul and another saint.[290]

Two very different contemporary artists illustrate well the differences between Jewish and Christian readings of this psalm: Moshe *Berger's image is of a bright white central orb out of which emanates Hebrew calligraphy, amidst deep blue rays; a crown is visible above the orb, and above that, the blue rays turn to red. The reference is from verse 29 (Eng. v. 28), translated here as 'I was kind to David when I made him King. This kindness will endure for ever. I entered into covenants with Abraham and David and I shall keep them forever.' This accords very much with the more positive reading of the psalm as a whole in Jewish tradition, which was discussed earlier.[291]

The second image is by Roger *Wagner, who, at the very end of Book Three of his *Book of Praises* illustrates verse 39 with an image of Christ on the cross, as the rejected Messiah, fitting with the tone of despair at the end of psalm, and giving it some correspondences with the visual exegesis of the end of Psalm 88 earlier (Figure 6). [292] This resonates with the more traditional view in reception history that the psalm ends on a negative note of despair.

Like Psalms 2, 45 and 110, the reception of this psalm points to key differences of Jewish and Christian reception, and their different interpretations of the everlasting or temporal nature of the Davidic covenant, and of the identity of the one who is to inherit the promises of an everlasting throne.

Before moving on to assess the reception history of the psalms in Book Four, it is important to finish with some observations about Book Three. One is to

---

[288] See http://www.bl.uk/manuscripts/Viewer.aspx?ref=add_ms_19352_f118r.

[289] See http://psalter.library.uu.nl/page?p=109&res=1&x=0&y=0.

[290] See http://warburg.sas.ac.uk/vpc/VPC_search/record.php?record=32193.

[291] See pp. 73–4 (on Psalm 89).

[292] This is taken from email correspondence with the artists in November 2015.

You have put an end	הִשְׁבַּתָּ
To his brightness	מִטְּהָרוֹ
And flung his throne	וְכִסְאוֹ לָאָרֶץ
Into the dust	מִגַּרְתָּה:
You have cut short	הִקְצַרְתָּ
The days of his youth	יְמֵי עֲלוּמָיו
And have covered him	הֶעֱטִיתָ עָלָיו
With shame	בּוּשָׁה

Selah סֶלָה:

FIGURE 6   *Roger Wagner, Ps. 89:44–45: The King and the Cross.*

Source: Wagner, R. 2013. *The Book of Praises: A Translation of the Psalms. Book Three*. Oxford: The Besalel Press.

note a very different tenor than that in Books One and Two, which through the collections of laments, thanksgiving and didactic psalms performed a prayerful and ethical guide to obedience and piety. Very few psalms in Book Three have been used in this way: other than Psalm 73, the only other obvious exceptions are Psalm 86, a 'Psalm of David', and perhaps also Psalm 84. Following from this, a second observation is that the reception history of Book Three, through the rich resources of liturgy, illumination, music and poetry, has been more concerned with theological questions about the character of God and his dealings with his entire people. A persistent concern, especially in Jewish reception, has been about making sense of a broken past in order to face the future. This 'backwards look' has been the key feature of Book Three: only in Books Four and Five is there a more decisive future perspective. Finally, because of this interest in the fate of the whole community, the memory is primarily focussed on the covenant made with Moses and the traditions of Genesis and Exodus (Psalms 74–78 [other than 78:67–72], 79–83), and only in the latter part of Book Three does the attention begin to focus more on David (Psalms 86 and 89). This dialogue between the covenants with Moses and David is a critical feature of Book Four, with its additional element of the 'High Kingship of Yahweh'. Psalm 90 thus returns to the interest in Moses and the vicissitudes of the people at a time of loss.

BOOK FOUR: PSALMS 90–106

Human Transience and the Everlasting God

Book Four, also a collection of seventeen psalms, could be read as a response to the more agonised psalms questioning the presence of God in Book Three. Book Four can be divided into four sub-groups, each comprising different themes which highlight different facets of the character of God, who here is presented as Refuge, King, Defender, Creator/Redeemer.[1] For example, the first three psalms (90–92) are quiet and reflective prayer; the focus is on God as Refuge, and the figure of Moses and the traditions of the Exodus and wilderness are prominent. All three psalms are connected by several linguistic motifs. The next eight psalms are jubilant praise (Psalms 93, 95–100), interrupted by a lament, reflecting on the judgement of God, in Psalm 94; throughout the emphasis is on God as King, both over his people and over the entire cosmos. Again, these psalms have several linguistic correspondences, and Moses and the Exodus again play an important part throughout. The following three psalms (101–103) return to the mood of reflective prayer, with personal complaints interspersed with declarations of faith: the theme is God as Defender, and although there are some echoes of Psalms 90–92, the focus is not on Moses, but on David as a paradigm of obedient faith, continuing the theme of kingship expressed in Psalms 93–100.[2] In the final collection (Psalms 104–106) the figure of Moses comes back in view: this collection starts with a psalm of praise, and the emphasis

---

[1] These sub-groups have some affinity to the divisions offered by Wallace 2007: 88–94.

[2] See McKelvey 2010: 3 and 15, who argues that although God's Kingdom is of paramount importance Moses and David are in different ways earthly expressions of it.

Psalms Through the Centuries: A Reception History Commentary on Psalms 73–151, Volume Three, First Edition. Susan Gillingham.
© 2022 John Wiley & Sons Ltd. Published 2022 by John Wiley & Sons Ltd.

is now on God as Creator (Psalm 104) and Redeemer (105–106), with Psalm 106, closely linked to 105, concluding Book Four with instruction and warnings on account of the peoples' failures. So whereas Book Three was a 'Book of Questions', Book Four offers some tentative answers, in four movements, twice progressing from quiet reflection to corporate praise. The conclusion is more solemn, as it was at the beginning, with a considered reflection of the peoples' inconstancy compared with the constancy of their God.

Moses is more dominant here than anywhere else in the Psalter. He is only mentioned once in the Psalter outside Book Four, but seven times within it.[3] The shadow of Moses is cast over the whole of Book Four, with his presence being specifically evident in the first and last psalm of the whole collection, as a reminder of what God has done for the people in the past.[4] By contrast, the Davidic title occurs in only two psalms in the Hebrew text; proportionally this is far less than in any of the other four Books of the Psalter. This alternative perspective is hardly surprising, given the dissolution of the monarchy which is expressed so vividly in Psalm 89 at the end of Book Three.

The *LXX translators countered this emphasis by adding more Davidic titles throughout the whole of Book Four: nine of the thirteen psalms over which the title *tō David* has been added are found in these seventeen psalms. Additions are made to 91 (*LXX 90); 93 (92); 94 (93); 95 (94); 96 (95); 97 (96); 98 (97); 99 (98); and 104 (103). The Davidic headings in Psalms 96 (95) and 97 (96) are oddly anachronistic, however, as they add further details about the rebuilding of the Temple (96 [95]) and the restoration of the land (97 [96]). Furthermore, the Davidic headings in Psalms 91 (90), 93 (92), 95 (94), 96 (95) and 97 (96), all untitled psalms in the Hebrew, contain other additions which suggest a more eschatological interest in David, making a link between the Kingship of God and a coming Davidic Messiah. In brief, the narrative impact of Book Four in the Hebrew develops a sense of community identity which is informed more by the covenant with Moses, and the narrative impact in the Greek develops a sense of community identity which is informed more by the covenant with David. We shall see how this is further developed in the commentary on the individual psalms.[5]

The story of Book Four can be perceived in another way. Just as Book Three overall bears witness to the downfall of the king, Psalms 90–106 reflect on what follows, chronologically, in Israel's history: the consequent experience of the exile. The repeated emphasis on Moses and the Exodus traditions throughout

---

[3] Outside Book Four, Moses is referred to explicitly only in Ps. 77:21. In Book Four, references are found in the title to Psalm 90 and in Pss. 99:6; 103:7; 105:26; 106:16, 23, 32.

[4] See Mournet 2011: 66–79.

[5] We shall see how this is further developed in the commentary on the individual psalms.

Book Four has affinities with other biblical texts such as Isaiah 40–55 which also suggest the effects of the exile. For example, Book Four begins and ends with pleas to God to 'take pity' on his people (90:13 and 106:45) and the beginning and ending of Isaiah 40–55 reflect the same theme (Isa. 40:1 and 54:11). At the beginnings of each work, in Ps. 90:5 and Isa. 40:6–8, human frailty is compared with grass. And in Pss. 96:1 and 98:1, as well as in Isa. 42:10, we read of the 'new song' which is a celebration of what God will later do for his people. Furthermore, the universal reign of God is defiantly declared throughout both works, for example in Ps. 96:4–5 and Isa. 40:18–23. Each denounces the worship of all idols, each playing on the Hebrew words for 'gods' (*elohim*) and 'nobodies' (*elilim*: see Ps. 96:5 and Isa. 40:17–18).[6]

The overall theological interest in Book Four is in the ephemeral nature of humanity and the everlasting faithfulness of God, who, as we have noted, is the Refuge, King, Defender, Creator and Redeemer of his people. As far as reception history is concerned, this overall emphasis on the character of God provides an opportunity to bring the two faith traditions more closely together, although the familiar controversies of 'Judaising' or 'Christianianising' a psalm will also become evident.

[6] See for example Creach 1998: 63–76. Other studies on the shape of Psalms 90–106 include Goulder 1975: 269–89; Zenger 1998: 238–57; Kim 2008: 143–58; Gelston 2010: 163–76; and Ngoda 2014: 147–59.

The *motif* of 'God as Refuge' is found in Pss. 90:1, 91:1–2, 9–10 and 92:12–13. Psalms 90–92 together are particularly preoccupied with the transitory nature of humanity, with Moses playing a central part in all three psalms. The importance of Moses in this and in the next collection is emphasised even more by later Jewish reception history: for example, in the *Midrash Tehillim* not only Psalm 90 is given Mosaic authorship, but also the next ten psalms, up to Psalm 100—one for each of the eleven of the tribes (Simeon is excluded on account of that tribe's disobedience as told in Numbers 25). So here Psalm 90 is for Reuben; Psalm 91, for Levi; and Psalm 92, for Judah. This contrasts markedly with the Davidic titles in the *LXX* tradition; it also explains the more Davidic/royal readings of these psalms in subsequent Christian readings because they were more dependent upon the Greek translation.

These three psalms move in an increasingly hopeful sequence from lament (Psalm 90) to divine promise (Psalm 91) to thanksgiving (Psalm 92), the latter preparing the way for the praise which follows in Psalms 93 and 95–100. The key theme is that, rather than depending on any human institution, God alone is now the refuge of his people, and his never-failing presence is to be found by 'night and day' (90:5–6; 91:5–6; 92:2).

Psalm 90: Lamenting Human Transience

Psalm 90 immediately refers back to Psalm 89, concerning the brevity of life (90:3–6; 89:47–48): the context seems to be of a people still living under the

Psalms Through the Centuries: A Reception History Commentary on Psalms 73-151, Volume Three, First Edition. Susan Gillingham.
© 2022 John Wiley & Sons Ltd. Published 2022 by John Wiley & Sons Ltd.

judgement of God (compare 90:7–10 and 89:46) and the question 'how long?' is found in Pss. 90:13 and 89:46. The inspiration of Moses is not only in the heading ('A Prayer of Moses, the man of God') but also in the use of parts of his 'speeches' of Deuteronomy 32, 33 and Exodus 32. The *Targum* heading over Psalm 90 is 'A prayer of Moses the prophet, when the people of Israel sinned in the desert', thus emphasising the mediating role of Moses throughout the psalm and the use of texts from Exodus and Deuteronomy. Verses 1–6 lament human mortality; verses 7–12 reflect on God's wrath.[7] Verses 13–17 petition God to restore his 'dwelling place' with his people.

Later Jewish interpretation continues the emphasis on Moses in relation to this psalm. He is 'the man of God' because he stood before the people 'as God' through the miraculous escape from Egypt and on Sinai: 'From his middle and above Moses was called "God"; and from his middle and below he was a man.'[8] A somewhat different reading of this psalm focuses on verse 4 ('a thousand years in thy sight are but as yesterday'), arguing that if a day is a thousand year period, then from Creation to Moses, and Moses to David, and David until the present day is 5000 years (that is, about 1000CE); the dawn of the Messianic Age will be at 6000 years (c. 2000CE) and will last for a final 1,000 years: so within this constructed 'world history', Moses plays a significant part, as revealed in this psalm.

The theme of transience in this psalm has resulted in a prominent liturgical use of this psalm in Jewish tradition. It is used at funerals along with Psalm 91, and sometimes with Psalm 92. Psalm 90 is prominent in the *Shiva (shib'ah)* service—i.e. the daily services lasting seven days at a mourner's home after the burial. It is also frequently used (along with Psalms 91, 92, 93 and 100 in Book Four) as *'Verses of Song'* (*Pesukei de-Zimra*) heralding the 'reception' of the Sabbath (*Kabbalat Shabbat*) on Friday evening.[9] The psalm is also used in a traditional morning *Shabbat* service to frame the 'Great Hallel' (Psalms 135 and 136) along with Psalms 19, 24, and 91 (Psalms 33, 92 and 93 were added at the end of it) and, the whole collection preceded the Daily Hallel (Psalms 145–150) to teach about Exodus, Creation and the world to come as preparation for the *Shabbat* prayers.[10]

Despite its theological emphasis on God as an eternal refuge, only verse four is alluded to in the New Testament. This is in 2 Pet. 3:8, but here the emphasis

---

[7] In v. 10 'seventy years' brings together the two themes of human mortality and also the years of exile (see for example Jer. 25:11, 12 and 29:10).

[8] R. Abin, cited in Braude 1959: 89. *Midrash Tehillim* also debates the tradition of Moses being called the 'spouse of God', acting like a husband who has authority over his wife to ratify or make void a vow: see, Braude 1959: 89–90, citing R. Simeon ben Lakish.

[9] In Orthodox liturgy, Psalm 90, along with Psalms 91–93 and 100, is used even more frequently, found in every morning service.

[10] Many of these details were taken from Boeckler: 2014 (unpublished paper).

is different. The context concerns the coming Day of the Lord ('with the Lord one day is like a thousand years, and a thousand years are like one day'). The verse is also used in this way in early Christian writings such as *Justin's *Dial.* (81:3) and the Epistle of Barnabas 15:4. Later Christian writers, such as *Basil the Great and *Athanasius, have commented on the theme of 'refuge in God' in this psalm, but also give it a more Christian apologetic twist: Athanasius, for example, uses this psalm against the *Arians in his defence of the 'eternity' of the Son.[11] A curious example of later reception is the way that Hebrew of verse 9 'our years come to an end *like a sigh*' (*kemō hegeh*) is found in the Greek and Latin respectively as *hōs arachnēn* and *sicut aranea* ('like a spider') so this verse reads as 'our years come to an end like a spider'. Commentators such as *Cassiodorus see this as a simile for the barrenness of our lives, as like a spider we weave what webs we can in the hope of catching passing flies.[12] The *Stuttgart Psalter* (fol. 106v) depicts the psalmist sitting and watching a huge spider spinning its web.[13]

In English liturgy, it is the theme of refuge in God which has given this psalm its popular appeal. The hymn by Isaac *Watts (composed in about 1719), originally entitled 'Man Frail and God Eternal', is frequently used at Remembrance Day services in Britain, as well as at State Funerals (for example, that of Winston Churchill in 1965) to commemorate the permanency of God over and against the futility of war and the fragility of life. Probably this public liturgical use explains its occurrence in Evelyn Waugh's *Decline and Fall* (1928) and in the film *Tom Jones* (1963).[14]

> O God, our help in ages past,
> our hope for years to come,
> our shelter from the stormy blast,
> and our eternal home.
>
> A thousand ages, in thy sight,
> are like an evening gone;
> short as the watch that ends the night,
> before the rising sun.
>
> Time, like an ever rolling stream,
> bears all who breathe away;
> they fly forgotten, as a dream
> dies at the opening day.[15]

---

[11] See Wesselschmidt 2007: 166–9: see Athanasius' *Discourses Against the Arians 1.4.12,13* in NPNF 2 4:313–14 (on 90:1–2 and 17).

[12] Cassiodorus trans. Walsh 1991a: 375.

[13] On the use of 'spider' in the Psalter see Gillingham 2018: 238–9 and 333.

[14] See Dowling Long and Sawyer 2015: 172. Unusually for Watts, no explicit Christian reinterpretation is evident.

[15] Bishop Edward Bickersteth's hymn 'O God the Rock of Ages' (1860) follows a similar theme, as does Francis *Bacon's poem 'O Lord, thou art our home, to whom we fly': for the latter, see Wieder 1995: 137–8.

In about 1781 Robert *Burns composed a non-liturgical interpretation in his 'The First Six Verses of the Ninetieth Psalm'; instead of Watts' emphasis on time and eternity Burns dwells on the theme of God our Creator:

> O Thou, the first, the greatest friend
> Of all the human race!
> Whose strong right hand has ever been
> Their stay and dwelling-place!
>
> Before the mountains heaved their heads
> Beneath thy forming hand,
> Before this ponderous globe itself
> Arose at thy command.
>
> That power which raised and still upholds
> This universal frame,
> From countless, unbeginning time
> Was ever still the same...[16]

Several musical performances of this psalm also develop this theme of time and timelessness. John Henry *Newman used this psalm (along with 31 and 148) at end of his 'Dream of Gerontius', composed in 1865. In *Elgar's version of Newman's text, this is sung by the souls in Purgatory:

> Lord, Thou hast been our refuge in every generation
> Come back, O Lord! How long: and be entreated for Thy servants
> Bring us not, Lord, very low: for Thou hast said,
> Come back again, ye sons of Adam...

This is followed by the final chorus of Angels singing what became a well-known hymn:

> Praise to the Holiest in the height
> and in the depths be praise;
> in all his deeds most wonderful,
> most sure in all his ways.

In 1921 Ralph *Vaughan Williams composed 'Lord, Thou hast been our Refuge', also developing the theme of human fragility and dwelling in God's presence. The choir (or sometimes a baritone soloist) chants the first verses, all explicitly on the brevity of life; this is followed by silence, and then the organ (or more arrestingly a single trumpet) breaks the hush with the first line of Watts' 'O God our Help in Ages Past', to its familiar tune of 'St Anne'. The two are performed

[16] See Atwan and Wieder 1993: 11–12.

in tandem until the end of the first verse of Watts' hymn, after which the psalm continues, interspersed with fugal instrumental echoes of 'St Anne', reaching a finale with the last verses, starting with 'The glorious majesty of the Lord be upon us'. This was sung by Westminster Abbey Choir at the 70th Anniversary Service of the Battle of Britain in 2010.[17]

A very different interpretation is by Charles *Ives, who set the words of the *KJV of Psalm 90 to music in 1923–24, reflecting that this was the only piece he had ever set which really satisfied him. The darkest parts, concerned with the threat of our destruction (verses 3–4) are intoned mainly in unison, whilst the more poignant prayers for God to deflect his anger (verses 12 and 13) mainly use tenor and soprano solo voices, and the resolution and submission to God at the end of the psalm (14–17) is sung as a chorale, with church bells and a gong contrasting with the threatening moods of the earlier verses. Pedal C dominates the organ throughout, as a symbol of God's omnipresence in life and death.[18]

The visual representation of this psalm is mainly depicted not so much in Christological terms but with a more universal appropriation. Even the image in the *Utrecht Psalter, despite its familiar depiction of Christ Logos flanked by angels, is dominated by a walled enclosure which represents the tabernacle which in turn represents the psalmist's refuge in God.[19] Only Byzantine Psalters such as the *Theodore Psalter are more Christocentric; the image there is of Moses, the purported author of the psalm, praying to Christ. More universal tendencies are continued in the *St Albans Psalter, some three hundred years later than *Utrecht*, where the initial 'D' for '*Domine*' at the beginning the psalm depicts a young man holding two sprouting branches ('In the morning he shall pass away like grass...') and facing him is a stooped old man, holding a crutch and another branch ('And in the evening he shall grow dry and wither').[20] A vast number of modern images of Psalm 90 are based on verse 4 ('a thousand years in your sight are like a year that is just gone by') and verse 12 ('teach us to number our days'), each without a specifically Christian emphasis.

In the *KJV* verse 3 reads: 'Thou turnest man to destruction; and sayest, Return, ye children of men'. The word 'destruction' rather than 'dust' is a more negative rendering of the Hebrew which is not found in more recent translations. The phrase 'children of men' at the end of this verse gave rise to a disturbing novel by the English crime writer P. D. James: *The Children of Men* was published in 1992 and adapted into a film in 2006 by Alfonso Cuarón. It opens with a record from the 2021 diary of an Oxford don, 'Theo' Faron, which

---

[17] See https://www.youtube.com/watch?v=R4vdOyc5Nnc.

[18] See Kirkpatrick and Smith 1970, on Ives' composition of Psalm 90.

[19] See https://psalter.library.uu.nl/page/113.

[20] See https://www.albani-psalter.de/stalbanspsalter/english/commentary/page254.shtml.

records that no births have been recorded for some twenty-five years, and the human race now faces extinction. The book explores the consequences of mass infertility not only in terms of human transience but of the limits of political power. The more positive emphasis in the psalm is alluded to when the possibility of the 'redemption' of humanity eventually emerges in the discovery of a baby boy. Humans might once again learn to praise God for being our eternal Refuge. In the light of the prominent use of this psalm (and indeed the two psalms following it) during the Covid pandemic, the use of this verse by P. D. James has an uncanny resonance.[21] Whether in liturgy, poetic imitation, musical interpretation or art, and whether in Jewish or Christian tradition, the most consistent theme is that of the contrast between human mortality and the eternal God as Refuge: but the experience of Refuge comes through dislocation of communities and destruction of human life. Small wonder it has appealed to threatened and fragmented Jewish and Christian communities over more than two millennia. It is 'everyone's psalm', for it teaches how an experience of human fragility can be transformed by knowing that although life is temporal, God is eternal. In the words of *Coverdale, still chanted today, '*O teach us to nonbre oure dayes, that we maye applye oure hertes unto wysdome*' (90:12).

Psalm 91: God's Promise of Protection

Psalm 91 also emphasises that God is a 'dwelling place' or 'refuge' (91:2, 9; see 90:1) but here the psalmist is preoccupied with some specific deliverance from evil. Psalm 91 can be read as three promises given in three parts of the psalm: vv. 1–8, 9–13 and 14–16. In the first part, after a confession of faith (vv. 1–3), the verses switch dramatically to address the reader in the second person and offer an extraordinary image of God as a mother eagle who protects his people from the 'snare and fowler' and night-time and noon-day pestilence and destruction.[22] The second promise of refuge (vv. 9–13), likewise beginning in the first person (v. 9a) and switching dramatically to address the reader in the second person (vv. 9b–13), refers to God sending his protective angels.[23] The third promise (vv. 14–16) consists of eight blessings, using eight verbs of protection: here, unusually in the Psalms, God speaks in the first person—taking on a persona more common to the prophetic literature.

---

[21] This commentary was in the process of being completed in 2021.

[22] This image is also found in Exod. 19:4 and Deut. 32:10–12 and here it may allude to the wings of cherubim in temple (1 Kgs. 6:23–28) suggesting God's everlasting care for his people despite the destruction of his 'dwelling place'.

[23] This may allude to other Mosaic passages such as Exod. 23:20, 23 and 32:34.

The attributions in the *Midrash Tehillim* of this psalm to Moses understand the 'secret place' in verses 1 and 9 to be the Holy of Holies or a reference to Moses' unique position before God.[24] By contrast, the *Targum* arranges this psalm as a dialogue between David and Solomon: in verses 2–8 David speaks to Solomon, in verses 9 Solomon responds, and in verses 10–16 God speaks. This is, however, an atypical understanding of the role of David in these three psalms: most later (post-*Septuagint) Jewish readings emphasise Moses, not David, with some understanding the psalm to be written by Moses for the tribe of Levi (probably on account of the reference to the sanctuary).

Although it is difficult to be sure of any direct correspondence, there are some intriguing similarities with a much earlier, possibly seventh-century, Phoenician text in Aramaic. The text is an incantation, seeking help from the deities Ashur, Horon and Shamash to keep the night creatures at bay until the sun rises.[25] Immediately we are reminded of Psalm 91:5–6 and the promises of protection from the 'terror of the night, or the arrow that flies by day, or the pestilence that stalks in darkness, or the destruction that wastes at noonday'. The Phoenician inscription, from Arslan Tash, is too large for an amulet, but it may well have been attached to a doorpost, following the ritual described in Exod. 12:22–27 and Deut. 6:4–9. An intriguing link with Psalm 91 is the use of similar verbs found in verse 13—'You shall tread (using the verb *d-r-kh*)) on the lion and adder, the young lion and the serpent you will trample (using *r-m-s*) under foot'. Another correspondence is the promise of rescue in verse 3 'He will deliver you (using the *hiphil* of *n-ṣ-l*,) from the snare of the fowler'.[26]

The correspondence of parts of this psalm with an ancient incantation text also fits well with its later apotropaic reception, particularly between the first-century BCE and first-century CE. For example, at *Qumran, in 4QPs[b] (vv. 5–8 and 12–15), and again in 11QPsAp[a] (vv. 1–4 and 16), Psalm 91 is included alongside three other non-canonical psalms as the 'Fourth Exorcism Psalm'.[27] The *Septuagint also reflects this reading: the difficult phrase in verse 6, 'the destruction that wastes at noonday' (*miqqeteb yashud ṣohorayim*), is translated as 'the noonday demon' (*daimoniov mesēmbrinos*). Here the Hebrew verb meaning 'destroy' (*'yashud'* from *sh-d-d*) is read as a demonic force, illustrating the tendency in the Greek to view the whole psalm as having the power to drive away personified forces of evil (cf. the name for God *shaday* in v. 1). This in turn throws some light on the ironic citation by Satan in his use of this 'anti-demonic psalm' in Jesus Christ's temptations. Ps. 91:11–12 ('For he will give his

[24] Braude 1959: 100–3.

[25] See Cathcart 2011: 87–100.

[26] See *ibid*.

[27] See Evans 2011: 541–45, also citing Josephus, *Ant.* 8:45–47.

angels charge of you... On their hands they will bear you up') is quoted by Satan in Matt. 4:6 and Lk. 4:11, as part of his last challenge to Jesus to throw himself from the pinnacle of the Temple. It is illuminating to see the way Christ rejects the magical use of this psalm in his response ('Do not put the Lord your God to the test', citing Deut. 6:16) both in Matt. 4:7 and Lk. 4:12. The magical associations of this psalm are however recognised in the citation of verse 13 ('you will tread on the lion and the adder...') in Lk. 10:19.

A magical reading of this psalm continues in Jewish reception. The *Talmud entitles Psalm 91 as 'A Song referring to Evil Demons' (*b. Shavu'ot* 15b) and *Midrash Tehillim* explains how Moses composed this psalm while ascending to heaven in order to defend himself against some demonic attack, a point on which *Rashi also agrees.[28] The *Targum* paraphrase of verses 5–6 is explicit: 'Be not afraid of the terror of demons that go about in the night, nor of the arrow of the angel of death that he shoots in the daytime, nor of the death that goes about in the darkness, nor of the company of demons that destroy at noon.'[29] In *Shimmush Tehillim*, a medieval text on the magical use of the psalms, Psalms 90 and 91 are to be recited over a person tormented by an evil spirit. In one fragment from the Cairo *Genizah*, Ps. 91:1 is interlocked word by word with Deut. 6:4, again suggesting some incantational use, giving a fascinating insight into the knowledge of both texts as in the Temptations of Christ. Parts of Psalm 91 are also found on several incantation bowls, written in Aramaic—in this instance the bowls were turned upside down, supposedly to trap the evil spirits.[30] There is also evidence that verse 16 of this psalm ('with long life I will satisfy him') served as a medical amulet in Hebrew.[31]

In Christian tradition, Psalm 91, through the Latin translation of the Greek in the *Gallican Psalter*, was also known, by the early Church Fathers, as an 'exorcism text'. One Latin translation at the end of verse 6 reads '*a morsu infidiantis meridae*' ('by the bite of the midday demon'). By the Middle Ages, in the *Ordinaria*, the marginal comment reads 'a hymn against demons'. A fourteenth-century Wycliffite version in Middle English actually translates the Latin word for demon as 'goblin'. In the medieval monastic tradition this 'midday demon' was popularised as one of the four vexations of the church, each assigned to a specific devil: this particular demon, disguised as an angel of light, plagued the monks with lethargy at noon-time.[32] Parts of this psalm are found on door lintels in Syria, Cyprus and in two Byzantine churches in Ravenna where again

---

[28] See Braude 1959: 101; and Gruber 2004: 583.

[29] See Stec 2004: 174–75.

[30] See Breed 2014: 298–303.

[31] Davis 1992: 174–75.

[32] See Kaulbach 2008b: 553–54.

they point to the apotropaic quality of this psalm. Most tellingly, at least twenty-five examples of verse 4–5 and verse 11 have been found on Byzantine amulets and rings from the sixth- to twelfth-centuries CE.[33]

This popular use of Psalm 91 in Jewish liturgy follows that of the previous psalm. In some Jewish traditions, it is read, along with Psalm 90, at funerals: as the coffin is carried to its grave, these two psalms are chanted between three and seven times along the way. In the *Ashkenazi tradition, it is read with Psalm 90 as one of the additional *'Verses of Song' in the morning services of Sabbaths and feast days.[34]

In Christian liturgy, at least by the sixth-century, Psalm 91 became one of the most frequently prayed psalms at *Compline, along with Psalms 4 and 134.[35] The association of Christ's protection over the night-time demons resulted in this psalm becoming, in Benedictine tradition, the first of the Compline Psalms, as those performing the *Opus Dei* sought protection through the night hours. For similar theological reasons it became an important psalm in Good Friday Liturgy in the Western churches, where it was often used with John 3, each with the *motif* of the serpent: the crucifixion was thus understood as the means whereby Christ trampled underfoot (see Ps. 91:13) the demonic forces.[36]

The imagery in this psalm has inspired diverse representations in art. The reference to Christ treading underfoot the lion and serpent is a typical image in many illuminated Psalters.[37] Sometimes this 'trampling' refers to the spiritual forces of evil: a striking example is found in the *St Albans Psalter*, where the illuminated initial 'Q' introducing this psalm depicts Christ stamping on the basilisk, asp, lion and dragon, prodding them with his crozier shaped as a 'tau' and clasping a book with verse 13 written on the cover.[38] A different example is found in the marginal illustrations in the *Theodore Psalter* (fol. 123v), where verse 12 is selected as an example of this psalm by Jesus Christ during his temptations: here he stands, resolute, on the roof of the Temple.[39] A similar image is found in the *Khuldov Psalter* (fol. 92v).

Other images depict trampling enemy forces in military terms. An early ninth-century example is from a *Carolingian Manuscript, comprising a Gospel Lectionary, made in Aachen at the court of Charlemagne. Known as *The Douce Ivory*, the ivory plaque on the cover depicts Christ in majesty, bearing a cross-

---

[33] See Breed 2014: 301–2. See also Maguire 1989, plates 134 and 136 (cited in; Holladay 1993: 190).

[34] Hertz 1942: 61–83.

[35] Neale and Littledale 1874–79: 3/162–3.

[36] Breed 2014: 303–7.

[37] For the *Eadwine Psalter, see https://bit.ly/2QaBDDn.

[38] See https://www.albani-psalter.de/stalbanspsalter/english/commentary/page256.shtml

[39] See http://www.bl.uk/manuscripts/Viewer.aspx?ref=add_ms_19352_f207v.

staff over his shoulder, carrying an open book inscribed 'HIS XPS' (*'Iesus Christus'*) and 'SVP[er] ASP[idem]' (*'super aspidem'* from Ps. 91:13). As the verse indicates, Christ's feet are trampling on a lion and a serpent-dragon. Given the associations between the Charlemagne as king and Christ as king, the physical and spiritual connotations of this victory over evil forces are obvious. This is represented here as PLATE 6.[40] The imagery of God as 'Shield and Buckler' (verse 4) further contribute to more military and physical readings: themes also used in heraldry.[41] The imagery is similarly developed in the circle of Andries Cornelis Lens (1739–1822) where the painting is of an angel and cherub with sword and shield, with the title *'Scuto circumdabit te veritas eius'*—'Truth will encompass you with his shield', taken from Psalm 91:4 (**Vulgate: 90:5).[42]

It is not surprising that several contemporary military interpretations of this psalm make the same point. Chuck Norris, for example, cited this psalm in the context of Islamic Fascism: 'God of 911, Psalm 91:1'.[43] Ps. 91:5 is one of the verses found on the telescopic sights of Accupin rifles made by the American firm Trijicon: 'Thou shalt not be afraid of the terror by night, nor of the arrow that flieth by day'. Furthermore, the camouflage bandana for the US Marines has part of Psalm 91 printed on it, with the slogan: 'Someone is watching over you.'[44] More poignantly, this psalm also occurs in *Dr. Zhivago*: Yuri Zhivago, escaping to meet his lover, Lara, but captured by the Reds, is obliged to treat a wounded young soldier: he is amazed to see that the bullet which struck just above the heart hit a locket with an amulet inside, thus saving the soldier's life. The soldier's mother had carved on the amulet the very same 'deliverance' passage from Psalm 91:5.

More spiritual artistic depictions of this psalm are found in the *kabbalistic tradition.[45] A recent Jewish illustrator, Irwin *Davis composed his own version of the psalm in 1992 to give it both literal and spirtual meanings. Verses 5–6 are depicted in both ways: on the right side, symbolising daytime, the literal reading of warfare depicted, with archers firing arrows into a burning castle, whilst on the left side, symbolising night time, a bird of prey hovers whilst watching pestilence attack a group of people in a ruined landscape. The spiritual reading arises out of the centre of the psalm: the obedient believer is lifted high by six angels, forming a star of David, and thus protected from the carnal sins of power (represented by the lion) and lust (depicted by the snake).

---

[40] See Hebron 2014: 174–75.

[41] See Huxley 1949: 297–305, citing verses 4 and 11 of Psalm 91 as popular mottos.

[42] See https://bit.ly/2RjlY5v.

[43] Breed 2014: 306–7.

[44] On Psalm 91 on Christian rifles, see https://en.wikipedia.org/wiki/Trijicon_biblical_verses_controversy. On the citation of this psalm on bandanas, see, for example, http://www.thepsalm91bandana.com.

[45] See http://themuseumofpsalms.com/product/psalm-91.

The diverse liturgical settings for this psalm have inspired its musical use. One of the most interesting is *Mendelssohn's rendering of 'He shall give his angels charge over thee' in his *Elijah* (first performed in 1846). Psalm 91:11 is found in Part One, Movement 7 (when Elijah raises from the dead a widow's son) set as a double quartet sung by angels.[46] A vast number of musical arrangements seek to portray the idea of God protecting the individual from the (spiritual) forces of evil. These could be compositions for the Catholic Sunday service in seventeenth-century Venice, as illustrated by Johann Rosenmüller's 'Qui habitat in adjutorio' (for two four-voice choirs and a small orchestra). Or they could be chants for Anglican liturgy using *Coverdale's version, such as the version by T. Tertius Noble (1867–1953), 'Whoso dwelleth under the defence'. Or they could even be arrangements for more contemporary Catholic liturgy, as in the version by Joseph *Gelineau, 'Those who dwell'.[47] Other modern examples include a recent Jewish rendering by Alon Wallach (b. 1980) for the Frankfurt 'Tehillim Project' which adapts an unusual 5/4 time to indicate the vicissitudes and instabilities found within this psalm. And finally, the Irish singer Sinead O'Connor chose 'The Lion and the Cobra' as the title of her debut album (1987) based on Ps. 91:13. One of the tracks, 'Never Get Old', is a recital by Enya, in Gaelic, from Psalm 91, again developing the theme of protection.[48] O'Connor produced a later version of this psalm as 'Whomsoever dwells'. Her lyrics also reflect on the quasi-magical qualities of the psalm:

> Whomsoever dwells
> In the shelter
> Of the most high
> Lives under the protection of the Shaddai
> I say of my lord
> That he is my fortress
> That he is my own love
> In whom I trust
> That he will save u
> From the fowler's trap

[46] Verse 7 ('A thousand may fall at our side') is also used in Part Two, after Elijah has faced Jezebel. We have noted the use of Psalm 88 in this oratorio (p. 69); Ps. 93:3–4 are also used as part of a choral setting after the defeat of the prophets of Baal. See 'Eljiah' in Stern 2011: 259–79; also Dowling Long and Sawyer 2015: 75.

[47] For Noble's version, see 'O Praise the Lord of Heaven' *The Psalms of David Volume 2*, Wells Cathedral Choir, directed by Anthony Crossland; Priory Digital Recording 337, 1990. For Gelinau, see *Psalms of David*, with the Cathedral Singers and Richard Proulx, Conductor. GIA Publications Inc. CD 357 at https://www.giamusic.com/store/resource/psalms-of-david-recording-cd357.

[48] Hear Enya at http://www.last.fm/music/Sin%C3%A9ad+O%27Connor/_/Never+Get+Old?autostart.

And he will save you
From any Babylonian crap
And he will lift you
All up in his wings
And you'll find refuge
Oh underneath those things
And his truth will be your
Shield and rampart
So u need not fear
What comes looking for you in the dark
And you need not fear
What comes looking for you in the day
And you need not fear
What takes everybody else away
Ten thousand may fall at your side
Ten thousand at your right
But it can't come near you
'Cause you're dealing with the most high
And he will send his angels to mind you
And they will lift u all up so that you
Won't strike your foot against no stone.[49]

Hence through the reception history of this psalm (whether expressed through popular use, liturgical adaptation, or in poetry, art and music) we find a consistent theme in both Jewish and Christian interpretation, which is closely linked to the psalm before it and to the psalm after it: God is (again) our refuge. In the case of Psalm 91, God is the one who protects more personally (those who trust him) and more specifically (from various described forms of evil). As was seen for Psalm 90, this is a universal theme, appropriate not only for a people exiled in the sixth-century BCE, but also for all those afflicted by the vicissitudes of life. This is neatly summed up in part of Richard Gwyn's Psalm 91 in Haiku form:

…He will cover you,
His pinions a shield for you
when danger threatens.

His truth your buckler
you will have no need to fear
the terrors of the night,

nor arrows by day;
nor pestilential darkness
and plagues at noonday…[50]

[49] See https://www.youtube.com/watch?v=5_CoCepMu7k.
[50] Gwyn 1997: 106.

Psalm 92: A Thanksgiving Song for the Sabbath

Psalm 92 is linked to 91 by its reference to God as 'Most High' (92:1; see 91:1, 9), by its witness of the downfall of the enemy (92:11; see 91:8) and by the ongoing theme of God as Refuge. There are also links back to Psalm 90, for example: the reference to God as 'eternal' (*le'olam*) in verse 8 (Hebrew verse 9) reminds us of Ps. 90:2 (*ume'olam 'ad 'olam*); similarly the reference to evildoers 'flourishing' (using the verb ṣ-ṣ) in verse 7 echoes the image of the grass flourishing in Ps. 90:6 (also using ṣ-ṣ), whilst the reference to God's 'steadfast love' (*ḥesed*) in verse 2 is found in Ps. 90:14, as also 'rejoice' and 'be glad' (ṣ-m-ḥ and r-n-n) in verse 4 in Ps. 90:14.

The reference to God being 'exalted on high' in verse 8 (the longest verse and the heart of the psalm) points ahead to the next Kingship Psalm, 93:4. The psalm is one of optimistic trust in the promises of God. Verses 1–5 are a thanksgiving song; verses 6–11 are a testimony to God's righteous judgement; and verses 12–15 testify to God's constancy.

Although there is no reference to the Sabbath in the text, the sevenfold use of the name of God (*Yahweh*) may have contributed to its title as 'A Song for the Sabbath'. The number seven is an important feature throughout Sabbath liturgy: this is seen, for example, in the seven benedictions in the **'Amidah* prayers for the Sabbath.[51] The Sabbath associations may also have arisen on account of the theme of divine order in creation as in Genesis 1, as well as the emphasis on the righteousness of God at the end of the psalm.[52] These associations are quite early—**Mishnah Tamid* 7:4, for example, refers to the Levitical singers using a special psalm (during the daily **Tamid* sacrifices) and Psalm 92 is assigned the Sabbath day: 'A song for the time to come, for the day that will be all Sabbath and rest for everlasting life'.[53] Psalm 92 is distinctive in the Psalter in that it is the only one to be given a title in the **MT* for a specific day of the week: four other psalms (24, 48, 94 and 93) have these titles but only in the Greek.[54] Because of its Sabbath associations, the ascription of authorship in Jewish interpretation is interesting: it is frequently ascribed to Adam, who, created on the sixth day, sang Psalm 92 and kept the Sabbath on the seventh, and so was saved from death in this act of obedience to Torah. The **Targum* superscription thus reads 'A Psalm and

---

[51] Hertz 1942: 448–69.

[52] See Sarna 1962: 155–68. The more unusual treatment of the 'socio-moral motif' of the Sabbath is on pp. 165–7.

[53] See Trudinger 2004: 14–18, 147–60.

[54] On the use of this psalm as preparation for Sabbath prayer along with the Great Hallel and Daily Hallel and six other psalms, see the commentary on Psalm 91 (p. 90). As with Psalms 90 and 91, this psalm is also used for funerals as mourners enter the synagogue.

Song which Adam offered on the Sabbath Day'. However, because the Torah and Sabbath command were not actually given until the time of Moses, Moses is more often viewed as the author. Hence Moses dedicated this psalm to the tribe of Judah, with the purpose of consoling those brethren who were enslaved in Egypt: the Exodus/Egypt and Exile/Babylon typology are particularly clear in this psalm.[55] *Rashi takes this idea of consolation even further: the psalm speaks of the world to come, at the seventh millennium, when there will be an unending Sabbath.

In subsequent Jewish liturgical practice, Psalm 92 is therefore read as part of the Friday evening prayers welcoming the Sabbath (*Kabbalat Shabbat).[56] In the *Ashkenazi tradition it is also read as part of the *Pesukei de-Zimra used on Sabbaths and feast days instead of Psalm 100 in the morning service: the mode is akin to the minor key, which makes the psalm seem more poignant and meditative. In *Sephardic liturgical tradition the chant used for Psalm 92 is in a mode suggesting a major key, creating a majestic dialogue between the cantor and choir, often with the organ, in order to give the impression that this psalm heralds in the 'Royal Bride' or the 'Queen of Days'. In both ways this psalm nevertheless enriches our sense of rest and peace and refuge in God. In *kabbalistic tradition, Psalm 29 is linked with the Kingship psalms (95–99): along with Psalm 92, these seven psalms represent the seven stages of ascent towards God's mystical presence: and because Psalm 92 is the seventh psalm of the seven, it takes pride of place amongst them.

To remember the Sabbath is to remember that we are all created in God's image—thus opening the psalm up for Christian as well as Jewish use with its universal themes of creation, redemption and God's returning to his people in the future. In terms of reception, Psalm 92 is first and foremost a Jewish psalm. It is not found in the New Testament; it is not as prominent in Christian liturgy as are Psalms 90 and 91.[57] Its main contribution in the commentary tradition is of a single verse. The first three words of verse 10 (verse 11 in the Hebrew) could be translated in many ways: one reading might be, 'You have raised up my horn like a wild ox'. The *LXX translation reads in English 'You have lifted up my horn like a one-horned beast' (*hōs monokepōtos). In *Jerome's Homily on verse 10 of this psalm he speaks of three one-horned animals being sacrificed in the Temple (the bull, the ram and the buck), and, comparing the cross to the horn on which Christ was also a sacrificial victim, he sees this verse referring to Christ, who by his cross raised us from earth to

---

[55] See Braude 1959: 108–114.

[56] This ancient practice is referred to by Maimonides and is also testified in the Palestinian *Genizah texts.

[57] Neale and Littledale 1874–79: 3/185–86.

heaven.[58] The Latin of the *Gallican Psalter* takes this one stage further and reads '*et exaltabitur sicut unicornis cornu meum*'. Both *Coverdale's Psalter and the *KJV translate this as 'But my horn shalt thou exalt like *the horn of a unicorn*.' The tradition of Christ as unicorn has already been referred to in Psalm 22, where it was recognised as an important medieval trope, influencing several illuminated Psalters.[59] Another possible reference to the 'unicorn' was also discussed in the commentary on Ps. 78:69.[60] So in Psalm 92, it is not surprising to find Christ also represented in art as a unicorn, in part influenced by Christian commentary tradition as well as the *Vulgate* translation: John *Chrysostom, for example, interpreting the unicorn as the Son of God, views this verse as a prophecy about Christ, although unlike Jerome this is about his incarnation not his crucifixion. Similarly, *Basil the Great identifies Christ as the unicorn whose one horn reveals he has one common power with the Father.[61]

This depiction of Christ is frequently found in Byzantine Psalters. The *Khludov Psalter* (fol. 93v), for example, offers a marginal illustration of the Virgin Mary and the unicorn, with a note 'Chrysostom interpreted the unicorn as the Son of God', thus viewing this verse as a prophecy about the incarnation.[62] The *Theodore Psalter* (fol. 124v) has only an image of the Virgin and Child, but it is from this same tradition. This representation is continued in Western Psalters, which sometimes display Mary and the unicorn together, or, as in the *Stuttgart Psalter* (fol.108v) the psalmist in conversation with the unicorn, with the finger of God pointing from the heavens that this is Christ himself.[63]

Another common motif in Christian art is of the believer rooted like a palm tree. The *Utrecht Psalter* (fol. 54r) places this in a broader context: the psalmist stands to the left on the steps of the Temple, with the walls of the city below him, safe against his assailants. Four musicians stand to his right, two playing the lyre and harp; across the heavens seven angelic beings cry out, and to the far right is the palm tree, standing firm.[64] The *St Albans Psalter*, by contrast, depicts in the first initial 'B' the just man, standing in a paradise garden, bearing a palm frond.[65] In a later interpretation (c. 1900) James *Tissot depicts Ps. 92:12 by way of the believer standing against a veritable forest of

---

[58] Jerome trans. Ewald 1963: 170–171. See also Balás and Bingham 1998: 77.

[59] See Gillingham 2018: 137–8. See also p.182 on Psalm 29:6. 'For the day....

[60] See pp. 26–27 for the discussion on Psalm 78.

[61] Wesselschmidt 2007: 177, citing Basil's *Homilies on the Psalms* 13.5 from *FC* 46:204–5.

[62] See Corrigan 1992: 25, 76.

[63] See https://bit.ly/3rNNHeP

[64] See https://psalter.library.uu.nl/page/115

[65] See https://www.albani-psalter.de/stalbanspsalter/english/commentary/page258.shtml

palm trees.[66] By contrast, Moshe *Berger offers a *kabbalistic interpretation with the psalmist against a tree, here depicted as a *menorah.

Poetic imitations of this psalm also describe the psalmist praying within a paradise garden. One example is Mary *Sidney's version (c. 1592). She assumes the psalm to be about the universal spiritual experience of a God who provides for all who trust in him; verses three and four take up so vividly the sound and sense of many of the fertility images of the psalm, and play upon the unicorn metaphor as well:

> The wicked grow
> Like frail though flowery grass;
> And, fallen, to wrack past help do pass.
> But thou not so,
> But high thou still dost stay:
> And lo thy haters fall away.
> Thy haters lo,
> Decay and perish all;
> All wicked hands to ruin fall.
>
> Fresh oiled I
> Will lively lift my horn
> And match the matchless unicorn:
> Mine eye will spy
> My spies in spiteful case:
> Mine ear shall hear my foes' disgrace.
> Like cedar high
> And like date-bearing tree,
> For green, and growth the just shall be.[67]

As for the musical arrangements, the Sabbath associations have resulted in several Jewish compositions. Salamone de *Rossi composed a version of this psalm which was first performed in Vienna in 1623.[68] Another example is Salomon Sulzer, a cantor and musical director in the synagogue of Vienna, who commissioned the prolific Austrian composer, Franz Schubert, to write a polyphonic choral arrangement for a baritone solo and two choirs of four voices, with organ accompaniment, for his collection 'Schir Zion' (1840–65). Schubert's piece is based on Ps. 92:1–8 and is called 'Tov l'hodos l'Adonai', evoking the theme of restfulness in the Most High God: it is an extraordinary blend

---

[66] See https://bit.ly/39Uez32.

[67] Taken from; Wieder 1995: 139–40.

[68] See Salamone de' Rossi, 'Mizmor Shir (A Psalm, a Song)' (eight voices, double choir) from The Songs of Solomon, Psalms, Songs and Hymns, Pro Cantione Antiqua, directed by Sidney Fixman, Carlton Classics 30366 00452. See https://www.youtube.com/watch?v=_ww7jyZJZSA.

of church and synagogue in its effects. Other similar Jewish arrangements include L. Lewandowski (1821–94) with his composition, also for *SATB voices, 'Tov Lehodoss l'Adonoj', for the synagogue in Berlin, and A. Grechaninoff, a Russian emigré who lived in New York, who composed 'Tov l'hodos' for the Jewish community there.[69] A more poignant version is by Eric Zeisl, entitled 'The Requiem Ebraica' (1945) in memory of his father and indeed of all Holocaust victims.[70]

In Christian tradition, from the Reformation onwards, renderings of this psalm, usually focussing more on a thanksgiving theme, include metrical versions by Louis Bourgeois, Hans Prince, Jean Berger, Paul Schwartz, and, in English, more recent arrangements by Maurice Greene, Michael Hurd and Martin Joseph. Edward *Elgar's *The Apostles* (1903), about the life of Christ as seen through the eyes of the apostles, adapts Ps. 92:1–12 to various Hebrew melodies as part of a morning psalm, just after the call of the disciples at the beginning of Part One.[71] A more traditional liturgical interpretation, to accompany Anglican chant sung to Coverdale's Psalms, is by Terence Albright ('It is a good thing to give thanks unto the Lord').[72] Perhaps the most notable is a more provocative and lively Jazz version, aimed at taunting the wicked.[73]

To conclude, in this first collection of three psalms in Book Four, the reception history of all three psalms, in various ways, evokes a spirit of prayer and reflection. There are two dominant themes: that of rest in God, and that of protection by God, in both cases using the metaphor of 'Refuge'. The psalms progress towards an increasingly confident expression of faith: Psalm 90 laments the fragility of life, whilst Psalm 91 expresses a more specific hope in God's deliverance from evil, and Psalm 92 is essentially a thanksgiving psalm because of its belief in the downfall of the wicked. The concern about the fragility of human life in relation to the permanency of God is a universal theme shared by both faith traditions in the reception of all three psalms.

---

[69] See Gorali 1993: 256 and 266.

[70] https://www.youtube.com/watch?v=y4tBkYJetec.

[71] Dowling Long and Sawyer 2015: 18.

[72] Recorded on *'Let God Arise':The Psalms of David Volume 7*, Norwich Cathedral Choir conducted by Michael Nicholas and organist Neil Taylor; Priory Records Digital Recording 409, 1992.

[73] See Daniel Richardson and Angel Napieralski, 'Though the Wicked Spring up Like Grass', Jazz Psalms, Calvin College, 2004: https://worship.calvin.edu/resources/publications/jazz-psalms.

Psalms 93–94, 95–100: God as King

Psalms 93–100 explicitly and implicitly testify to a greater king than David: God alone is King. Nevertheless, Moses and the idea of Torah continue to appear in these psalms.[74] The sovereignty of God over the entire cosmos dominates this collection: although Psalms 94 and 100 make less explicit references to God's Kingship, the whole collection may be presented as follows:

> Psalm 93: God's kingship is for ever
> Psalm 94: God will come to judge the nations of the earth
>
> Psalm 95: God's people are called upon to acknowledge God as king
> Psalm 96: 'Sing to the Lord a new song'
> Psalm 97: God reigns in Zion
> Psalm 98: 'Sing to the Lord a new song'
> Psalm 99: God reigns in Zion
> Psalm 100: All earth is called upon to acknowledge God as king

Psalm 93: God's Kingship is for Ever

Psalm 93 begins with 'The Lord reigns!' (*Yahweh malak*), indicating God's continual sovereignty over the cosmos. Verses 1–2 claim Yahweh has always

---

[74] Pss. 93:5 and 94:12 refer to 'decrees' and 'Torah' respectively, and Moses and Aaron appear in 99:7.

Psalms Through the Centuries: A Reception History Commentary on Psalms 73–151, Volume Three, First Edition. Susan Gillingham.
© 2022 John Wiley & Sons Ltd. Published 2022 by John Wiley & Sons Ltd.

been king from time immemorial, and now through the praises of his people he becomes their king. Verses 3 and 4 take up the myth of the cosmic sea, and verse 5 affirms that God's Temple ('thy house') is where God's eternal rule and earthly abode intersect. There are various similarities with the ancient Song of the Sea in Exod. 15:1–18, where the battle with the sea refers not to creation but to the escape through the sea; that hymn ends similarly with God celebrating his victory by making his abode in his sanctuary on earth, so this psalm is evocative of God's parting of the sea (as in Exodus) as well as God's victory over the sea (as in Genesis 1). The presentation of verses 3, 4 and 5 as three verses containing three short lines each could be said to evoke the rhythm of the rise and fall of the waves of the sea, whilst verse 2, with its two short lines, suggests, by contrast, the firm establishment of God's heavenly throne.

Despite Ps. 93–100 being a new collection, the placing of the collections of psalms in Book Four does not seem to be an entirely accidental early stage of reception. Links between Psalm 93 and Psalm 92 may be noted. The one who is 'on high forever' (92:8) is the one who is 'everlasting' and whose 'throne is established from old' (93:2), using *'olam* in each case; the 'house of the Lord' (*bet yahweh*) is found in both Ps. 92:13 and in 93:5.[75]

The use of this psalm at *Qumran is interesting. It follows Psalm 92 in 4QPs[a] but in 11QPs[a] it comes between the *Apostrophe to Zion* (a sectarian hymn addressed to Jerusalem) and Psalm 141. This might be partly due to the references in Ps. 93:5 to the sanctuary, and also to an eschatological reading of the psalm. It shows that Psalm 93 in the second or first-century BCE was not yet part of a universally fixed collection. The connections with Psalm 92, noted above as part of the reception of the *MT, may therefore have taken some time to be established. The *Septuagint (and later the *Vulgate) includes the heading. 'For the day before the Sabbath when the earth was inhabited. A praise song of David', probably on the understanding of Genesis 1:26–2:4a, as God completed creation before he rested.

Mishnah Tamid also assigns this psalm for use on a Friday (i.e. the sixth day) closely connected with Psalm 92, the Sabbath psalm. The *Midrash Tehillim*, somewhat anthropomorphically, reads verse 1 as God being 'clothed' in Sabbath finery—that is, in the garments he donned for the creation of the world. The use of the psalm on the 'sixth day' is thus about God's completion of his work and his becoming King over it.[76] *Rashi, also seeing the close connections with Psalm 92, understands that this psalm refers not only to God's kingship at creation but also to his establishing of his kingship in a future Messianic era, when all will see

---

[75] The links between Psalms 93 and 94 will be outlined in the following psalm.

[76] See; Braude 1959: 124–25; also Feuer 2004: 1157. On God establishing his kingship over creation, see Rashi in Gruber 2004: 590.

the majesty of God revealed and when the 'holiness of God's house' (v. 5) will again be restored as the third Temple is rebuilt. Because he assumes the tradition that Psalm 93 was composed by Moses for the Benjaminites, he argues that the Temple will be built in the territory of Benjamin in fulfilment of Deut. 33:12.[77] Like Psalms 90–92, Psalm 93 is also found in the additional *Pesukei de-Zimra* read on Sabbaths and feast days instead of Psalm 100; its special relationship with Psalm 92 is seen in the way it also follows 92 in introducing evening prayer on the Friday (*Kabbalat Shabbat*).[78] In the ancient *Tamid* service, Psalm 93 was the psalm to be used on the sixth day of the week.[79]

The musical expressions of this psalm also arise from its use in Jewish liturgy. The Polish/German composer of synagogue music, Louis Lewandowski (1821–94) wrote 'Adonai Moloch', using cantor, choir and organ, for the synagogue at Berlin. David Rubin (1837–1922) wrote 'Adonoj moloch' for the 'New Jewish Temple' at Prague; these are both compositions at a time when such arrangements were widely used in both Reform synagogues and concert halls. Recent Jewish arrangements, both from 2006, include Miriam Gideon's 'Adonai Malakh (Psalm 93)' and Robert Druckmann's 'Psalm 93'.[80]

Christian commentaries are less rich in reception. The imagery of the noise (and indeed the 'voice') of the flood waters in verses 3 and 4 may have influenced the imagery of the 'voice of a great multitude, like the sound of many waters' in Rev. 19:6, in a chapter which also emphasises the kingship of God, but the psalm is neither cited nor alluded to elsewhere in the New Testament. Its early use for the Feast of the Ascension, along with Psalm 47, was a means of understanding God's victory over the cosmic and chaotic waters (whether at creation or at the Exodus) as a description of Christ's victory over death, so that the phrase 'Christ is risen!' had the same connotation as 'The Lord is king!'—i.e. another redemptive event in the past made present in worship and praise. The Gospel reading for Ascension Day, often from Luke 24:44–53, became a typical lens through which this psalm was read.[81] According to *Athanasius, in his *Letter to Marcellinus*, '...if on a Friday, your words of praise are in the ninety-second (LXX; 93rd in NRSV), for it was when the Crucifixion was accomplished that the House of God was built ... so it is fitting that we should sing on Friday a song of victory, such as that Psalm'.[82]

---

[77] See Rashi (*ibid.*).

[78] See Donin 1980: 261; also Reif 2010: 193–214.

[79] See Trudinger 2004: 135–46.

[80] See *Psalms of Joy and Sorrow*, the Milken Archive of American Jewish Music; Gideon's composition is sung by the London Chorus, conductor Robert Corp; Druckmann's, by the Rochester Singers, conductor Samuel Adler, recorded on Naxos American Classics.
See https://www.youtube.com/watch?v=zBGlWeQAI3c.

[81] See discussion on the Feast of Ascension and Psalm 47 in; Gillingham 2018: 285–88.

[82] Taken from https://bit.ly/3ILPLtZ.

This psalm, as the start of the collection of the Kingship Psalms, represents for Martin *Luther an interesting change of emphasis in his first lectures on the psalms entitled *Dictata super Psalterium*. Up to this point Luther has consistently focussed on the superiority of the Christian reading of each Psalm, following *Augustine and *Cassiodorus. Here Luther begins to use the term 'faithful synagogue' as a positive term whereby the words of the (Jewish) psalmist representing that 'pre-Incarnational faith' are seen to have an intrinsic worth.[83] Luther still emphasises the incarnation as the watershed in interpretation, but phrases such as 'The Lord reigns' and the 'Lord being clothed in beauty and strength' (93:1) are read as genuine expressions of the 'faithful synagogue' which is later to become the voice of the 'faithful church'.

Early Christian liturgical use influenced several later musical compositions. Some of the earliest versions in English derive from metrical forms, for example from the *Genevan Psalter*. By contrast, music for the English royal court developed the kingship theology in this psalm: one such example is Henry *Purcell's 'The Lord is king, and hath put on glorious apparel'.[84] But this was also a psalm for the laity: an eighteenth-century example is Isaac *Watts' 'The Lord Jehovah Reigns; His Throne is Built on High'.[85] This might be compared with a near contemporary version by William *Boyce, with the same title, but using *Coverdale, for five voices (*SSATB) with a bass solo with organ accompaniment. Nineteenth-century arrangements include those by Henry Ley (again, using Coverdale, with the same title), and John *Keble's 'The Lord Reigns, He is Robed in Majesty' (1839) with a musical arrangement by Henry Thomas Smart (1867). A recent popular version, for performing not only in the church but also for a secular audience, and using the text of Mary *Sidney, is by Howard *Goodall (2010), as 'Though Rivers Roar/*Lavaverunt flumina*'.[86]

Artistic representations of Psalm 93 develop a similar kingship theme. The *St Albans Psalter* in its letter 'D' (for 'Dominus') depicts God himself reigning, flanked by two men and two women who seem to represent the whole world acknowledging God's sovereignty.[87] A fifteenth-century example is in a Book of Hours, the *Très Riches Heures du Duc de Berry*, kept at Musée Condé, Chantilly. The artists are the Limbourg Brothers; they depict the constancy of

---

[83] See German 2017: 98–105. German notes this change in Luther's emphasis began in the *Asaphite Psalms in Book Three, to be developed more explicitly here in Book Four, reaching its culmination in Psalm 119. See Luther's commentary on Psalm 119 on pp. 245–6.

[84] See https://www.youtube.com/watch?v=zGXzWTGzyIM.

[85] See http://www.hymnary.org/text/the_lord_jehovah_reigns_his_throne_is_bu.

[86] This is from *Pelican in the Wilderness: Songs from the Psalms*, with Enchanted Voices and Tippet Quartet; see https://www.youtube.com/watch?v=7GMJPnzxOkk.

[87] See https://www.albani-psalter.de/stalbanspsalter/english/commentary/page259.shtml.

God's throne in a time of change, and this time it is Christ who is sitting on that throne. A very different image is William *Blake's preliminary sketch, in 1805, for Ps. 93:1: '*Christ* girding himself with strength'.[88] An interpretation from a Jewish mystical perspective is Moshe *Berger's image of Psalm 93. The top portrays a purple and white streaked sky, at the peak of which, instead of the sun, is a tiny *menorah, and under this is a white canopy, protecting a city created out of Hebrew letters. Other letters topple down from the sky and canopy to create ice blue waves which form the sea; a bright rainbow banner cuts the image in half, whilst a mound, emerging from the sea, creates a fire whose flames of coloured Hebrew letters in turn seem to feed into the rainbow: 'In the future, God's sacred presence will be manifested so miraculously that it will become evident that God's holiness pervades every inch of this earth. This sanctity thus befits the Almighty for it displays His Omnipresence'.[89]

Despite the variety of cultural settings for Psalm 93 the overriding universal message is about the Kingship of God over time and space. Either this is about God, or it is Christ who is enthroned. Jews and Christians may differ in the identity of the one who is King, and on when, whether and what has or will take place, but neither would dispute that the Rule of God is central to this psalm.

Psalm 94: God Will Come to Judge the Nations of the Earth

Psalm 94 creates a very different tone with its emphasis on 'God of vengeance'. Nevertheless, the psalm picks up the theme in Ps. 92:15 (Heb. v. 16) of God as 'my Rock' (*ṣuri*); here in Ps. 94:22 God is the 'rock of my refuge' (*ṣur maḥsi*) and this in turn anticipates the reference to God as Rock (*ṣur*) in Ps. 95:1. Furthermore, the reference in Ps. 94:8 to dullards and fools (*bo'arim* and *kesilim*) echoes 92:6 (Heb. v. 7, *ish-ba'ar* and *kesil*). Psalm 94 also has some contrast-links with Psalm 93: in Psalm 93 we read of the exaltation of God, whilst Psalm 94 is about the self-exaltation of the proud and wicked. Hence in 93:2 we read of God's throne having been established from of old and in 94:20 we read of a throne of iniquity to describe the destructive power of wicked, each psalm using different contrasts of the word *kisse'* for 'throne'. The use of the verb *d-k-'* in 94:5 to describe the wicked 'crushing' God's people takes us back to 93:3 where the same root is used as a noun to describe the pounding of the waves of the sea. These two apparently different psalms may well have been brought together because of their contrasting themes.

---

[88] See Blake's image, see the preliminary pencil sketch held at the Tate, at https://bit.ly/3s81byE.
[89] See http://themuseumofpsalms.com/product/psalm-93.

Psalm 94 begins as a lament (vv. 1–7), pleading with God to inaugurate on earth the rule celebrated in Psalm 93; it then turns into a didactic psalm, reminding the congregation of the depth and extent of evil (vv. 8–15). It ends in the confidence that God will come to their aid, and by way of two rhetorical questions (vv. 16 and 20) it affirms that justice will prevail.

Because of its theme of the 'God of vengeance', Psalm 94 has a different reception history from 93. In Jewish tradition it is the only psalm between 90 and 99 not to be used in the Sabbath liturgy (Psalms 90–93 being added to the *'Verses of Song' for Sabbaths and feast days and Psalms 95–99 being used in *Kabbalat Shabbat-'). Psalm 94 is however assigned for use on Wednesdays towards the end of the morning service.[90] Here it is read along with Ps. 95:1, since the ending of Psalm 94 ('the Lord will wipe out their wickedness') was deemed too negative on its own, given the anticipation of the Sabbath in three days' time. The use of this psalm on the 'fourth day' as in the Greek heading to the psalm is an early tradition, also associated with the Levites and priests who, using this psalm on the fourth day, cite the psalm as a witness to 'A God of vengeance'.[91]

In some Jewish traditions the vindictive tenor of the psalm is explained by seeing the fear as not so much about God's coming Kingdom as about the state of chaos on the earth here and now and hence the need for the vindication of the good. This then takes on a future orientation, whereby Moses, the 'composer' of the psalm, is seen to be speaking of the Messianic age: just as Moses composed Psalm 93 for the tribe of Benjamin, with the promises of the restoration of the Temple; he composed Psalm 94 for the tribe of Gad, from which Elijah descended. Psalm 94 thus points to the bringing in of the Messianic Kingdom of which Elijah is the forebear.[92] Much is made of the use of *ashre hageber* ('blessed is the man') in verse 12: rather than linking this with the 'righteous man' as in Psalm 1, this is viewed as more like the figure of Job, suffering, tried and tested but ultimately vindicated as the *gibbor* (literally, 'warrior', or 'strong man').

The New Testament alludes to this psalm several times, and there are at least two specific citations taken from the didactic section in the middle. In 1 Cor. 3:20, in his debate about the nature of human and divine wisdom, Paul cites verse 11, from the Greek: 'The LORD knows the thoughts of men, that they are futile' (*kurios ginōskei tous dialogismous tōn anthrōpōn hoti eisin mataioi*),

---

[90] See also *b.Rosh HaShanah* 31a, which refers to this as the 'Song of the Day' for the fourth day of the Sabbath, when God created the sun and moon (and when he will punish those who worship astral deities rather than the Creator who made them).

[91] Trudinger 2004: 109–20; Hertz 1942: 224–27.

[92] See Feuer 2004: 1163–4; also Braude 1959: Vol. 2, 87.

but changes the Greek slightly so it reads 'The Lord knows the thoughts *of the wise, that they are futile.*' (*kurios ginōskei tous dialogismous tōn sophōn hoti eisin mataioi*). And Ps. 94:14 ('The Lord will not cast off his people') is cited and expanded in Rom. 11:2 ('God has not rejected his people *whom he foreknew*'), where it is now applied to the new considerations of the place of the Jews within the Christian covenant.

In Christian tradition the suffering theme, especially the reference to the condemnation of the innocent to death (v. 21), has been interpreted as referring to the passion of Christ.[93] *Athanasius' *Letter to Marcellinus* makes this clear: noting the superscription which in the Greek assigns the psalm to the fourth day, he observes 'So, when you read in the Gospel how on Wednesday the Jews took counsel against the Lord, seeing Him thus boldly challenge the devil on our behalf, sing the words of Psalm 93 (LXX; Psalm 94 in NRSV)'.[94] *Augustine, meanwhile, argues more generally that the psalm is really about the conflict between Divine Grace and Free Will (seen especially in verses 8–11) where God has to come to our aid.[95] Interestingly, *Jerome, commenting on the associations of this psalm with the fourth day, noted in his typically numerological commentary that this was a psalm, therefore, with three daily psalms on each side, reminding us of the Trinity.[96]

An early modern performance of Psalm 94 is found in Orlando *de Lassus' *Sacred Readings from the Book of Job* (in Latin: published in 1565): the psalm, sung in *plainchant, sets the scene for this motet cycle of texts and responses from Job, thus again reading the 'blessed man' as a paradigm of innocent suffering.[97] J. S. *Bach (1685–1750) also composed an arrangement of this psalm: 'Ich hatte viel Bekümmernis' was completed during his employment at the royal court of Weimar, and narrates the progress of the soul from mourning and doubt to confidence and joy.[98] A different arrangement is the metrical version of this psalm often credited to *Purcell, which omits verses 3 and 8–13 with their more negative tone, and makes the psalm more of a passionate cry for God's mercy: 'Wilt thou, who are a God most just/Their sinful ways sustain?'. Another interpretation by James *Turle (1802–1882) suggests a darker and more solemn mood: 'O Lord God, to whom vengeance belongeth' using *Coverdale's translation.[99]

---

[93] See de Solms 2001: 460.

[94] Taken from https://bit.ly/3ILPLtZ

[95] Wesselschmidt 2007: 181, taken from *Letter* 214 in FC 32:61–2. See also Augustine trans. Uyl 2017: 476–77.

[96] See Howell 1987: 189.

[97] Dowling Long and Sawyer 2015: 202.

[98] This serves as the Choral Prelude to Cantata BWV 21.

[99] See https://www.youtube.com/watch?v=3T75shbLh0c.

George *Herbert alludes to Ps. 94:9 ('He who planted the ear, does he not hear?/He who formed the eye, does he not see?') in his poem 'Longing', from *The Temple* (1633), most probably taken from Purcell's version noted above. This is set in the more optimistic context of an appeal to God as Creator rather than Judge, so lines 35–36 read: 'Lord heare!/*Shall he that made the eare, Not heare?*'

Psalm 94 has an underlying narrative which is often developed in early Christian art. The *Utrecht Psalter* (fol.55r) is a good example of this.[100] There we see the *Christ-Logos in a globe-*mandorla, held up by three angels: Christ seems to be teaching this psalm to a group to his right (verse 12). Three other angels hurl firebrands at a group of the 'wicked' who fall into pits which are dug out for them (verses 13 and 23). The personification of justice (verse 15), bearing a palm and a battle-axe, also takes part in this destruction. The personification of mercy (verse 18) offers a crown to the psalmist, who appears here to be captain of a band of soldiers (verse 21). He points down to wicked king enthroned on the hillside ('the seat of iniquity', verse 20), who is commanding other soldiers to murder the 'widows' and the 'fatherless' (verses 5–6). A wall surrounds this whole scene: God is the psalmist's refuge and a stronghold for the oppressed (verse 22).

Although this is a psalm with a more sombre and vindictive mood, it nevertheless fits into the collection Pss. 93–100 because of the universal appeal of its portrayal of God's just and sovereign rule despite the threats of the wicked. The personification of divine justice and divine mercy (verses 15 and 18) lies at the heart of this psalm; Christians and Jews may differ as to whose Kingship this celebrates, but the victory of God's rule again remains a constant in each tradition.[101]

Psalm 95: God's People are Called upon to Acknowledge God as King

Psalm 95 begins with a sequence of calls to the people to acknowledge God as King. As part of the first stage of reception through compilation, the placing of this psalm again is not accidental. Verse 1 is linked to Ps. 94:22 in its image of God as 'rock' (Hebrew ṣur), although in this psalm, verse 8 shows that this image is also to be read with the literal connotations concerning Meribah and Massa (Exodus 17). The 'people' are the focal point of Pss. 94:5, 8 and 14, and 95:7 and 10 (using the Hebrew word 'am in each case). The myth of the cosmic sea found in Psalm 93 is also alluded to in verses 4 and 5.

---

[100] https://psalter.library.uu.nl/page/117.
[101] See for example the discussion on Psalm 85:10–11 on pp. 57–8.

Psalm 95 consists mainly of invitations to praise (vv. 1–6) followed by prophetic exhortation to obedience by learning from the lessons of history (vv. 7–11).[102] The end of the first part marks another point in the reception history of this psalm: verse 6 in the Hebrew reads 'Let us *kneel* before the Lord our Maker', using the cohortative form of the Hebrew word *b-r-k*: 'kneel' in this case. The Greek, as well as adding the heading that this is a psalm 'of David', makes a significant change to verse 6: using the word 'weep' (*klaiō*, from the Hebrew word *b-k-h*), it reads the end of the verse more penitentially: the people are urged, 'Let us *weep* before the Lord our Maker'. The compilers also seem to have intended some connection with Psalm 100, thus delineating the first and last psalm of this run of kingship psalms that is Pss. 95–100. Compare, for example, Ps. 95:7 ('For he is the Lord our God and we are the people of his pasture and the sheep of his hand…') with Ps. 100:3, ('Know that the Lord is God … we are his people and the sheep of his pasture').[103] Again, the ordering of this collection of psalms, as the first stage of their reception, is not a random process.

Verse 6 is an important verse in Jewish liturgy. Using the Hebrew, this exhortation is used as part of daily prayer upon entry into the synagogue.[104] The whole psalm, along with Psalms 96–99, is also used every Friday evening at *Kabbalat Shabbat*. The call to prayer 'Come let us sing!' is an appropriate introduction to the Sabbath Praises. Jewish readings, as we have seen, take the role of Moses in this collection most seriously. This is the sixth of the eleven psalms composed by Moses, in this case this is to Issachar, the tribe apparently immersed in singing the songs of Torah.[105] *Midrash Tehillim* also notes that the use of *melek* in verse 3 implies a king who rules over his own people with consent: hence the response is in worship (v. 6): had the corresponding word *mashal* been used, this would imply a ruler who *imposes* his reign, i.e. over the Gentiles. Again using verse 6, the willingness to prostrate oneself before God (in the morning), and to bow down (in the afternoon) and to kneel (in the evening, in submission, before sleep) speaks of the ongoing response to God as King in the present moment.[106] By contrast, *Kimḥi argues for a future orientation in this psalm.[107] The reference to 'the day' in verse 7 is, in his view, about the eternal Sabbath: if only Israel were to keep one day of the Sabbath he would be saved, and the Messiah could

---

[102] Here the call to praise is to the assembled congregation, and contrasts with Psalm 100, which calls upon the whole world to praise God.

[103] See comments on Psalm 100, p. 126.

[104] Reif 1993: 211.

[105] See Feuer 2004: 1175.

[106] See Feuer 2004: 1177.

[107] See Feuer 2004: 1176.

then come.[108] Kimḥi also views the psalm as eschatological, to be sung at the advent of the Messiah, as the nations are gathered in and Jerusalem is about to be saved.[109]

A very different reading of this psalm is found in Hebrews 3–4. Heb. 3:7–11 cites Ps. 95:7–11—the third longest citation of any Old Testament text in the New Testament—with the interesting inference that the author of this citation is in fact neither David nor Moses but the Holy Spirit. The following three sections (Heb. 3:12–19; 4:1–5, 4:6–11) each cite a verse from Psalm 95 to illustrate its new Christological significance. The promise of rest for Christians is debated in Heb. 3:7–11, 15 and 4:3 and 7; Psalm 95 is juxtaposed with Gen. 2:1–4, also on the theme of 'rest', and the argument is that *now* Christians enter their 'rest' because this has been achieved by Christ: it was promised from the start of creation, but withheld from Israel on account of the people's complaints in the wilderness (95:11).[110] The author of Hebrews argues that from the time of Moses to Jesus the promise was offered to the people of Israel, but now it is the church of Christ who will receive their 'rest' which is to be a spiritual gift— this is no longer about 'rest' from the enemies, i.e. the physical gift of land. In the *LXX, the Greek of 94:10 (95:10) reads 'that generation' (*tē genea ekeinē*); in Heb. 3:10, the text reads 'this generation' (*tē genea tautē*), giving a contemporary appropriation: this is now about '*this* obedient generation' of the new covenant against '*that* disobedient people' of the old covenant.

Since this is the only psalm in the collection of Psalms 93–100 to be used in this prophetic way in the New Testament, it is not surprising that the Church Fathers seized upon this theme. *Augustine, for example, writing on verse 10, develops the phrase 'forty years' of Israel's disobedience in the desert to contrast with the different periods of 'forty days' which highlight Jesus's obedience to the Father—whether the forty days of temptations in the desert, or the period between the cross and resurrection.[111] This is just one example of the way in which Psalm 95 is read as about Jesus and then the Church, and no longer about Israel.[112]

In later Christian tradition the very first phrase, '*O come let us sing to the Lord*', and the dual themes of worship and obedient faith, with the final promise of 'rest' (verse 11), resulted in this being the key psalm which was recited at the

---

[108] See Braude 1959: 137.

[109] See Cohen 1992: 312; also *Rashi in Gruber 2004: 595 who sees this as a reference to the salvation of Jerusalem (as in Ps. 132:14).

[110] See Attridge 1987: 114–21; also Enns 1997: 353–63. See Human and Steyn 2010: Frevel (165–93) and Steyn (194–228) deal with the exegetical issues arising from the use of this psalm, whilst Human (147–64) intriguingly applies this psalm to a modern South African context.

[111] See http://www.newadvent.org/fathers/1801095.htm; also Augustine 2017:484.

[112] See Neale and Littledale 1874–79: 3/216–17.

beginning of Morning Prayer. It was prescribed daily in the *Liturgy of Hours, and, in the *Benedictine Rule (Chapter 9) for the very early morning hours of *Vigils.[113] What was quite probably once a call to worship at the Jerusalem Temple is now a call to Christians everywhere to praise God (95:1–6) and to listen to Him (95:7–11), so that, as Christopher Renz observes, the noise of praise gives way to silent awe in remembering 'today' (verse 7) the presence of God in His people's history.[114] Known as the *Venite* (from its first words in Latin, 'O Come…') it is to 'this day' a prominent psalm at Morning Prayer.

Because of its liturgical use, Christian musical compositions of Psalm 95 are prolific. One early example in English is by Thomas *Tallis, who used this psalm as the fourth of his eight for Archbishop *Parker's Psalter: 'O come in one to praise the Lord: The fourth doth fawn, and flattery playeth'.[115] Other metrical versions include *Tate and Brady's 'O Come, loud anthems, let us sing loud thanks to our Almighty King' (1628); Isaac *Watts' 'Come, let our voices join to raise' (1719); and Charles *Wesley's 'Father, in whom we live, in whom we are and move' (1747).[116] Interestingly, none of these musical versions develop the Christological re-interpretation found in the New Testament and Christian commentators: here, Psalm 95 is a more 'universal' psalm of praise. This is also the case in Ralph *Vaughan Williams' adaption 'Let all the World in every Corner Sing' (1911) and again in Herbert *Howells' arrangement in 1976.[117] This universal tendency is also evident in more contemporary versions such as those by Liam Lawton (1998), Marty Haugen (2000), James Chepponis (2004) and 'lechu neranena' by the Messianic Jewish Band Miqedem (2016).[118] There is however one well-known exception. The call to praise in verse 5, 'O come let us worship' apparently inspired the Christmas carol 'O Come all Ye Faithful', composed in about 1740; 'Venite adorate' is changed in the refrain to 'Venite

[113] The Byzantine use of this psalm as an invitatory prayer is actually at *Vespers.

[114] See Renz 1996: 140–53; here p. 142.

[115] This is found in John Day's *The Whole Psalter translated into English Metre* and is performed on *The Complete Works of Thomas Tallis*, Volume 6, Music for a Reformed Church, Chapelle du Roi, directed by Alister Dixon, Signum Classics B0000D9Y7T.

[116] These can all be heard on the Cyber Hymnal website. For Tate and Brady, see http://www.hymntime.com/tch/htm/o/c/o/m/ocomelan.htm; for Watts, http://www.hymntime.com/tch/htm/c/o/m/e/l/comelovo.htm; and for Wesley: http://www.hymntime.com/tch/htm/f/a/t/h/e/fatherin.htm. Several other metrical versions are also found on this site, focused on individual verses from the psalm (e.g. vv. 1, 2 or 6).

[117] Dowling Long and Sawyer 2015: 144.

[118] All are from GIA Publications. On Liam, see Liam Lawton 'Sing as Song to the Lord: Psalm 95' (1998) GIA Publications, found on http://www.giamusic.com/search_details.cfm?title_id=988; Haugen's 'Come let us Sing for Joy' is on http://www.giamusic.com/search_details.cfm?title_id=4576 and Chepponis' 'If Today you Hear the Voice of God' is on http://www.giamusic.com/search_details.cfm?title_id=1271. For Miqedem, see https://miqedem.bandcamp.com/track/lechu-neranena.

adoremus', or 'O Come let us adore him'. This is now about giving worship to Christ, the newborn King.

Musical arrangements of this psalm are also quite profuse. One striking version is a composition set to Hebrew cantillation by the composer David Mitchell, based upon the work of Haïk-Vantoura. Again, this also has no explicitly Jewish or Christian overlay, being an exercise in trying to replicate ancient Jewish worship. Mitchell writes about the poetic foot of each verse being adapted to musical bars, to indicate the rhythm of the psalm, whilst the 'bold confidence' of the psalm is represented by the scale of a major third.[119]

A completely different dimension to this psalm, partly on account of its familiarity in worship, was its use as a 'battle psalm' by the Knights Templar, the Spanish Armada, Oliver Cromwell, the Huguenots and the Cevenols.[120]

Psalm 95 is also alluded to by George *Herbert in *The Temple*. In the first stanza of 'Mattens' (1633) there are echoes of Psalm 95, the *'Matins psalm' which calls on people to hear God's voice 'today':

> I cannot ope mine eyes,
> But thou art ready there to catch
> My morning-soul and sacrifice:
> Then we must needs for that day make a match…[121]

As Herbert questions 'My God, what is a heart?' in the second and third stanzas, it reminds the knowing reader of the phrase 'Harden not your hearts' later in the psalm (verse 8; also verse 10).[122]

An extraordinary example of visual exegesis is found in *Les Très Riches Heures du Duc de Berry* (commissioned 1409). Psalm 95, as a Matins psalm, is the first to be illustrated (fol. 26v) in the Hours of the Virgin. The Limbourg brothers represent David as an oriental sovereign, leaning on his harp and pointing to the Infant Jesus—who hangs mid-air before the entrance to a place of worship. Two musicians, one playing the viol, the other the lute, kneel before him. The title below reads 'David summons the people and announces the coming of Christ'. Here the liturgical, the historical and the prophetic all elide in one image.[123]

Other than in early *Carolingian or Byzantine Psalters, the above example is exceptional in its explicit Christian overlay. Two Jewish readings and one

---

[119] See Mitchell 2013: 125–28. A suggested score of this psalm, using Haïk-Vantoura's work, is given on pp. 126–27.

[120] Prothero 1903: 80–81.

[121] See https://www.ccel.org/h/herbert/temple/Mattens.html.

[122] See Kinnamon 1981: 16–17.

[123] See Longnon and Cazelles (eds.) 1969:23 and 185.

Christian interpretation illustrate this. The first is from the thirteenth-century
Parma Psalter, in which a figure is blowing a long trumpet, set in the first
word of the psalm; the trumpet stretches over the entire text and the figure
signals to two figures on the left of the word, one who is singing and the other
who is playing a *shofar*: this is a reference to the call to rejoice and sing songs
of praise in verses 1–2. It is an extraordinary early depiction of Jewish art in a
sacred text, and is found as PLATE 7 in this work.[124] In a contemporary image
of verse 1 by Moshe *Berger (dated about 2000, in pen, brown and blue ink,
wash and pierre noire), the voice of praise in Hebrew emerges from what seems
to be the 'mouth of the deep'. The artist's comment is: 'This is an enthusiastic
appeal urging everyone to surrender his doubts and forget his preoccupation
with material concerns and illusions. The Psalmist urges *everyone* to join him
in singing God's praises.'[125] A similar interpretation is given by the contemporary English artist, Michael *Jessing. Jessing portrays swirling figures on a
rocky plain, with God's hands forming a rainbow connecting the 'deep places
of the earth' with the space 'above all gods'. The image evokes the invitation in
the psalm to receive the Creator and his gifts of life.[126]

So although in the commentary and liturgical tradition Psalm 95 has evoked
some most distinctive Jewish and Christian readings, in much of the poetic,
musical and artistic tradition the dominant concern is with psalm's more universal
interest in God's people everywhere joining to sing praises to their King. The
Oxford poet, Edward *Clarke, has a recent composition which is most apt in this
respect, as he views the psalm in the context of two paintings by Samuel Palmer
(*Pastoral with a Horse Chestnut Tree* and *The White Cloud*). The poem ends with
an allusion to the theme of 'rest for the people of God' as in Hebrews 4.[127]

> While someone exhorts us
> In song to sing to God,
> I've looked askance and asked, is he
> Among us here or not?
> And found that question, off its no-man's land
> Uptaken then in hand,
>
> Lies with sheep in shade,
> And takes its rest in space,
> Beneath a large-leafed chestnut, bright
> With burning candles, placed
> At intervals upon it, by that same hand,

---

[124] See *Parma Psalter*, fol. 136v. See also Metzger 1996: 87–88.

[125] See http://www.biblical-art.com/artwork.asp?id_artwork=15222&showmode=Full.

[126] See http://www.mixastudio.com/psalm-illustrations.php.

[127] Taken from email correspondence in July 2018. See Clarke 2020: 103.

Which forms from sea dry land.

Can it be we have
A second chance of rest?
I labour to hear a voice whose sworn
Obscurity you blessed,
Like a bright cloud above unharvested grain,
A clear heat after rain.

Psalm 96: 'Sing to the Lord a New Song' (i)

Psalm 96 begins 'O Sing to the Lord a new song'. Like Psalms 94 and 95, it regards other deities as nothing (vv. 1–6) and the call to 'sing to God' in 95:1–7 is like that in 96:1–6. In these verses it is possible to see the addressees as the exiles, who were tempted to worship what they could see and touch—Babylonian idols. The twin themes of the new song and the nothingness of other gods were also used in Isa. 42:10–12 and 43:16–21. This further suggests that the exile in Babylon was the context for this psalm. Psalm 96 continues by addressing other nations, with their deities 'dethroned', and calling upon to praise the true Lord (vv. 7–10); heaven and earth are also called upon to join in this praise to the God who has come and will come again (vv. 11–13).

The first stage of reception—that of compilation—is again fairly clear, for there are several links here with Psalm 95. The distinctive *hishtaphel* verb *hishta-h-v-h* (to bow down) is found in both Ps. 95:6 and 96:9. The theme of rejoicing is prominent at the beginning of Psalm 95 and at the end of Psalm 96 (95:1 and 96:12, both using the verb *r-n-n*). The God of 'salvation' is found in both Ps. 95:1 and 96:2; God is a 'great king' in Psalm 95 (verse 3), in Psalm 96 he is both great (96:4) and he reigns as king (96:10). Most especially he is superior to all other gods (*'al-kol-elohim*) in both Ps.95:3 and 96:4.

This psalm is one of the very few to be used in the Hebrew Bible itself. 1 Chron. 16:23–33 cites it, after citing Ps. 105:1–15. The Chronicler's account was probably written during the Persian period, after the writing of Samuel and Kings, so its description of David bringing the Ark to Jerusalem tells us much about the nostalgia for the past as expressed in Second Temple worship. So emphasis on the new song (*shir hadash*) in verse 1 takes on a new meaning, as do the references to the sanctuary (*miqdash*) in verse 6 and God's 'courts' (*hasrot*) in verse 8: these were all seen in the context of the restored Temple, and these references in Psalm 96 were interpreted as prophecies about God's coming to his people and hence judging the earth (v. 13) which were now in the process of being fulfilled in the Chronicler's time by the people returning to Zion. The additional superscription in the *LXX ('When the House was built after the Captivity: A Psalm of David') also bears

witness to this reading—despite the fact that David did not, in biblical tradition, build the Temple; it seems that the Greek was borrowing from the
Chronicles account where David, rather than Solomon, all but built it.

Jewish tradition records this song as written by Moses for the tribe of Zebu-
lun, who 'studied the Torah and rejoiced' (Deut. 33:18).[128] It was sung by David,
when he brought the ark to Jerusalem (using 1 Chronicles 16). The attitude to
Gentiles in this psalm has provoked discussions between Reform and Orthodox Jews concerning their conversion: are these the 'righteous of the nations'
in the Noachic covenant, or does this imply the need for a Jewish mission to
the Gentiles? The use of this psalm in relation to the Gentiles is debated by
Maimonides in *Mishneh Torah, Hilchot Teshuvah* 3:4, following the discussion
in *Tosefta Sanhedrin* 13:1 and *Talmud Sanh.* 105a.

In liturgy, the psalm is used in *Kabbalat Shabbat* as part of the collection of
Psalms 95–99. According to *Midrash Tehillim*, the threefold call to 'sing' in verses
1 and 2 indicates the importance of prayers three times a day, in the morning, afternoon and evening. *Kimḥi even argues that this threefold daily song would bring
in the coming of the Messiah.[129] Following the Jewish enlightenment movement
in the eighteenth and nineteenth centuries, Jewish musical arrangements of this
psalm emphasised the importance of this psalm being 'a song': these include *B.
Marcello's 'O Sing unto the Lord' in Hebrew for the synagogue in Venice in 1724;
*R. Da-Oz's 'Yissmechu Hashanaim' for the Jewish community in Haifa in 1929;
and Yehudi Wyner's 'Shiru Ladonai' recorded by the BBS Singers in 2006.[130]

One particular verse of this psalm caused later controversy, but this time not
only between Christians and Jews but between Christians and pagans. The reference to the 'dethroning' of deities resulted in verse 5 ('For all the gods of the
peoples are idols') was translated in the LXX as *daimonia* (demons) and in the
Vulgate as *daemonia*, thus discrediting pagan deities while still acknowledging
their possible power. It was a text used by *Ambrose when the Romans in Milan
wanted to restore to the Senate a statue and altar of the goddess Victory, and it
eventually led to the Emperor Theodosius banning all pagan rites in 392 and
then their images in 408. Some six hundred years later, the same verse appears in
an illustrated form in Byzantine Psalters: for example, the *Theodore Psalter* (fol.
128v) has a marginal image of the pagans worshipping their gods on two huge
plinths; in the context of the *iconoclastic controversies the marginal note 'all the
gods are devils' is most pertinent.[131]

---

[128] See Feuer 2004: 1185.

[129] See Braude 1959: 139; and Feuer 2004: 1186.

[130] For Wyner's version, recorded in *Psalms of Joy and Sorrow*, directed by Avner Itai for Naxos
American Classics, 2006, see https://www.naxos.com/catalogue/item.asp?item_code=8.559445.

[131] *See* http://www.bl.uk/manuscripts/Viewer.aspx?ref=add_ms_19352_f128v. The same image is
found in Khludov, fol. 96v.

Another verse also caused disputation but between Christians and Jews. An early Latin version of verse 10 reads 'The Lord reigns *from the tree (a ligna)*', probably because of a copying error in an earlier Hebrew version. *Justin Martyr, writing mainly in Rome in the middle of the second-century, knew of this addition and accused the Jews of erasing these words from an earlier translation, arguing that this was because it had a specific reference to the crucifixion of Christ. Justin's invective is found in his *Apology* 40–41 and his *Dial.* 73. *Tertullian, in his *Marc.* 3.19, similarly defends the addition in 96:10 as an accurate manuscript tradition. It was also used in a hymn attributed to *Venantius Fortunatus in the sixth-century:

> Fulfilled is all that David told
> In true prophetic song of old;
> Amidst the nations God, saith he,
> Hath reigned and triumphed from the Tree.[132]

*Cassiodorus, developing the commentary by *Augustine, also assumes this reading to be correct in a strident anti-Jewish passage: 'They must say among the nations that the Lord will reign from the wood of the cross; not from the wood of the tree in Paradise, by which the devil was seen to hold the human race captive... On that wood in Paradise hung the death caused by transgression, but on this wood shone the faith of confession. The first led to hell, but the second directs us to heaven'.[133] This tradition was also known in some illuminated *Carolingian Psalters: it is interesting that the *Stuttgart Psalter* for Psalm 96 has the folios torn out, but it is possible that here was an early depiction of Christ on the cross illustrating the reign of God in crucified form. This was after all one of the images used for Psalm 69.

An interesting representation of this psalm in art is found in a fourteenth-century Psalter made at Ramsey Abbey (fol. 105v): it is very different from other Gothic Psalters. Perhaps indirectly influenced by pseudo-*Bede, and also *Theodoret, who argued that Psalm 96 was about the need to free the Jews from Babylonian exile, the illustration has a more Jewish and historical emphasis than a Christian one. It depicts two singing monks, with the prophet Habakkuk between them; in the upper image he is being carried by an angel and in the lower image he has landed in a den of lions. The source is undoubtedly Daniel 14:32–43 (in Greek) where Habakkuk is commanded to visit and encourage Daniel in the lion's den; after Daniel's release, the Babylonian king praises Dan-

---

[132] See Neale and Littledale 1874–79: 3/234–35, arguing that the original might have been referring to the wood of the Ark of the Covenant, and the victories over the Philistines.
[133] See Cassiodorus in Walsh 1991a: 421.

iel's God in words very like Psalm 96. So the psalm is read through the lens of Daniel's miraculous escape in exile, which is a symbol of Jewish freedom from captivity. Its Hebraic tone may be due to the influence of Christian commentators such as *Herbert of Bosham and Nicholas of *Lyra who were known as 'Christian Hebraists'.

Christians have usually re-read Psalm 96 in the light of another fulfilment: God's Kingdom is always entering history, as we saw in the Chronicler's use of this psalm, writing in the Persian period, and the 'new song' is now the song of the Kingdom of God inaugurated through Jesus Christ. It is possible to read a series of allusions to Psalm 96 throughout Revelation 9–19.[134] *Jerome, for example, commenting on the Greek and Latin headings to this psalm, observes in his *Homilies on the Psalms*: 'Sing to the Lord a new song; Who is to sing? Sing to the Lord, all the earth. If this is to refer to the Temple in Jerusalem, O Jew, why is *all the earth* called to praise?' Jerome also read the 'day by day' in verse 2 to refer to the two testaments, and Christ reveals himself in both.[135] *Rashi, aware of this reading, and writing nearly seven centuries later, responds: 'This Psalm refers to the distant future and its end proves this, saying: "that he comes to judge the earth". Everywhere a "new song" refers to the future to come'.[136] According to Rashi this 'new song' can only be sung in full at the final act of restoration, when the Messiah comes, and, as in verses 7–10, all nations will acknowledge the God of the Jews.[137] By the sixteenth-century John *Calvin is making a similar observation, seeing this collection of psalms, with Ps. 96:7 as its focus, pertaining to the future Messianic kingdom—but one which is centred on Christ.[138]

In Christian worship the 'new song' has resulted in Psalm 96 being used along with Psalm 97 and 98 in the liturgy for Christmas Day, sometimes with the Old Testament reading from Isa. 9:6–7 (on a royal figure who will bring in the righteous rule of God) and the Gospel reading from Luke 2:1–14 (on the birth of Jesus). Arrangements of Psalm 96 include a version by Samuel *Wesley, 'Ascribe unto the Lord';[139] George *Handel's Chandos Anthem no. 4, 'O Sing unto the Lord a New Song' from 1718;[140] a version based on

---

[134] See Witherington 2017: 244–45.

[135] Jerome trans. Ewald 1963: 184–86. This is taken from Homily 23: 181–90.

[136] See Shereshevsky 1971: 76–86; also Howell 1987: 191.

[137] See Feuer 2004: 1186 and 1190, citing Kimḥi; also Cohen 1992: 315.

[138] See Bullock 2001: 194–95.

[139] See https://www.youtube.com/watch?v=p2n8QcGnk7o

[140] See several different performances at http://www.musicsalesclassical.com/composer/work/28695. Handel's Chandos Anthems were based on Psalms 93, 95, 96, 97, 99 and 103.

*Coverdale by John Naylor (1838–97), 'O Sing unto the Lord a new song';[141] and a version by Joseph *Gelineau, 'O Sing a New Song to the Lord'.[142] The well-known hymn, 'O worship the Lord in the Beauty of Holiness' is taken from Ps. 96:9. It is significant that those controversies inspired by particular verses in this psalm are no longer evident in their adaptation for worship.

A very different way in which the idiom of 'new song' has been used is for polemical purposes. In her *Music as Propaganda in the German Reformation*, Rebecca Wagner Oettinger describes the 'power of song', whereby popular melodies were given political and theological content.[143] We have noted elsewhere, for example for Psalm 46, how this works in metrical psalmody.[144] But in this case, this is about a trope from a psalm, carved into a contemporary song, for public oral distribution in the sixteenth-century, far removed from the *scholae cantorum*. These particular and biographical songs are about martyrdom and sainthood. So 'ein neues Lied', taken from Ps. 96:1 (also 98:1) is particularly pertinent:

> We raise a new song,
> may our Lord God help us
> to sing what He has done
> to His glory and honour
> in Brussels, in the Netherlands.
> Indeed, through two young men
> He has made His wonders known,
> and with his gifts
> He has adorned them richly.[145]

The second of the twelve strophes of the 'song' above indicates that this is about a certain 'John' and 'Heinrich'. The song describes how they were hounded by the Catholic authorities, the 'Sophists' from Louvain who 'belittled Scripture'. Hinting at the Fiery Furnace in the Book of Daniel, we read how they were condemned at the stake and burnt for heresy. This is far removed from the 'new song' in Psalm 96, except that it speaks again of new life emerging out of exile, death and judgement.

---

[141] This is recorded on 'Praise the Lord Ye Servants': The Psalms of David Volume 5 by Gloucester Cathedral Choir directed by John Sanders, organist Mark Lee, under Priory Records Digital Recording 387, 1991.

[142] This is on *Psalms of David, with the Cathedral Singers*, conductor Richard Proulx, GIA Publications Inc 1995, CD 357: see https://www.allmusic.com/album/psalms-of-david-mw0000903932.

[143] See Oettinger 2001: 27, 32.

[144] See Oettinger 2001: 46–47; and Gillingham 2018: 279–81.

[145] See Oettinger 2001: 61–69; here 64.

So Psalm 96 is often interpreted in different ways by Christians and Jews: a Christian might read this as about Christ as King, both in his earthly life and in his reign to come, and the summons of the nations to give glory to God in Ps. 96:7 is a call to the whole world including Jews to worship Christ. A Jewish reading is that the whole psalm refers to the rule of the Messiah at the end of time. Yet in art, music and poetry, the emphasis often shifts away from Jewish and Christian controversies to matters concerning a more universal hope.

Psalm 97: God Reigns in Zion (i)

Psalm 97 returns to a theme at the end of Psalm 93: God's rule in Zion. It is 'paired' most clearly with Psalm 99, which similarly develops this theme. Yet it is also linked to Psalm 96: the expression 'let the earth rejoice' (*tagel ha'areṣ*) is found in 96:11 and 97:1, and the polemic against other deities in 96:4–5 is found again in 97:7 (also referring to them as *elilim*—which is translated as 'idols'—although *elilim* sounds similar to *elohim*, it means 'worthless ones' or 'weak ones').[146] The compilers, in this first stage of reception, again chose with care the placing of the psalms in this collection. We see again the imagery of God as Lord of the storm gaining victory over other deities (vv. 1–7) with the consequence that Zion and the cities of Judah rejoice at his exaltation (vv. 8–12).[147]

In Jewish interpretation Psalm 97 raises similar issues to Psalm 96: the vision of the other nations throwing away their images (v. 7) is one which will come about when the Messiah comes.[148] The references to 'righteousness and justice' in verse 2, reminiscent of Ps. 96:13, also suggest that the age of the 'third Temple' is about to come.[149] The ascription of this psalm to Moses, and its purported dedication to the tribe of Joseph, results in interesting exegesis. Because Joshua descended from this tribe, and is accredited with taking over the land of Canaan, the assumption is that when the Messiah comes Joseph too will come to restore the whole land, from where the universal reign of God over the wicked will begin, and will end in his Temple.[150] Again it is appropriate that Psalm 97 is also used in *Kabbalat Shabbat* as part of the collection of Psalms 95–99.

---

[146] See the discussion on Ps. 96:4–5 on pp. 112–3.

[147] We may note how similar this is to the way the Babylonian god Marduk, after his victory over Tiamat, builds a sanctuary to dwell in; so too the Canaanite deity, Baal, celebrates his victory over Mot by building a palace.

[148] See Braude 1959: 141–2; Feuer 2004: 1203 and 1206.

[149] See Feuer 2004: 1194, citing Kimḥi.

[150] See Feuer 2004: 1193; and Cohen 1992: 318.

The psalm is not cited in the New Testament, although the idea of all peoples ('coastlands') rejoicing when they recognise God's kingship (verse 1) is taken up in Rev. 19:6–7. In Ps. 97:7, the Greek translates the word for 'gods' who 'bow down' before God in verse 7 as 'angels', so the imagery of 'angels bowing down' before God has correspondences with the Greek in Heb. 1:6 and Rev. 11:7.[151] The idea of God gaining victory over the earthly powers in the first part of the psalm, and of God dwelling among his people in the second part, was read by early Christians to refer Christ's second coming and to his incarnation. This is clearly seen in the metrical version of this psalm by Isaac *Watts, whose heading for verses 1–5 is 'Christ reigning in heaven and coming to judgement', and for verses 6–9, 'Christ's incarnation'. So the last verses are paraphrased as follows:

> The Lord is come; the heav'ns proclaim
> His birth; the nations learn his name;
> An unknown star directs the road
> Of eastern sages to their God.
>
> All ye bright armies of the skies,
> Go, worship where the Savior lies;
> Angels and kings before him bow,
> Those gods on high and gods below.
>
> Let idols totter to the ground,
> And their own worshippers confound
> But Judah shout, but Zion sing,
> And earth confess her sovereign King.[152]

Watts is taking up tradition in Christian commentaries as varied as *Augustine, *Cassiodorus, and *Luther. It is not surprising, therefore, that this psalm, along with 96 and 98, became an important part of the liturgy for Christmas Day. It is also used at Epiphany, which celebrates the coming of the wise men to worship the baby Jesus as King.

Several illuminated manuscripts take up both the themes of Christ as King and the Incarnation. Christ as King is represented in the *Stuttgart Psalter (fol. 111r) which illustrates the first part of the psalm as an image of Christ reigning in a globe-*mandorla, supported by two angels, with a righteous man below worshipping him and an idol worshipper disappearing into a pit with a devouring devil.[153] The initial 'D' in the *St Albans Psalter depicts verses 6–7: we see the contrast between two disciples (perhaps representing 'angels') adoring Christ

---

[151] See Witherington 2017: 245–46.

[152] See http://www.cgmusic.org/workshop/watts/psalm_97.htm.

[153] See https://bit.ly/3IBS4iU

as King in the upper part of the letter, and below three demons (undoubtedly representing 'idols') being struck with terror.[154]

Musical arrangements of this psalm by Christian composers rarely make any Christian overlay explicit. A very early version is by the Paris composer Pérotin the Great (c.1150–1200), one of the best-known composers from the School of Notre Dame, whose *Viderunt Omnes* developed the earlier two voice structure into a four-part polyphony. A later version is Henry *Purcell's 'Jubilate Deo', for chorus and ensemble, which was inspired by verse 12. Antonin *Dvořák* used verses 2–6 of this psalm ('Clouds and thick darkness are all around about him') as one of his ten biblical songs in Czech, composed in *1894*. Several arrangements of the whole psalm use *Coverdale's version, whilst more recent Catholic versions prefer the *Gelinau Psalter.[155] Perhaps the best-known arrangement is 'Hail, Gladdening Light', a third-century Greek hymn (*fōs hilaron*) based upon Ps. 97:11 ('light dawns for the righteous'). This hymn was particularly important in the *Tractarian movement, having been translated from the Greek by John *Keble. The setting by Charles *Wood (d.1926) relies on a dialogue within the double choir, a feature no doubt available to him in his work with chapel choirs in Cambridge.

So, like many psalms in this collection, Psalm 97 is used in a similar way by Jews and Christians when referring to the universal reign of God breaking into history, and also when refuting the worship of idols; the difference is in their understanding of how and when in history God's Kingship has been or will be made manifest. A contrast between the (Jewish) *Septuagint version and the (Christian) Syriac Psalter makes this clear. The *Septuagint adds an extra heading to this psalm ('*For David, when his land is established*') and gives a future tense to verbs in verse 3 ('Fire *will go* before him…') and verse 10 ('He *will rescue them* from the hand of the wicked…'). This is about the future reign of God as King. By contrast, one of the Syriac headings to this psalm reads '*A psalm of David, in which he predicts the advent of Christ (i.e. in the flesh), and through it his last appearing (i.e. to judgment).*'

Psalm 98: 'Sing to the Lord a New Song' (ii)

Psalm 98 is paired with 96 in its identical call to 'sing a new song' (vv. 1–3) and, again using imagery from the myth of the cosmic sea, calls on all the earth to

---

[154] See https://www.albani-psalter.de/stalbanspsalter/english/translation/trans266.shtml

[155] For 'The Lord is King', on *Psalms of David, with the Cathedral Singers*, conducted by Richard Proulx, GIA Publications,Inc. CD 357, 1995 see https://www.allmusic.com/performance/psalm-97-the-lord-is-king-mq0002095676.

worship the Lord as King (vv. 4–6); even the sea (*yam*) and rivers (*neharot*), symbols of primordial chaos, join in this celebration (vv. 7–9). Other links with Psalm 96 include the jussive appeals to praise in 96:11–13 ('Let the heavens be glad, and let the earth rejoice; let the sea roar, and all that fills it…') which are mirrored by those in 98:7–9 (Let the sea roar, and all that fills it; the world and those who live in it…). Psalm 98 is also closely linked to Psalm 97: in 97:4 his lightnings illuminate the world (*tebel*) to herald God's coming, whilst the same word *tebel* is used in relation to God's coming in 98:7 and 9. Similarly the more general word 'earth' (*ereṣ*) is personified in 97:1 and 4 as it 'rejoices' and 'sees', whilst in 98:3 and 4 all the (ends of the) earth also 'rejoice' and 'see' God's salvation. The mountains are also personified in each psalm: in 97:5 they 'melt' at God's presence, and in 98:7 they 'shout for joy'. The phrase *Yahweh malak* ('The Lord reigns') is found in 97:1 and in 98:6 we read *Yahweh hammelek* ('The Lord is king'). The twin themes of 'righteousness and judgement' also lie at the heart of each psalm (97:2; 98:9). If these three psalms are not by the same composer, the first stage of their reception history shows how the compilers have brought them together because of their close formulaic expressions of praise, perhaps editing them as well. It is not surprising that in Greek all three psalms are ascribed to David.

As with Psalm 96, much has been written about the meaning of the 'new song' in 98:1. *Rashi, for example, responding to *Jerome's reading that this song has been fulfilled in Christ, a theme developed by medieval scholars, believes that in both psalms this refers to the future.[156] Rashi argues that Israel cannot fully rejoice until the Messiah comes, so this psalm is about the *eventual* redemption of Israel from captivity.[157] *Midrash Tanchuma*, with its teaching on the Torah, speaks of the 'new song' in Psalm 98 as the last of the Ten Songs of Faith—the one to be sung at the end of time.[158] The date of the coming of the Messiah is known only to God (v. 2) but the tradition of the dedication of this psalm by Moses to the tribe of Naphtali, who were content in God's blessing (Deut. 32:34), offers a model of patient faith and hope. The references in verses 7–9 to the whole of the created order praising God at the end of time are either interpreted literally—for example Abraham *ibn Ezra reads verses 7–8 as sailors on the seas clapping their hands—but they are usually read as a metaphor of happiness and joy.[159] This is another psalm used at *Kabbalat Shabbat*.

---

[156] See Shereshevsky 1971: 78, on Ps. 98:8.

[157] See Gruber 2004: 601; Braude 1959: 143; and Cohen 1992: 320.

[158] See Feuer 2004: 1202. The others are the Passover song sung in Egypt; Exod. 15:1–21; Num. 21:17–20; Deut. 32; Josh. 10:12; Judg. 5; 2 Sam. 22/Psalm 18; Psalm 30; Song of Songs; and Psalm 98.

[159] So Rashi in; Gruber 2004: 601, see also Feuer 2004: 1206.

Again, the reading is very different in Christian interpretation. The allusion to a new song and the victory of God in verse 1 is found in Rev. 14:3 ('They sing a new song before the throne and before the four living creatures and before the elders…'). This new song now concerns the reign of Christ. The reference in Ps. 98:3 to all the ends of the earth seeing the salvation of God allows for the justification of the Gentiles' inclusion within the Christian community: the one who 'judges the earth with righteousness' (Ps. 98:9) is now not God alone, but God working in Christ as in Acts 17:31 ('he has fixed a day on which he will have the world judged in righteousness by a man whom he has appointed…'). Similarly, the Church Fathers read the references to the 'new song' as 'the church's song to Jesus Christ'. Following the New Testament writers, they too understood the universal application of the psalm, in that this is a song for Gentiles as well as Jews.[160] *Cassiodorus reads the psalm as celebrating both the first and second coming of Christ.[161] Not surprisingly, therefore, Psalm 98 is also part of Christmas liturgy, and here the Gospel reading is usually from John 1:1–14.[162]

Most Christian arrangements of this psalm also focus on the 'new song'. 'Puer nobis natus est', a *Gregorian Chant for Christmas day, is based on the first verse of the psalm and Isa. 9:6. Verses 4–9 were the inspiration for Isaac *Watts' Christmas hymn, 'Joy to the World' (1719). This was composed in praise of the First Coming and in anticipation of the Second Coming, with its arresting opening of descending notes to sound like pealing bells.[163] Heinrich *Schütz's seventeenth-century 'Singet dem Herr ein neues Lied' used *Luther's translation of Psalm 98.[164] Felix *Mendelssohn-Bartholdy created a different arrangement: 'Singet dem Herr ein Neues Lied' was performed in the new year of 1844 in Berlin Cathedral with two mixed choirs, and, unusually, a harp and organ. Recent versions include Benjamin *Britten's *The Prodigal Son* (1968) which uses verse 1 as a chorus sung by the servants on the return of the prodigal from a far country.[165] James *MacMillan's 'A New Song' (incorporating Psalms 96 and 98) also assumes a Christian theme, and was featured in the BBC Proms in

---

[160] See Wesselschmidt 2007: 200, citing *Eusebius, *Proof of the Gospel* 6.6 in POG 2:6–7. See also de Solms 2001: 473 on *Athanasius and *Augustine.

[161] Cassiodorus trans. Walsh 1991a: 430–31.

[162] See Neale and Littledale 1874–79: 3/251), which lists a number of other Christian festivals which used this psalm.

[163] Dowling Long and Sawyer 2015: 127.

[164] See *Psalmen Davids*, CD 2, Cantus Cölln and Concerto Palatino, directed by Konrad Junghänel, HMC 901652.53 harmonia mundi s.a. 1998.

[165] Dowling Long and Sawyer 2015: 189.

July 2000.[166] A contemporary meditative version by David Hurd, 'The Lord is King, let the Earth rejoice' is a chant in five voices, adapted from the *Anglican Chant Psalter* (1987). And an unusual jazz version by Daniel Richardson and Angel Napieralski, entitled 'Sing, Sing a New Song to the Lord God', is based upon words from the *Genevan Psalter.*[167]

In the *Benedictine Rule Psalm 98 is the first psalm to be read on Saturdays, and it also marks the seventh of the eight liturgical divisions in the Psalter as a whole (other major liturgical divisions are found at Psalms 1, 27 (Latin 26), 39 (Latin 38), 53 (Latin 52), 69 (Latin 68), 81 (Latin 80) and 110 (Latin 109).[168] This results in Psalm 98 often being given a larger illuminated initial 'C' (for 'Cantate', 'sing') in some Psalters. For example, a fourteenth/fifteenth-century Cluniac choir Psalter, known as the *Bromheim Psalter* (MS. Ashmole 1523), probably from a Cluniac Priory in East Anglia, with stylistic similarities with the *Ormesby Psalter*, has a striking illuminated initial for Psalm 98 (*Vulgate* 97) on fol. 116v (despite it missing the text from 98:4–102:2 (*Vulgate* 97:4–101:2). In the upper part of the initial 'C' is Christ, Architect of the Universe, holding a compass, surrounded by birds, animals and the fishes of the sea. In the lower part of the initial; King David, seated, points up to Christ, whilst listening to three monks singing from a book. A crowned figure, blowing two trumpets, separates the upper and lower parts.[169] For a representation of this image, see PLATE 8. The trope of three monks chanting is taken up in other illuminations to this psalm, but usually without the explicit Christological emphasis.

The thirteenth-century *Parma Psalter* also takes up the theme of 'sing to the Lord a new song' and its illustration to Psalm 98 has some connections with Psalm 95. Again set in the entire first Hebrew word of the psalm, a figure, with his right arm raised, points with his left to a musical stave with five lines and ten square notes. Three hybrids, one to the left, one above and one below, each with open beaks, represent the choir which the figure leads.[170]

An alternative but equally notable representation of Psalm 98 is a sculpture in the Tate Collection by Barbara Hepworth (1958), entitled 'Cantate Domino'. The upper of the two interlocking diamond shapes is open, and reminiscent of two outstretched arms held out in prayer, whilst the curve between them resembles a face in song. Hepworth wrote: 'My sculpture has often seemed to me like offering a prayer at moments of great unhappiness. When there has

---

[166] For a version sung by St John's College see https://bit.ly/319WjBq.

[167] See https://worship.calvin.edu/resources/publications/jazz-psalms.

[168] See (Gillingham 2018): for Psalm 27, see p. 173; for Psalm 39, see p. 239; and in this volume, for Psalm 81, see p. 40; and for Psalm 110, see p. 190.

[169] Solopova 2013a: 143–52.

[170] *Parma Psalter* fol. 139v; also Metzger 1996: 29–148, here 88.

been a threat to life ... my reaction has been ... to make something that rises up, something that will win. In another age ... I would simply have carved cathedrals.'[171]

Finally, an extract from another short poem by Edward *Clarke captures a contemporary reading of this psalm. This takes up the image of the 'withdrawing sea', a common biblical motif (see Isa. 11:11,15 and Exod. 14:21–30). Clarke sees the decaying culture of our world emblematised by the sea of space and time, and the stanza below enacts the crumbling of the walls as in a frescoed room of a Palladian farmhouse. But as the sea withdraws it leaves behind the things of tradition: the 'new song' which is both old and forever new.[172]

> Let the roaring sea, which is this world,
> Tumble, and all who sit inside
> Its vast and half-transparent walls shall stand
> And sing of that withdrawing tide;
> The things it hurled
> Behind it on the strand,
> Archaic words that still deceive the eye
> With their reality.

Again, the more specifically Jewish and Christian readings of this psalm in the commentary traditions are quite different from the more universal readings in music, poetry and art.

Psalm 99: God Reigns in Zion (ii)

Psalm 99 seems to have specific links with the first psalm in this collection, Psalm 93; with its opening words *Yahweh malak* (Yahweh reigns), its reference to keeping God's 'decrees' (*'edot* in 93:5 and also in 99:7), and to God being clothed with strength in 93:1 (*'oz*) and again in 99:4 where he is addressed as 'mighty king' (also using *'oz*).[173] Again noting that compilation is the first stage of reception, Psalm 99 also brings together another theme running throughout this entire collection (Pss. 93–100), namely that of God's holiness. Three times God is acclaimed as holy: verses 3 and 5 cry out 'Holy is he! (*qadosh hu'*) and verse 9 ends 'For the Lord our God is holy' (*ki qadosh yahweh elohēnu*). Similarly 93:5 speaks of God's house being holy, 96:9 calls on the people to worship God in 'glory of holiness', 97:12 ends with 'give thanks to his holy name' and

---

[171] See http://www.tate.org.uk/art/artworks/hepworth-cantate-domino-t00956.

[172] Taken from email correspondence with Edward Clarke in July 2018. See Clarke 2020: 105–6.

[173] See Hossfeld and Zenger 2000: 491.

98:1 begins with the affirmation that God's 'holy arm' has given him victory. Similarly the myth of God's victorious cosmic rule over the storm and the chaotic seas, expressed in different ways in Psalms 93, 95, 96, 97 and 98, is found again in Psalm 99: here, as in 97, this rule is particularised by God's dwelling in Zion (vv. 1–5). Moses the intercessor (as in Psalm 90) is recalled, along with Aaron and unusually Samuel (vv. 6–8), to illustrate again that God's Kingship pre-dates that of the inauguration of the Davidic monarchy. The Zion theme occurs again at the end of the psalm with a call to worship God in Zion (v. 9).

The *Septuagint has the additional heading 'Psalm of David': this might be to link the psalm with the same superscription in Psalm 98. Jewish commentary tradition understands that this psalm, partly because of its emphasis on 'justice and righteousness' (v. 4), refers again to the future day of judgement, when God will establish his universal reign. Again the Mosaic authorship is emphasised: this is a psalm by Moses dedicated to the tribe of Dan, 'the young lion, leaping from Bashan' (Deut. 33:22) its association with judgement is appropriate.[174] Much is made of the way that this psalm speaks of being released from ongoing exile—for example, the people trembling in verse 1 is seen to refer to the Jews, not yet at peace, and the reference to Mount Zion in verse 2 is seen as a promise of what is to come, and the reference to 'Jacob' in verse 4 refers to the Jews in exile being brought back to their land.[175] The reference to Aaron the priest alongside Samuel the seer (v. 6) is to emphasise the importance of the priesthood of the tribe of Levi and the role of non-Levites (Samuel is from the tribe of Ephraim) in the worship of Israel. As well as being part of *Kabbalat Shabbat*, along with four other psalms in this collection, Psalms 95–99, the psalm has been associated with the theme of 'waiting in exile' making it appropriate for use in the liturgy of *Tisha b'Av*, which mourns the destruction of the Temple and waits for God's coming again to his people.

The reference to the priesthood of Moses and Aaron also influenced Christian typology: Jesus, with the seamless robe of the high priesthood, becomes a high priest greater than Aaron (Heb. 7:11, 26–27) and even greater than Moses (Heb. 3:2–3). Christological readings were developed by the early fathers who viewed the psalm as a prophecy about Christ. For example, *Justin, in *Dial.* 37, cites at length both Psalms 46 and 98 (NRSV Pss. 47 and 99) to show that the rule of Christ is prophesied throughout the psalms: 'And in the ninety-eighth Psalm, the Holy Spirit reproaches you, and predicts Him whom you do not wish to be

---

[174] Rashi and *Kimḥi note some apocalyptic associations with Gog and Magog (Ezek. 38–39 and Zech. 14): see Feuer 2004: 1207 and Gruber 2004: 602.

[175] See Feuer 2004: 1207 and 1209; Braude 1959: 144.

king to be King and Lord, both of Samuel, and of Aaron, and of Moses...'[176] The psalm is cited again at length in *Dial.* 64, to make the same claim, that Christ as Messiah (king) is prophesied throughout Psalm 98 (99).[177] *Jerome, too, makes a similar point, that the three psalms beginning with 'The Lord is King' (93, 97 and 99) are a means of showing how *'the patriarchs and prophets are the garments of Christ'*. So 99:1, which speaks of the people trembling, is a reference to the Jewish people 'trembling' at their crucifixion of Christ. 'The Lord has suffered; the Lord has been crucified ... O the kindness of the Holy Spirit! He did not say, let them perish, but let them tremble. He wished to point out fault, not their punishment ...' It was this sort of Christian exegesis that impelled *Rashi to read all three psalms as within the life of the Jewish people, so Psalm 99 is a reference to the war of Gog and Magog at the end of time, when the nations (i.e. the Gentiles) will tremble.[178]

Some musical arrangements use the words of Ps. 99 without expanding them to give any particular Christian reading, although this is implicit from the liturgical context. Giovanni *Gabrieli's Motet for Six Voices, 'Timor et Tremor', first published in 1615, is one example. Another example with a very different arrangement is by Jan Pieterszoon *Sweelinck (1562–1621). He adapted his metrical version of this psalm from the *Genevan Psalter* as into a celebratory polyphonic composition, 'Or est maintenant l'Éternel regnant' in which the 'Eternal' is Christ the King.

Several Byzantine Psalters give an explicitly Christian representation of this psalm in art, particularly reading verse 5 ('Extol the LORD our God; worship at his footstool. Holy is he!') in the light of the cross. For example, the *Khludov Psalter* (fol. 98v) depicts verses 5–7 with Moses, Aaron and Samuel at the bottom of the page, but above them is a hill out of which emerges a book and an empty cross. A similar association is in the *Pantokrator Psalter* from Mount Athos (fol. 140r), where Golgotha is surrounded by a sanctuary. The eleventh-century *Paris Psalter* (fol. 6v) has an illustration of verse 5 with a miniature of the cross, and another miniature illustrates verse 9 with an icon of Christ with a cross. The origin in the eastern tradition may be a sermon from *Theodore the Studite (759–826) abbot of the Stoudios Monastery in Constantinople, in his *Homily 2, 'In adorationem crucis'*, which associated verse 5 of this psalm with the Orthodox liturgy of the Exaltation of the Cross in Lent. So it would seem that liturgical practice encouraged this visual interpretation of verse 5 ('worship at his footstool!') whereby the cross is now the 'footstool' for worship.[179]

---

[176] http://www.newadvent.org/fathers/01283.htm.

[177] http://www.newadvent.org/fathers/01285.htm.

[178] Shereshevsky 1971: 78–80.

[179] See Corrigan 1992: 5, 25, 41 and 93; also Walter 1986: 18.

Although Psalm 99 has a less rich reception history than the other Kingship Psalms it actually offers unusual and distinctive Jewish and Christian interpretations, not only within the commentary tradition but also in music and art.

Psalm 100: The Whole Earth is Called upon to Acknowledge God as King

Psalm 100, concluding this collection of eight psalms, is, as its title suggests, more of a particular thanksgiving psalm than the other hymns of praise in this collection. The thanksgiving focusses on the exilic theme of the people as God's flock and God as their Shepherd (vv. 1–3).[180] The psalm ends nevertheless with a hymnic call to all peoples to process together to the Temple (vv. 4–5). As a conclusion to this collection, Psalm 100 seems to have been placed here because it has links with all the other psalms within it. It has associations with Psalm 95 in its call to the whole earth to acknowledge God as King. It has correspondences with other more explicit kingship psalms such as 93, 97 and 99, for even though the Hebrew word *melek* is not used, verse 1 is similar to the calls of praise in those psalms.[181] It could be paired with Psalm 96 in its call to all nations to worship God, with the call to 'bless his Name' (96:2 and 100:4). It also recalls Psalm 98 in its pairing of God's love (*ḥesed*) and faithfulness (*'emunah*) in 98:3 and 100:5. Psalm 100 suggests what Zenger terms an 'astonishing universalism', a feature found in Isaiah 40–55 (e.g. Isa. 45:22) but which moves beyond the other kingship psalms, because it consistently includes 'all the earth' in its praise. So in several ways Psalm 100 was chosen as an appropriate psalm to conclude Psalms 93–99.[182]

In terms of later reception through translation, one verse is especially important. This is verse 3, where the Hebrew has an oral reading (**qere'*) 'It is he that made us *and we are his*', alongside a written reading (**ketib*) 'It is he that made us *and not we ourselves*'. The **Septuagint* prefers the written reading, as does the **Peshitta* and **Vulgate*. These variations caused some interesting issues for the reformers, as we shall see.

In Jewish interpretation this is the last of these psalms to be given Mosaic authorship, dedicated this time to the tribe of Asher, 'blessed in bounty' (Deut. 33:34): the psalm is one of gratitude to God for the blessings to come when the

---

[180] See for example exilic texts such as Pss. 74:1; 79:13; Jer. 23:1 and Ezek. 34:31.

[181] See the links between Psalms 100 and 95 on pp. 99 and 107 previously.

[182] See Hossfeld and Zenger 2000: 497–98.

Messianic Age dawns.[183] Jews have debated whether the word *todah* in the title and in verse 5 (Eng. verse 4) really means 'to confess' as in Ezra 10:11, or 'to give thanks', as in Ps. 26:7 and Lev. 17:11–18, where it concerns the thanksgiving sacrifice. *Rashi, noting the universalistic tone in this psalm, argues that for the Jews this means 'to give thanks' (for sins having been redeemed) and for the Gentile nations it means 'to confess' (in acknowledgement of their wickedness).[184] This led to further debates about verse 5 (Eng. verse 4) and whether all offerings, or indeed all prayers, will cease in the Messianic Age, other than that of thanksgiving.[185]

Because the theme of thanksgiving (past, present and future) dominates the psalm, it plays a prominent part in Jewish liturgy: in the *Ashkenazi tradition it is read as a Psalm of Thanksgiving at every morning service as an introduction to the *Pesukei de-Zimra except on Sabbaths and feast days.[186] An arrangement of this psalm for five voices ('Mizmor letoda: Hari'u l'Adonai, kol ha-aretz'), for the Italian synagogues in Mantua, first published in Venice in 1623, testifies to the prominence of this psalm in Jewish liturgy.

Despite its universal appeal and its obvious relevance regarding the place of the Gentiles both as made by God (verse 3) and recipients of God's steadfast love and faithfulness (verse 5), the psalm is never used in the New Testament. The appropriate translation of verse 3 was an ongoing issue, exemplified by *Luther and *Calvin. In his early lectures, *Dictata super Psalterium*, Luther argued that the Latin translation of verse 3 ('it is he that made us, *and not we ourselves*') was an ideal example of the teaching in the psalms on justification by faith alone.[187] Calvin, meanwhile, took a different approach, reading 'we are his people' as an invitation for (Reformed) believers to praise God, because he has chosen *them* to be his people, out of all the different nations. Christians are therefore to bless his name (verse 4):

> ...so that his glory be preserved unimpaired, and that no deity be opposed to him that might obscure the glory of his name. True, indeed, in the Papacy, God still retains his name, but as his glory is not comprehended in the mere letters of his name, it is certain that there he is not recognised as God. Know, therefore, that the true worship of God cannot be preserved in all its integrity until the base profanation of his glory, which is the inseparable attendant of superstition, be completely reformed.[188]

---

[183] See Feuer 2004: 1215.

[184] See Gruber 2004: 605; also Feuer 2004: 1216.

[185] See Braude 1959: 148 and Feuer 2004: 1216. Jewish debates have also been on the *ketib/qere* of verse 3, with Rashi preferring the *ketib*: Gruber 2004: 605.

[186] Hertz 1942: 60.

[187] See Hendrix 1974: 1–3. The thirteen psalms are 8, 15, 41, 44, 59, 68, 73, 79, 83, 88, 100, 110 and 121.

[188] See https://www.sacred-texts.com/chr/calvin/cc11/cc11008.htm.

It is interesting that the psalm whose potential universalism created such criticism in Calvin's commentary also inspired the sixteenth-century metrical psalm, 'All People that on Earth do Dwell', attributed to Louis Bourgeois of Calvin's church in Geneva, here translated from the French for the *Anglo-*Genevan Psalter* (1561) by William *Kethe:

> All people that on earth do dwell,
> Sing to the Lord with cheerful voice;
> Him serve with mirth, His praise forth tell
> Come ye before Him and rejoice.[189]

A later arrangement was the addition of a doxology: the best known, a century after Kethe's version, is that of Thomas *Ken, as the psalm became known as the 'Old Hundredth':

> Praise God, from Whom all blessings flow
> Praise Him, all creatures here below;
> Praise Him above, ye heavenly host;
> Praise Father, Son and Holy Ghost.

Latin motets also continued to be published: Christopher*Tye's 'Omnes Gentes' is a good example.[190] Other metrical versions include Isaac *Watts' 'From all that Dwell below the skies' and Charles *Wesley's 'O for a Thousand Tongues to Sing My Great Redeemer's Praise'. It was probably its liturgical familiarity which influenced George *Herbert's adaptation of Ps. 100:1–2 (as well as Ps. 95:1–4) as 'Antiphon I' in *The Temple*—a metrical poem which later was also used as a hymn:

> Let all the world in ev'ry corner sing,
> *My God and King.*
>
> The heav'ns are not too high,
> His praise may thither flie;
> The earth is not too low,
> His praises there may grow...
>
> The church with psalms must shout,
> No doore can keep them out:
> But above all, the heart
> Must near the longest part...[191]

---

[189] See https://hymnary.org/text/all_people_that_on_earth_do_dwell.
[190] See https://www.hyperion-records.co.uk/dw.asp?dc=W9262_GBAJY0870401.
[191] See Kinnamon 1981: 11; also https://www.ccel.org/h/herbert/temple/Antiphon1.html.

Other musical arrangements, not all in English but nevertheless well-known, include *Gabrieli's 'Jubilate Deo', omnis terra', a large-scale polychoral work probably dating sometime after 1605; *Schütz's 'Jauchzet dem Herrn, alle Welt' from his *Psalmen Davids*, from 1619; Johann Sebastian *Bach's 'Jubilate', written for Jubilate Sunday (Easter 3), and first performed at Weimar in 1714; and *Handel's 'Canticorum Jubilo' as part of his *Chandos Anthems* (1716–1718), where Psalm 100 is first. 'Give to God our Thankful Songs' was one of *Haydn's *Six Psalms*, performed during his second visit to England in 1794.[192] Ralph *Vaughan Williams arranged 'The Old Hundredth' for the coronation of Elizabeth II in 1953, a version which has been used for many state occasions since, including the fiftieth coronation celebrations again at Westminster Abbey in 2002.[193] Leonard *Bernstein also used this psalm in *Chichester Psalms*, composed for the Chichester Cathedral Three Choirs Festival in 1965, calling it '… the most B-Flat majorish tonal piece I've ever written': it used a mixed choir, boy solo, strings, three trumpets, two harps and percussion: Ps. 108:2 ('Awake psaltery and harp! I will arouse the dawn') begins the piece which concludes with Psalm 100 in entirety, in a dance-like 7/4 rhythm.[194] Other arrangements include Benjamin *Britten's 'Jubilate Deo in C', composed at the Duke of Edinburgh's request for St. George's Chapel, Windsor in 1961, and played during his eightieth and ninetieth birthday services; it was played once more at the Duke's funeral in May 2021.[195] Another memorable arrangement is William *Walton's 'Jubilate Deo', a multi-textural polyphonic piece premiered at Christ Church Cathedral, Oxford, in 1972.[196] Concerning its popularity as an anthem, motet, and hymn, J. R. Watson is quite right to observe that 'the survival of this psalm, when so many others have been forgotten, except in Scotland, is probably owing to the combination of words with tune, which carries them with dignity and grandeur'.[197]

Rather like Psalm 95, it is the liturgical and musical use of this psalm which has influenced its popularity in other ways. Parts of this psalm have even been used as mottos in Christian heraldry: 'Servite in laetitia' ('Serve the Lord with gladness') and 'Inservi Deo et laetare' ('Serve God and rejoice') are just two examples.[198]

---

[192] https://www.hyperion-records.co.uk/tw.asp?w=W11548.
[193] See https://www.youtube.com/watch?v=mj9w7IUQ5AU.
[194] Dowling Long and Sawyer 2015: 45.
[195] See https://www.youtube.com/watch?v=meKEf-x39uA.
[196] For Britten, see http://www.hyperion-records.co.uk/dw.asp?dc=W8476_GBAJY0764305&vw=dc; and for Walton, see http://www.hyperion-records.co.uk/dw.asp?dc=W2828_GBAJY0555705&vw=dc.
[197] See Watson 2002: 67.
[198] See Huxley 1949: 297–301, here, 300.

The liturgical use has also influenced many different visual representations. Some depict in literal ways the call to 'enter his gates with thanksgiving' as entering the gate of the Temple. A modern version is Annie *Vallotton's sketch in the *Good News Bible*, where the Temple is the church.[199] Moshe *Berger's extraordinary depiction of fire and light emanating from and hovering over an ice-blue entrance to a building is another such example, and this probably refers to the Jerusalem Temple.[200]

The most unusual artistic representation of all, because it 'upturns' so much of what is celebrated as good and positive in this psalm, is Philip *Evergood's painting of oil on canvas in 1938–39, now in the Jewish Museum, New York. Evergood's work (rather like that of Arthur *Wragg) was 'strongly influenced by social themes, such as political oppression and racism'.[201] In 'The Hundredth Psalm', the four menacing white-hooded figures circling a bonfire hardly seem to reflect the mood of this psalm, but here Evergood 'ironically contrasts the psalm's plea for mercy and justice with the inhumanity of a Ku Klux Klan gathering at a lynching.' PLATE 9 represents this image by Evergood. This is one of the most radical artistic depictions of any psalm in the Psalter, and the fact that Evergood chose 'The Old Hundredth', with its honest and open call for all peoples to give God the honour due to his name, makes it all the more arresting: it makes the viewer think again about the traditional reading of the psalm in the context of violence and oppression.

To conclude this collection of psalms from 93–100: we may note again that, outside the additional headings in the *Septuagint (in Psalms 93, 95, 96, 97, 98 and 99), the focus on David in later Jewish reception is rare. The covenant of the people under Moses is given more prominence throughout this collection, and this offers a more future orientation. The several references to God's choice of Zion, to which, after a victory over other nations and their deities, the Lord will return, are obvious examples.[202] In Christian reception, by contrast, the Kingship Psalms have been given a this-worldly orientation in the ways they were seen to witness to the birth, passion and resurrection of Jesus. The Kingship psalms have also provided a good deal of material for the development of Christian doctrine, particularly in the theology of Creation and of the Second Coming. Despite all this, Jews and Christians have together found in the use of these psalms shared concerns, not least in the ways they all testify to the relationship between the community of faith and those outside it.

---

[199] http://www.biblical-art.com/artwork.asp?id_artwork=26069&showmode=Full.

[200] http://themuseumofpsalms.com/product/psalm-100/.

[201] Taken from https://bit.ly/3EF2uv5.

[202] See Pss. 93:5; 96:6, 8; 97:8; and 99:2.

Psalms 101–103: God as Defender

The mood of confident celebration in Psalms 93–100 now takes on a more sombre tone. The figure of David returns briefly at this point, for in the MT both Psalms 101 and 103 have Davidic headings. Indeed Jewish readings sometimes continue the theme expressed in the Kingship psalms, emphasising David's return to herald in the Messianic Kingdom. However, the overall theme, developed in both faith traditions, is one of exemplary faith held within the compassion of God.

Psalm 101: David: The Model Servant

Psalm 101 speaks in the voice of one in authority aspiring to be a model servant of their people. The prayers for divine favour (vv. 1–2) are followed by seven promises of fidelity (vv. 3–8). The Davidic heading suggests that this is to be seen as an 'ideal David', who, like Moses, attends to the law: he resembles the figure of Josiah in 2 Kings 23, and to the 'idealised David' of the book of Chronicles. It could be an actual king, perhaps at a festival, or in later times, it could be religious leader who promises to walk in the ways King David once walked.

Here the linguistic connections with previous psalms are less specific: they include the reference to God's 'faithfulness' in 100:5 and the reference to the 'faithful' in the land in 101:6; and the reference to 'coming' into God's presence and gates in 100:2 and 4 and the psalmist asking God to 'come' to him in 101:2,

Psalms Through the Centuries: A Reception History Commentary on Psalms 73–151, Volume Three,
First Edition. Susan Gillingham.
© 2022 John Wiley & Sons Ltd. Published 2022 by John Wiley & Sons Ltd.

(literally, 'Oh when will you *come* to me?' in 101:2b). These are very general, however, suggesting that the compilers developed Psalms 101–103 as a separate but related collection.

The *Qumran Scroll 11QPs^a begins with Psalm 101, giving the emphasis on instruction and future hope typical of much of this scroll. It is followed by Psalms 102 and 103, then 112,109, 113–116 and 118, and then Psalm 104. Even though the order is so different from the MT arrangement, it is significant that Psalms 101–103 remain intact as a smaller collection.[203]

Despite the Davidic title noted above, in *Midrash Tehillim* the psalm is seen to refer back to Moses, who chooses the Levites as priests and sets up the Tabernacle (see 'my house' in verses 2 and 7), and so sets the psalm aside for reading at the Feast of Tabernacles (or Booths), to be read on the morning of the fifth day.[204] Other Jewish readings see David as the actual composer: for example, they note that the prayer 'O when will you come to me?' in verse 2b suggests David at the beginning of his reign, waiting to bring the Ark into Jerusalem.[205] Despite its vows of obedient service, the psalm is rarely used in Jewish liturgy: it is one of the few in Book Four not to be appropriated in this way.[206]

In Christian reception the psalm is seen to point to Jesus Christ as the obedient servant. A similar royal 'manifesto' of such service is also found in, for example, Luke 4:16–21, where Jesus applies a similar passage concerning an obedient servant from Isa. 61:1–2. *Augustine spoke of this psalm as a weapon against sin: following the example of Christ, those who receive pardon should also give pardon.[207] In his exposition of this psalm, Augustine discusses at length the theological tension between 'justice' and 'mercy' in verse 1, concluding these are balanced together in Jesus Christ, the obedient servant.[208]

Later Christian tradition also read the psalm in an instructional and practical way: the 'Oxford Martyr' Nicholas Ridley (1500–1555), when Bishop of London, understood the psalm as 'The Householder's Psalm', and apparently expounded it regularly to his household in Fulham; and Francis *Bacon termed it the 'Mirror for Magistrates', on account of the reference 'no one who practices deceit shall come into my house'.[209] Andrew Mein notes that the insistent and

---

[203] See Abegg, Flint and Ulrich 1999: 545–53. The order after Psalm 104 is also unique to this scroll (*ibid.* 553–70).

[204] See Braude 1959: 150–2. On the defence of its association with Tabernacles, see Rabinowitz 1936: 357. See also Goulder 1975: 283.

[205] See Cohen 1992: 326; also Feuer 2004: 1219.

[206] It is not ascribed for use in daily prayer, but in older *Ashkenazi traditions it is prescribed for use in the consecration of a house. See Singer 1892: 301.

[207] See Wesselschmidt (2007: 207–8) citing Augustine in *Letter* 167.20 in FC 30: 48–49.

[208] See Augustine trans. Uyl 2017: 506.

[209] See R. E. Prothero 1903: 139.

repeated appeals to the integrity of the suppliant (likely in his view to be originally a Davidic king) are evident in all the verses except the first; this suggests not so much stability and confidence in their authority but rather the anxieties involved in ruling over others. Whether the speaker is from a royal, or political, or religious context, he is actually dependent upon the integrity of others in order to maintain harmony and justice for those he serves.[210]

This didactic theme is also developed in the *Theodore Psalter* (fol. 133v): influenced by the use of this psalm during Lent, it depicts a poor young man, sitting on a rock and looking up to heaven, from where God's hand is seen to be offered in blessing. Other Byzantine Psalters with the same theme include the *Khludov Psalter* (fol. 100r), the *Pantakrator Psalter* (fol. 141v), and the *Bristol Psalter* (fol. 165v). The same instructional tenor is expressed in the *St Albans Psalter*, where in the initial letter 'M' of this psalm (starting in Latin with 'Misericordiam') Christ seems to spear with a fork two miserable sinners who attempt to come into his house, turning his eyes to the cross above rather than looking at them.[211]

The psalm has had a limited role in Christian liturgy, other than in Lent; hence musical arrangements are not prolific. Sydney Nicholson's arrangement of *Coverdale's 'My song shall be of mercy and judgement' at the beginning of the twentieth-century is one example; Stephen Pearson's 'I'll sing of your Justice and Love' is a more recent twenty-first-century version.[212]

Hence the didactic element in this psalm, which starts with a focus on David (or Moses) and later on Christ, ends up with a more universal appropriation: the figure in this psalm can be adapted by anyone. Even so, there are some who find the psalmist's claim to have integrity somewhat excessive (see for example verse 2: 'I will study the way that is blameless... I will walk with integrity of heart within my house...') and, placing it alongside Pss. 7:3–5 and 35:13, prefer not to use it as a practical and pious guide.[213]

Psalm 102: A Penitential Prayer of a Suffering Servant

Psalm 102 has no Davidic heading in either the *MT or the *LXX; it is an anonymous individual lament sung as 'A prayer of one afflicted, when faint and pleading before the Lord'. The first part is a plea for God to hear (vv. 1–11), followed by a statement of confidence in the eternal God who once ruled as

---

[210] See Mein 2010: 56–70.

[211] See https://www.albani-psalter.de/stalbanspsalter/english/translation/trans269.shtml.

[212] For Nicholson see https://www.hyperion-records.co.uk/dw.asp?dc=W9083_GBAJY1100809; for Pearson, see https://bit.ly/2Q7MjTA.

[213] See Brueggemann and Bellinger 2014: 430–34.

king from Zion and who will build up this city once again (vv. 12–22). The final part is a prayer for the psalmist's life to be spared (vv. 23–28). Here we find some correspondences with Psalms 90–92, at the start of Book Four, expressed in the sense of the permanence of Yahweh contrasted with the fragility of human life. The specific references to life as 'fading grass' in 90:5–6 (also 92:7) is taken up here in 102:4 and 11. The measurement of a lifetime in days and years as in 90:9–10, 12 and 14–15 is expressed as the passing of days in 102:3 and 11. Psalms 101 and 102 have a few associations: the references to the 'integrity of heart' in 101:2, the 'perverse heart' in 101:4, and the 'arrogant heart' in 101:5 have echoes with the 'stricken heart' in 102:4. The verb 'to cling' (Hebrew, *d-b-q*) is found in 101:3 and 102:5, in each case concerning a situation of distress. The 'earth' as the specific setting of God's activity is found in 101:8 and 102:15,19 and 25, and more specifically the 'city of the Lord' as the sphere of God's blessing features in 101:8 and is expanded on in 102:13–21. Hence these two psalms, very different from Psalms 93–100, have apparently been placed together because of their similar themes.

One of the issues in the reception history of this psalm is whether the 'affliction' is, literally, about an individual or a dramatic personification of Zion and/or the Jewish community itself, creating some affinities with the book of Lamentations. Later Christian reception in music (as we shall see) brought these two ideas together by adapting the personal elements for a public context.

Midrash Tehillim interprets 'Hear my prayer' in verse 2 (Eng. verse 1) as the voice of David, of the tribe of Judah, fulfilling the words of Moses in Deut. 33:7, 'Hear the voice of Judah!'. The psalm is understood in a further prophetic light, with David as the suppliant, 'afflicted' in foreseeing the sins of Ahaz, Manasseh and Amon.[214] A more general reading is to see David having composed the psalm to express the feelings of any poor person in misery.[215] 'The poor' might instead be a suppliant in exile: the initial themes of human misery and God's eternal care, ending with the restoration of Jerusalem and the ingathering of other nations make this 'the psalm of an exile'.[216] *Rashi, for example, notes that verse 14 (Eng. verse 13) refers to those in exile who have taken with them, as a memory of what they once had, the stones of Jerusalem.[217] The imagery of a lonely bird (longing to return to a permanent home, as in verse 7) further suggests this context. Following the reference in verse 18 ('let this be recorded for a generation to come'), the promise in verse 28 ('The children of your servants shall live secure; their

---

[214] See Braude 1959: 153–4.
[215] Feuer 2004: 1225.
[216] Cohen 1992: 328; also Feuer 2004: 1225.
[217] Gruber 2004: 610.

offspring shall be established in your presence') is recited on *Rosh HaShanah and at *Yom Kippur, alongside the first verse of Psalm 103.

Verses 25–27 of this psalm are cited in Heb. 1:10–12. There the 'Lord' (which is added in the Greek of verse 25) is taken as an address to Jesus Christ, stating his superiority over the angels, indicating also that the relationship between the exalted Son and creation was prophesied in this psalm. *Cyril of Jerusalem puts this in a slightly different way: he writes about how this world will perish (vv. 18–28) but how humans can receive the gift of immortality through Christ.[218] Few Christian commentators read the 'voice of anxiety' in this psalm as Christ himself speaking: even when reading this as a prayer rather than prophecy, the character of the 'afflicted and grieving pauper' is someone addressing Christ.[219] Nevertheless, Christ's incarnation, transfiguration and resurrection have all been understood as prophecies hidden in verses 12–28.[220]

Psalm 102 is used frequently in the Christian liturgical year: it is often read on New Year's Day, on Ash Wednesday, and after *Lauds on Fridays during Lent, in part because of its theme of the brevity of human life and the dependence of all humanity upon God. It was marked out, at least as early as *Augustine, as one of the seven *penitential psalms of the church.[221] Indeed, Augustine's *Confessions* use verses from this psalm many times, the most frequent being verse 27: 'But thou art the same, and thy years have no end' which is cited at least nine times.[222] *Luther, for whom the penitential psalms were a critical influence on the eve of the Reformation, argued in his early lectures, *Dictata super Psalterium*, that the promises for the rebuilding of 'Zion' were promises for the renewal of the Church.[223] Yet Luther also added to the title of this psalm 'the people before the advent of Christ', and so understood this as a 'pre-Incarnational' confession of a penitent psalmist. This is thus another example of the piety of the 'faithful synagogue' which we noted for Psalm 93, so it is both an early Jewish reading and a later Christian reading which is, unusually for Luther, applied here.[224]

Its use as a penitential psalm has resulted in many poetic paraphrases. One metrical version is by the nineteenth-century English poet John Clare (1793–

---

[218] See Wesselschmidt 2007: 209–10 citing Cyril's *Catechetical Lectures* 2.12 in LCC4:88.

[219] *Cassiodorus trans. Walsh 1991b: 1–2. A similar point is made by pseudo-*Bede, cited in Neale and Littledale 1874–79 3/285.

[220] de Solms 2001: 490.

[221] Of the seven penitential psalms (6; 32; 38; 51; 102; 130 and 143), Psalm 102 is the fifth. Set alongside the seven deadly sins, Psalm 102 is against the deadly sin of avarice.

[222] See Poque 1986: 155–66.

[223] https://www.ccel.org/ccel/schaff/hcc7.ii.ii.xv.html.

[224] See Luther's comments on Psalm 93 on p. 102; also German 2017: 110–18.

1864): the third stanza below displays in rhythm and metaphor the sheer fragility of human life:

> The wilderness's pelican,
> The desert's lonely owl—
> I am their like, a desert man
> In ways as lone and foul.
> As sparrows on the cottage top
> I wait till I with fainting drop.[225]

The penitential use of the psalm has also inspired a vast amount of music. Several composers have arranged all seven penitential psalms together: Orlando *de Lassus composed seven motets as *Psalmi Davidis Poenitentiales* for Duke Albrecht V of Bavaria in 1563. His 'Domine, exaudi orationem meam' takes the eight traditional liturgical modes as his overarching idea. Henry *Purcell's 'Hear my Prayer' (c. 1680–82) was originally for the organ and a cappella choir, set mainly to the first verse of this psalm; a recent public performance was given at St. Paul's Cathedral at Margaret Thatcher's funeral in 2013.[226] *Mozart's *Davide Penitente* was composed for Lenten liturgy in 1785, as a cantata for soloists, choir and orchestra.[227] The several metrical versions of this psalm, usually focussed on one verse (such as verses 11 or 25), include versions by John *Newton (for the *Olney Hymnbook*, 1779) and John *Whittier (1882). Modern versions based on older psalm texts include Howard *Goodall's poignant but insistent version, 'Pelican in the Wilderness/*Pelicano solitudinis*' (2010), which uses *The 1640 *Bay Psalm Book* version of this psalm.[228] This was the Psalter used by the pilgrim founders of America who arrived on the Mayflower in Plymouth Bay in 1620. Goodall's use of this version identifies the 'affliction' in this psalm with a displaced people: 'Like Pelican in the wilderness, like Owl in the desert so am I: I watch, and like a Sparrow am, on house top solitarily...' Each of the above examples illustrates how a psalm designated for personal penitence can also be an appropriate composition for solemn public occasions: indeed, it was a psalm used in Coronation services until 1603.

If the liturgical use inspired innumerable musical compositions, the actual placing of this psalm within the Psalter has similarly inspired a number of interesting illustrations. In the Latin text this psalm is numbered as Psalm 101,

---

[225] Atwan and Wieder 1993: 314–15.
[226] See https://www.youtube.com/watch?v=642mO-afvng.
[227] Dowling Long and Sawyer 2015: 59.
[228] See https://bit.ly/2OykLpQ.

and so marks the beginning of the third 'fifty' which was a common division in Latin Psalters. Very often this was marked by images of David at prayer, set in the initial 'D' (for **D**omine) at the beginning of the psalm.[229] A similar frequent trope, shared with other penitential psalms such as 26, is here based upon verse 1b ('Let my cry come to thee!') and is of David pointing to his mouth.[230] A variation of this is of a suppliant praying directly to Christ.[231] Sometimes the division between the Latin Psalm 100 and 101 (EV Psalms 101 and 102) is indicated by an image of a pious patron, whether monastic or secular: two such examples, from fourteenth and fifteenth-century English Psalters, are of a cleric kneeling at an altar with an open book, and of a female patron at prayer.[232] Sometimes this division is simply indicated by a much larger illumination of the first letter 'D': this is the case of the *St Albans Psalter*, which, following *Augustine's *prosopological reading of this psalm, depicts Jesus praying in the Garden of Gethsemane, taken from verse 1 of the psalm ('Lord …let my cry come to thee!').[233]

Other artistic representations are taken from the reference to the pelican in verse 7 (although the Hebrew is *qa'at* and the particular bird implied is unclear). The identification of Christ with the pelican may be dated as early as second-century Alexandria, in a Christian work entitled *Physiologus*: just as the mother bird nurtured her young with her blood, so Christ nurtures his Church. Thus the symbol of 'Christ as Pelican' became common in medieval art and architecture. So for example the *Theodore Psalter* (fol. 134r, opposite the illustration of the poor man being blessed by God) depicts a pelican on a nest of eggs on top of a column, with small birds flying around waiting to be fed. The image elides verses 6 and 7 of this psalm, but the medieval reader would see this as a symbolic reference to Christ protecting his church which is hidden in the psalm. A representation of this image is found at PLATE 10.

Hence this is a surprisingly rich psalm, particularly in the Christian tradition, although the theme of the fragility of human life and the enduring mercy of God is a universal theme throughout its varied reception history.

---

[229] See http://www.getty.edu/art/gettyguide/artObjectDetails?artobj=136158&handle=li.

[230] See https://www.abdn.ac.uk/burnet-psalter/text/197r.htm. (from the fifteenth-century Burnet Psalter).

[231] See https://bit.ly/2PGC9cL, taken from the twelfth-century Psalter of Eleanor of Aquitane, from the collections of the Koninklijke Bibliotheek, The Hague.

[232] Oxford, Bodleian Library, MS Douce 18 (c.1433, England) and MS Lit. 198 (thirteenth-century, NE England). See Solopova 2013b: 89–104, here 95 for MS Douce 18.

[233] https://www.albani-psalter.de/stalbanspsalter/english/translation/trans270.shtml. On the Church Fathers' readings of this psalm, see Brunert 1996: 21–30.

Psalm 103: God's Compassion is Everlasting

Psalm 103, also with a Davidic heading, continues the theme of divine constancy over human failure, but focusses on God's justice and compassion rather than his judgement and anger. Verses 1–5 speak explicitly about God's forgiveness of the individual, reminding us of the image of the eagle in Ps. 91:1–6; verses 6–14 are about God as healer of the nation, citing an early creed, also used in Psalms 86 and 147, which occurs in Exod. 34:6–7, and is about God's mercy being greater than his anger.[234] Verses 15–18 focus on human finitude, whilst verses 19–22 compare this with God's everlasting care, reflecting again on the creed of Exodus 34. Its 22 verses are a reminder of the 22 letters of the Hebrew alphabet; although this is not acrostic in form, it does suggest a sense of order and completeness in its account of God's mercy. For those in exile, this psalm, stamped with the authority of David in its heading, and the authority of Moses in its (Exodus) creed, would have been an important personal inspiration for those remembering the sufferings of the exile. The links with Psalm 102 are clear. In Psalm 102 the contrast is made between the psalmist's fleeting days (102:3, 11) and God's everlasting years (102:24, 27); in Psalm 103 the psalmist's days are like grass (verse 15) but God is everlasting (verse 17). The grass metaphor is also found in Ps. 102:11. Ps. 102:12 speaks of God being enthroned forever and 103:19 refers similarly to God's throne being in the heavens. God's tender love is expressed in Ps. 102:13 (Heb. verse 14) using the verb *r-ḥ-m* and this verb is also used with God as subject in Ps. 103:8 (twice). In Ps.102:15 (Heb. verse 16) the heathen are to 'fear' the name of the Lord, (using the verb *y-r-'*) and in Ps. 103:11, 13 his own people are also to 'fear him', also using the verb *y-r-'*.

Jewish tradition assumed Davidic authorship for this psalm because of the superscription. The fivefold reference to 'Bless the Lord, O my soul' in verses 1, 2, 22 and 104:1, 35 prompts a discussion about David symbolising the five stages of the development of the soul—from its embryonic state to birth, infancy, maturity and death.[235] In both Jewish and Christian tradition the psalm has sometimes been used to inspire penitence—where the emphasis is on the brevity of the human life in the psalm—whilst at other times it has been used to inspire praise, where the emphasis is more on the everlasting love of God. An example of the latter is the Prayer of Azariah—the song of the three men in the fiery furnace, a later Greek addition to Daniel 3—where Psalm 103, along with Psalm 148, is used as part of the call to praise. Similarly verses 11–13 ('For as the heavens are high above the earth, so great is his steadfast love to those who fear him…') are used frequently as blessings in Jewish liturgy. A more common use, however, is

---

[234] See Note 234 previously.
[235] See Feuer 2004: 1237.

in liturgies of penitence: *Sop.* 19:2 suggests Psalm 103 should be read along with Psalm 130 ('Out of the Deep') as a psalm of confession. Similarly Ps. 103:1 is used at **Yom Kippur*, and verses 15–17 are used at funerals (again reflecting the associations of this part of the psalm with Psalms 91 and 92). Louis Lewandowski's composition in 1878 for the new synagogue in Berlin ('Psalm 103: Preise, meine Seele, den Ewigen')—no longer in Hebrew, but in the vernacular—is for soloists, a mixed choir, and organ: this interprets the psalm as both penitence and praise.

Like Psalm 102, Christians have also associated Psalm 103 with sin and penitence. The link between healing and forgiveness is found in the account of the healing of the paralytic in Mark 2:1–12 which suggests an allusion to Ps. 103:3 ('who forgives all your iniquity, who heals all your diseases'), particularly in the words of Jesus as recorded in Mark 2:9–11. Verse 8 may have influenced the reference to God's compassion and mercy in James 5:11: if so, this is an interesting example of the complex trajectory of reception, insofar as the verse from the psalm seems to have drawn from Exod. 34:6–7: Pss. 86:15 and 145:8 also use the same expression, suggesting that this was some early formulaic creed used throughout Scripture.[236] More explicit penitential references include a reading by *Ambrose of Milan, some three centuries later, who took the imagery in verse 5 of the eagle—which renewed its plumage by flying near the sun and plunging into water—as a reference to new birth after baptism.[237] Related to this, in the liturgy for catechumens in the eastern churches, Psalm 103 is sung as the first of three *antiphons in the *typika.[238] As late as the sixteenth-century *Calvin's penitential liturgy for the Church in Geneva (1539) used Psalm 103 (not the more usual psalm of penitence, 102) as one of the psalms of confession and forgiveness (along with Psalms 32, 51, 130, 25 and 36). The psalm is used in Calvin's Eucharistic liturgy (1556) as an alternative to the *sursum corda* ('lift up your hearts!') and it also takes the place of a post-communion thanksgiving[239]

A very different version, but also focussing more on the penitential aspects of this psalm, is Mary *Sidney's poetic paraphrase which interprets verse 14 ('As a father has compassion for his children, so the Lord has compassion for those who fear him.') with particular intimacy and tenderness, to show how fond the father is of his stubborn child:

> And looke how much
> The nearly touching touch
> The father feeles towards his sonne most deare

---

[236] See Note 234 previously.
[237] Wesselschmidt 2007: 220, on Ambrose, *Concerning Repentance* 2.2.8 in NPNF 2 10:346.
[238] See Holladay 1993: 180.
[239] See Witvliet 1997: 278–89.

> Affects his hart
> At Ev'ry part
> Plaid by his child:
> Soe merciful, soe mild,
> Is he to them that beare him awfull feare (ll.57–64).[240]

Verses 15–16 ('As for mortals, their days are like grass… for the wind passes over it, and it is gone'), which are also found in Psalms 90 and 91, have similarly influenced a more reflective reading of the psalm: Margaret Mitchell's *Gone with the Wind* (1936), for example, was influenced by these verses. Similarly verses 13–17 are frequently used in Christian burial liturgies: they suggest the promise of God's mercy beyond the grave.

Several hymn-writers interpret the psalm in a more positive way, focussing not so much on human sinfulness and inconstancy but on divine mercy and on God's constant renewing power during this life. Heinrich *Schütz's 'Lobe den Herrn, meine Seele (SWV 39) and J. S. *Bach's 'Nun lob, mein Seel, den Herrn' (Choralsatz BWV 390) are two such examples, where the mood of the music is reflective praise rather than penitent lament. One well-known example in English is the metrical hymn by Henry Francis *Lyte (1834):

> Praise, my soul, the King of Heaven
> To his feet thy tribute bring;
> Ransomed, healed, restored, forgiven
> Who like me his praise should sing?

Similarly the translation of Joachim Neander's German chorale, *Lobe den Herren* as 'Praise to the Lord! The Almighty, the King of Creation' takes up the same theme. More recently, the St Albans composer Howard Blake (b. 1938) uses Psalm 103 in his *Benedictus* (1989), drawing from the Rule of Benedict and selected psalms, creating a mood of compassion and forgiveness.[241] By contrast, a more upbeat version is Stephen Schwartz's 'Bless the Lord O my Soul', from *Godspell*.[242] A more recent equally upbeat arrangement of verses 1–4 is by the Messianic Jewish Band Miqedem which was released in 2016.[243]

---

[240] See Fisken 1985: 177.

[241] See https://www.youtube.com/watch?v=HFvzVCezUL4. James *Macmillan's 'Domine non secundum peccata nostra' (2011) is a similar example, taken from verse 10. It was commissioned to mark the 500th anniversary of the founding of St John's College, Cambridge, with an eight-part choir and solo violin.

[242] This is sung in Part One, after the teaching of Jesus on serving two masters. *Godspell* was first performed in 1971, having a revival on Broadway from 2011–12.
See https://www.youtube.com/watch?v=19LP4qNYUD4.

[243] See https://miqedem.bandcamp.com/track/barchi-nafshi.

Zorada *Temmingh's organ improvisation interprets this psalm in an original way: initially this is as praise and of thanksgiving for God's care of all in creation, although the mood changes constantly throughout. Using the melody by John Goss (1869) to which Lyte's 'Praise my Soul the King of Heaven' is usually sung, the first verse uses the ascending scales to convey praise and tribute, whilst a chorale melody in the bass expresses God's constant faithfulness found in the second verse. The music of the third verse is light but serious as it interprets God's fatherly care towards his children; verse four is darker in and a minor key to demonstrate the frailties of human existence. The piece ends with a vibrant *toccata* in full chords to depict the praise of the angels with the whole cosmos in praise of God.[244]

Representations of this psalm in art have taken up both themes of penitence and thanksgiving. A cautionary image is in the *Utrecht Psalter* (fol. 59r).[245] There *Christ-Logos sits cross-*nimbed, in the heavens, his right hand raised in blessing; the sun and moon to the left and right suggest verse 12 ('as far as the east is from the west...'). The bearded psalmist stands to the lower left, beside a tree with an eagle on its branches (v. 5). An angel with a cross-staff offers a crown of 'mercy' to him (v. 4). The psalmist points to a fiery pit, at the opening of which there is a vast head representing Death (v. 4), beside which souls are being tormented by demons. Above the psalmist is a hill, covered with the 'grass' and the 'flowers of the field', which, like the psalmist, grow only to wither and die (v. 15). Moses is also depicted in this drawing (from v. 7); the small children on either side of him raise their hands to heaven, probably illustrating verse 13 ('As a father has compassion for his children...').

Psalm 103, as the final psalm in this small collection, serves a more universal purpose on account of its moods of both penitence and thanksgiving. Taken as a whole, Psalms 101–103 create a more reflective mood, focussing, like Psalms 90–92, on our shared human need for divine protection and forgiveness. Although the figure of the suffering David is present through the titles above two of the psalms (and above all three in the Greek version), reception history suggests that he is in fact not a dominant figure. Instead David seems to represent both the typical individual at prayer and the people as a whole, so that the personal 'I' in all three psalms can be read as the 'I' of everyone. He is the one who suffers, and sins, and yet remains faithful to God. This allows for a wide range of interpretation in the reception history of these psalms: the key theological motif throughout all three, however, is clear: the mercy of God is greater than his judgement.

---

[244] Zorada is an international composer and organist based in Stellenbosch. See https://zorada.co.za The information here is part of an email correspondence dated October 2016.
[245] See https://psalter.library.uu.nl/page/125.

Psalms 104–106: God as Creator and Redeemer

Although this starts a new collection, the first and last verses of Psalm 103 ('Bless the Lord, O my soul') are identical to the first and last verses of Psalm 104. Although the figure of Moses is now again dominant, the compilers intended there to be a clear connection between these two collections.

Taking the early stage of reception, namely Psalms 104–106 as a whole, the bringing together of these three psalms illustrates the art of narrating a story through the poetic medium. Psalm 104 acts as a prologue to this narrative by its focus on God as Creator, and brings into the Psalter, for the first time, the expression 'Hallelujah!' which is continued over the next two psalms as well. Psalm 104 also echoes the theme of the Kingship of God in Psalms 93–100. Psalms 105–106 speak of God as the people's Redeemer throughout their history, unusually, for the psalms, going as far back as Abraham. They both echo a key theme in Psalms 90–92 in their testimony to God as the refuge of his people and the one whose mercy outweighs his judgement. Psalm 105 celebrates what God has done and Psalm 106 highlights what the people have not done; the conclusion to Book Four is a prayer that God might gather his people from the nations (106:47).

Psalm 104: A Hymn to God as Creator

Psalm 104 is closely linked to Psalm 103 not only in the call to 'Bless the Lord, O my soul' but also in several other correspondences. 104:4 refers to the

Psalms Through the Centuries: A Reception History Commentary on Psalms 73–151, Volume Three, First Edition. Susan Gillingham.
© 2022 John Wiley & Sons Ltd. Published 2022 by John Wiley & Sons Ltd.

winds as God's 'messengers' (*mal'akayw*) whilst 103:20 calls upon God's heavenly 'messengers' (*mal'akayw*) to bless the Lord. Psalm 104:30 speaks of the earth being renewed (using the verb *ḥ-d-sh*) whilst Ps. 103:5 speaks of our youth being renewed, using the same verb. What is different, however, is that the image of God as the compassionate and healing parent in Psalm 103 has now been transformed into a hymn to God as the powerful cloud-rider and Creator of light and life. Verses 1–18 develop the theme of Yahweh as the storm god who defeats the forces of chaos, and who, like the Canaanite storm god Baal at *Ugarit, rides the cloud in a chariot (vv. 1–9) yet provides fertility for the whole world through the subterranean waters (vv. 10–12) and through rains from above (vv. 13–18). Verses 19–30 develop the theme of God as bringer of light and life into the world, using the same imagery as the fourteenth-century (BCE) Egyptian hymn to the sun god Aten as well as a demythologised reference, probably again from Canaan, to the fearsome sea monster, Leviathan, who is here just a toy used by God (vv. 24–26).[246] The psalm ends with a prayer for justice on earth (vv. 31–35).

In Jewish tradition, as evidenced by the additional heading 'of David' in the *Septuagint, this psalm was read as David's expansion of an earlier creation hymn, the 'Song of Moses', or the poetic account of creation in Genesis 1. Although the 'six day span' is more obvious there than in Psalm 104, David here is seen to make Genesis 1 more transparent, using the same order of God's creative acts. So, for example, the same attention is given to humans, made as the apex of creation on the sixth day (Gen. 1:26–27; Psalm 104:23–30).[247] The theme of God as the one who brings light and life influenced this psalm's association with *Rosh Ḥodesh*, the festival of the New Moon on the first day of each month, so that this psalm is called 'The Song of the Day'. Since the twelfth-century Psalm 104 has been used, with the Songs of Ascents (Psalms 120–134), on Sabbath afternoons in winter.[248] Verse 15 is particularly important: the reference to 'wine, to gladden the human heart' is a rationale for the use of wine at weddings, circumcisions, and this, along with the reference to the 'bread, which strengthens the human heart' is used at the *Kiddush* for the sanctification of the Sabbath.[249] Verse 24 ('O Lord, how manifold are your works!') and verse 31 ('May the glory of the Lord endure forever!') are especially important in morning prayers before the *Shema*, where God rejoices in his works before the light dawns.

---

[246] Aten imagery may be seen in 'when you dawn they live' and 'when you set they die' (vv. 22, 27–30). See Day 2013: 211–28. See also Dion 1991: 43–71.

[247] See Feuer 2004: 1251; also Braude 1959: 167–70.

[248] See Magonet 1994: 5; also Feuer 2004: 1251.

[249] See Donin 1980: 308.

Just as the Jewish psalmist adapted this hymn of creation from Genesis 1 and from Canaanite and Egyptian hymns about God as Creator, so Christians carried on the interpretive tradition and adapted the psalm in their own way, seeing parts of the psalm through a Christological lens. Psalm 104, like Psalm 8 (also a psalm of creation with links to Genesis 1), was used by both the New Testament writers and the Church Fathers to give this hymnic language of creation a Messianic emphasis. For example, in Heb. 1:7, the citation of the *LXX* version of verse 4, which refers to God's 'messengers' as 'angels', uses the psalm as a proof-text for the superiority of Christ over the angels—a theme taken up by the early Church Fathers, for example in the letter of *Clement to the Romans (36:3). The following summary of the psalm is offered by *Cassiodorus: 'Clearly the whole narrative is to be told of the Lord Christ, who in the beginning made heaven and earth'.[250] Another example is reading the references to the Spirit renewing Creation (vv. 24–30) to be about the Spirit restoring the human race through the Church. On this account 104 is often used as a 'Pentecost Psalm', along with Acts 2:1–21, with the Gospel reading as John 20:19–23. Hence several Church Fathers saw the expression of the Trinity here, in God the Creator, God the Word, and God the Spirit.[251]

Christians have used various verses as 'proof-texts' and come to many different conclusions. One example is verse 15, with its reference to the earth bringing forth wine, bread and oil: this suggested to the Fathers how ordinary things could be given sacramental significance.[252] Another example is verse 4, where the references to the angels in the Greek and Latin showed how the havoc on earth through storms and tempests was caused by (evil) angels sent by God.[253] This is a very different reading from the one in Heb. 1:7. Finally, in the sixteenth-century, verse 5 ('You set the earth on its foundations, so that it shall never be shaken') was used against the Renaissance astronomer Nicolaus Copernicus (1473–1543) to demonstrate that the earth did not rotate. By contrast, the Prussian geographer Alexander von Humboldt (1769–1859) saw in Psalm 104 'an epitome of scientific progress, a summary of the laws which govern the universe'.[254]

---

[250] Cassiodorus trans. Walsh 1991b:29. A similar citation is attributed to pseudo-*Bede in Neale and Littledale 1874–79 3/317.

[251] See Wesselschmidt 2007: 235–6, citing *Augustine, *Sermon* 223A.I, in *WSA* 3/6:212–13; and *ibid.*: 238–9, citing *Ambrose, *Spir.* 2.5.33, in NPNF 2/10:118–119, and *ibid.*: 239–40, citing Basil the Great, *Letter* 8, from FC 13:36–37.

[252] Neale and Littledale 1874–79 3/327–29.

[253] Wesselschmidt 2007: 229–30, citing John of Damascus, *Orthodox Faith* 2.3 from FC 37: 205.

[254] See Prothero 1903: 315.

The beginning of a fourteenth-century funerary text, on the tomb of Tirkhān Khātūn, a pious Mongol woman who wished to be buried close to Jerusalem, reads '*Kullu man 'alayhā fān*'. Taken from Q. 55:26–27 ('everyone on earth shall perish; but the Face of your Lord, full of majesty and grace, will abide'), this has close correspondences with Ps. 104:29,31: 'When you take away their breath, they die and return to their dust… May the glory of the Lord endure forever'.[255] Even if this might be seen as coincidental, given the similar views about mortality and the enduring glory of God, there are a number of other correspondences with Psalm 104 with *Surah* 55 (*al-Rahman*). The interest in the animation of nature, found in Psalm 104 (for example, the description of the winds as God's messengers in verse 4) is a theme also expressed in *Surah* 55, where for example we read 'The plants and the trees submit to His designs' (Q. 55:6). The myth of the separation of waters in Ps. 104:5–9 is also implicit in the description of the merging together of the two seas in Q. 55:19; so too the containment of cosmic forces in Ps. 104:9 is also found in Q. 55:20 and 33. More explicitly, we read in Q. 55:24 that 'His are the moving ships that float high as mountains on the sea', a theme also found in Ps. 104:25–26: 'Yonder is the sea, great and wide… There go the ships, and Leviathan that you formed to sport in it.'[256]

In Psalm 104 the list of the various natural phenomena of creation brought about by the deity also has correspondences with *Surah* 78 (*al-Naba'*). Ps. 104:13 reads: 'From your lofty abode you water the mountains', and in Q. 78:14 we read 'Did We not send water pouring down from the clouds?'. In Q. 78:13 the sun is personified as a 'blazing lamp', whilst in Ps. 104:19 the sun 'knows its time for setting'; in Q. 78:10 we hear how the night has been made 'as a cover', whilst at beginning of Psalm 104, God is covered with light 'as with a garment'. Each text recognises that humanity's subsistence depends on vegetation: in Q. 78: 15–16 the earth is 'to bring forth with it [rain] grain, plants, and luxuriant gardens', whilst in Ps 104:14 it is God who 'cause(s) the grass to grow for the cattle, and plants for people to use'[257] The poetic language is different, and Psalm 104 is more concerned about God's ongoing care of creation whereas in *Surah* 78 creation is an event in the past; but, given the popularity of Psalm 104 in both Jewish and Christian liturgy and commentary, some implicit reception through oral tradition is not impossible.[258]

---

[255] Neuwirth 2009: 733.
[256] See Neuwirth 2009: 756–59.
[257] See Neuwirth 2009: 740–45.
[258] I am grateful for the advice of Afifi Al-Akiti here. I have used his translation which is an adaptation of Haleem 2010.

This psalm about God's care for the natural order has undoubtedly lent itself to a good deal of poetic innovation. Perhaps the best-known Christian adaptation is the thirteenth-century 'Canticle to the Sun' by the *Franciscan Francis of Assisi, based on verses 19–20.[259] In the fifteenth and sixteenth centuries, Psalm 104 was frequently used as an experiment in English poetry. Mary *Sidney achieves this by developing the theme of creation somewhat radically, and with a surprising contemporary emphasis, personifying the earth and seeing Mother Earth as an aging mother, yet again pregnant, echoing the miraculous renewal of spring, and so encouraging the potential of regeneration in all of us:

> Earthe, greate with yong, her longing doth not lose,
> The hopfull ploughman hopeth not in vayne…
>   All things in brief, that life in life maintaine,
>   From Earths old bowells fresh and yongly growes.[260]

George *Herbert had a different emphasis. Given that Psalm 104 was sung at Pentecost, celebrating how the God who sustains us in history is also our Creator, the poem is called 'Providence'. Hence the brief call to praise, where the psalmist addresses himself at the beginning and the ending of the psalm, is developed and expanded into seven stanzas at the beginning of the psalm, and three at the end, so that over a quarter of the psalm is about praise in God's providential care. Compare this couplet with Mary Sidney:

> When th'earth was dry, thou mad'st a sea of wet:
> When that lay gather'd, thou didst broach the mountains…'[261]

According to Herbert, one crucial theme of the psalm is of God's providence of food for us all:

> Thy cupboard serves the world: the meat is set,
> Where all may reach: no beast but knows his feed.[262]

But whereas the psalmist speaks of wild asses, goats, and lions, Herbert uses images of pigeons, bees and sheep; instead of the cedars of Lebanon and fir trees, Herbert alludes to herbs and roses. The harsh realities of the ancient Near East are thus domesticated: this is an English country estate.[263] God

---

[259] https://www.catholic.org/prayers/prayer.php?p=183.
[260] Psalm 104, ll. 43–48. Taken from; Fisken 1985: 179.
[261] Ps. 104:6.8; ll.113–114. See Bloch 1992: 251–7.
[262] Psalm 104:14, 27; ll.49–50. See Bloch 1992: 252.
[263] See Bloch 1992: 252–3.

is homely and parochial in his providential care: there is little here of his clothing himself with light and walking on the winds, of his spreading out the heavens, laying the earth's foundations and rebuking the waters with his voice of thunder.[264] At the pinnacle of this providential created order stands Man.[265]

The metaphysical poet Henry Vaughan (1621–95) included Psalms 65, 104 and 121 in his *Silex Scintillans* because of the way each psalm spoke of God's care for the world of creation; he used 104:10–24 to depict this theme. The first part is in three pentameters, following a Sapphic style used often by the Sidneys; the last verse, part of a final trimester, is as follows:[266]

> O Lord my God, how many and how rare
> Are thy great works! In wisdom thou hast made
> Them all, and this the earth, and every blade
> Of grass, we tread, declare.

Whether Vaughan consciously played on the imagery comparing man's days to grass in Ps. 103:15–16 is difficult to tell; but the greatness of the Creator and the awesome but fragile nature of creation lie at the heart of this poem.

Psalm 104 has also inspired many metrical hymnic versions. William *Kethe's version (1561) from the *Genevan Psalter*, known as 'Old Psalm 104', was re-worked by Robert Grant (1779–1838). This is now the well-known hymn based on verses 1–10 and 24–33:

> O Worship the King all glorious above;
> O gratefully sing his power and his love;
> Our Shield and Defender, the Ancient of Days
> Pavilioned in splendour, and girded with praise...

Like Vaughan, Grant captures the imagery of the awe of God in the created order in verses 3 and 4 ('His chariots of wrath the deep thunder-clouds form/ and dark is his path on the wings of the storm') with God's mercy and care portrayed in verses 27–30 ('Thy mercies how tender! How firm to the end!/Our Maker, Defender, Redeemer and Friend').

A notable arrangement in English is Henry *Purcell's seventeen-minute composition during his time at the Chapel Royal: 'Praise the Lord, O my soul; O Lord my God' is for two violins and choir. Unusually for a psalm of praise,

---

[264] These images are taken from Bloch 1992: 253.

[265] Bloch here notes the links between Herbert's interpretation of this psalm and that of Psalm 8: see Bloch 1992: 256.

[266] See Hamlin 2004a: 136–7.

the composition starts in wistful and melancholy mood, which is interrupted by a triple-time section in a much lighter vein; after a more lively and forceful tenor interlude the psalm returns to a more characteristic and joyful tenor mode, returning to the theme of rest in God's majesty.[267] Some two centuries later, *Stanford's 'Praise the Lord O My Soul' is a briefer interpretation also for Anglican chant, using choir and organ.[268] A more contemporary arrangement (1993), composed by John Foley for string quartet and *SATB for Easter and Pentecost Liturgy, entitled 'God send out your Spirit' has a very different quieter and reflective mood: based on Ps. 104:30, it is a prayer for justice and healing to God who is Creator and Provider of all. John *Tavener's *Veil of the Temple* (2003) used verse 2 of this psalm in his adaptation of Orthodox Liturgy for the London City Festival: 'You mantle yourself in light, stretch out the heavens like a curtain…'[269] A more recent adaptation of this psalm was by the guitarist and composer William Loveday, who arranged parts of Psalm 104 at the request of the Duke of Edinburgh when it was sung at his seventy-fifth birthday in 1996; it was sung again at his funeral in May 2021.[270]

At least two arrangements have been influenced by the link between Psalm 104 and Akhenaten's 'Hymn to the Sun'. One is a distinctive Hebrew interpretation of this psalm, using a string quartet and two female voices, progressing to a mixed chorus and chamber orchestra; this takes up this ancient creation theme in its own imitation of the 'Hymn to the Sun'.[271] A second example is from the première of *Philip Glass's Opera 'Akhnaten', in Stuttgart, in 1984, under the guidance of Egyptologist Jan Assmann. It was intended to evoke 3500 years of tradition, and to show a possible precursor of monotheism in the context of the three monotheistic religions today. Psalm 104 was an important part of this opera and was performed by the *Tehillim Psalms Project* in Frankfurt in May 2016.[272]

Each year the *Tehillim Psalms Project* focusses on several performances of one psalm for an interfaith choir and audience: Psalm 104 was the focus in 2016. Another notable innovative use of this psalm was a performance by an Iraqi composer, Saad Thamir, who used an Ottoman Turkish translation

---

[267] See https://www.hyperion-records.co.uk/tw.asp?w=W7141.

[268] See C. V. Stanford, 'Praise the Lord O my soul', from *Hear my Prayer O Lord. The Psalms of David Volume I*, Hereford Cathedral Choir directed by R. Massey, Organist G. Brown: Priory Records Digital Recording 290, 1989.

[269] See https://www.youtube.com/watch?v=oXARpFeq8o4.

[270] See https://www.youtube.com/watch?v=CALiGDlLADE.

[271] See *The Psalms of Ra: New music set to Egyptian and Hebrew Texts*, at http://www.psalmsofra.com/cdcontents.html.

[272] See http://ircf-frankfurt.de/wp-content/uploads/2015/03/Tehillim_Konzert_Frankfurt.pdf. See also p. 92 (for the use of Psalm 91 in the same *Tehillim Psalms Project*).

alongside verses of the Qur'an to show the relevance of Psalm 104 for Moslems, Christians and Jews.[273] The Turkish translation was actually the work of Protestant Polish Ottoman prisoner, Wojciech Bobowski, who then became court musician in Constantinople and translated the entire Bible into Ottoman. For the psalms, he used the *Genevan Psalter*, given that it was familiar to him. He converted to Islam after which he called himself Ali Beg Ufki, but his version of the Bible became a cultural artefact pertaining to the Jewish and Christian faith. Hence the performance of Psalm 104 in Frankfurt in 2016 had an interesting trajectory: it came from a sixteenth-century Protestant Psalter which was then incorporated into a seventeenth-century Ottoman translation, to become part of a performance by an Iraqi musician now living in Cologne.[274]

As well as arrangements in sacred music, Psalm 104 lends itself to dramatic performance in the concert hall as well as the church. *Mendelssohn's *Elijah* picks up several of its themes. In the recitative in Theme 16, after the slaying of the prophets of Baal, and following an impassioned *Allegro con Fuoco* from the orchestra, with violins and violas, and some sixteen note arpeggios, Elijah sings from 104:4 ('O thou who makest thine Angels spirits') to praise Israel's one and only God: here using Jewish tradition about the angels and spirits and flaming fires descending from God and obeying him.[275] 104:4 is also alluded to in Ralph *Vaughan Williams' interpretation in *Job: A Masque for Dancing* (1948), which was inspired by *Blake's sketches of Job published in 1826. In Scene VII, following Elihu's 'Dance of Youth and Beauty', God answers Job from the whirlwind (Job 38:1–2) by way of reference to Ps. 104:3–4, which speaks of God riding his chariot on the clouds and wings of the wind.[276] Finally, *Elgar's *The Kingdom* (1906), following a similar theme found in *The Apostles*, uses Psalm 104:19 and 20 (with other psalms) which is sung by Mary after the death of Christ as she contemplates all she has seen and heard.[277]

There are many representations of this psalm in art. A distinctive depiction is in the Byzantine *Theodore Psalter* (fol. 137v) which, at the beginning of this psalm, shows David (following the *LXX heading) praying to an icon of Jesus: Christ is represented, implicitly, both as the Creator-Logos and as the

---

[273] Correspondences between Psalm 104 and the Qur'an include *Surah* 16 (*Surah An-Nahl*): see Speyer 1961: 475. Connections between Psalm 104:5ff. and *Surah* 78:1–16 have been proposed in; Neuwirth 2010: 740–45.

[274] This information is taken from the unpublished paper 'Das Frankfurter Tehillim-Psalmen-Projekt' given by Bettina Strübel for the 48th International Jewish-Christian Bible Week at Haus Ohrbeck July 2016. See https://bit.ly/31ZLAGD.

[275] See https://www.youtube.com/watch?v=kfOdEXTu-4c.

[276] See https://www.youtube.com/watch?v=GlGjFynWFUw.

[277] Dowling Long and Sawyer 2015: 134.

Redeemer-Sustainer in this psalm.[278] The image offers an interesting echo of the image of Moses praying to Christ, in the same Psalter, in Ps. 90:1 (fol. 121r).[279] A very different and striking image, also revealing the Christian reading of this psalm, is found in the *St Albans Psalter*, which depicts Christ (above the angelic host, as in verse 4) walking on the winds of the wind and breathing life into a naked body.[280]

The reception of Psalm 104 today has resulted in several ecological readings, not only from western 'First' World perspectives, but from several 'Third' World perspectives as well. In these world-views humans are merely one aspect of the 'Earth Community'; they are not to be seen in any hierarchical relationship over the world order. Psalm 104, with its more sympathetic view of the interdependent relationship between humans and the earth, is important. A reading from Fiji and another from Kenya make this point clear.[281] An ecological reading is also found in the recent image by Michael *Jessing, which depicts the cyclical nature of life, flowing between heaven and earth, water and rock, light and dark: this is about the creative spirit and the renewal of the earth (vv. 2–3, 14, 30: Figure 7). There are some similarities between this and the image for Psalm 95 referred to earlier.[282]

So along with Psalm 91, Psalm 104 is outstanding in Book Four as a most resonant psalm in terms of its reception history, both Jewish and Christian: it is rich in exegesis, in liturgy, as well as in poetic imitation and musical and artistic representation. Like many of the other psalms of creation (e.g. 8, 19A, 29, 33) it is a psalm whose universal themes raise issues about the power and the character of one God, not only in the cosmos but throughout all human history.

Psalm 105: A Thanksgiving Song: God as Redeemer in Israel's History (i)

Psalm 105 is less rich in reception history, but it has links with Psalm 104. Ps. 104:33 avows 'I will sing to the Lord'; Ps. 105:2 begins 'sing to him, sing praises to him!'. Ps. 104:31 speaks of God rejoicing in his manifold 'works' in creation whilst Ps. 105:5 speaks of the people remembering God's wonderful 'works' in history. In Psalm 104:13 the earth is 'sated' (using the verb s-b-ʿ) with God's provision, including bread to strengthen us, and in Ps. 105:40 the people in the desert are similarly satisfied (again using s-b-ʿ) with bread from heaven. So

---

[278] http://www.bl.uk/manuscripts/Viewer.aspx?ref=add_ms_19352_f137v.

[279] See p. 86 for the depiction of Moses praying to Christ in the *Theodore Psalter*.

[280] See https://www.albani-psalter.de/stalbanspsalter/english/translation/trans276.shtml.

[281] See Ntreh 2001: 98–108; and Walker-Jones 2001: 84–97.

[282] See http://www.mixastudio.com/psalm-illustrations.php.

FIGURE 7   *Michael Jessing: An Ecological Interpretation of Psalm 104.*
Source: http://www.psalms-mixastudio.com/psalms-101-116.php

although this psalm is more about history than creation, the two psalms are linked in that they both testify to God's activity in the world.

In Psalm 105 history starts not with the conditional promises of land made to Moses, but with the unconditional promises of land and progeny made to Abraham (vv. 1–6), who is also referred to again in verses 9 and 42. Having begun the story of Israel's ancestors with Abraham (vv. 7–11), this is followed by an account of the entry into Canaan (vv. 10–15). The emphasis on adversity and triumph allows for the development of the theme, 'a foreign land': so the psalm moves backwards to tell the story of Joseph in Egypt (vv. 16–22) and this is followed by the account of Israel in Egypt (vv. 23–38) and then of Israel in the desert (vv. 39–45—ignoring the rebellion tradition which is so clear in Psalm 106).[283] The overall focus is not only on the gift of the land but—following on from Psalm 104—also on the giving nature of Israel's God, who can always do new things, particularly for a people in exile.

The citation of Psalm 105 in 1 Chron. 16:8–36 implies that the Chronicler understood the psalm to have been composed on the day that King David brought the Ark into Jerusalem: Asaph apparently cited one verse which was then repeated by all the Levites.[284] This reading in turn influenced the tradition that the Levites sang this psalm every morning, looking back in praise to the covenant from Abraham and Moses, whilst they sang Psalm 96 every evening, looking ahead in expectation of God's coming kingdom.[285] So despite it being a didactic psalm teaching lessons from Israel's history, it was still a psalm which could be sung. This is illustrated further in the *Dead Sea Scrolls, 11QPs[a], where Psalm 105 is found before Psalm 146 and 148 and after Psalm 147, which in turn is preceded by Psalm 104. The fact that Psalm 105 follows such an obvious psalm of praise—and indeed is followed by Psalms 146 and 148, other hymns of praise—further shows that this psalm, even though it is a didactic psalm about history, had a liturgical use. Furthermore, the change of verse 2 ('let the hearts of those who seek the Lord rejoice') to 'let the hearts of those who seek *his favour* rejoice' matches the *LXX version of the liturgical song in 1 Chron. 16:10 (*eufranthēsetai kardia zētousa tēn eudokian autou*).[286] In 11QPs[a] the first verse is expanded to include 'for he is good … for his mercy endures forever', thus connecting the psalm with 106:1, 107:1 and 118:1, 29.

Further evidence of the psalm's liturgical usage is illustrated by the recitation of 1 Chron. 16:8–36 at the beginning of *Pesukei de-Zimra. Because of the citations in Chronicles, Psalm 96 and Ps. 106:47–48 are also used here, in addition to other verses from Pss. 99:5, 9 and 94:1–2. By the Middle Ages this psalm had also become part of the *Shimmush Tehillim, bearing witness to its magical use: it was 'against a quartan fever'.[287]

The re-use of this psalm in 1 Chron. 16:8–22 bears testimony to the ways in which 'God's renewal through history' was understood upon the actual return to the land; as was noted for Psalm 96, this shows the different reception of some of the psalms in later biblical tradition. Its partial citation by the priest Zechariah in Luke 1:72–73 points to another re-use, this time viewed through

---

[283] The paired psalms which celebrate the Exodus theme do so positively on the one hand (Psalms 77; 80; 105) and negatively on the other (Psalms 78; 81 and 106). See Gillingham 1999: 19–46.

[284] Feuer 2004: 1269.

[285] See *Kimḥi cited in, 2004: 1269; also Braude 1959: 180–81.

[286] See Hossfeld and Zenger 2008: 62–65.

[287] See Magonet 1994: 6–7.

the coming of Jesus Christ. Other examples might be found in Stephen's speech in Acts 7:10 (verses 20–23) and Acts 7:36 (verse 27). Knowledge of 105:39–41 is perhaps implied in Paul's use of the Exodus story in 1 Cor. 10:5.[288] Perhaps for this reason Psalm 105 is used in the lectionary at Pentecost—to refer to the history and journey of all God's people, bound together in their covenant faith.

By the time of *Aquinas, however, the psalm is read as anti-Jewish polemic: as the voice of the Apostles concerning the Jews, which is concluded in Psalm 106 which speaks of their wickedness.[289] Yet *Luther includes this psalm as another witness to his 'faithful synagogue', stressing this importance of verses 8–10 as pertaining to the 'eternal covenant' which began with the promises made to Abraham.[290] This radical reading, breaking with the more traditional 'Jewish/Christian duality' developed in the earlier Christian commentary tradition, is another important example of Luther's grappling with the piety of the psalms before the coming of Christ.

Perhaps the best-known musical arrangement of this psalm, along with 106, is found in *Handel's *Israel in Egypt*, which was written in all but a month in 1738. This is Handel's only oratorio, other than *The Messiah*, which is composed entirely from biblical texts, using choruses, airs and recitatives, with no named characters. An early version contains a thirty-minute dirge on the death of Joseph, reflecting a similar lament composed in 1737 on the death of Queen Caroline; the later version is in just two parts. In Part I, the librettist, probably Charles Jennens, combines verses from Ps. 105:23–28 with parts of Exodus to describe the plagues and events leading up to the escape from Egypt, with the last two choruses using Ps. 106:9–11 (Exod. 14:31) as God 'rebukes' the Red Sea. (Part II comprises entirely the Song of the Sea in Exodus 15).[291] So in this oratorio both psalms, despite their difference emphases, serve to point to how the grace of God is greater than his anger.

Illuminated Psalters usually give the psalm a more explicit Christian reading. One common theme, as in the *Theodore Psalter* (fol. 140r) is the depiction of Peter and John preaching to the nations, with an icon of Christ above them.[292] This contrasts starkly with a brown-ink etching by Marc *Chagall (from *Psaumes de David*, Plate 32, 1978), where Moses offers the commandments to the people watched by Aaron the high priest (105:26), as the people rejoice with their musical instruments.

---

[288] See Witherington 2017: 248–49.

[289] See Neale and Littledale 1874–79: 3/342–43; 366–67, citing *Eusebius of Caesarea, *Bede and Aquinas.

[290] See Luther on Psalms 93 and 102. See German 2017: 118–25.

[291] See 'Exodus' in M. Stern 2011: 89–100.

[292] See http://www.bl.uk/manuscripts/Viewer.aspx?ref=add_ms_19352_f140r.

This psalm actually provides an excellent example of the complex process of reception history within the biblical tradition. Adele Berlin's seminal article on Psalm 105 argues that the psalmist drew from the traditions of the Torah to create a new interpretation as a liturgical composition, with the unconditional promise of the land as its central theme.[293] She shows how the psalmist made selective use of allusions alongside citations and exegetical comments, thus creating something new whilst recalling known traditions. 'In allusion the new text is primary; the old text is the servant of the new. In exegesis the old text is primary; the new text is the servant of the old.'[294] So when we add to this the way the psalm is again 'received' and re-interpreted in 1 Chron. 16, we see that 'reception history' is not an exercise which begins *after* the text becomes part of a canonical collection, but the process is early and inherent in the ways in which the biblical writers themselves handled the texts.[295] So finding further exegesis and allusions in later Jewish and Christian traditions is continuing a way of reading texts that is found in Scripture itself.

Psalm 106: A Lament: God as Redeemer in Israel's History (ii)

Psalm 106 is a lament. Instead of the grace of God pervading the psalm, as we saw in Psalm 105, we now encounter God's anger (although vv. 4–5 and 47 do show some hope for God's compassion). Some themes are shared with Psalm 105, showing these psalms are to be read as a pair: of God's protection and, in the latter, as a sign of God's judgement. Moses is found three times in Psalm 106 (more than in 77, 90, 99, 103 and 105, where he is found once). In Ps. 105:26 it is 'Aaron' who is chosen, whilst in Ps. 106:23 it is Moses, who also appears in verses 16 and 32. There are also several correspondences with Psalm 90, for Exodus 32 which was used there is also used here (Ps. 106:23), with the same call to repentance and the same appeal to God's steadfast love (Pss. 90:14 and 104:45).

After a prayer for God's favour to return (vv. 1–6) the focus is on Israel's rejection of God: the rebellion at the Red Sea (vv. 7–12), the testing of God in the desert (vv. 13–15), the uprising against Moses and Aaron (vv. 16–18), the Golden Calf (vv. 19–23), Baal of Peor (vv. 24–31), the waters of Meribah (vv. 32–33) and even child sacrifice (vv. 34–46). The psalm ends with another plea for God to gather his people from the nations (v. 47), reminding us of the plea

---

[293] Berlin 2005: 20–26.

[294] Berlin 2005: 20.

[295] See Gillingham 2015: 450–75, which also brings Psalm 106 into this argument.

to restore the monarchy in Ps. 89:49–51. The final doxology sits as oddly with this psalm as does the doxology at the end of Psalm 89: their purpose is to show that each particular book of psalms is complete.[296]

A small part of this psalm has also been used in 1 Chron. 16:35–36. This is the doxology at the very end (verses 47–48), which acts as a prayer for redemption not only for the end of Psalm 106, but also for the end of Book Four as a whole.[297] It is interesting that the Chronicler chose not to use any of the accounts of Israel's rebellion under Moses. But because of this citation, early Jewish tradition understood David to have been the composer of both Psalms 105 and 106, on the day he brought the Ark to Jerusalem. The mediating figure in the psalm itself is of course Moses, and the interpretive text is Deut. 4:30–31, where Moses emphasises that God will not forget his covenant people (see Ps. 106:44).[298] Hence again the early reception of this psalm brings together Davidic and Mosaic traditions. As in Psalm 105, this is another psalm which is redolent with the experience of exile; this is expressed not only in the confessional element in the psalm, with its emphasis on suffering on account of disobedience, but also in the prayer for redemption in verse 47. The two psalms are held together in Jewish liturgy, for example at *Pesukei de-*Zimra, and also in the *Shimmush Tehillim*—this time, as 'against tertian fever'.[299]

Because of its links with Psalm 105, references to the history of Israel in the New Testament also allude to parts of this psalm. Luke 1:71–72 (the Song of Zechariah) alludes to verses 10 and 45, and Paul's lament on the people's stubbornness in Rom. 1:23 may have an allusion to verse 20.[300] Similarly the passage in 1 Cor. 10:1–13 suggests the use of verses 14–15. Like Psalm 105, the reception in Christian tradition is more pragmatic than doctrinal. We know from *Augustine's sermons that Psalm 106 was regularly used for the Octave (or eighth day) after Christmas, on 1 January. Psalm 106 is also frequently cited in later Jewish tradition, praying that God's people might be 'gathered from among the nations'. Augustine turns this idea on its head, arguing that the church is the new Israel, and the nations are now both Jews and Gentiles. He observes that Jesus' Great Commission (at the end of Matthew's Gospel) is the fulfilment of verse 47 of this psalm; and the Apostle Paul, sent to the Gentiles, brings about 'the incoming of the nations' who 'glory in God's praise' and also fulfil this

---

[296] On the different nature of this doxology compared with those at the end of Books One, Two and Three, see Gillingham 2015: 205–219.

[297] See Feuer 2004: 1285 and 1302; also Cohen 1992: 351.

[298] See Feuer 2004: 1286; also Braude 1959: 193–4.

[299] See Magonet 1994: 6–7.

[300] See Witherington 2017: 249 who argues that Rom 1:18–32 is indebted throughout to Psalm 106 regarding the 'universal scope of sin'.

psalm.[301] Psalm 106 was one of the eight psalms most frequently used by Augustine in his *Confessions*.[302]

Perhaps because of its more sombre tone, Psalm 106 has been interpreted by more composers than its 'twin' psalm. Christopher *Tye's *'Peccavimus cum patribus nostris'* was composed during the time of Mary Tudor to reflect the mood of repentance at the excesses of the early reformers. Henry *Purcell, more than a century later, composed 'O give thanks unto the Lord' in 1693; it is said that the scarcity of musical resources in the Chapel Royal, whose Protestant court institutions were largely starved financially by James II, accounts for the minimalist instrumental accompaniment (two solo violinists play at the end of the different sections). Again, the mood of the psalm served well its seventeenth-century context (although Purcell also focussed on the more hopeful verses, 1–3, combining these with Ps. 86:5, 9 and 10). Psalm 106 was interpreted variously for *SATB voices by, for example, James *Turle, Samuel Sebastian *Wesley, grandson of Charles *Wesley, and Hubert *Parry. The version by Parry, based upon *Coverdale's version, has been recorded in *The Psalms of David* series.[303]

In terms of art, this psalm which depicts so negatively the rebellion of the Jews has perhaps predictably been used in anti-Jewish polemic. The *Khludov Psalter* (fol. 108v) has graphic images of the worship of the Golden Calf and the Jews being thrown to the pit. Further pointed illustrations of the idolatrous practices of the Jews are also in *Khludov*, on the sacrificing of children to demons and the delivery of the Jews into the hands of their enemy, (fol. 110r, also found *Paris gr. 20* fol. 18r and the *Pantokrator Psalter* fol. 154v).[304] By contrast, the motif of God's judgement on idolatry is interpreted more universally—for Christians as well as Jews—in the 'Harrowing of Hell' motif, depicting Christ's descent into Hades, which is sometimes linked to this psalm. One example is from the *St Albans Psalter*. There, the illuminated initial 'C' is of Christ in the blue half upper of the letter, who reaches out to touch and spare a nun (presumably Christina of Markyate) and (behind her) four monks, all in the left-hand green 'earthly' half of the 'C'. The composition and the postures are remarkable similar to an illustration accompanying the description of the Harrowing of Hell (from the Gospel of Nicodemus) earlier in this Psalter, where

---

[301] See Wesselschmidt 2007: 249–50, citing Augustine, *Sermon* 77.5, from *WSA* 3 3:319–20. See also Holladay 1993: 167.

[302] See Poque 1986: 155–66.

[303] 'O give thanks unto the Lord' is taken from *The Earth is the Lord's: Psalms of David Volume 3*, sung by Durham Cathedral Choir, directed by James Lancelot, Priory Records Digital Recording 343, 1990.

[304] See K. Corrigan 1992: 20, 35–7 and fig. 45 (on p. 258) from the *Khludov Psalter*.

Christ reaches out to Adam, and behind him, to Eve, plucking them out of hell (presented as a gaping monster), with other figures behind, like the monks, begging for deliverance. The image for Ps. 106:1 is the only one in the entire Psalter to emulate explicitly this Harrowing of Hell motif.[305]

To conclude Book Four, the reception history of this collection of psalms raises some important observations. As we have noted, it offers several very different portrayals of the nature of God, as Refuge (90–92), King (93–100), Defender (101–103) and Creator and Redeemer (104–106) of his people. Secondly, Book Four has very different emphases on the figures of Moses, David and Christ. Jewish rabbinic interpretation tends to see that in Psalms 90–100 Moses is either the composer or the key influence behind these texts, whilst in Psalms 101–106 David is the composer, taking up the traditions of Moses himself: so even here Moses plays the most prominent part. The emphasis in the *LXX, by contrast, sees, through its headings, Psalms 90–98 and 101–103 as concerning David and his coming kingdom, with the role of Moses acknowledged explicitly only in the heading to Psalm 90, and in the text itself at Pss. 99:6, 103:7 and 105:26, and 106:16, 23, 32. Christian readings, using the *LXX, tend to read Psalms 93–100 and 104–106 more in the light of Christian doctrine ('psalms about Christ'), and Psalms 90–92 and 101–103 more in the light Christ as example ('psalms of Christ').

Thirdly, Jewish and Christian traditions agree on one other important theme in Book Four: loss and human fragility lived out in the knowledge of the permanence and sovereignty of God. In Jewish tradition this is initially associated with the exile in Babylon, but also relates to an experience of ongoing exile. In Christian tradition this is more associated with the ephemeral nature of humanity in general and the constancy of God's incarnate love for his people.

This leads to a fourth theme common to both faith traditions—whether these psalms (particularly 93–100) are about life in the here and now, or whether they should be interpreted in the light of the future and of eschatological hope. In Jewish reception, this discussion is founded upon Moses and the Torah and completed in David and the promise of a coming Messiah. In Christian reception, this is founded initially upon Moses and David, but its final consummation is in the person and work of Christ.

Because of these rich and diverse theological themes interwoven throughout the whole of Book Four, these psalms, taken together, offer a vital liturgical resource to Jewish and Christian traditions. Their adaptation in worship

---

[305] On the illumination at the start of Psalm 106, see https://bit.ly/3hn8ZJI; and for the illumination on the Harrowing of Hell, see https://bit.ly/340diaN.

has inspired a large repertoire of musical works, artistic representations, and poetic responses both Jewish and Christian, of which the above examples have been but a small selection of a vast reserve.

So although Book Four as a whole has inspired Jews and Christians in different ways, its essential message of repenting for broken faith in the past, of trusting in God's promises in the present, and of hoping for some restoration (both physical and spiritual) in the future is a shared concern in both traditions.

BOOK FIVE: PSALMS 107–151

Envisaging Restoration: The Divine Plan in History

Book Five comprises forty-four psalms (forty-five including Psalm 151, which will also be discussed) and so is the longest book in the Psalter. It is also the most diverse. As with Book Four, there are fewer superscriptions (especially in the Hebrew), so the final arrangement is again more thematic. It is possible to divide Book Five into Psalms 107–118, with Psalm 119 as a 'bridging psalm' anticipating Psalms 120–136, and Psalm 137 (albeit more connected with Psalms 135 and 136), as another 'bridging psalm' anticipating Psalms 138–150. We will examine these divisions shortly.

Books Four and Five stand out from Books One to Three in having several shared concerns.[1] Both books offer some answers to the questions raised in Book Three about God's justice and power, although the progression of thought in Book Four (which, we have noted, was a combination of quiet reflection and corporate praise) is not as clear in Book Five, mainly because of its complexity and size.[2] Nevertheless, the name 'Yahweh' dominates, over 300 times, within both books; Elohim is only found some 30 times.[3] The interest in God's Kingship, made so explicit in the heart of Book Four, is continued here, although given a different emphasis, as we shall see below, and this theme is spread throughout Book Five.

---

[1] See Wilson 1985: 209–28, 2005a: 391–406, esp. 391–96; also Auwers 2000: 27–42; Hensley 2018: 25–32.
[2] See pp. 79–80.
[3] Witherington 2017: 256.

Psalms Through the Centuries: A Reception History Commentary on Psalms 73–151, Volume Three, First Edition. Susan Gillingham.
© 2022 John Wiley & Sons Ltd. Published 2022 by John Wiley & Sons Ltd.

There are, however, at least seven thematic differences with Book Four, suggesting that Book Five is in fact an independent work. If Book Four is set within the context of the Babylonian exile, where the theological issues raised were expressed in the different views of God (as Refuge, King, Defender, Creator and Redeemer), so Book Five appears to be set more in the context of Persian domination (i.e. from the late sixth-century onwards) where the theological concerns were somewhat different.

The first distinctive feature is perhaps more about absence: here God is not explicitly called 'King'. There are no references to God sitting on a throne, and none to God ruling as King; instead he is depicted as residing 'in heaven'. The term 'God of heaven', also a Persian term, is frequently found in Ezra, Nehemiah and Daniel.[4] Although it occurs as an actual title only in Ps. 136:26, the references to God being in heaven and looking down on earth (not least to protect Zion) are more frequent here than in any other book of the Psalter.[5] So if Book Four focussed on the contrast between human transience and the everlasting God, Book Five focusses more on the violability of the actual community and the vulnerability of Jerusalem, and contrasts this with the constancy and inviolability of God In heaven above.

Another different theme, also with possible Persian influence, is found in the references to enemies, not only in the Psalms of Ascent, but also in psalms before and after this collection. The enemies are not only threats to individuals within the community, but they are foreign powers affecting the whole community's wellbeing. The adaptation of Psalm 118, which may originally have been a royal psalm, is a prime example in this respect.[6]

A third theme concerns the greater interest in David than that evident in Book Four. There are two royal psalms which refer explicitly to the role of the king (110 and 132), whereas Book Four had, possibly, one (Psalm 101). In Book Five we find two clear Davidic collections (108–110; 138–145) with additional Davidic headings, in the Hebrew text, over Psalms 122, 124 and 131.[7] Book Four had one small Davidic collection (101–103), although only two of these had Davidic headings. Fourteen of the forty-four psalms in Book Five reveal some concern about David and the future of that dynasty, seemingly at a period after that dynasty had ended. It is difficult to know whether these Davidic references are expressed as a future hope in the actual restoration of the dynasty,

---

[4] See for example Ezr. 1:2, (also 2 Chron. 36:8); Ezr. 5:11,12; 6:9,10; 7:21,23; Neh. 1:4–5, 2:4, 20; and Dan. 2:18, 27, 44.
[5] See for example Pss. 108:5; 113:5–6; 115:3; 121:2; 123:1; 124:8 and 134:3. See also Tucker 2014a: 142–153.
[6] See *ibid.*: 82.
[7] See Wallace 2014: 193–20; also Hensley 2018: 157–82.

or as a belief in some coming 'messianic' deliverer, or whether such references might be applied democratically, in the present, to the community itself, taking up a royal calling: this will be discussed in the relevant psalms.[8]

Related to this, a fourth theme which marks out Book Five from Book Four is a renewed focus on Zion. In several psalms the Temple is now standing again, creating an identity marker for the community even though the Davidic king is no longer present. This cautiously confident response to the Temple is very different from the judgement-orientated views in the *Asaphite psalms (50, 73–83) which contemplate the Temple's destruction, and it is also different from the more personal longing for God's presence in the Temple in the *Korahite psalms (42–49, 84–85, 87–89). There are frequent positive and corporate references to the Temple (for example in Psalms 120–134 and 137 and 138), and in Pss. 107:2 and 144:7, 11 the Temple focus is also clear; and in the final psalms of praise (Psalms 147, 149 and 150) God is praised in his sanctuary.[9]

We saw in Book Four the repeated focus on the role of Moses. Although Book Five has many allusions to the exodus tradition, both in a collection later known as the Egyptian Hallel (Psalms 113–118) as well as in Psalms 135 and 136, Moses is never referred to by name. And although Book Five contains the longest psalm in the Psalter, in praise of the Torah, Moses is never mentioned in any of its 176 verses. The interest is in what Moses represents—Exodus and Torah—rather than in the charismatic figure of Moses himself. This is another distinguishing feature of Book Five. David is named; but Moses is not.

Sixthly, Book Five not only has a specific didactic interest in the Torah but there is also more general instructional material, reminiscent of a more universal wisdom tradition. For example, Ps. 107:42–43 opens Book Five with an appeal to 'those who are wise' to give heed to its teaching.[10] Psalms 111, 112 and 145 take up an acrostic form to impart their instruction. Psalm 119 also has an acrostic format, although here the focus is on the importance of keeping of the Torah. By contrast, Book Four contains neither Torah psalms nor acrostic psalms, and although its didactic psalms (90–92; 101–103) suggest some wisdom elements, their concern with human ephemerality is very different from the more practical morality offered in Book Five.

A final feature which distinguishes Book Five from Book Four is the interest in God's care of the poor and needy (as in for example Psalms 109, 110, 112, 113, 119, 140 and 146). This is a theme which was noted at the end of Book One (Psalms 35–41) and it recurred in individual psalms in Books Two (e.g. Psalms

---

[8] See the literature review in Mitchell 1997: 15–65; also Snearly 2016: 57–78.
[9] See Gillingham 2005: 308–341.
[10] See Zenger 1998: 77–102, where Psalms 107 and 145 are seen as a 'wisdom frame'.

70 and 72) and in Book Three (e.g. 74 and 86). It is given a fuller expression in Book Five, in the context of economic as well as spiritual deprivation.[11]

So Book Five comprises many parts. It has an interest in David, but also in the earlier exodus traditions associated with Moses. It refers frequently to God's presence in the Temple and Zion, but also to God's presence in heaven. It has an interest in the specific commands of Torah, but also in the general precepts of wisdom. There is a concern about foreign oppressors, but there are clear universalistic concerns as well. Furthermore, Book Five has a strong liturgical element. This is expressed in Psalms 113–118 which are associated with Passover; in Psalm 119 with its later associations with the Feast of Weeks; and in Psalms 120–134 with their association with Tabernacles or the Feast of Booths (*Sukkot). So, given this diversity is it possible to divide up Book Five so that its *narrative impact* is also evident?

Two seminal suggestions have been proposed, first by Reinhard Kratz and, second, by Frank-Lothar Hossfeld and Erich Zenger. Kratz sees three collections: Psalms 107–117 are one collection, brought together under the theme of 'Ingathering'; Psalms 118–135 form another collection, under the theme of 'Pilgrimage'; and Psalms 136–150 suggest the final group, on the theme of 'Universal Worship'.[12] Kratz notes that the psalms which begin these three collections all have a similar introduction, in their calls to 'give thanks' to the Lord (Psalms 107, 118 and 136) and the psalms which close the collections also have similar conclusions, ending with 'Alleluia' (Psalms 117, 135 and Psalm 145, which is slightly different). The problem here is that the proposed divisions cut into already established collections.

Hossfeld and Zenger have a slightly different approach. They begin with three very obvious collections as the base of Book Five. These are Psalms 113–118, all starting with Alleluia; Psalms 120–134, all headed 'A Song of Ascent'; and Psalms 138–145, all with Davidic headings. Around these three main groups, smaller collections and individual psalms have emerged. So Psalm 107 stands on its own, linking back to Psalm 106 but announcing some of the key themes in the rest of Book Five; Psalms 108–110 form a small Davidic Collection; Psalms 111 and 112 create a pair of acrostic psalms. After Psalms 113–118 the compilers placed another independent psalm, 119, and this stands between the Hallel Psalms (113–118) and the Ascent Psalms (120–134). Psalms 135 and 136 form another pair, like Psalms 111 and 112, and they are very close to the Ascents in their pilgrimage concerns. Together they link back to Psalm 118 (135:19–21 are like 118:2–4; and 136:1, 26 are like 118:1, 29). Psalm 137, like 119, is another 'connecting' psalm, also with a concern for Jerusalem and anticipating

---

[11] See Zenger 1997b: 95–105, who sees this influence especially in the two Davidic collections. See also Tucker 2014a: 179–85 and 187; Bellinger (2019): 75–79 on the nature of complaint in Book Five.
[12] See Kratz 1995: 1–34.

some of the themes about suffering and divine justice in Psalms 138–145. Psalms 146–150 create a doxological conclusion, framing the entire Psalter along with Psalms 1–2.[13]

Hossfeld's and Zenger's overall structure will be used in the following commentary. It does justice to established collections whilst also recognising that individual psalms have been brought later into this book where they fitted theologically and linguistically with their neighbours. It will become clear that the first part of the overall narrative moves between the God of David and Zion (Psalms 108–110) and the God of the Exodus (Psalms 107; 113–118), and between general instruction and specific teaching through the Torah (Psalms 111–112; 119). The second part of the narrative then moves on to an expanded interest in the God of David and Zion (Psalms 120–134), although the God of the Exodus is again recalled in 135–136. Psalm 137, on longing for Jerusalem, introduces the last movement which is more concerned with David in relation to the community of faith (Psalms 138–145) and this opens into a final collection of psalms of praise (Psalms 146–150) reflecting on God not only within the community of faith but also the God of all peoples. There are still changing moods and emphases within these dominant themes: it is as if the compilers, creating the first stage of reception history of the Psalter as a whole, brought together most of the themes found within Books One to Four. Because Book Five offers not one dominant theological theme, but many, it is a rich resource for the study of reception history, both in Jewish and in Christian tradition.

[13] See Zenger 1998: 77–102; also Hossfeld and Zenger 2011: 2–7; also Koch 1994: 243–77.

As we have already noted, the doxology at the end of Psalm 106 is somewhat different from the other four doxologies marking off Books One, Two and Three, and this suggests that Psalm 106 and 107 were actually seen as quite close together.[14] The *LXX* places the 'Hallelujah' of this doxology at the beginning of Psalm 107, thus making Psalm 107 start in an identical way to Psalm 106: this is another example of a later perception of the close relationship between the two psalms. This is further confirmed by the fact that 'O give thanks to the Lord for [he is good]' (*hodu la'donay ki-tov*) is also found in 106:1 and in 107:1 followed by the phrase 'for his steadfast love endures for ever' (*ki le'olam ḥasdo*). The same words are also used as a refrain in Psalms 118 and 136, psalms which each conclude different collections in Book Five, indicating that this is a theme which links as far back to Psalm 106 at the end of Book Four.

Although many correspondences might be coincidental on account of the similar contents of each psalm, several more specific examples suggest more than coincidence. In many cases the contrast is made so that Psalm 107 is seen to focus on the more positive aspects of God's love for his people. The call to God to 'gather us from among the nations' in 106:47 anticipates the more confident thanksgiving 'he has gathered (the redeemed) from the lands' in 107:3 (in each case using the verb *q-b-ṣ* ('gather'). The reference to God's 'wonderful works' (in each case using a *niphal* feminine participle in plural form) is found

---

[14] See pp. 154-55. See also Hensley 2018: 64, citing Wilson, Hossfeld and Zenger, and Kratz as examples of those who see Psalms 106 and 107 linked together.

in 106:7 (*'your* wonderful works'; also in 106:22, where the people forget what God has done). The same formula is found in 107:8, 15, 21, 24 and 31 (in each case '*his* wonderful works') and here in the context of the people's response. Similarly the use of the verb *g-'-l* in 106:10 (where God is seen to have 'redeemed' his people) becomes a call of praise for the 'redeemed of the Lord' who have been 'redeemed from trouble' in 107:2. The contrast of the peoples' sorry state 'in the wilderness' (*ba-midbar*) and 'in a desert' (*bishimon*) in 106:14 is also found in 107:4 where the same two words occur together (*ba-midbar bishimon*), but in the context of God delivering them from their distress. Indeed, the refrain in 107:6, 13, 19, and 28 ('And they cried to the Lord in their trouble, he delivered them from their distress') is a telling example of the ways in which the hopes of the lament in Psalm 106 are fulfilled in Psalm 107.

One of the issues here is whether this refrain about God delivering the people from distress is an assurance to the people living under Persian rule.[15] The use of the imperfect in many of the Hebrew verbs, used here with a jussive sense, indicates that this is not an account of past history but a view of what God 'should' do in times of trouble (but has not finally done yet). This then is not so much a continuous thanksgiving psalm for a liberated people as a psalm indicating hope that God will act in favour towards his people once again. After the prelude (vv. 1–3) it comprises two main parts, of which the first (vv. 4–32) focusses on four kinds of people: pilgrims who have been in the desert but have now arrived 'home' (vv. 4–9); prisoners who have been set free (vv. 10–16); sick who have now been healed (vv. 17–22) and sailors who have been saved from a shipwreck (vv. 23–32). The four refrains noted above occur only in these four sections, alongside a second refrain ('Let them thank the LORD for his steadfast love, for his wonderful works to humankind') which is found in verses 8, 15, 21, and 31. The second part (vv. 33–43), with its imperfect tenses (translated as present tense in the NRSV) appears to be an addition, with some wisdom interests at the very end ('Whoever is wise, let him give heed to these things ...').[16]

One curious feature in the reception of this psalm is only noticeable in Hebrew codices. It seems that the later copyists needed to make a particular comment next to verses 21–26 and verse 40 by inserting at the end of the verse a letter 'n' which was written the wrong way round (the term used for this is an 'inverted nun'). It occurs elsewhere only in Num. 10:35–36. Some have argued that this is because the passages are not in the correct place, but it is unclear why this should be the case in Psalm 107, given that it is found in both parts of the psalm (vv. 4–32 and vv. 33–43). Sometimes we can know *that* various changes

---

[15] See Tucker 2014b: 181–83; also, 2014a: 59ff.
[16] See Beyerlin 1979 who sees the role of the Levitical singers in bringing this psalm together.

were later made in the literary reception of the text, but we cannot really know *why*: later Jewish tradition explained this as a sign of exclusion, implying that not all those who cried out would be heard once the heavenly decree is set.[17]

Turning to earlier Jewish reception, the presence of Psalm 107 in a collection of psalms found in Cave 4 at *Qumran (4QPs[f]) is interesting because it shows verses 2–5, 8–16, 18–19, 22–30 and 35–42 were combined with Psalms 22 and 109 and three sectarian psalms (including the 'Apostrophe to Zion'). It is possible that Psalm 108 was also included, but the proximity of Psalm 22 and other psalms not even in the Psalter shows how, despite the linguistic connections with Psalm 106 noted earlier, this placing was not fixed in the liturgy and teaching at Qumran in about 50 BCE, which is the approximate date of the scroll.[18] This is further illustrated in the way just one verse (107:27) is also alluded to in another scroll, part of the *Hodayot* (1QH III, line 14).[19] Similarly the book of Baruch, an apocryphal work imitating the prophets, which can be dated to perhaps the second-century BCE, summarises Ps. 107:4–9 in Bar. 3:1, and 107:3 is in part recalled in Bar. 4:36. So Psalm 107 was used outside its context in the *MT before the Christian era.

Later Jewish tradition frequently understands the psalm to be about the 're-gathering' of God's scattered people, using Isa. 11:11–12 as a parallel text, and emphasising especially the prelude and the first part of the psalm.[20] This reading is also evident in the *Targum*, where in verse 7 'Jerusalem' is explicitly added as the 'city of habitation'. Additional references to a return to the Torah resulting in God's restoration in verses 35 and 41 make clear the conditional nature of this restoration: for example, verse 41 reads '*But when they returned to the Torah*, he exalted the needy from poverty...'[21]

The exaltation of the poor and needy, a key theme throughout both parts of the psalm, is also a key theme in Luke's Gospel. In the *Magnificat*, or the Song of Mary (Luke 1:47–55), we read in 1:53: 'He *filled the hungry with good things*, and sent the rich empty away' which takes up the intentions and indeed some of the phraseology of Ps. 107:9: 'For he satisfies the thirsty, and *the hungry he fills with good things*'. Similarly, in the *Benedictus* (or the song of Zechariah at Luke 1:68–79) verse 79 speaks of those who sit in darkness and the shadow of death being given light: Ps. 107:10 and 14 take up the same theme.[22] Luke refers to this psalm again in Acts. In Paul's speech at Pisidian Antioch in Acts 13, the references in verses 35–37 to being saved from 'corruption' (here in relation to the resurrection) develop the theme of Ps. 107:18–21, where the people cry and

---

[17] See Feuer 2004: 1311, citing *Ros Has* 17a.

[18] See Abegg et al. 1999: 586–88.

[19] See Flint 1997: 220.

[20] See Braude 1959: 197.

[21] See Stec 2004: 199.

[22] See Witherington 2017: 258–67.

are saved from their distress (in the refrain of verse 19) and are then delivered from 'destruction'. The same Greek word for destruction (*diaphthora*) is used in each case—indeed, three times in Acts 13. Just as God saved the people of Israel from destruction/corruption and near-death (Ps. 107:17–22), Christ has saved his people from the corruption and death itself (Acts 13:35–37).

Later Christian reception is perhaps best summarised by the quotation from *Cassiodorus:

> After the confession of the Jewish people discussed in the previous psalms, the prophet passes to the Christian people who wandered through the tracts of the entire world … He reminds them they must confess the Lord's praises, for they have been redeemed by His precious blood, and have attained churches… he enjoins that the Father be thanked because the Lord Christ at His coming has broken down the bronze gates and iron bolts of the devil by the majesty of His omnipotence…[23]

The 'gates of brass' (107:16: 'doors of bronze' in the NRSV) are now seen as referring to Christ, having broken the gates of hell and conquered death, and so delivered all humanity, Jews and Gentiles alike, from 'corruption'.[24] The reference in verse 3 to the gathering of the people from the east, west, north and south (although the Hebrew reads 'sea', which again implies the west) is also often given a Christian reading. The heading over Psalm 107 in the *Peshitta* cites that first God gathered the Jews from Babylon, and then Christ gathered the nations from the four quarters of the earth through the teaching of Baptism and Faith.[25] This theme is also taken up by *Augustine who reads the 'redeemed of the Lord' in verse 2 as those Christians gathered from the four quarters of the earth.[26] *Jerome makes a similar point: he asks, what is it that the redeemed (in verse 2) actually say? He answers that Christ has redeemed with the price of his blood, gathered from many lands and from the power of the foe.[27]

*Gregory of Nyssa has perhaps the most original insights into this psalm. Nyssa emphasises that it is the first psalm in each book which announces the theme of the rest of that book, and so he focusses particularly on Psalm 107 which introduces the final book. Nyssa's view is that this is 'the most sublime step of contemplation', containing 'a complete consummation and recapitulation of salvation', revealing 'all the grace which we experience'.[28] Verses 2–3 are again

---

[23]Cassiodorus trans. Walsh 1991b: 82–83.

[24] See *Theodoret of Cyrus, Letter 151, in NPNF 2 3:328, cited in *ACCS VIII* 253; also *Eusebius of Caesarea. 'Proof of the Gospel 6.7' in *POG* 2:7–8, cited in *ACCS VII*: 254–55.

[25] See Neale and Littledale 1874–79: 3/409.

[26] Augustine trans. Uyl 2017: 547.

[27] Jerome trans. Ewald 1963: 238–44. This is taken from Homily 33:238–39.

[28] Heine 1995: 14–15, 67–68, 108–119.

critical, as also the verses at the end of the psalm. They suggest 'that all humanity will return to the goodness which is God and be redeemed from death...
Divine mercy is greater than human waywardness: we are called upon to be
wise enough to perceive it, not by inquiry but by retention of wisdom'[29] (I.111).

Much Christian exegesis views Psalm 107 primarily as about a plan of salvation for Christians, not Jews. Hence *Luther's comments on this psalm are quite
unexpected: he reads the psalm as 'divine praise concerning Christ and the
people redeemed by him *and of the synagogue converting to Christ, prophetically
foretold.'* This affirms that some of the godly could be Jews.[30]

In *Dante's *Purgatorio*, in the second part of *The Divine Comedy*, in Cantos
I:115 and especially Cantos II:13, 16, 19, 22, 25, 28 and 31, where the souls
of the dead arrive singing *In Exitu Israel de Aegypto*, parts of Psalm 114 and
107 are used. The theme of time in purgatory being like time on earth (unlike
heaven and hell, which are in eternity) is typified by the 'earth-clock' pointing
to time in relation to the four points of the earth's circumference: this specific
reference from 107:2–3, and the general theme of redemption through Christ
effecting release from the misery of sin to a state of grace, illustrate the importance of Psalm 107 to this part of Dante's poem.[31]

Moving from a fourteenth-century Italian poet to one from the eighteenth-
century, John *Newton's earlier experience of the slave trade and his previous
naval service made Psalm 107 an appropriate expression of redemption. 'When
Israel was from Egypt freed' is based on 107:6–7.[32] The imagery is from the
account in Exodus and Psalms 105 and 106; but the text is from 107, and the
last but one verse recalls the last verse of this psalm:

> The way was right their heart to prove
> To make God's glory known;
> And show his wisdom, pow'r and love
> Engaged to save his own.

In his childhood Newton could sing by heart many children's hymns by Isaac
*Watts, who died in the year of Newton's conversion from being a slave trader.
Watts is well known for the way he composed hymns with political connotations as well as Christian themes.[33] So his version of the second part of Psalm
107 (verses 33–43) is not so much spiritual as physical: it had the title 'Colonies
planted; or, Nations blessed and punished.' It was 'A Psalm for New England.'[34]

---

[29] Heine 1995: 67–68.
[30] See German 2017: 133–35.
[31] See De Solms: 519.
[32] This is found in *Olney Hymns Vol I* no. 49: 'He led them by a right way.'
[33] See Gillingham 2008: 159–61.
[34] See https://hymnary.org/text/when_god_provoked_with_daring_crimes.

The psalm became a warning to the Puritans that they should affirm God as the one who gave them the land and ensures its prosperity:

> Thus they are blessed; but if they sin,
> He lets the heathen nations in;
> A savage crew invades their lands,
> Their princes die by barb'rous hands.

> Their captive sons, exposed to scorn,
> Wander unpitied and forlorn;
> The country lies unfenced, untilled,
> And desolation spreads the field.

> Yet if the humbled nation mourns,
> Again his dreadful hand he turns;
> Again he makes their cities thrive,
> And bids the dying churches live.

It is surprising that this psalm plays very little part in Jewish liturgy, whether Orthodox, Liberal or Reformed.[35] One exception, although concerned more with private practice, is in the Hasidic tradition: the Ukrainian seventeenth-century writer, Rabbi Israel Baal Shem Tov, has been attributed with a mystical commentary on this psalm, called 'The Small Book', or 'a song of holy sparks', for recitation on Sabbath eve. The sparks are the souls of the dispersed of Israel, who will be elevated from a state of death to holy living: they are to be set free to give thanks to God (107:1). According to the Baal Shem Tov, these are the intentions the pious Jew should have in mind on Sabbath eve.[36]

In Christian liturgy the commentary tradition influenced the use of the psalm on Easter Eve as early as the *Ambrosian liturgy; this was the reference to Christ who 'shatters the doors of bronze' (107:16) through his death and resurrection. The 'sacrifice of thanksgiving' (verse 1) becomes the sacrifice of the Eucharist, and the four groups of people described in this psalm—pilgrims, prisoners, the sick and those in fear of death at sea—are read allegorically as part of the story of redemption achieved through the death of Christ.

Because this psalm is so rich in imagery, particular parts have been represented in Christian art. 'Some went to the sea in ships' is a popular theme, developed by (for example) such different artists as the nineteenth-century British artist James Shaw Crompton (1853–1916), the German nineteenth-century painter Hermann Hendrich (1854–1931), and the illustrator of the *Good News Bible*, Annie *Vallotton (1915–2013).[37] In the ninth-century *Stuttgart*

---

[35] Psalms 107–110 as a whole have little part in Jewish worship.
[36] See Zvi 2015: 298–99.
[37] http://www.biblical-art.com/biblicalsubject.asp?id_biblicalsubject=1457&pagenum=1.

Psalter (fol. 124r) one of its three images is of Christ stilling the storm, whereby 107:23–32 is received through this story (for example, Matt. 8:23–27).[38] Another theme is that of 'ingathering': in the initial 'C' in *St. Albans Psalter* (Confitemini Domino) we see Christ leading out four men with red cords; he grasps one by the hand. They have been gathered from the four areas from the rising and setting of the sun, and from the north and the sea (107:3).[39]

Other images in illuminated Psalters give special attention to Psalm 107 because it marks the beginning of Book Five. The thirteenth-century Italian *Parma Psalter* (fol. 155r) has an ornamental band separating Psalm 106 from 107, and to the left of it a figure lifts up his head and left arm: he is the singer calling all to give thanks to God. The figure to the right, with his mouth open, joins in the song. Between upper and lower decorated band, joining together the two figures, are the words, in Hebrew, 'O give thanks to the Lord, for he is good'.[40] The twenty-first-century *Saint John's Bible* also has a special illumination for the beginning of Book Five: its vibrant colours depict thanksgiving for God's redeeming love (107:1–2). This illumination is presented here as PLATE 11.

A different twenty-first-century example is Moshe *Berger's *kabbalistic interpretation. God's redemptive care is illustrated by the Hebrew letter *Waw*, symbolising an Arm, then the letter *He*, symbolising a giving hand (*He* having the numerical value of five), then a second *He* illustrating the receiving hand; the letter *Yod* illustrates the essential food for body and soul and lies between the two letter *He's* and above a mother bird feeding her nest-bound brood. Taken together, these letters spell out *wehayah* (and it/he will be), alluding to the meaning inherent in the sacred name 'Yahweh': this is represented in PLATE 12.

Two twenty-first-century images are larger and in a different medium. One is in stained glass to replace a vandalised window in the church of Whitburn in Durham Diocese. It was commissioned in 2005; the artist Thomas *Denny depicts Psalm 107 through the image of sailors reeling during a storm at sea. Its theme is, like one of the refrains, that God delivers us from our distress. This is found as PLATE 13.[41] Another large image is in a triptych wall mural; Psalm 46 is on the left, 104 at the centre, and 107 is on the right. The artist, Michael *Jessing, exhibited designs for this triptych in Edinburgh in June 2018; the project is to date still in the making. Its common theme is of God's sustaining of the earth, using 'eco-psalms' such as Psalm 107, which is used to show how the earth can be transformed by God's mercy and salvation. The power to trans-

---

[38] See https://bit.ly/3IBS4iU.
[39] https://www.albani-psalter.de/stalbanspsalter/english/commentary/page290.shtml.
[40] Metzger 1996: 43.
[41] See Gillingham: 2018: 79–80 (Psalm 8) and 220 (Psalm 36) for examples of other works by Denny in stained glass.

form takes up the last verse of the psalm: 'let those who are wise give heed to these things...'[42]

Musical arrangements of this psalm focus on similar themes. Three examples are, first, general thanksgiving (107:1); second, danger at sea (which, as in art, lends itself dramatically to musical representation); and third, the offer of redemption (107:2–3) seen through Christian eyes. In the first category, we might include Henry *Purcell's *SATB) version, using *Coverdale, based upon verses 23–32 and 21, which is a celebratory thanksgiving psalm, and *Beethoven's 'Give Thanks to God' (SAB: Op. 48 No 1) which combines Pss. 96:7–9 and 107:9–10, 20, 22. In the second category, one notable arrangement is William *Billings' *Euroclydon*, in *The Psalms Singer's Amusement* (1781), which is an *a capella* SATB chorus based on Ps. 107:23–30. But in this case it evokes Paul's shipwreck off Malta (Acts 27), with the music emulating the wind and storm, and the final stillness of storm (verse 29), finishing with a rousing conclusion, 'Welcome Home!'[43] A more recent composition imitating the storm is by Herbert Sumsion (1899–1995) who wrote 'They that Go Down to the Sea in Ships', in 1979, for Repton Preparatory School Choir, again taken from 107:23–30. The rocking accompaniment evokes the rise and fall of sea.[44] Another contemporary example is Sea Street's anthem 'Shipping Forecast', from 2011, with chorus, SATB piano, and strings.[45] In the category of compositions concerned with the redemption of God, one example is from *Elgar's *The Kingdom* (Op 51), which was premiered at the Birmingham Festival in 1906, re-using some of the work in the *Apostles*. In the first scene, in the upper room, the Apostles and 'Holy Women' are reflecting, after the Ascension, about the resurrection of Jesus. They use Old Testament texts as if spoken by Jesus, of which one is Ps. 107:2, concerning God's redemption of his people from trouble.[46]

This psalm might revolve around the theme of redemption, but the nature of that salvation (expressed in the fourfold refrain in verses 8, 13, 21 and 31) could not be more different in Jewish and Christian reception. Jewish interpretation thanks God for his wonderful works to humankind but still looks ahead at what is to come; the Christian emphasis thanks God for his wonderful works which have already taken place in the human life and death and resurrection of Christ. This first psalm of Book Five anticipates a good deal of dissension in the reception of these final forty-five psalms.

---

[42] Taken from email correspondence with the artist in June 2018.
[43] See Dowling Long and Sawyer 2015: 79.
[44] See 2015: 239.
[45] See 2015: 239–40.
[46] See 2015: 134.

Psalm 108: A Composite Psalm of Remembrance

Book Five has several examples of psalms which re-use other psalms, and Psalm 108 is one of these, in this case in a very obvious way. It uses the second part of Psalm 57 (thus omitting the violent imagery of 57:1–4) and similarly the second part of Psalm 60 (again omitting the brutal military imagery in 60:1–4). Furthermore, by omitting the superscriptions in Psalms 57 and 60 it seeks to 'tell a different story'. Its somewhat general heading 'A Song. A Psalm of David' also takes away the particularities of those earlier psalms. Verses 1–5, taken from Ps. 57:7–10, start with a paean of praise in music, and verses 6–13, taken from Ps. 60:5–12, end with a note of confidence of God's sovereignty over foreign powers. Psalm 60 in particular suggests pre-exilic battles for land, probably before the fall of the northern kingdom Israel, referring to the great enemies of Moab, Philistia and Edom (also referred to in early prophetic oracles against enemy nations, for example in Amos 1–2). By the time Psalm 60 was adapted and combined with Psalm 57, these nations had long been destroyed. Probably in the early Persian period, when hopes for independence from Persia were still high, they became symbols of God's universal victory over foreign powers, although there was a resistance to mentioning this power by name. The heading 'of David' is a nostalgic reminder of days when there was still a king and a nation.[47]

[47] Tucker 2014b: 183–85.

Psalms Through the Centuries: A Reception History Commentary on Psalms 73–151, Volume Three, First Edition. Susan Gillingham.
© 2022 John Wiley & Sons Ltd. Published 2022 by John Wiley & Sons Ltd.

So this psalm is an excellent example of reception history within the Psalter itself. A problem arises from this. It is difficult to know whether later examples of reception are using this psalm or parts of Psalms 57 and 60 in their earlier setting. For example, can we read George *Herbert's 'Rise heart; thy Lord is risen...', based on Ps. 57:8, also for Ps. 108:1–2? And is *Purcell's composition on 57:10–11 'For your steadfast love is as high as the heavens' also for Ps. 108:4–5?[48] Do we receive Roger *Wagner's image of the enormous blue angel astride a winding river, flinging a shoe to the viewer, not only for Ps. 60:8 ('on Edom I hurl my shoe') but also for 108:9?[49] And what of the use of Ps. 60:12 ('with God we shall do valiantly...') used in the Great *Compline of the Byzantine Church against infidel Jews and Arabs?[50] Is Ps. 108:13 part of this reception history too? The answer is probably not, because Psalm 108 has a different story and a different purpose, despite using the same psalm texts.

Although the Davidic heading links this psalm with 109 and 110, unusually there are few specific connections between these psalms, and there are no obvious linguistic correspondences with Psalm 107. The only witness in *Qumran is in 4PesherPsalms[a] (4Q171) which also includes parts of Psalms 107 and 109, where in fragmentary form the promise of God over Israel's enemies is remembered (verses 7–8). It is interesting that also found in the same scroll is an interpretation of Psalm 37, with its interest in the inheritance of the land.[51]

The *LXX makes some changes, including the doubling of 'my heart is steadfast' in the first verse; this is not in the Hebrew, but it is in the Hebrew of Ps. 57:7 (Hebrew, verse 8). The *LXX also follows more closely the text of Psalm 60 in the latter part of Psalm 108, namely in the idea of foreigners being made subject to God in 60:8 (Greek verse 10) and 108:9 (Hebrew and Greek verse 10) with a rather odd translation of the Hebrew word for 'washbasin' (*sir raḥṣi*) which reads now as a 'cauldron *of hope*' (*lebēs tēs elpidos*). The Aramaic in *Targum* reads, somewhat oddly again, 'I have trampled the Moabites like my washpot'. *Targum's* translation of 108:10 (Aramaic v. 11) is telling: '*And now because I sinned* who will bring me to the *wicked city of Rome?* Who will lead me to *Constantinople* of Edom?' Here is a very specific attempt to 'contemporise' even further the references to God's sovereignty over foreign powers, also showing that the date of this translation must have been some time after the founding of Constantinople in c. 330 CE. *Targum* associates the temporary period of disempowerment with the people's sinfulness again in verse 11 (Aramaic v. 12) by repeating '*is it not because we have sinned before Yahweh he has forsaken us?*'

---

[48] See Gillingham 2018: 334.
[49] See Gillingham 2018: 343.
[50] See Gillingham 2018: 341.
[51] See Gillingham 2018: 222.

Later Jewish tradition has two main emphases. One takes up yet again a motif from verse 2 (Heb. verse 3) concerning David's harp which was blown by the north wind so that David awoke to sing his psalms. *Rashi makes much of this, and it is taken up in later Jewish images of this psalm.[52] The other pertains to God's sovereignty over the nations: *Kimḥi opines that the reason behind taking up two older psalms was to use them to speak of the future deliverance of God's people by the Messiah.[53] He argues that because this composite psalm now refers to Israel as a whole (i.e. not only to David's flight from Saul and his conquest of Aram as in Psalm 60), it thus refers to the glorious time when the Messiah, son of David, will lead the Jews in a triumphant conquest of their enemies.[54]

The New Testament has nothing to say on this psalm, and because it does not readily provide much obvious doctrine, it is not excessively commented on by the Fathers. *Augustine popularised the view that Christ's Ascension and the coming of the Holy Spirit are hidden in verse 5: 'let your glory be over all the earth'.[55] *Cassiodorus typically expands this idea: Christ the Lord speaks through the entire psalm. Comparing the psalm to the way Psalms 96, 105 and 106 are used in 1 Chronicles 16,[56] Cassiodorus argues that in the first part (using some of Psalm 57) Christ appears as man, addressing God the Father, speaking of his passion and his rise to glory. In the second part, he again reveals his humanity and his sufferings in the flesh.[57]

This corresponds with the psalm's use in Christian Liturgy on Ascension Day. But in terms of Jewish liturgy, there is almost nothing: Psalms 108–110 are not used regularly in Orthodox, Conservative or Reformed traditions. The closest we get is a citation amongst many other psalms in Jewish 'Bibliomancy', where psalms are used for protective purposes as a fight against omens. Psalm 108 is used, somewhat puzzlingly, for happiness at home.[58]

The first two verses, as we have already noted, have inspired an interest in this psalm in music. Jim *Cotter, in his work of devotions for private and public prayer, focusses entirely on the importance of music in the psalm, so that all the metaphors have musical connotations. So his refrain reads:

> With the voice of song
> And the sounds of nature
> with the instruments of melody

---

[52] See Gruber 2004: 637. Because this is at the beginning of the psalm, more is made of it than in 57:8.
[53] See Cohen 1992: 364.
[54] See Feuer 2004: 1319.
[55] 'Tractates on the Gospel of John' 100. 3.4. in FC 90:232 *ACCS* VIII: 257.
[56] Cassiodorus trans. Walsh 1991b: 102.
[57] Cassiodorus trans. Walsh 1991b: 96.
[58] Magonet 1994: 6–7.

> with the strains of the heart,
> with the discords let loose
> and the cries unshaped,
> we seek to make music,
> the music of God.

His prayer at the end of the psalm reads:

> In the music of lament and celebration, of loyalties and questioning, of love and
> protest, of ballad and cantata, we seek to be your partners, Creator God, in the
> weaving of the patterns of glory. Inspire us, guide us, transform us.[59]

The psalm has inspired several classical musical arrangements, including
those by Heinrich *Schütz, based upon verses 1–2: 'Mit rechtem Ernst und
fröhlichem Mut' is included in his *Becker Psalter* (SWV 206), whilst another
very different metrical version in English, by Thomas Clark (1775–1859) for
*SATB, is entitled 'O God, my heart is fully bent' (1810).[60] Perhaps the most
popularised use, based in part on the tradition of David's harp, is from *Bernstein's *Chichester Psalms*: 'Urah, hanevel v'chinor: Airah shahar'. This focusses
on the psalm being sung at dawn, and was performed at the Southern Choirs
Festival in 1965.[61] A less well-known version arranged by Welsh singer and
song-writer Martin Joseph (b. 1960) is based on the first five verses: 'I will
awaken the Dawn' is for SATB and piano and was published in 1995.[62]

Several Christian images in art develop the theme of the Ascension of
Christ, both in *Carolingian and Byzantine Psalters. The *Theodore Psalter* (fol.
118r) presents Christ in a globe-*mandorla, with its central verse being 5: 'Be
exalted, O Lord...'[63] The *Utrecht Psalter* (fol. 63v) has a similar theme but typically develops it. At the left is a personified sun, indicating it is dawn, which
falls upon the psalmist who carries a harp and a lute (verse 2). King David
stands at the heart of the image: he is in a walled enclosure (verse 10) and holds
a pair of shoes, destined for Edom (verse 9). To his right sit three men: Gil-
ead, Manasseh, and Ephraim (verse 8). To the right Moab is holding up a cup,
which, following the Latin translation of the Greek, is here 'a cup of hope' (*lebes
spei meae*: verse 9). Over this scene Christ rules supreme: his mandorla is supported by four angels, and he holds a scroll in one hand and makes a speaking
gesture with the other.[64]

---

[59] Cotter 1993: 24.
[60] See http://www2.cpdl.org/wiki/index.php/O_God,_my_heart_is_fully_bent_(Thomas_Clark).
[61] See Gorali 1993: 270 (score on p. 271).
[62] See https://www.jwpepper.com/I-Will-Awaken-the-Dawn/1970458.item#myratebox2.
[63] See Corrigan 1992: 21–22. See also
http://www.bl.uk/manuscripts/Viewer.aspx?ref=add_ms_19352_f064v.
[64] See https://psalter.library.uu.nl/page/134.

I will Wake the Dawn is the title of artist Debra *Band's book of illuminations and commentary on thirty-six psalms.[65] Although the actual psalm is not one of those eventually used, partly because of its more negative views of other nations, the phrase itself indicated the sort of 'ecstatic inspiration' which brought the book together. Implicit here, too, is the tradition of David's Harp blowing in the wind.[66]

Finally, a pertinent comment on this psalm is by Edward *Clarke, whose reworking of this psalm is most telling: it uses the idea of its composite nature as a symbol of the complex and ephemeral nature of our lives, thus giving its message a universal application:[67]

> Just like this Psalm my mind's made up
> Of parts of other texts:
> Just like this Psalm I am determined,
> 'O God, my heart is fixed'.
> Book three was finished yesterday, book two
> Two days before, and now
>
> I find I have one hundred psalms
> In all, I thought to myself,
> Crawling on quasi-rhymes, to loot
> The harp from off the shelf:
> Picked up from off the table, struck with fear,
> Its words are in my ear.
>
> I struggled with their hope, these lines,
> Then raced to work, my route
> Across a park towards a cedar,
> My mind burdened with loot
> As I walked, when to my eye an eagle cropped
> That cedar, took its top-
>
> Most branch, its tender twigs, into
> An arid land of start-
> Up businesses, a four-square city
> With money at its heart:
> Majestic companies busy like Mammon
> Exiling its river's salmon.
>
> 'Vain is the help of man': I'll take
> That line and plant it firm
> In lofty soil of this one hundred-
> Year-old lyric form,
> The invention of a man, forlorn at fifty
> Counting what leaves us swiftly.

[65] See Band and Band 2007: xiii–xvii.
[66] This is part of email correspondence dated 26–10–18. For an illustration of Psalm 114, see p. 216 and note 248.
[67] Clarke 2020: 114.

Psalm 109: Living with Abuse

Just as 108 fell into two clear parts, taken from two psalms, it is probable that Psalm 109 is also composite. This decision depends on whether one sees the dreadful curses in verses 6–19 as the psalmist's own words, or as citations of the curses of the enemies, using a singular form directed against the psalmist. Much depends on whether one sees verse 20 ('May that be the reward of my accusers from the LORD, of those who speak evil against my life') as a summary of the psalm or part of verses 6–19. If verses 6–19 are intended to be read as the psalmist speaking, this is a unified psalm concerned with *lex talionis*, where violation is met with violence. If these verses are spoken by the enemy, the psalm is more concerned with the issue of justice and protection of the poor. Certainly the NRSV translation implies these are curses spoken by the enemies, with the addition, at the beginning of verse 6, of the words 'They say…' (which are not found in the Hebrew or Greek texts). This is also advocated by some Jewish commentators such as the nineteenth-century rabbis Malbim and *Hirsch, who also note that the enemies are plural, but the curses of vv. 6–19 are all directed to a subject who is in the singular. The view here is that this concerns David, pursued by Saul and cursed by his arch-enemy Doeg the Edomite.[68]

The psalm actually falls into four related strophes, comprising verses 1–5 (an appeal to God); verses 6–20 (offering a legal case to God); verses 21–25, 26–29 two pleas to God to intervene); and verses 30–31 (a promise to thank God when the prayer is heard). Its heading in Hebrew is curious: 'to the choirmaster' implies its place in worship, and indeed verse 1 refers to 'God of my *praise*'; that the curses were part of liturgy is possible (for example, the curses against foreign nations in the prophets might have had such a context), but it is odd in a psalm as personal as this. It rather suggests the curses were cited as words of the enemy directed against the suppliant, now seen through the experiences of David: this is indicated in Jewish tradition noted above but is actually not a major element of the psalm's reception history.

Psalm 109 is the second of a trilogy of Davidic psalms, although this collection has no obvious linguistic correspondences. There is a sequence of ideas, however: Psalm 108 is about the threat of a physical assault by foreign powers; Psalm 109 is about a more personal verbal attack on the psalmist; and Psalm 110, linked to the last verse of 109 in the reference to God standing at the 'right hand' (*yamin*) of the needy, speaks of a redeeming figure of authority who is at God's right hand (110:1 and 5, also using *yamin*).

---

[68] See Cohen 1992: 366.

Although a sequence works for the three psalms within the *Masoretic text, the evidence from *Qumran shows 109 linked with other psalms. In 11QPs^a (also known as 11Q5 or 'The Great Psalms Scroll'), dated as late as the mid first-century CE, Psalm 109 is placed after 103 (another psalm with a Davidic heading) and before 118 (although Psalm 110 and following psalms might simply be missing).[69] In 4QPs^f (or 4Q88), dating from about 50 BCE and comprising a series of fragments, it seems 109 is followed not by Psalm 110 but by a sectarian hymn of the community called 'Apostrophe of Zion'. Throughout Book Five the Qumran Scrolls reveal that the compilation of this work had a more unstable textual tradition; all that can be said is that the reception of Psalms 108–110 in the *LXX and MT does make some sense, even though this ordering was not unique.

The New Testament use of this psalm gave it the title *Psalmus Ischarioticus*—a psalm of Judas—mainly because of its citation in Acts 1:20, alongside Ps. 69:26. We have noted before the tendency to associate Judas with the curses on David's enemies in the psalms (for example in Psalms 52 and 55).[70] Earlier in Acts 1:16 we read how the psalms were often read as prophecies in the early church: '…the scripture *had to be fulfilled*, which the Holy Spirit through David foretold *concerning Judas* …'. The use of Ps. 109:8b in Acts 1:20 shows how this prophecy is about to be fulfilled: 'let another take his position as overseer' uses the more general Greek word *episkopē* in the *LXX to mean something more specific. Ps. 109:8 is now read in Acts as a prophecy fulfilled by Matthias, taking up Judas's 'office' amongst the disciples.[71] This then assumes the curses of verses 6–19 are the words of David about his enemy, not the words of the enemies about David.

This was just the beginning of the association of the psalm in general and the curses in verses 6–20 with Judas. For example, 109:6 reads 'let an accuser stand at his right hand'. In the Hebrew Bible, 'the Satan' is also known as 'the accuser' (e.g. Job 1:6–8; Zech.3:1) and so the figure of the accuser in Psalm 109 was understood as a personification of (the) Satan. *Augustine, for example, is quick to point out that the phrase can be read 'and let Satan stand at his right hand' demonstrating that this is about Judas who had the devil in him. Similarly the references to an ignominious death in 109:8a, 9–10, and to all remembrance of life being blotted out in 109:13, also allowed commentators such as Augustine to identify these words as a prophecy about Judas.[72] Judas became a type of the unbelieving synagogue, just as Peter was a type of the believing church.[73] *Origen, writing before Augustine, actually read the entire

---

[69] Noting again the references to the 'right hand' of God in 118:15–16.
[70] See Gillingham 2018: 318 (Psalm 52) and *ibid*. 325-6 (Psalm 55) where the same identification with Judas is made.
[71] See Witherington 2017: 310.
[72] Augustine trans. Uyl 2017: 547, 552–53.
[73] See Neale and Littledale 1874–79: 3/423.

psalm as about Judas: for example, verse 2 ('For wicked and deceitful mouths are opened against me, speaking against me with lying tongues …') also typified Judas' betrayal.[74] By contrast, *Jerome, more contemporaneous with Augustine, read the superscription in the Greek (*eis to telos*) as meaning, literally, 'unto the end' and saw the entire psalm as a meditation about Christ on the cross, with the role of Judas bringing that about.[75] *Cassiodorus also understood Psalm 109 as the fifth in the Psalter to be completely about the passion of Christ (the others thus far being 22, 35, 55 and 69).[76] Hence verse 31 at the end of the psalm ('For he [God] stands at the right hand of the needy, to save them from those who would condemn them to death') is about the promise of the resurrection.

Codex Palatino-Latinus 68 in the Vatican Library is a *Gloss* on the Psalms used perhaps as early as the eighth-century in the Irish Church. The tendency here is to read the psalms more historically, as the voice of David, although a few glosses offer Christological readings. The introduction to the commentary on Psalm 109 is first understood as the voice of David in remembrance of his son Absalom; it is then read as the voice of persecuted Jews during the time of the Maccabees. Nothing is made of Acts 1:16–20; but there is an interesting reference to the psalm having 'thirty curses', fitting for Judas the betrayer on account of the 'thirty pieces of silver'.[77]

Psalmus Ischarioticus led to some vivid images in Psalters which sought to bring out the moral lessons behind the curses on Jesus and the betrayal of Judas. The *Stuttgart Psalter* (fol. 126r) has a striking image of Judas, being taunted and attacked by the devil to his right and a sinner to his left.[78] Verse 19 ('may it [cursing] be like a garment that he wraps around himself') is illustrated on fol. 126v, and the pleas in verses 26–27 ('Help me O God …') are on fol. 127r, where a figure addresses the hand of God in the heavens.[79] The *Bertin Psalter* (written in 999 for Abbot Odbert of Saint-Bertin, and now held at the Bibliothèque Municipal at Boulogne-sur-mer) is one of several Psalters to have a striking image of Judas hanging by a rope from the letter 'D' ('Deus') introducing the Psalm.[80] For a reproduction of this image, see PLATE 14. The *Theodore Psalter* (fol. 150r) has an image of Judas hanging from a tree, with the rope held by a winged demon; standing behind the tree is either the Evangelist Matthew (the only Gospel writer to record this incident in Matt. 27:5) or the Apostle Matthias (as in Acts 1:23–26), holding a book which signifies the

---

[74] Origen, 'Against Celsus' 2.11 cited in *ACCS* VIII: 259.
[75] Howell 1987: 192.
[76] See Cassiodorus trans. Walsh 1991b: 115.
[77] See McNamara 2000: 415–416.
[78] See https://bit.ly/3Gq2dxp.
[79] See https://bit.ly/31HpWuc (fol. 126v) and https://bit.ly/3oFoEZf (fol. 127r).
[80] See Lafran 2018: 61–78, especially p. 71. The manuscript at the Bibliothèque municipal is MS 20: see https://bvmm.irht.cnrs.fr/iiif/75/canvas/canvas-104204/view.

fulfilment of prophecy.[81] The *Khludov Psalter* (fol. 113r) and the *Barberini Psalter* (fol. 190r) add to this an image of Christ in Gethsemane, with rays from the hand of God descending on him as he kneels amidst olive trees. In *Les Très Riches Heures du Duc de Berry*, for the Hours of the Passion, Jean Colombe includes an arresting illustration of Psalm 109 (fol. 147v) of Judas, strangled by a noose round his neck, his face in a dreadful grimace, and the buildings of Jerusalem behind him. His cloak lies at his feet. Verses 2–4 and 18 accompany this image.[82]

What few musical compositions there are focus on either verse 1 or verse 21: so Heinrich *Schütz's 'Herr Gott, des Ich mich rühmte viel' (SWV 207) is a chorale, based on verse 1; Orlando *di Lasso's version in Latin is based on verse 21; and Samuel *Wesley's version, using *Coverdale's text, is also from verse 21.

It is strange, given the psalm's heading and its first verse, that Jewish liturgy does not use this psalm at all. It has played a controversial part in more recent Roman Catholic and Anglican Liturgy which prefers to omit the cursing verses (6–20) as being inappropriate for worship. C.S. Lewis (1898–1963) views Psalm 109 as 'an unabashed hymn of hate as was ever written', agreeing to its inappropriateness for prayer and worship. Yet the congregationalist minister Robert Vaughan (1795–1868) attempted to 'redeem' the psalm for worship in the following Collect to accompany Evening Prayer 'of the 22nd Day':[83]

> O God of our praise, who was contented that thy Son Jesus Christ should be betrayed into the hands of sinners by one of his own Apostles, the Traitor *Judas*, and in punishment of so great impiety did'st suffer Satan to stand at his right hand tempting him to despair… let thy righteous judgements find out all those that are Traitors to their Prince, enemies to the Church, Apostates from Religion, Hypocrites under specious pretences, and beauteous titles; that they may be clothed with shame… that …they may be driven to a sharp and salutary repentance, and may be saved in the life to come. Deal thou with us, O Lord, according to thy mercy, take away thy curse, and let not thy blessing be far from us: let not our wickedness, nor the wickedness of our fathers be had in remembrance in thy sight…

The psalm has also found a contemporary voice. Beth LaNeel Tanner vividly imagines that the voice pertains to the unheard cries of women trapped in

---

[81] See http://www.bl.uk/manuscripts/Viewer.aspx?ref=add_ms_19352_f064v.

[82] Longnon and Cazelles 1969: 112 and 213.

[83] Vaughan 1702: 217.

a patriarchal society.[84] David Slavitt's *Sixty-One Psalms of David* uses it as a challenge back to God to deal with the problem of evil and innocent suffering:[85]

> O God where are You? In this silence
> all I hear is wicked lies,
> a villain's insults, threats of violence…
> I look up to empty skies
>
> for help, and turn in need to You,
> beset, despised for my good deeds.
> An empty unremitting blue
> glares down on me, and my heart bleeds.
>
> Set some crook upon him, and let
> that crook have lawyers. Let them sue.
> Let his odd virtues count against him.
> Number his days let them be few…

Perhaps the most evocative commentary is found in post-Holocaust writings. For example, in *Facing the Abusing God*, the post-Holocaust writer David Blumenthal (b. 1938) uses four psalms, of which one is Psalm 109, and presents them in four columns as if on a page of the *Talmud*, to illustrate the *mid-rashic nature of his commentary. 'Words' offer a philological exegesis of the psalm; 'Sparks' take up the more spiritual insights from Judaism; 'Affections' turn the outrage of the psalmist's emotions outwards; and 'Con-verses' capture the silent rage trapped within. The dialogue is between the faith of the received Jewish tradition and the experience of terrible suffering, where the theology and poetry within this psalm become a protest against God. The Christian hate against Judas is now Jewish hate against those who sought to eradicate their faith, and against the One who allowed it. Blumenthal ends: 'Is there really salvation? Can the broken pieces of abused relatedness really be put together? …W/who will save w/Whom? The question remains in con-vers[e]-ation.'[86]

Hence a psalm so associated with Judas the betrayer in early Christian tradition takes up the theme of God as betrayer in contemporary Jewish tradition. Jews and Christians have thus used it in different ways in relation to the problem of evil and innocent suffering.

---

[84] See LaNeel Tanner 1998: 283–301. See also Goldingay 2008: 288–89.
[85] Slavitt 1996: 92-93.
[86] Blumenthal 1993: 156.

Psalm 110: A Psalm about Abraham, David, the Messiah and Christ

We have already noted how the three Davidic psalms (108, 109 and now 110) cohere in their perception of God's victory over the enemy, and how the reference to 'right hand' links 109:31 to 110:1.[87] So in the first stage of reception, the compilers intentionally brought these three psalms together, despite their very different provenances and emphases.

Not only is the text of Psalm 110 one of the most difficult to understand in the entire Psalter, but also its composite nature makes it impossible to know when or why it was written. It seems that a royal oracle, and perhaps also an oracle concerning the ordination of a high priest, might have played a part: its royal associations suggest a date and setting close to Psalm 2, where the investiture of the king, God's protection of Zion, and the military threat of other nations also lie at its heart.[88] But what is clear is that after the failure of the restoration of the monarchy, from the Persian period onwards, this psalm, like Psalm 2, was adapted to speak about a coming figure, in this case both royal and priestly. It is also clear that there were moments in later history when the psalm was read as if that time had arrived: for example, in the second-century BCE, during the time of the *Hasmonean priest-kings.[89] A typical text citation is 1 Macc. 14:41. The view that the beginning of the psalm forms an acrostic 'To Simeon', the first of the Hasmonean priest-kings, is intriguing: the first letters of verses 1a, 1b, 2, 3, and 4 read *L-Sh-M-'-N*, which in Hebrew spells out 'to Simeon'. Even before the psalm was used in the New Testament (and it is used there more than any other psalm) it had accreted many layers of Jewish interpretation, most of which are hidden from us. This is what makes Psalm 110 such a challenge when writing about its reception history.

The seven verses fall into two clear parts. Verses 1–3, beginning with *ne'um Adonay* ('the utterance of the Lord'), form a divine oracle concerning the defeat of enemies (verse 1) and God fighting from Zion (verse 2). The references to the 'mighty sceptre' and 'rule' suggest that, again like Psalm 2, originally the king was being addressed: he is therefore 'my lord' addressed by the psalmist in verse 1. The end of verse 3 forms the second part of this oracle: if the *Masoretic vocalisation is interpreted differently, it could be read 'out of the womb of the dawn, I bore you as dew'. Verse 3 certainly assumes an intimate relationship between God and

---

[87] See p. 177.

[88] See Gillingham 2017: 25–27.

[89] 'Whilst the Hasmoneans probably did not compose the psalm, they probably did use it to defend their claims to priestly and royal prerogatives.' See Hay 1973: 24. See also Tucker 2014a: 79–81.

the king, with affinities with the father/son imagery in Ps. 2:7, where the king is 'begotten' of God. Verse 3 undoubtedly uses birthing imagery: the word *reḥem* means 'womb', and the word vocalised *yaledut* by the Masoretes means 'youth' or 'childhood' and is related to the verb *y-l-d* 'to give birth'. The Greek translation makes this birthing imagery clear: *ek gastros pro heōsphorou exegennēsa se* ('out of the womb of the morning star I have begotten you').

Verses 4–7 form a divine oath (*nishba' Adonay*) as found in other royal psalms such as 89:35, 49 and 132:11; but here this concerns, most unusually, the priesthood of the king. The themes of the subjugation of the enemies and of God as warrior (verse 5–6) echo verses 1–3. The last verse is an enigma: the difficulty of translation suggests this is an ancient psalm whose meaning has long been forgotten.

The Greek modifies the idea of divine utterance in the Hebrew of verse 1 to, simply, 'The Lord *said* to my lord' (*eipon ho kurios tō kuriō mou*), somewhat confusingly using the same word for 'Lord'. (In the masoretic vocalisation it is clear that God is the subject and the king is being addressed). The Greek undoubtedly led to some confusion between the subject and recipient in New Testament readings.

Three differences between the Hebrew and the Latin are important for later reception history, as we shall shortly see. The first is the translation of the word *'ad'* ('until', 'as far as', or 'up to') in verse 1; this becomes *heōs an* in the Greek, meaning 'as far as', suggesting a more specific passage of time. The Latin follows this by using *donec* ('as long as, until). The second is the word for dawn (*mishḥar*) in verse 3 which in the Greek is *heōsphoros*, often used to refer to the morning star; in the *Vulgate* this is now *ante luciferum*. Some interpreters see the Greek in particular as a reference to a pre-existent angelic being, a figure later associated with the Messiah;[90] this is probably taking the evidence too far. A third change is in verse 4, which the Latin refers to as *'secundum ordinem Melchisedech'*, which encouraged some Christians to read 'secundum' not as 'according to' but as 'inferior/subordinate to', thus indicating this priestly order was subordinate to that of Christ. We shall see shortly how these changes were understood in commentary, art and music.

Psalm 110 does not occur in the *Qumran scrolls: it probably did and has not been found, given that Psalm 2 is cited several times. But its lack of popularity might be due to the Melchizedek reference in verse 4, and the appropriation of this psalm by the Hasmonean priests (whose high priest was the 'wicked priest' according to the Qumran community). Interestingly Psalm 110:4 is not explicitly quoted in the Melchizedek Scroll (11Q13), but this is probably because of its fragmentary nature.

We now turn to the reception of this psalm in Jewish tradition, where the recipient of both the oracle and oath is firstly Abraham, and then David, and, occasionally, the Messiah. The interest in Abraham focusses mainly on verses 1

[90] Schaper 1995: 103.

and 4: Genesis 14 is the only other place in the Hebrew Bible where reference is made to Melchizedek, and this comes after Abraham's victory over the alliance of four kings from the East (Gen. 14:1–17). Melchizedek appears to Abraham at the King's Valley near Jerusalem (Gen. 14:17); he is the priest-king of Salem, or Jerusalem (Gen. 14:18). Abraham is blessed on account of his victory over the foreign kings (Gen. 14:19–20), and this is ratified by sharing bread and wine (Gen 14:18). Hence rabbinic tradition reads Ps. 110:1 as a dialogue between God and Abraham, 'the righteous man from the East' (*Sanh.* 108b) who came to Jerusalem. Abraham shared in the priesthood of Melchizedek (*Ned.* 32b), and indeed even took over that priesthood himself. *Midrash Tehillim* views the whole psalm as an ancient hymn which God recited to Abraham, and he was the only one who could call God his Lord.[91] *Midrash Tehillim* also identifies the recipient of the blessing in Psalm 110 as Abraham, 'the man from the east who roused up nations of the earth'.[92] Abraham is the one who was raised to sit at the right hand of God— the right hand where one day the Messiah will sit.[93] *Rashi also sees Abraham as the initial recipient of the words of this psalm: the battle imagery fits the context of Genesis 14, and in Gen 23:6 Abraham is again addressed as 'my lord'; moreover, verse 6 (concerning filling the earth with corpses) refers to the covenant ceremony in Genesis 15 when Abraham is given authority over all the nations.[94]

Nevertheless, the Davidic heading over the psalm and its place in the Psalter also allowed for a David-centred reading of the psalm, continuing the promise first offered to Abraham. *Targum reads the whole psalm in the light of David. He is 'the righteous king' (playing on the name Melchizedek, 'my king is righteous').[95] Not only in the Greek and Latin, but also in the Aramaic, is the word 'until' in verse 1 now read as a period of waiting, interpreted in the light of David's situation in 2 Samuel 2: '*Return and wait for Saul, who is of the tribe of Benjamin, until he dies; for you are not associated with a Kingdom that is near, and afterwards I will make your enemies a stool for your feet...*'[96] *Targum* then offers a somewhat anachronistic interpretation of verse 3: as David prepares for this battle, he will be assisted by those people *who have spent their time of waiting by reading the Torah.* By the sixth-century CE when *Targum* would have been used by Jews, Torah reading was seen as an act of devotion which could bring about victory over the Gentiles. *Ibn Ezra and *Kimḥi date the psalm early in David's reign, and view the enemies of verse 1 as the Ammonites, during the wars with the

---

[91] Feuer 2004: 1339.
[92] Braude 1959: 205.
[93] Braude 1959: 206.
[94] Gruber 2004: 645–50.
[95] Hay 1973: 31.
[96] Stec 2004: 202.

Philistines.[97] Rashi, following *Targum*, added his Davidic interpretation to his Abrahamic reading noted above: verse 1 refers to David's activities with Saul, and the phrase 'sit at my right hand' really means 'pause, and wait for deliverance'.

It is difficult to assess how early a Messianic reading of Psalm 110 took place. The New Testament writers assume, when they use this psalm (and it is really only verses 1 and 4 which are used) the ubiquity of a Messianic reading held by various Jewish parties. Certainly the appellation of Jesus as 'Lord' suggests some earlier Messianic reading of Ps. 110:1. As Hay notes, 'Was their [the New Testament writers'] exegesis… simply an extension of Jewish messianic interpretation?'[98] Certainly by the time of *Midrash Tehillim* the delay of the Messiah is read in the light of that word 'until' in verse 1: just as David taking his throne, subduing his enemies and (metaphorically) sitting at God's right hand had to be delayed, so too the time for the coming of the Messiah who will sit victorious at God's right has also to be delayed.[99] Nevertheless, in later Jewish tradition Psalm 110 is rarely cited in relation to the Messiah: it is quite likely that this is to counter Christian readings of these figures in relation to Christ, as we shall see below.[100]

If Jewish readings were mainly divided between seeing Abraham and/or David and occasionally the Messiah in Psalm 110, Christian reception is united in seeing this as a prophecy directly relating to Christ, although views are divided as to whether this confirms his humanity or his divinity or both (rather like in the reception of Psalm 2).[101] Despite its many interpretations by Jewish writers, this psalm was cited more times in the New Testament (some twenty) than any other, adding further to the diverse ways in which some of the verses might be read. The New Testament citations and allusions fall roughly into four categories: those appealing to Jesus as David's son ('my lord', using verse 1); those emphasising the divinity of Christ, sitting 'at the right hand of God' (also using verse 1); those taking up the motif of Jesus' subjugation of enemies (verses 2, 5 and 6); and those applying the title 'Melchizedek' to Jesus himself (taking verse 4). We shall deal with each of these in turn.[102]

Psalm 110 was used in the Synoptic Gospels to confirm both Jesus as the Messiah and the Son of David. Verse 1 is cited in Mark 12:25–37, Matt. 22:41–46 and Luke 20:41–44. In Mark this verse is used by Jesus himself, clarifying that,

---

[97] Cohen 1992: 371–72.
[98] Hay 1973: 15–16.
[99] Braude 1959: 206–7 (citing R. Yudan).
[100] Shereshevsky 1971: 84–86.
[101] See Gillingham 2017: 30–32.
[102] See for example Witherington 2017: 267–80 and 357–74, which focusses on the use of Psalm 110 in the New Testament; also; Dupont 1974: 419–22.

because David calls the Messiah 'Lord', the Messiah cannot be a son of David.[103] Matthew places this in a more hostile setting of disputes with the Pharisees. In Luke, meanwhile, the verse is cited, but in a less confrontational setting. There is a paradox here: Matthew is at pains to state in his genealogy that Jesus is from the house of David, albeit through Joseph (Matt. 1:1–17), but the Messiah is greater than David's son, given that God is his Father. The question is: how can Jesus be David's Lord and David's Son? Ps. 110:1 was read as resolving this tension.[104]

The Gospel of John never refers explicitly to Psalm 110. It is possible that this is because the psalm speaks of one who moves from a lower to a higher status, whereas Jesus in John has always been the pre-existent Logos 'equal with God' (John 5:18).[105]

Secondly, the expression 'the right hand' (sometimes 'of God') occurs some forty times in the psalms, often in relation to God's protection of the psalmist. But Ps. 110:1 is the only invitation to *sit* at God's right hand. In Acts 2:34–35 this becomes a means of speaking about the resurrection and ascension of Christ. So more general references to Jesus (or 'the Son of Man') *seated at the right hand of God* have also been influenced by this verse, combining it with others such as Dan. 7:13 and verses from Enoch. One example is Luke 22:69, spoken by Jesus during his trial before Caiaphas.[106] Others include Mark 16:19, Acts 5:31, Rom. 8:34 (where the phrase is linked to Christ's priestly intercession), Eph. 1:20, Col. 3:1, Heb. 1:3 (which adds that Christ is thus above the angels), and Heb. 8:1 (where Jesus is also called the 'high priest'). Heb. 10:12 plays on the use of the word 'until': Jesus dies, and through his resurrection was raised to God's right hand, but has now *to wait until* all his enemies are subjected under his feet).[107] Heb. 12:2 also makes use of the idea of the 'pause' between what Jesus has achieved and what is still to be achieved. 1 Pet. 3:22 is also indirectly influenced by Ps. 110:1 in its description of Jesus 'at the right hand of God'. Dunn makes the interesting point that although figures of antiquity are described at this time as having been raised to a throne with God (such as Adam, Enoch, even Melchizedek and the Messiah) it is unusual that someone in such recent memory should be described in this way.[108]

---

[103] On Mark's use of Psalm 110 see Watts 2004: 36–41.

[104] On Matthew's use of Psalm 110 see Menken 2004: 73–76.

[105] Daly-Denton 2000: 270–78. The church fathers interpreted verse 3 in exactly this way, as we shall shortly see.

[106] On Luke's use of Psalm 110 see Doble 2004: 96–97; also Marshall 1980: 56–57; also Dunn 1988: 504.

[107] It interesting that this idea of 'waiting' in Ps. 110:1 and in Heb 10:12 has influenced Christian views of 'Dispensationalism'—that Christ's world rule will finally break in after an allotted period of time.

[108] See Dupont 1974: 341–422.

Thirdly, the reference to Christ's subjugation of the enemies 'under his feet' (here taken from the expansion in the Greek) is another phrase in Ps. 110:1 which is frequently found in the New Testament. Sometimes this is combined with Ps. 8:6, as in 1 Cor. 15:25–27, where the inference is no longer foreign nations, but evil powers of a spiritual nature, and reference is made to the necessary pause 'until' the enemies are subjugated.[109] This use of Ps. 8:6 alongside Ps. 110:1 is also found in Eph. 1:20–23 to show the dramatic enthronement of Christ through his death and resurrection.[110]

The Epistle to Hebrews cites or alludes to Psalm 110 at least 12 times. Some examples have been cited above. One of the most intriguing, and indeed distinctive to Hebrews, is the number of Melchizedek references in chapters 5–7, for these are combined with several other theological motifs, such as Heb. 5:5–6, which combines Ps. 2:7 with 110:4 to develop the dual theme of Jesus as God's Son and Christ as the High Priest. In Heb. 7:17, Ps. 110:4 is again explicitly cited; Heb. 7:11, 15 and 21 all use Ps. 110:4 implicitly in the teaching about a heavenly priesthood, where Jesus intercedes between the earthly and heavenly sanctuaries and so transforms the role of Melchizedek: he is both the sacrificial victim (here other Old Testament texts are borrowed, as this is not in Psalm 110) and the great high priest.[111]

All these four different adaptations of Psalm 110 in the New Testament offer a theocentric reading: not one of them deals with the humanity of Christ. The psalm points to Christ's divinity, and verses 1 and 4 in particular work to that end.[112] It is not surprising that most of the early church fathers developed the same emphasis and indeed took it further still.

As early as the Epistle of *Barnabas (12:10–11) Ps. 110:1 is used to demonstrate that 'Jesus is Messiah, not as son of David, but as Son of God, whom David calls Lord'.[113] Similarly *Justin in *Dial.* 32:6 reads the whole psalm in the light of Jesus as God. *Hippolytus reads Psalm 110 in the light of the Incarnation, the Harrowing of Hell, and the Resurrection.[114] In his *Discourse against the Arians* (2.15.14), *Athanasius uses Psalm 110 to demonstrate that Christ is Lord and King Everlasting, fulfilling 'what he always has been'.[115] Even *Theodore of

---

[109] See Gillingham 2017: 74–75 (on Psalm 8).
[110] See Moritz 1966: 9–11; also, 2004: 184–87.
[111] See Attridge 2004: 197–99.
[112] It is possible that the birthing imagery in verse 3 and the drinking imagery in verse 7 could speak of the humanity of 'the Messiah', but these verses are not used by the New Testament writers.
[113] Cited in *ACCS* VIII: 261.
[114] See https://www.ccel.org/ccel/schaff/anf05.iii.iv.i.v.v.html.
[115] See NPNF 2 4:355–56 in *ACCS* VIII:262.

Mopsuestia counts this as one of the only four psalms (with 2, 8 and 45) capable of a thoroughgoing Christological interpretation.[116]

Here we see the use of the Greek and later Latin text of verse 3 enabled Christian commentators to read the psalm not only about the Incarnation, but also about the *pre-existence* of Christ. So for Justin, in *Dial.* (83), Christ is begotten in the womb (of God) before the morning star was created.[117] In *Proof of the Gospel* (4.16) *Eusebius make the same point, reading this alongside Ps. 2:7 where the 'Messiah' is begotten by God to subject all nations under him.[118] Athanasius, in *Defence of the Nicene Definition* (3:13) makes it clear that the 'womb' in 110:3 signifies a divine birth, not an earthly one, also citing Ps. 2:7.[119] John *Chrysostom makes this clearer still: the birth took place before the creation of the 'morning star': hence this is about Christ's pre-existence, not the Virgin Birth. The 'womb' refers to God, who begot Jesus before his earthly birth in the Virgin's womb. In the light of Jewish controversies, verse 3 is important in showing that Christ is the Son of God. And in the light of the *Arian controversies, this reading both opposes the third-century heretical Bishop, Paul of Samosata (because Psalm 110 makes it clear that the Son was generated from eternity) and it also opposes *Arius (because it is clear that the Son was generated, not made).[120] *Cassiodorus reads Ps. 110:1 in the light of John 1:1 as showing from Jewish scriptures that Christ is the pre-existent Word and co-equal with God.[121] And *Thomasius reads verse 3 as about Christ's birth from the spiritual womb of God before the morning star was made: this is the Birthday of the Lord which we should also celebrate at Christmas.[122]

So, as with the New Testament, the most prominent theme is that this psalm demonstrates the divinity of Christ: it is interesting to see how often verse 3 is now used to support it. But the same writers could just occasionally speak about the humanity of Christ. So Justin, in *Dial.* 33:3, speaks of the *kenosis*, or self-emptying of Christ, in the first and last verses of the psalm. Cassiodorus refers to the phrase 'rule in the midst of your foes' in verse 2 as about the humanity of Christ, and he reads verse 7 ('He will drink from the stream by the path') as about Christ's drinking in our mortality: hence Cassiodorus classifies this psalm as the seventh psalm to speak of Christ's *two* natures.[123] Earlier, *Jerome, writing in the context of the *Manichean controversies, also sees verses 3

---

[116] See Gillingham 2008:32.
[117] See FC 6:280–81 in *ACCS* VIII:264.
[118] See *POG* 1:204–5 in *ACCS* VIII:265.
[119] See NPNF 2 4:158 in *ACCS* VIII:266.
[120] See Cassiodorus trans. Walsh 1991b: 26–28 and 31.
[121] Cassiodorus trans. Walsh 1991b: 116–117.
[122] See Neale and Littledale 1874–79: 3/439.
[123] Cassiodorus trans. Walsh 1991b: 124.

and 7 as referring to Christ's humanity. In his view, the different Hebrew words for God in verse 1 also point to the divine and human Christ.[124]

Very few Christian commentators until *Calvin (with the exception of those in the Irish Church) refer to David alongside Christ in this psalm.[125] Calvin, however, sees the psalm as containing the whole sweep of Jewish and Christian history, from Abraham to David, who speaks on behalf of Christ, and so on up to Christ. David's kingship is again a type of Christ's kingship, but the references to the 'right hand' in verse 1 show that Christ is more unique even than David, and indeed in the Gospels we read that Jesus himself sees the psalm to be a prophecy about himself. So this entitled Calvin to see in Psalm 110 prophecies about Christ's *incarnation* (verse 3), where 'womb of the morning' is seen to refer to the Virgin Mary; prophecies about Christ's *passion* (where in verse 7 'drinking from the stream' illustrates Jesus' words in Gethsemane in Matt. 26:39; and where in verse 5, 'he will shatter kings' denotes Herod and Pilate); prophecies about the *ascension* (by using verse 1, 'sit at my right hand'); prophecies about his priesthood (verse 5, 'After the order of Melchizedek'); and, finally, prophecies about Christ's *kingdom* (by citing verse 2, 'rule in the midst of your foes', and verse 6, 'he will execute judgement among the nations').[126]

*Luther, who, earlier than Calvin, preached eight sermons on Psalm 110 between May and June in 1535, also saw that no other psalm refers to Christ's humanity and divinity as completely as this one. But Luther makes little reference to David; he also makes little reference to Abraham or Melchizedek, except to oppose the Roman Catholic view that Melchizedek's offering of bread and wine to Abraham prefigures the Mass; Luther stressed instead the eternal high priesthood of Christ who makes intercession for us, 'not for one hour or one day… as the private Mass of a popish priest'.[127] Christ's humanity is found in the references to the start of his ministry in Jerusalem in verse 2. Like Calvin, Luther sees references to Gethsemane in verse 7, where the image of 'drinking' signifies Christ's Passion. But it is Christ's divinity which, according to Luther, pervades this psalm: he is referred to as Lord, King and Priest: furthermore, 'sit at my right hand' affirms his divine power. Reading the psalm in the light of Rom. 1:4—which speaks of Christ as a descendent of David and the Son of God—Luther argues that in Psalm 110, above all other psalms, we see the unique nature of Christ's kingdom.[128]

---

[124] Jerome trans. Ewald 1963: 270–279. This is taken from Homily 36 on Psalm 109 (110).

[125] On Irish commentators see McNamara 2000: 407–409 who notes again *Pal. Lat 68* which reads the psalm as if by David speaking of Saul and himself. This is a rare example of a non-Christological reading in a commentary on the psalms for the Church.

[126] See Pak 2010: 16.

[127] Pelikan 1956: 325–26.

[128] See Luther 1956: 228, 265, 313, and 345. See also; Waltke and Houston 2010: 484–518, esp. 492.

It is not surprising that the psalm plays no obvious role in Jewish liturgy, whereas in Christian liturgy the reference to 'seated at the right hand' is, for example, the sixth article of the *Apostles Creed* and is also linked to the Ascension. Its use on Christmas Day testifies to the debates about verse 3 amongst Christian commentators.

From this, it should not be surprising that Psalm 110 is rich in Christian illustration but less easy to find in Jewish art. There are common motifs in Christian illuminated Psalters, particularly those church traditions which recognise a liturgical division at Psalm 110. The first represents Christ and the Father, in conversation, with Christ on his 'right hand'. A vivid example is from *The History Bible* (fol. 31r) by van Deventer of Utrecht, dating from 1443, and preserved at the Koninklijke Bibliotheek in The Hague.[129] This is represented as PLATE 15. A similar image interpreting Psalm 110 is found in MS. Laud Lat. 82, preserved in the Bodleian, Oxford, where the Father and the Son each wear golden crowns.[130] The *Ormesby Psalter*, also held at the Bodleian, shows the Father and Son as identical figures in prayer, although the figure on the left has his feet on a footstool. Above them a third head is found in the letter 'U', representing the Holy Spirit, whilst the struggles of England and Scotland are represented in the fighting wrestlers on a bear and lion below: hence the entire Trinity in this psalm oversees a political landscape.[131] Other Trinitarian interpretations include MS. Douce 118 (127r) and MS. Laud Lat. 114 (148r).[132] A remarkable example is found in MS. Canon. Liturg. 271 (55v), a fifteenth-century Psalter from northern Italy, where the Father actually holds against himself the crucified Son, with the Dove above his head.[133] Another memorable image is in the *St. Omer Psalter*, a fourteenth-century East Anglian Psalter preserved in the British Library, which depicts in the initial 'D' of the psalm ('Dixit Dominus') Christ seated in judgement, summoning the dead from their tombs, some outside the frame of the initial. The roundels around the margins of the page represent different scenes from the Passion of Christ.[134] This image is presented here as PLATE 16.

A quite different English example is from the *St. Albans Psalter*, again at a liturgical division: the letter 'D' portrays a haloed Christ in the bottom left, on earth, with a group of worshippers and holding a sceptre (verse 2); he is reaching up to God who is sitting on a throne, with his angels, holding a book inscribed with 'Sit at my right hand', and pointing to the throne on his right.[135]

---

[129] See https://manuscripts.kb.nl/zoom/BYVANCKB%3Amimi_69b10%3A031r_init.
[130] See Solopova 2013: fig. 25 and pp.152–56.
[131] Law 2017: 134–36. See https://bit.ly/3t0M4rQ.
[132] See Solopova 2013b: fig 49; pp. 297–305; Fig. 18; pp. 109–13.
[133] See Solopova 2013b: fig. 96; pp. 548–53.
[134] See Marks and Morgan 1981: 79–80.
[135] See https://www.albani-psalter.de/stalbanspsalter/english/commentary/page299.shtm.

Earlier Byzantine Psalters prefer more the typology between David and Christ, often using the figure of Melchizedek as a mediator between the two, and often therefore with a focus on the offering of bread and wine and the offering of Christ at the Mass. So in the *Khuldov Psalter* (114v), based on verse 1, David stands with his right hand raised to Christ on a throne, and God's hand emerges from heaven, shedding light on Christ. The marginal note is 'David prophesies the son of God'.[136] Another image on fol. 115r is based on verse 4, which is of David and Melchizedek together testifying that Christ will be in a new kingdom and a new priesthood. Christ stands behind an altar and distributes bread to Peter, with six other Apostles to his right, one of whom is drinking from a chalice. The note in the margin reads 'You are a priest forever according to the order of Melchizedek'.[137] A similar image is found in the *Theodore Psalter* (152r).[138]

Psalm 110 was also the first psalm of *Vespers on Sundays and on major Feast days. Hence there is a vast number of musical compositions for Vespers.[139] *Monteverdi created at least five versions entitled 'Dixit Dominus', of which the one for his 1610 *Vespro della Beata Vergine* is the best known. The Vespers are a monumental Venetian masterpiece with mixed chorus, soloists, solo violin, cornet, and ripieno, using not only verses from Ps 110 but also from Psalm 113, 122, 127 and 147:12–20.[140]

*Vivaldi also composed several versions of Psalm 110, as did *Haydn. So too did *Handel, who wrote *Dixit Dominus (for the Festival of our Lady on Mount Carmel)* when in Rome in 1707, again as part of the Roman Vespers. A better-known version by this composer was in his oratorio *Deborah,* premiered at the King's Theatre, London, in 1733. This work, on Judges 4–5, was actually a pastiche of other works, including his previous Vespers Psalm setting *Dixit Dominus.*[141] A similar work is attributed to one of Handel's students, John Christopher Smith, in 1769, called 'Gideon', based on Judges 6–8, which also uses Handel's *Dixit Dominus.*[142]

*Mozart composed several versions of this psalm, also for Vespers. One is 'Dixit and Magnificat', to be accompanied by organ or orchestra, which also included Psalm 111 *(Confitebur);* Psalm 112 *(Beatus Vir);* Psalm 113 *(Laudate Pueri);* and Psalm 117 *(Laudate Dominum).* Another, from 1779, is *Vesperae de Dominica* (Sunday Vespers) for soloists, chorus, orchestra and organ.[143]

---

[136] Corrigan 1992: fig. 54, pp. 44–45.

[137] 1992: figs. 56–58, p. 278.

[138] See http://www.bl.uk/manuscripts/Viewer.aspx?ref=add_ms_19352_f152r.

[139] The full extent of these compositions is on http://www2.cpdl.org/wiki/index.php/Psalm_110.

[140] See Dowling Long and Sawyer 2015: 255.

[141] See Dowling Long and Sawyer 2015: 61.

[142] See Dowling Long and Sawyer 2015: 91.

[143] See Dowling Long and Sawyer 2015: 254.

Later uses of this psalm are found in James *Montgomery's *Songs of Zion, being Imitations of the Psalms*, composed in 1822. His use of the well-known hymn 'Hail to the Lord's Anointed/Great David's Greater Son' borrows from 110 and 72.[144] A more contemporary version was composed by the American composer and parish musician Kenneth Kosche for the Festival of Three Psalms in 1998, using three octave hand-bells to symbolise the portentous content of this psalm.

Almost all these compositions focus on verse 1, with the emphasis on Christ as God who is to be worshipped. Although Vespers compositions mainly used the entire psalm, verse 3, celebrating the birth of Christ 'from the womb of the morning star', was often used as an appropriate allusion to the Virgin Mary. A hymn based on verse 4, by Isaac *Watts, focusses mainly on verse 4, and the relationship between Christ and Melchizedek.[145]

An appropriate last word on this psalm is an extract from a recent poem entitled 'Hapax Legomenon' by the Oxford poet Edward *Clarke, based on Psalm 110:[146]

> …Out of what might just be
> An old scribe's carelessness,
> The dittographic mess
> Of a hapax legomenon, I see
> A royal figure come: like night the day tricks,
> This ancient text's its matrix…

To conclude, the 'royal figure' in Psalm 110 could not be interpreted more differently in Jewish and Christian tradition. Indeed, alongside Psalm 2, its vast amount of reception history (especially in the commentary tradition, in art and in music) bears witness to the ways in which each faith tradition can read just seven verses in such distinctive and peculiar ways.

---

[144] See https://www.hymnal.net/en/hymn/h/968.
[145] See https://bit.ly/3wJqBWv.
[146] Clarke 2020: 118.

Psalms 111–112: Two Acrostic Psalms

Psalm 111: An Acrostic Psalm Concerning the Righteousness of God

Just as Psalms 108–110 were brought together by the compilers by way of a Davidic theme, and (as we shall see shortly) Psalms 113–118 were eventually bound together by their liturgical use, Psalms 111 and 112 are also intricately related. They are clearly twin psalms, taken together firstly by their message (about living wisely in the fear of the Lord, which occurs at the end of Psalm 111 and at the beginning of 112) and secondly by the medium of their ten-verse format (each is set in an acrostic form, creating short lines of three or four words after a word starting with each successive letter of the alphabet). The first eight verses of each are set as bicola and last two of each are tricola. Each psalm starts with 'Hallelujah'.[147] Two phrases even occur in the same place in each psalm. First, Ps. 111:3 (starting with the sixth Hebrew letter *Waw*) refers to God's righteousness enduring forever, and Ps. 112:3 (also starting with the letter *Waw*) refers to human righteousness enduring forever. Second, 111:4 (starting with the eighth Hebrew letter *Ḥet*) refers to God being 'gracious and merciful' (*ḥannun weraḥum*), a creedal formula associated with the Exodus as in Exod. 34:6), whilst 112:4 (also at the letter *Ḥet*) uses the same formula, whilst implying that humans should emulate this too. The key difference between the two psalms is brought out in

---

[147] Psalm 113 also starts with Hallelujah, whilst Psalms 115, 116 and 117 end in Hallelujah.

Psalms Through the Centuries: A Reception History Commentary on Psalms 73–151, Volume Three, First Edition. Susan Gillingham.
© 2022 John Wiley & Sons Ltd. Published 2022 by John Wiley & Sons Ltd.

these two correspondences: Psalm 111 is more concerned about God's righteousness, whilst Psalm 112 is more interested in how humans can live righteously. These twin psalms create a very different mood from Psalms 108–110: as John Goldingay has observed, instead of the violent images of God's rule, all is now about grace and mercy, and, albeit through stereotypical and general maxims, about the gaining of wisdom for right worship.[148]

In terms of later reception, the two key issues concern, firstly, the *message* of the psalm, not least whether its didactic teaching is more specifically connected with Torah or more generally connected with wisdom, and thus has a more Jewish or a more universal appeal; and, secondly, the *medium* of the psalm, where various later translations seek to imitate the acrostic form.

The psalm is absent from the *Dead Sea Scrolls, and there are no controversial changes in the Greek (although some manuscripts add a heading 'Of the Return of Haggai and Zechariah', indicating the later provenance of the psalm). Nor are there any obvious linguistic connections with Psalm 110. So our focus begins with more general Jewish reception. One early adaptation is in Wisdom 1:12, which in its interest in immortality borrows from Ps. 111:3, concerning God's righteous deeds enduring for ever. (Ps. 112:3 and 9, concerning human's righteous deeds enduring forever, is another possible source of reception). The expression in verse 8, 'faithfulness and uprightness' (*be'emet veyashar*), is taken up, for example, in *b.Berakoth* 10a, where these attributes are seen as pertaining to God's 'righteous principles'.[149] Traditionally these principles were applied to Torah study (even though the word Torah never occurs in the psalm).[150] By contrast, Marc Brettler considers Psalm 111 as an ambiguous 'riddle psalm', a little like Proverbs and hence more associated with wisdom, but for 'an in-group'.[151] So in Jewish tradition the psalm offers a more specific Torah reading as well as a more general didactic application.

As for Christian use, it is possible that in Luke 1:49, part of the *Magnificat*, the phrase 'and holy is his name' is an allusion to Ps. 111:9, a verse which also seems to be alluded to in Luke 1:68 (in his *Benedictus*) about God's redemption of his people. This practical 'wisdom' psalm receives little interest, however, in either the New Testament or later Christian reception. Mainly commentators reflect on 'the works of the Lord' in 111:4 in a more general and even political way, as illustrated in *Chrysostom's application of it to the brief resurgence of *Julian the Apostate from 361–63 and the killing of Maximin the persecutor by Licinius which led to the more tolerant rule of Constantine.[152] E. de Solms

[148] See Goldingay 2008: 307.
[149] See Cohen 1992: 374.
[150] See Feuer 2004: 1347, citing *Sforno.
[151] Brettler 2009: 141.
[152] See Chrysostom trans. Hill 1998: 44 and note 35 on pp. 51–52.

cites the medieval theologian Rupert de Deutz (c.1075–1129) as an exception, who reads 111:4 as about God's deeds through the body and blood of Christ, where God's faithfulness to his covenant (111:5) is most clearly seen.[153] *Augustine 'Christianises' 111:10, which links the fear of the Lord with wisdom, by noting that the former is the first of the sevenfold gifts of the Spirit and the latter is the seventh.[154] But the main Christian response can be summarised by *Luther, who noted that the memorial Christians should reflect on is 'eternal, not temporal, universal, not specific'.[155]

Despite this, the psalm is found in many places in Christian liturgy. Ps. 111:4–5 is frequently used as a communion prayer, applying God's 'works' to the Eucharist. it is also a *Proper Psalm of Easter.[156] The latter two uses resulted in it being used by several composers. In 1641 *Monteverdi completed 'Confitebor tibi Domine', the last of his three settings of Psalm 111, in C Major and in homophony, alternating between solo sections and *tutti* sections, where voices and instruments performed together. The climax is verse 9–10, capturing the holiness of God in single sustained notes and the fear and trembling before God in a sequence of semiquavers.[157] *Vivaldi composed another setting in 1732. In 1779 *Mozart composed 'Sunday *Vespers', using Psalms 110–113 and 117 and the Magnificat (or 'song of Mary', taken from Luke 2) in a work for soloists, chorus, organ and orchestra.[158] In 1780 Mozart used Psalms 110–113 and 117 in a great work called 'Solemn Vespers of the Confessor' (an unnamed saint) using soloists, mixed chorus, organ, wind and brass, for the court in Salzburg; whereas Psalm 110 has a more festive appeal, with drums and trumpets, Psalm 111 uses soloists in a more reflective and responsorial way.[159] Many other examples, also for Solemn Vespers, date from the sixteenth to the eighteenth centuries.[160] A much more recent example, capturing the lighter mood of the psalm, is by the American composer Richard Prouix (1837–2010) 'My heart is full today', with a two-part choir, triangle, tambourine and hand-bells: it was first performed in 1997.

Artistic representations tend to capture the didactic nature of the psalm, focussing on the works of God, sometimes combining this with a Eucharistic theme. The *St. Albans Psalter* is a good example of both.[161] David sits on

---

[153] See De Solms 2001: 537.
[154] Augustine, *Sermon* 248.5 in *WSA* 3 7:114, in *ACCS* VIII: 269.
[155] Taken from *WA* 31 1, 412 cited in Kraus 1989: 359–60.
[156] Gillingham 2008: 154.
[157] Dowling Long and Sawyer 2015: 522.
[158] Dowling Long and Sawyer 2015: 254.
[159] Dowling Long and Sawyer 2015: 254–55.
[160] See http://www2.cpdl.org/wiki/index.php/Psalm_111.
[161] See https://www.albani-psalter.de/stalbanspsalter/english/commentary/page300.shtml.

a throne holding an empty book which probably represents the covenant. He points to the words written in Latin in the right-hand margin above the first words of the psalm: 'He has sent redemption to his people, he commanded his covenant for ever'. On David's right is a tonsured priest, vested for mass and holding a chalice: he has already given food to those who fear him. Christ on the far left is similarly tonsured and vested, his hands sharing the chalice and blessing with the priest. This accords again with the use of 111:3–4 as a communion prayer.

Thus far we have focussed on the *message* of the psalm. We end with two examples which seek to convey the acrostic format outside the Hebrew medium. Mary *Sidney's sixteenth century translation focusses on the brevity and simplicity of the psalm. The first lines of the revised version read:[162]

> At home abroad, most willingly I will
> Bestow on God my praise's utmost skill:
> Chanting his works, works of the unmatchèd might,
> Deemed so by them, who in tier search delight.
> Endless the honour to his pow'r pertains,
> From end as far his justice eke remains…

Gordon Jackson's version, published in 1997, makes more changes to the syntax in order to create his own alphabetical structure:[163]

> All that I am I offer in praise of the Lord,
> Being in the band of the blessed, all good men and true.
> Can we give adequate, accurate praise of his works?
> Dearer and dearer he is to us, as we consider them.
> Exalt him as much as we may he is always more worthy
> For the meters of mortals are useless to measure his good with…

Finally, the phrase 'the fear of the Lord is the beginning of Wisdom' in verse 10 (found particularly in wisdom literature) is often used in English heraldry, particularly for educational institutions. It is the motto, for example, of Aberdeen University, and of several High Schools for Girls, such as those in Hull, Sutherland and St. Albans, encapsulating in brief the considered teaching of this psalm.[164] Ultimately, compared with its neighbour, Psalm 110, this is an

---

[162] Hamlin 2009: 217.
[163] Jackson 1997: 28.
[164] See Huxley 1949: 301.

innocent psalm, creating little controversy, used widely mainly because of its universal, didactic message.

Psalm 112: An Acrostic Psalm Concerning Human Righteousness

We have already noted the shared linguistic correspondences between Psalms 111 and 112, as well as their similar acrostic forms.[165] Indeed, the last verse of 111 ('The *fear of the LORD* is the beginning of *wisdom*; all those who practice it have a *good understanding*. His *praise* endures forever') has a counterpart in Psalm 112:1: '*Praise* the LORD! Happy are those who *fear the LORD*, who greatly delight in his *commandments*.' So it is not surprising that the two psalms share a similar reception history. Psalm 112 places more emphasis on the human response to God's righteousness, and its *ashre* formula ('Blessed is …') at the beginning places it close to the Torah Psalms 1 and 119 (cf. 1:1 and 119:1–2), and the acrostic forms link the two psalms with Psalm 119, when many of the terms used in 112 are also found in 119.[166] It is quite possible that this psalm influenced Psalms 1 and 119, although the *ashre* formula also occurs in other non-Torah Psalms (for example, 2:12; 32:1,2 and 33:12 and 34:8; 40:4 and 41:1; 84:4 and 84:5; 94:12; 106:3; 127:1 and 128:1; 144:15 and 146:5). So, given that this formula occurs frequently in neighbouring psalms, it is odd that Psalm 111 does not share it too: it would appear that the compilers placed the pair together intentionally, but they are also quite different. One of the key issues in the reception history of Psalm 112 is the importance of generous giving, a theme completely absent from Psalm 111 (but one very much developed in, for example, Psalms 15 and 36 and the proverbial literature, for example in Prov. 11:24; 21:26 and 25:21).[167]

Like Psalm 111, some themes from 112 appear in the *Wisdom of Solomon, not least verse 3 in Wisd. 1:12, concerning the unusual expression about human righteousness enduring forever, and verse 6, on the same theme, which is found in Wisd. 4:1. Also like Psalm 111, some Greek versions add, after the Alleluia, 'Of the Return of Haggai and Zechariah', again indicating this is a later psalm, being paired with its neighbour. Unlike Psalm 111, 112 does occur at *Qumran, albeit in a fragmentary form of which one example is just five words and four partial words (in 4QPs^b, whose fragments span Psalms 76–130). Here it seems that Psalm 112 follows 102. In the *Targum*, the acrostic form is lost in

---

[165] See pp. 193–94.
[166] See Zakovitch 2010: 218–20.
[167] See Gillingham 2017: 102–105 and 218–20 on generous giving in Psalms 15 and 36 respectively.

the Aramaic, as with 111; more is made of the Torah, as for example in verse 2 ('His descendants will be mighty in the land') which is changed to 'mighty in the Law'. In verse 5, the one who conducts his affairs with justice is now, in *Targum*, the one who 'supports his words with *halakah*' (i.e. teaching and instruction). Hence the result is a more Torah-orientated reading of the psalm.

Interestingly rabbinic commentators note that implicitly Abraham is the model of Torah piety, citing Gen. 26:5. Verse 2 is also read in the context of Abraham's obedience and his willingness to sacrifice Isaac in Genesis 22.[168] Little is made of Moses; Abraham is the recipient of the blessing of God (112:1: see Gen. 12:3, 18:18, for example, although a different word for 'blessing' is used here) and Abraham is the model of the one who 'fears' God (112:1: see Gen. 22:12) and Abraham is the one first given a promise of the land (112:2: Gen. 12:1–3). It is interesting to see how the interest in Abraham links Psalm 112 back to Psalm 110 in this respect.

The New Testament alludes to this psalm in just two ways. The first is the way that the same ethos is shared in the Beatitudes. For example, in Matt. 5:5 'Blessings' are also offered in terms of food, drink and clothing (see 112:3, 9). The second is the theme of the generous giver: it is possible that verse 9 is alluded to in 1 Cor. 9:9: (As it is written, 'He scatters abroad, he gives to the poor; his righteousness endures forever.'). This concerns the taking of the collection to the poor in Jerusalem and Judea, and here the reference to the righteous giver 'enduring forever' and the principle of blessings conferred upon those who are generous is endorsed—as in Psalm 112.[169]

The Church Fathers use this psalm mainly in relation to generous giving. *Clement of Alexandria adapts it in this way: he argues from the psalm that he who retains his wealth is not wealthy, but he who gives discovers that true wealth is in the soul.[170] In a sermon for the Feast of St. Andrew, *Gregory the Great uses this psalm in the context of Christ as the model for the just man, using verse 10 alongside Matt. 8:12, 13:41 and 24:50.[171]

*Luther's approach to Psalm 112 is less pragmatic and more theological. His concern with the teaching is about the 'deeds of the righteous man' enduring forever, as in verse 3; this, Luther notes, is about a prophecy awaiting fulfilment, as righteousness cannot be achieved fully before the time of Christ. Nevertheless, Luther argues that this psalm is a Jewish pre-Christian model upon which the Christian faith is built.[172]

---

[168] See Braude 1959: 210–11.
[169] See Williams 2004: 176–79; Witherington 2017: 112; Böhm 2017: 156–60.
[170] Sermon in *Christ the Educator* 3.6.35 in FC 23:228–29, as in *ACCS Vol* VIII: 273.
[171] De Solms 2001: 541.
[172] German 2017: 138–43.

In Jewish liturgy the psalm is used on the occasion of making collections for hospitals, again taking up its theme of generous giving. The Christian teaching about Christ as the model of generous service has some continuity here, and probably lies behind 112:1–3 being used as a Christmas *antiphon.

The liturgical use of this Psalm in the *Benedictine tradition as one of five psalms sung at *Vespers has resulted in a number of musical compositions, all of them based on the first verse concerning 'the fear of the Lord' rather than generous giving.[173] Some of the earliest are the well-known settings by Luis de *Victoria composed in about 1582 as part of a group of ten Vespers psalms.[174] In 1630 *Monteverdi completed his motet 'Beatus Vir' for soloists and a six-part chorus, with organ, *basso continuo*, and two obligato violins, borrowing music from his duet '*Chiome d'oro*' published in a book of madrigals in 1619: 'Beatus Vir' is a piece known for its repeated Glorias and its final amen.[175] Monteverdi composed another version in 1650 as part of a work for Vespers; this therefore also included Psalms 110, 111, 113 and 117. *Vivaldi composed several settings of 'Beatus Vir', two of which (from 1713 and 1719) are well known.[176] *Mozart's 1779 *Vesperae de Dominica*, referred to earlier, also included 'Beatus Vir' as one of five psalms.[177] His 1780 *Vesperae Solennes de Confessore* has yet another version of 'Beatus Vir'.[178] *Haydn similarly composed two versions in Latin, each known as 'Beatus Vir', as gradual psalms: one was composed in 1782, and the other in 1785, both for *SATB and using a variety of woodwind, brass and stringed instruments with organ.[179] Henry *Purcell composed a metrical version in English: 'O happy man that fears The Lord' was written in about 1688 for *basso continuo* and SATB, one of his several psalms composed beginning with 'O happy man' (the others include Psalms 128, 144, 41 and 32). *Mendelssohn also used verses 1 and 4 in his *Elijah*, first performed in 1846. Part One, after Elijah's raising a widow's son from the dead, is entitled 'Blessed are the men who fear him'.[180] The first verse of this psalm starts in the same way as Psalm 1, which has several Jewish compositions;[181] it is surprising that the only notable Jewish version of Psalm 112 is by Salamone *Rossi, entitled 'Halleluyah Ashre 'ish', written in Venice in 1622.[182]

---

[173] A range of compositions can be seen at http://www2.cpdl.org/wiki/index.php/Psalm_112.

[174] See https://imslp.org/wiki/10_Vespers_Psalms_(Victoria%2C_Tom%C3%A1s_Luis_de).

[175] See Dowling Long and Sawyer 2015: 27.

[176] See https://www.youtube.com/watch?v=Fs_vbS_bLUc.

[177] See Dowling Long and Sawyer 2015: 254.

[178] See Dowling Long and Sawyer 2015: 254–55.

[179] All of these are not to be confused with Latin arrangements of Psalm 1, also entitled 'Beatus Vir'. See Gillingham 2018: 22–24.

[180] Stern 2011: 264.

[181] See Gillingham 2018: 22.

[182] See https://www.youtube.com/watch?v=j-7klA6wr-Q.

If much of the music was inspired by the use of Psalm 112 in liturgy, much of the art was inspired more by the commentary tradition, based on the theme of giving generously. In Jewish tradition the generous giver is often dressed as a rabbi, and in Christian tradition, as a monk. A notable example is in the *Parma Psalter* (fol. 163r), which shows a figure in a prayer shawl with ritual tassels, holding a book on which are written the words, in Hebrew, 'Master of all worlds'. This illustrates 112:1, on the rewards for fearing the Lord and delighting in his commandments; the verse is in part enclosed by this image.[183] The *Khuldov Psalter* (fol. 116r) presents the image of verse 9 as Charity in monkish habit: there are clear similarities with the image of Ps. 37:36 (fol. 35r) here.[184] The related *Theodore Psalter* has a similar image on fol. 153v, where the rich man is again wearing monkish dress.[185]

In terms of the appropriation of the acrostic *form* of the psalm, in addition to its message, two examples must suffice. One is from an early English metrical version preserved in the eleventh/twelfth-century *Paris Psalter* (fols. 133v–134v). Francis Leneghan writes of the way this psalm has been presented to create a conscious aural patterning, with an emphasis on alliteration despite the loss of the acrostic form, a feature which is not found in the Latin.[186] Ps. 112:5, for example, reads in Latin '*iucundus homo qui miseratur et commodat disponet sermons suos in iudicio*' ('It is well with those who deal generously and lend, who conduct their affairs with justice.'). The *Paris Psalter* reads: 'Glæd man gleaw-*hy*dig, god and mildheort, seteð soðne dom þurh his sylfes word': here one sees not only the alliteration (the repetition of the 'gl'/'g' and the 's') but also the emphasis on letters taken from the Latin (the 'm' and the 's'). According to Francis Leneghan, the sophisticated plays on aurality enabled an easier recall by memory, producing a model of metrical psalmody that long pre-dated the psalmody of the Reformation with its greater emphasis on rhythm and rhyme. So the acrostic form is replaced by different aural plays on words and sense.

The sixteenth century saw not only the development of metrical psalmody with a memorability based on rhythm and rhyme, but also greater experimentation in the imitation of the Hebrew forms. Mary *Sidney eschewed any acrostic form, and instead for Psalm 112 focussed less on the beginning of each line and more on the verbal forms in each line of each verse:

---

[183] See Metzger 1996: 91.

[184] See Corrigan 1992: 128; for Figure 40 on Ps. 37:26 see 253. This was reproduced in Gillingham 2018: Figures 12 and 13.

[185] http://www.bl.uk/manuscripts/Viewer.aspx?ref=add_ms_19352_fl10r#.

[186] Leneghan 2017: 186–92 and 194–7. Leneghan analyses the whole of Psalm 112 in this way.

> Oh, in how blessed state he standeth,
> Who so Jehovah feareth,
> That in the things the Lord commandeth
> His most delight appeareth!...
>
> He is both good and goodness loveth,
> Most liberal and lending:
> All business wherein he moveth
> With sound advice attending.[187]

Hence whether through the message or the medium of the message, the didactic and universal purpose of this psalm, like that of Psalm 111, could not be more clear: its application in this psalm, whether in a Jewish or Christian context, is that God loves a cheerful giver.

---

[187] See Hamlin *et al.* 2009: 218.

Psalms 113–118: A Liturgical Collection (i)

In Jewish tradition Psalms 113–118, apparently purposefully set between Pss. 112:1 and 119:1 which both begin with *ashre* ('happy is …'), are all linked together because of their liturgical use (and parts of this collection are similarly linked together liturgically in Christian tradition as well). The call to praise, 'Hallelu-jah', is found in the Hebrew text at the beginning and end of Psalms 113 and 117, and at the end of Psalms 115 and 116, and the dominance of this term resulted in this collection being known as the 'Hallel'. (Psalm 114 itself has no Hallelujah in the Hebrew, and so initially stands outside this collection, and Psalm 118 is also different in that its beginning and ending, 'O give thanks to the Lord, for he is good' link it to Ps. 107:1 at the beginning of Book Five, and Ps. 136:1, which is known as the 'Great Hallel'.[188]) The collection consists of six psalms overall: this corresponds with the six Hallel psalms in 145–150 which praise God as Creator. The Hallel in 113–118 is usually termed the 'Egyptian Hallel', mainly on account of Psalm 114 with its theme of Israel leaving Egypt (verse 1), although the specific exodus theme actually only occurs in this one psalm.

The link between the Hallel and Passover is found in the *Haggadah (see for example, *Tosefta Pesaḥim 10:9*), where the whole collection is read on Passover eve (14 Nisan) and on the first day of Passover (15 Nisan). This tradition is also referred to in *Mishnah Pesaḥim* 115b and 116b. When the Festival was cele-brated when the Temple was still standing, it seems that the Levites were those who sang the entire collection (*Tosefta Pesaḥim 3:11*).[189]

---

[188] See pp. 347–48.

[189] See G.F. Willems, *BTFT* 51: 397–417, especially pp. 406–7.

Psalms Through the Centuries: A Reception History Commentary on Psalms 73–151, Volume Three, First Edition. Susan Gillingham.
© 2022 John Wiley & Sons Ltd. Published 2022 by John Wiley & Sons Ltd.

Tosefta Sukkah 3:2 refers to the Hallel also being used at the Feast of Booths (*Sukkot), and *Mishnah Sukkah* 3:9 and 4:1 again shows the role of the Levitical Singers in the Temple liturgy when the collection was sung every day during the eight-day festival. Similarly the Hallel was sung on each of the eight days of Hanukkah.[190] In the Babylonian *Talmud b.Arachin* 10a–10b we read that the first cup of wine accompanied the *Kiddush, the Grace after Meals was said after the third cup, so that the first part of the Hallel (Psalms 113–114) was sung over the second cup, and the second part of the Hallel (Psalms 115–118) over the fourth cup. Significantly the Hallel is not used on *Rosh Hashanah or *Yom Kippur, where the theme is more of repentance than rejoicing. Nor is it used at *Purim, partly because it contains its own hymn of praise, but mainly because the context is one of foreign rule. In contemporary Jewish tradition the Hallel is cited on Independence Day and Jerusalem Day, again because of its associations with the birth of the Jewish people out of the waters of Egypt.

In terms of the Christian liturgical reception history of this group of psalms, in the Roman Catholic and Anglican tradition they are used at the 'Watch' at the beginning of Maundy Thursday, when the Triduum—the three days of services leading up to Easter Sunday—starts. Readings from each psalm are interspersed with readings from John 13–17, creating a new Easter narrative. In the *Benedictine Rule Psalms 113–117 were read in sequence on Sunday and Monday *Vespers; this practice probably influenced the choice of some of them (110, 111, 112, 113 and 117 [EV]) for the Feast of Confessors and Martyrs. *Mozart's *Vesperae de Dominica*, performed in Salzburg in 1779, is one example of this.[191] The Vespers of our Lady also used five psalms, usually sung on the day before the Feast, but only one is taken from this collection. Typically they were 110, 113; 122; 127 and 147:12–20 (all EV numbering). This is what is used in Monteverdi's *Vespro della Beata Vergine*, composed in 1610 in Mantua.[192] *Handel's *Carmelite Vespers*, performed first in Rome in 1707, to celebrate the feast of Our Lady of Mount Carmel in Santa Maria di Monte Santo, is another example. Hence Christian tradition plays fast and loose with this collection, contrasted with Jewish liturgical practice which preserves them as a whole.

Psalm 113: God Elevates the Poor

Psalm 113 is a well-structured hymn in three sections: verses 1–3 praise the name of the Lord, verses 4–6 focus on his nature, and verses 7–9 focus on his

[190] *Ibid.*, 417.
[191] See Harper 1991: 159–61; also https://www.youtube.com/watch?v=jPOHTkX8qzU.
[192] See https://www.youtube.com/watch?v=3aX7eE1b_OY.

deeds. This links it both to Psalm 111, on the character of God, and to Psalm 112, which is about the righteous being compassionate to the downtrodden, whereas in Psalm 113 it is about God elevating the downtrodden and poor. The Hallelujahs at Pss. 111:1, 112:1 and 113:1 (as well as 113:9) also link these psalms together. There are also associations with 115, concerning praise of 'the name' of Yahweh (113:1–3, 4 and 115:1); the phrase 'heaven and earth' (113:6 and 115:15); the references to 'praise and bless' (113:2–3 and 115:17–18); and the phrase 'from this time on and for evermore' (in 113:2 and 115:18). In addition, the explicit critique of idols in 115:2–8 is implicit in 113:4–6. This suggests again that Psalm 114, with its specific exodus theme, and its lack of Hallelujah in the Hebrew, once stood outside this sequence.[193] Finally, the links between Psalm 113 and 118 on God's sovereignty over the nations (113:4 and 118:10–12) and the reversing of the fortunes of the lowly and rejected (113:7–9 and 118:22–24)—themes found only in these two Hallel psalms—illustrate the thematic concerns of those who created this collection, stressing at the beginning and end of it God's transcendence over all things. Hence the reception history of Psalm 113 starts with its reception into the collection as a whole.

Much has been made of the verbal and semantic links between Psalm 113 and the Song of Hannah in 1 Samuel 2. Ps. 113:7–9 speaks of raising the poor from the dust and lifting the needy from the ash heap, and making them sit with princes; so too does 1 Sam. 2:8. The reference to the barren woman ('*aqarah*) in 113:9 is also in 1 Sam. 2:5.[194] The shared interest is the reversing of the fortunes of the poor; the key difference is that 1 Samuel 2 is a thanksgiving psalm sung by Hannah herself, whilst Psalm 113 appears to be more a hymn sung by the entire congregation, whereby the 'barren woman' becomes a type for the whole people once enslaved in Egypt, or even, as in exilic thinking, a type for the restoration of Zion (see Isa. 54:1 and 66:8), whose restored fortunes are often referred to as a personified woman.[195] A link between Psalms 113 and the exodus tradition in 114 is in reading 'servants of the Lord' in 113:1 as referring to Israel's status as 'slaves' under Pharaoh, so that the imagery of raising the poor from the dust anticipates the escape from slavery in Egypt made more explicit in 114.

Verse 9 ('He gives the barren woman a home, making her the joyous mother of children') offers a problem of translation, whereby the definite article in Hebrew before 'home' is omitted in both the Greek and the Latin, so that this becomes a more universalised reading referring to 'any woman' and 'any home'. *Targum*, applying this to the people as a whole, waiting for fulfilment before

---

[193] The *LXX* actually places the Alleluia from the end of Psalm 113 at the beginning of Psalm 114.
[194] See Willis 1973: 139–54.
[195] See Cohen 1992: 378.

a period of pain and uncertainty, applies the verse to the community so that it reads 'Making the assembly of Israel to be like the barren woman, anxious in relation to the men of her house...'[196]

The New Testament makes two allusions to this psalm, both in the Gospels. Firstly, the theme of the barren woman is used in a different way, applying this now to the virginity of Mary and the miraculous conception. The imagery in 113:7, on the raising up of the lowly, and in 113:9, on the barren woman rejoicing over her children, is alluded to in Luke 1:48–49 ('for he has looked with favour on the lowliness of his servant ...'). This is no more than an allusion, but the use of 107:9 in Luke 1:53 and of 111:9 in Luke 1:68–79 does suggest that Luke had some of these psalms in mind.[197] The second allusion to Psalm 113 is in the celebration of the Jewish Passover during the Passion of Christ. If indeed Psalm 113 (and 114) was sung before the Passover itself, then these two psalms would to later Christians be portents of the death and resurrection of Jesus.[198]

Several Church Fathers read the psalm through the Passion of Christ, and from this, the martyrs of the church: *Ambrose, for example, uses the psalm to speak of how one cannot gain Christ until one experiences the hardship and suffering expressed in this psalm.[199] *Augustine, too, reads the essential message of the psalm as about humility and the need to submit to the yoke of Christ.[200] *Chrysostom focusses on verse 9 and the identity of the barren woman: citing Isa. 54:1, he sees this to be about the Church as once a barren mother, but now bringing forth many children.[201] In his commentary on Psalm 51, *Gregory the Great uses the phrase in 113:7 ('naked on a dung heap', also in Job 2:8) as a cry of penitence from one gravely ill by the wounds of sin: this leads back into Gregory's commentary on Psalm 51.[202]

The use of this psalm in Jewish liturgy has already been outlined with reference to the collection as a whole. Its later use at Christian Sunday *Vespers has also been made clear. A further unsurprising use is as a *Proper at Easter, partly imitating the Jewish use at Passover and partly on account of the commentary tradition associating it with the sufferings of Christ.

---

[196] See Stec 2004: 205.

[197] See p. 166 (Ps. 107:9 / Lk. 1:53) and p. 194 (Ps. 111:9 / Lk. 1:49, 68).

[198] Noting that Mk. 14:26 and Matt. 26:30 refers to the meal ending with 'a hymn' before the journey to Gethsemane, which might allude to the use of Psalms 115–118 *after* the meal. See p. 237 (on Psalm 118).

[199] See *Letter 61* FC 26:378, in *ACCS* VIII: 276–77.

[200] Hegbin and Corrigan 1960: 563–64.

[201] Chrysostom trans. Hill 1998: 73.

[202] See *PL* 79.582–83, quoted in Caruthers 2001: 216–18.

This psalm's reception has flourished in art and music. It is one of the first psalms to be illustrated in Jewish Prayer Books for Passover. One example is the *Prato *Haggadah*, a Spanish Sephardic prayer book dating from about 1300, with silver and gold leaf embellished with reds and blues: fol. 33r illustrates the opening 'Hallelujah!' to Psalm 113, the psalm to be sung at the beginning of the Passover meal, with birds and animals coming out of the two letter *Lameds* (l) in 'Hallelujah'.[203] Another example is the *Barcelona Haggadah*, preserved at the British Library, dating from between 1250 and 1350 and also from Spain: here the 'Hallelujah' of Psalm 113 is illustrated with a synagogue scene of the celebration of Passover. This image is presented as PLATE 17 here. The *Oppenheimer *Siddur* (Bodleian Ms. Opp. 776), an *Ashkenazi prayer book from the fifteenth-century, has a colourful tapestry image around the 'Hallelujah' of Psalm 113 on fol. 45v: two dragons are fighting a lion which is being attacked from behind by a bear.[204] A more unusual and contemporary version is by the Jewish artist, *Benn, whose illustration in 1953 of verse 3 ('From the rising of the sun to its setting the name of the LORD is to be praised') depicts God's glory radiating from heaven to cover the earth in a warm embrace. The presence of God is symbolised by two Hebrew letter *Yod's*.[205]

Christian imagery, taking its lead from the commentary tradition and from liturgical use, looks at the psalm through the trope of the raising up of the poor and lowly. The *Utrecht Psalter* (fol. 66r) depicts an angel helping a poor man 'out of the dust' (verse 7) to help him to sit on an empty seat in the middle of the scene where 'princes' sit. Below the chair is the 'barren woman' who has become 'a joyful mother of children' (verse 9). Christ sits in the heavens within a *mandorla, attended by six angels and by personifications of the sun and moon (verse 3). He is the one who now looks down on the low things in heaven and in earth in order to raise them up (verse 6).[206] The *Theodore Psalter* (fol. 154r) also focusses on the lowly being raised from the dust: using verse 7 alongside Job 2:8, the figure is Job, on his ash pile, with his wife offering him food in a gourd on a stick. Christ in an arch of heaven again surveys the scene.[207]

Perhaps one of the most unusual artistic depictions is in the fifteenth-century *Isabella Breviary* (BL Add. Ms.18851), fol. 354r.[208] Psalm 113 is one of the psalms used at the Vespers of our Lady, so it not surprising that the scene is of the Annunciation. Behind her is a *Tree of Jesse: with verse 9 and the Magnifi-

[203] See https://bit.ly/3wKpN3Z.
[204] See https://bit.ly/3sb2ooU.
[205] See Markus 2015: 275; Benn 1970: no page numbers; also https://www.artofbenn.com/biblicalimages.
[206] See https://psalter.library.uu.nl/page/139.
[207] See http://www.bl.uk/manuscripts/Viewer.aspx?ref=add_ms_19352_f154r.
[208] See Backhouse 1993: 51.

cat ('Song of Mary') as the interpretative lens, and Mary is the 'barren woman' who will give birth to a son. He comes from the line of David, and so here too we also have hints not only of David and Jesse but also of Samuel who anointed David as King, and so further back still to Hannah, mother of Samuel, and so to her psalm, in 1 Sam 2, very like the ethos of Psalm 113.[209]

Not surprisingly many Christian arrangements of this psalm have been for the Vespers Liturgy. Psalm 113 is used in Sunday Vespers, at the Vespers of Our Lady, and at the Vespers of the Apostles, Evangelists, Martyrs and Confessors—so it is a much used psalm.[210] We have already referred to works on Vespers psalms by Luis de *Victoria (1582), *Monteverdi (1630 and 1650), *Vivaldi (1713 and 1719) and *Mozart (1779 and 1780) where Psalm 113 always plays a part.[211]

Of Psalm 113 in Vespers collections two compositions stand out. One is in *Monterverdi's Vespers (1610), performed first in Venice and a major influence on Baroque style. Psalm 113 (*Laudate pueri*) is the fourth of thirteen parts, preceded by a versicle and response from Ps. 70:1, then Psalm 110, and then a passage from Song of Songs. In Psalm 113 the two choirs of four voices create a polychoral form of *Gregorian *plainchant: the bassline was originally provided by the organ.[212] The second composition of Psalm 113 is found in *Vivaldi's Vespers for the Virgin, probably also composed in Venice over a century later, and lasting twenty-four minutes. Vivaldi used soprano flute, two oboes, strings and continuo, in some places imitating the cantata form of J.S. *Bach, but with huge variety of melodic and metric and rhythmic details. Psalm 113 is treated as art music—its tempo and mood create a multi-faceted melody underscored with a volatile bass. Verse 1 is set in brisk tempo, in G major; verse 2 is in E Minor and more introspective; verse 3 portrays the rising sun in slow ascending line to the key of D major; verse 4 develops the theme of the Glory of the Lord in a quieter and majestic way, including some folk dance. Verse 7, on the theme of rescuing the poor and needy, is set in more agitated style, with vocal leaps and long-short-long rhythms on strings. Verses 8–9, which are about the poor raised to sit with princes, are in C Major and combine dignity with joy, so that the whole psalm is presented as a 'dance of life'.[213]

Two other works which are also well-known are Christopher *Tye's 'Praise the Lord ye children' (c. 1560–90) and *Handel's 'Laudate Pueri', part of his so-called Carmelite Vespers for the Virgin (1707) performed in Rome, along

---

[209] See https://www.moleiro.com/en/books-of-hours/the-isabella-breviary/miniatura/863.
[210] The list is extensive in http://www2.cpdl.org/wiki/index.php/Psalm_113.
[211] See Psalm 112, p. xxx.
[212] See Stern 2013: 110–15; also https://www.youtube.com/watch?v=m_qWg0dZRW4 (with score).
[213] Stern 2013: 99–109.

with Psalms 110 and 127.[214] Handel's work influenced the English composer John Christopher Smith (1712–1795) whose oratorio 'Gideon' in 1769 included works on Psalms 110 and 113.[215]

In addition to works influenced by Vespers liturgy, two other arrangements stand out because they are both by women, some eight hundred years apart, and are appropriate because one theme in the psalm is the raising up of women. The Benedictine Abbess and mystic Hildegard of Bingen (c.1098–1179) composed 'Benedictus es domine' from a Latin version of verse 2: it is an evocative and haunting interpretation of the praise of God at the start of this psalm: coming from the early twelfth-century it may well have been influenced by the Vespers of our Lady.[216] The South African/French composer, Pat Berning, offers an interpretation of verses 5–9 which dates from 2000; it focusses on the theme of social justice in the psalm and combines South African, Swiss and French influences.[217]

It is interesting that despite the use of Psalms 113–118 in liturgy, there is a limited number of Jewish compositions of this psalm until the twentieth-century. One Jewish composition stands out: this is by the Canadian singer and songwriter Leonard Cohen (1934–2016), whose version of Psalms 113–118 was originally published in his *Book of Mercy* (1984) and later released on a studio album called *Various Positions* (1984). Cohen takes the word 'Hallelujah' and develops the theme that unlike David his mystical harp could never please his lover. This is a love story which also takes in Bathsheba and Delilah, but the evocative defining word of the Hallel, Hallelujah, has here become the evocative defining word in quite a different composition.[218]

What to make of a psalm which semantically is so simple but nevertheless is so rich in reception, in part due to its role in Jewish and Christian liturgy? The poem by David Slavitt, published in 1996, which is a summary of the entire psalm is most appropriate here.[219]

> Praise the Lord! Oh, praise
> His name and His righteous ways.
> Now and forevermore,
> from first light to nightfall
> let us praise the Lord and adore
> Him who is ruler of all.

---

[214] Dowling Long and Sawyer (2015): 199.
[215] See p. 191.
[216] See https://gloria.tv/video/LE1QrMxDj1WU49bKjuyW6ZPsg.
[217] See https://patberning.bandcamp.com/album/psaumes.
[218] Dowling Long and Sawyer 2015: 97.
[219] Slavitt 1996: 96.

> To whom shall we liken our
> God who presides in the sky,
> raising the weak and the poor
> to seat them in glory by
> the sides of great princes and kings?
>
> To the barren woman, He gives
> children, a home—and she lives
> in comfort the rest of her days.
> For His works the universe sings
> to the Lord, in prayers of praise.

The distinctive contribution of Psalm 113 in terms of reception history is in part liturgical, because it is used in such different but complementary ways in both Jewish and Christian tradition. But in addition, its differences revolve around the identity given to the 'barren woman'. In Jewish tradition, this is a minor concern, and indeed can be a symbol of hope for personified Israel; whereas in Christian tradition, it is a major concern, because that woman is the mother of Jesus Christ.

Psalm 114: A Passover Psalm

One of the greatest issues in the reception history of Psalm 114 is to know whether to read it and Psalm 115 as one single unit, rather like Psalms 9–10 (although these are easier to understand on account of their shared acrostic form and similar themes).[220] Only in later Jewish tradition in the late Middle Ages are 114 and 115 independent psalms, partly because Psalm 115:1–11 was omitted from Passover liturgy to prevent too much rejoicing over the enemy. The *LXX, following the *MT, unites them (thus making the numbering of this psalm with the next one, in the Greek, Ps. 113:1–26). The Greek removed the 'Alleluia' from the end of Psalm 113 (where it is in the Hebrew) and placed it at the beginning of Psalm 114, thus making Psalms 111–114 each start with Alleluia. Psalm 115 had no such Alleluia; so it was combined with Psalm 114, with the odd consequence that the Greek then split up Psalm 116 (EV).[221] The Alleluia at the end of the previous psalm is now at the beginning of Psalm 116, and the second half, Ps. 116:10–19 (EV), was given an introductory Alleluia.[222] The *Vulgate also unites Psalms 114 and 115, as does the *Peshitta, as well as the tenth-century Aleppo Codex and the eleventh-century Leningrad Codex. But in Hebrew liturgy from the fourteenth-century onwards, Psalms 113–118

---

[220] See Gillingham 2017: 83–89 which comments on Psalms 9–10 as one unit.

[221] See p. 223.

[222] It is interesting that *Augustine, and before him *Origen, split Psalm 114 /115 in yet another way, so that Psalm 114+115:1–3 is Psalm 113 (using the Greek and Latin numbering) whilst Ps. 115:4–18 is 114, and 116 is not divided.

stand as separate psalms within one unit (although Psalms 117 and 118 have been combined in at least one Hebrew tradition).[223]

Despite this complicated reception history, because the content of Psalms 114 and 115 is very different, we will look at them as separate psalms. The links between 113 and 115 suggest that 114, the only psalm in the Hallel to have specific references to the Exodus, came from a different provenance, and perhaps was added later to Psalms 113–117, with Psalm 118 completing the collection.[224] If this is the case, it is Psalm 114 which has created the direct associations of this whole collection with the Exodus and hence the Passover. The psalm suggests four strophes. Verses 1–2 are a summary of Israel's origins, linking together the early exodus tradition of Israel in Egypt with that of Judah as God's sanctuary (i.e. Jerusalem). Verses 3 and 4 link together the two traditions of the crossing of the sea (from Exodus 14–15) and the crossing of the river Jordan upon the entry into the land (from Joshua 3–4). The personification of the mountain and hills rejoicing is typical of hymns of praise from the exile, as seen in Psalms 96:11–12, 98:7–8, and in Isa. 42:10–12, 44:23, 51:3 and 55:12–13. Verses 5–6 repeat verses 3–4 in question form. Verses 7–8 call on the earth to join in the dance of creation, using the same exilic motif. This is a compressed psalm: it uses Israel's own 'historical' traditions (with hints of Exodus, Sinai, Kadesh, the Monarchy, the fall of the north and the exile) alongside ancient Near Eastern mythological theophany traditions, especially those of the Canaanite myth of Baal's Victory over Prince River and Judge Sea, and the combat with chaotic waters. With a compression of so many traditions, it is likely to be a late psalm. The clear bicola and parallelism suggest it was created as a liturgical composition, applying the traditions about the escape from Egypt to the experience of the exile (see, for example, Isa. 41:8), reminiscent of what we saw in Book Four.[225]

One of the key issues in later reception is the discussion of the primacy of Judah in the traditions of the birth of Israel, and the meaning of the phrase 'the sea fled' (verse 3).[226] Commentators such as *Rashi argued that it was impossible that at the Exodus the tribe of Judah could have been chosen as the territory for the site of the Temple. Rashi then cites the *midrashic tradition which explains the reference to the 'sea fleeing' was on account of the infighting among the tribes, who each sought to demonstrate their great faith, and so inherit the best territory, by leaping into the water first; the contest was especially fierce between Judah and Benjamin, who threw stones to see who

---

[223] See *b.Berakhot 9b–10a*.
[224] See p. 231.
[225] See pp. 79–81.
[226] See Cohen 1992: 380.

could hurl furthest, and Judah succeeded in being given Jerusalem (and David's dynasty), and Benjamin was given Shiloh (and Saul's dynasty).[227] A more sanguine explanation of the 'sea fleeing' is that this is one of God's ten miracles of the sea (which included making the waters into a heap, flattening the seas, producing sweet water from salt water, and turning the sea into a dry valley) and here it 'fled' because it had seen Joseph's casket bearing his body out of Egypt.[228] Other commentators, preferring to emphasise that this psalm is about a new act of creation, explained that the reference to the mountains is about the giving of the law on Sinai, in addition to the escape from the sea, for Torah marks the climax of God's work in creation.[229] In Jewish reception, the common theme, nevertheless, is that Psalm 114 contains an aetiology for the primacy of Judah from early times.

The Christian commentary tradition takes up some of the same issues and gives them a different interpretation. 'The sea looked and fled' is now a reference to Jesus calming the storm, for example in Mark 4:39 ('He woke up and rebuked the wind, and said to the sea, "Peace! Be still!" Then the wind ceased, and there was a dead calm'). This expression later became an allegory, along with the references to the dancing mountains and hills, of the death and resurrection of Jesus, explaining the meaning of the term (with an eye to the use of this psalm in Jewish liturgy) of 1 Cor 5:7: '*Christ our Passover* is sacrificed for us'.[230] The early church read the two references to the river Jordan as about the waters of baptism: for example, 'Jordan turned back' was about the mysteries of salvation through water, whereby infants baptised at the beginning of their life and are 'turned back' from their state of original sin.[231] Commentators such as John *Chrysostom read the psalm not as about the birth of Israel and Judah, but actually about the obstinacy of the Jews, whose privileged status was a prelude to their infidelity.[232] *Augustine, however, reads the psalm through the Abrahamic covenant and thus as about Jews and Christians being from the same fold.[233]

In Christian liturgical reception, because the Greek and Latin texts are paramount, the liturgical use of 'In exitu Israhel de Aegypto' (Ps. 114:1) also includes part or whole of Psalm 115 (EV). This is why, for example, Psalm 114 (in Latin, Psalm 113) is used at burials for the commendation of the soul: there

---

[227] See Gruber 2004: 62. See also Gillingham 2017: 368, 371–72 on the place of Benjamin in Ps. 68:27.

[228] See Braude 1959: 219–220.

[229] See Feuer 2004: 1369.

[230] See Hill 1973: 111.

[231] This is from Ambrose in *On His Brother Satyrus* 2.74: see NPNF 2 10:185–86, as in *ACCS* VIII:279. See also Augustine in *Against Julian* 1.3.10, in FC 35:10, as in *ACCS* VIII:279.

[232] See Chrysostom trans. Hill 1998: 76, also citing Jer. 2:31.

[233] Augustine trans. Uyl 2017: 565–66.

is nothing in Psalm 114 (EV) to suggest this, but Psalm 115:17 ('The dead do not praise the LORD, nor do any that go down into silence') has influenced this particular use.[234] Psalm 114–115 also has a prominent use at *Vespers. As we noted in our discussion at the end of Psalm 112, Psalm 114/115 is mainly used for Sunday Vespers, along with 110–113, and with them 114/115 was included as a *Proper Psalm for Easter Vespers: this has given it a rich musical history of reception.[235] And because of its links with Easter, it was also an important psalm in Baptismal liturgy. Here, the two references to the river Jordan, as well as the liturgical use of this psalm from *Ambrose onwards, show just why Psalm 114/115 had such a prominent place, being sung during the procession of new converts to the threshold of the baptistry on Easter Sunday.

Musical reception of this psalm has a most interesting trajectory. Even in the fifth-century Augustine referred to this psalm, with the singing of Alleluia at the beginning of the Greek/Latin version, as 'an ancient custom of the church'.[236] The simple and clear parallelism in its poetry, even in translation, made this psalm an ideal model for *Gregorian *plainchant, with the many long vowels in the Latin encouraging *melismatic experimentation. By the ninth-century, we know that this 'Fifth Vespers Psalm' was regularly chanted to what later became known as the ninth mode, also the Aeolian mode; here the reciting tone changed from one half verse to the next, and this became known as 'Tonus Peregrinus', a sort of 'wandering tone'. This appellation was somewhat appropriate, given the psalm's contents describing the flight from Egypt. Given the importance of this psalm at both the Passover and Easter liturgies, it is likely that this mode of singing was originally borrowed from synagogue chanting; it is easy to see how the psalm could be used for basic *plainchant.[237] David Mitchell's score of the psalm in Hebrew, offered in Figure 8, illustrates a possible connection between the Hebrew chanting and (for example) Latin plainchant. Indeed, as Mitchell observes, when in the 1950s the musicologist Eric Werner worked on Abraham Idelsohn's earlier recording of the cantillation of Psalm 114, from immigrant cantors of both the *Ashkenazi and Sephardi (western European) traditions, it was not surprising to find similarities between the singing of this psalm in Hebrew and Latin plainchant.[238]

---

[234] See Balas and Bingham 1998: 78.
[235] See p. 203.
[236] See Stern 2013: 9.
[237] See http://llpb.us/MP3Hymns/OTCanticles-Psalms/226%20Ps%20114a.MP3.
[238] See Mitchell 2015: 138–40, on 'Restoring Temple Song', with two scores, one Ashkenazi and one Gregorian, of this psalm.

Psalm 114

FIGURE 8   *Interpretation of singing of Psalm 114 in its earliest setting.*

Reproduced with the kind permission of David Mitchell, Director of Music in Holy Trinity Pro-Cathedral, Brussels; website https://brightmorningstar.org/wp-content/uploads/2020/06/Ps-114.pdf.

Because, like Psalm 113, 114 has had a rich role in liturgy, composers as various as Josquin des Prez, William *Byrd, Heinrich *Schütz, Antonio *Vivaldi, Felix *Mendelssohn and Samuel Sebastian *Wesley have arranged this psalm in a variety of styles and languages: usually the Sunday Vespers plainchant tradition is both acknowledged and reinterpreted.[239] However, alongside these are pieces by, for example, the Dutch composer Jan Pieterszoon *Sweelinck, whose 'Quand Israel hors d'Egypte sortit' belongs to the legacy of French metrical psalmody; and similarly pieces by English composers of metrical psalms, from as early as *Sternhold and Hopkins, and later *Tate and Brady and Isaac *Watts, who each adhere to the simplicity of the poetry, using the rhyme and rhythm of Genevan metrical psalms rather than the plainchant of Rome. Watts' metrical version, below, is particularly interesting because of its contents: it divides the two Exodus and Settlement traditions compressed together in the text and it explicitly brings in the Sinai tradition as well:[240]

> When Isr'el, freed from Pharaoh's hand,
> Left the proud tyrant and his land,
> The tribes with cheerful homage own
> Their king; and Judah was his throne.
>
> Across the deep their journey lay;
> The deep divides to make them way.
> Jordan beheld their march, and led,
> With backward current, to his head.
>
> The mountains shook like frighted sheep,
> Like lambs the little hillocks leap;
> Not Sinai on her base could stand,
> Conscious of sov'reign pow'r at hand...

Although there are several fairly recent Jewish arrangements of this psalm, such as twentieth-century versions by the Israeli composer Yedidiyah Admon-Gorokhov (1894–1982) and by the Polish composer and cantor Moshe Koussevitsky (1899–1966), one of the most interesting contemporary examples of Psalm 114 is by John *Harbison. His *Four Psalms* (1998) was a response to an invitation by the Chicago Symphony Orchestra to compose psalms to commemorate the fiftieth anniversary of the State of Israel. Harbison went to Israel and learnt not only about the sufferings of the Jews but also about the plight of the Palestinians and Bedouins. His version of Psalm 114, as well as his third

---

[239] On Sweelinck's 'Quand Israel hors d'Egypte sortit', which is a very different contribution and part of the legacy of French metrical psalmody, see; Gorali 1993: 199. The range of other examples is evident at http://www2.cpdl.org/wiki/index.php/Psalm_114.

[240] See https://www.poetryfoundation.org/poems/50585/psalm-114.

psalm (137) is an expression of adversity; Psalm 126 is about new hope whilst the final psalm, 133, speaks of unity and peace for all.[241]

Not surprisingly Psalm 114 also has a rich reception history in literature and poetry, in part because of its liturgical prominence, and in part due to its links with Psalm 115, where verse 17 is often cited as an allegory of 'deliverance from hell'. *Dante's *Divine Comedy* is an interesting example of the use of Psalm 114 in the context of Psalm 115. In *Purgatorio* 2:46–48, in the description of the hundred souls escaping the slavery of worldly corruption into the freedom of heavenly glory, the company sings, verse after verse, with one united voice, 'In exitu Israhel de Aegypto': Dante notes 'they made the air rejoice'.[242] In his *Letter to Can Grande, part 7*, Dante explains further his interpretation of this psalm: it is to be read in part literally (about the liberation of the Hebrews), in part allegorically (about Christ's liberation of humankind from sin), in part morally (about man's deliverance from wrongdoing) and in part anagogically (about the soul's deliverance from the world).[243] The latter reading is the one applied in *Purgatorio*.

Some three hundred years later John *Milton, aged only fifteen years old, made a paraphrase of this psalm whilst still a student at St. Paul's School, London. Milton may well have studied some Hebrew at St. Paul's, but his version here relies heavily here both on the 1611 AV and the *Vulgate*. In 1634 Milton translated this psalm into Greek. Clearly he revered this 'exodus psalm'; still as a schoolboy, he translated another exodus psalm, 136: 'Let us with a gladsome mind' is perhaps better known because it became a hymn. Psalm 114 has more subtle classical and theological allusions. Hence the reference here to 'Tera's faithful Son' is Abraham: so like Augustine, Milton takes the origins of this psalm back to Abraham, the universal patriarch of Christians as well as Jews:

> When the blest seed of Tera's faithful Son,
> After long toil their liberty had won,
> And past from Pharian Fields to Canaan Land,
> Led by the strength of the Almighties hand,
> Jehovah's wonders were in Israel shown,
> His praise and glory were in Israel known...[244]

Christian illuminated Psalters tend, overall, to depict the themes from the psalm's liturgical use and from the commentary tradition. Hence the images of baptism are profuse, not least in Byzantine Psalters: the *Barbarini Psalter*,

[241] See https://www.allmusic.com/album/john-harbison-four-psalms-emerson-mw0001845807.
[242] See Stern 2013: 8–9.
[243] See https://bit.ly/3DFuLRJ.
[244] See https://milton.host.dartmouth.edu/reading_room/paraphrase_114/text.shtml.

for example (fol. 197r) offers a personification of the sea holding a cornucopia from which the 'river Jordan' (inscribed) flows. This leads to a depiction of John the Baptist baptising Christ. The *Khludov Psalter* (fol. 116v and fol. 117r) has similar images. So too the *Theodore Psalter* (fol. 154r, also with images of the previous psalm).[245]

The most striking examples are more recent Jewish interpretations, mainly because of the psalm's concern about the origins and preservation of the Hebrew people and its application to twentieth-century experience. Marc *Chagall's etching of Psalm 114 in his *Psaumes de David* shows a vast number of Hebrews escaping through a wall of water; above this is a figure, possibly Moses, and to the right of it the characteristic Torah and the star of David. The contemporary addition is the spires of churches, suggesting that persecution is not only an Egyptian experience but belongs to present 'Christian' persecution as well.[246] Another depiction is Moshe *Berger's version of Ps. 114:2. His commentary is that because of Judah's devotion to the Almighty, God entered into an intimate relationship with Israel, a relationship which resembled matrimony with God as the bridegroom and Israel as the Bride: a piercing white light emerges from a blue background, out of which a *menorah also materialises, as a mystical illustration of this relationship. A very different, even comic version is by *Benn, which is of a series of mountains and hills interwoven with skipping rams.[247] A contrasting and moving example is by Debra *Band, on a double page which sets side by side the Hebrew and English text, curving around the page as if swept along by the waves of the sea, representing letters attempting to formulate praise to God. The waters pour down the page from Red Sea, and across the foot of the page the damming of the waters of the river Jordan represent the second miracle alluded to in this psalm. The accompanying commentary observes that these miracles of water signify an ongoing act displaying God's creative power in the world and for his people.[248] These images are presented together as Plates 18 and 19.

Psalm 114 is short, but it is full of liturgical, musical and artistic reception. It offers the best example of the ancient shared origins of psalmodic chant in both Jewish and Christian traditions: in terms of its interrelated but distinctive liturgical and musical reception history it cannot be surpassed, not least because of the way it both brings the two faiths closer together and yet also reveals their distinctive features.

---

[245] See http://www.bl.uk/manuscripts/Viewer.aspx?ref=add_ms_19352_f154r.
[246] See https://bit.ly/3pMtymR.
[247] See Benn 1970: no page numbers.
[248] See Band and Band 2007: 136–40, taken also from email correspondence 13.12.18.

Psalm 115: A Liturgy: The Lifelessness of Idols and the Life-Giving God

The liturgical elements in this psalm are fairly clear. Verses 1–3 and 16–18 form short hymns. They share a common theme: given that neither foreign nations (verse 2) nor the dead (verse 17) can praise God, all the more should God's people give him the praise due to his name. In the heart of the psalm (verses 9–11) the thrice repeated imperative 'trust in the Lord!' suggests some *antiphonal liturgy addressed to different parts of the congregation.[249] On each side of verse 9–11 are didactic sections contrasting the lifelessness of idols (verses 4–8) with the life-giving God (verses 12–15). The psalm's closest linguistic links are not with Psalm 114, but 113 (the praise of the name of the Lord in 115:1 and 113:1–3; God in the heavens in 115:3 and 113:4; and the phrase 'from this time on and forevermore' in 115:18 and 113:2). This again suggests that Psalm 114 was a later insertion.[250]

Three groups of verses have been the main focus in the psalm's reception history: these are in the first hymnic section (verses 1–3), the section on idols (verses 4–8), and the final hymnic part on the dead (verses 16–18).

Starting with verses 1–3, one of the features of the *LXX is its stress on the transcendence of God: verse 3 (Greek Ps.113:11) speaks of 'our God of heaven above the heavens and the earth' (*ho de theos hēmōn en tō ouranō anō en tois ouranois kai en tē gē*), an expansion not taken up in the *Vulgate. *Targum similarly emphasises God's transcendence: 'Our God, his *residence* is in heaven' (115:3); the frequent references to the 'Memra' of the Lord in verses 9, 10, 12 and 14 also highlight this theme.

In the hymnic section on the silence of the dead (115:17; *LXX 113:25) the Greek now clarifies the place of 'silence' (in Hebrew, *dumah*) is 'Hades', which the Latin translates as *infernum* (hell). The *Targum* has 'the grave of the dead'. This is a place, according to *b.Shabbat* 30a, where the dead can no longer perform acts of Torah. We shall see shortly how this plays out in other forms of reception.

Although the versions do not make notable changes to verse 4–8, this section on idols has probably received the most attention. Wisd. 13:10 cites Ps. 115:4 (*LXX 113:12), and the whole idolatry section in Wisdom 13–15 has been influenced by this passage, even though the context is now Graeco-Roman

---

[249] Later Jewish tradition argues that verses 1–8 and 16–18 were sung by the Levites, and verses 9–15 were sung antiphonally by a precentor: see Cohen 1992: 382.
[250] See pp. 209–10.

idols.[251] The reference in 1 Cor. 12:2 to the Corinthians once being enticed and led astray 'to idols that could not speak' is probably also an allusion to 115:5 ('They have mouths, but do not speak') and similarly refers to Graeco-Roman idols. Rev. 9:20 ('[They] did not give up worshiping demons [*daimonia*] and idols of gold and silver and bronze and stone and wood, which cannot see or hear or walk' also alludes to this verse, paradoxically personifying the idols as 'demons'.[252] *Justin Martyr's *Dial.* 69:4 also cites this verse in his polemic against idols.

It is perhaps predictable that this satirical attack on idols in Ps. 115:3–8 is frequently illustrated in Byzantine Psalters in the context of *iconoclasm. For example, the *Pantokrator Psalter* (fol. 165r) has an illustration of the icono-clast John the Grammarian, associating him with the heretic and magician Simon Magus. Here John points critically to two idols, but David rebuts this by pointing to the Temple with its various liturgical objects of worship: David is defending the correct interpretation of the psalm.[253]

This satire is re-read in an interesting way in poetic imitation. Isaac *Watts, for example, entitles his metrical version 'Popish idolatry reproved', with the sub-title 'A Psalm for the Fifth of November'. Here the idols are those of the Catholic Church, and the people addressed are the Protestants in Britain who survived the Catholic plot in 1605 to assassinate the Stuart king James I.[254]

> The kneeling crowd, with looks devout, behold
> Their silver saviors, and their saints of gold.
>
> Be heav'n and earth amazed! 'Tis hard to say
> Which is more stupid, or their gods or they:
> O Isr'el, trust the Lord; he hears and sees,
> He knows thy sorrows and restores thy peace…
>
> [Vain are those artful shapes of eyes and ears;
> The molten image neither sees nor hears;
> Their hands are helpless, nor their feet can move,
> They have no speech, nor thought, nor power, nor love…]
>
> O Britain, trust the Lord: thy foes in vain
> Attempt thy ruin, and oppose his reign;
> Had they prevailed, darkness had closed our days,
> And death and silence had forbid his praise:
> But we are saved, and live; let songs arise,
> And Britain bless the God that built the skies.

---

[251] See Skehan 1948: 391.

[252] See Witherington 2017: 310–11.

[253] See Corrigan 1992: 27–29, 33–35; also Figure 44 on p. 257. For a similar image on the dispute about idols in the *Theodore Psalter*, see http://www.bl.uk/manuscripts/Viewer.aspx?ref=add_ms_19352_f140r.

[254] Taken from https://www.ccel.org/ccel/watts/psalmshymns.Ps.252.html.

Another more contemporary view is of the 'idols' as materialism and secularism, so that verses 4–8 have frequently been commented on by liberation theologians. A related version is by Jim *Cotter (d. 2004), who created his own paraphrases of the psalms:[255]

> Our idols are silver and gold,
> the gods of money rule in our land.
> They have mouths and utter platitudes.
> They have eyes and see not the poor.
> They have hears but hear no cries of pain,
> they have noses and keep themselves clean.
> Their hands touch no one with love,
> their feet never walk the streets.
> Keep us from growing to be like them,
> may we put on trust in possessions.

We now turn to the other verses which are also rich in reception, taking the hymnic sections (verses 1–3, 16–18) together, because here we see a more specifically Christian reading of this psalm. One example is *Augustine's interpretation of 'not unto us' in verse 1: this is about God's works for Christians, who are nothing without God's grace.[256] His commentary on verse 1 is as follows: 'For that grace of the water that gushed from the rock (now that rock was Christ), was not given on the score of works that had gone before, but of his mercy … For "Christ died for sinners", that men might not seek any glory of their own, but in the Lord's name'.[257] Augustine similarly redeems the negative tenor of verse 17 ('the dead do not praise the Lord') by contrasting the fate of the sinners with the fate of the righteous, so verse 18 is read in the light of the resurrection. His commentary reads: 'But we, who live, will praise the Lord, from this time forth *for evermore*'.[258]

Verse 1 has received many other interpretations, of which that of *Luther is perhaps the most interesting, because it is seen as part of his scheme of 'Three Advents', starting with a focus on God's advent to the Jews (whereby the 'faithful synagogue' is also deemed worthy of responding to God's love and mercy) and then a focus on God's coming in Christ (where God's 'pure mercy' is seen), and finally on the 'spiritual advent' of God's coming into our hearts, preparing us for Christ's coming at the end of time. This sense of God's mercy throughout

---

[255] See Cotter 1993: 37.
[256] *Sermon* 229.4 in *WSA* 3 6:329.
[257] Augustine trans. Uyl 2017: 566.
[258] *Ibid.*, 568.

all history is unusual in Luther's works, because it allows for the place of the Jews in God's plan of redemption, and is an extended interpretation of Augustine's reading.[259]

Augustine's and Luther's readings of 'Not unto us, O Lord, but to your name give glory', are theological; but the reception of this verse often has a political slant as well. Examples include the allusion in Shakespeare's *Henry V*, Act IV Scene 8, when the King gives thanks for the victory of the English army at Agincourt: 'O God, Thy arm was here; and not to us, but to Thy arm alone, Ascribe well all…' Likewise, after the Battle of Naseby in 1645, a critical defeat of the Royalists by the Parliamentarians, Cromwell also cited this verse 'Not to us, O Lord but to your name give glory…'[260]

Returning to Augustine, one of the psalm verses most cited in Augustine's *Confessions* was Ps. 115:16: 'The heavens are the Lord's heavens, but the earth he has given to human beings.'[261] But again we see how one verse can be viewed in such different ways. Arthur *Wragg, writing in the Great Depression in the 1930s, offers a more satirical comment. He turns the following verse on its head: 'But the earth hath he given to the children of men'. His black and white cartoon in Figure 9 shows how the 'children of men' seek instead to control the earth and abuse it for their own purposes.

Another comment we noted earlier in relation to Augustine was his redemption of the negative view of death in verse 17, by re-reading verse 18. A similar interpretation, written as a vitriolic comment after the Holocaust, is by Jacqueline Osherow. Her poem, 'Dead Men's Praise' (from 115:17) reflects on both the theme of silence and the call to praise God with Hallelujahs.[262]

> …this verse had festered in its psalm
> waiting to reveal its acrid heart…
>
> *The dead don't praise God*
> *Or the ones who go down to silence,*
> *but we'll praise God*
> *from now on forever*
> *hallelujah –*
>
> I'm not suggesting that we think about it:
> just sing it, during Hallel
> at synagogue, the next new moon
> and get in on a little

---

[259] See German 2017: 146–48.
[260] See Prothero 1903: 252.
[261] Poque 1986: 156.
[262] See Osherow 1999: 79–83.

FIGURE 9   Arthur Wragg, 'But the earth hath he given to the children of men'
(Ps. 115:16).

Source: Wragg, A. 1934: *The Psalms for Modern Life*. New York: Claude Kendall.

of its stubborn bravado,
its delirious proof
of itself—*hallelujah* –…

…and my *hallelujah*,
my precious, rising *hallelujah*,
doesn't have the stamina
I need it for
it has, in fact, been burned away
before it could adorn a single tongue

for countless generations of David's offspring
and I'm not talking about the ones who turned to ash –
they're around somewhere, singing *hallelujah* –

I'm talking about the other ones, numberless as stars,
who never got to sing a word at all…

Against such protests, the musical use of the entire psalm, both at Hallel and at Sunday *Vespers, creates a continuity which echoes an ancient context of worship. The influence of the Hallel is seen in the version entitled *Yisrael betaḥ ba-shem*, composed by the German 'singing Rabbi' Shlomoh Carlibach (1925–1994) (from 15:9, 'O Israel, trust in the Lord!') which was arranged for popular singing.[263] Christian composers, using Psalm 115 because in the Latin it was adapted along with Psalm 114 as part of the collection of Psalms 110–114 for Vespers, include *Byrd, *Schütz (whose version of Psalm 115 is notable for its use of disconnected staccato notes in the satire on idols), *Purcell, *Vivaldi and *Mendelssohn (whose version is based on verse 12, 'The Lord is mindful of his own'). One notable arrangement is Samuel Sebastian *Wesley's 'Ascribe unto the Lord', written for a Church Missionary Society service at Winchester Cathedral in 1853, combining contemplative worship of God from Psalm 96 (*BCP) with Ps. 115:3–8, this time sung as a lively fugue in its ridicule of idols, followed by Ps. 115:12–15, praising God as creator of heaven and earth.[264]

So Psalm 115 has inspired both theological reflection and social critique by Jews and Christians alike. It is not actually a controversial psalm dividing the two faith traditions; but its contents have caused divided opinions within each tradition. So the psalm is a good example of how a different cultural context can create a contrasting emphasis from the same verses.

Psalm 116: The Fate of the Dead and the Cup of Salvation

Psalm 116 is the first Hallel psalm to have a more personal appeal, although it still has elements of liturgy within it (for example, the congregational references in verses 14 and 17, and the reference to the Temple courts in verse 19). Primarily it is an individual prayer interspersed with confessions of trust.

---

[263] See Boulanger 2010: 209. This psalm also features in the Frankfurt *Tehillim* Project: see http://www.bettina-struebel.de/wp-content/uploads/Vorank%C3%BCndigung.pdf.

[264] See Dowling Long and Sawyer 2015: 20. Also https://www.youtube.com/watch?v=x2CVnviYYcA.

Its placing has not been accidental: there are clear links with Psalm 115, for example in the references to 'the name of the Lord' (115:1 and 116:4, 13 and 17) and to death and the dead (115:17 and 116:3, 8 and 15).

Three main issues have been the focus of this psalm's reception history. First, the fate of the dead, not least the death of the martyrs (from verses 3–11 and 15); second, the cup of salvation (verse 13) and payment of vows (verses 14 and 18) and from this, a theology of sacrament and word; third, the piety of the psalmist, especially his appeal for God's protection because of 'my affliction' ('*oniti*). These will be explored below.

We noted in our discussion of Psalm 114 that Psalm 116 has been divided into two in the **LXX* and an 'Alleluia' has been placed at the beginning of verse 10 (EV). This division, however, interrupts the flow of the testimony verses 1–11, and the extra two verses in the second half have little to do with the more ritual elements in verses 12–19. The Greek also omits verse 14 (on paying vows to God), as it is repeated in verses 18: it does not, however, omit verse 13b which is also repeated in verse 17b. So the reception of the psalm into Greek raises unresolved issues.

Jewish tradition mainly focusses on the personal elements in this psalm. *Rashi believed it was by David, after Saul's death, whilst the nineteenth-century Rabbi Malbim argued it was a thanksgiving by Hezekiah, after his illness.[265] One liturgical use of this psalm, taken from verse 16 ('I am your servant, the child of your servant girl …') is the Jewish tradition of praying for a sick person by naming their mother, on the basis that the mother's prayer would be the most sincere and effective.[266] Another view (*Ros Has.* 16b–17a) is that the psalm describes the day of Final Judgement at the time of the Resurrection of the Dead, a theme taken up in two contemporary Jewish paintings to be discussed below.[267]

Several New Testament allusions also concern the references to death in this psalm. Some see this psalm as a 'Gethsemane Prayer', based on Mark 14:36: this was one of the Hallel psalms to be sung after the Passover meal, and the plea 'Save my Life!' (verse 4) is seen as alluded to in Mark 14:36a. The cup of salvation (verse 13) now becomes the cup of suffering; hence the following verse 15 ('precious in the sight of the Lord is the death of his faithful ones') takes on a

[265] Cohen 1992: 385.
[266] Donin 1980: 53 and 86.
[267] Feuer 2004: 1385.

new meaning.[268] That the early church saw this psalm in the light of Jesus' death and resurrection might be seen in the use of the expression 'chains of death' (see verse 3) in Peter's speech in Acts 2:4, describing Jesus' resurrection.[269] Other allusions to the 'cup of salvation' and its association with Passover/the Last Supper, and so with the death of Christ, are suggested in 1 Cor. 10:16: 'the cup of blessing that we bless, is it not a sharing in the blood of Christ?'. Although this is now termed the 'cup of blessing' (*potērion tēs eulogias*) rather than 'cup of salvation' (*potērion sōtēriou*), the imagery of drinking from a cup which entails both suffering and redemption makes verses 14–15 quite appropriate.

The Church Fathers read this as Psalm 115 and divided it into two, in both the Greek and the Latin. So the division of verses 1–9 was about Christ's deliverance of souls from hell, rousing the living from worldly sleep, and verses 10–19 were concerned with the fate of the martyrs who had also drunk the cup of the Lord's sufferings.[270] *Cyprian, for example, understands verses 10–19 as about the martyrs of the church; *Augustine, in a sermon on the psalm, makes the same point.[271] *Basil of Caesarea (or Basil the Great) comments on 'the cup of salvation', seeing this as being thirsty for martyrdom.[272] Basil also tries to make sense of the Greek in verse 1 which simply states 'I loved' (*ēgapēsa*) without any object (the NRSV has 'I love *the Lord*...). He states: 'I have loved because the Lord will hear the voice of my prayer... who is the someone who is loved? We supply the thought "God of the universe from whom we can never be separated (Rom 8:35)."'[273]

One phrase which has created some controversy is in verse 11, with its citation 'all men are liars'. During the Reformation this was quoted as an indictment of the Pope. *Luther's account of this verse never makes this point explicit, though he is quick to note its use in Rom. 3:4, and to argue along with Paul that this encapsulated the 'Truth of the Gospel': all men are liars, so God alone is true. This has also been an important argument in medieval commentaries, including in the *Glossa Ordinaria*, and for Luther this was not so much a pessimistic anthropology as an optimistic assertion about the grace of God.

---

[268] Kiley 1986: 655–59.

[269] See Witherington 2017: 311, who notes this is a typical way of taking 'the sacred language about death' in the psalms.

[270] See Neale and Littledale 1874–79: 3/497, citing pseudo-*Thomas and pseudo-*Bede.

[271] For Cyprian, see *Letter 8* in MFC 17:128, used in *ACCS* VIII:293; for Augustine, see *Sermon 276.4* in WSA 3 8:31, used in *ACCS* VIII: 294.

[272] See De Solms 2001: 559–60.

[273] Basil, *Homilies on the Psalms 22* in FC 46 351–52, used in *ACCS* VIII:285.

People cease to be liars when they are claimed by God.[274] This type of exegesis is a good example of Luther's use of medieval exegesis within a sixteenth-century context: his theology was rooted in the past, and offers an interesting complement to his more positive exegesis of the threefold coming of Christ in the previous psalm.[275]

We have already noted the link between the 'chalice' in Ps. 116:13 and the death of Jesus. Hence the psalm became part of the liturgy of Maundy Thursday, Good Friday, Corpus Christi, and the Festival of the Martyrs.[276] It was also used in both the *Gregorian and monastic traditions at the Office of the Dead, using the *antiphon 'I walk before the Lord in the land of the living', and the antiphon 'Precious in the sight of the Lord is the death of his faithful ones'. It has been used at funeral services from late antiquity to the present day. Throughout western tradition the whole psalm (in its two parts in Latin) was assigned to Monday *Vespers, ratified in 1911 in the Roman Breviary of Pius X. Furthermore, the reference to the 'chalice' accrued eucharistic significance, being linked to the wine (and bread) at Passover; verses 10–16 are still recited by priests before the celebration of the Mass, with verse 13 being used as a prayer in its own right.

The association of this psalm both with death and the Eucharist is found in artistic and musical reception. For example, the *Hamilton Psalter* (fol. 205r) depicts two saints kneeling with their executioners close by. The *Theodore Psalter* (fol. 155v) portrays Christ blessing a sick man on his bed, with the personification of death rising out of his sarcophagus.[277] The *Utrecht Psalter* (fol. 67r) has a picture of the psalmist having escaped Hades, now appealing to Christ and three angels.[278] The *St. Albans Psalter* illustrates the second part of Psalm 116 (in the Latin, 115) with the psalmist holding up a book, inscribed with 'the chalice of salvation'; in his other hand is a chalice. Christ looks on as a wicked man shoots the psalmist with an arrow, illustrating verses 13 and 15.[279]

Two recent Jewish illustrations take up the commentary tradition about the psalm describing the final judgement and the resurrection of the dead. Moshe *Berger's painting has at its heart the walled city of Jerusalem with its Temple above it and with waters running downwards out of it, in a silver-white hue; at the top is the letter *Yod*, representing God, and first red flames of fire and the outer blue shafts of light emerge behind the city. The image gives the impression

---

[274] See Hagen 1997: 85–102.

[275] See pp. 219–20.

[276] See Neale and Littledale 1874–79: 3/498.

[277] See http://www.bl.uk/manuscripts/Viewer.aspx?ref=add_ms_19352_f155v.

[278] See https://psalter.library.uu.nl/page/141.

[279] See https://www.albani-psalter.de/stalbanspsalter/english/commentary/page307.shtml.

of a human face. Berger writes that this is about the day of final judgement, when God, the compassionate one, will forgive many. They will sing 'I love God for he hears my voice and supplications' (verse 1).[280] By contrast, *Benn's image of Psalm 116 (1969) depicts an extended figure in a yellow robe, lifting upwards a blue chalice to the heavens, where God is represented in yellow light. This is about both judgement and salvation: the figure's face is calling out in pain as much as joy.[281]

Several composers have arranged this psalm for Monday Vespers, basing this on the first verse of the second half of the psalm in Latin ('credidi') or 'I kept my faith'); they include Orlando *di Lasso, Tomás Luis de *Victoria and *Monteverdi. By contrast, the third and fourth verses of the first part of psalm ('The snares of death encompassed me ...') are often set as antiphon for the Office of the Dead.[282] An unusual composition is by Henry *Purcell, who (in about 1689) arranged Ps. 116:18–19 ('Praise the Lord, O Jerusalem') as a coronation hymn for William and Mary, performed at Westminster Abbey, an anthem still in popular use today.[283]

The theme of death and dying has encouraged its use in oratorios. *Mendelssohn's *Elijah* (Part One No. 8) uses verse 12 in a recitative between Elijah and the Widow, whose son has died and whom Elijah will bring back to life.[284] Another example is the one-act cantata by the American composer and organist Daniel Pinkham (1923–2006) entitled *Daniel in the Lion's Den*, premiered in 1973, which uses Psalm 116 to illustrate Daniel 6, where Daniel is threatened with death by being thrown into the lion's den, and Daniel 14, where Daniel is sentenced to death for threatening the cult of Bel and its sacred dragon. Pianos, percussion (including timpani and an electronic tape of lions growling) show this psalm in yet another light.[285]

One final theme which holds this whole psalm together is the emphasis on the psalmist as poor and 'afflicted', and so dependent only on God for protection. Two recent pieces bring out this theme. One is Marty Haugen's 'I will walk in the Presence of God' (1995) with woodwinds and guitar, based on 116:9.[286] The other is by the English composer Jonathan Harvey (1939–2012) whose 'I Love the Lord' (1976) is a more detailed setting of verses 1–4 and 7–9, for unaccompanied double choir and solo voices. It combines Anglican chant in the first section, expressing

---

[280] See http://www.biblical-art.com/artwork.asp?id_artwork=15122&showmode=Full.
[281] Benn 1970: no page numbers.
[282] See http://www2.cpdl.org/wiki/index.php/Psalm_116.
[283] See https://www.youtube.com/watch?v=oehzoLHMvQg.
[284] See Stern 2011: 264.
[285] See Dowling Long and Sawyer 2015: 56.
[286] See https://www.youtube.com/watch?v=pfRC4Ck2YSM.

trust in God, with discordant and agitated solo voices in the middle section, concerned with the fear of dying; the appeal by two solo trebles for God to 'deliver my soul' (verse 7) leads to some resolution, with the repeat of 'I Love the Lord'. Had Harvey also used the second half of the psalm, with its somewhat paradoxical views about death, the resolution would have been particularly poignant.

One of the most evocative reflections on this verse is the poem entitled 'Praise II' by George *Herbert. This poem, later a hymn, is entitled 'King of Glory, King of Peace, I will love thee'.[287] It too is concerned with the poverty of the psalmist, especially in terms of his faith. Although its focus is more on the problem of sin than of death ('Though my sins against me cried, Thou didst clear me ...'), the resolution of praise for 'seven whole days, not one in seven' accords with the resolve to give God a thanksgiving offering near the end of this psalm.

One of the most interesting aspects of this psalm, consonant with the other psalms from Psalm 113 onwards, is that there is little evidence of Jewish/Christian controversy. Although there is some Christological engagement with this psalm in the reference to the 'cup of salvation', there is little here which actually divides Jews and Christians. From the *Maccabean period onwards, first Jews and then Christians have used this psalm to speak of a martyr's death, to explain the importance of ritual and word in each of their liturgies, and, most of all, to highlight the importance of a personal faith which can triumph over adversity. Psalm 116 therefore is a psalm whose reception has universal concerns.

Psalm 117: Brief Praise with Abundant Implications

These two verses may comprise the shortest psalm in the Psalter, but the psalm has still received a great amount of reception, mainly because of the ways it conceives the relationship between Jews and Gentiles. On the one hand, verse 1 calls upon nations and peoples to praise God, imagining them, as in Ps. 98:3–6, as present. The Hebrew reads 'the' peoples, but the NRSV translation is 'you' nations and 'you' peoples: they are not Jews. On the other hand, verse 2 describes God's 'steadfast love' and 'faithfulness' as a gift to the present congregation ('For great is his steadfast love toward *us* ...'), perhaps recalling a short creed in Exod. 34:6, in the context of God's redemption from Egypt.[288] So this is a Jewish statement of faith. The simple hymnic form of this psalm—the imperative exhortation to praise in verse 1, addressed to 'you', and the reasons for it in verse 2, addressed to 'us'—goes to the heart of the question in the entire

---

[287] See Atwan and Wieder 1993: 316–17.
[288] These were also used in another Hallel psalm, 115:1–2.

Psalter as to whether or not the Gentiles are included into the Jewish faith. We shall see below how this is played out in the psalm's reception.

The reception of this psalm as an independent unit has not always been clear. Many Hebrew manuscripts and several Medieval Bibles combined this psalm with Psalm 116 (EV). Even in the fifth century, *Augustine wrote of a Latin tradition which united them. Furthermore, the *LXX* transferred the last Alleluia of verse 2 to Psalm 118, so that all the Hallel psalms began with an Alleluia. This tradition is followed in the *Vulgate*.

Jewish tradition is fairly consistent in its interpretation of the two groups of people in this psalm. One is the children of Israel, continuing to serve God through the 613 precepts of the Torah; the other is the Gentiles, fulfilling the seven Noahide laws. According to *Kimḥi, 'Its insertion in the Psalter is a witness to the universal aspiration of Judaism'. He argues that its brevity is in order to speak concisely of the conversion of the Gentiles after the advent of the Messiah.[289] *Midrash Tehillim* expands on this: it distinguishes between 'nations' (*goim*) and 'the peoples' (*ha-'ummim*) in verse 1: the former are the oppressors of Israel, the latter are those who did not oppress them.[290] A more liberal Jewish reading is to see 'the peoples' (*ha-'ummim*) in verse 1 as a term for the Jewish people(s). In this reading verse 1 is not about the Gentiles alone: Jews are included in the summons to praise, but this then leads on to the conclusion that the reference to 'us' in verse 2 must therefore mean both Jews and Gentiles together, who together share in the awesome responsibility of praising God. This Jewish reading is less typical, however.[291]

The Christian commentary tradition takes a different perspective. Rom. 15:9–12 is a *florilegium* bringing together the key themes of this Epistle about the place of the Gentiles in God's plan of redemption. Rom 15:11 cites the Greek of Ps. 117:1 (*LXX* 116:1): here, like the later Jewish tradition noted above, the implication is that 'all the nations' (*panta ta ethnē*) are the Gentiles, and 'all the peoples' (*pantes hoi laoi*) include the Jews, thus seeing the shared legacy of Gentiles and Jews, glorifying God together.[292] The reference to God's steadfast love or 'mercy' (*eleos*) in Rom. 15:8 might also be an allusion to the same word in the *LXX* in Ps. 117:2: if so this implies that the psalm speaks of Gentiles also

---

[289] See Cohen 1992: 388; Feuer 2004: 1397.

[290] Braude 1959: 230.

[291] See Jonathan Magonet, https://www.haus-ohrbeck.de/fileadmin/user_upload/02_Haus-Ohrbeck/Bibelforum/Bibelwoche/2016/Einfuehrung_Jonathan_Magonet_-_englisch.pdf.

[292] Other references used in this same passage include Deut.32:43 (from the Law) and Isa. 11:10 (from the Prophets) with Psalm 117 used as an example from the Writings. See Hays 1989: 70–71. See also Witherington 2017: 311.

experiencing 'mercy' of God. Hence the whole psalm is seen to be about Jews and Gentiles together glorifying God, rather than, as in the more prominent Jewish tradition, dividing this into two parts with the Jewish faith as superior.

The early fathers read this psalm as a testimony to the Gentiles being equal inheritors of the Abrahamic faith.[293] *Cassiodorus, somewhat typically, sees the psalm as about the collective praise of the whole catholic church throughout the world, making no reference to Jewish tradition.[294] All but a millennium later *Luther, who wrote a thirty-six page pamphlet on this psalm, argued by reference to Paul and Augustine that the privilege of praise of God was too great to be restricted to Jews alone.[295] *Calvin, however, took a more restrained reading: the psalm spoke about salvation *first* to the Jews, and *later* to the Gentiles.[296]

This was the third psalm in the Hallel to be used after the Passover meal, after 115 and 116 and before 118. And this was the last of the psalms to be used at the *Vespers of the Apostles and Evangelists and the Vespers of the Martyrs and Confessors, after Psalms 110, 111, 112 and 113. In Christian tradition Psalm 117 has a rich musical reception history: composers as diverse as *Byrd, di *Lasso, *Schütz and Liszt have all produced motets or cantatas on this entire psalm, sometimes, because of the theme of the Gentiles, for Vespers at Epiphany time.

A few specific examples must suffice. *Monteverdi's version (c. 1651) is set for five solo voices, two violins and a four-voice choir, with the possible addition of four violas or four trombones; it is full of vitality until the word 'misericordia' (mercy): here this is sung three times to a descending chromatic scale, evoking the sufferings of Christ. The French composer of Baroque vocal music, Marc-Antoine Charpentier (1643–1704) made six arrangements of this psalm; the best known (written in about 1674) was composed for three voices, choir and organ for the convent of Port-Royal in Paris; the first verse is sung by a solo voice, the second verse by two voices, and the doxology by three, with the first verse repeated after the doxology as progressive praise sung in the light of the Trinity.[297] *Vivaldi, by contrast, composed a piece lasting just two minutes; this was for Vespers, arranged during his first period at the *Ospedale della Pietà* in Venice from 1703 onwards; like Monteverdi's version, it is full of energy, with violins playing in unison against the choir, and again the surprise is the extended modulation on the word 'misericordia' which changes the praise to

---

[293] De Solms 2001: 561, citing *Athanasius, *Eusebius and Augustine.

[294] See *Exposition of the Psalms 116:1* ACW 53:160, cited in *ACCS* VIII 298.

[295] *Exposition of Psalm 117* [WA 31, first edition, 223–57]. See Fischer 1983: 83–86 on Psalm 118.

[296] See Calvin, https://www.ccel.org/ccel/calvin/calcom11.xxvi.i.html.

[297] See https://www.hyperion-records.co.uk/dw.asp?dc=W2887_GBAJY0080920.

a penitential mode appropriate for Vespers. J. S. *Bach's *Lobet den Herrn, alle Heiden*, for four voices and *basso continuo*, is his only motet based on an entire psalm (date unknown; published in 1821). The first verse is based on a double fugue; the second verse graduates from homophony to polyphony, and instead of a doxology the final 'Alleluia' is set to a simple dance-like fugue. The high point is the phrase 'the faithfulness of the Lord endures forever', where the first syllable of the word 'Ewigkeit' ('for ever') is extended into a lengthy melodic line to suggest eternity. The version in 1758 by German Baroque composer, Georg Philipp Telemann (1681–1767), entitled *Laudate Jehovam Omnes Gentes* is set in three movements with an *SATB chorus, two violins, *basso continuo* and ends with a festive alleluia.[298] *Mozart's version was composed in 1779 with the other four Vespers psalms. *Laudate Dominum* is also in three parts, with a 3:3 rhythm; it is set for a solo soprano voice with two violins, cello, bassoon and organ, the *Gloria* is taken up by a choir, with the final 'Amen' sung by the solo soprano. It is possible that this female ending is intended to evoke the part of the Virgin in being a 'light to enlighten the Gentiles' (Luke 2:32): the fact that Psalm 117 is followed by the Magnificat makes this interpretation quite likely.[299] Finally, the contemporary Taizé chant, *Laudate Dominum*, has been popularised as a haunting and meditative prayer sung in several parts or as a round.[300] In all these pieces it is interesting to see how the music evokes a specifically Christian overlay.

There are two unusual representations of this psalm in art. One, again developing the associations of Mary with the psalm, is by the Florentine portrait artist Alessandro Allori (1535–1607) and is dated 1598, entitled 'The Presentation of Mary in the Temple', where Mary is holding the text of Psalm 117, written in Hebrew, with verse 1 on the right side and verse 2 on the left. It is an altarpiece in the Duomo in Lucca (Cathedral of San Martino).[301] This has been included here as Plate 20. A second, from *Paris Lat.* 11560 (fol. 31v), part of the *Bible Moralisé* Vol II (made in about 1233 and now preserved at the Bibliothèque Nationale de France) includes, on a page of eight medallions of the psalms as examples of typology and prophecy, an image of Psalm 117 (*Vulgate* Psalm 116). This miniature is of Paul preaching the Gospel to the Gentiles, with a convert being baptised to his right. *Laudate Dominum* is written to the right of the medallion.[302]

By way of conclusion we might recall the universal nature of this psalm. This is admirably achieved by Mary *Sidney in her unique poetic imitation of

---

[298] See Dowling Long and Sawyer 2015: 141.

[299] For Charpentier, Vivaldi, Monteverdi, Bach and Mozart see; Decleir 2007: 399–401.

[300] See https://www.youtube.com/watch?v=vuVyoOc1luQ.

[301] I am grateful to John Sawyer for this discovery.

[302] See https://bit.ly/39XhojY.

Laudate Dominum.[303] The acrostic 'Praise the Lord' is an appropriate epithet for such a short psalm which has much potential in uniting Jews and Christians in a common faith.

> **P** raise him that aye
> **R** emains the same
> **A** ll tongues display
> **I** ehovah's fame
> **S** ing all that share
> **T** his earthly ball:
> **H** is mercies are
> **E** xposed to all,
> **L** ike as the word
> **O** nce he doth give,
> **R** olled in record,
> **D** oth time outlive.

Psalm 118: A Psalm with Many Voices

Psalm 118 may well have been incorporated as a conclusion to the Hallel because of its associations with all the previous psalms. The theme of God's sovereignty over the nations is found in 113:4–6 and 7–9 and 118:6–7, 10–12 and 22–24; and the exodus theme in Psalm 114 is found in Psalm 118, which borrows from Exod. 15:2 in verse 14 and 21, whilst verse 16 echoes Exod. 15:6, 11 and 12. The theme of trust in God, not idols, in Ps. 115:1–11 is taken up in 118:6–9 (trusting in God, not man); furthermore, the abbreviated name for God as 'Yah' is used in 115:18 and here in Psalm 118:5, 14, 17, 18 and 19, and three of the four references in the Psalter to the 'house of Aaron' occur in these two psalms (115:10, 12; 118:3). The theme of deliverance from death in 116:3–9 is found in 118:17–18, with the specific reference to 'salvation' (*yeshu'ah*) in 116:13 being taken up in 118:14 and 21. Finally, the call on all nations to praise the Lord in Psalm 117 is implied in Ps. 118:1, 4 and 29.[304]

What gives Psalm 118 its distinctiveness, however, is that underlying these themes there seems to be a liturgy which is centred not only on Exodus but also on the role of a king (or perhaps a religious leader). The psalm starts with a call

---

[303] Taken from; Hamlin *et al.* 2009: 224.

[304] On the integration of Psalm 118 with other psalms in the Hallel see Vaillancourt 2019: 167–71.

to all Israel, to the priests, and to all peoples to give thanks to the Lord, using the refrain 'His steadfast love endures forever' (verses 1–4). It is then possible to read the following narrative throughout the rest of the psalm. Verses 5–18 appear to be a thanksgiving prayer of the king, who was nearly overcome by his enemies but was then granted victory by God, whose 'right hand' is exalted (verse 15–16). Various repetitions are used for dramatic effect throughout (verses 6 and 7; verses 8 and 9; verses 10, 11 and 12). The figure then requests to be allowed passage through the gates to the Temple (verse 19), and is given an answer from within (verse 20). He then recalls his rejection by his people (verses 21–23) and the congregation offer thanks at his having been reconciled with them (verses 23–25). He is then admitted to the company who bless him (verses 26–27); his own final thanksgiving (verse 28) is concluded with the same refrain at the start of the psalm (verse 29).

Whether or not this psalm was once used by the king, or was constructed for worship in the Second Temple (where the 'enemies' in verses 10–11 could be those opposing the rebuilding of Jerusalem, as in Nehemiah 6, for example, or even, given the Exodus references, imperial powers), its liturgical and narrative form makes it distinctive; its 'royal' allusions also allow for a later 'messianic' reading, both in Jewish and Christian commentary tradition, as we shall shortly see.

Firstly, the *LXX has made a few changes to this psalm: the call to Israel in verse 2 is now 'house of Israel', following Ps. 115:12 (which also includes 'house of Aaron'), emphasising the lay and priestly participation in this refrain. The strange reference to being encircled by bees in verse 12 is expanded to explain the threat: these are 'bees [with] a honeycomb' (*hōsei melissai kēriov*). Finally, the reference to the stone becoming the 'head of the corner' (Hebrew, *lero'sh pinnah*) in verse 22 is translated *kephalēn gōnias* suggesting a coping stone— one used near the end of building process, rather than a foundation stone, used at the beginning. This emphasises its vital place in the building, a theme which is developed in later Jewish and Christian tradition, as we shall see.

The psalm appears in six scrolls at *Qumran. Twice (in 11QPs[a] and 4QPs[e]) it is placed after Psalm 116 and before Psalm 104, thus breaking its connection with Psalm 118 at the end of the Hallel. In 4QPs[a] the reference to the 'bees' in verse 12 is entirely missing, making sense because the refrain in verses 10, 11 and 12 ('they surrounded me!') is now almost identical. One interesting reference is in 4QPsalmsPesher[b], or 4Q173, where the 'Teacher of Righteousness' is described using language from Psalm 118: references include a 'broad place' (verse 5); 'gate' (verse 20); and 'light', 'festal branches' (verse 27). The most contentious use of Psalm 118 is in 11QPs[a] (and also in 11QPs[b]) where part of it is added on to Psalm 136. This might be because the refrain in Ps. 118:1 and 29 ('O give thanks to the Lord, for he is good, for his steadfast love endures forever') is the same as Ps. 136:26; so the addition of Ps. 118:15–16, 8–9 after 136:26 in column XVI (i.e. much later than the earlier use of Psalm

118 itself, before Psalm 104) is not a mangled version of the psalm but a deliberate addition of well-known liturgical material from this festal psalm, here connecting the psalm concluding the Hallel with the Great Hallel, that is, Psalm 136, as many recent commentators have done.[305]

The importance of Psalm 118 in Jewish tradition is found especially in *Targum*, where, following the narrative reading above, verses 21–28 become an *antiphonal commentary on how the youthful David was rejected by the builders (i.e. the religious leaders) to be the rightful king, taken from 1 Sam. 16:1–13. So in verse 23a the builders speak; in 23b the sons of Jesse reply; in 24a the builders speak again; in 24b the sons of Jesse reply again; in 25a the builders respond; in 25b Jesse and his wife respond; in 26a the builders answer; in 26b David replies; in 27a the families of Judah join in; in 27b Samuel the prophet speaks; in verse 28 it is David, and verse 29 concludes with Samuel.[306] This corresponds with our earlier observations about the distinct narrative and liturgical character of this psalm. Again, in *b.Pesahim* 119a we find a similar antiphonal narrative but with different assignments: David speaks in verse 21, Jesse in verse 22, David's brothers in verse 23, Samuel in verse 24, David's brothers then David in verse 25, Jesse then Samuel in verse 26, all those assembled then Samuel in verse 27, and David and the tribe of Judah in verse 28. In each case the central feature is the rejected stone—the Davidic king—which then becomes the head of the corner.

Midrash Tehillim, also concerned with associations between the Psalter and the Torah, argues that both verse 11 and the 'stone' imagery in verse 22 concern not David but Abraham; he is the 'foundation stone', the one whose righteousness endured forever (citing Ps. 112:9, but in the light of the refrain about God's steadfast love enduring forever in 118:1–4 and 29).[307] Nevertheless, verse 23 ('This is the Lord's doing') is seen as praise about David enabling Judah and Jerusalem together to rejoice in God.[308]

Other Jewish commentators prefer to read Psalm 118 as an early liturgy spoken by Israel as a whole, having escaped the annihilation of exile (for example verse 17: 'I shall not die, but I shall live, and recount the deeds of the Lord ...'). *Rashi, writing on this verse, paraphrases it as 'I the congregation of Israel shall not die a permanent death like the rest of the nations, but I shall live ...'[309] Given the Christian emphasis on resurrection, arguing that unbelieving Jews would suffer permanent death, this is Rashi's affirmation of the superiority of Judaism. There is some argument that the 'righteous' who pass through the gate in verse

---

[305] See Holladay 1993: 102; Hoenig 1968: 162–63; also Abegg et al. 1999: 569–70.
[306] See Stec 2004: 209–10.
[307] Braude 1959: 238.
[308] See Braude 1959: 244–45. For a more recent review of the reception of Psalm 118 in Jewish tradition see Vaillancourt 2019: 188–89.
[309] Rashi in Gruber 2004: 672–74.

20 could be righteous Gentiles; but the 'rejected stone' in verse 22 is undoubtedly Israel, despised by her enemies, but restored by God.[310] The balance is between the more personal interpretation, seeing the psalm as about Abraham, or David, or about the nation, whether Israel in exile in Babylon, or Israel reflecting on her final redemption, when she is to be returned to her former glory.[311] In all four interpretations the motif of the 'rejected stone' is central.[312]

We noted earlier that this could be read as about the processional entry of the King into Jerusalem. Such a view, evident by the time of Christ, afforded the New Testament writers new vistas of interpretation, much of it centred around Jesus' entry into Jerusalem, cited in all four Gospels (alongside Zech. 9:9, where the king rides on an ass, in Matthew and John). Thus we see another story line: in different ways they view Jesus as the young son of Jesse and the 'unrecognised king', whilst the opposing Jewish leaders become the builders rejecting the keystone, and the crowd becomes the receptive congregation at the end of the psalm. All four Gospels cite verse 26 ('Blessed is the one who comes in the name of the Lord …') and all but Luke cite the 'Hosanna' ('Save!') in verse 25. Verse 6, but especially verses 18, 19–20, 22–23 and 25–26, the subject matter of the recitations in *Targum* and the *Talmud*, are cited some sixteen times in the New Testament and very frequently by the early church fathers, who used these verses alongside others from, for example, Isa. 8:14 and 28:16, to demonstrate that Jesus is the Messiah.[313] We shall see below just how subtly each Gospel writer deals with this psalm.

Ps. 118:22–23 is cited in Mark at the end of a confrontation with the religious leaders about Jesus' authority (Mark 11:27–12:12), after his cleansing the Temple (Mark 11:15–26) which itself comes after Jesus' entry into Jerusalem (Mk.11:1–11), when Ps. 118:25–26 is sung by the crowds. Then, after the parable of the vineyard when the heir is killed, Ps. 118:22–23 is cited at Mark 12:10–11. Although these verses were written in Greek, there may be some intended word play between the term 'stone' (*'eben*, v. 22), referring to the building of the Temple, and the word 'son' (ben), referring to Jesus himself: Jesus, rejected by the religious leaders, becomes the corner stone in the new people-Temple (Mark 14:58).[314]

Like Mark, Matthew uses Ps. 118:25–26 as a hymn of praise sung by the crowds when Jesus enters Jerusalem (Matt. 21:9), although Matthew adds 'Hosanna *to the son of David*'. Then Matthew follows the same Temple disputes with the authorities

---

[310] See Cohen 1992: 289 and 392.
[311] Feuer 2004: 1401.
[312] Feuer 2004: 1411.
[313] See McLean 1992: 78–79.
[314] See Watts 2004: 30–35.

as in Mark, ending with the same stone saying from Ps. 118:22–23 (Matt. 21:12–42). Matt. 23:39 then cites Ps. 118:26 again, in the context of a lament for Jerusalem 'the city that kills the prophets and stones those who are sent to it' (Matt. 23:37–38). The inference is similar, albeit expanded, to that in Mark: Jesus will become a corner-stone in a new city not made with hands (see also Matt. 24:1–2).[315]

Luke follows a similar narrative, although Ps. 118:26 is recontextualised; it is found in Luke 13:35, and is spoken as part of the journey made by Jesus *before* he reaches Jerusalem: this then speaks of Jesus' destiny to die there. This makes the reference to Ps. 118:25–26, upon Jesus' entry into Jerusalem, in Luke 19:29–30, all the more poignant, where here Jesus is explicitly hailed as a *king*, ('Blessed is the king who comes in the name of the Lord …') perhaps also hinting here at Ps. 2:7–9.[316] The use of Psalm 118 after the parable of the vineyard is similar to Mark and Matthew, except in Luke only *the son* is killed (Lk. 20:9–16) and Luke cites only 118:22 (Lk. 20:17) thus linking this 'stone saying' to other passages such as Isa. 5:1–7 and Isa. 8:14, but in this context also alluding to Jesus' future vindication. Psalm 118 is important to Luke: verse 22 is also found in verse 11 of Peter's speech in Acts 4:1–31, where Ps. 2:1–2 is also cited (verses 25–26), reiterating the theme of the vindication of Jesus through his resurrection.

John 12:13, also narrating Jesus' entry into Jerusalem, similarly uses Ps. 118:26; here the use of palm branches by the crowd may well evoke the Feast of Tabernacles with which this psalm later became associated (see Ps. 118:27). Here Jesus is hailed as 'King of Israel' and Zech. 9:9 is also quoted. John emphasises that the disciples did not understand the meaning of this event until after the resurrection (John 12:16).[317]

Hebrews uses Psalm 118 too, although only verse 6 ('The Lord is my helper: I shall not fear what men shall do to me…') in Heb. 13:6, where 'the Lord' is now a reference to Christ himself. The only other detailed use of the 'stone saying' is found in 1 Pet. 2:4–10, where the motif of 'the stone' is developed further: Christ is the living stone (1 Pet. 2:4); the church is called to be living stones too (1 Pet. 4:5); Isa. 28:16 is then cited (1 Pet. 2:6) and is combined in 1 Pet. 2:7 with Ps. 118:22 and in 1 Pet. 2:8 with Isa. 8:4. This '*catena*' using stone sayings (see also Eph. 2:20–21, where Ps. 118:22–23 is also alluded to) shows just how significant Psalm 118 had become in the early church: along with Psalms 2, 22 and 110, Psalm 118 pointed to Jesus as the Messiah.

In the church fathers the 'stone sayings' are also prominent, but interestingly these are also combined with Ps. 118:20 ('This is the gate of the Lord…'). In this context the 'stone saying' is harsher than in the New Testament, being often used

---

[315] See Menken 2004: 70–75.
[316] See Wagner 1997: 163 and 175–76. See also Doble 2004: 84–86, 97–100.
[317] See Brunson 2003: 23–26.

along with Isa. 8:14–15 and 28:16 as an argument that God has rejected Israel and vindicated Christ: examples include Acts of Peter 24; Epistle of Barnabas 6:4; and *Justin in *Dial.*, 126:1. It is a strident theme in John *Chrysostom's commentary on this psalm, arguing for the place of the Gentiles in God's plan of salvation.[318] *Augustine, by contrast, cites Eph. 2:15–16, and, seeing Christ as the place where two walls connect, applies this to 'circumcision, to wit, and uncircumcision'.[319] The same view is taken by *Eusebius of Caesarea, who also uses 1 Cor. 10:4 to show how Christ as cornerstone brings the walls of Jews and Gentiles together.[320] Linking the motif of the stone with that of the gate, *Ephrem the Syrian sees the cornerstone as the stone which covered the tomb, which then became the gate of life through which the righteous Gentiles could enter.[321]

The interest in the 'gates' is found as early as *Clement of Rome, who sees that Christ is the one who opens the gate, through which the blessed can enter.[322] *Cassiodorus develops this: this is the gate of justice, and is not only about Jerusalem, but is our inheritance for which the prophets and apostles had received keys; it is also the gate of teaching and nourishment for the Catholic Church, and is indeed 'wonderful in the eyes' of all those who, like Peter, have seen and confessed Christ as the Son of the Living God.[323]

By the Middle Ages, the psalm was associated not only with the sufferings of Christ (as in verses 10–13) but as a psalm of praise because of all that Christ had achieved through his resurrection (verses 15–19) in opening up the gate for the righteous (verse 20), uniting the church (verse 22–23), announcing the days of the New Testament (verse 24) and encouraging the festivals of the church (verses 26–27). As for the bees: these were the Jews, the persecutors of Christ, surrounding him, and who Christ 'cut off' (verse 12). This is a common theme in the *Gloss, seen in the commentaries of Nicholas of *Lyra and *Lefèvre.[324]

This highlights just how different John *Calvin's approach to this psalm was. Taking, typically, the view that the figure of David lies at the heart of this psalm, as an example of true piety (and thus challenging those in the Catholic Church), Calvin equates 'the builders' in Ps. 118:22 with Roman Catholic leaders who lead the people astray: David is thus an exemplar of Protestant piety, promoting true worship of God. Hence rather than seeing the 'enemies' as the Jews, they are those Roman Catholics who deal cruelly and 'surround' the (Protestant)

---

[318] Chrysostom trans. Hill 1998: 124–25.

[319] Augustine trans. Uyl 2017: 574; also *Sermon* 4:18 in *WSA* 31:195 cited in *ACCS* VIII:308.

[320] Eusebius in *Proof of the Gospel* 1.7 in *POG* 1:45–46, cited in *ACCS* VIII:309.

[321] Ephrem, *Commentary on Tatian's Diatessaron* 21.21.

[322] 1 Clement 48 in *AF* 83, cited in *ACCS* VIII:306: see http://www.earlychristianwritings.com/text/1clement-roberts.html.

[323] Cassiodorus trans. Walsh 1991b: 169–71.

[324] See Pak 2010: 16.

people of God (Ps. 118:10–12): they, in fact, are 'like bees'. As for the Jews, Calvin reads Ps. 118:25–26 as actually promoting the piety of the Jews, exemplars of faith and trust whose words inspire us today.[325]

For Martin *Luther, 'I fell in love with this psalm. Therefore I call it my own. When emperors and kings, the wise and the learned, and even saints could not aid me, the Psalm proved a friend and helped me out of many troubles...'[326] A well-attested tradition recounts that Luther wrote the words and the plainsong notes of Ps. 118:17 ('I shall not die but live, and recount the works of the Lord') on the walls of his living quarters in Coburg Castle. He wrote an impassioned commentary on it during the Diet of Augsburg in 1530, calling it 'the beautiful *Confitemini*'. Surrounded by enemies, both in the church and outside it (i.e. Catholics and politicians: verses 10–12) but saved and protected by entering the gates of the church into the presence of Christ (verse 20) and then encountering Christ as the Cornerstone and Head of the Holy Church (verses 22–23) Luther found himself able to see the dawn of a New Day when he cried 'Hosanna!: Lord, Save Us!' (verses 24–25).[327] For Luther, this is the psalm which defeats all tyrants opposed to Christ. There is no better example of the effects of the narrative power of this psalm, as Luther reads it from the time of David to the time of Christ into his own day.

In the light of this vast commentary tradition, it is an understatement to observe that Psalm 118 is one of the richest liturgical psalms in the Psalter. As we noted in our introduction, the liturgical and antiphonal elements are embedded in the complex composition of the psalm: its refrains at the beginning, in the following lament, and in the calls to praise at the end all testify to this. It is the last of the Passover psalms, yet verses 26–27 have resulted in its use at *Sukkot as well (see *Mishnah Sukkah* 3.9 and 4.5). Temple liturgy forms its backbone, so when this was broken after the Temple's destruction in 70 CE and the psalm was used instead in the synagogue, it became an important resource for lamenting on its loss and hoping for its restoration.[328] Its antiphonal use found in the *Targum* and the *Talmud* bears further testimony to this.

As for early Christian liturgical use, Chrysostom's commentary refers to singing verse 6 as a refrain, encouraging his readers to manifest it not only in song but in their deeds.[329] Two other antiphons (verse 25: 'Hosanna' and verse 26: '*Benedictus qui venit in nomine domini*' have been used at Mass from at least the sixth-century, and the psalm as a whole is prescribed from about the same time in the *Benedictine Rule for *Lauds on Sunday. Verse 17 ('I shall not die,

---

[325] See Pak 2010: 90–93.
[326] Taken from *WA* 31:66, cited in Pak 2010: 157.
[327] See *WA* 31, and cited by Fischer 1983: 277–83.
[328] See Schonfield 2017: 145–57.
[329] See Chrysostom trans. Hill 1998: 118.

but live') and the later reference to the righteous passing through the gates (of death to life) resulted in its use at funerals; as early as the eighth-century it was used in processions from the church to the grave.[330]

Its later liturgical use from the sixteenth century onwards is evidenced in the vast number of compositions usually based on one to three verses (antiphons). Verses 16–17 were often composed for the offertory: Luther's version of verse 17 is one such example. Another example is William *Byrd's *Haec Dies* (1589), a motet for six voices, which sets verse 24 in honour of the Jesuit priest Edmond Campion who used it defiantly in 1581 when sentenced to death.[331] Verse 26 (*'Benedictus'*) is used by J. S. *Bach; originally intended for Christmas Day 1724 for a tenor voice and wind *obbligato*, it was incorporated into his Mass in B Minor. George *Wither published *Hymns and Songs of the Church* in 1623, which included melodies ascribed to Orlando *Gibbons: Ps. 118:24 is used in this case as an Easter antiphon.[332] *Handel arranged the same verse for the wedding of the Anne, the Hanoverian Princess Royal.

Interestingly, neither the controversial 'gate' in verse 20 nor the 'stone' in verses 22–23 received much attention in earlier Christian music. A number of contemporary hymns, however, use these verses: 'God is my Strength and Song' is based upon verses 14–17, and 22–24; and 'Open to me the gates of Righteousness', on verses 19–22. The hymn 'Christ is our Cornerstone', from an unknown author in the sixth or seventh centuries, and arranged by Samuel Sebastian *Wesley in 1839, is also based on verses 22–23. Isaac *Watts' 'Lo! What a glorious corner-stone/The Jewish builders did refuse' is an earlier version on the same theme.[333]

Jewish compositions mainly used verses from the very end of the psalm. Salamone *Rossi's *'Baruch Habah Beshem Adonai'*, published in about 1623, was a motet based upon verses 26–29 in *a cappella* style. It imitated an Italian Madrigal, and was composed to suggest what the Levitical singers might have performed at Passover for the Hallel. The leader declaims a verse and the congregation sings back using both polyphony and homophony.[334]

A more secular example is *Hava Nagila* (*'Let us Rejoice'*), based upon verse 24; this is a folk song and instrumental piece from Ukraine brought to Jerusalem and published in 1914 by the musicologist Abraham Zevi Idelsohn (1882–1932). This is about human solidarity, with no reference to God; it became the song accompanying the Balkan circle dance known as the 'Hora Dance', later known

---

[330] See Pickett 2002: 10.
[331] Dowling Long and Sawyer 2015: 96.
[332] Dowling Long and Sawyer 2015: 104.
[333] See https://www.ccel.org/ccel/watts/psalmshymns.Ps.263.html.
[334] See Stern 2013: 41–47; also https://www.youtube.com/watch?v=kYMEzX1w_O0.

as the Wedding Dance, and used in, for example, *Fiddler on the Roof* (1971), *The Jazz Singer* (1980) and the movie documentary *Hava Nagila: The Movie* (2012).[335] A very different arrangement, entitled 'Odecha ki anitani', of verses 21, 5, 17, 22 and 28, is by the Messianic Jewish Band Miqedem, released in 2016.[336]

One unusual jazz version which uses verses 19–23 is by the American jazz pianist and composer David Brubeck (1920–2012) whose *The Gates of Justice* (1969) was composed for the Union of American Hebrew Congregation, Florida. Intended to enable reconciliation between blacks and Jews, this was a mixture of Psalms, Martin Luther King's speeches, negro spirituals, and Jewish Hallel songs. Verses 19–23 are used in Part II, along with Isa. 62:10 and 57:4, using a Jewish cantor and spiritual blues singers. The gates here lead to the market-place, the bus station, the subway exit, and the shopping mall, deliberately imitating the same 'secular' audience the biblical prophets would have addressed.[337]

Conversely, artistic representations of the psalm focus more on the 'gate' and 'stone' motif. Byzantine Psalters, for whom verses 22–23 spoke of God's rejection of the Jews during the *iconoclastic controversies, used this image frequently. The *Theodore Psalter* (fol 157v), and also the *Barberini Psalter* (fol. 202r) for example, illustrate Christ riding an ass through the gates of Jerusalem with angry Jewish leaders looking on whilst palm fronds are raised in jubilation. The image here is very like that for Psalm 8.[338] This image is represented in PLATE 21. 'This is the gate of the Lord' is illustrated in the letter 'C' (for Confitemini, using the first letter of verse 1) of the twelfth-century *St. Albans Psalter*, where an angel opens the gates with one hand and hands a book inscribed with verse 20 to the psalmist.[339] A similar invitation to enter God's gates with thanksgiving is found in the *Oppenheimer *Siddur* (Bodleian Ms. Opp. 776 Fol. 79b): the colourful and lively illustration is of various instrumentalists praising God, and the word 'hosanna' is written under it. This is the only time this word comes in this form in the psalms (although Ps. 106:47 is close to it): so this is likely to refer to Psalm 118, given the *Siddur*'s associations with the Passover and its use of the Hallel: see PLATE 22 for a reproduction of this image. Finally, the twentieth-century artist *Benn similarly illustrates verse 20 with God appearing in the guise of a winged angel full of light.[340]

We noted at the beginning of this psalm that it might well have had a military background in the context of the king if it is a pre-exilic psalm or a religious leader if it is post-exilic. As far as an ancient setting is concerned, this has been

---

[335] See Dowling Long and Sawyer 2015: 98.
[336] See https://miqedem.bandcamp.com/track/odecha-ki-anitani.
[337] See Stern 2013: 177–85.
[338] See Gillingham 2017: 78–79 (on Ps. 8:2).
[339] See https://www.albani-psalter.de/stalbanspsalter/english/commentary/page309.shtml.
[340] Benn 1970: no page numbers.

developed in some detail by Dennis Tucker, reading the psalm in the context of deconstructing the empire of the Achaemenid dynasty (550–330 BCE).[341] Parts of Psalm 118 have frequently been used in this way: for example, verse 1 ('O give thanks unto the Lord, for he is good ...') was apparently sung by the forces of Henry of Navarre before the Battle of Coutras in 1587. More recently, when war in Europe ended in May 1945 with the surrender of Germany, Field Marshall Montgomery sent a message to all the troops under his command as Commander in Chief of the 21st Army Group: 'On this day of victory in Europe I feel I would like to speak to all who have served and fought with me during the last few years ... We all have a feeling of great joy and thankfulness that we have been preserved to see this day. We must remember to give praise and thankfulness where it is due: 'This is the Lord's doing and it is marvellous in our eyes' (Psalm 118:23).

The multivalent use of this psalm is thus proven: it serves a similar purpose in Jewish and Christin liturgy, but in the commentary tradition it has had an unsettling influence in Jewish–Christian relations. In music and art, however, and even in political rhetoric, the more universal aspect of its overall message— that God's steadfast love endures for ever—is better heard.

---

[341] See Tucker 2014a: 89–94.

Psalm 119: Reflections on the Formation of Character

Normally the compilers make connections between one psalm and its neighbour. Psalm 119, by contrast, has little in common with the collection of psalms before it (113–118) and after it (120–134). It lacks their liturgical references, and their acknowledgement of the people's history and the Temple: the means of entering the presence of God in Psalm 119 is through a personal encounter with the Torah. Yet even here (rather like Psalm 1) the interest in the Torah is distinctive: there are no specific references to the commands in the priestly and deuteronomic law codes, nor any particular models for obedience; furthermore, despite its 176 verses, the figure of Moses is entirely absent, and use of the word 'covenant' is eschewed. It is thus a 'Torah' psalm in an idealised sense: the supplicant rarely addresses the congregation directly by talking about God, but rather, unlike Psalms 1 and 19B, addresses God in the second person as his personal 'teacher'. Psalm 119 is thus a unique and independent psalm which knows of the Pentateuch but does not limit the Torah to this alone.[342]

And yet in terms of the first stage of reception of this psalm, the compilers surely inserted it here for a reason. Its acrostic structure links it back to Psalms 111 and 112, and verse 176 may be a redaction to connect the end of the psalm with the theme of the wanderings in 107:4 and 40, at the beginning of Book Five. The inference is that compilers placed this distinctive psalm here to break up the two different collections of 'Egyptian Hallel' (113–118), centring on the exodus traditions, and the Songs of Ascent (120–134), focussed on Zion.

---

[342] See Levenson 1987: 567.

Psalms Through the Centuries: A Reception History Commentary on Psalms 73–151, Volume Three, First Edition. Susan Gillingham.
© 2022 John Wiley & Sons Ltd. Published 2022 by John Wiley & Sons Ltd.

At first sight Psalm 119 has a very clear structure, whereby each of the eight verses contained within each of its twenty-two strophes begin with the same Hebrew letters, so that the words starting with the letter *Aleph* occur at the beginning of each of the eight verses in the first strophe, and the letter *Beth* begins each word at the beginning of the second strophe, and so on.[343] Furthermore, within each set of eight verses, seven loosely connected ideas are expressed, with the final verse acting as a summary, creating a 7+1 pattern which has various liturgical connotations of eight days festivals and the reading of the law (see Neh. 8:1–18). Eight key words are used to describe Torah: four are feminine (words mostly translated as 'promise', 'word', 'testimony' and 'commandment') and these often alternate with four masculine synonyms ('statute', 'instruction', 'ordinance', and 'precept').

But this apparently ordered structure has several anomalies. Other words for Torah are used as well—for example, other words for 'way' and 'path', thus breaking up the pattern and creating ten synonyms, not eight. Furthermore, the masculine/feminine convention is not rigidly maintained, and the '7 + 1' rule does not apply to every strophe; nor is there any obvious development of argument between one strophe and another. Finally, the individual verses offer little repetition or contrast of ideas ('parallelism'), a feature associated with conventional Hebrew poetry such as in Proverbs. See for example verse 1–8: they clearly demonstrate this irregularity, even in English translation. This is partly due to the constraints of the alphabetical arrangement and repetition of the synonyms for 'Torah'.

Partly because of this lack of inner coherence, and partly because of the length of the psalm, the following discussion of the psalm's reception will deal only with the psalm as a whole and a few familiar verses.

The reception of this psalm into Greek does not attempt to utilise any acrostic form, given that the alphabet has 24 letters, not 22, and an attempt at enumeration instead is evident in only one medieval manuscript, although the equivalent letter heads up each strophe (for example, α' αλφ at the beginning of verse 1). However, the Hebrew word *torah* occurs twenty-five times in Psalm 119 and in each case this is translated consistently by the Greek word *nomos* ('Law'). The **LXX* also develops the same emphasis in the Hebrew about a *relationship* with the Torah: it actually stresses the 'love' for the Torah more than in the Hebrew (verses 2, 22, 24, 70, 77, 85, 92, 98, 117, 143, 174).[344]

Turning to the psalm's reception at **Qumran*, one scroll offers some interesting insights into the more positive relationship of Psalm 119 with the Psalms

---

[343] It may even be that this whole psalm of 22 smaller parts corresponded with the 24 psalms comprising Psalms 120–34, and this may be another reason for its reception at this juncture in the Psalter.

[344] See Hossfeld and Zenger 2011: 284–85.

of Ascent. In 11QPsᵃ the sequence runs from Psalms 120–132, and is then followed by Psalm 119 (taking up nine columns and following the MT with a great degree of consistency), and then by Psalms 135–136. Psalm 119 thus concludes the Psalms of Ascent, instead of 133–134, which emphasised Temple liturgy: here the love of Torah is emphasised instead. This is one small example of the ethos of the community with its more negative response to the legitimacy of the Temple and its more positive response to the identity-marker of the Torah.[345]

Later Jewish tradition focusses on two key figures as typical models of the piety in Psalm 119: one is David; the other, Abraham. For example, in the *Talmud* it is David who is the figure praying in verse 62: 'At midnight David aroused himself to praise and pray ... inspirational to our prayer' (*b.Berakot* 3b, 4a); whereas in *Midrash Tehillim* the figure is Abraham, who is blessed and walks in God's ways (verses 1–4) by leaving his homeland (Genesis 12) and being prepared to sacrifice his son (Genesis 22).[346] *Rashi, by contrast, affirms the Jewish practices of his day by citing verse 164: 'Seven times a day I praise you for your righteous ordinances'. He adds: 'In the morning service I recite two benedictions before reading the *Shema*, and one after it, and in the Evening Service I recite two before it and two after it'.[347] Other Jewish commentators focus on the references to the numbers seven, eight, and ten, and the synonyms for 'Torah'.[348] Much is also made of the visual and semantic meaning of each of the twenty-two letters: for example, the sixth letter *Waw* symbolises being straight and upright, whilst the eighth letter *Ḥet* speaks of the importance of grace.

Remarkably, given its similar linguistic identity, the *Targum* focusses on translating the content of the text but again at the expense of an acrostic form, just like the Greek and, later, the Latin translations. *Targum* typically expands difficult phrases, so that in verses 2 and 10 'seek the Lord' becomes 'seek *instruction* from the Lord', thus also keeping God's distance from human activity; whilst in verse 135 'make your face to shine' becomes 'make the splendor of your face to shine'. Slightly different is the change to verse 130, where for clarity 'the righteous will see' becomes 'the righteous will see *your punishment*'. But here these are more technical changes typical of the *Targum* throughout the psalms and offer little for a new understanding of the psalm.

---

[345] Psalm 119 is found in fragmentary forms in five other scrolls. Holladay 1993: 109 notes how popular Psalm 119 was at Qumran, with verse 1 ('thou whose way is blameless') occurring seven times in the *Community Rule*.

[346] Braude 1959: 248.

[347] Gruber 2004: 686–7.

[348] Feuer 2004: 1416–17, citing Rashi.

One of the intriguing features of Christian reception of this psalm is the way it so often embraces a particular theology of 'Torah'. 'A tree of two and twenty branches, each with eight boughs, from which drops of sweetness continually fall' is *Neale and Littledales' summary of the use of the psalm by the early fathers.[349] The blessedness corresponds to the eight beatitudes; and the last eight verses in Hebrew all begin with the Hebrew letter *Taw* which in Greek is the letter *Tau* and so remind us of the mark of the cross, so that the whole psalm leads up to Christ.[350]

There are some fourteen allusions to Psalm 119 in the New Testament, but no citations. Part of verse 32 is found in 2 Cor. 6:11 ('our heart is wide open to you'); verse 89, on God's word being firmly fixed in heaven, may lie behind Luke 21:32–33; verse 103 is in part alluded to in Rev. 10:9 ('sweeter than honey'); and verse 160 may be hinted at in John 17:17 ('your word is truth'). None of these expressions, however, need to have come directly from Psalm 119. So like Psalms 1 and 19B this is another Torah psalm which is not prominent in the New Testament.

Nevertheless, Psalm 119 became one of the eight most popular liturgical psalms from the second-century onwards.[351] This fed into the Christian commentary tradition as well. One popular form of reception was to take the ten synonyms for the Torah and to show how, allegorically read, they pointed to Christ as the fulfilment of the Ten Commandments as part of the Law. *Origen, for example, does this with the word 'Way': this now refers to the 'Way of Christ' (as in John 14:6, Acts 9:2 and *passim*) or the Christian life of faith, following the example of Christ. So Origen reads in verse 46 the witness of Christ before Pilate ('I will speak of your decrees before kings') and similarly finds references to Christ's passion in verses 22–23, 28 and 161, as these speak of the persecution of the psalmist. Similarly, the resurrection is assumed in verse 91 ('If your law had not been my delight, I would have perished in my misery').[352]

*Hilary of Poitiers wrote a two-volume commentary on Psalm 119, divided into twenty-two sections for the twenty-two letters of the Hebrew alphabet, arguing that remembering points by way of letters was an aid to the memory for the less literate. His was a philological work, but was also close to Origen's allegorical method with reflections on what it means to be human, what it means to know the truth, and how knowing Christ as the 'fulfilment of the law' is a guide in our human imperfection.[353]

---

[349] See Neale and Littledale 1874–79: 4/3.
[350] See *ibid.*, 154. This is taken in part from the Epistle of *Barnabas: see Vesco 1986: 9.
[351] On the liturgical potential of Psalm 119, see p. 242.
[352] See Rose 1983: 218–22.
[353] See Rigolot 2017: 115–20.

Both *Ambrose and *Augustine used Psalm 119 frequently in their sermons—there are twenty-two known sermons by Ambrose, and thirty-two by
Augustine, the latter especially well-known in the context of the *Pelagian
controversies (the last one dating from 418). It was probably the trusting
obedience of the psalmist and Augustine's sense of Torah as 'grace' which
drew him to this psalm: his *Confessions*, for example, refer to different verses
some forty times—more than any other psalm (although one has to take into
account its length, as the next most cited, Psalm 18, is used twenty-one times).
In his Preface to Psalm 119, Augustine explains that he had put off writing
about this psalm because of its length and its profundity. He was pressed to
write by 'the brethren' and so decided to do this by means of sermons directly
addressing the laity.[354] Then follow the thirty-two sermons spoken 'from the
heart to the heart'.

*Cassiodorus' commentary on this psalm could not be more different.
Although he speaks about embracing the psalm, he is more concerned about
the various numerical schemas in it (ironically for such an anti-Jewish commentator, here he emulates much Jewish exegesis). He notes, for example,
that this is only the third of alphabetic psalms thus far to contain the entire
alphabet—the others being 111 and 112—and so it is to be given a Trinitarian
emphasis.[355]

If Augustine focussed on the way in which Psalm 119 could feed the faithful
in the here and now, *Luther gives this psalm a more future emphasis. Luther's
earlier medium is not sermons but lectures, not least those given between 1513
and 1516. There is a sharpness within his exegesis, even though he still follows
the Christological approach of Augustine. Luther's key issue is the difference
between the 'law of Moses' and the 'law of faith', and the extent to which the
'faithful synagogue' (verse 81) who are the people of Israel (verse 83) can be
included within the church (verse 163). So in seeking out a 'Gospel of Grace'
within this psalm, Luther emphasises the idea of the law as 'testimony', as this
looks ahead to the future. For Luther the literal, ordinary interpretation of the
piety of the psalmist is not enough: the prophetic reading of the psalm in terms
of its fulfilment in the life of the church (which then takes over the 'faithful
synagogue') is the truest meaning. The whole psalm only makes sense as a petition for the coming of Christ and his offer of Grace: if read otherwise it speaks
only of the temporary, provisional character of the Law of Moses.[356] It was as a
result of studying Psalm 119 that Luther offered three principles for studying

---

[354] See Augustine trans. Uyl 2017: 601 (note 518).

[355] The observation is correct since Psalms 25, 34 and 145 all miss out a single letter—this betrays a
remarkable knowledge of the Hebrew text: Cassiodorus trans. Walsh 1991b: 258–9.

[356] Preuss 1969: 176–99, especially p.178, citing *WA* 4.281.35–37.

the Bible: *oratio*, (prayer of a personal address *to* God), *meditatio* (meditation *about* God), and *tentatio* (a struggle against the trials of life *with* God).[357] Luther's lectures were delivered before the Diet of Worms: it is interesting that by 1542, four years before his death, Luther began to understand this psalm in a different way. Then he wrote in his Bible, against verse 92 of this psalm: 'If your law had not been my delight, I would have perished in my affliction'.

*Calvin's legally trained mind was critical of the way in which the psalmist spoke of various matters without dealing with any of them in great detail.[358] Consequently he read Psalm 119 very differently from Luther. If true religion was integrity of spirit 'from the heart', then this psalm was about true religion and dedication of all one's being to the grace of God. According to Calvin, the very beginning of the psalm made this point so clearly. Here we read that all aspire to happiness, but they look for it in the wrong place: living in the grace of God and being obedient to God is where true happiness is to be found.[359] Ironically, in this respect, Calvin's reading of this psalm is actually closer to Augustine's interpretation than is Luther's.

Given that this is such a long psalm, and given its popularity in the commentary tradition, it is not surprising that in Jewish liturgy several verses are frequently used. For example, verse 156 ('Great is your mercy, O Lord …') is used in the sixth benediction of the *'Amidah* and verse 153 ('Look on my misery and rescue me …') is used in the seventh benediction as part of the call to worship. Jewish liturgical practices in the Sephardic tradition customarily chant Psalm 119 after the Sabbath afternoon service, along with Psalms 120–134 and Psalm 91. More specifically the alphabetic structure encouraged the recitation of the strophes beginning with the letters *Beth, Resh, Kaph* and *He*—making an acronym for *Berekah* (blessing)—to be recited as a blessing in, for example, the consecration of a house.[360] In the *kabbalistic tradition the psalm was seen as a cure for illness, but when recited backwards, it was a curse on one's enemies.[361]

A similar pattern emerges in Christian liturgy. Verse 164 ('Seven times a day I praise you …') was seminal in the creation of the *Daily Office: *Benedict's Rule makes it clear that prayer is to be made seven times a day.[362] The psalm plays a prominent part in *Prime, and three parts are also used in *Terce, *Sext and *None on Mondays, whilst the recitation of other parts follows throughout the week. It plays a critical part in the Easter vestal liturgy (starting with verse 73) and it is also used in *Vigils. 'The Little Alphabet of the Monks in the School

---

[357] Lehman 1960: 279–88.
[358] See Brueggemann and Bellinger 2014: 519 citing Calvin trans. Beveridge 1979: 398.
[359] Quoted in Selderhuis 2018: 257, citing CTS II: 402–403.
[360] See Elbogen 1993: 42–43, 101; Holladay 1993: 146.
[361] See 1993: 288 and 184.
[362] This is cited in Chapter 16 of the *Rule*.

of Christ', attributed to the fifteenth-century spiritual writer German Thomas à Kempis, is taken from the didactic acrostic of 119. In some traditions this psalm marks one of the eight liturgical divisions in the Psalter, encouraging illustrations of its first letter 'B' (the Latin translation for 'Blessed' or 'Happy')—in imitation of Psalm 1.[363] So whether used in its entirety, or whether used by adapting isolated verses as *antiphons, this more personal and reflective psalm has become a key element in Christian as well as Jewish liturgy, in part because of its structure and in part because of its emphasis on Torah as a gift of God's grace.

Psalm 119 poses a problem for its representation in art. Did an illuminator use one image for the entire psalm, or did they illustrate each of the 22 collections of verses? The *Utrecht Psalter* (fol. 68v) provides just one image which is in fact of the first three stanzas (twenty-four verses). Four blessed men walk in the way of the Lord, whilst the hand of God blesses a man who is reading the Law in the Temple; the psalmist is prostrate in worship on the steps. Two men (Moses and Jeremiah?) preach to kings and princes (verses 21–23) whilst an angel hurls a battle axe towards them.[364] The related *Eadwine Psalter* (fol. 210v) makes these representations even more clear.[365]

The *Stuttgart Psalter* illustrates, by contrast, all twenty-two strophes, many read with a specific Christological emphasis. At the beginning, the artist offers an additional illumination of the letter 'B', for 'blessed' (fol. 132v), again reminiscent of the 'Beatus' illumination in Psalm 1. Several times the life of Christ is narrated: the most striking is the penultimate image (fol. 142r) of Christ being led out to be crucified (v. 161, following Origen *et al*: 'princes persecute me without cause…') whilst the very last image is of the vindication of Christ, protected by the hand of God emerging from a cloud (fol. 142v).[366]

The *Theodore Psalter*, typical of Byzantine Psalters, has marginal images, and these are not directly related to the eight-line stanzas. Hence fols. 158r–161v depict the importance of human piety—rather like the *Midrash Tehillim*, for example—but do so, as with *Utrecht*, through figures of saints. The first image is of five saints (fol. 158r), who here reflect not on the law, but upon an icon, and others include St. Paul and David, the latter also engrossed with an icon.[367]

Perhaps the most striking artistic representation of Psalm 119 is found in the *St. Albans Psalter*. This reads almost like a personal hand-produced Book of Hours, where the focus is on the piety of psalmist, and the twenty-two images are illuminations of the first Latin letter of each of the twenty-two stanzas. As

[363] See Solopova 2013b: 131.
[364] See https://psalter.library.uu.nl/page/144.
[365] See https://bit.ly/3fWWoO3.
[366] See https://bit.ly/3lOFMtR (for fol. 142r); and https://bit.ly/3Gwjh50 (for fol. 142v).
[367] See http://www.bl.uk/manuscripts/Viewer.aspx?ref=add_ms_19352_f158r.

in the *Stuttgart Psalter*, the first is an illumination of the letter 'B' ('Beatus') which here is of a naked soul raising his hands in prayer to the psalmist. David holds open a book, inscribed 'Blessed are the blameless in the way'. His right forefinger touches the soul's head and the text, as if to bring the two together in prayer.[368] Three particular themes are repeated throughout the other images. In several other places we see the naked soul before God (for examples, for verses 73 and 105); another theme is of Christ blessing the psalmist (usually David, as in verses 49 and 81); a third clear motif is of pilgrimage—both an inward journey of the soul and a literal journey as well, in preparation for the motif of Zion in Psalms 120–134 following. The illumination of verse 49, for example, has a barefoot pilgrim on crutches, offering to Christ a book with the words 'in place of my pilgrimage …'[369] Perhaps the most striking, because of its social commentary relevant to the Psalter's own setting, is of verses 25–33 ('Turn my eyes from looking at vanities') which is a full page image enclosed within the elongated initial 'A'.[370]

Almost a century later the *Parma Psalter* offers different Jewish illustrations. In this Psalter Psalm 118 has been divided into two, so 119 is actually Psalm 120.[371] The initial *Aleph* for the first letter of the first verse (fol. 171a) is illuminated in a similar style to Psalm 1, although not as lavishly decorated; but the word '*ashre*' is similarly contained in a box and illuminations are found around it. Every eight-verse stanza is then divided with markers, covering twenty-four folios (171v-182r) overall. Some images are of singing birds, or dogs; fol. 182b is of a dragon, head in the air, apparently singing his own praises to the Torah.[372] Clearly this psalm was seen as most significant in the Psalter as a whole.

When Psalm 119 is used in stained glass windows the instruction is more symbolic and universal, and the commentary often has more social implications. Typical is the use of Psalm 119 in *Chagall's windows at Sankt Stephan Kirche in Mainz, begun when the artist was 91. The whole work, worked out in ethereal deep blue glass, started in 1982 and was another example of Chagall's work which was designed to reconcile Jewish and Christian faiths after the Second World War (when St. Stephen's church was badly bombed). Chagall completed nine of the thirty-seven windows before he died. The Psalm 119 window depicts the psalmist David reading, with a golden *menorah to his left; the text of Psalm 119:105 ('Your word is a lamp to my feet and a light to my path') is above this, and a hovering angel holds open the book. The whole image

---

[368] See https://www.albani-psalter.de/stalbanspsalter/english/commentary/page312.shtml.
[369] See https://www.albani-psalter.de/stalbanspsalter/english/commentary/page317.shtml.
[370] See https://www.albani-psalter.de/stalbanspsalter/english/commentary/page315.shtml.
[371] Metzger 1996: 92.
[372] Metzger 1996: 92.

is in blue and gold glass, and the verse is used to represent the steadfastness of the Jewish faith after the Holocaust and the importance of the light of Scripture in drawing both faith traditions together.[373]

Another depiction of Psalm 119, arousing a different social comment, is by Arthur *Wragg. His black and white cartoon depicts a man with a suitcase; the verse offered as commentary is 119:9, taken from the *KJV: 'Wherewithal shall a young man cleanse his way?' (Figure 10). When asked where the man was going, Wragg added a large £ sign: this, rather than taking heed to God's word (as expressed in the latter part of verse 9) was what was leading the man on—to his destruction.[374]

A corollary of this image is provided by *Benn, for his figure is of one turning towards the Torah rather than walking away from it. Rather like Chagall's use of ethereal blue, but this time with silver-white as the contrast, a dark blue figure is set against a canvas of lighter blue. The verse under it is Psa 119:97 ('Combien j'aime Ta loi!') and the extended figure raises their hands towards a white Torah scroll above which is a figure of a dove throwing light back onto the suppliant.[375] The image is dated 1972 and again, given Benn's experience in a French concentration camp during the Second World War, this is about the power of the Torah to heal the individual rather than act as reconciler between the faiths.

Psalms with acrostic forms always provided a challenge for poets seeking to represent both the form and the content in their own translation: a psalm as long as Psalm 119 provides a peculiar challenge. The twenty-two letters in the Hebrew alphabet do not correspond with the twenty-six letters in our English alphabet so even if poets choose only to present the first letter of each of the twenty-two stanzas in the relevant letter, there is still the problem in knowing how to match the twenty-two stanzas. Mary *Sidney produced a poetic form in English which imitates the Hebrew acrostic in a more flexible way by matching only the first letter of each stanza. So the first starts 'An undefiled course who leadeth,/And in Jehovah's doctrine treadeth, /How blessed he!' The second stanza begins with 'By what correcting line,/May a young man make straight his crooked way?'. The third stanza commences 'Confer, O Lord,/ This benefit on me,/That I may live, and keep thy word'. To make each stanza distinctive, however, Sidney uses a different poetic genre in each of the twenty-two cases. And to make up for the difference in the letters, she omits the letters j, u, x and z. This is a remarkably creative work, especially when reading one stanza after another.[376]

---

[373] On Chagall's contrasting image of Psalm 150 at Chichester Cathedral, with its reds and golds, see pp. 440–41 and Plate 30. On this psalm in Mainz Cathedral, see Rosen 2013: 114–15.

[374] See Brook 2001: 57.

[375] See Benn 1970: no page numbers. See also https://www.artofbenn.com/biblicalimages (105/124).

[376] See Hamlin *et al*. 2009: 228–47.

FIGURE 10   Arthur Wragg, 'Wherewithal shall a young man cleanse his way?'
(Ps. 119:9).

Source: Wragg, A. 1934: *The Psalms for Modern Life*. New York: Claude Kendall.

Other poets have sought to focus only on the eightfold repetition of each letter and so create a complete stanza, like the Hebrew, in the repeated alphabetic form. Again four English letters have been omitted: Gordon Jackson's version (below) omits q, x, y and z. So under 'L' the first six verses read:

> Lord, your word is inscribed
> indelibly in the heavens;

> Laws that you laid the earth by
> keep faith with our generations;
> Lasting and life-giving logic
> that loyally follows your will.
> Lost I would be through affliction
> if love had not bound you to me.
> Life is the lot you supplied me,
> a lesson I tell your love by.
> Learning your will is my study;
> as I am your own, Oh save me...

The problem here is that the form dominates the content: although the verses capture something of the sense in the Hebrew, it can only be approximate.[377]

Hymnody—for public use, rather than for more private reading, as with the examples above—uses the psalm somewhat differently. In some cases the composer is influenced by only one verse. One such example is John Henry *Newman's 'Lead kindly Light, amid the encircling gloom,/Lead thou me on', written in 1833, before his conversion. The poem, which again echoes verse 105 ('Your word is a lamp to my feet and a light to my path') reflects the anxiety and uncertainty brought about in part by a recovery from illness and in part because of the political unrest of the times, as seen in the irregular meter which the familiar tune 'Lux Benigna' brings out so well.[378]

Few composers have set the entire psalm to music. *Coverdale's version was broken up into several parts—either a complete stanza or just one verse—and used by many different composers. Examples include William *Byrd's 'Teach me O Lord', and William *Boyce's 'Teach me O Lord the Way of Thy Statutes', both based on verses 33–38;[379] also Henry *Purcell's 'Thy Word is a Lantern' based on verse 105–111.[380] In 1671 Heinrich *Schütz arranged the psalm in a cycle of thirteen motets, creating a double chorus and *basso continuo*, calling the piece *Schwanengesang*—a 'swansong' of David and the Prophet—and concluded it with Psalm 100 (SWV 482–92). Schütz also wrote at least seven other arrangements of different stanzas from Luther's text, and verse 54 ('Your statutes have been my songs wherever I make my home') was sung at his funeral.[381] By

---

[377] See Jackson 1997: 141.
[378] See Watson 2002: 267–69.
[379] See https://www.youtube.com/watch?v=2FdkskCbBsA (William Byrd); also (for William Boyce) https://www.cpdl.org/wiki/index.php/Teach_me,_O_Lord,_the_way_of_thy_statutes_.
[380] See https://www.youtube.com/watch?v=kCQDtEN50s4.
[381] See http://www2.cpdl.org/wiki/index.php/Psalm_119 and concerning Schütz in particular, see for example http://www2.cpdl.org/wiki/index.php?curid=177108; also Dowling Long and Sawyer 2015: 1–2. Schütz's *Schwanengesang* is at https://www.youtube.com/watch?v=neSRx-biZbs.

contrast, Isaac *Watts divided the psalm into eighteen songs under connected themes, rather than working through each stanza:[382] Watts chose words such as gospel, word, truth, promise instead of law, commands, judgements, testimonies, and instead of the acrostic form he used rhyme and rhythm instead, thus contemporising the psalm within a Christian milieu and so creating a poem very different from the Hebrew original. There are several examples of parts of the psalm in contemporary popular music: 'Thy Word', taken from verse 105, by Amy Grant and Michael W. Smith (1984), is one such example.[383]

In contemporary discourse Kent Reynolds makes the point in his *Torah as Teacher* that the psalm is not about narrow-minded legalism but about 'formation of character'.[384] This approach is very much evident in Dietrich *Bonhoeffer's writings on Psalm 119. In 1939, having joined the resistance and having been co-opted to the *Abwehr*, Bonhoeffer began to write increasingly about the psalms, under headings such as 'Creation', 'Law', 'Salvation', 'The Enemy' and 'The End'. Psalm 119 was particularly important to him, both from his experience of it in liturgy (Mirfield being one particular influence during his time in England in 1933) and now also in personal prayer. Bonhoeffer wrote three moving meditations on this psalm: the first was on verses 1–4 ('praise'), the second in verse 5–16 ('guiltless') and the third, unfinished, on 17–26 ('with eyes wide open'). The last is especially poignant, as here Bonhoeffer writes that our security is the 'Word of God', and here we need to 'see' afresh, like blind Bartimaeus: 'The great wonder in the law of God is the revelation of the Lord Jesus Christ. Through him the Word receives life: contradictions are resolved, revelation of unimaginable depths. Lord, open my eyes!'.[385] The meditation, written in 1940, breaks off in the middle of a sentence some pages later, on verse 21. It is a reflection on the consequences of disobeying the Word of God. In July 1940 France had surrendered, and it is well-known that from this time on Bonhoeffer began to lead his double life: along with the cheering crowd in Memel, he gave the Hitler Salute, explaining to his companion, Eberhard Bethge: 'We shall have to run risks for very different things now, but not for this salute!'. The complexities of life and obedience to God had begun to overwhelm him. As far as we know, he never returned to writing any more of his commentary on Psalm 119.

[382] See https://www.ccel.org/ccel/watts/psalmshymns.cclxiv.html.

[383] See https://www.youtube.com/watch?v=a6LC8cu03Ig.

[384] See Reynolds 2010: 181–83. For a further resource, see https://thelongpsalm.wordpress.com/resources.

[385] Robertson (ed.) 2005: 89 and 97.

Psalms 120–134: A Liturgical Collection (ii)

The 'Songs of Ascent' (Psalms 120–134) form a collection of fifteen short songs averaging some seven verses for each psalm. Indeed, only one psalm in this collection (Ps. 132) extends to more than nine verses. Psalm 119 comprised twenty-two stanzas of eight verses: its 176 verses make the psalm far longer than the 105 verses of this whole collection. Whereas it was difficult to find a cohesive argument throughout Psalm 119, mainly because of the constraints of its acrostic form, the 'Songs of Ascent' exhibit a development of themes, despite the number of psalms from various hands in very different settings. The Zion (and, to some extent, Davidic) interests within this collection are very different from the groups on either side, where the Exodus/Torah themes dominate (Psalms 113–118, 119 and 135–136). So did the editors collect together these disparate prayers as a liturgical collection, perhaps for use at the autumn festival of *Sukkot in Jerusalem?[386] Or was this a literary and theological collection, perhaps with an ideology intended to counter imperialism and to foster social justice, in the context of Persian rule?[387]

Against this being only a literary collection, theology and ideology can be fostered through worship as well, as is the case with the so-called royal psalms. There are several indications that this might have been edited as a liturgical

---

[386] Mitchell 2015: 3–9 argues the collection was used at the autumnal festival as early as Davidic times. On the other hand, Goulder 1997: 28–30 argues the collection was created for Sukkot at the time of Nehemiah in the Persian period.

[387] See Albertz 1997: 95–108, also Tucker 2014a: 135–39.

Psalms Through the Centuries: A Reception History Commentary on Psalms 73–151, Volume Three, First Edition. Susan Gillingham.
© 2022 John Wiley & Sons Ltd. Published 2022 by John Wiley & Sons Ltd.

collection, rather like Psalms 113–118 in Jewish tradition. The repeated theme of blessing, the examples of repeated formulaic language, the changes of speakers, and the title over each psalm as a 'Song' all suggest liturgical concerns. So our working proposal here is that diverse psalms, some with elements of 'popular' piety (those using farming imagery in 126:5–6 and 129:3, 6–7; those concerned with hunting and warfare in 120:4–7 and 124:6–7; and those interested in family life in 123:2, 127:1, 3–5, 128:3–6, and 131:2) have been adapted to create a liturgical anthology of fifteen psalms, primarily focussed on David and Zion.[388]

The evidence from the first-century CE scroll 11QPs[a] suggests that this collection was known and adapted in different ways. The sequence in that scroll is Psalms 120–132, 119, 135–136 (with Psalms 133 and 134 not culminating the collection but appearing separately later in the scroll). Psalm 119 does not introduce the Ascents, but concludes it, showing nevertheless the close relationship between obedience to Torah (Psalm 119) and the God's blessing from Zion within the other Ascents psalms.

There are at least three main views about the overall structure of these fifteen psalms. Erich Zenger, for example, assumes three parts, comprising 120–124, 125–129, and 130–134. Both 120 and 130 begin a collection with a lament psalm; 125–129 is a collection comprising mainly familial and popular piety; and at the heart of each small collection is a psalm focussing on Zion (122; 127, with its Solomonic heading; and 132).[389] Klaus Seybold argues for five parts, whereby Psalms 120–122 and 132–134 depict arriving in and leaving Jerusalem; 127–129 focus on God's blessing from Zion; 123–126 progress from lament to confidence, and 130–131 progress from penitence to trust.[390] This places more emphasis on the theme of pilgrimage than on the relationship between more familial and more official religion, as seen in the threefold grouping. David Mitchell sees the whole collection as festal. He advocates it reveals a *chiasmus, with Psalm 127 at the heart and seven psalms on each side.[391] Psalms 120 and 134 mirror each other (on departing for Zion and leaving Zion); so too do Psalms 121 and 133 (on Zion as a place of blessing); so also Psalms 122 and 132 (on the arrival of the pilgrims into Zion [122] and also the Ark being brought into Zion [132]). Psalms 123 mirrors 131 (on humility, with eyes not lifted up in pride); so also Psalms 124 and 130 (on hostile waters and being redeemed from trouble); Psalms 126 mirrors 128 (with the fertility imagery) whilst Psalms 125

---

[388] See Limburg 2002: 84–86 especially. See also Crow 1996: 130–43; Mitchell 2015: 31; Goulder 1997: 25–26; Hunter 1999: 173–258, especially the table on p. 183.

[389] Hossfeld and Zenger 2011: 296. This is also found earlier in Auffret 1982: 439–531.

[390] See Gillingham 2005: 317–20, citing Seybold 1978: 69–75.

[391] Mitchell 2015: 12–13.

and 129 have similar concerns (on the hope for deliverance from foreign domination). Psalm 127, with its Solomonic heading, thus stands at the centre of this collection. This is an intriguing suggestion, which combines both literary and liturgical concerns, which works better with some pairs of psalms than with others. We shall adopt in the main Zenger's proposal that there are three overlapping collections, with more familial psalms being brought alongside those emphasising the central place of Zion, whilst also recognising that this seems to have been brought together as a pilgrimage collection.[392]

The theme of blessing dominates this collection; only Psalms 120 and 123 do not close with some sort of blessing.[393] Otherwise these psalms speak frequently of Israel blessing God and God blessing Israel. Indeed, phrases used in the 'Aaronic Blessing' in Num. 6:24–26 ('May God bless you/protect you/be gracious to you/give you peace') are interspersed throughout twelve of the fifteen psalms, being absent only in 124,126 and 131.[394] Blessing is a liturgical act; so again this points to a liturgical collection.

The step parallelism, whereby the end of one clause is repeated at the beginning of the next, is another unusual feature in this collection, contributing to a rhythm also suggestive of liturgical use.[395] For example, Psalm 120:5 speaks of 'dwelling' in Kedar; 120:6 takes up the idea of 'dwelling' and adds the motif of 'peace'; 120:7 focusses on the word 'peace'. Similarly, Ps. 121:3 speaks of God who does not 'slumber'; 121:4 adds to the idea of 'slumber' that God is the 'guardian of Israel'; and 121:5 focusses on the word 'guardian'.

Repetitions, words and distinctive phrases also suggest the formulaic language of liturgy. One example is 'the Maker of heaven and earth' (121:2; 124:8; 134:3; see also 113:6 and 115:15); another is 'from this time forth and for evermore' (121:8; 125:2; 131:3; see also 113:2 and 115:18). Suggestions of *antiphonal responses include 'Let Israel now say' in 124:1 and 129:1; and 'O Israel, hope in the Lord' in 130:7 and 131:3.[396]

The final indication of the liturgical purpose of this collection is in the title to each psalm: these are all '*Songs* of Ascent'. Interestingly only the last three psalms refer explicitly to Temple ritual: it is primarily through *singing* that the community of faith is renewed.[397] These are also 'Songs of *Ascent*': the Hebrew word *ma'alah* (singular, 'Ascent') could be a reference to some pilgrimage up to Jerusalem, and it is possible that this collection came together as early as the Persian period for this purpose.[398] *Ma'alot* (plural) is used in Exod. 20:26 to describe

---

[392] Auffret 1982: 439–531 stresses the Zion theme at the heart of each of the three collections.
[393] Mitchell 2015: 7.
[394] Gillingham 2005: 319, citing Liebreich 1955; Grossberg 1989.
[395] Mitchell 2015: 32–34; Goulder 1997: 25.
[396] Viviers 1994: see especially 278–83, for the use of distinctive repetitions in this collection.
[397] On Psalm 137 and the poignant impossibility of singing a song of Zion in exile, see pp. 359–62.
[398] Knowles 2006: 1–18 and 121–28.

the steps up to an altar; and in Ezek. 40:20 and 26, *ma'alot* describes the actual steps to the Temple. The *LXX odē tōn anabathmōn* also translates the Hebrew as a 'flight of steps'. This could therefore be the 'Fifteen Songs of the Temple Steps'.[399] According to Josephus there were *fifteen* steps in the Temple leading from the court of women to the court of men, and on these steps the fifteen psalms were sung.[400] The *Mishnah* agrees: its memory is that it was on these steps between the two courts that the Levites stood with their musical instruments to sing the fifteen Songs of Ascent (*m.Sukkah* 5.2–3,4; *b.Sukkah* 4:7–9).

This focus is on a physical and literal reading of the 'Songs of Ascent'. But early reception seems to indicate a more spiritual and metaphorical reading as well. Given that many Jewish communities in the Diaspora would not have found the opportunity to make a pilgrimage to Jerusalem, it seems that the familiar 'fifteen steps' of the Temple also took on a more imaginative adaptation; after the final destruction of the Temple in 70 CE this would have undoubtedly become the norm. The richness of the poetry, the emphasis on singing, and the absence, until the last three psalms, of reference to the Temple's liturgical rites, enabled a more internalised piety in 'imagining' Zion; this was about an inner journey to Jerusalem, which by the end of the first-century CE became a common theme in Jewish tradition.[401] This is why the 'Ascents' were so important for Diaspora communities at Sukkot, then Hanukkah, then *Purim, and in all the Sabbath services leading up to Passover. One might argue that no other collection in the Psalter had such extensive liturgical use.[402] Rabbi Saadia Gaon even argued that because the composer is not named, the songs might have had a divine source, offering continual solace to those in exile who longed for deliverance.[403] These fifteen psalms are still read, albeit with different emphases, in both *Ashkenazi and Sephardic liturgy, at afternoon Sabbath services from Sukkot to Passover.[404]

This self-contained collection, shaped for public liturgical use, is undoubtedly very different from Psalm 119, which is presented as a literary artefact for private reflection, and the overall work of one author. Yet Psalms 119 and 120–134 are closely related in their concern for obedient piety—Psalm 119 expresses this in terms of the Torah, and Psalms 120–134 is more focussed on Zion. The rabbinical tradition notes that the 22 divisions of Psalm 119 correspond to a

---

[399] Sawyer 1968: 33.

[400] The *Tosefta* makes the same point (see *T. Suk* 4.7–9). In early Christian tradition, *Hippolytus refers to these fifteen psalms once corresponding to the fifteen steps of the Temple: see Mitchell 2015: 32–33.

[401] See Zenger 2004: 84–114; also Hossfeld and Zenger 2011: 292–94.

[402] See Willems 1990: 411–17.

[403] See Cohen 1992: 417.

[404] Keet 1969: 112–33.

'universal design for human obedience', whilst the 15 Psalms of Ascent intentionally echo the name of God and the creation of the world. The divine name (Yahweh) begins with the letter *Yod* (also in Hebrew the number ten), and the world is fashioned with the letter *Heh* (also the number five), thus creating the number fifteen in all; this is expressed not only in the fifteen steps of the sanctuary, but also the fifteen words in the priestly blessing (Num. 6:24–26) and the fifteen songs celebrating the construction of the Temple.[405]

The Christian reception of the tradition of these fifteen songs and fifteen steps has one interesting interpretation. In the thirteenth-century *Golden Legend*, the Virgin Mary, aged about three, is brought to the Temple by her parents, Joachim and Anne: 'And there (were) fifteen steps of degrees to ascend up to the Temple, because the Temple was high set ... and Our Lady was set on the lowest step, and mounted up without any help as if she had been of perfect age ...' Having received the blessing from the high priest Zacharias, Mary is left in the Temple with the other virgins, and is ministered to by angels, confirming her early consecration as a chosen vessel to become a living Temple, offering a new creation, namely Christ incarnate.[406] This legendary account became a recurrent motif in Renaissance and Counter Reformation art. One well-known version is Titian's *Presentation of the Virgin* (c. 1535) kept in the Accademia Gallery, Venice.[407] An earlier and very different image is in *Les Très Riches Heures du Duc de Berry* (fol. 56v), to mark the beginning of *None: this is to illustrate the Purification of the Virgin, and immediately follows several texts and illustrations from the Psalms of Ascent (fols. 52v-56r). It shows Joseph, the Virgin Mary and the Christ Child standing with a group of onlookers at the foot of the Temple steps: a young woman, carrying two sacrificial doves, walks up them towards the High Priest at the summit.[408]

Jewish and Christian reception of each of these individual psalms is usually expressed in different ways, as the following commentary, based on a literal and an imaginative pilgrimage to Zion, will demonstrate.

---

[405] Feuer 2004: 1499–1501, noting many other instances of the number fifteen exemplified most in these Songs of Ascent.
[406] Cited in Hall 1979: 252.
[407] See https://www.titian.org/the-presentation-of-the-virgin-in-the-temple.jsp#prettyPhoto[image2]/0.
[408] Longnon and Cazelles 1969: 56, 195.

Psalm 122, at the heart of this collection, is the only actual 'Zion hymn', the other four having no explicit reference to Jerusalem. 120 is a clear diaspora psalm, and 121 also seems to be set away from Jerusalem. 120 and 121 are more individual, whilst 123 and 124 are more communal, the former a prayer for deliverance, and the latter a thanksgiving for restoration. 121 and 123 are connected by beginning in a similar way ('I lift up my eyes'). So, there seems to be some purposeful arrangement as the first stage of reception, moving from a personal pilgrimage (120 and 121) into Zion (122) where the community of faith is paramount (123 and 124).

Psalm 120: A Song from the Diaspora

One of the key issues in the psalm's reception is whether the prayer for deliverance is from verbal abuse or physical violence: verse 2 ('lying lips… deceitful tongue') implies the former, whilst the military imagery in verses 4 and 7 suggest something more physical. 'Arrows' (verse 4) may be simply a metaphor for a verbal attack (as in Ps. 64:4) but they also allude to violence (Ps.11:5).[409] The psalm as a whole is somewhat disjointed: verse 1 appears to be a thanksgiving, verses 2–4 consider the mortal and verbal threats of the enemy, whilst

[409] Tucker 2014a: 97.

Psalms Through the Centuries: A Reception History Commentary on Psalms 73–151, Volume Three, First Edition. Susan Gillingham.
© 2022 John Wiley & Sons Ltd. Published 2022 by John Wiley & Sons Ltd.

verses 5–7 (starting with the onomatopoeic *'oyah-li'* ['woe to me!']) is about homesickness caused by living in the Diaspora.[410] Meshek has associations with warring peoples in E. Anatolia or N.E. Asia Minor (Ezek. 38:2) and Kedar with tribal peoples in the Syro-Arabian desert (Jer. 2:10); but they are best interpreted metaphorically, as 'barbarians and heathens', the one in the far north and the other in the far south.[411] Hence this is a diaspora psalm where the psalmist seems to be living in a dangerous and violent place, far away from Jerusalem.

The *Septuagint presents the psalm in the past tense throughout, suggesting that the testimony to foreign oppression is looking back on a more difficult period. It interprets *meshek* as derived from the verb 'draw out, endure', thus reading verse 5 as 'Woe is me that my dwelling [in exile] has been so long' (*oimmoi hoti hē paroikia mou emakruthan*). The Greek nevertheless keeps Kedar as a place name, thus reading this literally as 'I have tented amongst the tents of Kedar' (*kateskēnōsa meta tōn skēnōmatōn kēdar*), implying the setting is the Syro-Arabian desert. The *Vulgate* reads these two place names similarly: for *meshek* the Latin reads *prolongatus est* (as in *heu mihi quia incolatus meus prolongatus est*), again making it clear that this is a 'diaspora psalm'.

At *Qumran, Psalms 120–132 maintain a coherence as part of the whole collection.[412] But Psalm 120 does not follow 119, for this long psalm instead follows 132. In 11QPs[a] 120:1 follows instead 148:5 (Column II), whilst in 4QPs[a] 120:6 follows 115:17 (the rest of 120 is missing). Although this Ascents collection comprises only thirteen psalms, Psalm 120 is therefore still the first.

Later Jewish tradition confirms the idea that 120 is a psalm composed under foreign domination and physical threat. The *Targum* reads verse 6 as 'My soul has dwelt *with Edom* who hates peace', interpreting Edom now as a symbol of Roman oppression.[413] This Edom/Rome reading is also taken up by *Rashi.[414] *Midrash Tehillim* assumes *meshek* to mean 'carried off' (from *memushshak* as used in Isa. 18:7) and Kedar to mean 'black people' (from *ke-derah*), this time stressing a more far-flung barbarian setting of the psalmist.[415]

Midrash Tehillim also develops the reference to 'the tongue', assuming the threat to be as much about verbal as physical abuse. Commenting on verse 4, the issue is that the 'tongue that is deceit slays three': the one who owns it, the one who listens to it, and the one of whom it speaks (here using the example of Doeg in 1 Sam. 22:1–23).[416] Libellous tongues are seen to be as painful an experience in exile as physical violation.

[410] Allen 2002: 200.
[411] Anderson 1972: 850.
[412] See p. 254.
[413] Stec 2004: 219.
[414] Gruber 2004: 698–99.
[415] Braude 1959: 292.
[416] Braude 1959: 291.

The psalm is not referred to in the New Testament, although there might be an allusion in 1 Peter 1:1–2 and 2:11–12 in the references to exiles who live as 'aliens' in this world. A change in Christian interpretation is not found until the later Fathers, who develop the idea of an 'imposed exile' being life here in this world, so that the hoped-for destination is not Jerusalem, but the heavenly city. *Chrysostom writes in his typically critical way that the Jews were possessed by their desire for earthly Jerusalem and were enslaved by that desire; to avoid their fate we need to be possessed by the love of heavenly things and of Jerusalem above.[417]

*Luther reads verses 3–4 as typical of the warfare faced by the church on earth. Hence the 'deceitful tongue' is just that—verbal attacks on the faith by the Roman church.[418] Related to this, it is likely that this is the psalm that Thomas *Sternhold composed in metrical form when he was released from prison for his support of Protestant martyrs in 1543: it was an ideal psalm for encouraging courage to stand up for one's beliefs when being unjustly slandered. So we read in Sternhold's version:

> In trouble and in thrall
> Unto the Lord I call
> And he doth me comfort
> Deliver me I pray,
> From lying lips alway,
> And tongues of false report.[419]

As for the Jewish liturgical use of this psalm, in later Sephardic tradition Psalms 120–134 were chanted along with verses from 119 and 102 at the conclusion of the Sabbath service at sundown. *Mishna Ta'anith* 2 prescribes 120 explicitly for this service, especially on fast days.[420] First come the *Zikronoth* (verses concerning remembrance of the past); then the *Shofaroth* (trumpets imitating God's voice of thunder), and then Psalm 120, and after it, Psalms 121, 130 and 102. This again associates the psalm with diaspora Judaism.

Christian liturgy continues the idea of an 'earthly exile' with a 'heavenly redemption': hence the association of this psalm with Lent. It was once recited daily in Lent, but now usually on Wednesdays and Maundy Thursday.[421]

In Christian art a few Byzantine Psalters interpret the psalm as about physical warfare. *Biblioteca Vaticana gr.*1927 presents Psalm 120 (*LXX*, Psalm 119) in fol. 233r with an image of a helmeted ruler, possibly Saul, holding a spear, flanked by two bodyguards, each holding a spear and shield (possibly

---

[417] Chrysostom trans. Hill and Chrysostom 1998: 132–33.
[418] *Lectures on the Psalms* 1513–1515 in LW II:538 and WA 4:396, cited in Selderhuis (ed.) 2018: 286.
[419] See https://hymnary.org/text/in_trouble_and_in_thall.
[420] Willems 1990: 415.
[421] Holladay 1993: 221.

referring to 1 Sam. 22:6); below is a beardless male figure, possibly the priest Abiathar, and other male figures (see 1 Sam. 22:20). If the association is indeed with the lying Doeg of 1 Sam. 22 there is an interesting association with the Jewish reading of this psalm in *Midrash Tehillim*, noted earlier.

*Carolingian Psalters such as *Utrecht (fol. 71v) and *Harley (fol. 64r) and *Eadwine (fol. 227r) also combine the motifs of physical warfare and lying tongues. The psalmist, standing on a small hill, is calling to Christ in the heavens. He is surrounded by three groups of men. The group in the upper right hold arrows whose tips seem to be on fire (verse 4). The foremost of the group is handing an arrow to the psalmist. In the lower right corner are the inhabitants of the 'tents of Kedar' (verse 5). A man is speaking to them (verse 5). To the left in a cave is the third group, the people with 'lying lips and deceitful tongues' (verse 2).

The artwork of the *Parma Psalter* (fol 184v) associates this psalm only with physical violence. A human figure, with hands joined, is attacked by two other figures, one with a dog's head and armed with sword, and one with a snake's head and armed with a pike.[422]

More recent contemporary illustrations by *Wragg (in the 1930s) and by *Benn (image dated 1965) also depict more literally the motifs of 'war' and 'peace' in verse 7. Wragg's cartoon is of three huge torpedoes, with a man with money bowing down before them; the subheading reads 'I am for peace, but when I speak they are for war'.[423] Benn's illustration is of three men in black, bearing swords and menacing the psalmist, whilst the suppliant, in yellow, is releasing a dove.[424]

Psalm 120 ('*Ad Domimum*') was used as a Gradual for the Sunday with the Octave of Corpus Christi, and *Palestrina and *Haydn each arranged Latin versions of the psalm for this purpose; the liturgical context meant that the psalm was now seen through the prism of the suffering and slander experienced by Christ. Some metrical versions are usually aimed at supporting others in persecution: as well as *Sternhold and Hopkins, noted earlier, *Tate and Brady, Isaac *Watts and William *Billings have all produced metrical versions which focus on the themes of slander and isolation.[425]

With its seven verses, this little psalm is not normally explicitly used in any Christological way: rather, it has a more pragmatic purpose. Nevertheless, its pragmatism is curiously inconsistent. John Goldingay has recently pointed out that although the psalmist appears to want peace whilst others are for war, the imagery he uses against them (for example, of warrior's arrows, sharpened and hot) reveals he does not want peace. As Goldingay pertinently observes, if we want

---

[422] Metzger 1996: 92.
[423] Wragg 1934: pages not numbered.
[424] Benn 2005: pages not numbered.
[425] See http://www2.cpdl.org/wiki/index.php/Psalm_120 for a collection of these texts.

to be delivered from the tongues of others, we need first to be delivered from our own.[426] It is significant that none of the examples we have seen make this point.

Psalm 121: A Song of Journeying

If the mood of the previous psalm was of confinement in exile, this psalm has more of a sense of movement out of captivity—still surrounded by dangers—but, implicitly, towards Jerusalem. In this context, the change of person from the 'I' form in verses 1–2 to the 'You' form in verses 3–8 probably suggests a dialogue between the psalmist and his soul. This dialogue form, and the reference to 'going out and coming in' made the psalm a good choice for later liturgical enactment at the Temple. Its slightly different heading—not 'Song of Ascents' but 'Song *for* the Ascents' (*shir la-maʿalot*)—suggests that this psalm was understood to be not only about the journey, but about the destination.

The psalm nevertheless has an internal literary unity: the references to 'come' in verses 1–2 and 8 (Hebrew root *b-w-ʾ*) frame the psalm, and the five-fold reference to the 'Lord' who both 'keeps' or 'guards' his people (Hebrew root *sh-m-r*, six times) provide an ongoing sense of security in God. Reception history has made a good deal of this journeying theme, as we shall see.

Much has also been made of the first verse, and whether the mountains are a place where God is *not* to be found (the use of the word *meʿayin* in verse 1 creates a question implying the answer 'no'), perhaps because of the associations of mountains with high places and idol worship; or alternatively whether the mountains suggest in part a sign of God's care, for he is the One who made heaven and earth (121:2). The plural form ('mountains') indicates this is not a reference to Mount Zion where God was indeed seen to dwell: these are mountains away from Jerusalem.

If slander and physical abuse were problems for the psalmist in 120, in 121 there is a sense not only of physical dangers (mountainous passes [verses 1–2], uneven terrain [verse 3], the heat of the sun and menace of the moon [verse 6]), but of spiritual hazards as well. Not only were the mountains associated with idol worship, but the sun and moon were also deified in the ancient Near East, and sometimes given a demonic force (as in Ps. 91:5–6).[427] In this context the reference to the Lord *not* sleeping (verses 3–4) compares him favourably with other deities, and the affirmation that God is a constant guardian (verses 6–7) similarly confounds the fear of idols, for these have to be made and God is the Maker of all. Reception history has also made much of the possible encounters with evil within this psalm, as will be seen shortly.

---

[426] Goldingay 2008: 453.
[427] For Psalm 91:5–6, see pp. 88–90.

Two notable changes made in the Greek translation are the active form of God as 'guardian' in verse 5 (the Lord is the one who guards [*kurios fulaxei se*]) and the reversal of 'going in' and 'coming out' in verse 8, which makes more sense if the journey is still pressing on towards Jerusalem. The *Gallican Psalter*, used in the *Vulgate*, follows the Greek in this respect.

Psalm 121 occurs in only one *Qumran scroll (11QPsᵃ) and the only change worth noting is its expansion of verse 4: the Lord 'will not slumber *in the night'*. *Targum*, meanwhile, expands verse 6–7 to emphasise the demonic aspect: '*When the sun has dominion by day the morning demons shall not strike you, nor the night demons when the moon has dominion by night. The Memra of* the Lord will keep you from all evil...'[428] It also demonstrates the use of the *mezuzah* as a sign of protection on the doorpost of house. Verse 5 reads: 'the Lord *will give shade over you, on account of the mezuzah that is fixed* at your right hand *at your coming in...*'[429] Verse 8 is now read as a prayer associated with God's protection of a Jewish house, still recited today upon entry and exit. The magical qualities of this psalm have been brought out in various examples of reception. One example is its use in Hebrew amulets (along with Psalms 6, 13, 30 and 91) whereby the psalm is a means of warding off disease and suffering. Verse 6 ('the sun shall not strike you by day') is used to ward off sunstroke, and verse 2 ('My help comes from the Lord'), somewhat surprisingly, is used to ward off seizures.[430] Jonathan Magonet notes its recitation in the medieval *Shimmush Tehillim*, which also deals with magical use of the psalms, as a protection when travelling alone at night. Hence in several ways this psalm was deemed to have apotropaic qualities.

Rabbi David *Kimḥi offers a very different reading, ignoring references to demonic forces and seeing the 'mountains' indicate the announcement of reinforcements in war, with the sun as a symbol of bright fortune, and the moon as a symbol of light amidst dark fortune.[431] *Midrash Tehillim* also subverts the demonic aspects; it compares the psalm with Abraham in Genesis 22, where God hears Abraham's prayer when he lifts his eyes to the mountains, and spares his son, thus reading the psalm as instruction about obedience.[432] Furthermore *Midrash Tehillim*, in its discussion of the theme of 'remembering', links this psalm with Psalm 137, thus now reading 121 as about the restoration of the whole people from exile, with a particular play on Edom /Rome.[433]

---

[428] Stec 2004: 220.
[429] Stec 2004: 220.
[430] Davis 1992: 178.
[431] Feuer 2004: 1513.
[432] Braude 1959: 295–96.
[433] Braude 1959: 95–96.

Here the personal and demonic reading has been supplanted with a more national emphasis.

The psalm is not prominent in early Christian reception. It is not found in the New Testament and references in the Fathers deal mainly with more problematic theological ideas, such as God not being sought in the mountains and God not sleeping. According to *Augustine, we need to be pointed to God, not to the mountains, just as the apostle John pointed others to Christ. Alternatively, the 'hills' indicate the Church's great and famous spiritual men and women: Augustine preached his sermon on Psalm 121 on the feast day of one of the martyrs of the African Church, Crispina. The martyrs of the church are those to whom we should lift up our eyes.[434] An explanation of a different metaphor is taken up by *Basil the Great: referring to verse 4, he clarifies that it is not God who sleeps, but us, and this is when we assume, wrongly, that he is sleeping too.[435] Overall, however, this psalm is not typically read from a Christological point of view.

Perhaps one of the most notable spiritual allegorising commentaries on this psalm is not from ancient times but from four sermons by H.C.G. Moule (Bishop of Durham, 1901–1920).[436] So, for example, 'the look upward' in verse 1 is towards a heavenly Jerusalem, the 'mother' of the true Israel's God. The 'hill' (noting his use of the singular here), from which our help comes, is 'the green hill of Calvary.'[437] Verse 6 ('the sun will not strike you by day…') is about receiving the gift of the Spirit which protects us from the heat in the daytime ('the sun') and from fear at night time ('the moon'): the Lord as our Keeper is the Lord in all the fulness of the Trinity.[438]

As for the psalm's liturgical use, the praying of verse 8 at the exit and entrance of a house is not only a Jewish practice but became a Byzantine one as well, albeit without the *mezuzah*. In Jewish tradition, this is also linked with a service at the dedication of a house.[439] Psalm 121 is an important Sabbath psalm, and like Psalm 120, this is in part because of its diaspora connotations, and in part because of its references to God as Israel's Keeper who never slumbers nor sleeps. So, for example, Psalm 121 is prescribed for the afternoon service of the Sabbaths from *Sukkot to Pesach, and it is also read in the Sabbath morning service; in Sephardic tradition Psalms 121–124 are read as part of *Pesukei de-Zimra*. Its liturgical use is not only during the Sabbath. It is also used as part of the night-time prayer with the *Shema*: verses 4, 5 and 8 are particularly apt

---

[434] Sermon 379.7 *WSA* 3 10:358–59) cited in Selderhuis (ed.) 2018: 340–41.
[435] This is found in Homilies on the Psalms 14.2 in FC 46:214–15, cited in Selderhuis (ed.) 2018: 341–2.
[436] Moule:, 1898.
[437] Moule:, 1898: 17 and 18.
[438] Moule:1898: 58–60 and 78–79.
[439] Keet 1969: 125.

for more personal night-time use.[440] In Sephardic tradition it is read, along with Psalms 150, at the liturgy of the 'Blessing of the Moon'. It is also prescribed in the *Mishnah* to be used at a time of drought: here the traditional *Eighteen Benedictions were used with six other blessings, among which were Psalms 120, 121, 130 and 102 (121 being the only psalm which is not a lament, and so chosen more for its content than its form of prayer).[441]

Christian tradition has a different trajectory. Its particular use is at funerals (on account of verse 7, 'The Lord will keep your life [soul]'), when committing the body to the grave.[442] In the Church of England's *Common Worship* the prayers to be used at home before a funeral focus on Psalm 121: '*Lord, be with us as we open the door. Come in with us, go out with us. Do not sleep when we sleep, but watch over us, protect us and keep us safe, our only helper and maker*'.[443] Psalm 121 is also used at weddings; here the blessing in verses 7–8 as seen to be about life, not death.[444] Its quasi-magical connotation influenced its earlier prescription, in the *BCP, for recitation during the ritual of 'churching', as a service of thanksgiving for women who had recently given birth (although the Puritans repudiated this because of its associations with Jewish purification laws, reacting against the magical connotations in cleansing the mother defiled by the blood of childbirth). Finally, and associating this with Jewish liturgical use, the psalm is also used frequently at *Vespers, when its associations are not with the end of life (verse 7b) but with the ending of the day (verse 6b).

The rich liturgical reception, in both traditions, contrasts with the less developed use in the Christian commentary tradition. This liturgical use might also be on account of the psalm's imagery (of mountains, of God not sleeping, of journeying with God as one's 'Keeper') which has also contributed to some interesting artistic depictions.

The *Parma Psalter* (fol. 185v) and *St. Albans Psalter* offer two typical examples of verse 1. The Jewish, somewhat earthy, representation is of a human figure with his face and arms raised, pointing to two heaps of rocks which flank the initial Hebrew word.[445] The Christian interpretation is of the psalmist looking up to the figure of Christ, standing in blessing, holding a book with the caption from verses 1–2: he is pointing at the words 'My help comes from the Lord'.[446] This reading is echoed in a much more recent citation of this verse in a stained glass window in the Church of St. Olaf, Wasdale, in the Lake

---

[440] Feuer 2004: 295 and 293.
[441] Holladay 1993: 142 and 146.
[442] Hossfeld and Zenger 2011: 331.
[443] Pickett 2002: 15.
[444] Gillingham 2008: 257.
[445] Metzger 1996: 92.
[446] See https://www.albani-psalter.de/stalbanspsalter/english/commentary/page333.shtml.

District: it cites 121:1–2 as a memorial to members of those in the Fell and Rock Climbing Club who were killed in the First World War.

The representation of journeying is depicted in two very artistic different works. The Catholic Elisabeth Sophie Chéron (1648–1711) produced a volume of Psalms in French which were illustrated as engravings by her Huguenot brother, Louis, and published in Paris in 1694. Chéron's selected texts are divided into psalms of prophecy, captivity, and penitence; Psalm 121, following 137, falls under the category of captivity. Her brother took this psalm (*'Levavi oculos meos in montes'*) to depict a lonely Israelite, in open country, arms outstretched, facing the mountains. Whether he is praying for help or welcoming its arrival is unclear. Louis used the same illustration for Psalm 64. The image might have been completed after he had escaped to England, with the hills, rather than the seas or Christian creed, symbolising the painful divide between the siblings.[447] A very different image, but also originally from France, is by *Benn, dated 1956 (Figure 11). This time, however, the mountains are vast and threatening, set against a grey and foreboding sky. The lone individual now appears to be flying; but the figure is trapped by the height of the mountains, which increase his sense of captivity and are dark and imposing. The figure and the mountains depict the way the outside world perceived the plight of the Jewish people taken by the Nazis.[448]

Two seminal poems also focus on verses 1–2. A shared motif is about whether the mountains (and so the natural world) can offer sustenance in prayer, or whether we have to look elsewhere. D. H. Lawrence believed the latter in his poem 'The Hills':[449]

> I lift mine eyes unto the hills
> and there they are, but no strength comes from them to me.
>
> Only from darkness
> and ceasing to see
> strength comes.

For very different reasons, David Slavitt also rejects this notion:[450]

> I look up to the hills where the locals
> worship their primitive gods, and I
> defy them, superstitious yokels,
> for my God made the earth and sky ...

[447] Taken from Prescott 2011: 247–49. The engraving is kept at Houghton Library, Harvard University, Typ. 615.94.276.
[448] See Benn 2005: pages not numbered; also Markus 2015: 274.
[449] See Atwan and Wieder 1993: 322.
[450] Slavitt 1996: 101.

1956

Psaume 121-1

Je leve les yeux vers les montagnes ;
d'où viendra mon secours ?

I lift up my eyes unto the mountains ;
from whence shall come help ?

FIGURE 11   R. B. Benn, 'I lift my eyes unto the mountains: from where shall my help come?' (Ps. 121:1).

Source: Benn, R. B. 1970. *Les Psaumes*. Lyon: Musée des Beaux-Arts.

> He does not ever drowse or doze
> but watches over us to keep
> us safe. We have nothing to fear from those
> tribesmen up there, for while we sleep
> the moon won't light their way. Awake
> under the sun's benevolent rays
> the Lord will protect us and will take
> good care of His people all their days.
> Our comings and goings He will note
> and to our lives His love devote.

Psalm 121 comes into its own in music, partly because of its rich liturgical use. Salamone *Rossi's version is notable because of it being such an early Jewish arrangement: it is a melancholy piece, set for five voices, giving the richness of the metaphors variety, colour and texture.[451] A contrasting version is by J. S.*Bach, which is set as a German chorale (BWV 427). More recently, Herbert *Howells composed a version, along with Psalm 23, in his *Requiem* (written in 1936 but not released until 1980). Howells elected that this 'funeral psalm' should be for a baritone and tenor solo, with four-part choir, thus creating, in elegiac style, a sense of transience and loss. Howells had lost his son in 1935 so this psalm had a particular resonance. Arvo *Pärt composed a different but equally evocative version in his *Ein Wahlfahrtslied: Psalm 121* (1984 and 1996).[452] John *Rutter's *Psalmfest* (1993) used Psalm 121 as one of nine well-known psalms, creating another wistful and reflective version.[453]

A more recent Jewish version is by the singer/composer Rabbi Schlomo Carlebach (1961). It is entitled *Eso Eni*, taken from 121:1–2: it combines popular folksong, voice and guitar with clarinet percussion and male chorus. Schlomo was known as the 'Jewish Troubadour', because he travelled the world encouraging Jews to return to traditional Judaism but set his appeal in a modern idiom. He used liturgically familiar psalms, like 121, which were known in the home, community and synagogue, in unconventional concert settings, sometimes imitating the styles of Bob Dylan and Pete Seeger and Joan Baez.[454]

Psalm 121 also tells a story, as its use in two oratorios testifies. In Felix *Mendelssohn's *Elijah* (op. 70), based upon 1 Kings 17–19 and 2 Kings 1–2, Psalm 121 is used in Part Two, no. 28, when Elijah flees to the wilderness after his confrontation with Ahab and Jezebel. Verses 1–3 are sung by a trio of angels who encourage Elijah in his despair: 'Lift up thine eyes to the mountains' is set in *terzetto* for female voices, with a *SATB chorus for verse 4 (and Ps. 138:7). Perhaps Mendelssohn was emphasising here the importance of this psalm as about journeying into the unknown.

A second oratorio which uses this psalm is by Arthur *Honegger (1892–1955). His librettist, Rene Morax, in *Le Roi David*, interwove the psalms of David with the various stages of his life, drawing from biblical historiography. Psalm 121 is in Part Three, which is about David in his old age, with Bathsheba, Absalom and Solomon, as at the beginning of 1 Kings: the psalm, sung by a tenor solo, becomes a prayer about the importance of prayerfulness as

[451] See https://www.youtube.com/watch?v=ZHqInE4Vso4.
[452] See https://www.youtube.com/watch?v=mYtHzpEuoog.
[453] See https://www.youtube.com/watch?v=eiLQcM75cJ4.
[454] See Stern 2013: 187–89. See
https://www.discogs.com/Shlomo-Carlebach-At-The-Village-Gate/release/14382959; the track is B2.

exhibited by David near the end of his life—redeeming him after his early adultery with Beersheba and preparing the way for his ascent into heaven.[455]

Against this rather serious reception of this psalm, a reference to its use by Maria in *Sound of Music* might seem a little strange. But its use raises some important questions about the relevance of Psalm 121 beyond its ancient setting. As the family von Trapp hides in a convent where Maria, now Mrs. von Trapp, once lived as a nun, and as the military police enter and apparently prevent the family any escape, Maria sings verse 1 of Psalm 121. Her prayer is heard: they slip away and cross the border to the Swiss Alps: perhaps these were the 'hills' Maria had in mind.[456] The question is thus posed: in the light of all that has been noted about the psalm's reception history, is it right to use it in this literal and positivistic way? Did Maria, the ex-nun, recognise that she was praying not really to the mountains but also to the one who made heaven and earth (verse 2)? This is after all, in the history of reception, a 'traveller's psalm', often imbued with magical qualities. Psalm 121 has had many twists and turns on its journey up to Jerusalem and over the Swiss Alps.

Psalm 122: A Song of Arrival

In Psalms 120 and 121 the psalmist was vulnerable; in this psalm we sense joy at being safe in Jerusalem. The peace which was hoped for in 120:6–7 is now a reality (verses 6–9); the fear of the feet stumbling (121:3) is now an experience of standing firmly within the gates of Jerusalem (122:2). The experience of being alone in Psalms 120 and 121 is now supplanted by being part of the community of faith ('the tribes of the Lord' [verse 4]). This is the third psalm in the collection and its focus is now clearly on Jerusalem, and, through its extra heading, in Hebrew, 'For David', also on the king. (This is absent in the *LXX, *Vulgate and *Targum.) In terms of its earliest stage of reception, this psalm has been given a significant place within the collection as a whole.

Psalm 122 is not about the city *per se*: the beginning and ending of the psalm make clear this is about 'the house *of the Lord*' (verse 1) and 'the house *of the Lord our God*' (verse 9). Like Psalm 121, the psalm has a repeated beginning and end.[457] The concrete images of the military defences of the city (its gates [verse 2], its walls and towers [verse 7]) are complemented by a more spiritual image, playing on the name 'Jerusalem' in Hebrew, with its meaning 'city of

---

[455] Dowling Long and Sawyer 2015: 142–3.
[456] Creach 1996: 47.
[457] See pp. 269–70.

peace' [verses 6, 7, 8]). The reception history of this psalm follows the two trajectories of military and spiritual readings.

The only pertinent point in the Greek translation, which could not play on
the name 'Jerusalem' as in the Hebrew in verses 5–7, is the expanded phrase
'pray for *everything that contributes to* the peace of Jerusalem' (*erōtēsate dē ta eis
eirēnēn tēn Ierousalēm*). The Latin reads in a similar way: '*rogate quae ad pacem
sunt Hierusalem*'. A second interesting feature of the psalm's reception into Latin
is found in verse two, which reads '*stantes erant pedes nostri in* atriis *tuis*'—where
the word '*atrium*' is also associated with the square before a church. We shall see
shortly how the associations of Jerusalem with the church are evidenced in the
later Christian commentary tradition and in Christian art and music.

Psalm 122 is found at *Qumran in 11QPsᵃ following 121 and before 123,
thus supporting here the same order as the MT. The psalm is also found in
the 4Qprophecy of Joshua (4Q522), where it is cited with a nationalistic bias
concerning Jerusalem.[458]

Overall, early Jewish commentary tradition interprets the imagery in a
concrete sense, whilst early Christian commentary tradition develops a more
spiritual reading. For example, *Targum* imagines a physical pilgrimage to the
city corresponding with the presence of God accompanying the tribes going up
to Temple (see Ps. 68:7–8, 17–18) thus reading verse 4: '... to which the tribes of
the Lord go up, *testifying to Israel that his *Shekinah dwells among them, when
they go* to give thanks to the name of YHWH ...'. In *Targum's* reading of verse 5
the thrones are no longer for judgement, but are more especially for 'Jerusalem'
and for the 'kings of the house of David'.[459] The psalm is read as a nostalgic
reflection on the past (verses 2–5) and a positive reflection specifically on Jerusalem's welfare in the future (verses 6–9).[460] *Rashi, aware of the problem of
attributing to David a psalm about the Temple, reads this as if David's prayer is
for the wellbeing of the city once Solomon had actually built it, adding to verse
1, 'I, king David, heard that people (were) saying, "When will that old man die
so that Solomon his son may become king and build the Temple?" And I was
happy ...'. Rashi's commentary on verse 8 states: 'Even I, king David, pray for
your wellbeing'.[461] In other Jewish writings verse 3 ('Jerusalem...bound firmly
together') is read as about the uniting of the earthly and heavenly Jerusalem,
and verse 6 is interpreted as a prayer for God to rebuild the city as 'an eternal
structure', so here the concrete and the spiritual combine together.[462]

---

[458] Concerning the fragments of Psalm 122 cited in this way, see Martinez and Tigchelaar 1995:
1046–49.
[459] Stec 2004: 220.
[460] Cohen 1992: 422–3.
[461] Gruber 2004: 703–5.
[462] Feuer 2004: 1517–18.

In early Christian tradition there is no such double reading: Jerusalem is only about the heavenly city. When Jesus weeps over Jerusalem in Luke 19:42–44, this is in the context of its future destruction. *Ambrose takes verse 2 to be about our soul (not our feet) standing ready to enter the heavenly city.[463] *Augustine argues that the psalm cannot refer to any earthly locality: 'The psalmist is someone who wants to ascend. And whither... if not to heaven? ... In heaven is the eternal Jerusalem, where dwell the angels, our fellow citizens ...'[464] *Chrysostom will have nothing to do with the physical focus on Jerusalem: 'This was a situation of the past.'[465] So too *Cassiodorus: playing on the phrase in verse 3, 'Jerusalem, built as a city', he comments: 'In the first section, the prophet rejoices that he has been told that he will attain the heavenly Jerusalem, where the saints now reside in untroubled prosperity ...'[466] By the Middle Ages, Richard of St. Victor reads the psalm as about the fallen Adam and Eve (and with them, all humanity), rejoicing that we have been recalled from exile to return to Paradise.[467]

It is interesting to see how Early Modern writers and Reformation commentators writers start to identify Jerusalem not only as the heavenly city but also as the church on earth. *Calvin reads the psalm as about a call for unity ('peace be within you' [verse 8]) within the universal church.[468] So to pray for the peace of Jerusalem is to pray for the church.[469] And according to *Luther, the references to 'the house of the Lord' are to the church, and indeed 'any place where God's word is heard by those who exhibit faith and repentance and grace'.[470] Nevertheless, the twofold reference in verse 5 to the 'thrones' is read as a critique of the church of Rome: those now sitting on the thrones are not the Pope, nor the Bishops, but the apostles, and, invisibly, Christ Himself.[471] This was one of the psalms from which Luther argued that even the 'Jews of the faithful synagogue' had more faith in God's grace than the church of Rome: faith is what is important, and on this account the psalm is thus for both the faithful synagogue and the faithful church (Rom 2:28–29).[472] Philip Melanchthon reads the psalm as a thanksgiving for the preservation of the church alone: so we bring our prayers for the church (the Protestant Church) to our highest priest who brings them to the eternal Father.[473]

[463] Ambrose: *On Virginity* 9.59 (AOV 28–29) in *ACCS* VIII:343.
[464] Augustine trans. Uyl 2017: 609–10.
[465] Chrysostom trans. Hill 1998: 147–49.
[466] Cassiodorus trans. Walsh 1991: 271.
[467] Neale and Littledale 1874–79: 4/180.
[468] See CTS 12:273 (cited in Selderhuis (ed.) 2018: 292).
[469] See CTS 12:277 (cited in Selderhuis (ed.) 2018: 293).
[470] Luther, M. *Lectures on the Psalms* 1532–33 in WA 40/3:84 (cited in Selderhuis [ed.] 2018: 291).
[471] See Hendrix 1974: 3,50, 285, noting that Luther referred to Ps. 121:5 in the Leipzig disputation in 1519.
[472] German 2017: 176–79.
[473] *Comments on the Psalms* in CR 13:1205, quoting John 17:11, 23 (cited in Selderhuis [ed.] 2018: 291).

It is odd that a psalm so explicit about Jerusalem has had a limited amount of reception in Jewish liturgy. Along with the other Songs of Ascent it is read in the afternoon service of the Sabbaths from *Simchat Torah* to Passover.[474] The psalm is alluded to in the fourteenth blessing for Jerusalem of the *Amidah: 'To Jerusalem Thy city, return with compassion, and dwell within it as Thou promised: Rebuild it soon in our days as an everlasting structure; and speedily establish in its midst the throne of David...'[475]

In Christian liturgy this is an important *Vespers Psalm: its anticipation of righteous judgement (verses 4–5) and peace (verses 6–8) in part influenced its use both at Vespers during Advent and at the Vigil of Easter, as well as at the Feast of St. Andrew (with its emphasis on building up the church of God). In the eighteenth-century compendium of collects on each psalm, that for Psalm 122 echoes much of earlier Christian exegesis of this psalm over the ages:

> O Blessed Jesu, who didst descend according to thy human Nature from the house of thy servant David, and hast planted a church, and defended it with a mighty hand and great assistances; be pleased to preserve peace within her walls... Take from her all schisms and divisions, that she may be like a city that is at unity within itself... that at last she may be removed to a fellowship of all those joys and felicities which are laid up for the inhabitants of the heavenly Jerusalem which is from above, and is the Mother of us all.[476]

The phrase 'For my brethren and companions' sake I will say '*Peace be within you*' (verse 8)—whether with respect to the earthly or heavenly Jerusalem—is not only expressed in Jewish and Christian liturgy. In the Qur'an (Q 6:54) we read: 'And when those who believe in our signs come to thee, say "*Peace be upon you.*"' The aspirations for peace, very possibly traced back to the formula used in this psalm, playing in the meaning of 'Jerusalem' as 'city of peace', are found in all three monotheistic religions.

The identification of the 'house of the Lord' as the church of God is found in an illustration in the **Stuttgart Psalter* (fol. 144r). This is of verse 5 and depicts the 'thrones for judgement' (*sedes in iudicium*) as the thrones upon which the Apostles sit in heaven, anticipating Luther here. The image also depicts the 'thrones of the house of David' (*sedes super domum David*) as the church on earth. There is also a figure of an unnamed apostle, hand raised in blessing, sitting on a throne next to a building which, by its cross on the roof, is clearly a church.[477]

---

[474] See pp. 256, 260, and 264.
[475] See *b.Megillah* 17b; also Donin 1980: 94–5.
[476] See Vaughan 1702: 258–59.
[477] See https://bit.ly/3dCI0Il.

A less explicit depiction is found in the *St. Albans Psalter*, but the context is clearly about rejoicing in Christian worship. The smiling psalmist, here clearly a monk, stands within a tower, looking up. The book he is holding reads '*We shall go into the house of the Lord*' (verse 1) and he points to the tag in the text outside the illuminated letter 'L' (for *Laetatus sum*: 'I was glad'). The tag reads '*I rejoiced in these things*' and alludes to verse 1.[478] But here the rejoicing is not about worshipping in Jerusalem; it is about worshipping in St. Albans Abbey, in England, somewhere between 1120 and 1140.

Three more recent images give insights into the very different way in which this psalm has been perceived in Jewish tradition after 1948. The first is by Marc *Chagall: his image is of David, seated on a throne, with the city of David in the near distance; he holds a *menorah and a crowd of worshippers is beneath him. A rooster is just above him—a symbol of new life, and, since the destruction of the Temple in the first-century CE, a substitute offering for the goat at the Day of Atonement.[479] This is clearly a literal and physical reference to Jerusalem, with a sense that the prayers for 'the peace of Jerusalem' are now in the process of being fulfilled. The second is Moshe *Berger's image, from the 1990s, whose reading of the psalm is about 'the reconstruction of the Third Temple that will be built through the efforts of the Messiah, the scion of David'.[480] The image shows the gate into the city, the pillars of the Temple, over which is the menorah: all this is depicted in ice blue with Hebrew lettering. The Hebrew lettering in purple to the right and red to the left give an atmosphere of a royal celebration. Finally, Debra *Band's two outlines of Zion, one in Hebrew, the other in English, depict an adept use of calligraphy: Jerusalem is 'knit together' in an outline of its buildings in English and Hebrew letters, using verses from Judah Halevi's hymn to the city, *Tsion ha-lo Tish'ali*. On the one hand, this is very clearly a Jewish encounter with the psalm: the Jewish representation, all in Hebrew, displays the star of David overlaid with head-coverings of different Jewish communities, both East and West. The second outline in English, however, displays not only the menorah, but also a Byzantine cross and an Islamic geometric motif. This double image is not only about the hope for the 'peace' and unification of all the different factions of Judaism, but the hope for 'peace' for the three monotheistic faiths which claim the city as their own. This is an incredibly rich, universal, and striking representation of the psalm, where Jerusalem is depicted as a city 'knit

---

[478] See https://www.albani-psalter.de/stalbanspsalter/english/commentary/page334.shtml.
[479] See https://www.gallery.ca/collection/artwork/psalm-122.
[480] See http://www.biblical-art.com/artwork.asp?id_artwork=15244&showmode=Full; also http://themuseumofpsalms.com/product/psalm-122.

together' because Jews and all religions are seen to offer prayer for the peaceful coexistence of the city.[481]

It is impossible to write about the musical reception of Psalm 122 without reference to Hubert *Parry, whose work has been performed over the last century as a processional anthem at British coronations and royal weddings, as well as at the Service of Thanksgiving for the Queen's Royal Jubilee in 2012. It was originally composed for the coronation of Edward VII in 1902, re-used for George V in 1911, and most memorably again for the wedding of Charles and Diana in 1981 and then of William and Kate in 2011.[482] But how do the words of such a Jerusalem-specific psalm speak to such modern state occasions? It is as if Parry imbues the words of every verse with a new meaning: the majestic introduction, played by the organ and orchestra, represents the entrance of monarch (the psalm is after all dedicated to king David); the entrance of the choir, with a six-part chorus based on the first words of the psalm ('I was glad') is about entering 'the house of the Lord' which is now not Zion but a Cathedral or Abbey; the imitative setting of 'Our Feet Shall Stand' (verse 2) evokes now not the majesty of Jerusalem, but, usually, of London, which is enforced by the two choir *antiphonal exchange: 'Jerusalem is builded as a city' (verse 3)—concluding on the tonic, signifying the solidity of the city. The *Vivat* ('*Long Live the Queen!*'), sung on royal occasions, is clearly not part of the psalm. The solemn reflective conclusion, 'O Pray for the Peace of Jerusalem' (verse 6) which is sung by a semi-chorus, and the climax rising to the sopranos' high B flat: 'Peace be within thy walls' (verse 7) together express hope in a secure political as well as spiritual future.

Although Parry's is the best-known version, other composers have interpreted the psalm in similar ways. Tomás de Luis Victoria's '*Laetatus sum*' ('I was Glad') (1583) is set as a motet for a triple chorus, and the polychoral structure captures the psalm's joyful mood. Henry *Purcell's 'I was glad when they said unto me' is set for a five-part choir, with two treble voices. It was written, somewhat ironically, in 1685, at the time of the accession of James II and the revival of Catholicism. Marc-Antoine Charpentier, Antonio *Vivaldi, Domenico Scarlatti and William *Boyce are just a few examples of seventeenth- and eighteenth-century composers who also used this psalm for great public occasions. But the psalm also inspired compositions of a metrical nature for lay people: the heading to Isaac *Watts' Version I is '*Going to Church*':

---

[481] See Band and Band 2007: 170–74.
[482] Dowling Long and Sawyer 2015: 107.

How did my heart rejoice to hear
My friends devoutly say,
'In Zion let us all appear,
And keep the solemn day!'

I love her gates, I love the road;
The church adorn'd with grace
Stands like a palace built for God
To shew his milder face...[483]

After Parry's arrangement, perhaps the next most memorable is Herbert *Howells' 'O Pray for the Peace of Jerusalem', the first in his *Four Anthems* (1941), a restrained and melancholy piece which was composed a year after Howells had to leave his family home after it had been bombed. Psalm 122 evokes both transience and loss, but also hope and faith, even in the middle of the Second World War.[484] The same psalm inspired the American singer Paul Wilbur in his 'Shalom Shalom, Jerusalem' on the album *Shalom Jerusalem* (1995), and later his 'Pray for the Peace of Jerusalem' (2002), in each case reflecting not metaphorically but literally on Jerusalem whose name means 'city of peace'.

We have already seen that this psalm had a liturgical role in the Office of Vespers. In terms of the use of particular psalms at various occasions associated with Vespers we noted earlier how Psalms 110–115 were used for Sunday Vespers, and Psalms 110, 113, 122, 127 and 147 were used at the Vespers of Our Lady.[485] So Psalm 122 is prominent in compositions for this latter occasion: its arrangement for Monteverdi's 'Venetian masterpiece' is perhaps the best known. In 'The Vespers of 1610' (or 'The Vespers for the Blessed Virgin Mary') it is the third psalm, scored for six voices, with solo interludes.[486] Here the city of Zion personifies the Virgin Mary, testifying again to the multivalent use of this psalm in music.

Psalm 122 is charged with political as well as theological overtones. David Mitchell reminds us how on 7 June 1967 a crackly radio voice announced that the Israel Defence Force had taken the Temple Mount, and then Psalm 122 was read out over the radio waves.[487] After prayers for the fallen the Jewish populace erupted in celebration, singing *Yerushalayim shel zahav* ('Jerusalem the Golden'). This was a moment in Jewish history when, after 1900 years of waiting, Psalm 122 was used as a 'liturgy of the moment'—and the fulfilment

---

[483] See http://www2.cpdl.org/wiki/index.php/Psalm_122 for this version by Watts and an extensive list of other composers.
[484] Gillingham 2008: 299; also, Dowling Long and Sawyer 2015: 175.
[485] See p. 203.
[486] Dowling Long and Sawyer 2015: 255.
[487] Mitchell 2015: 171.

of prophecy. But what is a celebration for some is defeat and shame for others. Psalm 122 gives us ongoing challenge: we cannot long to visit Jerusalem until it becomes a city of peace. All we can do is use this psalm, perhaps with the images by Debra Band in our mind, to *pray* for its peace.

Psalm 123: A Song Praying for Mercy

After the focus on Jerusalem in 122, Psalm 123, like 120 and 121, and indeed like 124, reflects on trust in God without reference to the city. The experience of ridicule and mockery (verses 3–4) has correspondences with 120:3–4, with the sense of having had enough (verses 3 and 4) like 120:6. The psalmist lifts up his eyes to God (verse 1); this echoes lifting up one's eyes to the hills in 121:1, but here the psalmist who seeks out God's mercy (verses 2–3) is no longer 'on pilgrimage'. The movement is more internal, within the psalm's given structure, particularly through the extended use of 'staircase parallelism'. Four times in verses 1–2 the psalmist refers to 'eyes'; twice, in verse 2, to 'hands'; the verbs 'look to' and 'have mercy' occur three times in verses 2–3, and the verb 'have enough' is found twice in verses 3–4. Repeating words in new phrases intensifies the development of thought as the psalm progresses. This is, fortunately, a feature which can be translated into other languages.

Compared with the previous psalm, 123 lacks a rich reception history. It registers little, on its own, in Jewish or Christian liturgy, even though it is cited regularly with other psalms.[488] There are also no outstanding pieces in music. Images in art tend to focus mainly on eyes lifted upwards to God, as for example in the *St. Albans Psalter.[489] The most interesting reception history is actually that which wrestles with the language and some of the paradoxical ideas in this deceptively difficult psalm.

Some of the most notable examples actually occur in the early stages of reception through translation. The *Septuagint, for example, alternates between two translations of the Hebrew word *'el* (meaning 'to') so that it becomes *pros* when God is addressed (verse 1: '*To* you I lift my eyes' and verse 2: 'our eyes look *to* the Lord…') and *eis* when it concerns the master or mistress (verse 2: 'as the eyes of servants look *to* the hand of their master…'). This differentiates between trust in God and trust in humans. Interestingly the *Targum* also interprets 'looking to God' differently, albeit here somewhat negatively: the Aramaic

---

[488] Holladay 1993: 142 and 176.
[489] See https://www.albani-psalter.de/stalbanspsalter/english/commentary/page335.shtml.

reads the verb 'look' in the Hebrew as coming from a verb 'look with anxiety', so its version of verse 1 is '*our eyes look with anxiety* toward the Lord our God...'[490]

Turning to the *Septuagint, the Greek doubles the singular hand (in Hebrew, *yad*, in verse 2) so that it becomes the plural *cheiras*: 'eyes' then look to 'hands'. The Greek in verse 4 changes the sense of the Hebrew word *hasha-anannim* 'the ones at ease' (i.e. free from trouble), to *tois euthēvousin* 'those who prosper', and this is taken up in the *Vulgate as well (as *abundantibus*), thus changing the nature of the hostility towards the psalmist. The very last word of verse 4 has also produced several variants: the text is written (*ketib) as one word (*la-geyonim*, of the proud ones?) but vocalised to be read (*qere') as two (*lige yonim*, of proud oppressors?) probably alluding to foreign oppression. *Rashi in fact re-reads this as 'valley of the doves' (*lege' yonim*), taking up a rabbinic tradition that the return of exiles was like doves returning to their cotes.[491]

These may be details but they clearly illustrate the malleable nature of the text, a feature which gives poetic imitations of the psalm a creative freedom. Mary *Sidney's version captures well the idea of a heavy soul and a stoical sense of waiting:[492]

> Unto thee, oppressed, thou great commander of heaven
> Heav'nly good attending, lift I my earthy seeing.
> Right as a waiter's eye on a graceful master is holden;
> As the look of waitress fixed on a lady lieth:
> So with erected face, until by thy mercy relieved,
> O Lord, expecting, beg we thy friendly favour.
> Scorn of proud scorners, reproach of mighty reproachers
> Our sprites clean ruined fills with an inly dolour.
> Then friend us, favour us, Lord, then with thy mercy relieve us,
> Whose scornful misery greatly thy mercy needeth.

Christopher *Smart, by contrast, imagines the psalm taking place in a liturgical context, but his portrayal of oppression and persecution is even more intense. We read of the temple, the holiest of holies, God's 'footstool', and comforting angels; but we also see a clear distinction between the vulnerable community of faith and the oppressors who are outside it.[493]

---

[490] Stec 2004: 221.
[491] Gruber 2004: 706.
[492] See Hamlin *et al.* (eds.) 2009: 249.
[493] Wieder 1995: 191.

To thee from thy temple I lift up mine eyes,
And breathe from my heart-strings the passionate sighs,
O thou that with goodness and glory replete,
Hast fixed in the holiest of holies thy seat!

The looks of a servant his master revere,
The damsel her mistress with meekness and fear,
Thus elder and matron, and all our whole race
Attend at thy footstool for strength and for grace.

O Lord, let thine angel of comfort descend,
With blessed compassion our woes to befriend,
For in this dejection and wretched estate
They make us their object of scorn and of hate…

This was probably written during the period in the 1760s when Smart was confined to an asylum because of impossible debts and concerns about the emotional intensity of his faith. So in Psalm 123 the 'suffering David' and the 'suffering Smart' coincide: this is not so much about confidence and hope, as about protest and complaint.

Jim *Cotter's re-reading of this psalm offers us another moment of insight: 'looking' on God, and in return being seen by God, allows for a range of metaphors connected with 'seeing and looking', in the first instance aggressive and threatening, but by the end accommodating and offering hope:[494]

DELIGHT AND DEVASTATION

Will I survive the piercing eye?

Refrain: *We will not be trapped by the eyes of oppression:*
    We will see with the eyes of God.

The haughty look of the powerful,
the contemptuous stare of the wealthy,
the cutting glance of the clever,
the mocking glint of the cowardly:

Burdened by eyes that enslave us,
cast down by eyes of derision,
oppressed by eyes that pursue us,
held fast by eyes that never relent:

---

[494] Cotter 1993: 69.

The eyes of the cameras following us,
the shadow of spies in the dark,
the screen displaying the data,
the silent satellite unseen:

Fiery eyes, angry for justice,
compassionate eyes, warming the poor,
courteous eyes, attentive and waiting,
steady eyes, calm and courageous:

A reverent look awed and still,
a ready glance, willing to obey,
a look of hope, expectant of good,
a look of trust, as between friends.

What is notable in these examples is that, although it could be imitated, there is none of the 'staircase parallelism' in the English. Furthermore, in a psalm which, most unusually, speaks of women as expressions of obedient piety, most poets make little of this trope. This is particularly evident in Anderson's compilation which includes this psalm:[495]

To you enthroned in heaven
To you we turn our eye,
Like servants with their masters
As maids to mistress sigh.
To you we look O Lord God
Our master in the heavn's
Until you give us mercy
Until our hardship ends (italics mine).

The male re-casting of the female imagery takes an interesting twist in early Christian commentary tradition. *Augustine's commentary, for example, reads 123:2 not as about women *per se* but as about the church as the female embodiment of Christ. The people are the servants and the Church is the maid; this is therefore about the 'one-flesh' union between the church as bride and Christ as bridegroom: 'We are both servants, and a handmaiden: He is both our Master and our Mistress … the Power and the Wisdom of God … lift up thine eyes to the hands of thy Master, lift up thine eyes to the hands of thy Mistress, for thou art both servant and handmaiden; servant, for thou are a people; handmaiden, for thou art the Church … betrothed: and hath received a mighty pledge, the blood of the Spouse …'[496] Here the image of Christ as Mistress is undoubtedly a radical idea, and one rarely developed further.

[495] Anderson 2016: 187.
[496] Augustine trans. Uyl 2017: 613.

Another image, of lifting one's eyes like a servant /slave to one's master or to one's mistress, creates an odd paradox in a psalm which pleads for mercy (and with this, freedom) from God. Arthur *Wragg's black and white cartoon of this psalm makes an interesting comment on this paradox: its subtitle is 'Unto thee lift I up mine eyes, O thou that dwellest in the heavens' (Figure 12).[497] The image is of a man in prison, holding one of the bars and looking upwards with a face full of fear and despair. The other hand is on the sill of the prison window,

FIGURE 12   *Arthur Wragg, 'Unto thee lift I up mine eyes, O thou that dwellest in the heavens'* (Psalm 123:1).

Source: Wragg, A. 1934: *The Psalms for Modern Life*. New York: Claude Kendall.

[497] Wragg 1934: pages not numbered.

as he seeks out a small patch of sky from his prison cell, with the light falling on his hands and part of his face. Perhaps this is what 'waiting for God's mercy' is all about: the longing for the reversal of the *status quo* of both literal and spiritual oppression and captivity.

Psalm 124: A Song about National Deliverance

Psalm 120 was a prayer for peace—from both verbal and physical abuse—and the last of these five psalms is a thanksgiving for peaceful restoration, using two metaphors (being saved from drowning in the flood waters and escaping being caught in the hunter's snare) to describe the manner of deliverance. The psalm has a clear structure: verses 1 and 2 start with two 'if' clauses (*luley* in Hebrew) whilst verses 3–5 begin with three 'then' clauses (*azay* in Hebrew), describing with some emotional intensity what might have happened had God not acted, with verses 6–7 and 8 as thanksgiving and praise (although God is not addressed: the audience is the assembled congregation).

The psalm has some continuity with 123 in its use of 'staircase parallelism' in verses 4–5 and 7, and the two may have been brought together on that account. This parallelism is especially clear in the use of the two key metaphors: 'the *torrent* would have *gone over us*; then *over us* would have gone the *raging waters* ...' (verses 4–5, although the word for 'raging' at the end of verse 5 is hard to translate, as this masculine plural noun is a *hapax legomenon*). Similarly verse 7: 'We have *escaped* like a bird from the *snare* of the fowlers; the *snare* is broken, and we have *escaped*'. Verse 8 also has a clear link with 121:2 ('My help comes from the Lord, who made heaven and earth'): here we read 'Our help is in the name of the Lord, who made heaven and earth'. The name of the Lord is important in both psalms: it is used four times here and five times in 121.

In terms of the contrast with Psalm 120, the military overtones are clearer here than in 124. The use of *adam* (singular) in verse 2, which is often translated as 'enemies' or 'men', could refer to a specific human agent—an army led by one such as Sargon II or Sennacherib of Assyria, or Nebuchadnezzar of Babylon. The image of a bird shut in a snare is a stock image for military oppression: it appears in the fourteenth-century BCE 'El Amarna Letters' found in Egypt, and is used in the Annals of the eight-century BCE King Sennacherib, in his description of the siege of Jerusalem: '... As for Hezekiah the Judean...I locked him up within Jerusalem, his royal city, like a bird in a cage ...' The escaping from the snare here describes the lifting of the siege.[498] Similarly floods and torrents of

---

[498] See Tucker 2014a: 103; also https://bit.ly/3u7m7aH.

water are frequently used to describe not only the fear of death by drowning (see Ps. 69:2–3), but also the fear of national annihilation by military attack. (Examples include Jer. 46:8 and 47:2, concerning the judgement on the Philistines; Isa. 8:7–8, describing the Assyrians bearing down on Israel and Judah, and Isa. 17:12–13, about the nations roaring like mighty waters as they turn against Israel.) The additional Davidic heading, here not only in the Hebrew but also in the *LXX and the *Targum, adds to these nationalistic connotations.

Jewish tradition consistently re-affirms that this psalm is a thanksgiving for national victory: whatever the context, the enemies, like deep waters, can never utterly overwhelm the Jewish people.[499] The association of this psalm with the Jewish people's deliverance from Haman in the book of Esther is a theme developed in the *Talmud and perpetuated in other Jewish tradition.[500] This is typified in Salamone *Rossi's stately 6-part unaccompanied arrangement of the psalm for the Norsa synagogue in the Jewish ghetto in Mantua, published in 1622 with his other thirty-three psalms, hymns and *canticles. The arrangement exudes a quiet confidence. The tragedy is that in 1630 Mantua was over-run by the Austrian troops of Ferdinand II and the whole ghetto was razed to the ground, and the 2000 inhabitants were expelled or slaughtered. No record has even been found of Rossi's death: in this case the waters did overwhelm, and the bird did not escape the fowler's snare.

Two images painted after the Holocaust create a sense of defiance, and they each use the picture of the bird caught in the trap and so each indicate that there was some escape for the few. The first illustration is by Marc *Chagall, completed in 1957 for the church at Assy (a place often called a 'pantheon of religious art, Jewish and Christian').[501] Chagall first produced a tiled mural for the baptistry wall. Its theme was the Exodus, with Moses holding an uplifted staff preventing the waters drowning the Israelites; the crucified Christ observes the scene in upper right of composition, also suffering; this symbolises the typology between the rescue from the Reed Sea and the waters of baptism. Chagall's second contribution was two stained glass windows, flanking the mural on the east and west sides: one is of an angel holding a vessel of holy water, the other of an angel descending with candelabra and flowers towards the baptismal waters. A third contribution was of two plaster bas-relief sculptures, placed next to the windows, each again playing on water symbolism; one is of Ps. 42:7 and the other, of 124:7. The verse of the latter is written in French along the perimeter of the image, and takes up again the theme of the Exodus and the 'narrow escape': a small bird is struggling to free itself from a trap, whilst another bird is perched, free, on a tree to the right of the picture; in the middle is a very large bird,

---

[499] Feuer 2004: 1527.
[500] *BT Megillah* 11a, cited in Rosen 2013: 111.
[501] See https://bit.ly/3xBSv7t.

clearly in distress, encouraging the captured bird to escape. On the ground, a figure lies prone, presumably dead; and above in the heavens, also beating its wings, is typical sketch of Chagall's protective angel. This is a disturbing scene: it is again symbolic of that 'bittersweet deliverance which dominated Chagall's imagination in the wake of the *Shoah*.'[502]

*Benn's image, also of a bird breaking free from the fowler's trap, is again about the fate of European Jewry as Hitler's deadly net was cast over the Jews of Europe. The mixture of relief, sorrow and joy over the survival of the Jewish people is again evident: a blue bird, against a blue sky, has just broken free from its cage; below, against a sandy background, three figures in white dance together—partly in fear, partly in celebration. Again, we see that 'narrow escape': it speaks of the millions of Jews who were (literally) caged like birds, when only a few escaped: liberation is celebrated, but with great sadness (see PLATE 23 for a reproduction of this image).[503]

The idea of a 'narrow escape' has a very different connotation in Christian tradition. By the fifth century, according to *Augustine, the tropes of both the bird in a snare and the escape from raging waters spoke of the death of the martyrs of faith: 'And this (psalm) the holy Martyrs have sung: for they have already escaped, and are with Christ in joy about to receive at last incorruptible bodies... let us all sing together, and say, "If the Lord Himself had not been for us..."'.[504] The same theme was popularised in Byzantine Psalters, where the 'narrow escape' is often symbolised by Daniel in the lion's den. The eleventh-century *Barberini Psalter*, fol. 218v, depicts verse 6 ('Blessed be the Lord, who has not given us as prey to their teeth') with Daniel as the subject, wearing Persian dress, in the lion's den, along with Pantaleon of Nicomedia, martyr during the Diocletian persecution in 305 CE. The earlier ninth-century *Pantokrator Psalter*, fol. 182r, has almost the same scene, with two lions fawning at Daniel's feet; so too the eleventh-century *Theodore Psalter*, fol. 169r has another similar image, although in this manuscript the lions are badly damaged.[505] A different example is from the sixteenth century, when *Calvin interprets the metaphors of being swallowed up and drowning as also about the trials of the faithful in the church. Referring to the Davidic heading, and seeing this as applying not only to Jewish periods of persecution but also to the church's sufferings, Calvin notes: 'David then represents as in a mirror the uncertain and changeable condition of the Church ... to teach the faithful that its stability had not been owing to its own intrinsic strength, but that it had been preserved by

---

[502] Rosen 2013: 110–111; the citation is from p.111.
[503] See pp. 281–82; also Markus 2015: 281.
[504] Augustine trans. Uyl 2017: 615 and 616; Augustine's Sermon 335F.2, in *WSA* 3 9:240, is cited in Wesselschmidt (ed.) 2007: 346–47.
[505] See http://www.bl.uk/manuscripts/Viewer.aspx?ref=add_ms_19352_f169r.

the wonderful grace of God ... David here extends to the state of the Church in all ages that which the faithful had already experienced ...'[506]

Sometimes the bird which escaped the snare of the hunters is identified not as the martyrs of the Church but as Christ himself, breaking the snares of death. *Athanasius writes of the psalm as about the celebration for the victory of Easter.[507] *Aquinas (or pseudo-Aquinas) reads the psalm as about Christ breaking the snare of death, with the voices of apostles and martyrs praising his name.[508] Annie Sutherland notes that the fourteenth-century *Midland Prose Psalter* inserts, most unusually, the name of Christ into 124:7 (*Vulgate* 123:7): 'Þe trappe of Þe fend is to-broke wyÞ Þe deÞ of Crist, & we ben deliuered fro dampnacioun.'[509] ('The enemy's trap has been broken through the death of Christ and we have been delivered from damnation'). The use of 124 as a *Vespers and *Compline psalm is primarily because of its associations with Christ's victory over the power of evil, illustrated by the use of the *antiphon from verse 8, 'Our help is in the name of the Lord'.

Jews and Christians unite, however, in their military use of this psalm, albeit for different reasons: in Jewish tradition, the enemy is without, but often in Christian tradition it is the enemy within. The European Wars of Religion, for example, between the sixteenth and eighteenth centuries, testify to several uses of this psalm by Protestants and Catholics alike. William Reid argues that Psalm 124 was the most popular psalm of the Huguenot armies, such that 'by 1562 it had apparently become a recognised means of Huguenot self-identification.'[510] So when the Prince of Conde arrived in Orleans at the beginning of the civil war the people sang in the streets 'If it had not been the Lord who was on our side, now may *Orleans* say...'[511] And in the eighteenth-century *Parish Clerk's Guide*, compiled by Benjamin Payne, clerk of St. Anne's, Blackfriars, it is Psalm 124 which is assigned to the Fifth of November in memory of the Gunpowder Plot in 1605—another 'narrow escape'.[512] In 1719 Isaac *Watts wrote a metrical psalm for the same event, perhaps also alluding to the 'Glorious Revolution' of 1688 when the Catholic king James II was overthrown and his Protestant daughter Mary and her Dutch husband, William of Orange acceded to the throne.[513]

---

[506] See Calvin trans. Anderson 1849: 85, 88; also, CTS 12:86–87 (cited in Selderhuis [ed.] 2018: 298).

[507] Athanasius, *Festal Letter* 10.11 NPNF 2 4:531–32 (cited in Wesselschmidt 2007: 347).

[508] Neale and Littledale 1874–79: 4/191.

[509] Sutherland 2015: the discussion of *The Midland Prose Psalter* is taken from 'The Practice of Translation: Complete Psalters' (86–135). The citation is from p. 133.

[510] See W. S. Reid 1971: 47.

[511] See W. S. Reid 1971: 47; also, Gillingham 2008: 156–57. See also similar comments on the military use of Psalm 46 (2018: 279–80) and Psalm 68 (*ibid.* 371–72).

[512] See Gillingham 2008: 229.

[513] See https://www.ccel.org/ccel/watts/psalmshymns.Ps.289.html.

A Song for the Fifth of November.

Had not the Lord, may Israel say,
Had not the Lord maintained our side,
When men, to make our lives a prey,
Rose like the swelling of the tide;

The swelling tide had stopped our breath,
So fiercely did the waters roll,
We had been swallowed deep in death;
Proud waters had o'erwhelmed our soul.

We leap for joy, we shout and sing,
Who just escaped the fatal stroke;
So flies the bird with cheerful wing,
When once the fowler's snare is broke.

For ever blessed be the Lord,
Who broke the fowler's cursed snare,
Who saved us from the murdering sword,
And made our lives and souls his care.

Our help is in Jehovah's name,
Who formed the earth and built the skies:
He that upholds that wondrous frame
Guards His own church with watchful eyes.

It is ironic that, as Andrew Mein points out, during the First World War it was the Germans who saw the 'God of the Germans in a special sense and [ourselves] as the chosen people', with psalms such as 124 being read as about 'the Lord who [is] on *our* side.[514] This could not be further removed from the Jewish use of the psalm we noted earlier. A psalm of thanksgiving for national deliverance? Much depends on the identification of the victor and the victim. On VE day, 8 May 1945, at the service attended by the House of Commons in St. Margaret's, Westminster, after Winston Churchill's speech to the nation at 3.00pm, William *Whittingham's metrical version of Psalm 124 was sung at the service of thanksgiving and dedication.[515] It came shortly after the national anthem:

E'en as a bird out of the fowler's snare
Escapes away, so is our soul set free:
Broke are their nets, and thus escaped we…

---

[514] Mein 2019: 172, citing Kittel 1916.
[515] See https://bit.ly/3gWm3qr.

Psalms 125–129: Blessings from Zion

Psalms 125 and 126 have some parallels with the first psalm in the first collection, with their imperative appeals to God (120:1 and 125:4; 126:4) and indeed with both Psalms 120 and 121 in their sense of being oppressed by other peoples. 125:1–2, on the theme of the mountains surrounding Jerusalem, also takes us back to 121:1–2. Psalm 127, like 122, lies at the heart of this second collection, and its Solomonic heading is a reminder of the Temple in Jerusalem, just as Psalm 122, at the heart of the first collection, reflected on the importance of Jerusalem for the pilgrim. Psalms 128 and 129 reflect more confidently, like Psalms 123 and 124, on God's protection, with the more specific emphasis here on God's blessings for Zion (128:5 and 129:5). What is distinctive about this collection is its emphasis on familial piety and the home, especially in Psalms 126–128. So just as the first stage of reception in Psalms 120–124 was marked by the organisation of different psalms into a loose collection, so too Psalms 125–129 mark an early stage of reception in a different but clear arrangement.

Psalm 125: A Song about Restoration (i)

The theme of protection emanating from Zion (verses 1–2) announces the confidence in Zion throughout this entire collection (see 126:1; 127:1; 128:5; and 129:5). There is a connection with Psalm 129 in the references to 'the

Psalms Through the Centuries: A Reception History Commentary on Psalms 73–151, Volume Three, First Edition. Susan Gillingham.
© 2022 John Wiley & Sons Ltd. Published 2022 by John Wiley & Sons Ltd.

sceptre of wickedness' in 125:3 and 'the cords of the wicked' in 129:4. Each psalm moves from confidence to petition, and each uses contrasting terms for the 'wicked' and the 'righteous' (125:3; 129:4). The end of 125 ('Peace be upon Israel') is identical with the end of 128, again illustrating some inner coherence of this collection of psalms. It is quite possible that the threat of foreign powers lies behind 125, in which verses 1–3 serve as an expression of confidence in the God of Zion and verses 4–5 as a prayer for help. The 'sceptre of wickedness' in verse 3 may well suggest the oppressive foreign rule (as used for example in Isa. 9:3 and 14:5); the setting is likely to be Persian times.[516]

Psalm 125 is found along with all of Psalm 126 in 11QPsᵃ. It also occurs in a fragmentary form in 4QPsᵉ. In each scroll the differences are small (for example, in 4QPsᵉ 'their hands' is 'their hand' in verse 3, and in 11QPsᵃ 'evil doers' in verse 5 is 'all evil doers'). These changes do not affect the semantic sense of the psalm. The changes in the Greek, however, are more significant. In verse 1, the additional *ho katoikōn Ierousalēm* (the inhabitants of Jerusalem) applies to those who will never be moved: the use of this third person masculine participle is now not about the permanency of Mount Zion within the city, but about the security of the people who live there. The Greek translation in verse 3 renders '*shebet haresha*' not as 'the sceptre of *wickedness*' but as 'the sceptre of *the sinners*' (*tēn rabdon tōn hamartōlōn*). It is another more personalised rendering of the Hebrew. These are small changes, but they suggest an increased tension in the conflicts between Jews and Gentiles at the time of the translation. In the *Targum this tension is more intense still: verse 5, also referring to the wicked, adds '… the Lord will lead them away *to* **Gehenna: their portion will be with those who deal falsely …*'[517]

Jewish writings nevertheless emphasise that it is Mount Zion which 'cannot be moved' (verse 1). The focus is on a utopian Jerusalem, stripped of its protective walls, to which the dispersed will return at the ingathering of the exiles, and where they will nevertheless experience the security of divine protection.[518] This is quite different from Christian readings. *Chrysostom, for example, reads the 'mountain' as a metaphor for 'the irreversible character of hope in God, its stability, its invincibility, its impregnability … much more secure than a mountain, after all'.[519] And reading the Greek, Chrysostom sees 'the inhabitants of Jerusalem (who) will not be moved forever' as Christians who are enjoying the heavenly Jerusalem.[520] *Cassiodorus argues that the

---

[516] See Tucker 2014a: 104–106.
[517] Stec 2004: 223.
[518] Feuer 2004: 1531 and 1532 (with reference to *Sforno).
[519] Chrysostom trans. Hill 1998: 164.
[520] *Ibid.*: 165.

meaning of the word 'Sion' is 'watching'—'an apt activity for the Lord Jesus Christ our Shepherd'.[521] Noting that Jerusalem was indeed destroyed and its inhabitants exiled, thus showing that its dwellers were hardly immovable, Cassiodorus opines that the psalmist could only be referring to the heavenly city. Hence his reason for seeing that '… the Sion here is the Lord Jesus Christ who shall not be moved: it is He who is denoted here.'[522] Christ is the one who surrounds his people 'like mountains' (verse 2); he is the one who puts down the sceptre of the wicked with his own rod of righteousness (verse 3); he is the one who promises the 'true Israel' the gift of peace (verse 5).[523] A millennium later *Calvin takes a similar view, but now Zion describes not Christ, but the Church, 'emblematically described by the situation of the city of Jerusalem'; the mountains surrounding it are like a mirror, reminding all those who 'dwell' in the church (verse 1) that she is defended by God on every side.[524] Calvin is then able to read the rest of the psalm as about the afflictions which the church must nevertheless suffer, and about the purging of hypocrites from the church.[525]

This Christian and ecclesial ethos is similarly presumed in the use of the psalm at Christian *Vespers, which addresses Christ as 'Mount of Strength'. In the *Liturgy of Hours, Psalm 125 is used at Monday Vespers in the third week of the month, and it is one of Vespers Psalms arranged in a madrigal style by Giovanni Gastoldi (1607). An implicit Christian theme, assumed by the context of an intended performance in the liturgy, is also evident in Philippe de *Monte's *a capella* motet, 'Qui confidunt in Domino' (1574) and Heinrich *Schütz's a capella chorale 'Die nur vertrauend stellen' (in the *Becker Psalter* 1628, revised 1661).

The differences between Jewish and Christian readings are also evident in visual representations of this psalm. The thirteenth-century *Parma Psalter* offers an illustration (fol. 187r) which is very like Psalm 48, a Zion Hymn. The towers and palaces are enclosed by a round crenellated wall, in turn surrounded by four mounds which surround the initial word. This illustrates, literally, verse 2 of the psalm ('as the mountains are around Jerusalem…'). To the left, a human figure sings praises to Zion on what looks like a lute.[526] By contrast, the image next to this psalm in the Byzantine Psalter *Vat.gr.1927* (fol. 236v) illustrates verses 1–2 by ways of rays of light descending from a bust of *Christ-Logos, casting a radiance over a group of people gathered around a tower which

---

[521] Cassiodorus trans. Walsh 1991b: 288.
[522] *Ibid.*: 288.
[523] *Ibid.*: 288–90.
[524] Calvin trans. Beveridge 1979: 89–91.
[525] *Ibid.*: 92–95.
[526] Metzger 1996: 93.

represents Jerusalem. Verse 3, concerning the retribution of the wicked, is illustrated by a half-figure of an angel taking away the rod of a wicked man who is beating a group of righteous men around the head: God will protect the persecuted saints of the church. A similar theme is found in a very different twelfth-century work: the *St. Albans Psalter* depicts a *nimbed Christ in the top part of the letter 'Q' at the beginning of the psalm (for **Q**ui confidunt) who reaches down to bless the psalmist in the lower part of the letter. The psalmist points to Christ with his right hand, and with his left he points to a group of believers who are surrounded by Mount Zion, illustrating verse 2: 'As the mountains surround Jerusalem, so the Lord surrounds his people...' Here the Lord is Christ, and the people are the monastery at St. Albans.[527]

Poetic imitations of the psalm are a key medium for communicating both the physical and the spiritual meanings in the psalm. Amongst the best is the version by Mary *Sidney, in a sapphic mode, of which two verses, corresponding with verses 1–2, must suffice:[528]

> As Zion standeth very firmly steadfast,
> Never once shaking: so on high Jehovah
> Who his hope buildeth, very firmly steadfast
>   Ever abideth.

> As Salem braveth with her hilly bulwarks
> Roundly enforted: so the great Jehovah
> Closeth his servants, as a hilly bulwark
>   Ever abiding.

Psalm 126: A Song about Restoration (ii)

Although this psalm has a theme in common with 125, on the prayer for restoration (see 125:4–5 and 126:4), it also shares themes with the other three psalms in this collection, with its agricultural and familial imagery. Verses 1–3 look backwards, with gratitude, because of the (partial) 'restoration of the fortunes of Zion' (verse 1), whilst verses 4–6 look forwards to being completely restored to the land, alluding also to a time of bad harvest (verses 5–6). The motif of 'restore' (from the root *sh-w-b*) is found in both verses 1 and 4, linking both

---

[527] See https://www.albani-psalter.de/stalbanspsalter/english/commentary/page337.shtml.
[528] Hamlin *et al.* 2009: 250–51.

parts of the psalm together. This is not so much a psalm for a diaspora Jew making pilgrimage to Jerusalem (as for example Psalms 120 and 121) as a prayer for ongoing restitution of those living in or near Zion. The Syriac translation also reads the psalm in this way: its heading is 'Word of David on Haggai and Zechariah when they came back from deportation'. The concern with 'restoration', both national and agricultural, gives it many associations with Psalm 85, also possibly from the post-exilic period.[529] Psalm 126 has links with the post-exilic prophet Joel (verses 2–3 'The Lord has done great things' is repeated in Joel 2:21, which is about failure of crops during a time of famine); its later links with Haggai in the superscription together suggest the early restoration period when the people, under Persian rule, also experienced failed harvests (see Joel 1:15–20 and Hagg.1:6, 10–11).

The Hebrew of verse 1 is difficult. It reads literally 'At the returning of Yahweh in a return to Zion we were like dreamers'. The Greek changes this more positively to read 'At the returning (of) the Lord (after) the *captivity* (of) Zion we became like those who were *comforted*' (*en tō epistrepsai kurion tēn aichmalōsian Siōn egenēthēmen*) and the Latin offers a similar reading (*in convertendo Dominum captivitatem Sion facti sumus sicut consolati*). The *Qumran Scrolls also have variant readings for this verse: in 11QPsᵃ the reading of *keholemim* ('like dreamers') has an additional vowel letter so that the Hebrew reads (rather like the Greek) as 'like those renewed in health' (*kehelumim*). By contrast 4QPsᵉ, which also contains this psalm, retains the same vocalisation as the MT and so reads 'like dreamers'. Hence in terms of 'reception as translation' this is a psalm open to a variety of slightly different meanings, all of which nevertheless emphasise the hope for further 'restoration'.

This hope for complete liberation, whether military or agricultural, is also brought out in verses 5–6, where sowing is associated with tears and reaping a good harvest is associated with laughter. Yet even here the Hebrew is again difficult: *meshek ha-zara'* in verse 6 literally might be translated 'the leather bag of seed': the Greek omits it, the Latin paraphrases it to read 'seed for sowing' and *Targum translates it as an 'ox' that bears the loads of fertile seeds: 'The ox that bears the seed along shall go out with weeping …'[530]

Despite these relatively small uncertainties in later translation, this psalm has a rich reception history. For example, the rabbis read verse 4 ('restore our fortunes, O Lord') as about the need to subdue any intensity of celebration, 'even at a wedding': this verse in part inspired the custom of breaking a glass at

---

[529] See pp. 56–57.
[530] Stec 2004: 223–4.

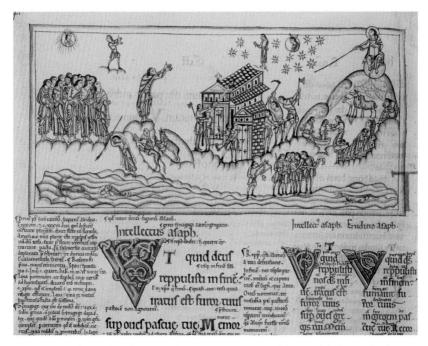

PLATE 1   Psalm 74: 'God works Salvation in the Midst of the Earth: The Birth of Christ.' From *The Eadwine Psalter*, Trinity College M.17.1, fol. 128v. (with permission from the Master and Fellows of Trinity College).

Psalms Through the Centuries: A Reception History Commentary on Psalms 73–151, Volume Three, First Edition. Susan Gillingham.
© 2022 John Wiley & Sons Ltd. Published 2022 by John Wiley & Sons Ltd.

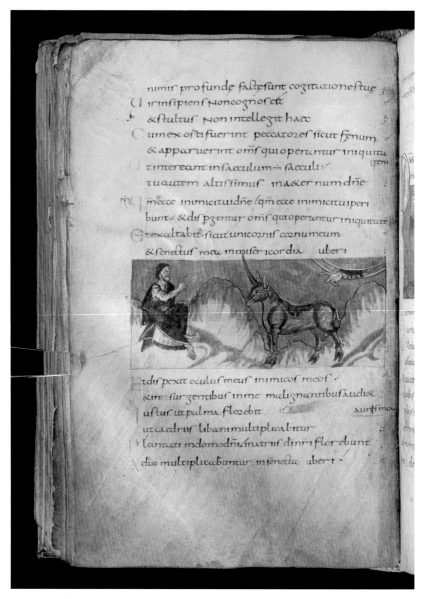

nimif profunde factefunt cogitacionef tug
Uirinfipienf Honcognofcet
& ftultuf Non intelleget haec
Cumexofti fuerint peccatoref ficut fenum
& apparuerint omf qui operantur iniquita
Uintereant infaeculum saeculi
tu autem altiffimuf inaeternum dne
Mecce inimicitui dne qm ecce inimicitui peri
bunt & difpgentur omf qui operantur iniquitate
Et exaltabit ficut unicornif coenumeum
& fenectuf mea inmifericordia uber i

Et difpexit oculuf meuf inimicof meof
& inufurgentibuf inme malignantibuf audiet
uftuf ut palma florebit
ut cedruf libani multiplicabitur
lantaci indomodni inatruf dinri florebunt
dae multiplicabuntur infenecta uber i

Plate 2   Psalm 78: David and the Unicorn. From *The Stuttgart Psalter*, Württembergische Landesbibliothek Stuttgart, Cod. Bibl M 23, fol. 108v. (with permission from
Württembergische Landesbibliothek, Stuttgart).

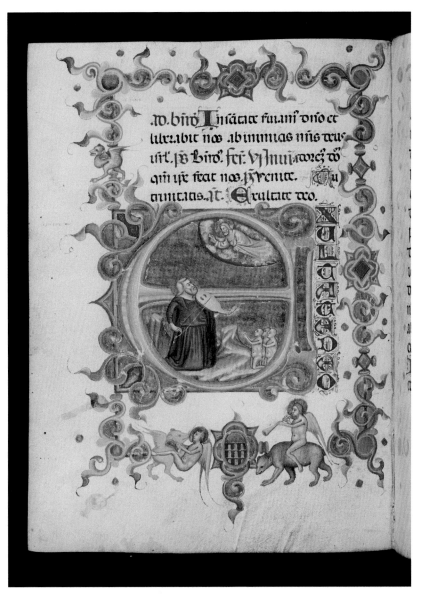

PLATE 3   Psalm 81 (Latin 80) as the Sixth Liturgical Division: a Rotund Psalmist plays
his Vielle to God. MS Canon Liturg 151, fol. 146v. (with permission of The Bodleian
Libraries, University of Oxford).

PLATE 4 Psalm 84: A Figure points to Jerusalem's Palaces and Towers. From *The Parma Psalter*, Biblioteca Paletina, Parma, MS Parm 1870 (Cod. De Rossi 510), fol. 119v. (with permission from the owners of the facsimile of *The Parma Psalter*, at www.facsimile-editions.com).

PLATE 5   Psalm 85: 'Mercy and Truth are Met Together...'. William Blake, c.1803, ©
Victoria and Albert Museum no. 9287 (with permission from the Victoria and Albert
Museum, London).

PLATE 6   Psalm 91: Christ tramples on a Lion and Serpent-Dragon: a Political Reading. Cover of *The Douce Ivory*, MS Douce 176 (with permission of The Bodleian Libraries, University of Oxford).

PLATE 7   Psalm 95: Calls to Praise on a *Shofar*. From *The Parma Psalter*, Biblioteca Paletina, Parma, MS Parm 1870 (Cod. De Rossi 510), fol. 136v. (with permission from the owners of the facsimile of *The Parma Psalter*, at www.facsimile-editions.com).

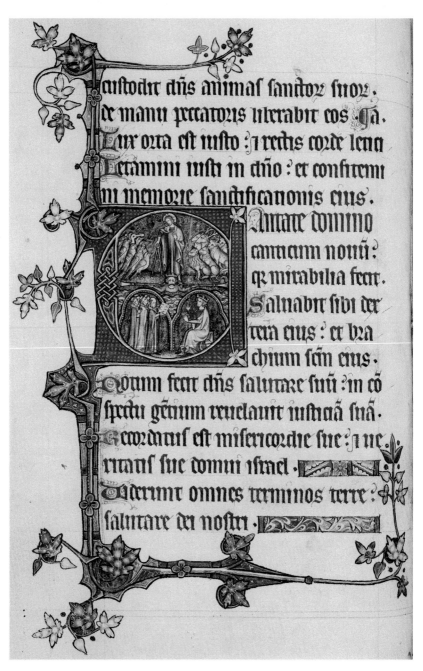

PLATE 8 Psalm 98:1: Illuminated Initial 'C'. Christ the Architect of the Universe, holding a Compass from *The Bromheim Psalter* MS Ashmole 1523, fol. 116v. (with permission of The Bodleian Libraries, University of Oxford).

PLATE 9   Psalm 100 Reversed: The Ku Klux Klan deny Mercy and Justice. Philip Evergood, 1938-9, Jewish Museum New York No. 27477 (© *Photo SCALA, Florence*, with permission of Scala Group S.p.a.).

PLATE 10   Psalm 102:6: The Pelican Feeds her Young as Christ feeds his Church. From *The Theodore Psalter*, British Library MS 19352, fol. 134r. (with permission from the British Library Board).

BOOK V

Psalm 107

O give thanks to the LORD, for he is good;
    for his steadfast love endures forever.
Let the redeemed of the LORD say so,
    those he redeemed from trouble
and gathered in from the lands,
    from the east and from the west,
    from the north and from the south.

Some wandered in desert wastes,
    finding no way to an inhabited town;
hungry and thirsty,
    their soul fainted within them.
Then they cried to the LORD in their trouble,
    and he delivered them from their distress;
he led them by a straight way,
    until they reached an inhabited town.
Let them thank the LORD for his steadfast love,
    for his wonderful works to humankind.
For he satisfies the thirsty,
    and the hungry he fills with good things.

Some sat in darkness and in gloom,
    prisoners in misery and in irons,
for they had rebelled against the words of God,
    and spurned the counsel of the Most High.
Their hearts were bowed down
    with hard labor;
    they fell down, with no one to help.
Then they cried to the LORD in their trouble,
    and he saved them from their distress;
he brought them out of darkness and gloom,
    and broke their bonds asunder.
Let them thank the LORD for his steadfast love,
    for his wonderful works to humankind.
For he shatters the doors of bronze,
    and cuts in two the bars of iron.

Some were sick through their sinful ways,
    and because of their iniquities
    endured affliction;
they loathed any kind of food,
    and they drew near to the gates of death.
Then they cried to the LORD in their trouble,
    and he saved them from their distress;
he sent out his word and healed them,
    and delivered them from destruction.
Let them thank the LORD for his steadfast love,
    for his wonderful works to humankind.
And let them offer thanksgiving sacrifices,
    and tell of his deeds with songs of joy.

PLATE 11   Psalm 107: *Psalms Book V Frontispiece*. Donald Jackson, Scribe with Sally Mae Joseph. © 2004, *The Saint John's Bible*, Saint John's University, Collegeville, Minnesota, USA. Used by permission. All rights reserved.

PLATE 13 Psalm 107: God's Deliverance from Storms at Sea. Thomas Denny: a
stained glass window at the church of St. Mary, Whitburn, Durham Diocese (with
permission of the Vicar and PCC of St. Mary's Church, Whitburn).

PLATE 14 Psalm 109: Illustrated Initial 'D'. Judas, betrayer of Christ, hangs himself. From *Le Psautier de Bertin*, BMB MS 20 fol. 122v. (with permission of Bibliothèque municipal de Boulogne-sur-Mer).

PLATE 15   Psalm 110: Christ at the Right Hand of the Father, in Conversation. From *The History Bible*, KB69B 10 fol. 31r. (with permission of the Koninklijke Bibliotheek, The Hague).

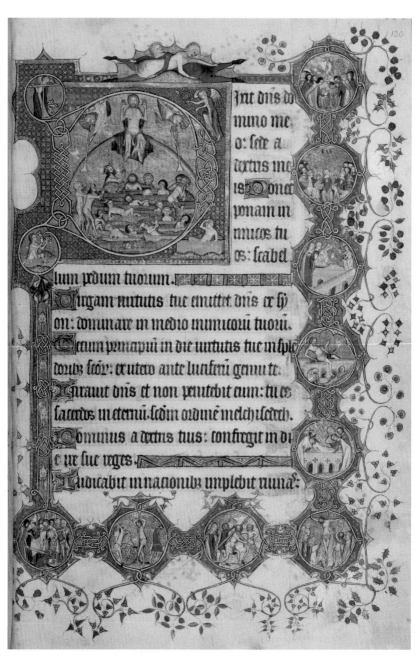

PLATE 16   Psalm 110:1 Illustrated Initial 'D'. Christ in Judgement Summons the Dead from their Graves. From *The Omer Psalter* MS 39810 fol. 120r. (with permission from the British Library Board).

PLATE 17 Psalm 113: A Synagogue Scene illustrating the Celebration of Passover. From *The Barcelona Haggadah*, Catalonia, Add 14761 fol. 65v. (with permission from the British Library Board).

PLATES 18 AND 19   Psalm 114: The Parting of the Waters, with English and Hebrew text: God's Creative Care. © Psalm 114, Hebrew and English illuminations, from *I Will Wake the Dawn: Illuminated Psalms*, by Debra Band. Jewish Publication Society, 2007 (with permission of the author).

PLATE 20   Psalm 117: A Vespers Psalm: The Presentation of Mary in the Temple, holding the Hebrew text of Psalm 117. Alessandro Allori (1598). Altarpiece in the Duomo in Lucca. (© simonemphotography123.com).

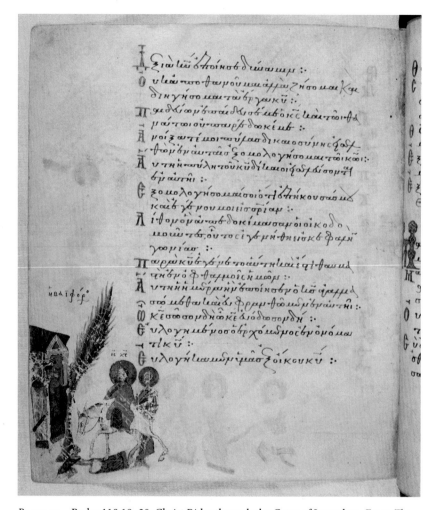

PLATE 21 Psalm 118:19–20: Christ Rides through the Gates of Jerusalem. From *The Theodore Psalter*, British Library MS 19352, fol. 157v. (with permission from the British Library Board).

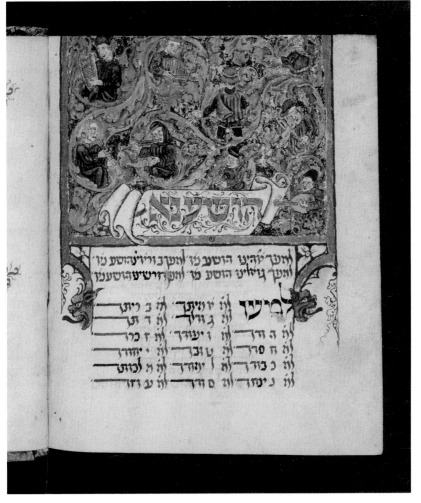

PLATE 22   Psalm 118: An invitation to Enter God's Gates with Thanksgiving. From *The Oppenheimer Siddur* (Bodleian Ms. Opp. 776 Fol. 79b it).

1957

Psaume 124-7

Notre âme, comme l'oiseau, s'est échapée du piège de l'oiseleur, le piège est brisé et nous sommes libérés.

PLATE 23   Psalm 124:7: Our Soul is Escaped like a Bird out of the Snare of the Fowlers. © Benn, *Les Psaumes*. Lyon: Musee des Beaux-Arts, 1970 (no page numbers).

PLATES 24 AND 25 Psalm 126, with English and Hebrew text: © Psalm 126, Hebrew and English illuminations, from *I Will Wake the Dawn: Illuminated Psalms*, by Debra Band. Jewish Publication Society, 2007 (with permission of the author).

PLATE 26 'By the Waters of Babylon'. From *The Eadwine Psalter*, Trinity College M.17.1, fol. 243v. (with permission from the Master and Fellows of Trinity College).

PLATE 27　　Psalm 137:5 'If I forget you, O Jerusalem…'. Mosaic of Psalm 137 in the Chagall State Hall, Knesset (© ADAGP, Paris and DACS, London, 2020).

PLATE 28   Psalm 148 fol. 41v: 'Christus Rex'. From *Les Très Riches Heures de Duc de Berry*, Musée Condé Chantilly (© with permission from the Agence Photographique de la Réunion des musées nationaux).

PLATE 29   Psalm 149:1: 'Sing to the Lord a New Song'. From *The Parma Psalter*, Biblioteca Paletina, Parma, MS Parm 1870 (Cod. De Rossi 510), fol. 213b (with permission
from the owners of the facsimile of *The Parma Psalter*, at www.facsimile-editions.com).

PLATE 30   Psalm 150: 'Praise the Lord!'. Marc Chagall's stained glass window at Chichester Cathedral (© ADAGP, Paris and DACS, London, 2020).

a Jewish wedding as reminder of the need for some solemnity.[531] Furthermore, the rabbis saw this psalm as marking Israel's *ascent* from exile, contrasting it with Psalm 137 which was read as Israel's earlier *descent* into the depths of exile: so Psalm 137 is recited prior to *Birkat HaMazon* (Grace after meals, on weekdays) to remind the people of the destruction of Temple even when they appear to be sated and well, whilst Psalm 126 is recited before *Birkat HaMazon* on Sabbaths and festivals, in order to give a glimpse of some future promise of a final release from captivity.[532] 'On the Sabbath, the sorrowful Psalm 137, which contains the traditional oath of allegiance to Jerusalem, is replaced by an optimistic and joyous one that looks forward to God's salvation and redemption.'[533]

The same Jewish hope is expressed in Moshe *Berger's recent image of this psalm, which suggests a people emerging from fire and water.[534] Berger writes: 'Since the destruction of the Second Temple, the most important event is the third return of the people to the Holy Land. Their ingathering to Jerusalem and the return to Zion is an essential act of faith…'[535] This is also what lies behind *Benn's image of this psalm, dated 1953, encountering the beginning of reparation after the Second World War. Relief and thanksgiving for survival are seen in the figure bearing golden sheaves, whilst a smaller, darker figure clearly sowing seeds in pain and grief begins to disappear from view.[536]

The psalm has a similar interpretation in Jewish music. Salamone *Rossi's *Shir Hama'a lot: Tehillim 126* was composed to be sung, without instrumentation, in synagogue ghetto communities in Italy in the early seventeenth-century.[537] The longing for integration and restoration was remarkably relevant. Over three and half centuries later, in 1986, the Christian musician Adrian Snell composed an oratorio called *Alpha and Omega*, based on texts from the Prophets and Psalms, reflecting on the tragedy of the *Shoah*. Psalm 126, 'Streams in the Desert', is used alongside texts from Joel and Isaiah.[538] This concern is continued in 1998, when Philip Glass was commissioned by the American Symphony Orchestra to celebrate the fiftieth anniversary of the State of Israel in 1998. Psalm 126, about the longing for the restoration of Israel, was spoken by a narrator and accompanied by a wordless chorus and orchestra: a recording is

[531] Feuer 2004: 1538. This is found in the *Talmud*, b.Berkat 31a.

[532] 2004: 1535; Cohen 1992: 427.

[533] Donin 1980: 301. See also (for a similar reception in Psalm 137) pp. 354, 357–8.

[534] See http://themuseumofpsalms.com/product/psalm-126.

[535] See http://www.biblical-art.com/artwork.asp?id_artwork=15248&showmode=Full.

[536] See Benn 2005: pages not numbered; also Markus 2015: 280–81, who links this psalm with Benn's image of 124:7.

[537] See https://www.youtube.com/watch?v=tmNprE98fUg; also Gorali 1993: 229, with a score of this psalm.

[538] See https://www.youtube.com/watch?v=Zo0houYxvmE.

available on *Psalms of Sorrow and Joy* (2005), released by Naxos as part of the Milken Archive of American Jewish Music.[539] In 1999, John *Harbison's *Four Psalms*, with *SATB soloists and SATB chorus and orchestra, was performed also to celebrate the founding of the State of Israel. Psalm 126 was again one of four psalms chosen, along with Psalms 114, 137 and 133. Yet again the theme of this psalm, concerned with the hope for the ultimate restoration of Zion, was remarkably relevant for that occasion.[540]

The Christian reading of this psalm is predictably different. Firstly, in the commentary tradition, the first three verses of the psalm are read allegorically. *Augustine, for example, sees this as about living between Babylon (symbolising confusion) and Sion ('the eternal Son') and is an anticipation of joy on arrival in the heavenly city.[541] *Basil agrees: this is about our future, *heavenly* joy.[542] *Cassiodorus also reads the psalm as containing a vision of the eternal Jerusalem: the first part concerns the believer freed from unbelief and sin, and the second part concerns those not yet freed: overall it is about the hope for the resurrection, expressed more fully in Psalm 127, with its ending about 'resurrection peace'.[543] *Bede offers a similar reading: this is about believers striving for heavenly joy, for there is no lasting happiness on earth.[544]

Secondly, Christians tend to read the last three verses of the psalm in part literally and in part allegorically. In Christian liturgy these verses are sometimes sung with a literal application at harvest-time. The *antiphon 'The Lord has done great things for us, we are glad' is often used at thanksgiving services. The hymn 'Now Thank we all our God', translated from the German by the nineteenth-century hymn writer Catherine *Winkworth, in part influenced by verse 3, is also used at harvest thanksgivings.[545] Another nineteenth-century songwriter, Knowles Shaw, composed 'Bringing in the Sheaves' as a Gospel Song, inspired by the last verse of Psalm 126. It was arranged to the tune 'Harvest' by George Minor and was used as a Sunday School song: its dotted rhythms, upbeat tempo and repetitions and short phrases contributed to it becoming a 'work song', popularised by Tennessee Ernie Ford in his *Hymns (1956)* and featured in *The Beverley Hillbillies, The Little House on the Prairie*

[539] Dowling Long and Sawyer 2015: 190.

[540] See pp. 214–15 (Psalm 114); p. 337 (Psalm 133); and p. 364 (Psalm 137).

[541] Augustine in Wesselschmidit 2007: 352; also Augustine trans. Uyl 2017: 620.

[542] Basil, *Homilies on the Psalms* 14.4 (FC 46:220), cited in Wesselschmidt 2007: 352.

[543] Rigolot 2017: 267–72.

[544] Bede, *Homilies on the Gospels* 2.13 (CS 111:119), cited in Wesselschmidt 2007: 353; also, Neale and Littledale 1874–79: 4/201.

[545] Some of this psalm is also from Sir. 50:22–24. See https://hymnary.org/hymn/CH4/182; see also Gillingham 2008: 215.

and even in an episode of *The Simpsons*.[546] The same focus on 'harvest' is also found in Christian art. A striking example is in a stained-glass window in Thunov Chapel, part of St. Vitus Cathedral, Prague, created between 1929 and 1934 by Kysela František (1881–1941), which portrays scenes of natural disasters such as floods, hail storms, fire, death, injury and old age, based primarily on Psalm 126:5.[547]

The harvesting theme is also developed allegorically in Christian illustrations with reference to 'the harvest of souls'. The ninth-century *Stuttgart Psalter* (fol. 146r) has a graphic image of one figure sowing and another making away with his sheaves, apparently rejoicing: but the hand of God from the heavens extends over both.[548] And in the twelfth-century *St. Albans Psalter*, the letter 'I' (from the first word, *In convertendo*) is divided into three tiers; in the top tier the psalmist points to the tag: *They that sow in tears*, and holds the book with the caption: *They shall reap in joy*. The second tier has a man reaping with a sickle, and in the third tier another man scatters seeds from a bag. This is about humans who are sowing seeds and then harvesting the fruits in their lives.[549]

Allegorical readings of Psalm 126 have also influenced musical arrangements, whether specifically Christian or less so. *Brahms' *German Requiem* (1865–8), with its fascination with mortality and immortality, uses in its first movement a passage from Matt. 5:4 ('Blessed are those who mourn, for they shall be comforted...') alongside Ps. 126:5–6—one of three passages used from psalms taken from *Luther's Bible—about the experience of all humanity needing comfort in sorrow.[550] A more explicitly Christian interpretation is found in Isaac *Watts' metrical psalm, with the title 'The Joy of a Remarkable Conversion', or 'Melancholy Removed'.[551] The more contemporary version by singer and song-writer Graham Kendrick entitled 'When the Lord brought us back' makes a similar point.[552]

A more pragmatic social and political appropriation of Psalm 126 is also evident in its reception history. Francis *Bacon's account of this psalm, in a work of selected psalms published in 1625 and dedicated to George *Herbert, has clear autobiographical allusions to Bacon's own rise and fall in power:[553]

[546] Dowling Long and Sawyer 2015: 36.
[547] See https://bit.ly/3vy2BnW.
[548] See https://bit.ly/3rM0rTb.
[549] See https://www.albani-psalter.de/stalbanspsalter/english/commentary/page338.shtml.
[550] See Gillingham 2008: 223.
[551] See https://www.ccel.org/ccel/watts/psalmshymns.Ps.293.html.
[552] See https://bit.ly/3vzFrhg.
[553] See Wieder 1995: 192–3.

When God returned us graciously
Unto our native land
We seemed as in a dream to be,
And in a maze to stand...

O Lord, turn our captivity
As winds that blow at south
Do pour the tides with violence
Back to the river's mouth.

Who sows in tears shall reap in joy,
The Lord doth so ordain;
So that his seed be pure and good
His harvest shall be gain.

William Holladay tells the story of Dorothy Day (1897–1980) who was a pioneer for the Catholic Worker movement in America. Having been nourished by the Psalms in her Episcopalian Church as a child, at university she left the church and became a socialist, fighting especially for women's suffrage, for which she was imprisoned. She asked for a Bible in prison; she speaks of how reading the Psalms gave her a warm familiarity with her childhood, along with new hope and joy. It was Psalm 126 which spoke to her in its entirety. After citing the whole psalm, she ends her reflections as follows: 'If we had faith in what we were doing, making our protest against brutality and injustice, then we were indeed casting our seeds, and there was the promise of harvest to come.'[554]

Perhaps one image above all others brings together the various aspirations, both Jewish and Christian, both spiritual and material, which have arisen from this psalm. This is by Debra *Band, who presents a double page representation of the psalm, first using English calligraphy and then using Hebrew (see PLATES 24 and 25 for a reproduction of these images).[555] The Hebrew page illustrates a flaming menorah, arising out of a dream-like image of a pool of sparkling blue water, surrounded by patches of gold which fall over the Hebrew letters below. The English page presents the text within a cloud of gold and blue patches. Band's commentary on the psalm notes its importance in the Jewish memory because of its recitation before grace after meals on Sabbaths and Festival holidays; two key words in the psalm are *shub* ('restore') in verses 1 and 4 and *rinnah*, a cry of joy, in verses 2, 5 and 6. Taking the Hebrew in verse 1 to refer to being as if in a *dream*, Band's Hebrew illustration is to present the psalm with

---

[554] Holladay 1993: 225–26, citing Dorothy Day, *The Long Loneliness* (New York: Harper & Row, 1952), 28 and 29.
[555] Band and Band 2007: 176–80.

a dream-like quality, encouraging the people to 'wake from sleep' to the joy of their future restoration which will come about with the return of the Messiah. The Christian reading of the psalm is also given a dream-like quality: its hope is also in the future return of Messiah (who is Christ) and its use at Advent reinforces a Christian memory perpetuated through worship. This psalm, fixed in the belief system of both Judaism and Christianity, uses imagery of victims of war (verses 1–3) and victims of famine (verse 4–6), and so 'builds upon memories of the past (and) attempts to shape the actions of the future'.[556]

Psalm 127: A Song about Security in the Home (i)

The hope for restoration in Psalm 126:4–6 is now expressed more specifically in 127:1–2; and the promise of progeny in 127:3–5 is continued in 128:1–4, with the particular use of the macarism 'Happy' in 127:5 and 128:1. Psalm 127 stands at the heart of 125–129, and also at the centre of the Ascents as a whole.

The Solomonic heading (found only elsewhere over Psalm 72) may be because of the association of the 'building of the house' (verse 1) and the 'building of the Temple'. The promise of sons is then read as a promise of a Davidic dynasty, from Solomon onwards. The 'city' and the city 'gate' feature at the beginning and ending of the psalm, so this is not only about family life but fits with that wider interest in Zion in most other Ascent psalms. The 'sleep' for the 'beloved' (verse 2) is then read as about Solomon (2 Sam. 12:24: 'And the Lord loved him') and about the dream at Gibeon (1 Kings 3:2–15) where Solomon was promised the gift of wisdom. Wisdom influence is evident in the proverbial teaching throughout the psalm, which is addressed not to God but to an audience, with two-line aphorisms in verses 1 and 3–4, as well as staircase parallelism in verse 1 ('Unless the Lord...' and 'in vain' being repeated twice). Even the two themes within the psalm have some alliteration: we read of builders (*bonim*) and God building (*yibneh*) in verse 1 and sons (*banim* and *bene*) in verses 3–5.

The Solomonic heading is a later stage in the psalm's reception: the likely date of the psalm is probably post-exilic, with its interest in genealogies and the gift of children (see for example, the book of Ruth). Some Greek manuscripts do not even have this heading, although 11QPs[a] at *Qumran does. The Syriac Psalter, like Psalm 126, has a heading referring to Haggai and Zechariah and the need to build the Temple (i.e. to take the focus away from building their own houses, as in Haggai 1:4), so it also places the psalm not in Solomonic times but in the post-exilic period.[557]

---

[556] Band and Band 2007: 179.
[557] Neale and Littledale 1874–79: 4/210.

Two interesting additions in the *LXX* suggest concerns of the Diaspora community, possibly from Alexandria. The first is the translation of the 'sons of one's youth' (*bene ha-ne'urim*) in verse 4 as 'sons of the expelled' (*hoi huioi tōn ektetinagmenōn*), or 'sons of the Diaspora', a phrase taken up in the Latin as well (*filii excussorum*). The macarism about descendants ('*Happy* is the man who has his quiver full of them', in verse 5) becomes in the Greek 'Happy is the man who *fills his desire* from them' (*Makarios anthrōpos hos plērōsei tēn epithumian autou ex autōn*) alluding to the hope for progeny, especially in the Diaspora. The Latin follows the Greek. Another telling addition is *Jerome's translation of verse 2 in the *Hebraicum*, where 'eating the bread of anxious toil' becomes 'eating the bread of idol worship' (*manducatis panem idolorum*). This is strikingly different from the more socially inclined paraphrase offered in the *Targum* on this verse: 'It is in vain that you *take pains to* rise early *in the morning to commit robbery*, that you go late to rest *in order to commit fornication*, that you eat the *foods of the poor, who toiled for them honestly...*'[558]

The Jewish commentary tradition is particularly explicit about sons; they not only protect their father in a military context (verse 4) but also in matters of justice, defending him in lawsuits (verse 5). This probably explains why daughters are not given any specific reference.[559] *Rashi, by contrast, focusses on Solomon and the Temple, reading the psalm as an explanation for the destruction of the Temple on account of his marrying an Egyptian princess of whom God disapproved (verse 4), reading verse 1 as a prayer of David: 'Why, my son, should you build the Temple and turn aside from the Omnipresent?'. This is very different from Rashi's commentary on Psalm 122, where David, Solomon and the Temple are seen in such a positive light.[560]

The New Testament again has no reference to this psalm. *Cassiodorus is probably the most notable commentator to develop a thoroughly Christian interpretation. Noting it is the 'eighth psalm' in the Psalms of Ascent, he sees this as a reference to the resurrection, whereby Solomon (meaning 'man of peace') is a type of Christ. Hence in verses 1–2 the 'house' is the church, and in verses 3–5 the 'sons' refer to Jesus Christ and his Apostles.[561] This was partly expressed earlier by *Hilary of Poitiers, who, in his commentary on Psalm 126 (MT 127) argues that the house for God is built on justice and holiness, on the solid rock of the Prophets and Apostles; the 'sleep' of death is transformed through Christ, our Peace, into our resurrection.[562] Building on this, pseudo-Thomas reads the

[558] Stec 2004: 224.

[559] Cohen 1992: 429.

[560] See p. 270 (Rashi, on Psalm 122); also Feuer 2004: 1541–42; Gruber 2004: 710–11.

[561] Cassiodorus trans. Walsh 1991b: 295–96; *Augustine also identifies Solomon with Christ in Augustine trans. Uyl 2017: 622–63.

[562] Taken from Rigolot 2017: 126–27.

psalm as about 'the Voice of the Church, built upon the resurrection; and the Voice of Christ.'[563] A more reflective development of Christian thought is found in the fourth-century *Scholia on Psalms* by *Evagrius Ponticus, which, from Ps. 127:1, compares the soul first to a house, where Christ is the Master; secondly to a city, where Christ is King; and thirdly, to a temple, which Christ possesses, as the living God.[564]

Yet again a shift occurs by the time of the Reformation, where now the psalm is seen to be about Christian leadership and the 'city' in verse 1 is now the 'Christian State': the Geneva Gloss on verse 1 identifies the city as 'the public State of the Commonwealth' and verse 2 as 'the rulers and magistrates of the city'. *Calvin notes from verse 1 that prosperity cannot flourish unless God blesses the proceedings.[565] *Luther is even more specific: 'Psalm 127 is a doctrinal psalm. As such it teaches that both governmental and domestic rule are gifts of God and are in God's keeping ...'[566] Philip Melanchthon reinterprets verse 5: 'Blessed is the state to whom God gives such governors. Therefore let us acknowledge that without the help of God no governance is possible.'[567]

The first part of verse 1 has been given several other political connotations. 'Unless the Lord builds the house, the builders labour in vain' is written in the floor of the Central Lobby in the Palace of Westminster, where the Houses of Parliament now convene. The Latin translation (*Nisa Dominus frustra*) is frequently used on coats of arms, for example the University of Bristol and the City of Edinburgh.[568] The commonly used liturgical *antiphon taken from this psalm 'Except the Lord keep the city, the watchman waketh in vain' (*KJV* of verse 1) can be interpreted in many different ways—familial, ecclesial, social and political.

'Building' is undoubtedly the central motif in many illustrations of this psalm. In Byzantine Psalters the builder is frequently King David, not Solomon, although he is usually symbolised as a Byzantine Emperor. *Biblioteca Vaticana, gr.752* (fol. 395v) depicts David, crowned, before a building with a balcony, and behind him is a priest, apparently celebrating the Mass, beneath a canopy. In *Carolingian Psalters such as *Utrecht* (fol. 73v), and also

---

[563] Neale and Littledale 1874–79: 4/209.

[564] These three comparisons are concerned with *praktikē*—about right living; *physikē*—about living in the world Christ has created and redeemed; and *theologia*—about contemplation of Christ as God. See Dysinger 2015: 110–11.

[565] Calvin, CTS 12:104–5 (CO32:321) cited in Selderhuis (ed.) 2018: 307.

[566] Luther, *Summaries*, WA 38:59–60, cited in Selderhuis (ed.) 2018: 306.

[567] Melanchthon *Comments on the Psalms*, CR 13:1210, cited in Selderhuis (ed.) 2018: 308.

[568] Huxley 1949: 302, citing many other heraldic uses of this verse.

in later related Psalters, such as *Harley* (fol. 66r) and *Eadwine* (fol. 233r), it is Christ who is the builder.[569] In all these Psalters we view a wall running across the entire image, behind which is a tabernacle, to the right of which is the bearded psalmist with a group of believers (verse 3). He points to Christ, attended by three angels, standing to the right on the other side of a hill. He holds a shield and spear in his left hand, and a trowel and plumb line in his right, suggested by: 'Except the Lord build the house … except the Lord keep the city' of verse 1.

The *Parma Psalter* (fol. 188v) also uses an image of building, again with the theme of 'unless the Lord builds the house…' A figure is laying bricks with a trowel, creating a wall, this time probably of the Temple. Another figure with a crown and fur tipper raises his eyes and his arms point upwards, as if to God: this is presumably Solomon, whose name, as part of the heading, appears to the right of the bricklayer.[570]

Musical arrangements are quite different. Three examples demonstrate a 'Marian' interpretation of this psalm. We noted earlier how both Psalms 122 and 127 in the Ascents are used in the Office of *Vespers of our Lady, along with 110 and 113.[571] So in Monteverdi's 'Vespers of 1610' (or the 'Vespers for the Blessed Virgin Mary'), composed during his time at Mantua (where Salamone *Rossi also worked), Psalm 127 is the fourth psalm used.[572] It might have been chosen because of its reference to sons being a reward of the fruit of the womb (verse 3). It follows a motet by three tenors entitled 'Duo Seraphim' (taken from Isa. 6:2–3 and 1 Jn. 5:7) and uses ten voices. It is followed by another motet, 'Audi Coelum', and then Psalm 147, and finally an 'Antiphon to Mary and the Magnificat'.[573] A century later *Handel included this psalm in his 'Carmelite Vespers', composing the music in Rome in about 1707. Part I includes the first three psalms (110, 113 and 122) along with motets, *antiphons and arias on Marian texts, whilst Part II adapts Psalm 127 in six different movements (including the Gloria).[574] Thirdly, Vivaldi's 'Nisi Dominus' is an independent composition, dating about 1710, perhaps written for the Pietà; it is set in nine movements, and is his most extended piece for one solo (alto) voice. One of its pieces ('Cum Dederit') plays on the reference to 'sleep' (verse 3) with slow and ascending chromatic lines. Its liturgical setting concludes with a joyous Amen, followed by a more sombre

---

[569] See https://psalter.library.uu.nl/page/154.

[570] Metzger 1996: 94.

[571] See p. 203.

[572] See p. 275.

[573] See https://www.youtube.com/watch?v=j10Quxg6fhY; also Dowling Long and Sawyer 2015: 255; Gillingham 2008: 184.

[574] See https://www.youtube.com/watch?v=-FkmbufxzxQ; also Dowling Long and Sawyer 2015: 199; Gillingham 2008: 188.

'Gloria Patri'.[575] Of the other Renaissance, Baroque and Classical settings of this psalm—inspired by its liturgical associations—the most notable is a chorale by J. S. *Bach (BWV 438).[576]

An interesting connection between this psalm and 126 is the image of dreaming and sleep, whereby in 126 the dream was a means of expressing hope.[577] Although the reference to 'sleep' in verse 2 creates problems for translation, the Hebrew reads, more literally, 'He provides (for) his beloved while they are asleep', the contrast with 126 is nevertheless interesting. Elizabeth Barrett Browning (1806–61) composed her poem, 'The Sleep', using the translation in the *KJV* where sleep itself is the gift of God. It is based on 127:2:[578]

> Of all the thoughts of God that are
> Borne inward into souls afar,
> Along the Psalmist's music deep,
> Now tell me if that any is,
> For gift of grace, surpassing this:
> 'He giveth his beloved—sleep?' …
>
> O earth, so full of dreary noises!
> O men, with wailing in your voices!
> O delved gold, the wailers heap!
> O strife, O curse, that o'er it fall!
> God strikes a silence through you all,
> And giveth his beloved—sleep. …
>
> And friends, dear friends, when shall it be
> That this low breath is gone from me,
> And round my bier ye come to weep,
> Let One, most loving of you all,
> Say, 'Not a tear must o'er her fall!
> He giveth his beloved—sleep'.

Over two centuries previously, at the very end of the sixteenth century, another female poet delivered the entire psalm into English verse, skilfully imitating its parallelism at the beginning as well as other poetic forms. Avoiding the identification of the 'house' with the Commonwealth, which from the Geneva Gloss she would have known about at this time, Mary *Sidney adopts a more familial and personal reading of the psalm. God's gift of children, for

---

[575] See https://www.youtube.com/watch?v=1WdX5uBFadM ('Cum Dederit'); also Dowling Long and Sawyer 2015: 168; Gillingham 2008: 190.

[576] For a further list see https://www2.cpdl.org/wiki/index.php/Psalm_127.

[577] See p. 294 and Plates 24 and 25.

[578] Hamlin *et al.* 2009: 323–4.

example, with its gendered rhetoric (verse 3) is interpreted with care, though not from an overtly female point of view:[579]

> The house Jehovah builds not,
> We vainly strive to build it;
> The town Jehovah guards not,
> We vainly watch to guard it.
>
> As unto weary senses
> A sleep rest unasked:
> So bounty cometh uncaused
> From him to his beloved.
>
> No, not thy children hast thou
> By choice, by chance, by nature;
> They are, they are Jehovah's,
> Rewards from him rewarding...

Psalm 127 is richly layered because its interpretation is so dependent upon the context of the reader—whether Jewish or Christian, male or female, ecclesiastical or political, liturgical or secular, or interested in family or state. It provides another good illustration of the way in which reception history tells us as much about the context of the interpreter as the psalm itself.

Psalm 128: A Song about Security in the Home (ii)

Psalms 127 and 128 were probably brought together because they have several features in common. The macarism (*ashre* 'Happy is …') in 127:5 is repeated in 128:1, although here the language has been more influenced by wisdom in its additional focus on 'the fear of the Lord', and the theme of blessing becomes more liturgical in verses 4 and 5 (to be discussed below). Psalm 128 ends with a more specific reference to God's blessing *from Jerusalem*, but this too has links with the Solomonic heading and building 'the house' at the beginning of Psalm 127. The reward of progeny is paramount in

---

[579] See Clarke 2012: 171; poem taken from Hamlin *et al.* 2009: 252–53.

both 127:3–5 and 128: 3–4,6, with the same Hebrew root (*g-b-r*) being used to depict the husband as a mighty warrior (*gibbor*, 127:4) and as the recipient of many children (*geber*, 128:4). Originally verses 1–4, beginning and ending with 'fear of the Lord', and focussed mainly on family life, might have been separate from the more liturgical verses 5–6, which changes both the speaker and addressee, being interested now in God's blessing from Zion. On the other hand, verse 4 ends with a reference to 'blessing' with a different word from that used in verses 1 and 2 (*yeborak*: the piel passive of the verb *b-r-k*, 'Thus shall the man *be blessed* ...') and the same verbal form of *b-r-k* begins verse 5: (*yebarekeka*, 'May the Lord *bless* you').[580] Whether or not Psalm 128 was an originally unified psalm, it is clear that the first stage of reception, in bringing both 127 and 128 together into the overall collection, was not accidental, with their joint interests on blessings in family life and blessings from Jerusalem.

The later Syriac heading connects the figure in verses 1–4 with 'Zerubbabel, Prince of Judah' on account of his role in the re-building of the Temple. This again presumes a post-exilic setting and again links this psalm with 127 before it.

The reception history of each psalm is, however, quite different. Psalm 127 is rich in reception, being open to a wide range of meanings, whilst Psalm 128 is less multivalent. The church fathers find little explicit Christology in 128, for example—other than a tendency to view the 'wife' and the 'children' in verse 3 as the Church.[581] Reformation commentators read home, family, and industry in a more literal way, rather than re-reading these as images about the Christian State as in 127. Hence for *Luther, this is a 'marriage song' *par excellence*. Jewish commentary tradition also has little new to add to this psalms, other than one unusual feature in reading both verses 1–2 and 6 as about promises not only now but about the life to come: *Targum, for example, paraphrases verse 2 as 'blessed shall you be *in this world*, and it shall be well with you *in the world to come* ...'[582] Verse 6 is read as about the resurrection at the end of time, when Moses and Aaron will appear, and then the Messiah appears to rebuild the Temple before the final judgment.[583] But these are exceptions: normally Jewish tradition, like Christian commentators, reads this psalm as about family life.

Images in illustrated Psalters also endorse family life. The *Utrecht Psalter* (fol. 73v) for example, depicts Christ blessing a family at table (perhaps a king

---

[580] The *Vulgate* makes this distinction clear: 'beati' is used in verse 1, 'benedictetur' in verse 4 and 'benedicat' in verse 5.

[581] For example, *Augustine trans. Uyl 2017: 625–27.

[582] Stec 2004: 225.

[583] Feuer 2004: 1555, citing Radvaz, *Responsa* II:644.

and queen) with a vine growing on a trellis and two olive trees illustrating the fecundity of wife and children as expressed in verse 3.[584] The *Stuttgart Psalter* (fol. 146v) offers a similar interpretation: God's hand emerges in blessing over a family of four at table: the father holds a cross, the wife holds vine leaves, and the children carry olive leaves, whilst to the right three naked figures—probably a women and two children—who clearly do not 'fear the Lord' are driven down to hell.[585] A seventeenth-century landscape painting by G. Donck, now in the National Gallery, has a similar image: it is of Jan van Hensbeeck and his wife and child, and his wife holds a basket of grapes, again an allusion to Ps. 128:3 ('your wife shall be a fruitful vine …').[586]

As for the liturgical use of this psalm, its inclusion in the *BCP marriage service, along with Psalm 67, testifies to the way that homely image of the blessings of family life are read into this psalm. Psalm 128 is used for weddings in Catholic, Anglican and Methodist services.[587] Its use in circumcision ceremonies in the Sephardic liturgy again testifies to its familial connotations within the Jewish home.[588]

Many of the musical settings are on account of the psalm's associations with weddings and the household. Salamone *Rossi's *Shir HaMa-a-lot Ashrei Kol Yerei* is set for three voices, with contrapuntal play between the trebles and bass parts, perhaps suggesting the relationships between father and children; its quicker triple metre for verse 3 is an intentional expression of joy at family life.[589] By contrast, the use of Psalm 128 in Nuptial Masses has resulted in a number of compositions originally for use in Catholic liturgy, for example by Giovanni *Gabrieli and Orlando *di Lasso; there are similar examples in Anglican Liturgy, such as by Orlando *Gibbons, Henry *Purcell and Henry *Lawes.[590]

It is perhaps not surprising that a more radical reception of this psalm is a more recent phenomenon. This has been in part a reaction to metrical versions of verse 3 such as that by George *Sandys:[591]

> Like a fair and fruitful vine,
> By thy house, thy wife shall join.
> Sons, obedient to command,
> Shall about thy table stand…

---

[584] See https://psalter.library.uu.nl/page/154.
[585] See https://bit.ly/3EHkPs7.
[586] See https://bit.ly/3t7C6UL.
[587] Gillingham 2008: 256–57.
[588] Keet 1969: 123.
[589] See https://www.youtube.com/watch?v=yXrk6Yh5Kiw; also Gillingham 2008: 166.
[590] See https://www2.cpdl.org/wiki/index.php/Psalm_128.
[591] https://www.cpdl.org/wiki/index.php/Psalm_128#Metrical_version_by_George_Sandys.

Contemporary reception has been in part a reaction to this teaching, which is found in both Jewish and Christian commentary tradition. For example, the *Soncino* commentary notes that this verse speaks of the wife who is to bear children for her husband, staying in the privacy of her home and reserving herself for her him.[592] Or again, *Gunkel's commentary on Psalm 128 (first published in 1929) notes without any aberration that the one who upholds religion is the father of the family.[593]

More recently, however, John Goldingay writes that this psalm is a stumbling block to those who are celibate, as it is also 'for those whose wife is more than a womb and daughters count as much as sons.'[594] Marc Brettler follows this view even more radically. Noting that 'the man' (*geber*) is the one who is blessed in verse 4, he suggests that the 'wife' and 'children' in verse 3 are not the recipients of blessing but rather the results of it, on account of the man's piety and industry (verse 2). So verse 3 is about the wife as a reward for the God-fearing man. Brettler comments especially on the image of the wife as a 'fertile vineyard on the sides of your house' (*eshteka kegefen beyarkete beteka*): this depicts the man and his children around the table, whilst the woman is peripheralised in the corner, or rear, or sides (Hebrew, *yarkete*) of the house. This might be in the kitchen, the bedroom, or the stable for animals: whichever image one associates with woman's work, hers is not the central place at the table.[595] Although the vineyard can be used positively for female sexuality (as in Song 1:6) in this psalm its application to the woman signifies her worth is dependent upon what she produces, rather than her intrinsic worth. If this is the ethos of the psalm it is not to be commended.[596]

David Blumenthal comments similarly in his *Theology of Protest*, which was forged out of the experience of the Holocaust. Noting that this is a psalm purportedly upholding the virtue of human happiness, as expressed by the macarism in verse 1 ('Happy is everyone…'), Blumenthal argues that 'everyone' in this case is the man addressed in verses 1–2, and 'happiness' here is not so much about the 'fear of God', but a way of actually exploiting ideas of oppression, terror, power and danger for women.[597] Like Brettler, Blumenthal notes how verses 3–4 read as if the woman is the tool which makes man's blessings possible. He cites two poems by Michele Foust and Naomi Janowitz.[598] One

---

[592] Cohen 1992: 430.
[593] See Gunkel 1929: 557, cited in Brettler 1998: 37.
[594] Goldingay 2008: 513.
[595] Brettler 1998: 32–33.
[596] Brettler 1998: 30.
[597] Blumenthal 1993: 70–83, referring on p. 75 to Rosenwald's comments, based on the Jerusalem *Talmud y.Kil'ayim* 1:7: 'When she remains in the intimate recesses of your house, she will be a fruitful vine'.
[598] Blumenthal 1993: 78–79.

re-reads the psalm to speak of the woman being independently blessed by God (Foust), and the other focusses on woman's work—her agonising pain in bearing children for God, not for man (Janowitz). According to Blumenthal, the psalm defies the reality of human experience, not only in relation to the woman and the man, but in relation to God's blessing of future generations of Jews in Jerusalem. We need to re-read it so '... That which is on the margin is displaced to the centre, and the centre is overturned toward the margin, and hope hangs between them caught in the interval'.[599]

We have seen how reception history so often 'goes with the grain', expanding the essential meaning of a psalm as it does so. But there are times when a psalm has also to be read 'against the grain'. These readings of this psalm are one such example, because the contents, from a contemporary perspective, necessitate it.[600] This extract from Marchiene Rientsra's *Swallow's Nest* is one way of allowing the 'marginalised' to become 'central', as she views the psalm as a blessing of a mother at her daughter's wedding:[601]

> You will surely enjoy the fruit of your labor,
> You will grow in happiness and enjoy wellbeing.
> Your husband will be like a fruitful seed in your garden.
> Your children will flower in beauty around your table.
> Receive the blessing of El Shaddai, my devoted daughter!

Psalm 129: A Song about Restoration (iii)

Psalm 129 has much in common with the first psalm of this collection, Psalm 125.[602] It is certainly very different from 127 and 128; here Zion is a focus of hate (compare 128:5 and 129:5) and blessing is absent (compare 128:5 and 129:8). The compilers perhaps included this psalm here on account of this contrast, or perhaps because of its agricultural imagery. There is some link back to 127:1–2 with similar 'staircase parallelism' in verses 1–2. But compared with these two previous psalms, Psalm 129 is not so much about blessings on home and family (127) or about fertile vines and olive trees (128), but about the infertility of

---

[599] Blumenthal 1993: 83.
[600] See p. 181 (Blumenthal on Psalm 109).
[601] Rienstra 1992: 189.
[602] See pp. 286–87.

ploughing, sowing and harvesting: ploughing is about disempowerment (verse 3) and the images of withering grass and bad harvest are used by way of a curse on the enemies (verses 6–7).

The reception history of 129 is very much influenced by different translations of particular Hebrew words into Greek and Latin. Just three examples will be highlighted here and their implications will be brought out later.

Firstly, in verse 1 the word *rabbat* is used as an adverb to describe the verb 'to attack' or 'to distress' (*ts-r-r*). This word could be translated as 'greatly/sorely' and is also found in 123:4, also used in 'staircase parallelism'. But the consonants could equally well have been vocalised *rabbot* and the word would mean instead 'many times' (so, for example, Ps. 40:6). This is how the Greek interprets it; the translation also interprets the verb 'attack' in a military sense, as 'wage war' so it reads 'they have *waged war* on me *several times*' (*pleonakis epolemēsan me*). The psalm is found at *Qumran (11QPsª) and in column 5 the word has a vowel letter to give the vocalisation *rabbot*.

Secondly, another re-reading is found in verse 3. The expression 'the ploughers ploughed' reads *ḥareshu ḥoreshim* in Hebrew, the sounds of which resonate with the Hebrew word for 'the wicked' (*resha'im*) as used in verse 4. The *LXX translates the 'ploughers' as '[wicked]sinners' (*hoi hamartōloi*).[603] It also transforms the agricultural imagery into a metaphor for metalwork: the sinners now hammer (or forge, strike) the suppliant's back. This is made even more clear in the Latin: '*supra dorsum meum fabricabantur peccatores*'. The Greek then continues to avoid the other agricultural imagery of verse 3: instead of furrows being lengthened, it is 'lawlessness' which is 'extended' or 'prolonged' (*emakrunan tēn anomian autōn*). Agricultural imagery is thus again minimised in the Greek.

Thirdly, in verse 4 the Hebrew might read 'The Lord is righteous; he has cut off the cords of the wicked'. In its context of ploughing, the 'cords' probably pertained to the lines held by the oxen who are ploughing; God will cut them free so they can no longer oppress the psalmist.[604] The *LXX, again removing the agricultural imagery, interprets the Hebrew words for 'cut off' as 'break up' or 'destroy', and reads the word for 'cords' or 'ropes' (*'abot*) as 'neck' (*'oref*), perhaps identifying the ropes as 'yokes' around one's neck. Whatever the reason, the Greek could be translated as 'he breaks the necks of sinners' (*sunekopsen auchenas hamartōlōn*). The Latin takes this up too: '*concidet* cervices *peccatorum*' or 'he cuts off [severs] the necks of sinners'.

Small letter changes between one ancient language and another might seem to be of very little consequence in the vast history of reception, but in the case of

---

[603] At Qumran (again, in 11QPsª) the word *ḥaresh'im* is also used instead of *ḥoreshim*, with the meaning 'wicked', although here the other agricultural imagery is retained.
[604] See Hossfeld and Zenger 2011: 407.

this psalm these changes have had a notable impact on the differences between Jewish and Christian reception, where the received Christian text (both Greek and Latin) is no longer about ploughing and oxen but about backs being beaten and necks being broken.

Jewish reception, reading the *Masoretic Text, maintains the more literal reading of the imagery of ploughing, so verse 3 is seen, for example, as a prophecy of the time when the Roman governor Turnus Rufus, having destroyed the Temple, had it 'ploughed over' so that not a trace remained.[605] The more general appropriation of being ploughed and released from oppression (verse 3–4) is also seen as describing the people's suffering and escape from Egypt; and not only Egypt, but also other periods of oppression and restoration. Another related reading, appropriate for the Psalms of Ascent, is to see this as a description of suffering in exile, under the yoke of heathen rulers, and the yearning for Zion, the city which the wicked despise (verses 5, 8).[606]

Christians tend to read verse 3 somewhat differently. In the Easter Vigil it is combined with one of the 'Servant Songs' in Isa. 50:6, which reads 'I gave *my back* to those who struck me...I did not hide my face from insult and spitting'; so 129:3 is also about the striking of *the back* (as in the Greek and Latin). So this verse is read liturgically, along with Isa. 50:6, as a prophecy about the sufferings of Christ by flagellation.[607] A seventeenth-century Easter Evening Collect for Psalm 129, also adapting the original imagery of ploughing, reads:

> O most blessed Jesus, who for our sins suffered the plowers to plow on your back, and make long furrows, suffering shame and whipping for our sakes... deliver us and all your holy church from those that fight against us; ...let the designs of those who have evil will at your church be like grass growing on the housetops, withered and blasted before it comes to maturity...[608]

What was seen in Jewish reception as a psalm about the many sufferings of the Jewish people throughout their history is now seen in Christian reception as a psalm about the sufferings and vindication of Jesus, and the sufferings and vindication of the 'the Triumphant Church'. Maturing through the righteous of Israel 'from her youth' up (verse 1) the Church thus inherits the Gospel of Christ. This is very much to the fore in *Augustine's commentary on this psalm, which speaks of the church 'being of ancient birth', from Abel to Enoch to Noah to Israel and so to the Lord Jesus Christ.[609] *Cassiodorus is even more direct: in

---

[605] Feuer 2004: 1558, citing *Sforno in *b.Ta'anit* 29a.

[606] Cohen 1992: 431–32, citing Hirsch; also, Feuer 2004: 1557.

[607] Neale and Littledale 1874–79: 4/223.

[608] Jeremy Taylor, 'Collect for Psalm 129' in *Works*, 15:186–87, cited in Selderhuis (ed.) 2018: 312.

[609] Augustine, 'Explanations of the Psalms' 129:2 in NPNF 1 8:611, also in Selderhuis (ed.) 2018: 312 and in Augustine trans. Uyl 2017: 627–28.

his first sentence of the commentary on verse 1 he states 'Israel, in other words, God's Church, is urged to say that she has often been warred on even from her early youth.'[610]

This Christian overlay is very clear in Reformation commentaries: this is no longer about Israel's history but about God's power working through the vicissitudes of the church. Both *Calvin and Melanchthon read Psalm 129 in this way, as did David Dickson, in a commentary on Psalm 129.[611] Martin *Luther re-reads the imagery more personally than in relation to the church, but the 're-reading' in terms of a Christian experience is the key here:

> When sin and death come and appear so immense that they seem to be the one and all, then just say: Mrs Sin, you are a powerful mistress, but you should know that you are like grass on the roof. Mr Death, it is horrible to see you, but actually you are just like grass on the roof. Mr Devil, you make me sad, but you should know you are just grass on the roof, just a water bubble.[612]

In Christian art, it is perhaps the *Utrecht Psalter* (fol. 74r) and related works, namely the *Harley Psalter* (fol. 67r) and the *Eadwine Psalter* (fol. 234v), which illustrate best how this psalm speaks not only to the church but also to the sufferings of the Jewish people.[613] In the image for Psalm 129 we first view Zion, personified, standing on a small hill; three faithful Jews appeal to Christ, in a *mandorla and served by two angels. He hands a sword to another angel who with others attacks a group of men who are approaching the figure of Zion on the hill from behind their backs (verse 3) and are about to attack (verses 1–2). To the left others cut grass, gathering it up to be burned within a thatched building (verses 6–7).

The *Stuttgart Psalter* (fol. 147r) offers an even more universal, and hence irenic, interpretation of this psalm, in that it seems to assume that the basic teaching in this psalm about reward and punishment.[614] To the left two men are building a wall.[615] 'Behind their backs' (verse 3, reading the Latin) two sinners are apparently seeking to attack them. To the right the hand of God reaches from the heavens, in order to cut off one of the sinner's head with a sword: this

---

[610] Cassiodorus trans. Walsh 1991b: 307–308.

[611] See Calvin on Psalm 129 in CTS 12:119, Melanchthon, *Comments on the Psalms* in CR 13:1213, and David Dickson, *Commentary on Psalm 129* in *The Last Fifty Psalms*: 263, all cited in Selderhuis (ed.) 2018: 313.

[612]*Lectures on the Psalms* 1532–33 WA 40/3:333, cited in Selderhuis (ed.) 2018: 314.

[613] The website for the *Eadwine Psalter* offers a clear image: see https://bit.ly/3vy6BEY.

[614] See https://bit.ly/3DEcfct; also Bessette 2005: 265–67.

[615] This is probably due to a literal reading of the Latin 'the wicked have built upon my back' (*supra dorsum meum fabricabantur peccatores*).

is an even more literal reading of the Latin of verse 4, 'he severs the necks of sinners'. Another sinner, to the right, lies on the ground, actually decapitated, his head rolling out of the frame of the image. The impact of this image is therefore confident, and even strident, in its teaching about God's severe punishment of the wicked who 'plot behind our backs'.

Attention given to individual words can cause friction in the reception of this psalm, but they can also serve to heal and illuminate the inner meaning. Yet again it is Mary *Sidney's version, transforming the conventions of the Hebrew poetry into English metre and rhyme, and carefully representing the voice of the psalmist, which offers a measured interpretation of the psalm's universal teaching about God's protection from evil. The ability to incorporate into this the agricultural metaphors in verses 3–4 is most striking:[616]

> Oft and ever from my youth,
>> So now Israel may say;
> Israel may say for truth,
>> Oft and ever my decay
>>> From my youth their force hath sought:
>>> Yet effect it never wrought.
>
> Unto them my back did yield
>> Place and plain (oh, height of woe)
> Where as in a ploughed field,
>> Long and deep did furrows go.
>>> But, O just Jehovah, who
>>> Has their plough-ropes cut in two!
>
> Tell me you that Zion hate,
>> What you think shall be your end?
> Terror shall your minds amate:
>> Blush and shame your faces shend.
>>> Mark the wheat on house's top:
>>> Such your harvest, such your crop...

---

[616] Hamlin *et al.* 2009: 254–55.

Psalms 130–134: Departing from Zion

Of these five psalms, 130 and 131 fit well together, not only because of their general themes of penitence and divine compassion (neither referring explicitly to Zion), but also because of the shared refrain 'O Israel, hope in the Lord!' in 130:7 and 131:3. Psalms 133 and 134 similarly form a pair with their shared theme on Zion as a place of blessing, with 134 acting as a short blessing in preparation for leaving the Temple. Psalm 132 stands at the heart of this collection as a lengthy composite psalm, possibly made up of ancient fragments of some ritual, celebrating God's protection of Zion through the king and the Ark. In brief, the first stage of reception testifies to some overall arrangement, ending, as the whole collection began, with a concern for Zion. This may be contrasted with 11QPs[a] at *Qumran, where the final three psalms have a very different arrangement. Psalm 132 is followed by 119, thus ending the 'Ascents' not with an interest in Zion, but with a Torah psalm.[617] Psalm 133, meanwhile, is found between 141 and 144, and Psalm 134 before Psalm 151 and after Psalm 140.[618] We shall note this again in the relevant psalms.

---

[617] See pp. 242–43.
[618] See Sanders 1965: 23; also, Wilson 1985: 110.

Psalms Through the Centuries: A Reception History Commentary on Psalms 73–151, Volume Three, First Edition. Susan Gillingham.
© 2022 John Wiley & Sons Ltd. Published 2022 by John Wiley & Sons Ltd.

Psalm 130: A Song from the Depths: The Soul and God (i)

Despite the similar address to Israel in 129:1 and 130:7 (see also 131:3), and despite the similar length of each psalm, the contrast with the language of protest expressed in Psalm 129 is notable; furthermore, here God is addressed more personally and directly.[619] And instead of familial images of work and agriculture, Psalms 130 and 131 focus only on the soul before God: even the step-parallelism in verses 5–6a and the repetition in verses 6b-8 reinforces the intensity of the psalmist's search for peace with God.

Psalm 130 was marked at least as early as *Augustine as one of the seven *penitential psalms, in this case to be used against the sin of envy. It is hard to see how this is a particular sin in the psalm, and even harder to find within the psalm a specific *confession* of sin (a motif which is lacking in four others of the seven, namely Psalms 6, 38, 102 and 143). Nevertheless, the psalmist is confident that God is forgiving (verse 4). So the structure might be as follows: verses 1–2 serve as a cry for help; verses 3–4, rather than describing the psalmist's plight, offer a note of confidence in God's ability to forgive; and verses 5–6, 7–8 offer expressions of hope, increasingly using liturgical language concerned with Israel rather than the individual. Unlike Psalm 51, for example, there is no suggestion that forgiveness has actually been received: the emphasis is on waiting (verses 5–6) and hope (verses 7–8). Despite all this, it is the attribution 'penitential psalm' which has given the psalm such a rich reception history—in commentaries, liturgy, art, music, and especially in poetry and theological discourse. What follows is a drastic distillation of its vast reception, using the theme of forgiveness as a focus.

Although there are not as many conundra as a result of difficulties of translation as in Psalm 129, verse 4 provides a critical problem in understanding the nature of forgiveness, because of the variant versions. Much depends on how the three consonants *t-w-r* in the Hebrew are understood and, as a result of this, how God's mercy and forgiveness are also understood. The *masoretic vocalisation reads the Hebrew (literally) 'for with you there is forgiveness, so that *you are feared*' (*ki 'immeka ha-seliḥah lema'an tiwware'*). The word for 'forgiveness' is only ever used of God, and the word for 'fear' has a broad spectrum of use, from 'terror' to 'awe/ reverence', so this is broadly about God's initiative and our response. The *LXX* reads 'forgiveness' more particularly as 'expiation' (*ho hilasmos*) and verse 4 ends here. The Greek in verse 5 begins with '*lema'an tiwware*' except the letters *t-w-r-* are read as 'your Torah': 'on account of *your Law* my soul waits ...' (*heneken tou nomou sou*).[620] The Latin divides the verse up

---

[619] This might be termed 'a God-centred psalm': God is addressed as Yahweh in verse 1, as Adonai in verses 2 and 3 (where he is also addressed as Yah), and is again spoken of as Yahweh in verses 5, 7 and 8, and as Adonai in verse 6.

[620] Although Psalm 130 is found in two scrolls at *Qumran (11QPsᵃ and 4QPsᵉ) the contentious phrase in verse 4, discussed here, is missing. The *Peshitta apparently intentionally omits verse 4b.

differently again, thus reading for the whole of verse 4 as follows: *quia apud te propitiatio est propter legem tuam sustinui te Domine sustinuit anima mea in verbum eius* ('But with you there is propitiation; because of *your law* I wait for you, Lord; my soul waits for *his word.*'). This places in parallelism the New Testament terms of 'law' and 'word (Gospel)'. The *Targum* reads the consonants *t-w-r* as if from the verb *r-'-h*, which means 'to see', as follows: 'For with you there is (the) forgiveness: *so that you will be seen.*' So is forgiveness a quality to evoke fear, as in the Hebrew? Or is it about expiation as a reward for obeying God's Law, as in the Greek? Or is it more harshly about propitiation, as in the Latin? Or is it a way of revealing the character of God, as in *Targum*? It is not surprising that, depending on the version being used for reading and translation, a variety of views about forgiveness emerges from the reception history of this psalm.

The only other notable change in translation is in verse 6, which in Hebrew, in the context of waiting for God, twice repeats the phrase 'more than those who watch for the morning'. The *LXX* and *Vulgate* change this to '… from the morning watch even until night' (Latin: *a custodia matutina usque ad noctem speret Israhel in Domino*). As will be seen, this has had some consequences for the later liturgical and artistic use of the psalm.

Jewish reception of this psalm offers some interesting comments on verse 1: apparently 'out of the depths' is about praying from a *low place*—never on a bed, or bench, or stool, or any other high place, 'for there must be no haughtiness in the presence of the Lord'.[621] This is why, in *Ashkenazi synagogues, the *amud*—the lectern between the *bimah* and the Holy Ark—is to be on a lower level, out of deference to Psalm 130:1 (*b.Berakoth* 10b).The psalm is recited in illness, at death, and in times of drought.[622] As for the word 'forgiveness' in verse 3, the reason for the word 'fear' is because there can be no forgiveness between the 'Ten Days of Repentance' between New Year's Day and the Day of Atonement, in order to teach us the fear of the Lord.[623] This relates to the book of Jonah, which is read in the afternoon service of the Day of Atonement: he too, taken to the 'depths' of the sea, had to be taught the fear of God before he could understand any offer of forgiveness.[624] Several questions are raised about whether forgiveness comes *only* when redemption arrives, for forgiveness is in the hand of the Lord alone, and no human nor divine agent (such as angels) can forgive sins (citing Exod. 23:20–23).[625]

---

[621] Braude 1959: 315.
[622] Holladay 1993: 146.
[623] Braude 1959: 315, citing R. Abba. *Leviticus Rabbah* XXX.7, discussing this ten-day period, cites Ps. 130:4 in this respect. See Coakley 2011: 38.
[624] 2011: 39. This also accounts for images of Jonah connected with this psalm.
[625] Feuer 2004: 1565; *Rashi in Gruber 2004: 716; also, Baker and Nicholson 1973: 27 for *Kimḥi on 130:5.

This explains the outrage at Jesus' claim to offer forgiveness of sins in Mark 2:5–12. It also explains why the New Testament is in fact so forceful about Jesus' ability to forgive sins, sometimes alluding to Psalm 130 in doing so. For example, 'You are to name him Jesus, for he will save his people from their sins' has echoes of 130:7 ('... It is he who will redeem Israel from all its iniquities') and it is cited to Joseph in Matt. 1:21, *by an angel*, in a dream.

Turning to the Church Fathers, we will focus on the western commentaries by *Hilary of Poitiers, Augustine, and *Cassiodorus, because these develop some seminal views on the meaning of forgiveness in this psalm.

Only Psalms 130 and 143 have survived of Hilary's commentaries on the seven penitential psalms. That on Psalm 130 exudes a confidence in the life of the Trinity, alongside the Pauline doctrine of justification and forgiveness: this is a good example of the way in which Hilary reads the psalms as a means of ratifying Christian doctrine.[626] So 'out of the depths' in verse 1 is read through Rom. 11:33–36, which speaks of 'the depths of the riches of the wisdom and knowledge of God', so that the psalmist's (apparently) confident faith in God's forgiveness breaks through in verse 2 ('Let your ears be attentive to the voice of my supplications!'). Verses 3–4 are read through the lens of Ps. 32:1, 5, which distinguishes between 'iniquity', as an act of disobedience, and 'sin', the state of human 'fallenness': to this is added Rom. 2:12, where the law is our judge on 'sin'. Hence using the Latin for verse 4, Hilary sees Jesus as the 'Word' of God, who has replaced the 'Law' of the Old Covenant, and so brings out 'forgiveness of sin'.[627] Such forgiveness is the direct work of the Trinity in the life of the individual.

In the light of Novatianism, which prevented lapsed Christians returning to church after the Decian persecution, Augustine was keen to urge that Christians should be able to receive forgiveness: hence verse 3 'who could stand?' was used as both a threat and promise for those who might waver. It is, however, verse 4 which takes up most of the commentary. Augustine examines the reference to 'propitiation' in the Latin and connects it to the idea of the sacrifice of Christ. 'What is this propitiation, except sacrifice? And what is sacrifice, save that which hath been offered for us?'.[628] Hence there is a law of the mercy of God—a law of love—but also a law of fear. The law which was given to the Jews was to make them feel guilty, and this was the law of fear. But there is also 'the law of the mercy of God, the law of the propitiation of God'. All this is ratified by the one through whom our sins have been remitted, who rose again from the dead in the 'morning watch' (verse 5).[629] There is much here which is

---

[626] Gillingham 2008: 36.
[627] Waltke et al. 2014: 241.
[628] Augustine trans. Uyl 2017: 630.
[629] *Ibid.*: 630.

confusing: the psalmist, whose words Augustine commends and uses, speaks from the time of the 'law given to the Jews' which apparently encourages guilt; the psalmist also believes that *Israel* will be redeemed from all iniquities, which in Augustine's view can only be brought about from the time of Christ.[630]

Cassiodorus' commentary is similar in scope and emphasis. Like Augustine he reads the reference to 'the depths' in verse 1 in the context of Jonah, although Cassiodorus views the depths not as a negative place, but one where there is the opportunity for spiritual growth in learning lessons of humility. Affirming Augustine's understanding of verse 4, Cassiodorus makes it even more clear that the reference to the 'word' is the '*law of the New Testament*', so that 'the word itself, in other words, God's Son, is set down here'.[631] Like Augustine, Cassiodorus also reads the 'morning watch' in verse 6 as a reference to the resurrection appearance of Jesus, 'offering mercy and plenteous redemption'.[632] It is interesting to see how both commentators can bring so much Christology into the psalm.

By the sixteenth century Psalm 130 not only influenced a positive Christian theology of the law, but paradoxically, and increasingly throughout the Middle Ages, a theology of *repentance* as another aspect of 'works'. This might explain *Luther's account of the psalm, which leads to a certain amount of anti-Jewish and anti-Catholic polemic. Luther reads Psalm 130 as 'the height of the Old Testament gospel', a kind of 'Pauline hymn': although divine judgement and human fear are unavoidable, he understands that there is always the possibility of salvation through the grace of Christ. It is interesting to see how, building on Augustine, Luther brings together the emphasis on 'fear' in the Hebrew text with the emphasis on the 'new Law of Christ' through using the Greek and Latin texts. So on the one hand the psalmist is seen as a prophet speaking about the work of Christ, but on the other hand the psalm is read as if from a pre-Christian context.[633] Only by being 'in the depths' and knowing what it is to 'fear God' can a (Christian) suppliant be driven to seek God's mercy and forgiveness offered in Christ; this creates similar difficulties to those we noted in Augustine's work, for the psalm has to be read as a CE, not BCE, prayer. Luther's views are best illustrated in his four-verse metrical hymn on this psalm, *Aus tiefer Not* (1524). By 1853 Catherine *Winkworth had made at least two versions of it; the second, more resonant of Luther's original, had more emphasis

---

[630] It is interesting to read *Calvin's much later commentary in the light of this, for his initial David-centred reading allowed him to be much more empathetic to the Jewish understanding of forgiveness and redemption: see https://ccel.org/ccel/calvin/calcom08.titlepage.html, especially pp. 127–38.
[631] Cassiodorus trans. Walsh 1991b: 314–15.
[632] Cassiodorus trans. Walsh 1991b: 315.
[633] See Preuss 1967: 153.

on God's grace in forgiveness, so that the hymn is actually far more paraphrase than translation:[634]

> Out of the depths I cry to Thee;
> Lord, hear me, I implore Thee!
> Bend down Thy gracious ear to me,
> My prayer let come before Thee!
> If Thou remember each misdeed,
> If each should have its rightful meed,
> Who may abide Thy presence?
>
> Our pardon is Thy gift;
> And grace alone avail us.
> Our works could ne'er our guilt remove,
> The strictest life would fail us.
> That none may boast himself of aught.
> But own in fear Thy grace hath wrought
> What in him seemeth righteous...

One difficulty in Luther's emphasis is the suggestion that prayer alone can bring about forgiveness, even though there is no actual prayer of repentance in the psalm. It is as if the *exposition* of the psalm, rather than the ancient meaning behind it, becomes the means of meditation for sin and so, through repentance, the gift of forgiveness. This is what the Calvinist Theodore Beza's 'Meditation on Psalm 130:1–2' also attempts to do.[635]

The search for forgiveness is also what the seventeenth-century Puritan *John Owen sought to achieve in his 325-page commentary.[636] Like Luther, Owen sees the psalm as a four-stanza account of the soul before God; having had a near-death experience from which he recovered by praying earnestly 130:4, Owen argues that it is only from the depths, and without any self-deception, that the guilty sinner can be forgiven and 'made righteous' by God.[637] Owen uses both the idea of 'fear' and 'the law' in verse 4 to demonstrate the different ways of discovering divine mercy and forgiveness. Owen concludes, 'there is with God, mercy ... redeeming from all iniquity; I have found it so, and so will everyone that shall believe.' A century later, in 1738, this is what John *Wesley discovered from the same psalm: it was on 24 May at St. Paul's Cathedral that Wesley heard the choir sing Psalm 130, and this led on to the

---

[634] See https://www.hymnologyarchive.com/aus-tiefer-not-schrei-ich-zu-dir.
[635] See Beza, *Upon the Pentiential Psalms*, G4v-G7r. cited in Selderhuis (ed.) 2018: 315.
[636] Gould and Quick (eds.): 1865.
[637] Waltke *et al.* 2014: 241–44.

same intense conversion experience that his brother Charles had had some three days earlier.[638]

Charles Spurgeon, the nineteenth-century non-Conformist preacher and writer, also had a high view of Psalm 130: he termed it the most excellent of the penitential psalms and argued that verses 3–4 contained the entire sum of Scripture. 'The Evangelical doctrine of the gratuitous forgiveness of sins does not of itself beget carelessness, as the Papists falsely allege; but rather a true and genuine fear of God … Forgiveness is the smile of God, which binds the soul to God with a beautiful fear.'[639]

The 'Papists' and Roman Catholics nevertheless had their own appreciation of this psalm. This was the prayer for the souls in purgatory in the Middle Ages.[640] In services of penitence it was almost as popular as the Lord's Prayer: '*De profundis, bivore pe pater noster*: '(Pray) Psalm 130, before the Lord's Prayer.'[641] By the sixteenth century, countless musical arrangements testify to its popularity in worship, especially in liturgies of penitence 'in the morning watches of the night', especially on Ash Wednesday at the start of Lent. Most of its verses have been set, several times, to countless *antiphons, which have become compositions for Lenten and Christmas liturgies, for funeral processions, and for *Lauds and *Vespers in the Office for the Dead.[642] Whether for private personal piety or in public worship, Psalm 130 seems to have a multivalent appeal.

The same multivalency is evident in artistic representations of this psalm. A common motif in Medieval Psalters is the identification of the 'deep' with the 'waters of the deep' and, following the commentaries of Augustine and Cassiodorus noted above, to link the figure of Jonah with the psalmist.[643] The *Stuttgart Psalter* (fol. 147v) has an image of a figure caught between the teeth of a huge sea monster, with a devil hovering above the waters. It is unclear as to whether he is being swallowed by the beast or has been vomited out of its mouth: the former is more likely, with Jonah being trapped and unable to escape. Nevertheless, the connection with Jonah 3, whose prayer resulted in his being disgorged, and the links between Jonah's fate and the resurrection of Christ (Matt. 12:39–41; Luke 11:29–32) suggest that the viewer is offered some hope.[644]

---

[638] See Gillingham 2008: 207.

[639] See https://www.christianity.com/bible/commentary.php?com=spur&b=19&c=130. The article finishes with an extraordinary collection of sermons and meditations based upon Psalm 130.

[640] Sutherland 2015: 220–24.

[641] Kaulbach 2008a: 185–86.

[642] For the vast collection of musical arrangements, in Latin, English, German, French, and Italian, many by Catholic composers, see https://www2.cpdl.org/wiki/index.php/Psalm_130. We shall attend to some of these shortly.

[643] See Gillingham 2018: 377 and Plate 26 (where the figure is David in danger of drowning, like Jonah). There the imagery is clearly of water (verses 2–13), but here it could imply mean a chasm, or a waterless abyss, such as is interpreted by the artist *Benn 1970: no page numbers.

[644] Bessette 2005: 267–30.

Hope from the depths is a shared motif in several Psalters, of which *St. Albans* is another good example, which depicts the psalmist looking up to Christ as he holds a book with the words 'Let your ears be attentive', pointing to Christ's listening ears above him.[645] And of the much more recent Jewish image of verse 8 by Moshe *Berger, which is of two beams of light radiating from a red centre at the heart of a pink and blue feathered sky, the artist writes, 'The Psalmist explains that prior to the redemption, God will encourage Israel to repent, fully, so that the people will be redeemed from all of their iniquities.'[646]

On the other side, the psalm has also been illustrated as an expression of profound despair. Georges Rouault used this psalm at least twice as a means of depicting the horror of devastation after two World Wars. *De Profundis* (1927), an etching in aquatint, is from his collection *Miserere et Guerre* (Plate 47).[647] His *Bella Matribus Detestata (War Hated by Mothers)* is perhaps his best-known image of the Madonna and Child, as Mary looks into the eyes of her son and sees his fate. Roualt's depiction of Psalm 130 also has a 'Madonna and Child' association: a grieving mother lies out on a cold slab, as through a grey door-way her son is about to die (or has died already) and above her is an icon of the dying Christ, but bathed in light. *De Profundis* (1947) is another different colour sketch, of a mother and child visiting a war grave.[648]

The psalm is also interpreted through images which are despondent, yet have a hint of hope. In the website *The Visual Commentary on Scripture*, Michael Banner chooses three strikingly different images to illustrate this psalm.[649] The first by Michael Arad and Peter Walker, entitled *Reflecting Absence* (2011), is of pools set in two cavernous spaces where once the Twin Towers stood. The water drains out into further spaces, as if disappearing into nothingness, representing 'the unfathomable depths of loss and despair opened up by... untimely death'.[650] The second image is Philip *Evergood's *Dance Marathon* (1934), depicting a dance context in its forty-ninth day, suggesting the participants are now in the throes of death rather than passion.[651] Here the 'depths' are like a spider's web, woven by the dancers themselves, and represented on the floor.[652] The third of this triptych is of one of Rembrandt's pen and brown ink sketches of the

---

[645] See https://bit.ly/3Gumyli.
[646] Psalm 136 has a very similar image, also concerned with the redemption of Israel: see http://themuseumofpsalms.com/product/psalm-136.
[647] See https://bit.ly/3aUKwsx.
[648] See https://bit.ly/3nC7idV.
[649] See https://thevcs.org/out-depths.
[650] Banner's commentary, with image, is on https://thevcs.org/out-depths/depth-dimensions.
[651] See p. 130 and Plate 9.
[652] See Banner, https://thevcs.org/out-depths/who-shall-stand. See p. 130 for how Evergood illustrated Psalm 100 with a radical rhetoric.

Prodigal Son—here, as he sits amongst the swine. This is called 'At First Light', as if this represents not only 'the depths of abjection' but also 'the possibility of forgiveness and so of hope ...' Banner imagines the prayer is from Psalm 130:4: 'There is forgiveness with thee'.[653]

Of all these examples, few of these images suggest the theme of immediate forgiveness. Despite this being a penitential psalm, the image of suffering and waiting is more intense than the act of repentance and receipt of pardon. This is not so in music, where the liturgical context of penitence was uppermost. Orlando *de Lassus, in about 1563, arranged music for all seven penitential psalms, each motet set in one of the church modes; Psalm 130 is sung in five parts, using a range of techniques to imitate its range of emotions.[654] Mozart also included all seven penitential psalms in his *Davide Penitente*. It focussed, through Psalm 51, on David's grief over the Bathsheba affair, and was for a Lenten concert in Vienna 1785. Much of the music for Psalm 130 was taken from the Kyrie and Gloria of the C Minor Mass, finishing with a joyful cadenza which presumed restoration with God.[655]

A sixteenth-century example of a musical composition designed to elicit repentance is Mary *Sidney. Having first translated the psalm, Sidney composed the music for it to be sung 'with low voice and long measure' to a lute accompaniment. This version is notable for its melodic leaps from heights to depths, both in the lute introduction and in the solo voice that follows.[656]

Psalm 130 was used by J. S. *Bach in one of his earliest cantatas (BWV 131), probably for a penitential service after the great fire in Mühlhausen in 1707. Unlike a painting which explores one image in one verse at one point in time, Bach's arrangement of the entire psalm, like that of Lassus, shows how the heights and depths can be expressed through different techniques. There are five movements based on verses 1–2, 3–4, 5, 6 and 7–8, mainly using G Minor, with the fourth movement in C Minor. 'Word painting' frequently occurs, for example in the *melismatic interpretation of 'waiting', in verses 5–6. The ending ('Israel, hope in the Lord') offers some resolution: an oboe *obbligato* and elaborate choral fugue anticipate the final 'he will redeem Israel from all its iniquities'.[657]

Other more recent penitential works are often anguished. They include an arrangement for the organ by Herbert *Howells in *Three Psalm Preludes Set 2* (1938), which was composed after the death of his only son in 1935. 130 is the first psalm, scored in D Minor and echoing the psalmist's cries of despair

[653] Banner, https://thevcs.org/out-depths/first-light.
[654] Dowling Long and Sawyer 2015: 191.
[655] See https://www.youtube.com/watch?v=0cFodyJ0PnE; also, 2015: 59.
[656] See Stern 2011: 106–109, with the musical score.
[657] Dowling Long and Sawyer 2015: 21.

to God (v. 1), interspersed with prolonged rests as no resolution is found. The piece ends in D Major, so there is some suggestion of resigned tranquillity.[658] By contrast Schoenberg's Hebrew work, for a six-part *a capella* chorus, composed in 1950, is a continuously troubled, dramatic and complex interpretation of the psalm. This was the last work before his death a year later.[659]

Arvo *Pärt's arrangement (1980) uses only male voices, and the percussion and organ interpret the psalmist's desperate prayer of supplication in an unfolding meditative piece which dies slowly away as the sound of a singular tubular bell captures the atmosphere of impending doom.[660] John *Rutter's *Requiem*, first performed in Dallas in 1985, and composed in memory of his father who died the year before, comprises seven movements using the text of the Latin *Requiem* Mass. The second movement, however, is from Psalm 130 alone. The first part is in C Minor, and changes to C Major at verse 4 where, as with Howells, some hope is expressed. Rutter uses a solo cello throughout, and its measured rhythm and occasional use of *rubato* have given it the nickname 'Anglican Blues'. There may be hope, but no resolution; verse 1 is repeated at the end, again with the solo cello weaving in and out of the human voices.[661]

A very different piece by the Irish singer and songwriter Sinead O'Connor, on her album *Theology* (2009), is based on Ps. 130:1–4. The lyrics compare the sinner crying out for mercy with the sufferings of Christ, also God-forsaken, heartbroken and alone: the whole performance is both sensual and prayerful.[662] Another poignant and contemporary representation of Psalm 130 is by the American composer Debra Scroggins.[663]

A most unusual arrangement of Psalm 130 is by Andrew Mackay (of Roxy Music) who presented his 'World Premier of 3 Psalms' at Southbank Centre in November 2018. Here three psalms—90, 130 and 150—were performed as a 'post-rock symphony', the product of twenty-five years of rock and roll experimentation, for which the present author provided some programme notes. Psalm 130, 'Deep', is an autobiographical psalm: it is sung in English and repeated in Hebrew, starting with a cacophonic electronic and musical collage of the soul 'in the depths'. Some resolution is achieved through the chanting and through the arpeggiated intricacies of a soprano sax solo near the end.[664]

---

[658] See https://www.youtube.com/watch?v=t0G7nsJPWC4; also, 2015: 242. See Gillingham 2018: 203 (on Psalm 33:3 which completes this piece); also, in this volume, p. 383 (on Ps. 139:12 which follows Ps. 130:1 here).

[659] See https://www.youtube.com/watch?v=RyU2DnIBXh0; also, 2015: 60.

[660] See https://www.youtube.com/watch?v=zJKWgnkBquk; also, 2015: 60.

[661] See https://www.youtube.com/watch?v=awe4OEEbPgQ.

[662] See https://www.discogs.com/Sin%C3%A9ad-OConnor-Theology/release/6684707; also, 2015: 81; also Goodman 2012: 38.

[663] See https://www.debrascrogginscomposer.com/sacred.

[664] See https://www.youtube.com/watch?v=eFtDcxeUrkc.

Despite this being a psalm with clear communal overtones at the end, much interpretation—in art and music not least—comes from reading it as the individual soul's conflict of faith and experience in prayer. In many cases this is neither specifically Jewish nor Christian; it comes out of a more universal experience of despair. Its universal appeal is why Psalm 130 is also rich in literary allusion and in poetic experimentation. It is sometimes used in novels: in *Ring and the Book* (1968), Robert Browning narrates how Count Guido Franceschini hears the intonation of Psalm 130 by the 'black fellowship' (of chaplains) when he is about to be executed, having confessed to the murder of his wife.[665] In *The Nine Tailors* (1934), the crime novel featuring Lord Peter Wimsey, Dorothy Sayers describes how the tailors cry for help using the *BCP version of De Profundis* as the sluice begins to give way.[666] And perhaps most famously of all, Oscar Wilde's later named 'De Profundis' was written in a cell in Reading Gaol in 1897, where he had been incarcerated for two years on charges of 'gross indecency'. In the last four months of his sentence, for cathartic purposes, the Governor allowed Wilde to write an open letter addressed to 'Bosie' (Lord Alfred Douglas), although he could not send it to him. This was Wilde's cry 'from the depths', agonised at the sense of injustice, although there is little penitential element here. The first half reflects on his destitution on account of his life with Douglas, and the second half is in part a means of identifying his sufferings with those of Christ. Wilde writes as an agnostic: 'Agnosticism should have its ritual no less than faith'.[667] In 1905, five years after Wilde's death, his friend and ex-lover Robert Ross published extracts and gave it the title 'De Profundis'.[668]

More specifically, Psalm 130 has been frequently imitated in English poetry. One example is the Elizabethan poet George Gascoigne's eight stanza poem 'De Profundis' (1575), which is a reinterpretation of the actual psalm, rather than, as Wilde, simply using the title.[669] Gascoigne composed this as a public statement of moral reformation: 'the prodigal son had returned'. The poem weaves together the psalmist's address to the God of Israel and Gascoigne's reading of the psalm an offer of forgiveness through Christ. Insisting first on his need and, at the end, emphasising God's gift of forgiveness, the first verse starts with the word 'from', repeated four times, and the last verse ends with 'He will', repeated eight times:[670]

---

[665] Kaulbach 2008a: 186.

[666] Kaulbach 2008a: 186.

[667] Taken from I. Murray (ed.), *The Soul of Man, De Profundis. The Ballad of Reading Gaol* (Oxford: OUP 1999), 98 and cited in Lemon *et al.* (eds.) 2009: 590.

[668] Kaulbach 2008a: 185–86.

[669] Another example is Christina Rosetti's four stanza poem also called 'De Profundis', which considers the constraints of being human and so 'from the depths' being unable to reach the stars or heaven: 'For I am bound with fleshly bands,/Joy, beauty, lie beyond my scope./I strain my heart, I stretch my hands,/ And catch at hope.' See https://www.poetryfoundation.org/poems/44994/de-profundis.

[670] Hamlin 2004a: 118; also; Atwan and Wieder 1993: 325–7.

From depth of doole wherein my soule doth dwell,
From heauie heart which harbors in my brest,
From troubled sprite whych sildome taketh rest,
From hope of heauen, from dreade of darkesome hell,
O gracious God, to thee I crie and yell …

He wylle redeeme our deadly, drowping state;
He wylle bring home the sheepe that goe astray;
He wylle helpe them that hope in him alwaye;
He wylle appease our discorde and debate;
He wylle soon saue, though wee repent us late;
He wylle be ours, if we continue his;
He wylle bring bale to ioye and perfect blis;
He wylle redeeme the flocke of his elect;
                    From all that is …

Finally, and perhaps most graphically, this psalm, once sung by thousands of Hasidic Jews —the elderly, women and children—as they were made to walk to the gas chambers, has been found inscribed, in German, on the walls of a memorial chapel at Dachau:[671]

From the depths, I cry to you, O Lord!
I cry in the night from the prison cell
and from the concentration camp
From the torture chamber
in the hour of darkness
hear my voice
                    my S.O.S.

The abundance of reception arising out of such a short penitential psalm actually matches the length of the commentary on the much longer penitential Psalm 51.[672] Whether, when read and sung in Jewish tradition, Psalm 130 is about the hope for redemption, or whether, when interpreted in Christian tradition, the psalm is about the belief in forgiveness through repentance, its most basic appeal, like Psalm 51, is ultimately about it being a universal cry of despair from the human heart seeking reconciliation with God.

---

[671] Goldingay 2008: 524 and 531, citing; Cardenal 1976: 39–40; Limburg 1999: 119.
[672] Gillingham 2018: 304–316.

Psalm 131: A Song of Childlike Trust: The Soul and God (ii)

Like Psalm 130 this is a personal psalm ending with the call to Israel to 'hope in the Lord' (131:3; see 130:7). The word 'my soul' (*nafshi*) is prominent in both psalms: it is found twice in 130:5 and 6 and again twice in 131:2. Psalm 131 has an additional heading 'Of/to David': this is odd in the light of the next more obviously royal psalm, 132, which has no such heading. Perhaps it hints at the children (literally, 'fruits of the body') promised to David in 132:11. It is another example of the way Davidic piety is continued intermittently in parts of Book Five, although this heading has been omitted in some versions in Greek.

Much of this psalm's reception is a response to the word *gamul* ('weaned') used twice in verse 2. The Hebrew could read, literally, *'But I have levelled and calmed down my soul, like a nursed child upon its mother, like a nursed child upon me is my soul'*.[673] Most translations use the word 'wean' (as in 1 Sam 1:23 and Is. 28:9): if this is correct, the image of a child no longer being breastfed, and yet being still, and not fretful, is puzzling. In the ancient world a child would have been weaned at perhaps three: it is possible that by this age 'wean' might mean acceptance and stillness. Yet even so, 'weaning' is about the loosening dependence upon the mother, but the psalmist speaks of the reverse—a calm dependence upon God.[674]

The reception of this verse in the **LXX* translation is quite confusing. It reads the Hebrew word *wedomamti* (a poel verb form, meaning calm down/ silence [one's soul]) as *weromamti* (a poel verb from meaning 'to raise up'), reading the Hebrew letter 'd' as an 'r'. This phrase is then *hupsōsa tēn psuchēn mou* ('I have lifted up my soul'). The Greek then translates the second use of the word 'wean' (*kegamul*, 'like a weaned [child]') as *kegemul*, 'as a correction', so that the whole verse in Greek reads, literally, 'If I was not humble, but exalted (lifted up) my soul, like a child weaned upon its mother, may there be correction on my soul.' This implies that the mother has weaned her child as an act of discipline, and again the image of the calm dependency of the soul upon God, like the baby upon its mother, has disappeared. The **Vulgate*, following the Greek, is equally confusing: *si non humiliter sentiebam sed exaltavi animam meam sicut ablactatum super matrem suam ita retributio in anima mea*—'If I was not humble-minded but raised up my soul, so may retribution [fall upon] me [as upon] one who has been taken from the milk upon its mother'. Again the implication is that just as a weaned child is a burden to its mother so retribution is burdensome to the soul.[675] Many later writers have proposed that

---

[673] A similar image is the image in Ps. 22:9: 'You kept me safe on my mother's breast'.
[674] Grohmann 2010: 515–16 asks the same questions.
[675] Ladouceur 2005: 123–4.

the mother/child imagery in this psalm suggests the influence of a woman: the translations, however, suggest a somewhat masculine approach to 'nursing' and 'weaning' and its effects on the afterlife of the small child. This paradox is brought out in later reception.

The *Targum* is confusing because it views the child as initially restless upon the breasts of its mother, and then interprets the psalmist's sustenance as not milk but the law: 'Surely I have placed *my hand on mouth* and quieted my soul *until I have sucked the word of the Law; like* a weaned child (*sic*) upon *the breasts of* its mother, *I have grown strong in the Law…*'[676] *Midrash Tehillim* also interprets the image as about 'sucking' and so continued dependence, rather than of weaning and hence independence: 'Just as a child is eager to suck the breasts of its mother, so am I eager to learn Torah from the least in Israel…'[677] *Kimḥi, by contrast, reads the word *kegamul* as 'like a *weaned* child'; but *Rashi reads the word as '*sucking* child', seeing it as a cognate from *gumel*, 'to perform kindness', which is what the mother gives to her child through her milk. In line with the questions raised earlier, Rashi also sees that a weaned child, no longer expecting nourishment from the mother, would be at odds with the psalmist's claim to be totally dependent upon God.[678]

The early Church Fathers so allegorised this psalm that they avoided the problem. *Jerome, using the Greek and Latin, sees the psalm is about true humility, which is not about making a show of being humble whilst being proud inside.[679] *Augustine, viewing the psalm as about the incarnate Christ, speaking as one of us and hence for us, reads verse 2 as about weaning, but this is really about the Christian moving from drinking milk to eating meat (see 1 Cor. 3:2) and so growing in faith.[680] *Cassiodorus reads this similarly, adding that the Latin does not necessarily imply that the mother is cruel, for she does it for our growth.[681]

Two sixteenth-century commentators, both women, use the psalm in a more practical way. Catherine Regina von Greiffenberg reads verse 2 as about seeking peace by keeping the Sabbath, because this day of rest brings repose and quiet which are essential for the Christian soul.[682] Arcangela Tarabotti reads verses 1 and 2 as condemning those parents who force their daughters into religious vocations; our renunciation of the world has to be voluntary, just like the voluntary rest of the child with her mother.[683] This again implies the image

---

[676] Stec 2004: 226.
[677] Braude 1959: 316.
[678] Feuer 2004: 1572; for Rashi see Gruber 2004: 717.
[679] Letter 22:27 in NPNF 2 6:33–4, cited in Wesselschmidt (ed.) 2007: 363.
[680] Augustine trans. Uyl 2017: 631–2.
[681] Cassiodorus trans. Walsh 1991b: 319–20.
[682] *Meditation on the Passion and Death of Jesus Christ*, p.133, cited in Selderhuis (ed.) 2018: 321.
[683] *Paternal Tyranny*, 61 cited in Selderhuis (ed.) 2018: 321–2.

is of a weaned child. The same is evident in a comment by Martin *Bucer, who emphasises especially the word 'if': 'If I had not composed and humbled my soul, so that I would be like a small infant just weaned, God would have sent this or that evil on me'.[684] Writing in the nineteenth-century, Charles Spurgeon also reads this as about the 'weaned child', noting, along the lines of Augustine, that even to the weaned child his mother is his comfort, even though she has denied him the comfort of her breasts. It is thus a mark of growth out of spiritual infancy when we can forego joys which once seemed to be essential, to find our solace in him who denies them to us: this is about mature discipleship, when every childish complaint is hushed. Overall this is a curious exposition of a psalm which exudes a confidence in the maternal provision of God.[685]

In light of this it is interesting to see just how many images in art are actually of breast-feeding, not weaning. The *Utrecht Psalter* (fol. 74v) has an image of Christ raising His right hand in a gesture of benediction: on the ground to the left of the psalmist is a mother suckling her child (verse 2).[686] The *Stuttgart Psalter* (fol. 148r) displays a rather large baby, but the mother is still feeding it, whilst the psalmist, perhaps connecting that relationship with his bond with God, looks on.[687] The *St. Albans Psalter* has a similar image in a very different style: Christ is looking at the humbly kneeling psalmist, who is pointing to a mother who is holding her child against her breast, and he points also to his heart or soul: the text next to it reads 'Lord my heart is not lifted up: neither are my eyes raised high' (verse 1). By this stage of psalm illustration there may be hints of the Madonna and Child here.

In poetic imitations of this psalm, the last verse in George *Herbert's poem 'The Pulley' is telling, because it shows how humanity, never satisfied, finds 'rest in God' difficult to attain. So if the reading of Psalm 131 is about the *weaned* child, this gives us insights into the tension the child and its mother, with the child disappointed by being taken from mother's breast and yet still seeking out her love. We too are restless in our search for God's love. The last verse in 'The Pulley' reads:[688]

> Yet let him keep the rest,
> But keep them with repining restlessness.
> Let him be rich and weary, that at least,
> If goodness lead him not, yet weariness
> May toss him to my breast.

[684] *Holy Psalms. Sacrorum Psalmorum*, 441–42, cited in Selderhuis (ed.) 2018: 321.
[685] See https://archive.spurgeon.org/treasury/ps131.php.
[686] See https://psalter.library.uu.nl/page/156.
[687] See https://bit.ly/3oBcOzt.
[688] See https://poets.org/poem/pulley; also Neale and Littledale 1874–79: 4/236–7.

Musical arrangements tend to avoid over-defining verse 2, assuming (like Jerome) that the whole psalm is about humility and calm trust. For example, *Bernstein's *Chichester Psalms* (1965), at the beginning of the Third Movement, uses Psalm 131 alongside Ps. 133:1. Beginning with a somewhat tense instrumental introduction, the first verse ('Lord, Lord, my heart is not too proud ...') is sung first in Hebrew and then in English. This is a gentle hymn-like chorale, in asymmetrical 10/4 metre, swaying at the concept not of the baby and mother but of the entire *community* dwelling together in unity and hope (verse 3). This fades away into the choral unison 'Amen'.[689] It is clear why Bernstein has linked this with Ps. 133:1, which celebrated the unity of the whole community.

A more personal interpretation of this psalm is Alexander Massey's 'I Trust in You'. A composer, singer and founder of 'Jewish Music UK', Massey's musical rendering of these three short verses combines a close reading of the Hebrew text with a theological interpretation about the need to discover humility (using here the figure of Joseph in Egypt as an example). Suggested uses include for a *Shoah* memorial or *Parshat Va'yeshev* (Joseph in the pit and in prison).[690]

Hence it is interesting that some feminist writers claim this might be a psalm placed on the lips of a mother—for example, of Hannah or Ruth.[691] We might ask, what 'mother-as-psalmist' would use weaning as an example of quietude and mature independence of the child and its mother? And even if we read the image as about breastfeeding, what mother-as-psalmist could claim that a baby really waits patiently and quietly for the milk at its mother's breast?[692] This is a difficult psalm because of its use of this dominant image: it rather suggests a less intuitive male psalmist throughout (i.e. 'David', as imagined in the psalm heading). The use of this image also raises questions about corresponding texts such as Gen. 21:8, where the father, Abraham, actually celebrates Isaac's 'weaning' as a sign of his becoming a boy, and 1 Sam. 1:22–24, where the mother, Hannah, experienced weaning as total separation between her role as mother to the child Samuel.

Overall this is a psalm whose reception history raises universal questions about how we attain a relationship of quiet trust in God. As M. Grohmann notes, 'The waiting of the thirsty and hungry throat for food is compared to the waiting of the soul of the individual and of Israel for YHWH. The rela-

---

[689] Stern 2013: 174–75.

[690] See https://alexandermassey.com/trust-in-you-ps-131.

[691] For example, Anderson 2016: 196; Farmer: 142–43; Davison 2001: 166. By contrast, Brettler 1998: 39–40 sees this cannot be a woman's psalm.

[692] See Knowles 2006: 385–89, especially note 14. Knowles concludes (389) how, if the female voice is present in the Hebrew of the psalm, it is still taken over by the appeal to the wellbeing of the entire nation at the end.

tionship between YHWH and Israel oscillates between nearness and distance like the relationship of a toddler to his mother, running away and coming back.'[693] Hence the metaphor of the mother/child relationship, whether implying breast-feeding or weaning, does not really suggest quietness and calm, but rather yearning and hope. This certainly makes sense in the light of the final verse addressed to Israel: 'Hope in the Lord'.

Psalm 132: A Song of the Temple and the Messiah

This is another psalm in the Songs of Ascent whose reception history shows very clear differences between Jews and Christians, and the issues raised place it alongside Psalms 110 and 118, also in Book Five. Psalm 132 is an extraordinary psalm: its eighteen verses differ starkly from Psalm 131, 133 and 134, of 3 verses each. Some of its vocabulary is not found anywhere else in the Psalter, including the 'Ark' (*aron* in verse 8) and God as 'the Mighty One of Jacob (*abir ya'aqov* in verses 2 and 5). The first part of the psalm, with its explicit references to David, is also unique in the Psalter.

And yet there is a clear structure. Its two parts mirror each other in several ways: it is likely that verses 1–10 use material from pre-exilic Temple liturgy, whilst verses 11–18 reflect a setting in the post-exilic Temple: if so, the psalm itself provides an example of two stages of reception history within the composition of the psalm.

Verses 1–10 form one unit, beginning and ending with a specific reference to David (verse 1: 'David's favour'; verse 10: 'David's sake') and it is clear that he is the 'anointed one' (verse 10). Verses 2–5 are concerned with the oath (*shebua*') which David swore (*nishba*') to God, and verses 6–10 are David's speech with a recitation of a liturgy for the Ark (using parts of Num. 10:35–36).[694] Verses 11–18 form a second unit, again beginning and ending with David (verses 11 and 17) who is again called the 'anointed one' (verse 17). Verses 11–12 are similarly concerned with an oath (*shebua*') but in this case it is the oath which God swore (*nishba*') to David about the permanency of the monarchy. Then follow two 'divine speeches': one about David (verses 11–12), the other about God's dwelling in Zion (verses 13–18) which intentionally echo the language in verse 8–10 concerning the Ark. Verse 8 refers to a 'resting place' (*menuhah*) for God and his Ark, which is repeated in verse 14 in relation to Zion, albeit without

[693] Grohmann 2010: 522.
[694] See Kruse 1983: 291–94.

reference to the Ark itself. Verse 9, referring to the priests being clothed with salvation and the faithful shouting for joy, is all but identical to verse 16. Hence David's promises to God in the first half of psalm reinforce God's promises to David in the second half: the unifying theme is the close relationship between the founding of the Davidic monarchy and the founding of Zion, and between the founding of the first Temple in Zion, before the Ark was taken to Babylon, and the re-founding of the second Temple in Zion.

2 Chronicles 6:41–42 uses verses 8–10 in the first part of this psalm, which suggests this part of the psalm pre-dates the Chronicler. Conversely, verses 11–12 utilise parts of 2 Sam. 7:1–7, concerning the Davidic covenant, suggesting that these verses are later adaptations of earlier royal traditions from Samuel (like the way the same chapter is used in Ps. 89:19–37). The personification of Zion as a female figure in verses 13–14 and Zion as a place for the protection of the poor in verse 15 further suggest a post-exilic understanding of the Temple and the city. In brief, first Temple liturgy from verses 1–10 is thus reinterpreted in the light of second Temple liturgy in verses 11–18, and the priests and the faithful people (verses 9 and 16) are the continuity between the two.

Jews and Christians follow two very different trajectories in their reception of this psalm. The Jewish tradition works in continuity with the reception history we have noted above; Christian interpretation is more discontinuous. So, in Jewish tradition, the figure of David, both past and future, is usually central. David is the founder of the Temple: Ephrathah (verse 6) is seen as another name for Bethlehem, David's birthplace (as seen in Ruth 4:11 and Mic. 5:2) and this links David both with the Ark and pilgrimage to Jerusalem.[695] Despite the fact that after the exile there was never again a monarchy or an Ark, Jerusalem still lies at the heart of God's continued plans for his people. Just as verse 12 shows the line of David will never cease, so verse 14 indicates that the sanctity of the Temple will endure for ever.[696] The psalm is thus a rallying call for belief in the restoration of the line of David and of an independent Temple: whilst the first part of the psalm looks back to the earliest origins of David and Zion, the second part takes on a Messianic and future significance.[697] So in terms of reception, we move from first Temple liturgy, to second Temple liturgy, to an interim period which is looking ahead to the formation of another liturgy in a 'third' Temple.

---

[695] See Cohen 1992: 437, noting that *Kimḥi prefers to read 'Jerusalem' instead of 'Bethlehem'.

[696] Feuer 2004: 1573, also citing Rambam on p. 1583.

[697] Stec 2004: 227, on verse 17: 'There I will make *a glorious king* sprout for *the house of* David...'

Just occasionally the actual absence of king and Temple results in Psalm 132 being also closely associated with the Torah, which continues forever. At *Qumran, for example, Psalm 132:8–18 is found on only one scroll, 11QPs^a, where it is followed not by Psalm 133 but by Psalm 119:1–6. This might in part be the link between the Ark in Psalm 132 and the Torah in Psalm 119, linking also the covenant with David with that with Moses. And at Qumran, as has already been noted for Psalm 119, the Zion traditions are frequently interpreted in the light of Torah.[698] The connection between this psalm and Torah is also found in *Midrash Tehillim*, which contrasts the *conditional oaths* of land, Temple and especially the king (noting that verse 12 starts with '*If* your sons keep my covenant…') with the *unconditional* gift of the Torah and the covenant with Moses and Aaron: so again, Zion and David are about hope, whilst the security of Torah is an ongoing reality.[699] *Targum* also expands verse 8 to '… you and the Ark *in which there is your Torah.*'[700]

Christian reception replaces this reading with Christological allusions. This begins early, as Psalm 132 is the only psalm in the Ascents to have an actual citation in the New Testament. Verse 5, concerning King David's desire to find a 'dwelling place' for God, is cited in Acts 7:46, which is part of Stephen's speech which argues that God does not in fact dwell in houses made with human hands (citing Isa. 66:1–2), implying that it was wrong, therefore, for Solomon to have built a house for him (Acts 7:47–50). Already the discontinuous reading of this psalm in Christian tradition is evident.[701]

This negative view about any dynastic continuation of the Davidic monarchy and about the restoration of the Temple is found repeatedly in Christian tradition. Expressions such God's 'dwelling place' and 'resting place' in verses 6–7 and 8 and 14, and the promise of an enduring Davidic covenant in verse 11, for example, take on a new meaning, as we shall see below. This is the only Ascents Psalm where both allegory and typology focus particularly on Christ himself: in other psalms the emphasis has been more on Christian living. In this psalm, by contrast, we find several references to the Incarnate Son, and to Jesus as King and High Priest. A few examples must suffice. Ireneaus, in his *Against Heresies* cites verse 11 to complement his reading of Isa. 7:14 as a testimony to Jesus' Davidic heritage, his kingship, and, most importantly, his birth at Bethlehem from a virgin.[702] In his *Answer to the Jews*, *Tertullian refers to Ps. 132:17 ('I have prepared a lamp for my anointed one') as

---

[698] See p. 241.
[699] Braude 1959: 317.
[700] Stec 2004: 226–27.
[701] There is also an allusion to verse 11 in Peter's speech in Acts 2:30.
[702] *Against Heresies*. 3.21.5, cited in Balas and Bingham 1998: 76.

referring to Christ, not David.[703] The Egyptian monastic, *Evagrius Ponticus, argues that 'Ephratha' is in fact the Virgin Mary, where the true Ark, the flesh of Christ, is found.[704] *Cyril of Jerusalem reads verse 11 as not about Solomon or his sons, for the dynasty did not endure, but about 'The Virgin Mary's Royal Lineage'; this meant that '... the Lord has chosen Zion' (verse 13) could be read as about Christ choosing the church.[705] *Augustine, like Tertullian, reads the imagery of the 'lamp for my anointed one' in verses 17–18 as prophecies about Christ (and moreover about his forerunner John) clothing his enemies with confusion.[706] *Jerome was particularly interested in Ephrathah: citing Gen. 35:19 in a sermon delivered at Bethlehem, he compared the birth of Jesus in a stable at an inn with his congregation, who, as monks, at least had their cells for their home. The phrase 'Behold we heard of her in Ephratha!' (verse 6) Jerome believes this refers to Mary; the masculine pronoun in the Hebrew is simply a means of referring also to her Son.[707] *Cassiodorus sees that the entire psalm 'describes the mysteries of our Lord's Incarnation'. In the first part we hear the prophet speak about Christ's promise to God, and in the second part the prophet says that what had been promised has now become known, and he awaits future fulfilment 'so that the fruits of the Virgin's womb may sit on the eternal throne of dominion'.[708] A fuller exposition, accorded to pseudo-Thomas, argues that this cannot be about David as he never fulfilled the promises in the psalm: for example, the Ark never had a permanent abode in Zion, and David's dynasty did not endure. Hence it was Mary's body which became the sacred and animate 'Ark', bearing the Creator in her womb. The children who 'sit on the throne for evermore' (verse 13) cannot be David's descendants, who came to an end, but they are rather the Apostles. The 'horn of David' and the 'anointed one' can only be Christ, for as Lk. 1:69 states, 'God raised up a horn of salvation for us in the house of his servant David'.[709]

This Christological reading continues into the early Modern and Reformation period. Konrad Pellikan, for example, taking issue with Abraham *ibn Ezra, continues to develop the view that Ephrathah points to the truth of the coming of the Messiah, the true Ark, from out of Bethlehem, 'in which the fulness of divinity which dwells bodily is none other than Jesus Christ, born in

---

[703] See https://www.ccel.org/ccel/schaff/anf03.iv.ix.i.html.

[704] Dysinger 2005: 167.

[705] See Catechetical Lectures 12.23 in FC 61:241–42 cited in Wesselschmidt 2007: 367.

[706] See Sermon 308A.1 in *WSA* 3 9:55, cited in, 2007: 368. See also Augustine trans. Uyl 2017: 637–38. For Augustine, however, the 'Ark' is not only the body of the physical Jesus but also the 'Body of Christ which is the Church' (634).

[707] See Jerome trans. Ewald 1963: 329–32.

[708] See Cassiodorus trans. Walsh 1991b: 321–22.

[709] Neale and Littledale 1874–79: 4/239–49.

Bethlehem, which has also been called Ephrathah …'.[710] *Calvin reads Mount Zion as referring now not to the city of Jerusalem, but to the whole earth: '… the whole world became an enlarged Mount Zion upon the advent of Christ …').[711]

This typology is also reflected in Christian art, where several Byzantine manuscripts illustrate the Church of the Nativity in Bethlehem as an interpretation of verse 6.[712] For example, in the *Khludov Psalter* (fol. 131v) David stands pointing to the church as a fulfilment of his oath to God. A similar image is found in the *Pantokrator Psalter* (fol. 184v) and in the *Barberini Psalter* (fol. 223r). The *Theodore Psalter* (fol. 172r) shows David in prayer, raising his right hand to an icon of *Christ-Logos, whilst fol. 172v, illustrating verse 6, shows David crowned and standing before an altar in a building at Ephrathah, which represents Church of the Nativity at Bethlehem; verse 7 ('let us worship at his footstool') is of the crucifixion, with two worshippers at Christ's feet.[713]

*Carolingian Psalters also offer variations of a David/Christ typology. The *Utrecht Psalter* (fol. 75r) displays the wall of the city of Zion, with the tabernacle (i.e. the Ark) approaching it to the left (verses 7–8). The bearded psalmist, with a crown and horn, points to a lamp (verses 17–18) and looks out at the Christ-Logos standing on a hill and blessing a man worshiping at his feet (verse 7). Below the hill, widows (suggested by 'vidua' in the Latin of verse 15) and 'poor' people are eating at a table, being 'satisfied with bread' (verse 15).[714]

Jewish images of this psalm are very different. The *Parma Psalter* (fol. 191r) has a figure in regal dress and wearing a crown who places his left forefinger to one of his eyes (verse 4), with his right hand on an open book on which pages the first two commandments are written. The figure is David (verse 1) and the book illustrates the 'covenant' and 'decrees' (verse 12). In this interpretation David and Torah are brought close together.[715]

*Benn's image of Psalm 132 is dated 1985. It too depicts King David, this time wearing simple white robes and a golden crown and bathed in light. In the background five figures clad in brown bow their heads in shame. This is of verse 18: '*Je revêtirai de honte ses enemies, et sur lui brillera sa couronne*.' In the context of the humiliation of the Jews in the Second World War, this statement about a Davidic hope is a political as well as a theological statement.

---

[710] See Pelikan's *Commentaria* 185r, cited in Selderhuis (ed.) 2018: 323, 326–7.

[711] See Calvin's Commentary, CTS 12:158, cited in Selderhuis (ed.) 2018: 327.

[712] See Corrigan 1992: 24–25. See *Khludov Psalter* (fol. 131v) and Figure 97 (p. 297), where the inscription 'David prophesies at Holy Bethlehem' is faintly seen. A similar image in the *Pantokrator Psalter* (fol. 184v) is illustrated as Figure 98 (also p. 297).

[713] For the *Theodore Psalter,* see https://bit.ly/32CmFwH and http://www.bl.uk/manuscripts/Viewer.aspx?ref=add_ms_19352_f172v.

[714] See https://psalter.library.uu.nl/page/157.

[715] See Metzger 1996: 95–6.

In a psalm with a limited liturgical use in either tradition, it is significant
that the use of Psalm 132:8–10 in Sephardic worship occurs after the reading
of the reading of the Law and the Benedictions when the scroll is replaced in
the Ark, following the recitation of Psalm 24. Again, Torah and David are thus
brought together in the Jewish liturgical use of this psalm.[716] Meanwhile in
Christian tradition the psalm is used at Christmas *Vespers, again showing its
links with the Virgin Birth at Bethlehem.

Composers such as William *Byrd and Thomas *Weelkes implicitly gave
verse 9, with its reference to 'the anointed one', a Christian interpretation.[717]
John *Newton, the eighteenth-century composer of hymns for the *Olney
Hymnbook*, incorporated a Christian reading of verses 11–18 in his 'Glorious Things of Thee are Spoken', although Isa. 33:20–21 and Ps. 87:3 were other
prominent texts.[718] Isaac *Watts created a Christian narrative running throughout the psalm. Watts' Christological overlay is usually predictable. But in the
case of Psalm 132 Watts creates two versions, one based upon verses 4, 5, 7, 8
and 15–17, on the establishment of a church:

> …The Lord in Zion placed his name,
> His Ark was settled there;
> To Zion the whole nation came
> To worship thrice a year.
>
> But we have no such lengths to go,
> Nor wander far abroad;
> Where'er thy saints assemble now,
> There is a house for God.
>
> Arise, O King of grace, arise,
> And enter to thy rest!
> Lo! Thy church waits with longing eyes
> Thus to be owned and blessed.

The other, based upon verse 5 and verses 13–18, is also for the ordination of a
Christian minister:

> …The God of Jacob chose the hill
> Of Zion for his ancient rest;

---

[716] Keet 1969: 118–19.
[717] See https://www.cpdl.org/wiki/index.php/Arise,_O_Lord_(William_Byrd) and
https://www.cpdl.org/wiki/index.php/O_Lord,_arise_(Thomas_Weelkes).
[718] See https://hymnary.org/text/glorious_things_of_thee_are_spoken.

And Zion is his dwelling still,
His church is with his presence blessed...

Here will I meet the hungry poor,
And fill their souls with living bread;
Sinners that wait before my door
With sweet provision shall be fed.

It is not surprising that the psalm was also used as a hymn for a reigning monarch. William Child composed a coronation anthem for two choirs based upon verse 18 (and Ps. 61:6–7) for the coronation of Charles II in 1661. It was called 'O Lord, Grant the King a Long Life' and ended with an exuberant Hallelujah. Henry *Purcell wrote a more sombre version when Charles II was gravely ill in 1685. And Thomas Atwood wrote a version for the coronation of William IV in 1831.[719]

This is the last psalm in the Psalter to receive such a thorough Christological interpretation, creating a certain amount of conflict between Jewish and Christian readings of the same psalm. To summarise briefly: in Jewish reception, Psalm 132 is in fact about *three* Temples—the pre-exilic first Temple, the post-exilic second Temple and the Temple to be rebuilt in the future—and *two* Messiahs: David, who is the anointed one, and the future Messiah. In Christian reception the *three* Temples are the physical Temple in Zion, now destroyed, and the spiritual Temple, which is first Christ's own body, and then, later, the physical body of the Church; and here the *two* Messiahs are David and the one born of the house of David in Bethlehem, namely Jesus Christ.

Psalm 133: 'Hinneh Ma Tov': A Song about Unity in Zion

'Oil' (Hebrew, *shemen*) and 'dew', (Hebrew, *tal*), are two striking similes of fecundity expressed in this psalm. The juxtaposition of these images is not unique: the word-pair occurs for example in Ugaritic poetry, where the goddess 'Anat celebrates her victory by bathing in 'the dew of heaven' and the 'oil of the earth'.[720] Within the context of a psalm about the unity of the community at Zion, probably after the repopulation of Jerusalem after the exile, the oil is given a sacerdotal quality, 'running down the beard ... of Aaron' whereas 'the dew of Hermon which falls on Mount

---

[719] See Dowling Long and Sawyer 2015: 173.
[720] See Dahood: 1966, p.251, who cites 'Anat IV:87. In Deut. 11:14 is it the 'light rain' which bring about the harvest of the grain and oil.

'Zion' offers a more natural everyday image, also meaning 'light rain'. We will see shortly how these two images have been used in the psalm's reception history.

Noting that the first stage of reception is the particular placing of psalms, here we see how the compilers have created a link with the Zion theology in Ps. 132:13–14 (133:3) and with the priestly clothing in Ps. 132:8 (133:2), although in 133 the Davidic hope has been overtaken by a theocratic one, through the high priest 'Aaron'. Other connections with Psalm 132 are the use of *hinneh* ('Behold!') in 133:1 (see 132:6, and also 134:1) and the importance of 'dwelling' in 133:1 (see again 132:13–14) and 'blessing' in 133:3 (see 132:15, also repeatedly in 134:1, 2, 3). The Zion theme also brings these psalms close together. Psalm 133 might be called an 'Ode to Zion'.[721]

This is a psalm about unity, and the Jewish folk song 'Hinneh ma tov' has given this psalm a universal appeal since at least the 1960s, as we shall note later concerning the psalm's reception in music.[722] The psalm offers a unity of form as well as of content. The oil 'runs down' Aaron's beard; 'running down' on the collar of his robes, the dew 'falls down' onto Mount Zion (in each case using the Hebrew present participle *yored*), and God commands his blessing similarly to come down on Zion and her people. The movement in the psalm, leading downwards to the giving of God's blessing in verse 3, is also enhanced by its staircase parallelism—the repetition of *mah* ('what, how') in verse 1, *tob* ('good') in verses 1 and 2, the repetition of 'it is like' in verses 2 and 3, and of 'running down' in verses 2 and 3, with the expansion of the 'beard' in verse 2 to be specifically 'Aaron's beard'.

The reception history of this short psalm has focussed mainly on the two similes of oil and dew (the former more than the latter, as we shall see), but also on the words 'Aaron' and 'Zion', and on the theme of unity expressed at the beginning of this psalm.

Whereas in the MT the connections between Psalm 133 with 132 and 134 are clear, this is not so at *Qumran. 11QPs^a includes it, as does 11QPs^b, and each scroll offers an additional ending to 133: 'Peace be upon Israel'. But more importantly, in both scrolls the psalm is set between the two 'Davidic' Psalms, 141 and 144, the conclusion to the Ascents having been replaced by Psalm 119.[723] The word 'there' in the MT of verse 3 is now 'to this place' in 11QPs^a (the Hebrew is *shamah*, not *sham*) suggesting that the recipients of blessing are no longer in Zion but are the community at Qumran. The title 'Song of Ascents' is preserved

---

[721] See Berlin 1987: 146.

[722] Francis Boulanger calls this 'le mondialement connu…Psalm 133:1': see Boulanger 2010: 209.

[723] See pp. 242–43.

in 11QPs^a, suggesting that the psalm has been extracted from Psalms 120–134 to be re-used elsewhere. Placing 133 after 141 might be due to the same words 'head' and 'oil' in 133:2 and 141:5, and the use of the word *na'im* ('pleasant') in 133:1 and 141:6. But it is really not clear why this new order has come about.[724]

The interest in blessing away from the Temple at Qumran contrasts with the paraphrase in **Targum* which reads 'Behold how good and pleasant it is *for Zion and Jerusalem to dwell like two brothers together*.'[725] Other Jewish commentators have different approaches to the role of Aaron in this psalm: according to **Kimḥi*, the 'brothers' in verse 1 are both Aaron and David (linking this to the previous psalm), bringing the nation into harmony by ruling together as King and High Priest.[726] Elsewhere, however, Aaron is read as accompanied by Moses, as a literal example of 'brotherly love', where the diarchy is of Moses as King and Aaron as High Priest.[727]

Not surprisingly Christian reception relocates the references to Zion: now they refer to a pilgrim people in a new Zion, which is no longer the city of Jerusalem itself. Although the psalm is not directly cited in the New Testament, it is frequently used by the Church Fathers. **Jerome* reads 133 as 'truly the psalm of convents and monasteries. It may even be applied to the churches, although … there does not in the Christian assembly appear to be the same degree of harmony'.[728] **Augustine* also calls it 'a little psalm which begat monasteries'— where 'monos' echoes the sense of the 'oneness' in this psalm, and where Christ both rules and serves as King and High Priest'.[729] The 'oil' is the Holy Spirit, descended from the Head (who is Christ) to the Beard (the Apostles) to the garments (the churches and the monasteries).[730] **Cassiodorus* affirms and develops this.[731] Indeed, a **Vespers* prayer attributed to **Alcuin* reads 'Christ the Lord, Whose holy name is as ointment poured out: grant, we beseech Thee, that the ointment of the head may be poured down by Thee, so as to descend to the beard of Thy people, and come to the very edge of the garment of this mortal life …'.[732] Pseudo-Thomas takes up the same idea: Christ himself anoints us and wears the crown of both king and priest.[733] Interestingly nothing much is made here of the image of 'dew'.

---

[724] See Chyutin 1994: 376, who argues that the community at Qumran preferred a liturgical collection of thirteen, not fifteen, psalms for Holy Days.

[725] Stec 2004: 228.

[726] Cohen 1992: 439.

[727] Feuer 2004: 1588–89. This is also found in Christian reception, as seen in the **Peshitta*'s superscription: 'Uttered of Moses and Aaron, living in a tent of the house of the Lord'.

[728] Jerome trans. Ewald 1963: 333.

[729] Augustine trans. Uyl 2017: 622–23.

[730] De Solms 2001: 369–70, citing Letter 142 in FC 20:149.

[731] Cassiodorus trans. Walsh 1991b: 332–36.

[732] Neale and Littledale 1874–79: 4/360.

[733] Neale and Littledale 1874–79: 4/257.

The emphasis on the *church* in the patristic and early modern period becomes an emphasis on *unity and order* in the Reformation period—but by no means, according to *Calvin, extending this to the Roman Catholic Church.[734] Calvin wrote in his commentary on this psalm: 'Should it so happen in the providence of God that the Catholics should return to that holy concord which they have apostatised from, it would be in such terms as these that we would be called to render thanksgiving to God, and in the meantime we are bound to receive into our brotherly embraces all such as cheerfully submit themselves to the Lord ... The peace that David recommends is such as begins in the true head, and this is quite enough to refute the unfounded charge of schism and division that has been brought against us by the papists ...'[735] Christian readings are as diverse as is Jewish reception of this psalm.

The lesser interest in 'dew' and the greater interest in 'oil' continues in artistic reception. An amusing literal representation of the psalm is in the *Stuttgart Psalter* (fol. 149v) where the surprised psalmist watches the hand of God emerging out of a cloud to pour out oil, from a *shofar*, upon the head of Aaron. 'Dew' is perhaps represented here in the mountains behind, where the one large mountain might be either Hermon or Zion.[736] The *St. Albans Psalter* is also unusual in using the psalm as a warning against dissension in a monastic community. In the upper register of the letter 'E' beginning the psalm in Latin ('Ecce quam bonum...') we see Christ blessing a band of happy and united Christians, but one looks on in resentment. Below the psalmist is instructing 'Aaron' (with a tonsure but with stubble, not a beard)) to observe the factions above. 'Aaron' is not receiving unction. He seems defensive, with one arm wrapped around his body and the other raised in dialogue with the psalmist. Some see this as pointing to the factional strife caused by Abbot Geoffrey, whose high-handedness and spending money at the church of Markyate had made him unpopular.[737]

A modern example of the visual exegesis of this psalm is in a Presbyterian Church in Chicago, which in 2006 commissioned twelve sanctuary banners created by Laurie Wohl, a Jewish textile artist interweaving texts using Arabic, Hebrew, Greek, Latin and English calligraphy, often, like *Chagall once did, for Christian churches. Psalm 133 is woven in green, representing the seasons especially during the summer months called 'Ordinary Time'. The psalm's message of unity, woven within the diversity of the warp and weft in the fabric,

---

[734] Selderhuis (ed.) 2018: 329.

[735] Cited in Selderhuis (ed.) 2018: 331, from Calvin, Commentary CTS 12:164–65.

[736] See https://bit.ly/30aBTb9.

[737] Geddes 2005: 109. See also
https://www.albani-psalter.de/stalbanspsalter/english/commentary/page345.shtml.

offers another intriguing insight into the way the underlying message of the psalm crosses interfaith barriers.[738]

The fecund imagery of dew has been infrequent in the reception of this psalm, but it does emerge in poetry. David Rosenberg's poem re-uses the images which speak of the unity of community of faith, and he also captures its staircase-like movement:[739]

> It's so good, the turn of a season
> people living for a moment as equals
> secure in the human family
>
> as sweet as spring rain
> making the beard silky
> Aaron's beard
>
> his robes sparkle
> rich with heaven's simple jewels
> like the crown of dew
>
> on Lebanon's Mt. Hermon
> shared equally on the hills
> of Israel
>
> where the Lord graces our eyes
> fresh from reborn wonder
> as if we'd live forever.

Within musical reception, this short psalm is frequently used at occasions marking the unity of the church.[740] But its use as a Jewish folksong has made it better known, as it appeals for unity within the family, the community, the cosmos, and even between Jewish and Christian communities of faith. In this musical medium Psalm 133 is thus given a more universal meaning. The best example is the song which uses only the first verse, '*Hinneh ma tov uma na'im/Shevet achim gam yachad*', repeated twice, and also forming the chorus. Familiar because of its use at *Shabbat* afternoon celebrations, *Hinneh ma tov*, originally arranged by Moshe Jacobson, was popularised and used to accompany folk dances. Harry Belfonte recorded a version for *Belafonte Returns to Carnegie Hall* (1960), and in the 1960s the rock band Spirit created a version for their *The Family that Plays Together*. *Hinneh ma tov* was used in the film *Raid on Entebbe* (1977), when Yonathan Netanyahu and Sammy Berg sang it

---

[738] Rosen 2013: 116, n. 27.
[739] Taken from Wieder 1995: 197.
[740] See https://www2.cpdl.org/wiki/index.php/Psalm_133.

with Israeli commandos while flying to rescue the hostages, and it was played again in the closing credits. Since the release of the album *Stand Up* (1999) the version sung by the Miami Boys Choir, arranged by Yerachmiel Begun, along with a folk dance choreographed by Silvio Berlfien, has become known for its use in flash mobs worldwide.[741] The arrangement by Paul Wilbur, on his album *Shalom Jerusalem*, is played to an audience of hundreds who leave their seats to join in a theatrical flash mob—a chain dance.[742]

Each of these examples was influenced by the original version by Jacobson. Two different Jewish examples are arrangements by Leonard *Bernstein and John *Harbison. Bernstein's *Chichester Psalms* (1965) uses Psalm 133 in the Finale, after 131 which comprises the third Movement.[743] In this instance *Hinneh ma tov* exudes a calm melody, but, perhaps imitating the by then popular folk song, adapts difficult time signatures, such as 10/4, 9/2 and 12/2. It is sung first in Hebrew and then in English; a haunting intonation by an unaccompanied chorus rises to a crescendo, which finishes in unison on the Hebrew word *yaḥad*, 'together', emphasising a message of peace; and then a trumpet plays the opening theme one more time.[744]

We have already noted John Harbison's use of Psalms 114 and 126 in *Four Psalms* (and will do so again for 137). Performed in 1998 to celebrate the fiftieth anniversary of the founding of the State of Israel, Psalm 133, as with the previous psalms, juxtaposes ancient Hebrew song with contemporary reflections from Jews, Arabs and Palestinians reflecting on the State of Israel. Psalm 133 is actually the last psalm, used in the hope for peace and future unity.

Bernstein's *Chichester Psalms* is a Jewish composition performed in a Christian Cathedral. Harbison's *Four Psalms* is both Jewish and inter-faith, including both Christians and Muslims. By contrast, Bob Marley's album *Survival* (1979) which also uses Psalm 133, has an even more universal appeal, evident in the use of the first verse in reggae form, calling for Africa's liberation from its own Babylon (Western Governments): 'How good and pleasant it would be before God and man, yeah, to see the unification of All Africans!'.[745] Following this track are words from both Garvey and Selasse, supporters of the call for African unification. There are clear connections here in the call to 'come out of exile' and the Rastafarian call for liberation in Psalm 137. Mbongeni William Skosana sang 'Hinne Ma Tov' as the opening act for the Wailers,

[741] Dowling Long and Sawyer 2015: 102.

[742] See https://www.youtube.com/watch?v=FkRgDPUyCLQ.

[743] See p. 324 (Psalm 131).

[744] See Dowling Long and Sawyer 2015: 45; also Stern and Leneman 2015: 265–66. See also https://www.youtube.com/watch?v=GmA3iT4wMfw (Psalms 131 and 133).

[745] See https://www.youtube.com/watch?v=psm68xZPZTA&list=RDEyrpNfcNCz8&index=2; also Dowling Long and Sawyer 2015: 10.

Bob Marley's original backing band, at The Emperors Palace in April 2012: like Psalm 137, Psalm 133 'shouts down' the liberation of all oppressed peoples.

The reception history of Psalm 133 has much in common with Psalm 137, to be discussed shortly. It is not surprising that both John Harbison and Bob Marley brought both psalms together, albeit in very different ways. The two similes of sacral anointing with oil and ordinary mountain dew encapsulate well the double reception of this psalm, which has been used both for the faithful and more universally. This psalm, like 137, has been used in both the synagogue and church, but has also been adapted for a worldwide call for unity and freedom from oppression.

Psalm 134: 'Hinneh Baraku': A Song of Blessing from Zion

Psalm 134, another psalm of just three verses, has a very different reception history from 133. Yet as a text it has a good deal in common with Psalm 133. Examples include the use of *hinneh* (behold!) in 133:1 and 134:1; the importance of blessing in 133:3 and 134:1,2,3; the focus on Zion as an agent of blessing (133:3, 134:3); and the peculiar use of a 'direct object marker' (Hebrew, *'et*) before definite nouns and names ('*the* blessing' in 133:3 [*'et ha-berakah*] and '*bless the* Lord' in 134:1,2 [*beraku'et adonai*]). It too assumes the unity of the pilgrim community, and its two references to the sanctuary ('house of the Lord' in verse 1, and 'holy place' in verse 2) correspond with the sacral interest in the 'brotherhood' and 'Aaron the priest' in the previous psalm. Thus we see again how the compilers placed another psalm with careful consideration. Nevertheless, 134 is different: it lacks the resonant similes in 133, where the words 'oil' and 'dew' resulted in a rich reception. It also has a more conventional structure, with a hymnic exhortation in the first two verses, suggesting it is a psalm to be sung at night, and with a blessing at the end from Yahweh (who is referred to five times in this psalm, compared with just once in Psalm 133). The ending is important: God who blesses Zion, also evident at the end of Psalm 133, is seen here as also the 'maker of heaven and earth'. Its straightforward hymnic nature, and its emphasis on the interrelationship between blessing God, and the Creator God blessing from Zion, suggests that 134 serves as a doxology for the other fourteen Ascent psalms. We proposed earlier that the theme of arriving at Zion and leaving Zion dominated this collection: if so, it is possible to see 134 as the final night blessing, imagining those now about to leave the city.[746]

---

[746] See p. 258.

Yet despite its significance in being placed at the end of the collection in the MT, Psalm 134 does not have a rich reception history. Amongst the great Jewish and Christian commentators, most manuscripts of *Rashi's commentary do not even have an entry for this psalm, and *Augustine, most unusually, offers only half a page on it, without any of his usual Christological emphasis. Mostly the commentary tradition is more about changes in words and phrases, such as the addition in the Greek to verse 1, which now reads '*in the courts* of the house of the Lord'. Perhaps it has been expanded to make it fit Psalm 135:2, thus making blessing apply not only to the priests but to the laity as well. The Greek also adds 'In the nights' (*en tais nuxin*) to verse 2, following the reference to the night in verse 1; this might suggest some regular nocturnal liturgy known to the translators.

Other small details focus on just on one word or phrase. 'Lift up your hands' in verse 2 is the best example. *Midrash Tehillim* sees this as about the priest lifting up his hands in order to wash them before giving the blessing.[747] Other rabbis see this as about lifting up the hands to read: they assume the priests would be meditating on the Torah throughout the night.[748] *Targum*, implying by its additions that the servants 'assigned to the night watch of the sanctuary' are priests, reads the phrase 'lift up your hands of holiness, you priests on the platform of holiness …', associating this with the actual liturgical accompaniment to blessing. By contrast, Christian commentators such as *Cassiodorus see the lifting up of hands as about giving alms 'faithfully and richly'.[749] *Luther reads the phrase as about the work of 'the ministers of the Gospel, whose role is to teach and admonish by day and by night'.[750] *Calvin makes this clearer still: it may be about the priests and Levites who bless the people, but they are 'servants of the Lord' and they lead the way for the *laity* to practice the results of that blessing in their homes, for God is creator of the heaven and earth and not only of Zion and the priests of the church.[751] It is evident that interpretation of verse 2 depends much on the liturgical context of the interpreter.

Perhaps the most significant aspect of the psalm's reception is its placing in Column XXVIII at the end of 11QPs[a] (the only *Qumran scroll in which this psalm is found). The actual order is 2 Samuel 23, then a summary of David's compositions, then Psalm 140, and then Psalm 134, so that Psalms 151a and 151b form the actual conclusion. Hence Psalm 134, which has no reference to David

[747] Braude 1959: 321, citing R Simoan ben Pazzi.
[748] Feuer 2004: 1594, citing *b.Menaḥot* 110a.
[749] Cassiodorus trans. Walsh 1991b: 339–40.
[750] Luther, *Summaries*, WA 38:62, cited in Selderhuis (ed.) 2018: 332.
[751] Calvin, *Commentary on 134*, CTS 12:168–69, cited in Selderhuis (ed.) 2018: 333–34.

but only to the servants in the Temple, is set between two pieces which have Davidic concerns: Psalm 140 has a Davidic heading, and Psalm 151 concerned with David's defeat of Goliath. Nevertheless, despite the loss of some six words at the beginning of the psalm, the title 'Song of Ascents' is preserved; like Psalm 133, it seems as if this psalm has also been removed from its original place in Psalms of Ascent.[752] The question is—why has it been moved to this particular setting? Not only was Psalm 134 once clearly linked to Psalm 133, as we have noted, but it also has many correspondences with 135—the continued interest in blessing, especially from Zion (134:2 and 135:21); those praying 'standing' in the house of the Lord (134:1 and 135:2); and the acknowledgement of Yahweh as 'maker of the heaven and earth' (134:3 and 135:6). One explanation might be the final reference to Zion as the agent of God's blessing in verse 3, although the Qumran community was interested more in Zion as a place of *future* blessing rather than anything in the present. Perhaps if Psalm 134 provided an appropriate doxological conclusion to the fifteen Psalms of Ascent in the proto-*Masoretic text, it could be used to provide a similarly apt conclusion to the very different Great Psalms Scroll, although in this respect it does not end the scroll but has to be seen alongside Psalms 151a and 151b. So as with Psalm 133, its relocation in 11QPsᵃ is not entirely clear.[753]

There is very little in artistic reception that adds any new reading of this psalm. Byzantine Psalters such as *Barberini* (fol. 225r) and *Theodore* (fol. 173v) illustrate verse 1 as the personification of the church, seated, crowned and holding a roll, with the marginal inscription 'Queen of the Christmas'.[754] But there is little evidence of anything explicitly Christological: the use of the psalm at *Compline in the western churches has resulted instead in illustrations of people at prayer against a night sky, as in the *Utrecht Psalter* (fol. 75v) and the *St. Albans Psalter*.[755]

One of the best ways of re-reading the psalm is again through poetic imitation. Mary *Sidney's paraphrase captures the quiet night-time mood of worship so well, in both form and content:[756]

> You that Jehovah's servants are,
> Whose careful watch, whose watchful care,
> Within his house are spent;
> Say this with one assent:

---

[752] See pp. 332–33.

[753] See Armstrong 2012: 492–96.

[754] For the *Theodore Psalter*, see http://www.bl.uk/manuscripts/Viewer.aspx?ref=add_ms_19352_f173v.

[755] See https://www.albani-psalter.de/stalbanspsalter/english/commentary/page345.shtml.

[756] Hamlin *et al.* 2009: 260.

'Jehovah's name be praised'.
To holiest place
Where holiest grace
Doth aye
Remain:
And say
Again,
'Jehovah's name be praised'.
Say last unto the company,
Who tarrying make
Their leave to take,
'All blessing you accompany,
From him in plenty showerèd
Whom Zion holds embowerèd
Who heav'n and earth of naught hath raised'.

The use of this psalm at evening prayer in Jewish tradition and at Compline in Christian tradition has inspired a few notable musical arrangements in each tradition. One Jewish example is from the mid-nineteenth-century: Solomon Sulzer used Psalm 134, set to an old Jewish folk melody, for the *Ashkenazi synagogue in Vienna. By contrast, Christian arrangements of this psalm in Roman Catholic and Anglican Liturgy are more plentiful.[757] One example particularly memorable for its contemplative appeal is Tomás Luis *de Victoria's *Ecce nunc benedicite Dominum (Hearken, bless ye the Lord)*, from late sixteenth-century Spain.[758] A very different composition is by Louis Bourgeois, who wrote a hymn tune for the paraphrase of Psalm 134 in the second edition of the *Genevan Psalter* (1551). This was the same tune later chosen by William *Kethe for the Old 100th, 'All People That on Earth Do Dwell'. Originally in French, Psalm 134 is sung to this tune in metrical psalmody in the Scottish church today.[759] Another different and contemporary version of the psalm, often used as an 'action song' for children, is 'Come Bless the Lord, all ye Servants of the Lord'.[760] David Mitchell, whose composition is seen in Figure 13, provides an example of how the text might have been used musically in worship in ancient Israel.[761]

---

[757] See https://www2.cpdl.org/wiki/index.php/Psalm_134.
[758] See https://www.youtube.com/watch?v=jGsdLSISpHE.
[759] See https://www.youtube.com/watch?v=X_O4uYFbVKo, sung in 2017 for the Psalms Project at St. John's Kirk Perth, Scotland.
[760] https://www.youtube.com/watch?v=2di1Qmf3qPQ.
[761] See also pp. 212–13, on David Mitchell's arrangement of Psalm 114.

FIGURE 13   *Interpretation of singing of Psalm 134 in its earliest setting.*

Reproduced with the kind permission of David Mitchell, Director of Music in Holy Trinity Pro-Cathedral, Brussels; website https://brightmorningstar.org/wp-content/uploads/2020/06/Ps-134.pdf

Psalm 134 has not had a rich reception in commentary tradition, as is the case for many of the Psalms of Ascent, nor is there much in artistic representation. It has mainly been an inspiration in music and worship, particularly at evening prayer. But because liturgy and pilgrimage best account for these Fifteen Psalms as a collection, Psalm 134 is an appropriate 'finale': this is not about blessing only for Israel, but on God's blessing offered outwards from Zion.

Psalms 135–137: A Trilogy of Psalms Concerning Restoration

This trio of psalms really comprises a pair and a related psalm; all share the theme of God's victory over Israel's enemies. We will discuss Psalm 137 on its own because it forms a 'bridge' between 135–136 and 138–145 and has different themes. Psalms 135 and 136 form a pair and each 'narrate' the story from the Exodus to the occupation of Canaan, with 135 recalling the occupation to the west of the Jordan and 136 ending earlier with the territory gained only in the east. Both psalms have a similar structure, starting and ending with praise, with the main body, following an almost identical outline, offering the reasons for it. Both psalms combine the theme of God in creation (135:6–7; 136:4–9) with God active in the history of his people (135:8–12; 136:10–22). Both psalms, placed by the compilers to anticipate Psalm 137, focus on 'the God who Strikes': he puts down imperial powers (135:8, 10 and 136:10, 17) in defence of the weak (135:14; 136:23–24).[762] Both psalms focus on God's uniqueness above all other gods (135:5; 136:2–3). The difference is that Psalm 135 is another 'praise psalm' starting and ending with 'Hallelujah', linking it back to Psalms 113–118 (and 104–106), whilst Psalm 136, starting and ending with 'O Give Thanks to the Lord' is a 'thanksgiving psalm', and its constant refrain 'For his mercy endures forever' links it back to Psalms 107:1 and 118:1–4, 29.[763] The theme of God's gift of the land has obvious links

---

[762] Hossfeld and Zenger 2011: 493 and 501.
[763] The Greek typically places the Alleluia at the end of Psalm 135 at the beginning of 136, as with Psalms 104/105 and 114, 116 and 118, thus giving the psalm an 'Alleluia' title.

Psalms Through the Centuries: A Reception History Commentary on Psalms 73–151, Volume Three, First Edition. Susan Gillingham.
© 2022 John Wiley & Sons Ltd. Published 2022 by John Wiley & Sons Ltd.

with God's dwelling in Jerusalem in the Ascents, made explicit in 135:21, on God's blessing emanating from Jerusalem.[764] In the Babylonian *Talmud*, Psalm 136 has the title 'Great Hallel' (*b.Pesach* 118a), to be sung at the last cup of blessing after Psalm 118; some rabbinical sources, however, imply that Psalms 135 and 136 together form this Great Hallel.[765]

Psalm 135: Praise of the Uniqueness of the Lord

Psalm 135 has been called a 'tessellation from other parts of Scripture'.[766] Its store of quotations and allusions is another example of its difference from Psalm 136. These come from the Torah (e.g. Exod. 18:11 in verse 5, Exod. 3:15 in verse 13; Deut. 32:36 in verse 14) and the Prophets (e.g. Jer. 10:13–14 and 51:16–17 in verse 7) as well as the Psalms (e.g. Psalms 113; 115; 118; 134; 136) and so suggests a late date for this psalm.

It is obvious why the compilers placed 135 next to 136.[767] But its juxtaposition with 134 is also intentional. Verses 1–2 have several similarities to 134:1, although the emphasis here is on 'praise' rather than 'bless' (although see 135:19–21, where the call to bless is repeated four times). Another additional phrase is 'courts of the Lord' (an interest in both Jewish and Christian commentary, as we shall shortly see). The calls to praise at the beginning and the calls to bless at the end, each with an emphasis on the divine name, form an *inclusio* for the two passages denouncing idols. The specific reference to the Levitical singers in verse 20 might suggest they might have been the editors of this psalm and the compilers in placing Psalms 135–136 at this juncture in the Psalter.[768]

These verses of idol polemic, especially 15–18, have interesting correspondences with Ps. 115:4–8, although there seven organs are highlighted, and only four here.[769] The comparison between idols and Yahweh implies that God too has a mouth, eyes and ears, which are invisible to humans. This is refined in *Wisdom of Solomon 13–15: there the emphasis is entirely on the futility of the idols and on those who make them (Wis. 13:10; 14:11) and on those who fall down to pray to them (Wis. 13:17, 15:5–6, 15–16). No contrast is made with God's organs: instead, the more abstract qualities of kindness and truth, and patience and mercy (Wis. 15:1).

---

[764] The Lucian Greek recension actually adds 'Alleluia: A Song of Ascents'.

[765] For example, R. Acha ben Jakob: see; Braude 1959: 324; Hossfeld and Zenger 2011: 491.

[766] See Neale and Littledale 1874–79: IV/277.

[767] See pp. 342–3 on the linguistic similarities between each psalm.

[768] See Hossfeld and Zenger 2011: 494 and 496; also; Gillingham 2010: 91–123; 2017: 35–59.

[769] The *LXX*, however, adds the other three.

Psalm 135 is found in 11QPs[a] at *Qumran, where it follows Psalm 119 (although precedes 136:1–16). The order of the three cola in 135:1 is now 1c, 1b and 1a. An addition to verse 2 uses a liturgical formula common to Kingship Psalms such as 99:5, 9: 'Exalt the Lord!'. Other changes similarly emphasise the uniqueness of Israel's God. In verse 2 the expansion is 'there is none like the Lord... none that acts like the King of Kings in the sea and all their depths'. Psalm 135 is also found in a fragmentary form in 4QPs[k] where it is followed by an hitherto unknown *Catena, and then by Psalm 99, again suggesting the anti-idolatry polemic has influenced these additions. Fragments of 135 are also evident in 4QPs[n], where verse 12 is followed by 136:23, although the rest of 136 follows 135:21, suggesting a close relationship between 135 and 136.

Jewish commentary tradition sometimes gives this psalm a future emphasis: it looks forward to the Messianic era when all will praise *Ha-Shem for directing history for the wellbeing of Israel.[770] The Messiah will establish himself in Jerusalem (verse 21).[771] The two references to the 'house of the Lord' and 'courts of the house of the Lord' in verse 2 testify both to worship in Jerusalem and in heaven above.[772] The reference to 'you that fear the Lord' in verse 20 is thus read as a reference to the Gentiles, as in Ps. 115:9–11), whose fear is so great that some will convert to Judaism.[773]

It is not surprising that the idea of an earthly and heavenly Temple was also developed in Christian commentaries. *Ambrose, for example, writes that verse 2 is about the outer courts being those of the church below, and the house of the Lord being the eternal Temple in the heavens.[774] Verses 19–21 are also about the church below: the 'house of Israel' is the body of Christian believers; the 'house of Aaron' concerns bishops and priests; the 'house of Levi', other ministers; whilst those who 'fear the Lord' are now the faithful laity.[775] A future reading is taken from verse 21: Christ who first appeared in Jerusalem, born of Bethlehem in Judah, will again appear from where he dwells in Jerusalem above.[776]

Some Christian commentators, such as *Chrysostom, read the psalm from a more historical point of view, seeing it as about God's provision for the Christian church, given that the Jews were those who had 'spurned him' by worshipping idols.[777] Others take up the allegorical interpretation of

---

[770] Feuer 2004: 1597 and 1598 (citing *Sforno).
[771] Feuer 2004: 1606.
[772] Feuer 2004: 1598.
[773] So *Rashi, in Gruber 2004: 724 and 725, note 11; also *Kimḥi, cited in; Feuer 2004: 1606.
[774] Neale and Littledale 1874–79: IV/277.
[775] Neale and Littledale 1874–79: IV/285.
[776] Neale and Littledale 1874–79: IV/285; also Cassiodorus trans. Walsh 1991b: 350.
[777] Chrysostom trans. Hill 1998: 221–22; also 231.

Ambrose: God's slaughter of the 'firstborn' in Egypt is about his victory over our original sins through the rite of baptism.[778] Sihon, the Amorites ('the lofty ones') and Bashan symbolise the works of Satan which God will punish and destroy.[779] Alternatively, *Cassiodorus views the whole psalm as about praise to God as Trinity, beginning with the threefold call to praise in verse 1.[780]

Given that the teaching against idolatry was particularly pertinent in the Reformation period, verses 15–18 received frequent comment. Richard Hooker, for example, in *Laws of Ecclesiastical Polity*, cites verse 18: 'Those who make them and all those who trust them shall become like them'.[781] Martin *Luther cites from these verses to make a similar point against ritualism.[782]

Psalm 135, like 136, with its calls to praise and references to the Temple personnel, is a psalm with liturgical potential. It is used in Jewish worship at the morning service for Sabbaths and festival days, being read after Psalms 19, 34, 90 and 91 and before 136, 33, 92 and 93, and the call to 'bless' is sometimes used with the two doxologies at the end of Psalm 72 and 89 as part of the Daily Hallel.[783] It is used along with Psalm 83 for the first day of Passover and for the following weekdays of this festival (*Sop.* 18:2).

Psalms 135 and 136 have a special place in Christian Orthodox liturgy, where they are called 'Polyeleos'—psalms of 'Many Mercies' (partly because of the refrain in 136), and used at *Matins on Feast Days, often with candles and peals of bells and the censing of the church. They are also frequently used at *Vigils, when the call to 'praise' is accompanied by the opening of the church doors and, again, the censing of the church.

As we have noted previously, artistic representations often focus on one striking word or phrase. In this case, in Byzantine Psalters, it is the image of the personification of the wind in verse 7 ('[he] brings out the wind from his storehouses…'). This is found in the *Barberini Psalter* (fol. 225v), the *Khludov Psalter* (fol. 133r), and the *Theodore Psalter* (fol.174r) where in each case the wind itself seems to be blowing a trumpet.[784] Perhaps understandably in the light of the *iconoclastic controversies, little is made here of the harsh critique of idols in verses 15–18. This is a key theme in western Psalters, however, which

---

[778] Neale and Littledale 1874–79: IV/282, again citing Ambrose; also Cassiodorus trans. Walsh 1991b: 345–46.

[779] Neale and Littledale 1874–79: IV/283.

[780] See Cassiodorus trans. Walsh 1991b: 343. According to Neale and Littledale 1874–79: IV/276 this is also found in the Syriac tradition.

[781] *Works* I:90–91, in Selderhuis 2018: 337.

[782] *WA* 46:494.37–495.2.

[783] Hoffmann 1997: 152.

[784] See http://www.bl.uk/manuscripts/Viewer.aspx?ref=add_ms_19352_f174r. See also Wragg 1934, who also uses this image: washing, pegged out on a line to dry, billows in the wind.

link this with the image of the 'striking God' in a rather bloodthirsty way. The *Stuttgart Psalter* (fol.150v), for example, depicts in its upper miniature the be-heading of Og, and in its lower miniature a satire on idol-making with wor-shippers paying homage to those who have made them.[785] Another theme is that of God as Creator of the cosmos and the heavens. An eighteenth-century Russian Orthodox triptych from Karelia uses Psalms 103 (MT 104), 147 (MT 147:12–20) and 134 (MT 135), with the latter psalm as the centrepiece; in the upper part Christ as *Pantokrator* sits enthroned, dressed as a High Priest and surrounded by angels, with the sun and moon in the upper left and right cor-ners. Below are scenes from the dream of Jacob (verse 4) and from the escape from Egypt (verses 8–9).[786]

Another interpretation of the 'striking God' is found in metrical psalms. Isaac *Watts' paraphrase of the psalm ends his paraphrase of the invective against idols with the following verse:[787]

> O Britain, know the living God,
> Serve him with faith and fear;
> He makes thy churches his abode
> And claims thine honors there.

In America, John *Mycall's 1787 edition of the psalms revised the end of Ps. 135:19 ('O house of Israel, bless the Lord') to 'New England, know thy living God'.[788]

In music, the creation theme within this psalm is found in John Beckwith's 'Jonah' (1963), a chamber cantata in four parts. Here verses 5–7 are important, which refer to God doing his will in 'heaven and earth, in the seas and all deeps' (verse 6) as Jonah is thrown into the sea. This is followed, also using the theme of Psalm 136, by 'he hates nothing he has made, his mercy is our shade'.[789]

The overall reception of this psalm is therefore evident in two particular ways: those who focus on God as 'Striker' (of the enemies of Israel and of those who worship idols), and those who emphasise God as Creator in the heart of this psalm. It is ironic that a 'psalm of praise' can elicit such ethnic and patriotic zeal as well as such universal hope.[790]

---

[785] See https://bit.ly/3EIDV1g.
[786] This was exhibited in a private collection in Amsterdam: see https://www.morsink.com/home.
[787] See https://bit.ly/3xEpacr.
[788] See Gillingham 2008: 161–62.
[789] See Dowling Long and Sawyer 2015: 124.
[790] See Brueggemann and Bellinger 2014: 567, who argue that the more negative aspects need to be subjected to the voice of some of the prophets.

Psalm 136: Thanksgiving for the Kindness of the Lord

Given that we have already noted the many connections between 135 and 136, it is surprising that the linguistic correspondences are not as precise as links between other neighbouring psalms. Some are fairly close, including 'for the Lord/he is good' (135:3; 136:1); 'land as a heritage… a heritage to his people/ servant Israel' (135:12 and 136:21–22); 'Sihon king of the Amorites' (135:11; 136:19) and 'Og king of Bashan' (135:11; 136:20). But other phrases with similar meanings use different expressions. We read that God is above all gods in 135:5 and 136:2–3, but the Hebrew words are actually quite different; and even 'God the striker' of the firstborn of Egypt (135:8) is different in 136:10 ('who struck down Egypt through their firstborn…' [with no reference to Pharaoh]). The creation imagery focusses on the sun, moon, and stars in 136:7–9, but on the clouds, lightnings, and wind in 135:6–7. Psalm 136 has a close affinity with the creation account in Genesis 1: verses 4–9 resemble Gen. 1:6–8, 9, 10 and 14–18, and this affinity accounts for the differences with 135:6–7. Psalm 136 also reflects the influence of the Persian period whereby Yahweh in verse 1 becomes 'the God of heaven' in verse 26.[791] So in this first stage of reception it is apparent that the compilers brought together two similar psalms but by two different hands.

The key difference in the actual reception history of Psalms 135 and 136 is the extensive influence of the latter in Jewish liturgy. This is in part due to its *antiphonal nature, where the congregation could participate with the refrain 'for his steadfast love endures for ever'. So for example the *Septuagint expands verse 16 with a citation from Deut. 8:15 and another antiphon; and at the end of the final verse, the first verse is repeated to emphasise before the final refrain that God is not only 'God of heaven' but the 'Lord of lords'.[792]

Similarly, at *Qumran, additions indicate a role in liturgy. The key scroll is again 11QPs[a]: apart from an odd repetition of the 'sun and the moon' at the beginning of verse 8, the psalm has few variations. Its placing is, however, different. Verse 26 is followed by verses from Psalm 118 (1, 15–16, 8–9, 29, and an unknown verse) which in turn is followed by another psalm of praise, 145. All four psalms which occur here together (135, 136, 118 and 145) are about victories over Israel's enemies; they may have been sung together as praises anticipating the future victory of the community at Qumran.

---

[791] See also Ezr. 1:2, 5:11, 6:9, 7:12; Neh. 1:4, 2:4; Dan. 2:18; Jon. 1:9; and 2 Chron. 36:23.

[792] Although there is no explicit polemic of idols as in 135:15–18, the concern to show God's uniqueness is illustrated in verse 7 which reads 'to him who *alone* made the great lights', following verse 4 ('who *alone* does great wonders').

The interest in the liturgical nature of this psalm is also found in Jewish commentators who emphasise the numerical nature of this psalm: its twenty-six verses, each repeating an identical refrain, correspond to the number 26, the total when adding together the value of each of the letters Y-H-W-H, the Hebrew name for God.[793] It was understood as 'The Great Hallel' because of its twenty-six-fold invocation of the name of God.[794] The number also corresponds with the twenty-six generations between creation and the giving of the Law on Sinai (year 2448), who until then were sustained instead by God's 'steadfast love'.[795] This, in turn, apparently explains why Sinai is not referred to here. It also shows that the climax of the psalm is *not* the miraculous parting of the Red Sea (verses 13–15, absent from Psalm 135), but the penultimate verse 25, 'who gives food to all flesh', showing God's provision through the mundane as much as the miraculous: 'What is more difficult, dividing the Sea or giving food to men?'.[796] This is another reason why this psalm is called the Great Hallel, for it is about God's provision of our daily bread, celebrated especially in the Passover *Seder* (b.Pesachim 118a). Another view is that it was the very song the priests and Levites were called to sing, along with the congregation ('those who fear the Lord'), at the end of Psalm 135: it was composed for the liturgy of the founding of the second Temple (Ezr. 3:10).[797]

The repeated refrain is not unique to Psalm 136; indeed it is found in a different form in *Surah* 55 (*al-Rahman*) in the Qur'an. The refrain, from Q. 55:13 onwards, is most unusual, for it is framed not as a statement, as in Psalm 136, but as a rhetorical question, perhaps addressed to mythic deities: 'So which, then, of your Lord's blessings do you both deny?' Like Psalm 136, Surah 55 also has its own narrative account, starting with the primordial act of creation and ending with a (double) description of a future Paradise. The key difference is that in Psalm 136 the narrative, from verse 10, concerns specific references to the salvation history of the people, whilst *Surah* 55 is concerned mainly with creation and moves in a more eschatological direction with its final emphasis on the coming Paradise. Nevertheless, the repetition of images and the use of dual forms is like Psalm 136, and each text evokes through the language and form a sense of order, in each case implicitly brought about by the counsel and might of God. Both texts start with an invocation to praise God, and each ends with similar praise of God. Ps. 136:26 ends 'O give thanks to the God of heaven,

---

[793] Feuer 2004: 1607, citing *Pesachim* 118a.
[794] Markus 2016: 280a.
[795] Feuer 2004: 1608; also Braude 1959: 324.
[796] 1959: 327–28, in a discussion as to whether the Red Sea was divided into 'ten parts' according to different Jewish tradition, or, as here in verse 13, just two.
[797] Neale and Littledale 1874–79: IV/287.

for his steadfast love endures for ever' whilst in Q. 55:78 we read 'Blessed be the name of your Lord, full of majesty, bestowing honour'.[798] The prominent part played by Psalm 136 as the Great Hallel in Jewish liturgy could have caused this psalm to be widely known, in oral form, and this might account for some of these general correspondences, especially in structure and form.[799]

Christian tradition has also emphasised the repetitive liturgical nature of this psalm. The threefold praise to God 'the Trinity' is found in verses 1–3: he is first called Yahweh (verse 1), representing the Father, then Elohim (verse 2: 'God of Gods'), representing the Son, then Adonai (verse 3: 'Lord of Lords'), representing the Spirit.[800] This is often read in the light of 1 Cor. 8:5–6.[801] Similarly the end of the psalm, 'he gives food for all flesh' is read as a reference to the participation in Holy Communion, rather than, following Jewish interpretation, either as about God's creative bounty or the Passover meal.[802] Finally, Christian commentators differ as to whether this is a thanksgiving psalm or a psalm of confession (the Greek has the imperative form of the verb *exomologeo* in vv. 1–3 and 26 and this can be read as 'give testimony'). *Chrysostom reads it as thanksgiving.[803] *Jerome, however, reads it penitentially: 'The prophet urges us to confess our sins, for God is good'. *Cassiodorus also reads the psalm as about penitence.[804]

Whereas there was little overt Christological commentary for Psalm 135, Psalm 136 is quite different. There is extensive reference to the splitting of the Red Sea in 'two parts' (verse 13) which is quite different from Jewish interpretation. Here the Sea represents, typically, Baptism, and the 'two parts' represent those who continue in that faith and those who fall from it.[805] The Red Sea also contains all the heresies attacking the Christian church, such as Sabellianism, *Arianism, and *Nestorianism, which God 'drives back' and allows the faithful to pass through.[806] This may have been behind the association of Psalm 136 with *Athanasius, when, at Alexandria, Syrianus and his troops burst into the church of St. Theonas, in order to disperse the Catholics and take control of the Patriarchy. Psalm 136, as we have seen, along with Psalm 135 was a popular liturgical psalm in the Eastern church. It was sung for protection against the Arians and to claim the perpetual mercy of God.[807] Another Christological

---

[798] Afifi Al-Akiti has clarified some of my thinking here. I have used his translation which is an adaptation of Haleem: 2010.

[799] See Neuwirth 2009: 746–69.

[800] Neale and Littledale 1874–79: IV/288, citing Bellarmine. See also Jerome trans. Ewald: 1963: Homily 47, p. 353, and the commentary on verse 2.

[801] *Augustine trans. Uyl 2017: 645; Jerome trans. Ewald: 1963: Homily 47, p. 354.

[802] Neale and Littledale 1874–79: IV/294.

[803] Chrysostom trans. Hill 1998: 234.

[804] Jerome trans. Ewald 1963: Homily 47, p. 353; also Cassiodorus trans. Walsh 1991b: 352–53.

[805] Neale and Littledale 1874–79: IV/293.

[806] *Ibid.*

[807] Neale and Littledale 1874–79: IV/288.

interpretation centred on verse 5: 'who by his understanding made the heavens'. This was read in the light of Prov. 8:22–31, where wisdom brings out the ordering of the cosmos; since Christ is the wisdom of God (following Col. 2:3), so 136:5 is a reference to the wisdom of Christ in creation.[808]

It is interesting that when we read commentaries from Reformers such as *Calvin, over a thousand years later, so little is made of the Christian overlay in this psalm. Calvin reads the praise of God in creation in verses 4–7 as '…statements not intended to foster scientific investigation but rather to lead the hearer to worship…' And as for verse 7 '…The Holy Spirit had no intention to teach astronomy…'[809] The context for Christian apology has completely changed. Similarly, the reference to God's 'outstretched arm' in verse 10 is simply a sign of God's power: Calvin, from his own more historical reading of the psalms, finds nothing about the cross in the text of Psalm 136.[810]

John Eaton notes that the liturgical quality of Psalm 136 is in its rhythmic nature (in the Hebrew, usually three beats for each half of the verse) but especially in its repetition: 'While the responsive or antiphonal style of Hebrew praise can be discerned in a number of psalms, only here is the method fully recorded'.[811] In Jewish liturgy, Psalm 136 is used both on the seventh day of Passover and during the Passover meal on the first day (*Sop.* 18:2). It is also an important Sabbath morning psalm, read, like Psalm 135, after Psalms 19, 34, 90, 91 and 135, and before 33 and 92, 93, all of which contain creation themes, at a time when the seven days of creation and Israel's election are considered. In addition, and perhaps curiously, the psalm is also used at *Purim: here the Persians are a type for the Egyptians, and Haman, for Pharaoh. The 166 words in the psalm correspond with the 166 verses of the Hebrew scroll of Esther, and the psalm's repeated response to God's mercy for his people gives it a theological relevance, with verse 24, rather than 25, marking the high point of the psalm.[812]

In Christian liturgy, as well as its use alongside Psalm 135 at *Vigils and *Matins, 136 (on its own) is one of the common psalms for Easter, because of its repeated emphasis on God's mercy.[813]

We noted that one of the common depictions of Psalm 135 in Byzantine Psalters was the personification of the wind.[814] Psalm 136 does not use a met-

---

[808] See for example Augustine trans. Uyl 2017: 646.
[809] Calvin trans. Beveridge 1979: 184.
[810] Calvin trans. Beveridge 1979: 185–86.
[811] Eaton 2003: 452.
[812] Markus 2016: 282a.
[813] See p. 345.
[814] See pp. 345–46.

aphor for the wind, but it does anthropomorphise the 'rule' of sun, moon and stars (verses 7–9). So it is not surprising to find the personification of the sun and moon evident in some Byzantine Psalters. In the *Kiev Psalter* (fol. 188r) the sun and moon are represented by figures drawing chariots: here this follows Russian folklore, that night and day are heralded in by horsemen wearing red and black respectively. The *Hamilton Psalter* similarly also personifies the sun, but in a large wagon, drawn by oxen (fol. 229r); the moon is also personified overleaf (fol. 229v). *Carolingian Psalters, such as *Utrecht and, later, *Harley, also personified the sun, holding a torch, whilst in the right corner the moon is personified and surrounded by stars (fol. 76v).[815] The *Stuttgart Psalter* (fol. 151v) is much more explicit. Here, in each top corner, both the sun (Latin *sol*, here with golden tresses imitating the god Apollo) and the moon (Latin *luna*, imitating the goddess Diana) have faces and bodies: the moon, personified as a woman, also holds a torch (rather than a horn). Most of the image is dominated by the representationt of the earth (Latin *terra*) as a woman: this refers to verse 25 ('who gives food for all flesh) and she is holding vines in her mouth and a sheaf of wheat in her hands, giving this a clear Eucharistic reading.[816]

A famous poetic imitation of this psalm is by John *Milton: his 'Let us with a gladsome mind' was a translation in 1623 of Psalm 136 into 24 couplets, taken mainly from the Latin. He was at St. Paul's School at the time, aged fifteen. It was published in 1645 in his *Poems*, along with Psalm 114, also composed in 1623.[817] Verses 4–9 and 25 in particular became a well-known hymn (again noting the liturgical potential of the antiphons), often sung to the French tune 'Midi'.[818] In the light of the comments about the personification of pagan deities noted in art, we may note how Milton's paraphrase of verses 8 and 9 has similar connotations:

> And caus'd the golden-tressèd Sun
> All day long his course to run;
> For his mercies aye endure,
> Ever faithful, ever sure.

> The hornèd Moon to shine by night,
> Among her spangled sisters bright;
> For his mercies aye endure,
> Ever faithful, ever sure.

---

[815] See https://psalter.library.uu.nl/page/160.
[816] See https://bit.ly/3EIDV1g.
[817] See pp. 214–15. It is interesting to see both psalms contain both creation and exodus themes.
[818] See https://hymnary.org/text/let_us_with_a_gladsome_mind.

Although Milton—composing in the wake of the Renaissance—intended these classical deities to be seen as *created* by God, it is interesting that some hymnic versions change the first line to 'the glorious Sun' and the fifth line above to 'the Moon' (although capitals and masculine/feminine pronouns are preserved). Henry *Baker's composition of this psalm in 1861 ('Praise, O praise our God and king! Hymns of adoration sing…') had a note that it was set 'following John Milton (1623).[819] A more recent version of Milton's text is by Bob Burroughs (2005), by GIA Publications.[820]

Another musical composition of this entire psalm is Heinrich *Schütz's *Danket dem Herrn*, SWV 45, performed at the BBC Prom 25 in 2017, conducted by Sir John Eliot Gardiner and sung by the Monteverdi Choir and the English Baroque Soloists to celebrate the 500th anniversary of the Reformation. This version is one of Schütz's large-scale works in his *Psalms of David*, composed after his time in Venice, with a typical combination of *Lutheran piety and Catholic (Counter Reformation) opulence. It was composed at the beginning of his fifty-five-year period as Kapellmeister in Dresden. Using the schema of the two galleries of choirs in St. Mark's Venice, Schütz has two solo choirs, one lighter, the other heavier, singing alternate half verses with a massed choir singing the refrain. It is in five parts. Part One (verses 1–5) is of the lower voice choir and the massed choir, with verse 5 sung by both; Part Two (verses 6–12) are of the higher voice choir and massed choir, again with both choirs singing verse 12. The roles of the 'sun' and 'moon' in this case are interpreted with a good deal of contrapuntalism. Part Three (verses 13–15), on the parting of the Red Sea, has more polyphony, with the lighter voice choir offering an ethereal quality to suggest the miraculous nature of God's action. Part Four (verses 16–25) leads up to verse 25 ('all flesh') with solo voices and a *tutti* ensemble from both choirs as well as the massed choir. This is the climax of the piece. Part Five (verse 26) is a clever evocation of the Trinity in its final hymn of praise, with *tripla* rhythms. The celebrative tone, with additional trumpets and timpani, gives the sense of worship not only on earth but of the massed angelic choirs in heaven.[821]

By seeing the climax as verses 25 and 26, Schütz's reception reverses (or perhaps sometimes tempers) the more violent and political elements of this psalm found in verses 10–22. We are left understanding better the observation by Zenger, that the violence expressed in both Psalms 135 and 136 is ultimately to eliminate unjust powers and defend the poor and vulnerable.[822] This

[819] Gillingham 2008: 206; Dowling Long and Sawyer 2015: 145.
[820] See https://www.giamusic.com/store/resource/a-song-of-praise-print-g6383.
[821] Stern 2013: 79–97. A version can be heard on https://www.youtube.com/watch?v=SOjjSrASDJg.
[822] Hossfeld and Zenger 2005: 501.

understanding is 'contemporised' by John Goldingay as 'bad news for the major powers of Europe, North America and Asia, but good news for the little peoples whom the big powers dominate':[823] Schütz prepares us for attraction and repulsion the reader might find in Psalm 137, where God's *hesed*, repeated twenty-six times here, seems to be in short supply.

Psalm 137: To Sing or Not to Sing? Waiting for Justice from God

Psalm 137, despite its very specific details, has without doubt the richest reception history in the Psalter. Even Psalms 1, 2, 8, 51, 110 and 118 come nowhere near it, mainly because 137 has been adapted not only by traditional believers, Jewish and Christian, but by many outside an orthodox faith tradition.[824] What follows is necessarily selective, focussing on the theme of its *multivalent appeal* in political and spiritual crises.

Jews and Christians have read this psalm in very different ways. Jews read it as a 'meta-narrative' about a community in exile whose eyes are fixed on Jerusalem as a sign of God's presence. Its appeal is primarily material, and about national identity.[825] Christians rarely read Psalm 137 as a whole: they have isolated various verses and applied them in a spiritual and personal way, usually reading 'Jerusalem' as a heavenly city and a symbol of a pilgrim faith. Others have read the psalm in the light of slavery and oppression and as a call for social justice.

Taking compilation as the first stage of reception, Psalm 137 links well with 135 and 136, with their similar emphasis on Jewish identity and the threat of other nations. It also has correspondences with 120–134, for these would be the very songs for Zion which the psalmist of 137 longs to sing. And its placing before 138 is also explicable, where we read about prayers *and songs* apparently being offered in a foreign land:

> I give you thanks, O LORD, with my whole heart;
> before the gods (*neged elohim*) I sing your praise…

Psalm 137 has three clear strophes. Verses 1–3 all are in the first-person plural—'*we* sat down'; '*we* wept'; '*we* remembered'; and '*we* hung up *our* lyres'. We also read of '*our* captors', '*our* tormentors' '*our* tormentors' who taunt 'sing *to us*'.

---

[823] Goldingay 2008: 597.
[824] In Stowe 2016, the author aptly terms the pool of settings and allusions as 'virtually infinite' (p. 183).
[825] See Berlin 2005: 66–85; Kugel 1990: 173–213; Gillingham 2013a: 64–82.

In Hebrew both forms give *-nu* endings to the words so the nine *-nu* endings create phonetically the impression of mourning. The plaintive plea in verse 4 is 'how shall *we* sing?' (*nashir*) thus stands out in reply. And then by contrast, verses 5–6 are in the first-person singular: 'if *I* forget you let *my* right hand wither' (the latter word 'wither' being a *piel* form of the root *shakach* [to forget]); 'if *I* do not remember you let *my* tongue cleave to *my* palate...' This self-imprecation on the hands (for playing the lyre) and the mouth (for singing) is addressed to the city of Jerusalem, vowing to sing there upon return. In verses 7–9, the verbal forms are second- and third-person masculine plurals (or third feminine singular, in reference to Babylon). The taunts of the Edomites are first recalled: directed to Jerusalem as a woman, they cry, 'Strip her naked!'. The devastating effects of 'mistress Babylon, the destroying one' are then remembered. The final dreadful curse, that both Babylon and her offspring should be destroyed, implies that Babylon is still standing.

Yet the psalm has an internal unity. The taunts of the Babylonians in the first part correspond with the taunts of the Edomites in the third part; and the self-curse in the second part anticipates the curse on Babylon in the third. Babel, 'city of confusion' frames the psalm: the two tricola in verses 1 and 8, display, first, anger at Babylon's abuse, and then the joy at Babylon's defeat. It is no coincidence that the word 'remember' (*zakar*) is found in all three parts: the 'remembering' of Zion in verse 1; the 'remembering' of Jerusalem in verse 6; and the plea to God to 'remember' in verse 7.[826] So in what follows we will consider the reception history of the psalm *as a whole*.

We have noted several times the curious arrangement in 11QPs[a] of many of the later psalms in Book V, and Psalm 137 is no exception. After Psalm 136 we find the sectarian Plea for Deliverance, then Psalm 139 (also known for its closing vitriolic curses), followed by 137 (verses 1 and 9; the rest is missing), then 138:1–8 (also with a concern about worship in a foreign land). In 11QPs[a] and in the Bible Hebrew, Psalm 137 has no Davidic heading (unlike the *LXX* which adds 'To – or By – David'). In the Hebrew Bible collection, however, it prefaces the last Davidic collection (138–145). Perhaps the interest in Jerusalem made this another 'Davidic' psalm.

One of the first references to Psalm 137 is in 4 Baruch (*Paraleipomena of Jeremiah*), which explains how a letter from Jeremiah highlighted the people's grief which gave rise to his composition of Psalm 137.[827] 4 Baruch dates between 70 and 135 CE. The context is therefore not the fall of Jerusalem between 597 and 587 BCE, but its final fall in 70 CE/135 CE. Both Babylon and Edom

---

[826] See Magonet 1982: 365–76, here 373–76.
[827] See 4 Baruch 6:4–6 and the discussion in Kugel 1990: 195–97.

later became synonyms for Rome—whereby Titus and the Roman Empire were deemed to be Edomite in origin—so Psalm 137:7–9 became an invective not only against Babylon, but also against Rome.[828]

*Targum reads Psalm 137 as a metanarrative but transforms it into a different drama of several speakers. Usually in Jewish interpretation the drama stays on earth but here, by the middle of the psalm, it moves up to heaven. By verses 5–6 it is 'the voice of the spirit of holiness', not the psalmist, who vows loyalty to the memory of Jerusalem, and in verses 7–9 it is the angelic protectorates of the nation who cry out in vengeance against their enemies.[829] The expansion in verse 3 to 'the songs *you used to utter*' is about the fall of the second Temple after 70 CE when once again the songs of Zion were silent. In verse 4 the psalmist is called a *Levite* (i.e. not David, nor Jeremiah, nor Baruch). This refers to a Jewish tradition about the Levites maiming their thumbs in order to disqualify them from any enforced blasphemy in singing about Zion in an alien land: *Targum* thus warns those in their present exile not to capitulate to Gentile demands.[830] The additional reference to Edom in verse 7, '*who laid waste Jerusalem*' again has a double connotation—literally, the Edomites, but later, the Romans. The fact that the speakers of the curses in verses 7 and 8–9 are '*Michael prince of Jerusalem*' and '*Gabriel prince of Zion*' is not only an unusual reference in *Targum* to named angels, but also raises this cry of vengeance to a supernatural level: this is not just a human curse on the enemy.

In *Midrash Tehillim* another meta-narrative emerges: its detailed comments intensify the peoples' suffering. The use of 'there' (*sham*) in verses 1 and 3 is because the Jews were allowed no rest-stop until they arrived in Babylon.[831] The reference to weeping by ('*al*) the Babylonian waters (v. 1) is on account of ('*al*) the people and their children actually being poisoned by ('*al*) the waters of the river Euphrates.[832] The use of 'also' (*gam*) in verse 1 is an indication that the pain was so great that God Himself wept with them too.[833] David is the 'prophetic' composer who foresees not only the destruction of both Temples, but also the pain of the ongoing exile. Whereas in the *Targum*, the emphasis is on the initiative of God who will soon vindicate those in exile, the emphasis in *Midrash Tehillim* is on the accountability of the people in their need to repent. Hence more is made of the self-mutilation of the Levites in verse 5, as well as the anger of Nebuchadnezzar, and the Levites' exemplary response. Verse 6 univer-

---

[828] There is a reference to this in the Babylonian *Talmud*, b.Gittin 57b; also Kugel 1990: 174–75.
[829] See Bernstein 1994: 326–45, especially pp.338–43; also Stec 2004: 231.
[830] The tradition of the self- mutilation of the Levites is found in *Pesikta Rabbati* 136a; see also Braude 1959: 334 and Edwards: 108–111.
[831] See *Pesiqta Rabbati* 130b, 1959: 331–32.
[832] See *Pesiqta Rabbati* 135a, 1959: 332.
[833] See *Pesiqta Rabbati* 131b, 1959: 334.

salises the vow concerning the memory of Jerusalem: every Jew is now to do the same. 'If a man covers his house with plaster, he must leave uncovered a small space as a mourning reminder of Jerusalem… If a woman is adorning herself, she must leave off some small thing as a reminder of Jerusalem, for it is said *If I forget thee, O Jerusalem, let my right hand forget her cunning* (Psalm 137:5)'.[834]

Rabbi Kimḥi's commentary has a similar emphasis. Verses 8–9 refer to God's vengeance on those who brought about the destruction of the first Temple, the Babylonians, but verse 7 refers to those 'of Edom' who brought about the destruction of the second Temple, 'for it was brought about by Titus who belonged to the Roman empire which was of the Edomites'.[835] The cry of vengeance in verse 7 is thus directed against the Romans, and by implication against *all* Gentile persecutors of the Jews.

Christian interpreters have been reluctant to associate this psalm, with its passion for the physical place of Jerusalem, and its violent hatred of the people's enemies, as 'about' or 'to' or 'of' Christ. Psalm 137 is never cited in the New Testament. The only verse alluded to is verse 9, in Luke 19:44. There the Greek word *edafizo* for 'They will *crush* you to the ground, you and your children with you…' is the same Greek word used in the *LXX* for *crushing* the children in 137:9 (136:9). In Luke 19:41–44 disaster is prophesied not on Babylon but on 'the city' (Jerusalem) which rejects the Anointed One. So Psalm 137 is up-turned: instead of 'remembering' Jerusalem the city is forgotten and destroyed. The very curse in verses 7–9 which is against the 'enemy nations' is now given against Jerusalem itself: the song for Zion will never be sung.

Despite its vast reception history elsewhere, Psalm 137 is used infrequently by the Church Fathers, and then usually by allegorising particular words. *Jerome begins his commentary by saying that Psalm 137 is understood in three ways—about the exile of the Jews in Babylon, about the expulsion of sinners from the church, 'and about the superior exile, whenever we wish it, by which a sometimes noble company is led forth into the vale of tears'.[836] Hence 'the waters of Babylon' are a metaphor for spiritual exile. *Cassiodorus, who from personal experience knew about physical exile in a hostile land, prefers to see here an exile in Jerome's spiritual sense, with Babylon as 'the devil's city… proud, flour-ishing, most joyful, watered by the vices of this world as by mighty waters'.[837] A second example is the 'harps': they denote the extent of the bitterness of grief, and the need to avoid compromise with the world; hence they are to be hung upon the tree, which is the cross.[838] Thirdly, 'captors' and 'tormentors' are nei-

---

[834] See *Pesiqta Rabbati* 1959: 335–36.
[835] Baker and Nicholson: 79–83.
[836] See Holladay 1993: 172 quoting Morin 1959: 165–242.
[837] See Cassiodorus trans. Walsh 1991b: 360.
[838] Cassiodorus trans. Walsh 1991b: 361; also Methodius, *Symposium or the Banquet of the Ten Virgins* 4.3 cited in Wesselschmidt 2007: 379.

ther Babylonians nor Romans; they are, according to *Augustine, 'the devil and all his minions, who have inflicted us with the wounds of sin'.[839]

Fourthly, Jerusalem is never the city itself. It is the Heavenly City, which forms a neat antithesis to Babylon, the worldly city and place of all confusion. This was a theological reality with political implications: Augustine preached a sermon on Psalm 137 in Carthage in December 412 (after the sack of Rome in 410) which stated that Rome, a 'descendent' of Babylon, was, like Babel, transitory and destined for destruction; meanwhile Jerusalem, the 'heavenly city', transcended worldly cares.[840] The challenge to the church was to escape its 'Babylonian captivity'. The phrase 'The Babylonian Captivity of the Church' became a byword, and from the fifteenth-century onwards Psalm 137 was frequently associated with it, where 'exile' was seen not only as physical displacement but as an experience of disenfranchisement without ever having 'moved' anywhere.

Fifthly, 'Edom' is read with a difficult anti-Semitic bias. Edom is Esau, the 'false kinsman', set against Jacob, the true Israel, *which is now the Church*. This is a theme in Augustine's sermons on the psalms—odd, one might argue, given that the real enemies in the church in Carthage were not so much Jews as imperial (pagan) rule, with the Theodosian Code creating religious intolerance towards the church. But Edom is now the Synagogue, 'the elder church which sought the life of the younger.'[841]

Sixthly, the 'children of Babylon' are 'sins of the flesh born of a wretched mother (Babylon)'; they inhabit our minds, and have to be prevented from growing to adulthood lest they will take us over; so in infancy they have to be dashed against the Rock which is Christ himself.[842] Following *Midrash Tehillim*, this gives attention to individual words, but at no point do we find a simple 'meta-narrative' being read into this psalm.

In Jewish liturgy Psalm 137 is traditionally recited at *Tisha B'av* usually in late July or August, commemorating the destruction of the first and second Temples. It is used before the Grace at meals on weekdays, as a way of solemnly remembering the loss of the Temple, '...symbolising that when the body is full, the heart must still grieve.'[843] This contrasts with the more celebratory use of Psalm 126, which is used before Grace for Sabbaths and holidays.[844] The memory of Jerusalem's destruction is preserved in family rituals: verse 6 is recited by

---

[839] Kirschner 1990: 254.

[840] See https://www.newadvent.org/fathers/1801137.htm.

[841] Augustine cited in Neale and Littledale 1874–79: 4/301.

[842] See *Origen, *Against Celsus* 7.22, cited in Wesselschmidt 2007: 379. See also Jerome trans. Ewald 1963: 59–60. Their text is 1 Cor. 10:4.

[843] Feuer 2004: 1624 and 1619.

[844] Donin 1980: 301.

the bridegroom at his wedding, with symbolic ashes on his head to represent the devastated Jerusalem, remembering 'Jerusalem, my *highest* joy'.

Liberal, Conservative and Reformed Jews often recite only the first six verses, although more orthodox *Ashkenazi and Sephardic Jews tend to use the whole psalm. The Christian monastic tradition recited it all but allegorised the last verses as about evil thoughts.[845] More recently, when Psalm 137 is used at *Vigils and *Vespers the Roman Catholic Church has advised that the final three verses be omitted.[846] This practice is followed in some Anglican and Reformed traditions, evidenced for example in *The Alternative Service Book* (1980) where the final verses are preserved but kept in brackets. Psalm 137 is not deeply engraved in Christian liturgical memory.

In artistic representations of Psalms 135 and 136 we noted the personification of the wind (135) and the sun and moon (136). Byzantine Psalters continue this theme by personifying the river in Psalm 137. It is portrayed as a stream pouring from an urn in the *Bristol Psalter* (fol. 223r),[847] in the *Theodore Psalter* (fol. 135r),[848] and in the ninth-century *Khludov Psalter* (fol 135r), where the context is the *iconoclastic controversies between Christians and Jews, so that the taunting by the waters is seen as no longer against Jews but Christians.[849]

The *Carolingian *Utrecht Psalter* (fol. 77r) depicts the river in a harsh line running across the bottom of the image: it symbolises the chaotic forces contained within this psalm.[850] The focus is on a 'hidden' prophecy: on a hill next to what is apparently the Temple is the figure of Jesus, with three disciples. They point to his lips. This appears to be a reference to the prophecy of Christ concerning the destruction of Jerusalem (in Matt 23:27; Luke 13:34, 21:20–24 and John 2:19–22). This reading reminds us of Luke 19:45–48: as Edom and Babylon fell and so vindicated the Jews, so the sack of Jerusalem by Rome in 70 CE vindicated Christians who inherited a new, spiritual Jerusalem. A more clear image, taken from the *Eadwine Psalter, fol. 243v, is produced as PLATE 26.[851] This Psalter is important, because, from the context of the Crusades, the battles were not just between the Jews and Edomites and Babylonians: they were about battles between contemporary kingdoms, focussed on Jerusalem. This is the beginning of a political as well as spiritual understanding of Psalm 137.

---

[845] Stowe 2016: 136 refers to the Rule of Benedict's Prologue explicitly interpreting Psalm 137 in the light of Augustine's teaching.
[846] As in the *Apostolic Constitution* 1970. See Holladay 1993: 304–311.
[847] See http://www.bl.uk/manuscripts/Viewer.aspx?ref=add_ms_40731_f223r.
[848] See http://www.bl.uk/manuscripts/Viewer.aspx?ref=add_ms_19352_f176r.
[849] See https://commons.wikimedia.org/wiki/File:Chludov_rivers.jpg.
[850] See https://psalter.library.uu.nl/page/161.
[851] See https://commons.wikimedia.org/wiki/File:Eadwine_psalter_-_Trinity_College_Lib_-_f.243v.jpg.

The *Stuttgart Psalter* has two images. The first (fol. 152r) is of verses 1–3, with another personified river: two ducks paddle out of the frame of the picture.[852] The second (fol. 152v) is actually of verses 7–9, where two men are holding two children and are about to dash them against a giant rock. To the left is a woman with various wicked thoughts emerging from her head: so these are thus not real children, but they echo the commentary tradition of Augustine and Cassiodorus about dashing our wicked thoughts against the Rock which is Christ.[853]

The *St. Albans Psalter* uses the body of the Letter 'S' ('**S**uper Flumine') to create a river filled with fish. Down both sides of the upper curve of the 'S' we see a grieving congregation of women and men, homesick in a foreign land. In the inner side of the bottom curve a group of people are apparently planning some form of retaliation. This is not only about the Jews and the exile: it is about all who suffer for their faith.[854]

Grieving women—mothers without their children—feature frequently in nineteenth- and twentieth-century depictions of this psalm. Kate Hastings' painting 'By the Waters of Babylon they sat down and wept' (1853) has four women, all in different postures of grief—the central figure with a defiant gaze, refusing to succumb to distress. Behind them is a wall, where the Babylonians feast and drink, making clear the separation between those who are free and those who are captive.[855] The central figure in the Copping Bible (1910) is also a defiant woman, sitting by the water and holding her harp.[856] Other images depict the exile as social oppression of women: one, of singing women shows how whose voices actually bring about their liberation.[857]

A musical example of women's voices in this psalm—literally—is Howard *Goodall's 'Super Flumina' (2010). The chorus ('Enchanted Voices') is all female: the quartet, also female, provides a 'string soundscape'.[858] So instead of a more typical and often heavy male lament, the psalm starts with a haunting solo soprano voice; here is a grief which is intensely personal. The strings—which we hear, *sotto voce*, immediately—remind us of the harps which were once denied, but they are now the means of expressing the memory of pain and loss. The soprano voice sings a high F sharp, then G sharp, then drops back to the low A—just a semitone less than the octave—emulating the rise and fall of

---

[852] See https://bit.ly/31zon1v.

[853] See https://bit.ly/31I4jtB.

[854] See https://bit.ly/3yh9v3r.

[855] See http://www.christies.com/LotFinder/lot_details.aspx?intObjectID=5127322.

[856] See https://bit.ly/3e1KzEO.

[857] See http://www.templemount.org/secondtmp.html.

[858] 'Super flumina' is from *Pelican in the Wilderness* (Classic FM Records CFMD13; solo: Grace Davidson). It can be previewed on
http://itunes.apple.com/gb/album/pelican-in-wilderness-songs/id369907442.

the distress. Gradually other female voices join in: 'As for our harps, as for our harps, we hanged them up…' The wistfulness (in singing what once could not be sung) continues to the end of the psalm, with its fading harmonies: 'How shall we sing?… How shall we sing?'. This is a composition whose wistfulness intentionally undermines the anger in so much of the (predominantly male) reception history of this psalm.

Returning to artistic representations, another image, with a very different social comment, is by Arthur *Wragg, from the 1930s Depression, at a time when poverty, unemployment, and the threat of war were stark realities. Wragg's image is of two tenement block windows, the top one with a withered plant on the sill and a birdcage with a hazy image of a bird inside. It is unclear whether it is dead or alive. The bottom window is closest to us: we can see through the curtains into the blackened room. A second birdcage hangs there: this time the white upright silhouette of the bird is clearer, but it is hard to know whether, being caged, it is unable to sing, or whether it is attempting some choked warbling. The overall impression is silence. The caption under it is simply 'How shall we sing the Lord's song in a strange land?' (see Figure 14).[859]

A more recent image is by an Oxford artist, Roger *Wagner. *In a Strange Land* (1988) is a series of poems and engravings, many of which are of the then deserted docklands of East London. The image of Canning Town is just one of the images which recalls Psalm 137. The colours of blue, black and beige create a sense of utter barrenness, as do the empty cranes, piers, wharves, ladders and warehouses criss-crossing our view: this physical and spiritual desolation recalls Psalm 137.[860]

Jewish art, by contrast, tends to interpret the psalm more literally. The *Parma Psalter* is an early thirteenth-century example. Psalm 137 would have been a highly charged psalm against the background of Jews in Italian society at this time, living with the consequences of the *Fourth Lateran Council in 1215, with forced conversions and burning of Jewish books. Here we see two figures, weeping, but compelled to draw the waters from the river which would eventually, according to tradition, poison them. Willow leaves frame the text, upon which are hung the lyres.[861]

The pogroms in late nineteenth-century Eastern Europe inspired several images based on Psalm 137, using the location and dress of that period. Maurycy Minkawski's 'After the Pogrom' (1905) depicts a group of Jews sitting at the corner of a village. Behind them is a line of Jewish figures, still completing their reportage. The dark painting and the shadowy but defiant faces take us back to the rivers of Babylon.[862] In the same mode, a wall plaque in Jerusalem by Zalman

---

[859] Taken from Wragg 1934 (no page numbers).
[860] Produced in Gillingham 2019: 460.
[861] See the image in Gillingham 2008: 71 and in Gillingham 2013a, Plate 1 (centre of book).
[862] See https://bit.ly/3eHpmix.

FIGURE 14   *Arthur Wragg, 'How long shall we sing the Lord's song in a strange land?'*
(Ps. 137:4).

Source: Wragg, A. 1934: *The Psalms for Modern Life*. New York: Claude Kendall.

Zwieg, dating from 1910 and recalling verse 1, is of a group of Jews imagining they are looking over to Jerusalem: the psalm again symbolised national mourning.[863]

After 1948 Psalm 137 sometimes offered more hopeful associations. One example is in the *Chagall State Hall of the Knesset. On the north side, set amidst Marc Chagall's wall tapestries with themes of diaspora and return, and amidst the floor mosaics which represent the love of the land, is a large wall mosaic, six metres high and five and a half metres wide, which is of the first and fifth verses of Psalm 137. Chagall's setting is prayers at the Western Wall (still under Jordanian control in 1966, when this was completed), with the Old City

---

[863] See http://www.freerepublic.com/focus/religion/2634882/replies?c=15.

and Tower of David in the background. Instead of harps we see a menorah, and above, echoing the angelic tradition expressed in the *Targum* and *Midrash Tehillim*, is an angel calling the people below to return to Zion, with the star of David in the top left corner. This is yet another 'meta-narrative' in visual form and is found as PLATE 27 in the centre of the book.

Psalm 137 is a powerful vehicle for expressing a sense of loss through music. Salamone de *Rossi's *Al Naharot Bavel* (1622) is an early example, taking advantage of the new tolerance of Jewish culture. Given the ban on music in synagogue liturgy, in memory of the destruction of the second Temple, Psalm 137 is set as unaccompanied *melismatic chant. The psalm itself is about 'not singing what should be sung', so the chorus, sung by low and heavy voices, is set to dissonant chords creating darkness and tension. A chromatic progression represents the Hebrew word 'wept', and a flowing passage in unison the Hebrew word 'river'. The hanging up of harps is achieved first by lowering the key by a semitone, with an unexpected F sharp in the soprano part at the end of the phrase. The call for revenge at the end of the psalm ('Destroy it! Destroy it!') is set to harsh, grinding chords.[864]

Psalm 137 has performative power as a 'meta-narrative' in the concert hall as well as the synagogue. The nineteenth-century Italian opera composer Giuseppe Verdi uses it in his third Act of *Nabucco*, first performed in Milan in 1842. The 'Chorus of the Hebrew Slaves' relives the Jews' time in exile, when the Babylonians threatened to kill them. Sometimes called the 'unofficial Italian anthem', Verdi imbued this arrangement by the librettist Temistocle Solera with contemporary social comment, influenced by the play from which it came, published in 1836 by Bourgeois and Cornue:[865]

> Arpa d'or dei fatidici vati,
> perché muta dal salice pendi?
> Le memorie nel petto raccendi,
> ci favella del tempo che fu!

> Golden harp of the prophetic seers,
> why dost thou hang mute upon the willow?
> Rekindle our bosom's memories,
> and speak of times gone by!

---

[864] See https://www.youtube.com/watch?v=HubKpEPkkYw.
[865] See https://www.youtube.com/watch?v=HY79yY247Eo.

The early twentieth-century Russian composer and conductor Zavel Zilberts also arranged Psalm 137 for a concert hall performance; this piece too captures a sense of national suffering and alienation. It started as a concert piece in Poland in 1905 and was then reworked with choral effects and contrapuntal experimentation for a performance in Carnegie Hall in 1923.[866] Similarly, William *Walton's 'Belshazzar's Feast' (1931) performed 137 as a concert piece. The oratorio begins with Isaiah's prophecy on doom for the people of Babylon, and is followed by this psalm. First the chorus, then a baritone soloist, then again the chorus evokes the emotions of melancholy, anger, pain and rage: the finale achieves a catharsis as the hubristic abuse of power eventually gets its due desert.[867]

Few composers have associated the sufferings of Christ with this psalm. One exception is Stephen Schwartz's 'Godspell' (Broadway, 1971), a musical based upon the Gospel of Matthew. The piece before the finale, sung by the band before Jesus goes out to Gethsamane, is 'On the Willows': this is deliberate recall of Psalm 137:2, with the '*weeping* willows' and the play on 'hanging (lives, not lyres) on the tree':[868]

> On the willows, there
> We hung up our lives
> For our captors there
> Require
> Of us songs
> And our tormentors mirth
> On the willows, there...

Moving from the concert hall and theatre to radio opera, Robert Saxton, Professor of Composition at the University of Oxford, brings together an extraordinary Jewish and Christian understanding of Psalm 137. It is used in the first of his eight-scene 'The Wandering Jew' (2010). The psalm is sung in a Nazi death camp, as the prisoners work and an old man is beaten and a protesting inmate is taken to her death. The 'Wandering Jew' stands by but is impotent to save. The psalm is sung again as a 'ghost chorus' at the end of the opera, in the same death camp, where both the 'Wandering Jew' and Jesus bear witness again to pain and death.[869] Here Jesus, the suffering Jew, is united with his people in their suffering.

---

[866] See https://bit.ly/33fAX3f.
[867] See https://www.youtube.com/watch?v=1DT9MJYFIHE.
[868] See https://www.youtube.com/watch?v=WFmGFWqAr68.
[869] See R. Saxton (composer), *Wandering Jew (The Opera)*, NMCD170 (2012).

The American composer John *Harbison used Psalm 137 in his 'Four Psalms' (1998/99) with a political comment.[870] Here it is prefaced by Jewish voices recorded by Harbison in Israel/Palestine: we hear a visitor drawn to the land they thought they would hate, a tour guide pacifying a group of Americans, another visitor who breaks down at the wailing wall, a second tour guide who confesses fear of the car bombs, and a third visitor who sees children in a music school and is reminded of the dark-haired children at his home town in Poland, 1934. Psalm 137, sung by a chorus, follows these voices, in Hebrew. We then hear other voices: a politician, a Palestinian, an Arab driver, a scholar who longs for unity in the land, and a Bedouin who fears his tears. By setting Psalm 137 amidst multivalent voices, an unexpected unity emerges from the human cries of despair.

We noted earlier that from Augustine onwards, this psalm, with its call to the church to escape its 'Babylonian captivity', took on Christian political implications: some have been seen in the musical arrangements above. A striking example took place between 1413 and 1414. The setting is the court of the Lancastrian Prince of Wales, later Henry V, where John Lydgate's poem, 'In Defence of the Holy Church', had been written to attack the 'Babylonian Captivity of the Church' during the *Lollard rebellion against the king in 1413. Lydgate uses the image of hanging lyres on the willows and the taunts of the enemy to identify 'Babel' with Lollardy, whose heretical opinions were preventing true worship in the church. Lydgate reiterates the theme of 'remember!' to encourage the 'true church' in exile to preserve the traditions of the past. He applies the last three defiant verses to the Lollards. Henry V he identifies with David, for like the prophetic figure behind this psalm, he must take action to recapture the church from its Babylonian captivity to Lollard heresy.[871]

Just over a century later, the same phrase was used in a completely different way. Martin *Luther's second treatise of 1520, against the church's teaching on the seven sacraments, refers to Psalm 137. Now it is the Roman *church* which is like Babylon, creating captivity and confusion, whilst the origin and destiny of the true Church is the heavenly city, Jerusalem. In the section on the 'Sacrament of Penance', Luther quotes the first two verses, adding: 'The Lord curse the barren willows of those streams!' as he highlighted the barren inefficacy of the sacraments of the Roman (Babylonian) church.[872]

The phrase 'Babylonian Captivity of the Church' was applied to all disenfranchised Christian groups, Catholic and Protestant. Psalm 137 became 'the quintessential psalm of the Renaissance and the Reformation.'[873] Miles *Coverdale and William *Whittingham were Protestants when England was officially Catholic;

---

[870] See https://www.allmusic.com/album/john-harbison-four-psalms-emerson-mw0001845807. See also pp. 214–15 (Psalm 114); p. 292 (Psalm 126); and p. 336 (Psalm 133).

[871] Kuczynski 1995: 161–64.

[872] Taken from Steinhauser *et al.* 1970: 209.

[873] See Hamlin 2002; 2004b.

Richard Crashaw was a Catholic when England was officially Protestant. All three spent time in exile on the Continent, and all three made metrical paraphrases and commentaries on this psalm.[874] Coverdale's version (preserved in the *BCP) was made in the 1530s, a speedy production of an English Psalter which would suit both Archbishop and King, done with the knowledge that the threat of exile was never far away. So Coverdale paraphrased with some feeling: 'How shall we synge the Lordes songe in a straunge lande?'. William Whittingham, by contrast, composed his version of Psalm 137 whilst in exile in Geneva during Queen Mary's reign. The reference to the 'king' in verse 4 scarcely disguises the political reference: the problem for Whittingham is not the impossibility of a 'Song of Zion' in a strange land, but that it has to be sung under a strange queen:

> Alas (sayd we) who can once frame,
> His sorrowfull hart to syng:
> The prayers of our loving God,
> Thus under a straunge kyng?[875]

Meanwhile, Richard Crashaw, exiled first to France and then to Italy in the mid seventeenth-century, plays on the interplay between music and memory:

> Ah thee Jerusalem! Ah sooner may
> This hand forget the mastery
> Of Musicks dainty touch, than I
> The Musicke of thy memory.[876]

In his *Psalm Culture and Early Modern English Literature*, Hannibal Hamlin quotes many other examples of verses in Psalm 137 being used to describe both spiritual and physical exile, by sixteenth and seventeenth-century writers such as Francis *Bacon, George *Sandys, Edmund Spenser (known as the 'poet's poet'), and the poet and politician Lord Byron.[877] Even Shakespeare uses this psalm in his *Richard II* (Act 1 Scene 3): England is in ruins, and seems to be in exile from its own self, and Mowbray has been banished from the realm: he laments 'And no my tongue's use to me no more/Than an unstringed viol or harp'.[878]

---

[874] Hamlin 2004b: 241–43.

[875] Hamlin 2004b: 244, from W. Whittingham's *Whole Booke of Psalms*, 1562.

[876] Hamlin 2004b: 237, citing R. Crashaw's *Poems English Latin and Greek*.

[877] Hamlin 2004b: 220–27. A. C. Swinburne's 'Super Flumina Babylonis', comparing the suffering of the exiles and of passion of Christ with the suffering in Italy at the time of the Franco-Prussian wars, is a further memorable example. See https://www.bartleby.com/336/435.html.

[878] A further reference in Act 5 Scene 3 is when Aumerle seeks Bolingbooke's forgiveness with the words 'My tongue cleave to my roof within my mouth / Unless a pardon 'ere I rise or speak...' See Hamlin 2004b: 242–4.

John *Milton, too, used Psalm 137, but very differently from Psalm 135.[879] Sonnet 18, 'On the Late Massacre in Piedmont', captures the horror of the Waldensians, living out their Protestant faith in the Italian and French Alps, who suffered most intense persecution under the Catholic forces of the Duke of Savoy. Milton's final line, 'the Babylonian woe', is an allusion to Psalm 137, but the lines '… the bloody Piedmontese … rolled Mother with infant down the rocks' are more graphically specific. Contrast this with Christopher *Smart's unusual reversal of these last verses:[880]

> But he is greatest and the best
> Who spares his enemies profest
> And Christian mildness owns;
> Who give his captives back their lives,
> Their helpless infants, weeping wives,
> And for his sin atones.

In Christian music, too, Psalm 137 served a political purpose. One example is by the Flemish composer Philippe de *Monte in his eight-part 'Super flumine Babylonis'. Having served in the court under Mary from 1554–55, where he worked with William *Byrd, de Monte was exiled on the continent on account of his Catholic faith. On hearing of the state of Catholics in England in 1583, de Monte's 'Super flumina Babylonis' was a motet on verses 1, 3, 4 and 2 of Psalm 137, with the emphasis therefore on being *coerced* into singing in a 'foreign' land: this was a covert gesture of support of the Catholic-inclined Byrd, who was now composing in the Protestant court of Queen Elizabeth I. The piece was addressed 'To Mr. Byrd, 1583.' Byrd's response was 'Quomode cantabimus', addressed, in turn, to 'Mr. Philip de Monte, 1584', on verses 5–6, with the emphasis on 'not forgetting' the past ('I will remember') and longing for restoration ('Remember O Lord'). It too was arranged in eight parts and in the same key.[881]

A very different political appropriation of Psalm 137 in music is in American metrical hymns. Isaac *Watts' *Psalms of David* (1719), known for its contemporary British comment, was edited with American colouring in eighteenth-century Congregationalist Churches in New England.[882] Timothy *Dwight produced two settings of 137. The political version spoke of the Church's captivity not within Babylon, or indeed England, but within America:[883]

---

[879] Psalm 135, Milton, pp. xx.

[880] Cited in Hamlin 2002: 248.

[881] For a performance of de Monte's and Byrd's motets,
see https://www.youtube.com/watch?v=hJk5HGrSGPg (de Monte) and
https://www.youtube.com/watch?v=GIZuFiihlVo (Byrd).

[882] Stowe 2016: 140 makes the interesting observation that Watts actually excluded Psalm 137 from his 1719 edition, seeing it as 'foreign to the spirit of the Gospel'.

[883] Taken from Stackhouse 1997: 43–70.

> Lord, in these dark and dismal days,
> We mourn the hiding of thy face;
> Proud enemies our path surround,
> To level Zion with the ground.
>
> Her songs, her worship, they deride,
> And hiss thy word with tongues of pride,
> And cry, t'insult our humble prayer,
> 'Where is your God, ye Christians, where?'

William *Billings also produced a hymn with political rhetoric. The enemy 'Babel' is now the British forces during the American Revolution in 1776. This metrical paraphrase was written during the British occupation of Boston:[884]

> By the waters of Watertown we sat down and wept
> When we remember thee, O Boston...
> For they that held them in bondage requir'd of them
> to take up arms against their brethren.
> Forbid it, Lord. God forbid! ...
> that those who have sucked Bostonian Breasts
> should thirst for American Blood!...
> If I forget thee, if I forget thee,
> yea if I do not remember thee,
> let my numbers cease to flow,
> then be my Muse unkind;
> then let my tongue forget to move
> and ever be confin'd...

The version survived: the 'Billings Round' is apparently still sung in Free Churches in the Deep South today, as evidenced in the round popularised by Tom Paxton.

It is largely due to the way the Rastafarians adapted Psalm 137 that it has become so familiar in contemporary popular culture. From their origins in Jamaica in the 1930s, the Rastafarians' belief in black liberation came from a Messianic use of the Hebrew Bible, especially the Psalms. 'Yah' of the psalms is name of their God, Jah Rastafari, and their Messianic founder was Emperor Haile Selassie I. Psalm 137 is crucial here. 'Babel' refers to those from the west who sold the people of African ancestry into slavery in the Americas and the 'exiles' are the disenfranchised black Jamaican masses. The genre of the psalm is reversed: it is no longer a lament but a protest song, not wallowing in self-pity,

[884] Taken from *op. cit.*: 83–85.

but defiantly 'chanting down', in reggae rhythms, 'Babylon's might. The actual process of 'singing that which is forbidden' can now effect social change. The 'call to war' (what was interpreted as the 'jihad') at the end of the psalm, against Babylonian domination, becomes the revolutionary call for liberation and justice, turning the mockery of African slaves entertaining American audiences by song and dance into their own act of defiance. The song is for 'King Alpha'— Haile Selassie, and the chorus inserted after verse 2 makes it a freedom song quite unlike any other.

> By the rivers of Babylon,
> Where we sat down,
> There we wept
> When we remembered Zion.
>
> Cause, the wicked carried us away in captivity,
> Required from us a song.
> How can we sing King Alpha's song
> In a strange land?
>
> Sing it aloud, ah, ah, ah
> Sing the song of freedom, sister, ah, ah, ah
> We gonna sing and shout it, ah, ah, ah …

There are several notable variants of this version, some using different lyrics as well. One adaptation was performed by the Melodians in 1969.[885] Another was used by Don McLean in his *American Pie*, immortalised in the folk club scene in the television series *Mad Men*.[886] One of the most iconic performances—and again different, albeit also familiar—is by Boney M.[887] More recently the Jewish protest singer Matisyahu, combining Jewish ideas with reggae, rock and hip-hop, also produced two versions. 'Jerusalem if I forget you' (2006), with its memorable lyrics about 'milk and honey' and 'ovens and gas', is the slower more haunting version.[888] Sinead O'Connor produced a more wistful version on her album 'Theology' (2007).[889]

Psalm 137 has repeatedly been used at times of national crisis. Andrew Mein writes of it receiving particular attention during the First World War.[890]

---

[885] https://www.youtube.com/watch?v=9BOa-tLeS3o.

[886] Stowe 2016: 48. See https://www.youtube.com/watch?v=JsqSNIR5DsU.

[887] See https://www.youtube.com/watch?v=2FgDles4xq8.

[888] https://www.youtube.com/watch?v=UVBzMQvCslU.

[889] https://www.youtube.com/watch?v=xncY5WP12BQ.

[890] Mein 2019: 163–85.

One approach denouncing the violence in the psalm, despite an atmosphere of demands for reprisals after the sequence of air raids on London in 1917, is seen in the decision of the Convocation of Canterbury which (controversially) concluded that verses such as 137:7–9 should no longer be sung in Christian worship. Theologians such as Alfred Bertholet, Old Testament Professor at Göttingen, expressed similar concerns at using the words of the psalm to justify extreme violence, although Bertholet was more disposed to acknowledge the relevance of this psalm in times of war. Isidor Hirsch, in his *Die Kriegspsalmen und die jüdische Volkseele* (1916) argued that the vitriol at the end of Psalm 137—which admittedly he saw as atypical in the psalms in its disproportionate view of violence—was in effect an appeal to God's justice. So, given the symbiotic relationship between war and religion during the First World War, the psalm was not without its relevance.

After the Second World it was used more frequently to address the misery of suffering. Karl Plank recalls Claude Lanzmann's film *Shoah* where the film opens with Simon Srebnik singing, as he walks along the Narew River, parts of Psalm 137. This anticipates the time of Srebnik's captivity when he too is forced to sing to amuse his captors: 'he sang, but his heart wept'. Much of Plank's article is on the paradox of singing what should not be sung, both in the Babylonian exile and during the Holocaust, where so often Jews had also to sing and dance to amuse their captors.[891] Rodney Sadler interprets the last three verses as an *actual* defiant song, subversively sung and intending to denigrate the captors (in Hebrew, which they would not understand): this would explain some of the subtle word play in these last verses. The ethos is therefore: 'You want a song of Zion? I'll *give* you a song of Zion!'.[892] Abraham Cohen's observation enables us at least to identify with the pain of those denied land, freedom and justice: '... if we think of him [the psalmist] as an exile recently back from Babylon, viewing with horror the havoc wrought in the city he dearly loved ...Refugees from Europe, when they returned and saw how their native cities had been turned into masses of rubble by the Germans, surely shared this mood'.[893]

Psalm 137 is about profound loss, when all that is left is to hand everything over to the justice of God. It is therefore not only appropriate for national crises but also for individuals coming to terms with trauma and grief: some of the greatest composers have used this psalm in this way, from the sixteenth-century Giovanni Pierluigi da *Palestrina, who composed 'Super flumina Babylonis'

---

[891] See Plank 2008: 180–84; also Stowe 2016: 152–57.
[892] See Sadler 2014: 456.
[893] See Cohen 1992: 447.

upon the death of his wife in Rome in 1580; to Antonin *Dvořák*'s version in his *Biblical Songs* (1894), at a time of grief over deaths of musical friends and the critical illness of his father; to the British composer Herbert *Howells, who in 1917 composed (but never published) a version of Psalm 137 at the time of severe ill-health and the death of a close friend in the war.[894]

This commentary on 137 has been written during lockdown from COVID-19. We know all about being unable to sing together, for that very act will increase the infection. Our instruments have been kept at home or locked up in synagogues and churches. We have tried to 'sing that which could not be sung' through creative technology, with each soloist in isolation creating the chorus in a digital space. In our impotence we have become acutely aware of the mockery of an invisible enemy which we might still name 'Babel', or confusion, because we can neither fully understand nor control it, and it threatens simultaneously our individual and global wellbeing. Perhaps in the light of this we might better understand the curse at the end of the psalm. Coronavirus has taken thousands of lives: we long for it to be annihilated, both it and its future mutations: we long for it all to be crushed to the ground. And as the psalm takes us through mourning to nostalgia to sheer anger, we can only sing in our isolation a united protest to God.

---

[894] See https://www.youtube.com/watch?v=HNBU-W0UmUU (Palestrina) and https://www.youtube.com/watch?v=ltbi8–Ds0E (Dorak) and https://www.youtube.com/watch?v=8XFWYiqMCLM (Howells).

Psalms 138–145: A Final Davidic Psalter

The placing of this last Davidic collection after Psalm 137 suggests a means of reaffirming the Kingship of God and obedient faith, using Davidic laments as examples of piety.[895] Psalms 138 and 145, both containing praise and thanksgiving, create an *inclusio* in this collection, with 138 implicitly recognising God as King (over the gods [verse 1] and over the kings of the earth [verse 4]) and 145 explicitly praising God as King over all space and time. The four psalms of lament (140–143) form a small collection with their shared theme of God's care for the poor and a retributive morality. Psalms 139 (a prayer in four parts) and 144 (an anthology) are more difficult to assess in terms of genre, although they share the themes of the four laments. In terms of the first stage of reception, the editors recognised some cohesive theme in uniting together these psalms each with a Davidic superscription.

This recognition, however, was not in the minds of those who received these psalms at *Qumran. The key scroll is 11QPs^a. The order (some psalms being in a more complete form than others) is as follows: firstly, Psalm 145:1–7, 13. X,[896] 14–21, X, on cols. XVI–XVII, which comes after a *catena* of verses from 118 and before 154; next is 139:8–24, on cols. XIX–XX, after 154 but before 137; next is 138:1–8, on cols XX–XXI after 137 and before Sirach 51; next is

---

[895] See Ho 2019: 249, citing Van Grol 2010: 336.
[896] Where 'X' is a hitherto unknown verse.

Psalms Through the Centuries: A Reception History Commentary on Psalms 73–151, Volume Three, First Edition. Susan Gillingham.
© 2022 John Wiley & Sons Ltd. Published 2022 by John Wiley & Sons Ltd.

141:5–10, on cols XXII–XXIII, after 93 and before 133; next is 144:1–7, on cols. XXIII–XXIV, after 133 and before 155; next is 142:4–8 and 143:1–8 on cols XXIV–XXV, 142 following 155 and 143 before 149; and finally 140:1–5 on cols. XXVI–XXVII, after David's Last Words (using parts of 2 Sam 23:1–7) and followed by 134. No scholar has yet found a convincing answer for this radical rearrangement.[897]

Psalm 138: In Praise of God before Gods, Kings and Angels

In terms of the psalm's associations with earlier psalms, the verbs *y-d-h* (thank) and *z-m-r* (sing), found in 136:1–3 and 135:3 respectively, are also used in 138:1. Psalm 138 has no explicit polemic against the gods, as in 135:15–18, and also holds a generous view of other kings compared with 136:17–18, for in 138:4 the kings are invited to praise God. The greatest difficulty is linking this psalm with 137, other than in the references to 'singing' in 137:3 and 138:1. It could be that 138 serves as the song of praise which was forbidden in 137, where instead of offering curses against the nation's enemies the kings of the earth are invited to join in God's praise (verse 4). Hossfeld terms the psalm 'a responsory counterpoint to Psalm 137'.[898]

The psalm begins and ends with reference to God's steadfast love (verses 2 and 8). The first three verses form a personal thanksgiving, whilst verses 4–6 have a more universal vision, intentionally using the name Yahweh four times. Verses 7–8 take up again a more personal note of confidence in God delivering the psalmist from his enemies. This might explain the additional heading to the Lucianic text of the Greek 'of Zechariah': it reads the psalm as about personal faith beset with foreign powers.

In terms of later reception history, the first two verses are most significant in that they act as a gateway to the way the rest of the psalm is understood. The most contentious is a phrase in verse 1, translated in the NRSV as 'before the gods' (*neged elohim*). The *LXX and *Jerome's *Gallican Psalter* translate the Hebrew word 'gods' as 'angels': 'I give you thanks, O Lord... before the angels I will sing to you.'[899] Much depends on whether one assumes the psalmist is acknowledging the existence of other deities (as in Pss. 82:1, 86:8 and 96:4), which suggests an exile away from the Temple, but in his commit-

---

[897] See Flint 1997: 361–2 for an outline of the arrangement of psalms in Books Four and Five in 11QPS[a].

[898] Hossfeld and Zenger 2005: 532.

[899] Jerome's Hebrew Psalter preserves 'before the gods'.

ment to Yahweh he bows down in its direction (see 1 Kgs 8:48; Dan. 6:11 [in Aramaic]; and Jonah 2:5, 8). Another assumption might be that the psalmist is in the Jerusalem Temple precincts, but in this case the phrase 'before the gods' is somewhat strange. The well-preserved text in 11QPs[a] has the vocative appeal to Yahweh that is absent in the *Masoretic Text. The text then continues 'before Yahweh Elohim I will sing to you' (*neged yhwh elohim azammereka*) which makes very clear how *elohim* should be read here.[900] Furthermore, the placing of 138 *after* 137 (despite the very different placing of other psalms which we noted above) suggests that at *Qumran this was seen to be a psalm also coming from the exile.

Jewish commentators preferred to read this phrase as 'before the judges' (**Targum*)[901] or 'in the presence of princes' (*Rashi),[902] reading the Hebrew 'gods' in verse 1 to refer to human leaders, especially in the light of the more universal connotations in verse 4. The Davidic heading encouraged a future Messianic interpretation with political connotations: 'The psalm captures the triumphant spirit that will pervade the Jewish nation at the advent of the Messiah.'[903]

Christian commentators have preferred the *LXX and *Vulgate versions: 'before the angels I sing your praise': this is the reading used by *Hilary[904] and Jerome's *Gallican Psalter*.[905] *Augustine writes: 'My song is joy, but my joy in things below is before men, my joy in things above before the Angels … God dwelleth in the Angels … Therefore … that very assembly of Angels is the Temple of God…'[906] *Chrysostom also observes: 'I shall do all in my power to sing in the company of angels, and shall strive to compete with them and join the powers on high in choir.'[907] *Cassiodorus argues that this is proof that angels not only hear but also attend to the song.[908] *Bede similarly urges: 'It is no surprise that angels are frequently present, invisibly, at the side of the elect, in order to defend them from the snares of the cunning enemy and uphold them by the great gift of heavenly desire.'[909]

*Calvin's reading corresponds with *Midrash Tehillim. 'Before kings' anticipates verse 4, which acknowledges the kings of the earth praising God.[910] Psalm

---

[900] The scribe has placed dots above and below the letters of YHWH here possibly to indicate that this is a scribal addition.
[901] Stec 2004: 232.
[902] Gruber 2004: 730–31.
[903] Feuer 2004: 1627.
[904] De Solms 2001: 639.
[905] Jerome trans. Ewald 1963: Homily 49, 361–2. Jerome's Iuxta Hebraicum reads *deorum* (gods).
[906] Augustine trans. Uyl 2017: 650.
[907] Chrysostom trans. Hill 1998: 246.
[908] Cassiodorus trans. Walsh 1991b: 367.
[909] Wesselschmidt 2007: 381, citing Bede's Homilies on the Gospels 2.10 (CS 111:91–92).
[910] Calvin trans. Beveridge 1979: 347–8; also Selderhuis (ed.) 2018: 199.

138 (as well as the Song of Simeon, or the *Nunc Dimittis*, in Luke 2:25–38, which like Ps. 138:4–5 sees God as the one who cares for all peoples) was used in the 1542 Geneva liturgy, and in the 1545 Strasbourg liturgy the psalm was sung as a thanksgiving ('before kings') during the distribution of the elements.[911]

Verse 2, also providing a gateway to the rest of the psalm, is another contentious verse in its reception, because of the different views on how to read 'I bow down to your holy temple and give thanks to your name'. Predictably (following the emphases we have seen in the Ascents) the Jewish reading is to see this about the literal Temple in Jerusalem, with a promise implied therefore that God's name will again be glorified in its future rebuilding (verse 8: 'Do not forsake the work of your hands').[912] *Sforno argued that verse 8 was also about Gog and Magog at the end of time, after which battle the Temple would be rebuilt and the Messiah would come.[913]

Christians often understood verse 2 as about the heavenly Temple, linking this with the praise of 'the angels' in verse 1: Jerome and Augustine make this point. Cassiodorus, by contrast, following *Hilary, sees this as about 'Christ, the blessed incarnation which Christians worship every day', so the references to the 'name' and the 'word' in verse 2 are to Christ.[914] Calvin's more typically pastoral concern is to interpret the 'holy temple' as referring to the body of believers, because the temple and its ceremonies were abolished by Christ's coming: the 'holy temple' is about those who worship God in spirit and in truth.[915] *Luther sees the temple as a reference to Christ's kingdom, where the powerful are to care for the vulnerable.[916]

These differences illustrate overall that there are two approaches to this psalm: to see the thanksgiving as concerned with matters spiritual and theological, or to see it as having a practical and political bias. This is borne out in Christian art. Byzantine Psalters predictably focus on the kings giving praise to God. The *Barberini Psalter* (fol. 229v) illustrates the psalm through verse 4: against the marginal inscription 'kings of the earth' two kings raise their hands to an icon inscribed IC XC ('Jesus Christ, Conqueror') which is of Christ with a crossed *nimbus holding a book. The *Theodore Psalter* (fol. 176v) has an almost identical image, with Christ raising his right hand in blessing.[917] Several Latin Psalters depict instead a heavenly Temple with the psalmist praising Christ along with the angels. In the *Utrecht Psalter* (fol. 77v) Christ is sitting in a globe-*mandorla flanked by eight angels. The psalmist is receiving God's

---

[911] Witvliet 1997: 287–9.
[912] Braude trans. 1959: 1629.
[913] Braude trans., 1959: 1631.
[914] Cassiodorus trans. Walsh 1991b: 367; on Hilary, see De Solms 2001: 640.
[915] Calvin trans. Beveridge 1979: 348.
[916] Selderhuis 2018: 347.
[917] See http://www.bl.uk/manuscripts/Viewer.aspx?ref=add_ms_19352_f176v.

blessing whilst the demons below attempt to threaten him with spears and bat-tle-axes.[918] The *St. Albans Psalter* has a nimbed psalmist pointing to the cap-tion 'I shall sing praises to you in the sight of the angels'. He gestures to two angels, praising Christ with their hands raised: Christ gives his blessing to all.[919]

Musical arrangements, especially those using the Latin, are about angelic praise: Sebastian de Vivanco's *In conspectu angelorum* is a case in point, as also Orlando *di Lasso's version: both use only the first verses of this psalm.[920] In *Mendelssohn's ora-torio *Elijah*, after the prophet's conflict with Jezebel, Ps. 138:7 (about God's protec-tion of the psalmist from his enemies) is used along with 121:4 in the *SATB chorus of angel voices.[921] By contrast Arthur Honneger's composition *Les Trois Psaumes* (1940–41) takes Psalm 138 (as well as 34 and 140) from the Huguenot Psalter, using the texts of Clément *Marot and Théodore de Bèze: its Calvinist associations mean that the reading concerns kings and princes giving tribute to God.[922]

To conclude, the following poem by Edward Clark is a recent and com-pelling version of this psalm combining many of the themes in its reception history.[923] The first two verses ask questions of 138:4: why do so few kings of the earth in effect praise God and who rules our future today? The last verse cites, part in doubt, part in faith, 138:1. Here 'Jack-by-the-hedge' (the name for Hedge Garlic) is a composite figure of Jack and the Beanstalk, and of Jacob and his Ladder. Jacob's dream is of ascending and descending angels (Gen. 28:10–17), and when he awakes, he realises (like David) that this place is 'the house of God … the gate of heaven'. The gods are also silently present through the figure of the giant in the fairy tale. So, in this poem kings, angels and gods all bear witness to David's efforts to give God due praise.

Psalm 138: The Song of the Frog[924]

Of David

The future is immense,

Some time ago, a poet said,

And David prophesied once,

'All kings of the earth shall praise thee, God.'

Where are these kings today? Art thou in space?

Who or what has taken thy face?

---

[918] See http://psalter.library.uu.nl/page?p=161&res=1&x=0&y=0.

[919] See https://www.albani-psalter.de/stalbanspsalter/english/commentary/page351.shtml.

[920] See https://www.cpdl.org/wiki/index.php/In_conspectu_angelorum_(Sebastian_de_Vivanco) and https://www.cpdl.org/wiki/index.php/Confitebor_tibi_Domine_a8_(Orlando_di_Lasso).

[921] Dowling Long and Sawyer 2015: 75. See also pp. 268–69 (Psalm 121).

[922] See https://www.youtube.com/watch?v=jVAB03eLea8.

[923] See Clarke 2020: 144. Notes provided through email correspondence with Edward Clarke 22–30 June 2020.

[924] A reference to *Perek Shira* where the 'Song of the Frog' is 'Blessed be the name of the glory of His Kingdom forever and ever' – the same words which Moses hears the angels sing on his ascent

I thought that there must be
Some kind of answer in the tale
Of David silenced by
The frog a Sea-beast swallows whole,
Whose song surpasses his. I write it out
And have, like God in man, no doubt.

'I will praise thee with my
Whole heart', with lines that burst through cracks
Along my days. I cry
As pungently by night. Like Jack-
By-the-hedge or ancient herbs in railway cuttings
Thy lines decultivate in my muttering.

Psalm 139: Knowing and Being Known by God

A key word throughout the psalm is the Hebrew verb *y-d-'* ('to know') recurring in verses 1, 2, 4, 6, 14 and 23. Apart from verse 14 God is always the subject of this verb. A key issue in the psalm's reception history is an emphasis on God's omniscience and omnipresence in the creation of the individual, and this has been complicated by the variant readings in translation, particularly in the Greek versions and the *Targums*. Some of these have influenced the commentary tradition as well as doctrinal and ethical discourse: verse 16 ('Your eyes beheld my unformed substance. In your book were written all the days that were formed for me...') is a key verse in this respect.

The first stage of reception—placing this psalm after 138—reveals several links between the two psalms. God is both transcendent and universal (138:4 and 139:7–12), and he 'knows' both the proud and the psalmist 'from afar' (138:6 and 139:2, both using *y-d-'* [know] and *r-ch-q* [far]). His 'right hand' delivers (138:7) and holds us fast (139:10). He deserves our thanks and praise (138:1–2, 139:14, in each case using the root *y-d-h*). Each psalm ends with reflecting on God's care into perpetuity (138:8 and 139:24, both using *'olam*).

The order is quite different, however, in 11QPs[a] at *Qumran. Psalm 139 is followed by 137 and 138 and is preceded by the sectarian prayer 'Plea for Deliverance'.

---

to heaven, and the same song which David, too proud of his own voice, is told that even the frog can sing better than he can. See Feuer 2004: xlviii–xlix. Clarke is making the point that singing in humility (138:6) is what pleases God: angels and frogs, and even the kings of the earth, can set us an example in this.

In part a plea for forgiveness, this non-biblical psalm has similar themes to both Psalms 139 and 51, about God's personal care in creation with plea to be given a spirit of 'truth and knowledge', and so it is not out of place here.[925]

Psalm 139 has three clear strophes, with verse 1 ('you have searched me and known me') having correspondences with verse 23 ('test me and know my thoughts'). Verses 1–6 focus on God's omniscience, and verses 7–12, on God's omnipresence. These have a high incidence of binary contrasts, such as 'sitting down' and 'rising up' (verse 2), walking (on a 'path') and 'lying down' (verse 3), being contained 'behind' and 'before' (verse 5), 'ascending' and 'descending' (verse 8), 'heaven' and *'Sheol'* (verse 8), 'darkness' and 'light' (verse 11), and 'night' and 'day' (verse 12).[926] Verses 13–18 praise for his formation of life before birth. Verses 19–22 create a stark contrast in the expressions of hatred for God's enemies, and verses 22–24 form a final short strophe, echoing the start of the psalm.

The *LXX* is one example of the different ways to vocalise and thus punctuate the Hebrew text. The resulting translation emphasises the temporal nature of God's knowledge: verses 4 and 5 are re-divided to read 'You Lord have known all things, the *first and the last*. You have fashioned me and laid your hand upon me' instead of, as in the *Masoretic Text, 'You Lord have known all things. You hem me in, behind and before and lay your hand upon me'. This links to the difficult verse 16 with its similar use of the verb *plasso* ('fashion' in verse 5) to describe the 'forming' of our days which are written in the book of life.

If the tone of the Greek is overall more positive, the *Targum* has a different emphasis.[927] One example is in verses 2 and 17, where the Aramaic (and Jewish commentators such as *Rashi) read the noun *re'a* ('thought') as 'friendship'. The NRSV reads verses 2b as 'you discern my thoughts from far away') but the *Targum* translation is 'you understand my friendship in your assembly from a distant people'.[928] The *Targum* also suggests a more oppressive view of God's knowledge, however, as in the book of Job. So verses 2 and 3 read: '...But now when I walk in the way and when I lie down to occupy myself with the Law you have become a stranger'.[929] Verse 5 reads: 'You press me in behind and before, and

---

[925] See Abegg et al. 1999: 573. This is verse 15.
[926] Many of these word-pairs provided ideal material for the Christian reading of the 'two natures' of Christ in this psalm, for example, 'ascending' and 'descending' (verse 8), as will be seen later.
[927] Stec 2004: 232–34.
[928] Rashi reads this as 'you make me a companion from afar' and verse 17 (in the NRSV 'How weighty to me are your thoughts, O God!') he reads as 'how precious to me are your friends'. See Gruber 2004: 732–37.
[929] Reading z-r-h (scatter, winnow) as z-w-r ('be a stranger'). Kimḥi's translation views this as not from the point of time but of space: maintaining the verb 'scatter' (citing Ezek. 12:4) he states: 'the psalmist means to say: in this respect thou hast arranged... my affairs...thou hast spread them abroad for me in every direction...' (taken from Baker and Nicholson 1973: 91).

let loose upon me the stroke of your hand.' Verse 7 ('Where can I go from your spirit?') has also more negative connotations: it reads 'Where shall I go from before your raging?' The Hebrew word *ruach* is thus read not as 'Spirit' but as 'wind', and here as a raging storm of wind. Verse 11 is not about the confidence in God's knowledge, but about the fear of darkness and of not being known: 'Surely the darkness *obscures me* and the night is *dark* for me'. (The NRSV, by contrast, translates the Hebrew *velaylah 'or ba'adeni* more positively: 'the night is *light* around me'.[930]) A final telling translation is of the contentious word *golem* in verse 16 (a word which occurs nowhere else in the Bible, known as a *hapax legomenon*). Whereas the Greek recreates the idea of 'formlessness', the *Targum* reads 'Your eyes saw my body (*goshmi*) and in your book of remembrance all my days were written in the days when the world was created at the beginning...' Here one is reminded of the 'formless void' (Gen. 1:2) at the beginning of all creation rather than the 'formless embryo' at the beginning of each human life.[931]

These examples are important, because a good deal has hinged upon the interpretation of these verses in later reception. In *Midrash Tehillim* the author of Psalm 139 is seen as Adam, once 'formless' and then 'fashioned' from clay and dust (139:16). The 'book' in verse 16 is the outline of human history etched in the flesh and bone of Adam, father of all mankind, referred to in Gen 5:1 as the 'descendants of Adam'.[932] So Adam revealed to David in this psalm the lessons of Eden—the enigma between man's free will and the divine plan, where there is no escape from God and yet one seeks to be free.[933] The reference in verse 11 'night will be light for me' is about Adam's creation on the sixth day: light was preserved through that night and so continued into the Sabbath day. Adam's creation lasted twelve hours: he was taken from the dust, kneaded into form, given limbs, given a soul, made to stand on his feet, and named the animals; in the seventh hour Eve was created, the eighth hour was their procreation, the ninth, the command not to eat from the fruit of the tree, the tenth, their sin, the eleventh, God's pronouncement of judgement, and the twelfth hour was their expulsion from Eden.[934] All this takes place in one day—before God's Sabbath rest.

---

[930] Kimḥi helpfully notes that this is about God's ability to see through the darkness and night which he also created, so that the all-seeing God can perceive the psalmist by night as well as by day. See Baker and Nicholson 1973: 95.

[931] Kimḥi understands *golmi* as akin to a piece of rough-hewn wood (Golem) before it is carpentered into some form. He reads 'day by day they are formed', as even though to God this is as one day, it is to human life many days. Kimḥi reads the difficult Hebrew, translated as 'not one of them', in the corrected form: he argues that God who has created them all in an instant ('one day') can perceive them all before they come into full existence. See Baker and Nicholson 1973: 99.

[932] Braude 1959: 1633.

[933] Braude 1959: 1634.

[934] Braude 1959: 1641–2.

This could not be more different from a Christian reading of this psalm, which centres not on Adam, but on Christ: the psalm is seen to witness especially to his two natures. For *Origen, Psalm 139 was about the invisible and eternal nature of the Godhead and his intimate dealings with humanity, now understood in Jesus Christ as the Word made flesh.[935] *Hilary of Poitiers wrote at length on this psalm: verses 13–16 speak of Christ's conception and incarnation; verse 8 ('If I ascend to heaven... if I make my bed in Sheol') refers to his divine and human nature; verses 17–18 speak of his resurrection (citing the Latin *exsurrexi* in verse 18) and verses 9–10 refer to his ascension, where Christ sits at the right hand of God.[936] Much of Hilary's writings were carefully worked out in the context of *Arian heresies about the nature of Christ, using Psalm 139 to speak of Christ as God before his Incarnation, of God and man in the Incarnation, and of Christ transformed by his Exaltation.[937]

*Augustine affirms the Trinity in this Psalm, defending, against Arianism, the co-equal natures of the Trinity, especially in verses 7–12.[938] He uses his typical *prosopological approach to defend the two natures of Christ in the psalm: so verses 1–2 are the voice of Christ the Head, speaking in intimacy to his Father, whilst verses 3–4 are the voice of Christ the Body, referring to his time on earth. Verses 7–9 concern Christ's death and resurrection (his 'downsitting' and his 'uprising'); and, following Hilary, verses 13–16 are about his incarnation, and 17–18, his resurrection.

*Cassiodorus reads the title 'unto the end' as confirmation that the psalm is about Jesus Christ, although in his view the whole psalm is about Christ the Head: the Church does not speak at all.[939] So the first section is Jesus Christ recounting to his Father his forthcoming death and descent to hell and his resurrection, knowing all his thoughts are already known to the Father. In the second section Jesus expounds the Father's power of divinity and speaks of himself sheltering in the womb of his mother (Cassiodorus has in mind here *Nestorian heresies).[940] Following Augustine, he reads verse 7 ('Where can I go from your spirit?') as about the Trinity.[941] The third section is Jesus speaking of his role as a servant praising his Father and preaching, and in the fourth section

---

[935] Origen, *Against Celsus* Chapter VII.42.
[936] See Wesselschmidt 2007: 646, citing *Tractatus super psalmum CXXXVIII, 22 (CSEL 22*: pp. 745–47*);* also De Solms 2001: 463–4.
[937] See Rondeau 1985: 329–333, especially p. 331, citing Hilary (*CSEL* pp. 757–8.). See also Rigolot 2017: 130–68, especially pp. 132–134, 138–9.
[938] See Wesselschmidt 2007: 387, citing Augustine, *On the Trinity* 2.5–7 FC 45:59; also De Solms 2001: 643–44, and 646–7 (where Augustine cites Hilary). See also Waltke et al. 2014: 522–4.
[939] Cassiodorus trans. Walsh 1991b: 371.
[940] Cassiodorus trans. Walsh 1991b: 378.
[941] Cassiodorus trans. Walsh 1991b: 375.

he bids all the wicked to depart from him, for they are beyond being saved by humble repentance.[942] This is the eighth, and last, of the psalms Cassiodorus believed demonstrated the two natures of Christ (the others are 2, 8, 21, 72, 82, 108 and 110)[943] but in this psalm above all others we see most clearly how he is both perfect man and perfect God.[944]

In the early Middle Ages *Gilbert of Poitiers also uses the different views of both Augustine and Cassiodorus now in the *Gloss.[945] His commentary on verse 18 follows Hilary: the Hebrew *heqitsoti* could mean 'I awake' but the Greek *exēgerthēn* is also used of the resurrection, in for example 1 Cor. 6:14, and the Latin *exsurrexi* has similar connotations. So Gilbert reads verse 18b as 'I rose and am with you still'. Gilbert follows Cassiodorus in the main, albeit in a briefer form. The ongoing commentary tradition concerning the two natures of Christ in this psalm continued into Peter *Lombard's work on the same psalm.[946]

This is not to deny that other writers took a more pastoral[947] and mystical[948] view. Moving forwards, *Luther surprisingly neither wrote nor lectured much on this psalm; but John *Calvin did, because for him this psalm gave vital insights into what it means to 'know' God who 'knows' and 'sees' us in all we do. This is not so much a Christological commentary as one which wrestles instead with the Augustinian problem of predestination and free will.[949]

Turning to liturgy, the *Ashkenazi tradition uses Psalm 139 in times of sickness. The *Midrash* on Adam and his creation before the sabbath day has resulted in the association of verse 12 ('the night is as bright as the day') being associated with the blessing over the sabbath candle to remember how Adam created light from fire on that first sabbath night.[950]

In the Methodist and Anglican tradition this psalm is one of those prescribed for Christian funerals.[951] Not surprisingly, given the way that the Christian commentary has associated so much of this psalm with the death and resurrection of Jesus, it is also used as part of the Introit on Easter Day: one ancient

---

[942] Cassiodorus trans. Walsh 1991b: 372.

[943] See p. 44 (Psalm 82); p. 174 (Psalm 108); and p. 188 (Psalm 110).

[944] Cassiodorus trans. Walsh 1991b: 384. The same reading is found in pseudo-*Bede: see Neale and Littledale 1874–79: IV/311.

[945] See Gross-Diaz 1996: 138–48.

[946] See Gross Diaz 1996: 147–48.

[947] For example, John *Chrysostom's commentary, with its focus on divine grace and human effort in the practice of virtue: see Chrysostom trans. Hill 1998: 252, 260, 262.

[948] For example, Richard Victor, who sees this psalm is about the contemplative life under the all-seeing God: see Waltke et al. 2014: 528–9.

[949] See Selderhuis 2018: 206; also Calvin trans. Beveridge 1979: 185; also, Waltke *et al.* 2014: 529–31.

[950] Feuer 2004: 1638–39.

[951] Gillingham 2008: 256–57, especially footnote 4.

prayer is 'Glory be to the Father, who knoweth the Son; glory be to the Son, who went down into hell, and ascended up into heaven; glory be to the Holy Ghost, the Spirit of the Lord which filleth the world'.[952] A more recent *antiphon envisages the risen Lord addressing his Father: 'I have risen, I am with you once more, alleluia. O God, you laid your hand upon me, alleluia. How marvellous your wisdom, alleluia!'.[953] The Easter associations also have baptismal connotations: as early as the time of *Cyril of Jerusalem in the fourth-century we read of the Saturday 'holy fire' and candles burning all night, where 139:12 ('… for the night is as bright as day …') is another appropriate antiphon for those catechumens receiving 'enlightenment' at their first baptism.[954]

How can art capture both the ineffability and the intimacy of God expressed in this psalm? Moshe *Berger does so by an illustration of Elijah's chariot of fire, where the 'dazzling light' takes up something of 'God's pervasive presence encompassing the entire globe'.[955] Mostly the focus is on human life—not on Adam, nor on Christ, but on each of us. The *Hamilton Psalter* (fol. 232r) depicts verse 10 of the psalm with a hand of God emerging from rays in an arc of heaven, above a man lying on the personification of hell. The hand of God is also used in the *Stuttgart Psalter* (fol. 153v), where the psalmist views two figures thrown in hell, but here the hand rests on his head (verse 10) giving him the power to pray (verses 11–12).[956]

Another Jewish contemporary image, very different from Berger's, is that of Irwin *Davis, who depicts the presence of God in a three-decker universe: at the bottom is cold and barren 'Sheol' where a deathly figure is lit by the moon and stars (verses 11–12); at the top is a figure taking the wings of the morning and flying over the sea towards the rising sun (verse 9); in the middle is a baby still in its mother's womb, and next to it an adult figure, 'fearfully and wonderfully made'. Other similar images take up a more ethical stance: Amanda Patrick's painting has the words of parts of verses 13–16 written in calligraphy over a coloured quilt, with a black and white image of a foetus dominating the heart of the psalm.[957] We shall return to this interpretation later, but its presentation in this artwork is to show that this is a complex issue.

Many poetic imitations of this psalm, emphasising the theme of an all-knowing God, tend to focus on the rhythm and stress of the words, as if the attempt to escape God's presence is to run as fast as possible in another direction. Per-

---

[952] Neale and Littledale 1874–79: IV/324 and 327.

[953] Daly-Denton 2010: 201–202.

[954] Waltke et al. 2014: 521.

[955] See http://themuseumofpsalms.com/product/psalm-139/.

[956] See https://bit.ly/3IzQ9vb; also Bessette 2005: 243–44, note 6.

[957] See https://fineartamerica.com/featured/psalm-139-amanda-patrick.html?product=poster.

haps the best known is Francis Thompson's 'Hound of Heaven' (1891) which speaks of the inescapable presence of God.[958]

> I fled Him, down the nights and down the days
> I fled Him, down the arches of the years;
> I fled Him, down the labyrinthine ways
>   Of my own mind; and in the mist of tears
> I hid from Him, and under running laughter...

Thomas Stanley's 'Paraphrase upon Part of the CXXXIX Psalm' is another example: its effect is somewhat ponderous, as if escape from God is impossible:[959]

> Great Monarch, whose feared hands the thunder fling,
> And whose quick eyes, all darkness vanquishing,
> Pierce in a moment earth's remotest parts,
> The night of futures, and abyss of hearts;
> My breast, the closest thoughts which there reside,
> From thy all-seeing knowledge cannot hide;...

The Oxford theologian Paul Fiddes argues that Gerard Manley *Hopkins's 'Wreck of the Deutschland' opens with a weaving together of themes from Psalms 18 and 139.[960] The poet considers God's hidden presence throughout the world, as in Ps. 139:7–12, and in the third stanza seeks, like a bird in flight, Christ's presence in the eucharistic bread ('I whirled out wings that spell/And fled with a fling of the heart to the heart of the host'). This brings to mind 138:9 ('If I take the wings of the morning ... even there your hand shall lead me'). Most especially the poet's exclamation 'Thou hast bound bones & veins in me, fastened me flesh' reminds us of 138:13–16 with its praise about God fashioning him in secret. So the first verse, with its sacramental overtones, reads:[961]

> Thou mastering me
> God! giver of breath and bread;
> World's strand, sway of the sea;
> Lord of living and dead;
> Thou hast bound bones and veins in me, fastened me flesh,
> And after it almost unmade, what with dread,
> Thy doing: and dost thou touch me afresh?
> Over again I feel thy finger and find thee.

---

[958] See https://www.youtube.com/watch?v=gToj6SLWz8Q for Richard Burton's reading of this poem.
[959] Atwan and Wieder 1993: 331–32.
[960] Fiddes 2009: 572–73.
[961] Gardner and MacKenzie 1967: 51.

Hymns have a more public performative intention, as versions of Psalm 139 make clear. *Purcell's haunting 'Thou knowest O Lord' (139:1-2) was sung at Queen Mary's funeral in 1695, and then at Purcell's own funeral some six months later. Samuel Sebastian *Wesley's 'Thou wilt keep him in perfect peace' (1850) begins with Isa. 26:3, sung by basses ('the darkness is no darkness with thee'), and then 139:12 ('the darkness and light to thee are both alike'), sung by tenors and altos, ending with words from the Lord's Prayer: it was included in the order of service for coronation of Queen Elizabeth in 1953.[962] *Howells also used Ps. 139:12 in his *Three Psalm Preludes* (Set Two) after the death of his son Michael in 1935: Psalm 139 is the second of the three psalms and exudes quiet reflection in contrast to the cry of despair in 130:1 and the 'loud noise' of 33:3. Composed out of private grief, this is now performed in concert halls.[963] The popularity of this psalm in Calvinist and Lutheran liturgies is found in arrangements by Claude *Goudimel (for the *Genevan Psalter*), by Heinrich *Schütz (in the *Becker Psalter*), by J. S. *Bach's cantata on the final verses, and by the lengthy composition by Ernst Pepping (1901–1981).[964]

An extraordinary feature of this psalm is the way that the *hapax legomenon* 'Golem', in verse 16, has created such a vast amount of reception history, especially in Jewish tradition. Just as Adam was an inanimate substance given form from the dust of the earth, so 'Golem' is a creature given form—usually, like Adam, from mud and clay—by human hands, and then brought to life, using various magical incantations, to be controlled by their maker. Parts of the *Book of Creation* (*Sefer Yetzirah*) in the Middle Ages refer to 'forming' of different Golems. The Golem was a popular feature in sixteenth-century Polish folktales from Chelm and Prague, where his creation became a mixed blessing: initially servile—one particular feature was the ability to protect the Jewish community from anti-Semitic attacks—he also had a capacity for enormous destruction directed even to the Jewish people (hence echoes of Adam here). This trope is found in a vast amount of literature and film.[965] One example of the latter is Paul Wegener's *Der Golem. Wie er in die Welt kam*, a macabre silent horror film

---

[962] Dowling Long and Sawyer 2015: 241.

[963] Dowling Long and Sawyer 2015: 242.

[964] See Oeming and Vette 2016: 224–5 (on Psalm 139). For both personal and public examples of the arrangement of this psalm see https://www2.cpdl.org/wiki/index.php/Psalm_139.

[965] The hubris theme is found in, for example, *Frankenstein, The Sorcerer's Apprentice, The Terminator*, and even in children's literature such as *The Gingerbread Man* (see M. Ginsburg, *Clay Boy*, New York: Greenwillow 1997). Chaim Potok's novels, for example *In the Beginning*, also feature the Golem in young David's fears and dreams.

from Berlin, 1920.[966] In the Jewish Ghetto of sixteenth-century Prague, Rabbi Löw creates a 'Golem'; this huge clay figure is animated by the spirit Astaroth and performs acts of heroism in defending the Jewish people against the Holy Roman Emperor. When the rabbi's assistant tries to manipulate the Golem for his own ends it becomes a force of destruction, rampaging throughout the entire ghetto. Löw reverses the spell and the Golem dies, although the film ends with it being carried back to the ghetto in some triumph: the Star of David is the final still. The 'Golem trope' ultimately asks questions about our own potential to be manipulated in ways which transgress the Maker's intentions.

This ties in, finally, with other ways in which modern discourse has adapted 139:16. On the one hand, pro-life activists have used this verse as a means of illustrating God's protection of our 'unfinished form' in the womb: we are 'fearfully and wonderfully made' from conception onwards.[967] On the other hand, LGBTQ + communities read this verse and indeed much of Psalm 139 in a very different way: 'You know my lying down and rising up … I am fearfully and wonderfully made' is about God's knowledge and acceptance of us, from conception onwards: the psalm is about God's acceptance and embrace.

Reception history exposes the multivalent readings in texts, and Psalm 139 is an excellent example of it. The 'knowledge' which the psalmist speaks of here is multi-dimensional: it is about knowing with both the mind and the heart.

Mary *Sidney's poem deserves the last word, in part because of her uniquely female account of the role of the mother in giving life in verses 13–16:[968]

> Each inmost piece in me is thine:
>   While yet I in my mother dwelt,
>   All that me clad
>   From thee I had.
>   Thou in my frame hast strangely dealt;
>   Needs in my praise thy works must shine
>   So inly them my thought have felt.

---

[966] This has been restored digitally on DVD and Blu-ray by Masters of the Cinema (UK) and Kino Lorber (US) in 2019 and 2020 respectively. See https://www.youtube.com/watch?v=FSTH0lGYqJ0.

[967] The Southern Baptist Convention has termed its funding initiatives for ultrasounds in pregnancy the 'Psalm 139 project'.

[968] See Hamlin 2004a: 128–31, citing lines 43–63 of the poem. The extract is from Hamlin, Brennan, Hannay and Kinnamon 2009: 267–70, here, 269.

Thou, how my back was beam-wise laid,
  And raft'ring of my ribs dost know:
    Know'st ev'ry point
    Of bone and joint
  How to this whole these parts did grow,
In brave embroid'ry fair arrayed,
  Though wrought in shop both dark and low.

Nay, fashionless, ere form I took,
  Thy all and more beholding eye
    My shapeless shape
    Could not escape:
  All these, with times appointed by,
Ere one had being, in the book
  Of thy foresight enrolled did lie.[969]

Psalm 140: Poisoned Tongues

Psalms 140–143 form a unity in that they are all personal prayers for deliverance against enemies. The word *selah only comes four times in Books Four to Five (occurring some sixty-eight times in Books One to Three) and three of the four are in 140:3, 5 and 8 (4, 6 and 9 in the Hebrew); the other is in 143:6.[970] The references in Psalm 140 to the 'poisoned tongue' have affinities with Pss. 52:2, 4, 64:8 and 120:2, 3. Furthermore, Ps. 52:4 and 6 (vv. 5 and 7 in Hebrew) also have *selah* corresponding to those of Ps. 140. The 'pause' for reflection makes sense in Psalm 140 which cries out against the effects of a malevolent curse: the third occurrence of *selah* in verse 8 (Heb. v. 9) is followed by similar curses thrown back to the enemy, suggesting some evil plot (verse 8; Heb. v. 9) as a context for the psalm, which now needs reversing by a similar malediction.

In terms of its association with other psalms, the lexeme *pach* ('bird trap') in 140:5 (Heb. v. 6) is also found in 141:9 and 142:3 (Heb. v. 4). In this psalm it links to the 'evil plot' of 140:8 (Heb. v. 9) brought about by the 'evil-doers' (verse 1, Heb. v. 2). The language of the curse against the enemies in verses 9–13 (Heb. vv. 10–14) has links with the curse at the end of Psalm 139: the 'wicked' (139:19; 140:8 [Heb. 140:9]) are violent in deed as well as in word (139:19–20; 140:1–3, 11 [Heb. 140:2–4, 12]).

---

[969] The 'book' (139:16; see also Ps. 56:8) is a motif also found in the Qur'an: 'With Him are the keys of the Unseen; none knows them but He…Not a grain in the earth's shadows, not a thing, fresh or withered, but it is in a Book Manifest' (Q. 6:59).
[970] Hossfeld and Zenger 2005: 549–50.

In 11QPsᵃ at *Qumran, the first verses of Psalm 140 follow a short fragment of 'David's Last Words' (2 Sam 23:1-7), included to emphasise the Davidic character of this Psalter, and a psalm recounting 'David's Compositions', again ratifying Davidic authorship and the prophetic nature of 11QPsᵃ. Psalm 140, with its Davidic heading, might serve the same purpose: it occurs at the end of 11QPsᵃ followed by Psalm 134, with its emphasis on blessing from Zion and then 151 (another Davidic psalm not in the MT summarising his life work). Psalm 140, with its fearful tenor until the last two verses, undoubtedly had an interesting early history of reception.

This tenor has resulted in its being associated with the conquering of all evil. The 'day of battle' in verse 7 (Heb. v. 8) is interpreted in later Jewish tradition as the time of the war of Gog and Magog, when the 'poor and needy (verse 12, Heb. v. 13) who are the dispersed of Israel will be vindicated.[971]

In Christian tradition this 'day of battle' is read in two ways: firstly, it is the voice of Christ during his passion.[972] *Hilary sees the ungodly traitor as Judas, 'the man of tongue' as in Psalm 109.[973] The wicked evildoers are the soldiers and the priests.[974] Secondly, it is the voice of the church under persecution. *Augustine, in a sermon addressed to an assembly of bishops, reads the psalm as the Church, set in the midst of the wicked, pouring out her heart to God.[975] *Cassiodorus also reads this as the Holy Church entreating the Lord to free her from the wicked devil who undermines the devotions of the faithful.[976] Earlier, *Athanasius suggests that the wicked are demons, who attack especially the monks at prayer, placing stumbling blocks in the way of their progress.[977]

The psalm has made little impact in liturgy: it is one of the psalms whose words of cursing (verses 9-11, Hebrew vv. 10-12), like those in 139:19-22, are often omitted from Christian recitation of the psalms. There is little of consequence in Christian art, although the *Stuttgart Psalter* (fol. 155r) has two vivid images of two evildoers running to plot the downfall of the psalmist, who as he turns to God in prayer is surrounded by their ropes attempting to bind him and trip him up: these illustrate verses 4 and 5.[978]

---

[971] Feuer 2004: 1647, with reference especially to *Sforno.

[972] Neale and Littledale 1874–79: IV/328.

[973] See pp. 178–80.

[974] 1874–79: IV/ 331, 333 and 336. See also Rondeau 1985: 348–53, where this is seen as the voice of Christ representing the sufferings of all humanity; De Solms 2001: 654 notes that the church fathers identified Psalms 140–143 all as references to the attacks on Christ during his passion.

[975] Augustine trans. Uyl. 2017: 658.

[976] Cassiodorus trans. Walsh 1991b: 386. The words of the workers of evil are now identified as the words of the many heretical groups in his day (p. 388).

[977] See Wesselschmidt 2007: 391, citing Athanasius, *Life of St. Anthony* 23:1–6 in CS 202:111,113.

[978] See https://bit.ly/3IzLeuo.

The most interesting aspect of the reception of this psalm concerns a spider. Verse 3 (Heb. v. 4: 'They make their tongue sharp as a snake's, and under their lips is the venom of vipers') creates a memorable double image of poison on the tongues of the evildoers. The MT uses *nachash* ('snake') and *'akshub* (viper). The Greek also uses the same parallelism (*ofis* and *aspis*); and when this verse is cited from the **LXX* by Paul in Rom. 3:13c, in his description of human depravity, this is also about 'the venom of vipers… under their lips'. The Latin preserves the same parallelism: *acuerunt linguam suam sicut <u>serpentis</u> venenum <u>aspidum</u> sub labiis eorum*. Qumran, however, reads the Hebrew *akshub* (viper) as a spider (*akkabish*): the evildoers have a *spider's* poison beneath their lips. **Rashi* also takes the verse in this way, using Isa. 59:5 and Job 8:14, and noting that the root *b-b-sh* ('conquer') is like a spider in its web. The **Targum* also reads 'the venom of a spider is under their lips'.

Why is this interesting? Because in Ps. 39:10 we noted how the Greek and Latin translated the Hebrew word for 'moth' as spider, weaving its net of destruction, and how the *Stuttgart Psalter* depicted a spider wasting itself away in its own web of destruction;[979] in Ps. 57:3 we noted how the legend of the spider weaving its web across a cave resulted in a **midrash* on this verse;[980] furthermore in 90:9 we read how the Greek and Latin replaced 'our years come to an end *like a sigh*' as '*like a spider*', resulting in an illustration again in the *Stuttgart Psalter* depicting the psalmist watching a spider spin its web.[981] All other examples concern the spider's web, rather than its poisonous tongue, although its ability to destroy is also evident in Psalm 39. It is difficult to know why this tradition emerged: but in the context of entrapment and fear which the psalm evokes, the image of the spider is fitting. To date no illustration has been found.

Eugene Peterson's contemporary version of these verses makes the same point but in a more striking way:[982]

> Yahweh, get me out of there, away from this evil;
> Protect me from these vicious people…
> They practice the sharp rhetoric of hate and hurt,
> *Speak venomous words that maim and kill…*

---

[979] See Gillingham 2018: 238–39 (Ps. 39:9).
[980] See Gillingham 2018: 333 (Ps. 57:3).
[981] See p. 84 (Ps. 90:9)
[982] Peterson 1994: 188.

Psalm 141: Guarding the Tongue. An Evening Prayer.[983]

The most obvious association between Psalms 141 and 140 is the fear of the destructive power of speech, although here the psalmist asks for a watch to be set over his own lips (verse 3). There are several verbal parallels: again, the awareness of the trap (*pach*) which has been set for the psalmist in 140:5 (Heb. v. 6) and 141:9; the plea for protection (root *n-ts-r*) in 140:1, 4 (Heb. vv. 2, 5) and 141:3; and the prayer for God to 'guard' (root *sh-m-r*) the psalmist in 140:4 (Heb. v. 5) and 141:3, 9. There is the emphasis on lips (140:3, 9 [Heb. 140: 4,10] and 141:3) on hands (140:4 [Heb. 140:5] and 141:2)—in 140, those of the enemy; in 141, those of the psalmist. Psalm 140 ends with a reference to God's face, or presence (*paneyka*, your presence) in 140:13 (Heb. v. 14) and 141 begins with a similar vocabulary (*lepaneyka*, verse 2). Finally, there is a similar contrast between the 'wicked' in 140:4, 8 (Heb. 140:5, 9) and 141:4, 10 and the 'righteous' in 140:13 (Heb. 140:14) and 141:5.

One of the puzzles in the early reception history of this psalm is why it is found in 11QPs[a] between Psalms 93 (a psalm about God's Kingship) and 133 (a psalm praying for the unity of the worshipping community). It is argued that perhaps the reference to the anointing of oil on the head (affirmed by Aaron in 133:2, and, in one reading of the Hebrew, refused by the psalmist in 141:5) might be one connection but it is difficult to find any obvious reason for this arrangement at *Qumran.

Verse 5, with its reference to the righteous striking the psalmist is difficult to ascertain, and not least the reference to 'Never let the oil of the wicked anoint my head' (NRSV) which requires reading the first Hebrew word for 'head' (*ro'sh*) as 'the wicked' (*rasha'*). In the context of the 'evildoers' and 'wicked' in verses 9 and 10, it could be about refusing to be enticed by those who work magic spells. The fact this psalm has been found in the early Christian catacombs as an evening prayer for warding off evil might support this reading.[984] In later Christian reception *Jerome read this as about avoiding heretics who (metaphorically) attempted to anoint the heads of men with balm.[985]

Most of the psalm's reception is based on verse 2: 'Let my prayer be counted as incense before you, and the lifting up of my hands as an evening sacrifice'. This raises questions about whether the psalmist is speaking at or away from the Temple, and so whether prayer is *instead of* incense, and the raising of hands is *instead of* sacrifice. In Jewish tradition, because the setting is seen to be David fleeing from Saul, far from Jerusalem and perhaps even driven out by Absalom,

---

[983]For the equivalent prescribed 'morning prayer', see the commentary on Psalm 63 in Gillingham 2018: 349–52.

[984] Prothero 1903: 11–12.

[985] Jerome trans. Ewald: 1963, Homily 51, 370.

it is understood that prayer is instead of incense (although a good deal is never-theless made of the importance of incense in crushing arrogance and slander).[986] The Fathers also made much of this being about personal piety in antithesis to ritual, arguing that Christ accepts our prayers *as* 'sweet incense', using 1 Tim. 2:1 as evidence.[987] Similarly the reference to the lifting of hands was seen to be Christ as the new sacrifice with his hands outstretched on the cross, dying at the ninth hour before the evening of the Sabbath.[988] Writers such as John *Cas-sian understood that the 'lifting of hands' here in the context of sacrifice was either a reference to the Last Supper (Matt. 26:26–29) or to Christ at the end of time raising his hands for the salvation of the whole world.[989] *Chrysostom argues that this was spoken at a time when the Temple was standing in all its glory, yet the psalmist preferred prayer and the lifting of hands: so how much more should those who worship without a Temple approach God in this way?[990] *Augustine understood that this was about Christians raising their hands when they recognise the sacrifice of Christ on the cross.[991] There is little suggestion that incense and sacrifice are a requirement: prayer and the lifting up of hands are sufficient in pleasing God.

By the middle of the third-century *Eusebius of Caesarea refers to the reg-ular use of Psalm 141 at evening prayer, whilst John Chrysostom, in his com-mentary on Psalm 141 affirms 63 as a regular psalm at morning prayer and 141 at evening prayer.[992] Similarly, by about 380 CE, the *Apostolic Constitutions* affirm the same use of both psalms. By about 420 CE John Cassian's *Institutes* concur that Psalms 63 and 119 are to be used in the monastic tradition at the sunrise service, whilst Psalm 141 is an evening psalm. *Ambrose of Milan, in *Hexameron V* 12:36, also affirms this.[993] This shows how just one verse in a psalm gives can give rise to a regular liturgical use in both eastern and western Christendom. The association of darkness and the threat of evil would have also affirmed its use, as is made clear in Egeria's observations of *Vespers in Je-rusalem, from which Taft has reconstructed the basic structure beginning with the lighting of lamps, then a hymn of light, and then Psalm 141—offered with incensation—followed by an evening collect.[994]

---

[986] See Feuer 2004: 1655–56. The Hebrew word *qetoret* is read as an acrostic of the Hebrew words for holiness, purity, mercy and hope, and because smell was the only one of the five senses Adam did not use when he took the fruit, so the nose was seen as the least sullied organ.

[987] Neale and Littledale 1874–79: IV/338.

[988] Neale and Littledale 1874–79: IV/324, citing Augustine, *Cassiodorus and Bellarmine.

[989] See Wesselschmidt 2007: 394–95, citing the use of verse 2 by John Cassian, *Institutes* 3.3.8–10, ACW 58:62.

[990] Chrysostom trans. Hill 1998: 279–80.

[991] See Wesselschmidt 2007: 394, citing Augustine, *Sermon* 342.1 *WSA* 3 10:34.

[992] See Gillingham 2008: 40.

[993] See Gillingham 2008: 40.

[994] See Taft 1986: 42–45.

Early artistic representations of this psalm use the trope of people (probably sinners) falling into a net held by two winged demons: in the Byzantine tradition the *Hamilton Psalter* (fol. 235v) depicts this with just one man held in the net, whilst in the *Barberini Psalter* (fol. 234v), the *Khludov Psalter* (fol. 140r) and the *Theodore Psalter* (fol. 180v) there are two figures.[995] The earlier Latin *Utrecht Psalter* (fol. 79r) also depicts two demons tying up a large net in which several people have been caught.[996] The *Stuttgart Psalter* has two illustrations: the first (fol. 155v), of David playing the *cithara*, sitting on a throne between two horses is inexplicable, as David nowhere *sings* in the psalm and the *cithara* (an instrument like a harp) is usually an instrument for praise, which this psalm lacks. The second illustration (fol. 156r) however, is again of the net with figures inside, tied up by two demons.[997] The *St. Albans Psalter* has a different image: Jesus leans out from heaven to place a curb on the lips of the psalmist, who in one hand is actually holding a censer wafting his prayers to heaven.[998]

Despite its liturgical setting, musical arrangements of this psalm are surprisingly few. A number of evening hymns use the imagery of incense and calling out to God found in this psalm. The Scottish Psalter is one such example, where the sense of verse 2 is somewhat contorted to create rhythm and rhyme:[999]

> As incense let my prayer be
> Directed in thine eyes;
> And the uplifting of my hands
> as th' ev'ning sacrifice.

This contrasts with the more reflective version by Thomas *Merton, who begins and ends his poem with the same image, and so avoids finishing with image of the net capturing sinners in the last verses:[1000]

> Lord, receive my prayer
> Sweet as incense smoke
> Rising from my heart
> Full of care
> I life up my hands
> In evening sacrifice
> Lord, receive my prayer....

---

[995] For *Theodore*, see http://www.bl.uk/manuscripts/Viewer.aspx?ref=add_ms_19352_f180v.

[996] See https://psalter.library.uu.nl/page/165.

[997] See https://bit.ly/3dBy8i0; also https://bit.ly/3y9v8Tq.

[998] https://www.albani-psalter.de/stalbanspsalter/english/commentary/page357.shtml.

[999] https://hymnary.org/browse/scripture/Psalms/141.

[1000] Atwan and Wieder 1993: 334–35.

And receive my prayer
Sweet as incense smoke
Rising from my heart
Free of care.

In a psalm which is so preoccupied with the power of words, perhaps the image by *Benn (1974) summarises Merton's poem and indeed Psalm 141 as well as any (Figure 15).

1974

Psaume 141-2

Que ma prière soit à tes yeux comme de l'encens,
mes mains tendues comme l'offrande du soir.

FIGURE 15   R. B. Benn 'Let my prayer be set forth before thee as incense; and the lifting up of my hands as the evening offering' (Ps 141:1-2).

Source: Benn, R. B. 1970. *Les Psaumes*. Lyon: Musee des Beaux-Arts.

Psalm 142: Prayer for Deliverance. Another Evening Prayer

It is ironic that a psalm with the most expansive title in this Davidic collection should have a somewhat meagre reception history. 142 is entitled a *maskil* (for use in teaching?); also a *tefillah* (prayer); and it has the first biographical comment since Psalm 63, making a specific connection with David 'when he was in the cave'.

A theme which links this psalm to the two before it is its confidence that God protects those who are oppressed and in need: the Hebrew word *pach* ('trap') common to 140:5 (Heb. v. 6) and 141:9 is also found in 142:3 (Heb. v. 4). The Psalmist takes refuge in God in 141:8, whilst God is a refuge in 142:5 (Heb. v. 6); he cries with his 'voice' to the Lord in 141:1 and 142:1, and sees himself in the company of the 'righteous' in 141:5 and 142:7 (Heb. v. 8). Again, we note the early reception in the intentional placing of the psalm in this collection.

As with most other psalms in the Davidic collection, it nevertheless has a different placing in 11QPs^a at *Qumran. Only verses 4–8 (Eng. vv. 3–7) are extant; the psalm follows 155, perhaps because of the common theme of a prayer for deliverance. 142 is in fact followed by 143 as in the MT, perhaps for the same reason.

In Jewish commentary tradition the same theme of praying for deliverance is evident: verse 2 (Heb. v. 3: 'I pour out my complaint before him…') is to be cited as a preface before the recitation of the *Eighteen Benedictions of the *'Amidah.[1001]

In Christian tradition the prayer for deliverance is linked to the sufferings of Christ or the Church. *Hilary of Poitiers, for example, sees verses 7–8 as a prophecy about the Passion of Christ,[1002] whilst *Augustine reads verse 5 ('you are my portion in the land of the living…') as a spiritual promise of the Christian's inheritance of heaven after a life of suffering.[1003] *Cassiodorus reads this first as David's prayer, hidden in a cave, in danger of Saul taking his life, which then becomes Christ's prayer, made in the flesh, before his passion: in the first part of the psalm Jesus cries to his Father recounting his persecution by the Jews, and in the second part he prays to be delivered from the prison of hell knowing that the trust of the faithful hung on his resurrection (verse 7).[1004] Cassiodorus reads verse 6 as words from the cross, whereby Jesus commends his spirit to God and tells the thief he will soon be with him in Paradise.[1005]

[1001] *B.Avodah Tsarah* 7b, citing R. Eliezer. See Markus 2016: 290b.

[1002] De Solms 2001: 658.

[1003] Wesselschmidt 2007: 400, citing Augustine, *Sermon* 4.13 *WSA* 3 1:193.

[1004] Cassiodorus trans. Walsh 1991b: 399–400. This interpretation is also used by pseudo-*Bede: see Neale and Littledale (1874–79): IV/349 and 351.

[1005] Cassiodorus trans. Walsh 1991b: 402.

Again, the prayer for deliverance makes this an appropriate prayer in evening liturgy in the eastern churches. Psalms 141, 142, 119:105–112, and 117 are part of a fixed evening psalmody in the East Syrian (Assyrian) Church, and 141/142 are in the Evening Office in the Byzantine and Armenian traditions.[1006] In Western Christendom the psalm is associated with Evening Prayer, partly because of its close proximity to Psalm 141, and in the liturgies of Maundy Thursday and Good Friday in the Roman Catholic tradition, with the *antiphon taken from verse 5.[1007]

Byzantine Psalters take up the image of the cave of Adullam, where the inference is that this is in fact Christ 'in prison' at the time of his Passion. This is found in the *Hamilton Psalter* (fol. 235v), the *Khludov Psalter* (fol. 140r), the *Pantocrator Psalter* (fol. 195v), the *Barberini Psalter* (fol. 235r, where a hand of God appears from heaven), and the *Theodore Psalter* (fol. 180v, also with the hand of God emerging from a starred arc of heaven).[1008] In the *Utrecht Psalter* (fol. 79v), and also the *Harley Psalter* (fol. 72v) and the *Eadwine Psalter* (fol. 250v), it is the psalmist who is kneeling within a prison, raising his right hand to the *Christ-Logos, standing on a hill attended by three angels and four righteous men. He points to the trap two men are spreading for him at the bottom of the steps of the prison, whilst an angel points out to the Christ-Logos the urgency of the psalmist's situation.[1009]

Two more recent images offer a social comment about the more general state of poverty. Arthur *Wragg's black and white cartoon depicts a figure hunched in an overcoat next to a bin, sheltering under a possible railway arch. Ironically the caption is from verse 5, which speaks of the Lord as the psalmist's refuge and portion in the land of the living (Figure 16).[1010]

Charles Knowles' image, completed in 1957, is a woodcut in black and brown paper, where a skeletal David stands with bent head within the stylised walls of a cave: there are allusions here to the experience of the Holocaust.[1011]

Howard *Goodall arranged this psalm for a choral-orchestral work, *Invictus: A Passion* (2018). This is a contemporary 'passion narrative' illustrating how the sufferings of Christ mirror all our human suffering, particularly the sufferings of women. Psalm 142 is in the Fourth Movement, 'Compassion', which is about a Polish nurse, Irena Sendler, who saved the lives of some two and a half thousand children in the

---

[1006] Spinks 2004: 210.
[1007] Holladay 1993: 221. The sequence follows various antiphons from Psalm 116,120, 140, 141, followed by the Magnificat and Psalms 51 and 22.
[1008] See http://www.bl.uk/manuscripts/Viewer.aspx?ref=add_ms_19352_f180v.
[1009] See https://psalter.library.uu.nl/page/166.
[1010] See Wragg 1934: no page numbers.
[1011] The woodcut is kept at the National Gallery of Art, Washington DC.

FIGURE 16   Arthur Wragg, 'I cried unto thee, O Lord: I said, Thou art my refuge and my portion in the land of the living' (Ps. 142:5).

Source: Wragg, A. 1934: *The Psalms for Modern Life*. New York: Claude Kendall.

Warsaw ghetto. The psalm is preceded by excerpts from Lamentations, and the text is from the *Psalterium *Gallicanum*: the association with Christ's sufferings is in the ending, which uses the antiphon '*Ubi Caritas*' for Maundy Thursday.[1012]

The fragile condition of the psalmist has communicated to countless individuals over the centuries. It is said that St. Francis of Assisi died with the words of Psalm 142 on his lips.[1013] The eighteenth-century collection of Psalm Collects has as its heading for 142 'A Prayer in all Sadness, and in the hour of Death'. The Collect begins, 'O Lord God, thou art our hope, and our portion in the land of

[1012] See http://www.howardgoodall.co.uk/works/choral-music/invictus-a-passion; also https://bit.ly/31GKa7w.
[1013] Prothero 1903: 92.

the living; consider our complaint and misery...' It ends '... assist us with the strength of thy grace, that our temptations and our enemies not being above our strength derived from thee, our souls may with confidence go out of prison, and give thanks unto the Name in the companies of the righteous.'[1014]

Psalm 143: God's Righteousness and Human Unrighteousness

This is the last psalm of a group of four psalms (140–143) whose subject is the triangle of relationships between the enemies, God, and the psalmist, although the lexeme *pach* ('bird trap') is absent here, with the focus as much about a spiritual deliverance as a physical one. That this is a late psalm is evident from its quotations of words from, for example, Psalms 18, 25, 69, 77, 86 and 119.[1015] Its earliest reception history shows that nevertheless it has been intentionally included into this collection: it has links with Psalm 142 in the reference to the fainting spirit (142:3 [Heb. v. 4]) and 143:4, each using the hitpael verb *hit'attaf* (to faint, grow weak) with *ruchi* (my spirit). The 'pursuing' enemy is found in 142:6 (Heb. v. 7) and 143:3 (both using the verb *r-d-f*). The word *nafshi* ('my soul') is found in 143:3, 6, 8, 11 and 12 and 142:4 and 7 (Heb. vv. 5 and 8); this is also found in 138:3; 139:14; 141:8 (that is, in every psalm from 138 to 143 except 140). The importance of praising and honouring God's *Name* explicit in 142:7 (Heb. v. 8) is also found in 143:11. 'Save me (*hatstsileni* using the *hiphil* imperative) from my persecutors' in 142:6 (Heb. v. 7) becomes 'Save me (also *hatstsileni*) from my enemies' in 143:9. That the *LXX* saw a link between these two psalms is evident in its additional historical heading: 'when the son pursued him', perhaps also connecting this with Ps. 3:1, when David is also said to be fleeing from Absalom.

Like Psalm 140, the use of *selah* at the end of verse 6 divides the psalm into two clear strophes; verses 1 and 7, in their pleas for God to hear, are similar, as also the plea for God to act in 'righteousness' towards the psalmist in verses 1–2 and 11–12. It is this theme—divine, not human, righteousness—which has characterised much of the psalm's Christian reception history, focussed especially on verse 2 ('Do not enter into judgement with your servant, for no one living is righteous before you'). This is expressed primarily by the Apostle Paul, *Augustine, and *Luther, as we shall shortly see. The same theme probably resulted in it being assigned as the seventh *penitential psalm: it has little to say about actual penitence, but a good deal to offer about God making us righteous.

[1014] Vaughan 1702: 286–87.
[1015] Hossfeld and Zenger 2005: 572–76, especially 577.

The main point of interest in early Jewish reception is why verses 1–8, found in 11QPS^a, follow a sequence of prayers for deliverance (144, 155, 142) and why the next psalm is 149, a Hallel psalm: only 149:7–9 is extant in this scroll, about God's vindication of the righteous by binding kings in chains. This sequence has some intrinsic consistency, concerning deliverance. The Jewish commentary tradition does not associate this psalm with repentance. It is more concerned about the original setting from its heading, discussing whether this is about David still trapped in the cave by Saul (so, *Kimḥi), or whether it is about David's flight from Absalom and the potential destruction of his kingdom (*Sforno).[1016] There is less detailed discussion about the theme of 'God's righteousness' in the psalm than in the Christian tradition.

When we turn to the New Testament—noting that there has been no New Testament reception in this Davidic collection up to this point—it is verse 2, referred to earlier, which is key. It is cited in Rom. 3:20 (adapting the Greek 'no human being will be justified in his sight') and Gal 2:16 ('no one will be justified by the works of the law'). This defends the Pauline doctrine of justification by faith, not works. In Romans 3 the 'righteousness of God' is contrasted with the failed 'righteousness of all humanity' (Jew, Gentile or pagan) and in Galatians 2 it is about the difference which faith in Jesus Christ, as the expression of the righteousness of God, makes to human failure. Interestingly in Psalm 143 God's righteousness both condemns the psalmist (v. 2b) as well as being the hope for his salvation ('answer me in your righteousness' [v. 1] and 'in your righteousness bring my soul out of trouble' [v. 11]). Ps. 143:2 is an important verse in the formation of the Christian doctrine of grace. As Hays concludes: 'Paul's proclamation presents the righteousness of God not as some unheard-of soteriological novelty but as the manifestation of a truth attested by Scripture from the first'.[1017]

Augustine does not only use 143:2; he views it within the psalm as a whole. He notes that this is a prophetic psalm, announcing Christ before his incarnation, and foretells his sufferings. Jesus is persecuted by Judas (v. 3), as David was by Saul; hence David becomes a type of the sufferings of Christ.[1018] The psalm also announces that Christ's sufferings bring about justification for sinners (v. 2). Verse 11 is important to Augustine: this might be summarised as 'For thy name's sake, O Lord, *Thou shalt quicken me in your righteousness*', which Augustine claims tells us that God's righteousness is not about what we deserve but *what God gives us*.[1019] The argument takes place in the midst of the *Pelagian heresies, and perhaps for this reason Augustine has less to say about Psalm 143 as the seventh penitential psalm and more about its significance as a prophecy of what Christ in God has done

---

[1016] Feuer 2004: 1670.
[1017] Hays 1989: 53; also, 1980: 107–115.
[1018] Augustine trans. Uyl 2017: 668–69.
[1019] Augustine trans., 2017: 670.

for us and will continue to do. *Jerome also emphasised verse 2: 'no one living shall be justified': it means that our salvation depends entirely on the work of God.[1020]

John *Chrysostom also never explicitly attests this as a penitential psalm, although he does emphasise the importance of confession within verse 2.[1021] Because of the links with Psalms 141 and 142, he sees this as a morning psalm as well. It is *Cassiodorus, at the end of his commentary on this psalm, who, building upon the number seven, really develops the view that this is the seventh penitential psalm, arguing that the enemy is not only Judas (as Christ's enemy, taking a prophetic interpretation here) but also, our sins.[1022] Like other penitential psalms this begins in hardship and ends with hope and even joy, where Christ speaks as the Body of the Church.[1023]

But because Jesus himself could not plead penitence and forgiveness there is also a tendency to read this as the Voice of Christ to God the Father during his Passion, and at the same time to see it as a prophecy about Christ foreshadowed by David. This is certainly the position taken by pseudo-Thomas and pseudo-*Bede, the latter who sees the reference to the 'I stretch out my hands to you' (v. 6) as about Jesus on the cross and the plea 'Answer me quickly, O Lord; my spirit fails' (v. 7) as Jesus' dying prayer.[1024]

A penitential reading was re-emphasised in the late medieval period. Not surprisingly it is particularly evident in those seeking to revive monastic spirituality. Denys the Carthusian, writing in the fifteenth-century, is a typical example, focussing on David as the author of the psalm and a model of true repentance and faith, as in his prayer he moves from despair to hope.[1025]

The Reformers also used this psalm to demonstrate the state of universal unrighteousness from verse 2, and from this the primacy of grace over works (verse 11).[1026] Luther's discussion in his *Penitential Psalms* follows a predictable trajectory: this is also where his teaching on 'the faithful synagogue' is clearly seen.[1027] Originally Luther read this, along with Augustine, as the voice of Christ the Body appealing to God's righteousness; but later he re-read this as a prophetic prayer of the 'faithful synagogue', waiting for the forgiveness of God and his Messiah. The two readings are not mutually exclusive, but to speak of the faithful synagogue means that the earliest level of actual meaning is found in

---

[1020] Wesselschmidt 2007: 401, citing Jerome, *Against the Pelagians* 1.15 FC 53:253.
[1021] Chrysostom trans. Hill 1998: 308.
[1022] Cassiodorus trans. Walsh 1991b: 406.
[1023] Cassiodorus trans. Walsh 1991b: 412–413.
[1024] Neale and Littledale 1874–79: IV/357, 358–60, 362–63.
[1025] Waltke et al. 2014: 261–63.
[1026] Selderhuis 2018: 366.
[1027] 2018: 366, citing Luther, *Penitential Psalms* LW 14:196 (WA 18:522).

the centuries before Christ and hence (unusually for Luther) enhances the status of the Jews before God—a meaning Paul also sought to provide in Romans 3.[1028]

*Calvin's take on this psalm is to read it, as usual, through the life of David, but with an interesting criticism of the way that the Papists read this psalm, far from following the humble example of David, who five times in the psalm cast himself wholly on God's mercy. The Papists invented a 'third way', partly dependent on their own works, and partly dependent upon God's mercy.[1029] For this reason, perhaps, he does not refer to Psalm 143 as a penitential psalm of the Catholic Church.

Nevertheless, because it was the seventh such psalm, 143 played an important part in Christian liturgy. In the Medieval Church all seven psalms were recited after *Lauds on Fridays during Lent and also on Good Friday, as well as at *Compline at the Commemoration of All the Faithful Dead. For catechetical purposes they were each associated with the seven deadly sins, and Psalm 143 was against sloth. In the *BCP Psalm 143 is appointed as a *Proper Psalm, with 130 and 102, at Evensong on Ash Wednesday. It was also used until 1603 with the other six in the Coronation service.[1030]

The popularity of the penitential psalms in Medieval Books of Hours resulted in a proliferation of illustrations in these works. In *Les Très Riches Heures du Duc de Berry* (fol. 74v) we see a typical image of David praying as a penitent before a covered altar behind which are statuettes.[1031] On the opposite page (fol.75r) is an extraordinary miniature by Jean Colombe of a bloodstained 'Jesus the Man of Sorrows', before whom the patron and his wife kneel, completing the theme of penitence maintained through the previous seven psalms.[1032]

Several musical arrangements of this psalm are from compositions of all seven penitential psalms and have been discussed previously. Orlando *de Lassus' *Psalmi Davidis Poenitentiales* was performed in Rome 1563; Psalm 143 was composed in the seventh (mixolydian) mode, with Psalms 148 and 150 added to create the eighth mode, thus giving the collection a wide range of emotional expression.[1033] In *Mozart's *Davide Penitente*, written for a Lenten

[1028] Preuss 1967: 153–56, 1969: 172–75; also German 2017: 183–85. For Luther and the 'faithful synagogue' in other psalms, see p. 271 (on Psalm 122).

[1029] Calvin trans. Beveridge 1979: 248–51, 258.

[1030] Jeffrey 2008: 596.

[1031] Longnon and Cazelles 1969: 74 and 200.

[1032] Longnon and Cazelles 1969: 75 and 200.

[1033] https://www.hyperion-records.co.uk/dc.asp?dc=D_CDD22056; also Dowling Long and Sawyer 2015: 191.

concert in 1785, the last movement, which is of this psalm, is a joyful cadenza for soloists.[1034]

By contrast, metrical psalmody, with its setting in the reformed tradition, offers a good deal about God's righteousness (here, 'justice') but, following the lines of the psalm, rarely is there a specific prayer of penitence. Isaac *Watts' version is a typical example. The following is a paraphrase of verses 2–3:[1035]

> Let judgment not against me pass;
> Behold, thy servant pleads thy grace:
> Should justice call us to thy bar,
> No man alive is guiltless there.
>
> Look down in pity, Lord, and see
> The mighty woes that burden me;
> Down to the dust my life is brought,
> Like one long buried and forgot.

Ironically this version is more akin to Jewish readings, in seeing Psalm 143 as another psalm of deliverance following on from 140–142. There is little specific about repentance here. It is only when Psalm 143 is viewed within the collection of seven penitential psalms, taken from different places in the Psalter, that the penitential aspect is foremost, but this reading is very different to what might be expected from its setting in and within Psalms 138–145. The reception of this psalm is thus multi-dimensional, dependent not only upon the syntax of the psalm itself, but the theological and literary context from which phrases such as 'the righteousness of God' are read. Perhaps *Benn's simple but evocative image yet again captures the essence of the psalm. It is of verse 6: 'I stretch out my hands to you; my soul thirsts for you like a parched land'. The suppliant, dressed in brown, set against parched grass and a blue sky, offers his hands up to the image of a white dove.[1036] In this case deliverance—spiritual as well as material—is dependent both on the faith of the psalmist and God's *Shekinah* above. Although repentance is implied, Psalm 143, in the context of Psalms 140–143, is essentially about trust and hope.

[1034] The entire collection can be heard, with musical score, at
https://www.youtube.com/watch?v=cWC8oPr1LL4. See also Dowling Long and Sawyer 2015: 59.
[1035] See https://www2.cpdl.org/wiki/index.php/Psalm_143.
[1036] Benn 1940 (no page numbers).

Psalm 144: Of Giants and Unicorns

If Psalm 143 cited a few word phrases from Psalms 18, 25, 69, 77, 86 and 119,[1037] Psalm 144 is really little more than an anthology of other psalms, and so provides a good illustration of reception history within the process of the *composition* of new psalms as well as through its later compilation position within this Davidic collection. We noted how Psalm 108 offered a similar illustration, readapting parts of Psalms 57 and 60 for a new situation.[1038] Psalm 144 provides an even more interesting example, not least in its use of Psalm 18 (which itself is linked to the almost identical 2 Samuel 22), and Psalm 8 (with its distinctive links with Genesis 1). Hence this is a psalm with an interesting earlier compositional reception history—reworking earlier psalms rather than creating citations *verbatim*. It has a fairly rich afterlife as well.

Significant citations include the *baruk tsuri* ('Blessed be my rock') formula in verse 1, very similar to 18:46 and 18:35. Other images of protection (fortress, stronghold, deliverer, shield, refuge) clearly link 144:1–2 with 18:1–3 (Heb. 18:2–4). The theophany account in verses 5–8 again suggests some borrowing from 18:7–19 (Heb. 18:8–20), where verse 5 echoes 18:9, verse 6, 18:14, and verse 7, 18:16. Another link is verse 10 with 18:50 (Heb. 18:51), where king David's archetypal dependency on God for protection is clear in each case. The use of Ps. 8:4 (Heb. 8:5) and 90:5–6 in verses 3–4 ('what are human beings that you regard them?') serves to democratise the royal promises: this is a psalm for blessing on all humans, not only God's people (as in verse 15, with its use of the 'happy' (*ashrei*) formula and content following Ps. 33:12). Now the 'servant David' (verse 10) is a distant memory and the prayer in verses 12–14, rather like Psalms 126–129 in the Ascents, is for fertility, peace and justice for the entire community.

The movement in the psalm from the 'blessedness' of God in verse 1 (using *baruk*) to being 'blessed' by God (using *ashrei*) in the final verse gives the psalm some structure in its movements from praise (verse 1–4) to petition (verses 5–8) and again from praise (verses 9–10) to petition (verses 11, 12–14, 15), with another movement being from 'I' (verses 1–2, 7–8, 9–10) to 'we' (verses 12–14, 15).

The psalm appears at *Qumran in both 11QPs^a (which contains verses 1–7 and 15) and in 11QPs^b (containing only verses 1–2). In 11QPs^a 'Yahweh' is changed to 'Elohim' in verses 3 and 5. In both scrolls 144 follows Psalm 133, perhaps because of the prayer of blessing for all the people. Despite the loss of its Davidic heading in both scrolls, it is followed by a Syriac Psalm, 155, itself

---

[1037] See p. 395 (Psalm 143).
[1038] See pp. 172–73 (Psalm 108).

another prayer for deliverance by 'king David'. These changes are not altogether clear, but again they show alternative processes of compilation in the proto-MT and Qumran Psalters.

Two specific themes emerge from the later reception history of this psalm. One is more political, following the reinterpretation of Psalm 18. Although this is no longer about military warfare Psalm 144 is still about opposition to imperial powers, based on verses 1–2 and 10–11. The other theme concerns the 'new song' (verse 9, also in Pss. 33:3, 40:3, 96:1, 98:1 and 149:1) of hoped-for restoration throughout all creation, from verses 3–4, 12–14 and 15. It will become evident below that these two themes have been reinforced by the additional tropes of Goliath and the Unicorn.

Firstly, the more political reception of Psalm 144 is evident in several ways. The *LXX*, for example, adds the superscription 'against Goliath' and so gives the psalm a greater Davidic emphasis than is found, for example, at Qumran. This might be due to the imagery of the hands and fingers used for warfare in verse 1 (1 Sam. 17:49), the 'sword' in verse 11 (1 Sam. 17:45, 51), and the imagery of deliverance in verses 6–7. Just as King David took on the Philistine 'giants' threatening the people, so now the people will be given the strength to take on imperial 'giants' of their own day.

Early rabbinic tradition makes similar connections, setting the psalm at the beginning of David's reign, either after David's victory over his enemies (so Abraham *ibn Ezra and *Kimḥi) or as seen above, after his defeat of Goliath.[1039] The 'fingers' in verse 1 thus allude to David's picking up five smooth pebbles and his fingers on his sling. The attitude to warfare here is to imitate 'servant David' who thought not about his own victory and reputation, but about giving glory to God. 'In this psalm David expresses the authentic Jewish attitude towards war and warriors ... Glory and fame are not for David, because it is God who grants salvation to kings (v. 10) ... The sword is needed to combat hostile powers, yet it should be deplored. Thus, David desires to compose a new kind of song to God (v. 9), not only about muscle and might ...'[1040] On this account the psalm is often cited in the Saturday evening service as an introduction to the end of Sabbath prayers (*Motsa'ey Shabbos*), being thus the first prayer of a new week and teaching that all our efforts at overcoming the 'enemy' are not about us but about God.

Predictably, in Christian reception the warfare is not so much physical as spiritual. So *Augustine sees verse 1 as about God training us for spiritual warfare in our inner battle with sin, which is about curbing our greed, crushing our pride, stifling our ambition, and slaughtering lust.[1041] *Chrysostom makes

---

[1039] Feuer 2004: 1677, citing *Midrash Tehillim*.
[1040] *Ibid.* 1677, again citing *Midrash Tehillim*.
[1041] Wesselschmidt 2007: 40–6, citing Augustine, *Sermon 9:13* in WSA 3 1:270–71.

a similar point, using the *LXX heading as further evidence of the battle imagery: this time the warfare is also about human effort, which results in a sense of worthlessness, and an awareness of divine mercy.[1042] De Solms, referring back to Chrysostom, argues that a change of mood takes place between Psalms 140–143 and 144: just as Psalm 18 is a prophecy about the victory of Christ over evil, so too Psalm 144 promises us Christ's victory, whereby verse 15 is Christ's prayer after his ascension for all believers.[1043] *Cassiodorus opines that the reference to Goliath in the Greek (and Latin) is a prophecy of Christ's struggle with evil and his victory over death: 'Just as David laid low Goliath by using a rock as the weapon of war, so the power of the devil was overcome by the Rock which is the Lord Jesus Christ'.[1044]

Reformation writers tend to see the warfare imagery and the promise of deliverance in more physical terms. *Calvin makes much of the final verse which he sees as a promise of God's providence when we are surrounded by enemies.[1045] Lancelot Andrewes, preaching during the critical period of the Church of England during the reigns of Elizabeth I and James I, used his 'Sermon on Psalm 144:10' to make particular reference to verses 9–11, where God is seen to save kings from the destroyer: given that both Pharaoh and Nebuchadnezzar acknowledged God, this leads Andrewes to offer prayer for all kings, recognising this can only be done by 'the servant'—the queen or king who is as humble and faithful as David, also taking up the promise 'I will deliver them'.[1046]

This political and military reading is found in illustrated Psalters both in the west and the east. The *Carolingian *Stuttgart Psalter (fol. 158v), using the *Vulgate which also attributes the psalm to the battle between David and Goliath, makes full use of the battle imagery in this psalm, with warriors with swords and shields and David with his stones and sling. The heading reads 'Goliath attacking David and David beheading the dead Goliath'.[1047] The Byzantine *Hamilton Psalter (fol. 237v), following the *LXX heading, shows David slinging at Goliath, holding his sword and shield, surrounded by an army of Philistines. The *Khludov Psalter (fol. 141v) and the *Barberini Psalter (fol. 237r) have a similar scene. The *Bristol Psalter (fol. 231v) adds an inscription

---

[1042] Chrysostom trans. Hill 1998: 332, note 25.

[1043] De Solms 2001: 665 and 666.

[1044] Cassiodorus trans. Walsh 1991b: 413. This is also found in *Ambrose *Exp in Ps* 118.11: see Walsh *ibid.* p.19.

[1045] Calvin trans. Beveridge 1979: 270–71.

[1046] Selderhuis 2018: 373–74, citing Andrewes *Works* 5:239, 249–50.

[1047] See https://bit.ly/3dGy28B.

with David as the 'Personification of Might' and Goliath as the 'Personification of Pride'.[1048] The same theme and inscription is found in the *Theodore Psalter (fol. 182r).[1049]

Musical arrangements also found in this psalm testify to the might of God through his vulnerable servants, opposing the imperial powers of their day. Kurt Weill's arrangement of Franz Werfel's libretto is a case in point: *The Eternal Road* (translated from the German *Der Weg der Verheissung*) was to alert the public to Hitler's persecution of the Jews. The six-hour production was premiered at Manhattan Opera House in 1937, directed by Max Reinhardt with 245 actors and singers on a five-tiered stage. Set in an imagined synagogue with raging pogrom outside, the terrified Jewish community shelters all night, whilst the Rabbi recalls biblical stories of faith and courage from Abraham to Jeremiah. Psalm 144—as a Sabbath psalm—appears in three of the four acts (Patriarchs; Moses; Kings; Prophets). This is 'David's Psalm', set to traditional *Ashkenazi liturgical music. The opera was performed again in Germany, America, Israel and Poland in 1999.[1050]

Dennis Tucker Jr. has written about this psalm several times, arguing that it is about praying for deliverance from oppressive rule. He identifies the phrase 'from the hand of the aliens' (Hebrew: *miyyad beney nekar*) in verses 7 and 11 as an esoteric reference to a threat by imperialist powers, probably Persia, claiming that this is how the phrase is read in other instances (for example Isa. 56:3, 6; 60:10; 61:5; 62:8). It is in poetic parallelism with the phrase 'from many waters', here suggesting the chaotic force of the foreign powers. Psalm 18 is an important point of reference in order to play down the more militaristic overtones (noting for example the absence of 18:37–40, 42 [Heb. vv. 38–41, 43] in Psalm 144). The psalmist is calling on God alone to bow the heavens (144:5) and overturn Persian rule.[1051] Hence it is the fading memory of the Davidic dynasty which is the means of seeing instead the ongoing might of God as King, and the democratised role of the people embodying royal rule in taking up arms against imperial power. In this way Psalm 144 is a subversive text: its use by Kurt Weill in *The Eternal Road*, noted above, is a good example of this in the musical reception of the psalm today.

This first theme of reception is about God's deliverance from oppressive rule. The second theme is about the renewal of creation and the restoration of family and community life (verses 12–14) as a consequence of this act of deliverance. *Rashi emphasises that this also relates to the rhetorical question 'What is man?' in verse 3, noting its *universal* significance. This includes both Esau

---

[1048] http://www.bl.uk/manuscripts/Viewer.aspx?ref=add_ms_40731_f231v.
[1049] http://www.bl.uk/manuscripts/Viewer.aspx?ref=add_ms_19352_f182r.
[1050] Dowling Long and Sawyer 2015: 79.
[1051] Tucker 2014a: 129–135; also 2014b: 188–89.

and Ishmael as representatives of the (Roman) Christian and (Arab) Islamic world.[1052] Both belong to 'Adam', the family of man, which in this psalm are an object of God's concern.

Linked with this is the singing of a new song of deliverance 'upon a ten-stringed harp'. Augustine argues that the ten strings represent the ten commandments, and the song is new because it could not be sung under law, but under grace which is the fulfilling of the law.[1053] *Cassiodorus argues similarly in his difficult anti-Semitic rhetoric that the 'Psaltery' here is the Decalogue, but that the new song is no longer for the Jews but has passed over to the Gentiles: this song introduces the songs of praise (145–150) which follow this psalm.[1054] Pseudo-*Bede notes similarly that Goliath's slaughter puts an end to lament so the Psalter can be completed by praise.[1055]

Just as the giant Goliath featured many times in Byzantine Psalters as a symbol of the might of external imperial power, so too we find several depictions of the Mythical Unicorn as a symbol of the power of inner temptation. If the Goliath trope takes its point of reference from the links with Psalm 18, the Unicorn image is read from verses 3–4 which use Pss. 8:4 and 90:5–6. In the *Kiev Psalter* Archdeacon Spiridon's account of the 'Fable of the Unicorn' is written in a tiny vermilion script along the top margin of the folio to Psalm 144, which is illustrated by a Unicorn in the illustration to the psalm itself.[1056]

The Greek version of this fable has been attributed to one of the fathers of the eastern churches, John of Damascus (675–749), and concerns one of the parables told by St. Barlaam to Ioasaph, a newly converted son of a pagan king. A man tries to escape a unicorn, represented here as a symbol of death, and attempts to climb a tree, an apparent symbol of life, whose branches are laden with honey; betrayed by the seduction of sweetness the man little knows that at the base of the tree, by day and night, a black mouse and white mouse are gnawing at its roots. Soon the tree and the man will fall into the pit of hell which is a gaping hole beneath them. The story has links with Genesis 3 and the seduction of the fruit of the tree (in this case, of knowledge, although the tree of life is also present); here the unicorn's role is similar to that of the serpent. The fable is linked to Ps. 144:3–4, because of its teaching on human fragility and divine permanence. The account of this fable can be seen faintly on the damaged manuscript of the *Theodore Psalter* (fol.182v). In the faded illustration

---

[1052] Gruber 2004: 749.

[1053] Wesselschmidt 2007: 407 citing Augustine's *Sermon* 33.1 in *WSA* 3 2:154. See also Augustine trans. Uyl and Augustine 2017: 672.

[1054] Cassiodorus trans. Walsh 1991b: 418 and 422.

[1055] Neale and Littledale 1874–79: IV/368, citing pseudo-Bede.

[1056] See N. Toranova and E. L. McGuire, *The Kiev Psalter of 1397: An Analysis*, published online 2003 at https://www.medievalists.net/2009/06/the-kiev-psalter-of-1397-an-analysis/.

the unicorn is inscribed, and the pursuit of the man has next to it the words 'Personification of Luxury', whilst the tree is described as 'Personification of Deceit'.[1057] The day mouse and night mouse gnawing under its roots can also be seen, as also the dragon in the pit, which is inscribed 'Personification of Hell'. The *Barberini Psalter* (fol. 237v) is almost identical in this respect.

At first sight it might seem incongruous to find in the reception history of this psalm references both to the threat of imperial powers, represented by the legendary giant Goliath, and to the deceits of personal pleasure, represented by the mythical Unicorn. Both can be brought together in the motif of the 'New Song' which lies in the heart of this psalm. This New Song is about the recognition that God alone gives victory over foreign dominion (verse 10); it is also in praise of God who alone is the source of everlasting life and blessing for his people. Domination, both external and internal, can only be released by singing this 'New Song', itself a medley of many other older songs, and in the case of this psalm this song can be sung not only by Jews and Christians but, as seen in verses 3–4, by all creation.[1058]

Psalm 145: A Song of Praise at the Beginning of the End of the Psalter

Psalm 145 not only has a Davidic heading, but also announces that it is 'A Song of Praise' (Hebrew, *tehillah*). This might have been taken from verse 21 ('My mouth will speak the *praise* of the Lord'), or might have been added later in anticipation of the Hallel collection (Psalms 146–150); nowhere else, however, is *tehillah* used as the actual title for a psalm. This acrostic psalm is also regarded as unique in rabbinic tradition because it contains 150 words and so embodies the 150 Psalms.[1059] Like Psalm 119, also an acrostic, it might once have served as a further final psalm in the emergent Psalter, this time ending not on a note of quiet reflection, like Psalm 119, but of considered praise. It might thus have once completed not only the Davidic Collection of Psalms 138–145, but also the Psalter as a whole. This makes its use of the ancient formula about God being 'gracious and merciful, slow to anger and abounding in steadfast love' most fitting, and is a reminder of the reception of the same phrase in Psalms 86 and 103 as well.[1060] This description of God is not unique to

---

[1057] See http://www.bl.uk/manuscripts/Viewer.aspx?ref=add_ms_19352_f182v.

[1058] There are some interesting associations here with other references to the unicorn, for example in Ps. 22:21, where the psalmist is released from 'the horns of the unicorn' and also performs a song of praise (22:25). See Gillingham 2018:137–38.

[1059] Feuer 2004: 1690.

[1060] See p. 60 (Psalm 86) and p. 138 (Psalm 103).

the Psalms, nor even to the Hebrew Bible as a whole: it occurs in the first phrase of every *Surah* in the Qur'an, save one (*Surah* 9; *al-Tawba*), which also ascribes God as being 'Most Gracious', Most Merciful' (Q. 1:1). This liturgical formula is seminal in both Jewish and Christian liturgy: it is remarkable that it is such an important feature in the Qur'an as well, and that it is found in several psalms.[1061]

Psalm 145 undoubtedly fits with the rest of this Davidic Collection. Like the other psalms it gives honour to the name of God (verses 1, 2 and 21), found also in 138:2; 140:13; 142:7 and 143:11. It is particularly concerned with the kingship of God (for example, verse 1: 'I will extol you, my God and King'; and verse 13 'your kingdom is an everlasting kingdom …'), a theme noted in a different form in 144:10–11 and 138:4.[1062] It develops further the theme of universalism (for example, in verses 8–9, 10–13, 21) expressed in 144:15.[1063] Furthermore, the twofold *ashrei* saying ('*Happy* are the people…') in 144:15 fits well with the twofold *'abarak* formula ('I will *bless* your name…') in 145:1–2. A key change in emphasis is that enemy oppression, exemplified by specific references to 'the wicked' (*rasha'*), found in 139:19; 140:4, 8 and 141:4, 10, is only briefly referred to at the end of the psalm (verse 20: '… all the wicked he will destroy…'). 145 is more a psalm of praise, and hence anticipates Psalms 146–150. Indeed, as we shall see with Psalm 146, several of the themes about God's universal provision have been taken up from this psalm and developed there.[1064]

The most important aspect of the psalm's later reception history is in Jewish liturgy. Its acrostic form and its overall structure have been important as an *aide memoire* in this respect.[1065] Verse 1 (starting with the Hebrew letter Aleph) and verse 21 (ending with the Hebrew letter Taw) stand as **inclusios*, both concerned with the praise of God's name for and ever. It is possible to see verses 2–10 as primarily concerned with the transcendence of God over creation and verses 11–20 with God's immanence within creation.[1066]

Before we attend to the liturgical adaptation of the psalm, it is important to note a somewhat quirky aspect of its reception. This is the various explanations for the loss of the letter 'N' ('nun') between verses 13 and 14, making it in effect an 'incomplete acrostic', rather like Psalms 25, 34 and 37, each with Davidic headings as well.[1067] At **Qumran, 11QPs^a adds a verse starting with 'N': 'God is

---

[1061] I am again grateful to Afifi Al-Akiti for his corrective advice, and his recognition that this is an interesting area for future research on the psalms in the context of Islam.

[1062] See p. 400 (Psalm 144) and p. 372 (Psalm 138).

[1063] See p. 400 (Psalm 144).

[1064] See p. 414 (Psalm 146).

[1065] For different views on the structure of the psalm, see Kimmelmann 1999:32; Magonet 1994:41.

[1066] Hossfeld and Zenger 2005: 594.

[1067] The complete acrostics 111, 112 and 119 do not have Davidic headings.

faithful (the Hebrew here is *neeman*) in his words and gracious in all his deeds'. This is almost identical to verse 17. The **LXX* and the Syriac Psalter also include this verse, but it is absent from Hebrew versions, with the exception of one medieval manuscript, Kennicott MS 142 (a thirteenth-century part-Bible). Rabbinic commentators offer several reasons for this, arguing that the letter 'N' starts the Hebrew word for 'fallen' (*naflah*) which is found in Amos 5:2 ('Fallen, no more to rise, is maiden Israel'). One reading holds that this letter has been omitted to state by implication that Israel will *not* fall (*b.Berakot* 4b).[1068] Others argue that since Israel has fallen, the praise is incomplete. Or this may be to create three strophes of seven verses which give the psalm a mystical reading, amounting to one hundred and fifty words.[1069] Moshe *Berger's illustration of this psalm, depicting the Merkava, or chariot with wheels of fire, with the word 'Shem' (for the name of God) emerging from each wheel, develops this theme, noting: '... When a person comes to recognise that every bit of his energy and vitality are a perpetual gift from the Almighty, he will dedicate his existence to drawing ever closer to his Creator. Such a person, thereby, belongs to the World to Come'.[1070]

The liturgical use of Psalm 145 is first evident at Qumran, where in 11QPs^a a refrain is added after each verse: 'Praised is Yahweh and praised his Name forever and ever'. In 11QPs^a the psalm follows 136, which also has a repeated refrain, so it seems that the *antiphonal elements of both psalms suggest the roles of a cantor and congregation. (Quite why 145 is followed here by Psalm 154, another Syriac psalm not in the Hebrew or Greek Psalters, is less obvious: it might be because of the themes of the grace of God and the rewards for the righteous, important themes in both psalms.) Interestingly the psalm's heading '*tehillah*' ('praise') is now '*tefillah*' ('prayer'). The psalm is given an additional ending ('This is for a memorial') and followed by several Hallelujahs: this might be read in the manner of Ps. 72:20 ('The prayers of David son of Jesse are ended'), thus signifying the end of a particular collection, or it might simply suggest it should be *memorised* on account of its contents, its acrostic format, and its liturgical use.[1071]

In mainstream Judaism the psalm has played a critical part in daily liturgy—not once, but three times. In *b.Berakot* 4b we also read 'Whoever says the *Praise of David* three times a day is assured of being a child of the world to come'. It is used twice in the morning prayer service, firstly after the **'Amidah* (or 'Standing Prayer') which comprises the recitation of the Eighteen Benedictions (the **Shemoneh esreh*,

[1068] Feuer 2004: 1694.

[1069] See Neale and Littledale: IV/ 383, citing Hengstenberg.

[1070] See http://www.biblical-art.com/artwork.asp?id_artwork=15265&showmode=Full.

[1071] On the implication of the use of this psalm in 11QPs^a, see also Kratz 2011, especially on its proximity to 136 (pp. 237–8).

actually numbering nineteen blessings), and secondly in *Pesukei de-Zimra* where the key element is Psalm 145 followed by 146–150. In the *Pesukei de-Zimra*, Psalm 145 is actually preceded by Pss. 84:4 (Hebrew 5) and 144:15, both of which contain an '*ashrei*' saying, reminding the people of their happy state in the 'house of God'. On this account Psalm 145 itself is called 'the Ashrei'. It is followed by Ps. 115:18, with its 'Hallelujah' at the end, and then Psalms 146–150, the Great Hallel. Near the end of the service 'the Ashrei' (preceded again by 84:4 and 144:15), is read a second time. It is also used without being followed by the Hallel, but with Pss. 84:4 and 144:15, at the beginning of the afternoon service.

Verses from 145 are also found in the *Kaddish* and *Shemoneh Esreh*, and the psalm plays a part in preparations for *Yom Kippur*. But why is this psalm so universally known in Jewish worship, unlike any single psalm in Christian liturgy? The *Talmud* (*b.Berakot* 4b, cited above) using the words of R. Eleazar b. Abina, asks the same question. 'What is the reason? Shall I say it is because it has an alphabetical arrangement? Then let him recite, Happy are the upright in the way, which has an eightfold alphabetical arrangement [Ps. 119]. Again, it is because it contains, 'Thou openest Thy hand and satisfiest every living thing with favour'? [145:16]. Then let him recite the great Hallel, where it is written: 'Who givest food to all flesh!' [136:21]. Rather, [the reason is] because it contains both.'[1072] The alphabetic form thus offers us an orderly programme for our lives, giving us a model of comprehensive praise, whilst at the heart of the psalm (verse 16) we learn that all creation is dependent upon God for everything.

Christian liturgical use is less apparent. There have been attempts to read the psalm as a prototype for the Lord's Prayer, with the phrase 'Our Father, who art in heaven, hallowed be your name' being alluded to in verses 1–2, 11–13 and 21; with 'Give us this day our daily bread', in verses 15–16; and 'Forgive us out trespasses …', in verses 8, 14, 18–20.[1073] A more obvious liturgical use, however, is in the petition in verses 15–16. The words 'The eyes of all look to you, and your give them their food in due season' have been sung as a grace over midday meals in monastic communities from at least the sixth-century onwards.[1074] Several illuminated manuscripts, both from the east and the west illustrate this tradition. For example, *Biblioteca Vaticana gr.1927* (fol. 256v), illustrates verse 15 by way of four monks sitting at a stone table in front of a low wall. The western *Utrecht Psalter* (fol.80v) and the later *Eadwine Psalter* (fol.254v) also illustrate verse 15, but in a more universal way: at the bottom left of each image is a group of men, women and children sitting at table laden with food, looking up (not to God but) to the *Christ-Logos.[1075]

[1072] Feuer 2004: 1687.
[1073] See Zenger 1997a: 2.
[1074] De Solms 2001: 669.
[1075] For *Utrecht*, see https://psalter.library.uu.nl/page/168.

The psalm has no explicit references in the New Testament.[1076] It is, however, read by the fathers as the first of the Alleluia Psalms (145–150), and so represents the praises of Christ after all he had achieved in his suffering, death and resurrection.[1077] *Augustine, for example, notes the title 'Praise to David himself' should really read 'Praise to Christ himself'—Christ, who was born of the seed of David—who rules as our King and brings us into his kingdom.[1078] The same theme is noted over a millennium later by the Augustinian friar, *Luther, who reads the psalm as a thanksgiving for the future kingdom of Christ, and notes the importance of praising God for the present kingdom which is hidden under the cross of Christ.[1079]

*Calvin uses this psalm, like 144, to correct the theology of the 'Papists', who are incapable of seeing the graciousness of God as expressed, for example, in the familiar *credo* in verse 8 ('the Lord is gracious and merciful, slow to anger and abounding in steadfast love …'): 'Papists represent him a dreadful God, from whose presence all must fly, whereas the proper view of him is that which invites us to seek after him.'[1080]

Another verse used frequently by the Church Fathers is verse 4 ('One generation shall laud your works to another …'). It was used by *Ambrose, for example, to defend Christian orthodoxy against *Arianism, which argued that the Incarnation could be compared with human generation, and that the Son was not eternal, as the Father had to exist before him. For Ambrose, this verse shows that God is unsearchable, and that although human generation takes place at a point in time, divine omnipotence is over all these things.[1081]

Given its liturgical use, Psalm 145 also has a fairly rich tradition in music—both Jewish and Christian, and both sacred and secular. One contemporary example is from Pinner Synagogue, London, showing the congregation's involvement in the calls and responses.[1082] A further example is from the orthodox Jewish Chabad tradition.[1083] The 'Blue Book', also known as '*The Voice of Song and Prayer*', presents the *Ashrei* in a traditional United Synagogue setting, and the score in Figure 17 again shows how Ps. 144:15 and Psalm 145 are sung.[1084]

The psalm's designation for use on Whitsunday in the *Book of Common Prayer* lectionary has resulted in compositions by, for example, Thomas Adams,

---

[1076] See, however, Witherington 2017: 302–309, on the possible allusions to verse 15 in Matt. 24:45 and to verse 8 in Lk. 6:27–38, and to verse 18 in Phil. 4:4–6.

[1077] De Solms 2001: 667.

[1078] Augustine trans. Uyl 2017: 673.

[1079] Luther, 'Summaries' in WA 38:65, cited in Selderhuis 2018: 375–76.

[1080] Calvin trans. Beveridge 1979: 275. On the importance of this verse ('the Grace Formula') within 145 as a whole, see Hensley 2018: 244–53.

[1081] Ambrose, *On the Christian Faith* 1.10.63 NPNF 2 10:211–12 in Wesselschmidt 2007: 411.

[1082] See https://alexandermassey.com/ashrei-yoshvei-veitecha/.

[1083] See https://www.chabad.org/multimedia/music_cdo/aid/692801/jewish/26-Ashrei-Song.htm.

[1084] I am grateful to Alexander Massey for these resources and for the score of *Ashrei*: see https://alexandermassey.com/.

Figure 17   *A Liturgical Score of the Ashrei (Psalm 144:15).*

Taken from F. L. Cohen (ed.) 1993:181. *Source*: Massey, A., website
https://alexandermassey.com/ashrei-yoshvei-veitecha)

John Church, and Orlando *Gibbons. The seventeenth-century composer, Marc-Antoine Charpentier, arranged some six settings of this psalm, the best known of which is a polyphonic motet in D Major: his rondo prelude from which, by an odd accident of reception history, became the signature theme of the Eurovision Song Contest.[1085] Another non-sacred use of this psalm is in *Belshazzar*, an Oratorio in 3 Acts (first performed in the King's Theatre, Haymarket, London 1745). This is based on Daniel 5, and the very last chorus, by captive Jewish slaves, is a victory song after Cyrus of Persia defeated the Babylonians, using the first two verses of Psalm 145.[1086]

There have been several attempts to present the psalm in an English alphabetical form. Here (setting aside whether or not to include the line with the letter 'N') the problem is capturing 21 verses in 26 letters. Gordon Jackson faces this challenge by paraphrasing the whole psalm, of which verses 1–2 are offered below:[1087]

> **A**ll worthy God, I honour you as my king,
> And as long as I have breath it will praise your name;
> **B**e my days many or few, each one will bless you,
> Each one be a holy day as I give it to you…

By contrast, Adam's speech, almost at the end of John *Milton's *Paradise Lost*, captures the spirit of this entire alphabetic psalm in just a few lines. Repentant and chastened, Adam addresses the angel:[1088]

> Henceforth I learne, that to obey is best,
> And love with feare the onely God, to walk
> As in his presence, ever to observe
> His providence, and on him sole depend,
> Merciful over all his works, with good
> Still overcoming evil, and by small
> Accomplishing great things…

Adam's speech condenses a psalm which in its praise asks nothing of God, but by implication asks everything of humanity in their grateful response to a God known both as King and Provider. As L. Allen observes, two lines of Robert Grant's hymn 'O Worship the King' are an appropriate summary of this psalm: 'O Tell of His Might, Sing of His Grace'.[1089]

[1085] Dowling Long and Sawyer 2015: 233.
[1086] Dowling Long and Sawyer 2015: 29. This is in Act Three, Scene Three, no. 64.
[1087] Jackson 1997: 162–63.
[1088] *Paradise Lost*, Book 12, Lines 561–67: see https://bit.ly/3ujwUyz.
[1089] Allen 2002: 374.

Psalms 146–151: The End of the Psalter

Psalms 146–150: The Final Hallel

In the MT Psalms 146–150 are united by the Hebrew word Hallelujah which begins and ends each one and is written as two words (*hallelu yah*). Psalm 150 forms an appropriate conclusion, using in the body of the psalm ten other such calls: 'praise him' (*halleluhu*).[1090] In Jewish liturgy, these five psalms (as well as 145) are recited in the preparatory material of the daily morning service, including the Sabbath, as part of *Pesukei de-Zimra*: this emphasises the importance of praise of God at the start of every day.[1091] In monastic liturgy, every morning, Psalm 148–150 are used at *Lauds (alongside Psalms 67 and 51). This is prescribed, for example, in the Rule of Benedict, and the tradition has continued in the *Divine Office to the present day: it is a reminder of praise of the risen Christ at sunrise on the third day.[1092]

Psalms 146–150 cohere as a theological collection. Firstly, they develop further the theme of the kingship of God found in Psalms 144 and 145, although now without any specific reference to David or to any human king: God alone is King.[1093] This theme is explicit in Pss. 146:10 and 149:2, particularly in relation to God's rule in Zion. A second shared theme, again especially evident

---

[1090] The first of these in 150:1 is actually 'praise God' (*halelu'el*).
[1091] See pp. 407–08 (Psalm 145). See also Scheindlin 1993: 72–76; Hoffman 1997: 107–46.
[1092] See Gillingham 2008: 40, 50.
[1093] See pp. 401and 403 (Psalm 144) and p. 406 (Psalm 145).

Psalms Through the Centuries: A Reception History Commentary on Psalms 73-151, Volume Three, First Edition. Susan Gillingham.
© 2022 John Wiley & Sons Ltd. Published 2022 by John Wiley & Sons Ltd.

in Psalms 144 and 145, is opposition to any imperial powers. Dennis Tucker has argued that, in the context of Persian rule, each of these psalms combines praise to the God of heaven and earth with a resistance to *any* human kingship: 'Through various means, the Persians sought to create a political ideology that reinforced a sense of imperial power ... there is an unmistakeable rhetoric within book 5 that "denounces the destructive, imperial structures and systems, and holds firmly that the biblical God will put an end to these systems".[1094] So in Psalms 146–150 praise to God is expressed as an act of defiance. Related to this, a third shared theme, also evident throughout much of Psalms 138–145, is the importance of justice for the poor and oppressed: unlike foreign kings, Yahweh's cosmic rule is to raise the weak and depose the mighty, and this theme is also found in Psalms 146–150.[1095] The following commentary will clarify just how frequently these three themes occur throughout the collection, suggesting that they are a coherent whole, illustrated further by the several verbal correspondences which link each psalm with its neighbour.

There is also evidence of a progression of participation in the way these five psalms have been organised. For example, 146:1–2 is the only psalm which speaks in personal terms of 'my soul' praising God (as also 145:1–2); 147:12 refers to the entire congregation being part of this praise; then in 148:1–3, 7–8 the whole cosmos, heaven and earth, is drawn into an act of praise; 149:1–2, the most explicitly political psalm in the collection, refers to the role of 'Israel' as part of the 'assembly of the faithful'; whilst 150:1 echoes briefly the expanded vision in 148, that heaven and earth are being brought into a repeated paeon of praise. It is possible that, like the Songs of Ascent, Psalms 146–150 originated from different times and places.[1096] The cohesiveness in the Hebrew version, however, indicates the work of the compilers marking this as the first stage of their reception history.

The *Septuagint maintains the same order but has different emphases. It splits Psalm 147 into two (verses 1–11 and 12–20) in the same way it split up Psalm 116. It creates a unity between Psalms 145–148 by presenting the 'Hallelujah' in the first verse of the Hebrew as an actual title for each psalm followed by the additional superscription 'Of Haggai and Zechariah'. Psalms 149 and 150 thus form a separate pair. Psalm 151 is added as an afterword about the *Davidic* inspiration of the whole.[1097]

[1094] See Tucker 2014a: 196, also citing Zenger 1997b: 97; see also Zenger 2003:139–55.
[1095] Tucker 2014a: 190, note 6. See also Hossfeld and Zenger 2011: 606.
[1096] Brodersen 2017: 21, 28–30, 270–78.
[1097] Hossfeld and Zenger 2011: 607. See p. 452 (Psalm 151).

In 11QPsᵃ at *Qumran, meanwhile, the collection is split up completely: we have already seen how this occurred with the Psalms of Ascent. Psalm 147 is found between Psalms 104 and 105, followed by Psalms 146 and 148; Psalm 149 follows 143, and although Psalm 149 is followed by 150 this is eclipsed by the following sectarian *Hymn to the Creator*.

As a collection, Psalms 146–150 thus have an interesting reception history. The group is also linked to Psalms 138–145, with 145 acting as a 'bridge psalm' between the two collections, as we noted earlier.[1098]

Psalm 146: Praise for God's Sovereignty and His Provision for All People

All three of the above themes come together in this psalm: God is King in Zion (verse 10); imperial powers are denounced (verse 3: 'Do not put your trust in princes'); and a large part of the psalm is concerned with justice for the oppressed (verses 7–9).[1099]

The macarism in verse 5 ('Happy is he whose help is the God of Jacob') divides the psalm into two: verses 3–4 are concerned with the abuse of power, and verses 6–9 with God's protection of the powerless, whilst verses 1–2 and 10 form the frame. There are clear links with Psalm 145: each psalm opens in the first person praise of God (145:1–2; 146:1–2); the proclamation of the kingship of God is 'throughout/for all generations' (145:13; 146:10); God is the one who 'lifts up' (*zoqef*) the 'bowed down' (*kefufim*) in 145:14 and 146:8; and God is the 'giver of bread' (*noten lechem*) to all, especially the hungry (145:15 and 146:7).

One early reception of this psalm is in 1 Macc. 2:49–70 as verse 61 ('And so observe, from generation to generation, that none of those who put their trust in him shall lack strength') alludes to Ps. 146:3–4 ('Do not put your trust in princes…') in the context of the *Maccabean revolt. The political use of this verse is frequently found in the psalm's reception, as we shall see.

We have already noted that the *Septuagint reinterprets the psalm by giving it a title: *allēlouia aggaiou kai zachariou. ainei hē psuchē mou ton kurion.* This comprises the 'Alleluia' taken from verse 1a, then an accreditation to 'Haggai and Zechariah', followed by verse 1b (here using the imperative form of another verb of praise (*aineo*) to read 'praise, my soul, the Lord'). The contextualisation of the psalm within the Persian period by attributing the psalm to Haggai and Zechariah makes sense of verses 7–9 about economic deprivation and support

---

[1098] See p. 414 (on Psalm 145 as a 'bridging psalm').
[1099] McPolin 1989: 90; also Magonet 1994: 141–45.

of the poor (verses 7–9). The roles of Haggai and Zechariah were later represented in several Byzantine Psalters which used the *LXX: the *Theodore Psalter* (fol. 185r) and the *Barberini Psalter* (fol. 241r) both depict these restoration prophets swinging a censor as if in Orthodox liturgy, whilst the *Khludov Psalter* (fol. 144r) illustrates them holding a scroll.[1100]

In 11QPs^a the psalm (which here begins at verse 9) included an additional passage between verses 9 and 10. This concerns God's power in creation: '*Let all the earth fear the Lord, let the inhabitants of the earth revere him … in his being known through all his works which he created … his mighty works…*'[1101] In some ways this is reminiscent of (the missing) verses 5–6: in refuting powers and dominions, and in supporting justice for the poor, an acknowledgement of God's ordering the cosmos is essential. Another allusion to this psalm is found in *4QMessianic Apocalypse* 2ii, where line 8 speaks of a new age when captives will be released, the blind will have their sight restored, and those who are bowed down will be raised up: 146:7–8 is the only text which contains all three elements. Further allusions to this 'new age' occur in the Gospels, but they do not cite this list in quite the same way as *4QMessianic Apocalypse* and Psalm 146.[1102]

Jewish reception reads verses 1–2 as evidence of our inability to praise God when dead (as in Ps. 115:17). Partly due to its familiarity as a morning prayer, the view that 'the psalmist does not expect people to live after death' is found in several commentaries.[1103] It is not surprising that Christian exegetes such as *Augustine refute this, interpreting the 'for ever' (Hebrew *be'odi*, Greek *heōs huparchō*) in verse 2 to refer not to this life (which is certainly what the Greek and Latin imply) but to life beyond death.[1104] Another Jewish emphasis is on God's restoration of Jerusalem (146:10), taking the *LXX heading about Haggai and Zechariah literally. Christian interpretation, as found for example in *Jerome, is about Christ's restoration of the new Jerusalem, the church, when the captives will be set free and the wicked will be destroyed, and Christ will reign forever.[1105]

Verses 3–4, on not trusting the 'princes' or 'mortals' of this world, have received a good deal of Christian commentary. *Eusebius applies the verses to the

---

[1100] For the *Theodore Psalter*, see https://bit.ly/3FKe7Cm.

[1101] Reconstructed in Abegg et al. 1999: 556.

[1102] See for example Matt. 11:5 and Luke 7:22. Brooke 1996 notes the correspondences between 4Q521 (4QMessianic Apocalypse) and the Gospel tradition, also noting here 146:7.

[1103] See for example Braude 1959: 361; Hoffman 1997: 124.

[1104] See Sermon 33A.I, in *WSA* 3.2:160, cited in Wesselschmidt 2007: 415; also Augustine trans. Uyl 2017: 678–9.

[1105] Jerome trans. Ewald 1963: Homily 55, pp. 392–990.

time when God brought about a reversal of fortunes for persecuted Christians through the Edict of Milan in 313, when Constantine and Licinius finally permitted religious freedom for all.[1106] These verses are also frequently interpreted in art. One example is in *Les Très Riches Heures du Duc de Berry* (fol. 85r), where the image is of David kneeling before an altar, in the choir of a church with huge pillars and gold altar hangings, intoning 'Put not your trust in princes'.[1107] Here David is a type for all Christian leaders of the Medieval church. Reformation commentators similarly focussed on verses 3–4 and 'trusting in God alone'. *Bucer, for example, notes that the princes and nobles are but 'children of men' (the Latin reads 'nolite confidere in principibus **in filiis hominum**'): they may be rich and powerful, but they are but human beings, mortal and miserable.[1108] *Calvin, too, found comfort in this verse, citing it with Is. 31:3: the 'princes' may be furnished with power, money and troops of men but they create a 'vain safety': we are under a different rule, in the safe keeping of a king who reigns expressly for our salvation.[1109] The black and white cartoon by Arthur *Wragg offers a more contemporary satirical sketch of these two verses: we see two hills full of crosses, set against a black sky, with a vast white question mark cutting through the middle of the image (Figure 18). Whether the deaths represent those in power, or those having suffered from those in power, is hard to know; but that it is a commentary on the First World War and the later Depression is quite clear.

The teaching on care for the poor and needy is also expressed in art. The *Utrecht Psalter* (fol. 81v) depicts the psalmist standing upon a hill and pointing to a group of 'the hungry': a table of food before them illustrates that this is the reward for trusting God rather than princes (verses 2, 3 and 7). An angel with a cross-staff is healing the blind and crippled (verse 8). At the extreme right the 'widows and fatherless' are raising their hands to heaven (verse 9).[1110]

Musical arrangements focus primarily on the theme of praise in the psalm. Salamone *Rossi's *Halelu-Yah*, composed in 1628 for a four-voice *a cappella* choir, is based on the first two verses, intended as a polyphonic chant for morning prayers in the synagogue of Mantua.[1111] In 1876 Louis Lewanowski's *Kedushah* was performed in the Berlin Reform Synagogue: it was to be sung on the evening of *Rosh Hashanah. This is a more serious piece, with an interplay between cantor, congregation and—by that time—the organ; everything leads up

---

[1106] *Ecclesiastical History* 9.11 *ECH I* 336–7, cited in Wesselschmidt 2007: 415.
[1107] Longnon and Cazelles 1969: 79.
[1108] Bucer, *Holy Psalms (Sacrorum Psalmorum)* 462, cited in Selderhuis 2018: 382.
[1109] Calvin trans. Beveridge and Calvin 1979: 291.
[1110] See https://psalter.library.uu.nl/page/170.
[1111] See https://www.youtube.com/watch?v=g8xxIJL6fOg.

Figure 18   *Arthur Wragg, 'Put not your trust in princes, nor in the son of man, in whom there is no help. His breath goeth forth, he returneth to earth; in that very day his thoughts perish'* (Ps. 146:34).

Source: Wragg, A. 1934: *The Psalms for Modern Life*. New York: Claude Kendall.

to the *thrice holy* in Isa. 6:3, followed by parts of Ezek. 3:12 and Deut. 6:4. The piece ends with Ps. 146:10, where God's rule in Zion is recalled and praised.[1112]

Christian composers mainly focus on individual verses of praise rather than the psalm as a whole. Examples include Dieterich *Buxtehude's *Lauda anima mea*, based on the first two verses.[1113] Similarly in *Lobe den Herrn, meine Seele*

[1112] See https://www.youtube.com/watch?v=lc2KrWxHHZQ; also Stern 2011: 311–13.
[1113] See https://www.youtube.com/watch?v=sibpIHnpFCM.

(BWV 143) J. S. *Bach uses verses 1, 5 and 10 as part of a New Year Cantata. By contrast, John *Rutter uses the whole of Psalm 146 ('Praise the Lord, O my Soul') as the third of nine psalms in his 1993 *Psalmfest*, selected in part because of its humanitarian concerns.[1114]

The psalm has also served political purposes. Max Stern's modern oratorio *Prophet or King* was performed at Ben Gurion University in 2007 as a critique of popular mass protests and of the power of kingship. The libretto is taken mainly from 1 Samuel 8 and 12, which describes the problematic origins of kingship in Israel when the people reject the voice of the prophet Samuel and seek an expression of earthly power. 1 Sam. 8:19–20 is a key choral text: 'Place a king over us that we also may be like other nations'. Ps. 146:10 is sung as the finale, highlighting by way of a traditional Sephardic melody the people's con-trition: 'The Lord will reign for ever and ever'.[1115] The use of this verse here corresponds with Dennis Tucker's observations, noted earlier, about the 'anti-imperialist' stance implicit in this psalm of praise. As John Goldingay observes, the praise of God is here held alongside the adage 'Never Trust Politicians'—at least, not for any sort of political, social, national or individual *salvation*, for they are mere humans like the rest of us, whilst God keeps faith forever.[1116] This is the theme which has most dominated the use of this psalm in both Jewish and Christian reception history.

Psalm 147: Praise for God's Sovereignty and His Provision for Israel

Again, the three themes of God's Sovereignty (verse 5), God's power over other nations (verse 10), and his provision for the poor and outcast (verses 2–3 and 6) are evident, especially in the first half of this psalm. The links with Psalm 146 are also particularly clear in this first part (147:1–11). The verbs *z-m-r* (sing to music) and *h-l-l* (praise) are found in 147:1 and 146:1–2; and God as the 'giver of bread', each using the masculine singular participle form (*noten*) is found in both psalms (147:9 and 146:7—also in 145:15—noting that in 147:9 this is for the animals). Other more common words or phrases occur, such as 'Jacob' (verses 147:19 and 146:5), the 'wicked' being brought down (147:6 and 146:9),

---

[1115] Stern 2011: 205–215, which discusses both the text and music.
[1114] See https://www.youtube.com/watch?v=eKec-kRseMk; also Dowling Long and Sawyer 2015: 191.
[1116] Goldingay 2008: 713–714.

but most telling of all is the address 'your God, O Zion' (*'elohayik tsion*) a phrase unique to 147:12 and 146:10.

Of all the examples, only the unique phrase noted above is found in the second part of the psalm. It is quite possible that Psalm 147 originally comprised two psalms (1–11 and 12–20), with the first part referring to Jerusalem in the third person (verse 2) and the second part directly addressing Zion. Only verses 1–11 are concerned with the weak and needy; verses 12–20 focus entirely on Yahweh's power. And as Zenger has shown in detail, verses 1–11, like Psalm 146, have far more intertextual references than verses 12–20.[1117] Perhaps the motif 'Israel' in verses 2 and 19 brought both parts of the psalm together— although in the first part this is the 'outcasts of Israel' and in the second this is about the nation Israel being given Gods 'statutes and ordinances'.

Whatever the reason, the *Septuagint split this psalm into two (as it did for Psalm 116), giving each the same title (*allēlouia Aggaiou kai Zachariou*) as for the preceding psalm (MT 146, *LXX* 145).[1118] Psalm 147A (MT; 146 in the *LXX*) is thus read as an announcement of God's restoration of Jerusalem, protecting the poor and needy, and Psalm 147B (MT; 147 in the *LXX*) as about the completion of the building, exhibiting God's power.[1119] A few small changes are evident: these include the change in verse 4 from God as the decider (Hebrew, *moneh*) of the number of the stars to God as the one who actually counts (Greek, *arithmōn*) them; and the addition in verse 8 of God's provision of 'green plants for human labour'. But the key change is the division of the psalm into two resulting in Psalms 148–150 finally having the same numbering in the Greek as the Hebrew.

Psalm 147:1–2, 18–20 is preserved in a fragmentary form in 11QPs[a] at *Qumran, and it is likely that here this marks the beginning and ending of just one psalm. 147 is placed between Psalms 104 and 105, perhaps on account of the creation theme in both 104 and 147. 11QPs[d] also contains some of 147 in fragments, and here Psalm 147 precedes 104, rather than following it; in verse 1 the word *na'vah* ('it is fitting') is repeated, to give the conjectured reading '[*Praise to*] *our God is fitting, and a song of praise is fitting and pleasant*'.[1120] The end of the psalm, although incomplete, has another emphatic addition: '*he has not revealed* [*any*] *ordinances to them*'.[1121]

As far as reception through the commentary tradition is concerned, the key verses include 5 (on God's 'understanding'), 9 (on the 'ravens' being given

---

[1117] Hossfeld and Zenger 2005: 621.
[1118] See pp. 414–15, on the LXX headings for Psalm 146.
[1119] Hossfeld and Zenger 2005: 627.
[1120] Abegg et al. 1999: 553.
[1121] Abegg et al.1999: 554.

food), 10 (on the 'strength of a horse'), 18 (on God's 'word' being sent out) and 20 (on whether or not other nations 'know' God—a view which is explicitly negated in the Qumran addition mentioned above). More generally, the references to the building up of Jerusalem (verse 3) and Zion (verse 13) are also dealt with differently by Jewish and Christian commentators, along the lines we noted for Psalm 146.[1122]

Verse 5 speaks of God's 'understanding' (Hebrew, *tevunah*), a word often associated with wisdom books such as Proverbs). Early Christian commentators read this as referring to Christ, the 'wisdom of God', through the lens of 1 Cor. 1:24: so this is about Christ equal to God and working together with him.[1123] This could not be more different from the Jewish emphasis on God's wisdom being seen in creation, taking a more literal reading of this verse.

Verse 9 is interesting because in the *LXX* it is the *young* ravens which God feeds. This verse is alluded to in Luke 12:24 ('Consider the ravens: they neither sow nor reap… and yet God feeds them.'). The *Talmud* refers to the ravens as contemptable birds, comparing them with dogs.[1124] *Young* ravens who 'cry' for their food are nevertheless an example of vulnerable dependence on the parent bird, and God feeds even them. This theme is depicted in several Byzantine Psalters: the *Khludov Psalter* (fol. 145r) has insects flying to the mouths of young ravens, as also the *Barberini Psalter* (fol. 243r), and the *Hamilton Psalter* (fol. 240r). The *Theodore Psalter* (fol. 186r) depicts a nest of ravens in a tree;[1125] whilst the *Biblioteca Vaticana, gr.1927* has three ravens and four sheep feeding on a hillside. *Carolingian Psalters also highlight this trope: the *Utrecht Psalter's* image of Ps. 147:1–11 (fol. 81v) shows animals grazing in a field, as it rains, whilst in the trees outside a city wall the ravens 'cry out' for food.[1126] The *Eadwine Psalter* (fol. 257v) has a very similar image.[1127]

*Coverdale's translation of verse 10 in the *BCP* is an acceptable translation of the Latin, but in contemporary language sounds somewhat odd: 'He hath no pleasure in the strength of a horse: neither delighteth he in any man's legs'. The English paraphrase of the *Targum* reads: 'He does not delight in the might of *those who ride on* the horse, *nor does he* take pleasure in the legs of men *who run*.'[1128] The Jewish commentary tradition explains that this cannot mean that God does not approve of the strength of a horse, as Job 39:19 makes it clear that

---

[1122] See p. 415, on the reading of Jerusalem in Psalm 146.

[1123] For example, Augustine, cited in Neale and Littledale 1874–79: IV/410. See also De Solms 200: 677.

[1124] B.*Baba Bathra* 8a. See also Gruber trans. *Rashi; 2004: 758.

[1125] See http://www.bl.uk/manuscripts/Viewer.aspx?ref=add_ms_19352_f186r.

[1126] See http://psalter.library.uu.nl/page?p=169&res=1&x=0&y=0.

[1127] See https://bit.ly/33oAFdQ.

[1128] Stec 2004: 242.

God gives the horse its strength; following Ps. 146:3–4, it is placing one's trust in this strength which is wrong (Isa. 31:1 and Ps. 33:17).[1129] This is the same conclusion *Augustine offers: horses carry us aloft and encourage us to think too highly of our own power and worth: we must resist pride.[1130] *Calvin also notes that this verse is about people trusting in their own strength rather than that which is given them from above.[1131] Mary *Sidney's poetry captures the same idea:[1132]

> The stately shape, the force of bravest steed,
> Is far too weak to work in him delight;
> No more in him can any pleasure breed
> In flying footman, foot of nimblest flight.
> Nay, which is more, his fearers in his sight
> Can well of nothing but his bounty brave...

The artist Eric Gill takes verse 10 in a completely different direction. In his relief entitled *Crucifixion* (1910), now in the Tate Gallery, a verse from Matt. 19:12 (which refers to eunuchs being examples of renunciation for the sake of the Gospel) runs across the right and left of the upright of the cross; underneath the upright, at the foot of the cross, under Christ's legs and feet, as it were, Ps. 147:10 is inscribed in Latin. This relief is one of a pair: the other, of a nude woman and an inscription from Swinburne's *Hymn to Proserpine*, lines 35 and 23–4, is intended to be a symbol of acceptance, whilst *Crucifixion* symbolises renunciation: in this image of powerlessness, this is perhaps where real power lies.[1133]

Two other verses creating debate between Jews and Christians are found in the second part of this psalm. The first concerns the identification of 'the word' which in the psalm is partly identified with God's work in creation (vv. 15–18) and partly with the law (verse 19), and this is how Jewish commentators have read this verse. *Eusebius, however, argues this predicts the spread of Christianity: God's word 'runs swiftly' (verse 15) and 'melts' the Gentiles (verse 18, although the reference here is surely to the snows).[1134] *Gregory, followed by *Cassiodorus, argues that this refers not only to the spread of the Gospel, beginning with Christ himself, but also to the Word of God in incarnation.[1135]

[1129] See Markus 2016: 301a.
[1130] Augustine trans. Uyl 2017: 685.
[1131] Calvin trans. Beveridge 1979: 298.
[1132] Wieder 1995: 218.
[1133] https://www.tate.org.uk/art/artworks/gill-crucifixion-n03563.
[1134] *Proof of the Gospel* 2:10, cited in Wesselschmidt 2007: 421.
[1135] Neale and Littledale (1874–79): IV/417. Cassiodorus trans. Walsh 1991b: 446–448 also reads the Trinity into verse 15 (p. 446).

On account of this reading Psalm 147:12–20 has been frequently associated with Christmas.[1136] This might in part explain why 147:12–20 was chosen as one of the five psalms texts for the *Vespers of the Blessed Virgin Mary* (Psalms 110, 113, 122 and 127 being the others, as well as portions of the Song of Songs), celebrating Mary as the bearer of the Word. The personification of Zion (verse 12) would also have contributed to this choice, where Mary becomes a 'type' of Zion. We have already referred to Monteverdi's use of the other four psalms for his own arrangement of the Vespers.[1137] A very different interpretation is found in the *St. Albans Psalter*, which has an extraordinary image of God facing upside down towards the earth; a bird flies out of his mouth down a shaft to the earth, which is depicted as a block of ice, surrounded by melting water.[1138] The identity of the bird is unclear: is it a symbol of Christ, or of the mission of the church? The image is certainly not about God's melting the earth's icecaps, but, rather like the Gill image of verse 10, the purpose of the bird, undoubtedly representing God's word, is somewhat ambiguous.

The other controversial verses conclude the psalm. These refer to God declaring his word to Jacob and Israel (verse 19) whilst other nations do not know his 'ordinances' (verse 20) and this has again produced very different Jewish and Christian responses. Jewish commentators affirm that the ordinances, or 'judgements' (*mishpatim*) refer to the Torah (or more specifically, the Decalogue): hence only Jews can understand the inner interpretation of God's judgements, even though Gentiles might understand something about the literal interpretation of the law.[1139] *Chrysostom, Augustine and Cassiodorus, for example, each refute this. Augustine argues that 'Praise the Lord' (in verse 12, as well as verse 1) is spoken to all nations: and although the word was indeed first given to Jacob and Israel, Jn. 1:11 makes it clear that they rejected that Word. 'The new Jacob supplanted his brother and the Gentiles came in.'[1140] Chrysostom argues that even if other nations were given a natural law, and the Jews the written law, the fact that they rejected the 'word' makes them all the more culpable.[1141] Cassiodorus, following Augustine, argues that Israel represents the Jewish people who rejected the word, and Jacob ('the supplanter') represents the new people of God, the church.[1142] Paradoxically, verse 19 was later used in Calvinism to

---

[1136] Anderson 2016: xix—xx, noting its use on the second Sunday after Christmas.

[1137] See p. 191 (Psalm 110); pp. 203 and 207 (Psalm 113); p. 275 (Psalm 122); and p. 298 (Psalm 127). See also Dowling Long and Sawyer 2015: 255.

[1138] See https://www.albani-psalter.de/stalbanspsalter/english/commentary/page368.shtml.

[1139] Feuer 2004: 1719.

[1140] Augustine trans. Uyl 2017: 681; Neale and Littledale 1874–79: IV/419.

[1141] Chrysostom trans. Hill 1998: 358–9.

[1142] Cassiodorus trans. Walsh 1991b: 444–49.

argue that not *all* people could obtain salvation, but only those who believed in the free gift of God through grace: this verse was cited at the Calvinist Synod of Dort in 1618 in Holland to condemn any tendencies towards universalism and to protect the belief in the predestination of God's elect.

This psalm also offers very different readings for Jews and Christians as to what was intended by Jerusalem or Zion (verses 2 and 12). As we have seen so frequently in other psalms which refer to the restoration of the city, the Jewish emphasis is on the promise of the physical reconstruction of the city which will become a spiritual centre for all those who seek to praise their God.[1143] This is what the *LXX headings to vv. 1–11 and 12–20 intended, with Haggai and Zechariah representing the physical work of restoration, and the psalm has primarily been used in this way throughout Jewish tradition. Again, as with Psalm 146, the Christian emphasis is not on the earthly Jerusalem, but on the heavenly reality. *Hilary of Poitiers writes about this;[1144] so too, *Origen, and of course Augustine;[1145] whilst *Jerome's Homily 57 on verses 12–20 focusses entirely on entering Jerusalem through the 'gates' of the Old Testament, but the city we then encounter is the spiritual city of Christ.[1146] The image in the *Stuttgart Psalter (fol. 159r), of 'children of Jerusalem' being blessed by the hand of God emerging from a cloud (verse 13) might suggest a physical city with walls and three towers, but it really denotes a spiritual reality which is the heavenly Zion.[1147]

Musical arrangements frequently divide this psalm into two: *Lauda Dominum* refers to Hebrew verses 1–11 (Psalm 146 in the Greek and Latin versions) and *Lauda Jerusalem* refers to Hebrew verses 12–20 (now Psalm 147 in all the versions, but with different verse numbers). Orlando *di Lasso, for example, composed a six- and seven-voice Latin setting respectively based on each part. Haydn composed a version based on the Latin of the first half-psalm; whilst Vivaldi's *Lauda Jerusalem* and Monteverdi's version, for his *Vespers*, used the second half-psalm, as was also the case with *Purcell's arrangement, *Praise the Lord O Jerusalem*.[1148] These different titles indicate the themes in the psalm as a whole: the first half-psalm (where as we noted earlier Jerusalem is referred to in the third person) focusses on the universal God who both cares for the oppressed (verses 2, 3, 6) and refutes all competing powers (verses 10–11), whilst the second half-psalm (where Jerusalem/Zion is addressed) focusses on the particular place from which God will restore his people. There is little disagree-

[1143] Feuer 2004: 1709; Braude 1959: 371–74.
[1144] De Solms 2001: 666.
[1145] Neale and Littledale 1874–79: IV/408–15.
[1146] Jerome trans. Ewald 1963: Homily 57, 408–15.
[1147] See https://bit.ly/33jlbYp.
[1148] See https://www2.cpdl.org/wiki/index.php/Psalm_147.

ment between Christian and Jews on the first half-psalm: this tells us about the nature of God. The difficulty, as we have seen in the commentary tradition on the second half-psalm especially, is knowing how and why and for whom God will act.

Psalm 148: Praise Has Cosmic Implications

Like 150, Psalm 148 has ten exhortations to praise, eight using the imperative form of the verb *h-l-l*, and two which could be read as jussive in form.[1149] Here the praise is directed to the entire cosmos, which is slightly different from Psalm 150 which is to all the musicians of the Temple. In 148 the Hebrew word *kol* is used ten times (verses 2, 9 and 11 twice; verses 3, 7, 10 and 14, once): hence the praise of the order in creation is mirrored in the ordering of the psalm. The praise in verses 1–7 moves from the heavens downwards (angels, hosts, sun, moon, stars) to the sea monsters and waters of the deep. Verses 8–13 start within the earth and end with human life, thus beginning with the elements of fire, hail, snow, frost and wind, then mountains, hills, trees, to the beasts, creeping things and birds, and finishing with humans—first kings, princes and rulers, and then all their subjects. The general order of this cosmogony has some associations with Genesis 1.[1150]

Each of our three themes is more implicit in this psalm. That of God's kingship is implied through the motifs of God as sovereign creator. That of the demise of foreign powers is evident, but more radically in that they are called to praise God (verses 11–12, 13), whilst the nation Israel is raised above them (verse 14). Although there is nothing on the care of the poor and needy, the emphasis is on the order of the cosmos upon which such decrees for an ordered society are based (verses 5–6).

The early reception history of this psalm is seen through the work of the compilers, and the associations with Psalm 147. These include the references to the stars (named in 147:4, called to praise in 148:3), to the elements of snow, frost, hail and wind and waters (147:16–18 and 148:7–8), to the provision for beasts and birds (147:9 and 148:10), and to the specific emphasis on Israel's role at the pinnacle of the created order (147:19–20, 148:14).

As for the next stages in reception, the **LXX* maintains the relationship with Psalms 146 and 147 by its repeated superscription (the 'Alleluia' and the

---

[1149] See pp. 435–36 (Psalm 150). The two Hallelujahs at the beginning and end make 12 in all.

[1150] Hossfeld and Zenger 2005: 631 and 638.

details about Haggai and Zechariah), thus implicitly continuing the theme of the rebuilding of Jerusalem. The *LXX* also adds other details: for example, in verse 3b the light is addressed as a separate entity, and verse 5 has the addition 'for he, he spoke and they came to be'. Verse 6a has a longer formula in the description of God establishing the cosmos 'for ever': it reads 'He made them stand fast for eternity, and from age to age'.

Psalm 148 is evident in 11QPs^a at *Qumran, where all the verses are found, but only their first lines, due to the damaged scroll. It is preceded by 146, whose creation themes connect it with God's provision of the hungry, and it is followed by most of the Psalms of Ascent (120–132): perhaps this paeon of praise ending with Israel's place in the cosmos in 148:14 made it an appropriate introduction to this collection.

Two early Greek texts which suggest the influence of this psalm are Sirach 43 and the 68-verse addition between Daniel 3:23 and 24 ('The Prayer of Azariah and the Song of the Three Jews'), known in Christian tradition as the *Benedicite*. In Sirach 43, the order of the wonders of creation are the sun, moon, stars, snow, winds, frost, and the deep (and sea monsters). Here the purpose is not so much to elicit liturgical praise, as in Psalm 148, but to encourage the godly to reflect on God's wisdom in creation: 'He is the all' (Sir. 43:27, 33).[1151] In the additions to Daniel the actual 'Song of the Three Jews' is most relevant (verses 29–68 of the addition). The movement of praise from heaven downwards, followed by the movement of praise within the earth, has many affinities with Psalm 148: we read of the sun, moon, stars, winds, fire and snow and frost; the mountains and hills, the beasts of the field, and the people on earth. The 'Song of the Three Children' arranged by Charles Villiers *Stanford, dedicated to Queen Victoria in 1885, makes use of both Daniel 3 and Psalm 148, with its impressive double chorus as a finale.[1152]

We have noted how the *Septuagint reads the psalm through the theme of the building up of Jerusalem, and how the placing of the psalm at Qumran, before the Ascents, suggests a reading which includes the restoration of Israel. In later Jewish tradition both these interests are continued: the whole universe is addressed to praise because they are about to witness Jerusalem's restoration.[1153] *Kimhi, for example, sees the reference to the 'horn' (*qeren*) in verse 14 as a metaphor for the strength of the Messiah, who will bring together all leaders of nations and all ranks of people to acknowledge Israel at the heart of this act of redemption.[1154]

[1151] Nitzan 1994: 184–89.
[1152] Dowling Long and Sawyer 2015: 241.
[1153] Feuer 2004: 1721.
[1154] Cited in, 2004: 1726. It is interesting to read how *Calvin uses the idea of 'the horn' to symbolise God's blessing on his church, which flourishes only through his strength: see Calvin trans. Beveridge and Calvin 1979: 309.

The association between God as Creator of the Universe and God as Creator both of Israel and the Church is found in the early Church Fathers. Frequently we read of how the belief in Christ as 'Logos' brings these two together. *Origen uses this psalm in his arguments about the first principles of the universe, relating these to his understanding of Christ as Logos from verse 5 ('for he commanded and they were created').[1155] *Augustine cites the psalm to discuss ranks of angels and categories of beings, and again relating this to 148:5, identified the 'he' ('He commanded…') as Christ the Logos: everything comes about by the word, and that word is Christ.[1156] *Jerome, using the psalm to show (against the *Manicheans) God's sovereignty over the sun and moon who give praise to him, argues from 148:5 that God's command is to the Son: he does the creating.[1157] *Chrysostom, noting how the psalm draws together that which is created in the heavens and that which is created on earth, opines that this is about creation of the visible and invisible, brought together by the Father and the Son.[1158] This argument is taken further by pseudo-*Ambrose, who relates it to the Blessed Sacrament: just as the Word of Christ makes efficacious things that are invisible and visible in earth and heaven, and just as that Word can bring things non-existent into being, so too that same Word can bring about change in things already visible and existing (the bread) so that it becomes the Body of Christ.[1159] Overall, like Psalms 8 and 104, this is a psalm which encourages Christian commentators to connect creation with redemption: praise to God as Creator is closely related to praise to Christ as Logos, and so to the work of Christ in salvation as well as in the cosmos.

This emphasis is also evident in illuminated Psalters, both from the West and East. In the *Utrecht Psalter* (fol. 82v), for example, the *Christ-Logos sits in a globe-*mandorla, supported by two angels. The sun and moon, each held by huge figures personifying the heavens, contrast with the tiny band of stars and the personified wind. Below are the mountains, hills, trees, beasts, cattle, creeping things, and birds: the kings of the earth and young and old below, with the 'deeps' and dragons underneath. Christ-Logos is central.[1160] The *Stuttgart Psalter* (fol.162r) has a similar focus: Christ-Logos here is at the centre of the image, between the personifications of the sun, moon, and wind, and below him are the beasts of the field, and a writhing serpent falling out of the frame.[1161] The *Theodore Psalter* (fol. 187r) and the *Hamilton Psalter* (fol. 241r) also por-

---

[1155] McGuckin 2011: 99–100.

[1156] See *Enchir.* 15.58 in FC 2:418–19, cited in Wesselschmidt 2007: 423; also Augustine trans. Uyl 2017: 689–93, especially p. 690.

[1157] See Jerome trans. Ewald 1963: Homily 58, pp. 413–23, especially 418–19.

[1158] See Chrysostom trans. Hill 1998: 364–50 and 372–74.

[1159] See Neale and Littledale 1874—79: IV/424–25.

[1160] See https://psalter.library.uu.nl/page/172.

[1161] See https://bit.ly/31I6Vrp.

tray the Christ-Logos praised by angels, with his right hand in blessing.[1162] This is followed in *Theodore* (fol. 187v) with a controversial image of an icon of Christ who is worshipped by kings and princes and people of the realm (verses 11–12).[1163] *Hamilton* (fol. 241v) also has an image of verses 7–12, and not only depicts figures from the created order but also Constantine the Great and the Empress Helena, each holding sceptres, apparently giving praise to the icon of Christ-Logos above (verse 11).

A memorable image is the portrayal by the Limbourg brothers of 'God in Majesty' in *Les Très Riches Heures du Duc de Berry* (fol. 41v). This follows an image of the three men in the fiery furnace and a selection of verses from the *Benedicite*; both are found in the earlier section on 'The Prayers of the Hours to the Virgin'. Here 'God in Majesty' is very clearly Christ. Christ's hand is on a globe and he is surrounded by angels with unfurled wings. The heavens are symbolised by a personified sun and moon; the earth and seas are represented by a small wood and body of water with two small ships. Here Christ seems to hover between heaven and earth, suggesting the wonder of the incarnation.[1164] See PLATE 28 for this image.

Psalm 148 has inspired many motets and hymns, mainly on account of its potential for visual and aural reception. Orlando *di Lasso's *Laudate Dominum* is a four-part motet published in 1584, along with Psalm 150, actually arranged to accompany the seven *penitential psalms. George *Sandys' translation, composed in the mid seventeenth-century, is set in tetrameter couplets to a hymn tune by *Lawes. It imagines all creation joining in the praise:[1165]

> Let the Earth his Praise resound:
> Monstrous Whales, and Seas profound,
> Vapours, Lightning, Haile, and Snow,
> Stormes which when he bids them blow...

A contrasting version is 'O Praise the Lord of Heaven', a metrical anthem for an *a capella* chorus, with an exuberant ending, which was one of five versions of this psalm published by William *Billings (c. 1794).[1166] William Draper's rendering of St. Francis of Assisi's hymn 'Canticles of the Creatures' or 'The Canticle of Brother Sun' (composed shortly before his death in 1226) was partly inspired by Psalm 148 and was first published in a hymn book in 1919. The hymn 'All Creatures of our God and King', sung to the tune *Lasst uns erfreuen*

[1162] For *Theodore*, see http://www.bl.uk/manuscripts/Viewer.aspx?ref=add_ms_19352_f187r.
[1163] See http://www.bl.uk/manuscripts/Viewer.aspx?ref=add_ms_19352_f187v.
[1164] Longnon and Cazelles 1969: 190.
[1165] Hamlin 2004a: 69–72.
[1166] Dowling Long and Sawyer 2015: 175.

(1623) is best known for its harmonisation by *Vaughan Williams, first published in the revised *English Hymnal* of 1933.[1167]

This call on the personified forces of nature is not unique to Judaism and Christianity. We have noted that Psalms 104 and 136 have some associations with two different *Surahs* in the Qur'an on account of the same poetic device.[1168] A similar correspondence might be evident here. Ps.148:9–10 calls on the mountains and hills to praise God, and also intriguingly, 'flying birds'. In *Surah 34 (al-Saba')* we read: 'We graced David with Our favour. We said, "You mountains, echo God's praises together with him, and your birds, too."' (Q. 34:10). The citation of the inspiration of David, and the unusual juxtaposition of the mighty mountains and tiny birds found in two texts which each encourage complete faith in God, suggest this correspondence is more than a coincidence, not least given the several other psalm verses which are alluded to in the Qur'an.[1169]

Non-liturgical performances of the psalm include the twentieth-century French composer Olivier Messiaen's *Visions de l'Amen*, the fifth in a suite of seven pieces for two pianos, composed in 1943, with its imaginative and complex play on the enlisting of the universe to sing God's praise;[1170] and John *Rutter's 1993 *Psalmfest*, along with Psalm 146.[1171]

The psalm has been the subject of much poetic imitation. Anne Finch, Countess of Winchilsea, wrote a paraphrase of Psalm 148 in November 1703. 'Upon the Hurricane 'was a version of this psalm: its focus was verse 8 ('... fire and hail, snow and frost, stormy wind fulfilling his command!'). This was a more personal composition, using a five-line Pindaric form. By setting the destructive force of the hurricane within a psalm of praise to God, it is the Creator, not the creature, who is in ultimate control. The following verses (of fourteen in all) starts with 148:8:[1172]

> Praise Him, ye waters petrified above,
>   Ye shredded clouds that fall in snow,
> Praise Him, for that you so divided move;
>   Ye hailstones, that you do no longer grow,
>   Nor, in one solid mass, oppress the world below...

[1167] 2015: 13.

[1168] See p. 149, especially note 273 (Psalm 104) and pp. 348–49 (Psalm 136). Again, I am indebted to Afifi Al-Akiti's counsel in what follows.

[1169] The assimilation of psalm texts is likely to be through liturgical associations, although one of the problems is knowing how the verse might have been used through either Jewish liturgy (in Hebrew) or Christian liturgy (in Greek) and then cited in Arabic. See W.A. Saleh 2014: 287–91; also Neuwirth (ed.) 2009: 734–39.

[1170] See https://www.youtube.com/watch?v=BvHDHN8LSvU; also Terrien 2003: 922.

[1171] Dowling Long and Sawyer 2015: 191.

[1172] Atwan and Wieder 1993: 335–37.

> But now, you storms, that have your fury spent,
>   As you his dictates did obey,
> Let now your loud and threatening notes relent,
>   Tune all your murmurs to a softer key,
> And bless that Gracious Hand, that did your progress stay.

A public and dramatic citation of the psalm is T. S. Eliot's use of it at the end of *Murder in the Cathedral*: this is by the chorus, as the choir, at a far distance, is reciting the *Te Deum*. Thomas Becket is dead, but life must go on:

> We praise thee, O God,
> for Thy glory displayed in all the creatures of the earth,
> In the snow, in the rain, in the wind, in the storm;
> In all of thy creatures, both the hunters and the hunted.
> For all things exist only as seen by Thee, only as known by
>   Thee, all things exist...[1173]

The psalm's more contemporary reception in art focusses mainly on the creation theme. The interpretation by *Benn (1969) depicts a deep turquoise sky with a mystical representation of the name of God in a white angelic form; the sun, moon, stars and angels all turn towards this sign to give him praise: this is praise 'in the heights', and it invites those who are 'in the depths' to raise their eyes to heaven.[1174]

Perhaps the most stunning of all images is the triptych of stained glass windows by Thomas *Denny, in the South Ambulatory Chapel at Gloucester Cathedral, part of the nine hundred anniversary celebrations of the founding of St. Peter's Abbey in 1089: the windows were completed in 1993. The central glass is of the artist's namesake, Thomas, meeting the risen Christ, and on each side, at bayed angles which give a sense of space to draw the viewer in, are two magnificent windows taken from Psalm 148, in the deepest of blues splashed with white and silver, gold and red: the whole chapel is bathed in blue light, and here we are challenged to see the risen Christ not only in personal encounter but in the mysteries of creation.[1175]

This is a psalm which displays so much vitality: it is full of sounds, including the seven voices of praise after verse 1 and has a rich reception in music and

---

[1173] This is from Part Two, final scene; see also Allen 2002: 395.
[1174] Benn 1940: no page numbers: Psaume 148:1–3.
[1175] See https://bit.ly/3oLkFdX.

poetry. It is also a visual psalm, in its many personified images from the created order which have inspired a good deal of art. By way of conclusion, it is perhaps appropriate to consider what has been done to the cosmos since the composition of this psalm. Celebration of 'planet earth' should also lead all humanity, of whatever faith tradition or none, to considered reflection upon the abuse of our environment. In the words of David Attenborough, '(The earth's) survival could not be more important to us. We depend on the natural world for all the food we eat, for the very air we breathe. Its health is our health. Its survival is essential for ours'.[1176] It is not coincidental that Psalm 148 is followed by a psalm of praise with more explicit pragmatic and political implications.

Psalm 149: Praise Has Political Implications

The three themes binding this collection together are most explicit in Psalm 149. God's Kingship is affirmed in verse 2 ('let the children of Zion rejoice in their King'). The political aspects of this kingship are seen in the contrast between God as King in Zion at the beginning of the psalm and the binding of foreign kings with fetters at the end of it. Thirdly, God's preference for the 'humble' (*'anavim*) in verse 4 can be read with social implications, for the Hebrew word can mean those who are physically poor as well as spiritually poor.[1177]

In terms of the first stage of reception, namely the work of compilers, Psalm 149 takes up where Psalm 148 leaves off. In 148:13 the praise of the cosmos ends with the praise of 'the people of Israel', 'his faithful', and Psalm 149 refers similarly to 'Israel' (verse 2), 'his people' (verse 4), and 'the faithful': the Hebrew word *hasidim* which is used in 148:14 occurs three times in 149, in verses 2, 5 and 9. The phrase 'for all his faithful ones' (*lekol hasidayw*) is actually unique to 148:14 and 149:9.[1178]

One of the key issues in the reception of this psalm is *the overlap* between the use of cultic and military language. The word 'assembly' (*qahal*) in verse 1 could mean a 'levy' as well as 'congregation'. The word for 'bed' (*mishkab*) upon which the faithful celebrate their 'victory' in their assembly (verses 4–5) could mean a simple bed, but also a prayer rug, or somewhere to sleep in a soldier's billet: there are also different meanings in the word *yeshuʿah* at the end of verse 4, which can mean 'victory' as well as 'salvation'. So the celebration of songs

---

[1176] Moss and Attenborough 2016: 11.

[1177] Gillingham 1988: 15–19.

[1178] See Auwers 2000: 91. I am grateful to Danny Crowther for his insights here.

and dances (verse 3) might not just be general acts of praise and worship, as in Psalm 148, but could also refer to a specific victory using the ideology of ancient warfare—a theme which is used for example in Ps. 118:15.[1179] This is why the psalm's reception history has had so many political and military overtones, and why in Jewish tradition Israel is seen as God's instrument for this act of restoration, albeit in future times.

In 11QPs[a] Psalm 149 follows 143, a prayer 'of David' (for deliverance). Although only 149:7–9 are extant, the addition 'for the sons of Israel, his holy people' is evidence for this Israel-centred reading in an early period.[1180]

Another phrase with clear military overtones is *veḥereb piphiyyot*, in v. 6, translated literally as 'and a sword with a double edge'. This is what the 'faithful', singing praises to God in their throats, carry in their hands (in v. 6). *Kimḥi and *Rashi read the two edges as about both military strength and the Torah: so the following verse, concerning the vengeance on the nations, is read in the light of the battle with Gog and Magog at the end of time, but also about the recitation of the Torah in bringing about the victory of God.[1181] More contemporary Jewish readings, however, react against the violence against other nations espoused in this psalm: the *Gates of Prayer* from Reform Judaism, as also Marcia's Falk's *Book of Blessings*, delete verse 6–9, and Havurat Shalom's *Siddur Birkat Shalom* substitutes here two verses on the coming age of peace from Is.60:18 and 5:16. Ellen Frankel notes in her commentary on this psalm in *Pesukei d'Zimrah*: 'History has taught us that, more often than not, swords are indeed *pifiyot*, literally "double-edged", frequently turning back upon those who brandish them'.[1182] This psalm is used weekly for morning prayer: Frankel offers an important woman's voice here. And given the liturgical use of verses 5–6 ('the bedtime *shema*') which introduces the reading of the *shema*' before going to sleep, as protection against all harm, the need to reinterpret the violence in this psalm is all the more pressing.[1183]

The other phrase interpreted frequently in Jewish tradition is the 'new song' (*shir ḥadash*). It is used in verse 1, and the whole psalm could be read as the content of this song. In Jewish tradition this is the eschatological song of the Messianic age, to be sung by 'the faithful'.[1184] This is illustrated in the *Parma Psalter* which depicts a figure, to the right of the Hallelujah written in Hebrew, who is conducting a five-voice choir in the upper left, just below the text of Psalm 148. A choir book is open, showing four or five staves of music, in red

---

[1179] Hossfeld and Zenger 2005: 642 and 645–46. On Psalm 118, see p. 232.
[1180] Abegg et al. 1999: 581. The psalm is probably also in *MasPs*[b] where it follows 148.
[1181] Feuer 2004: 1732.
[1182] Hoffman 1997: 138–41.
[1183] See Markus 2016: 304b, citing *b.Berachot* 5a.
[1184] See Markus 2016: 304a.

ink, with black musical notes—coincidentally giving us insights into Jewish choral accompaniment in thirteenth-century Italy when the Psalter was made. Underneath is a text from Ps. 86:8 ('There is none like you among the gods')— the verse which introduces the Torah reading on sabbaths and festivals, along with 148:13–14.[1185] This is reproduced in PLATE 29.

Christian reception, somewhat predictably, could not interpret these last two phrases more differently. *Augustine's view of the 'two-edged sword' is that it is the word of God, both the Old and New Testaments, but comprised of both temporal (Jewish) and eternal (Christian) promises. Hence (using here Matt. 10:34) Christ's sword brings division between Christians and Jews and Christians and the world.[1186] *Jerome notes how in Rev. 1:16 we see this divisive sword coming from the actual mouth of Christ. He reads its two edges as the historical and allegorical ways of reading Scripture, one through the letter and the other through the spirit.[1187] By the Reformation the reading is different again: the Italian Jesuit Cardinal Robert Bellarmine, for example, reads the sword as having both a political and eschatological meaning. It is about the judiciary power entrusted to the saints at the end of time, when (with reference to 'binding kings in fetters' as in verse 8) 'they will pass sentence on the Pryeres, the Herods, the Neros, the Diocletians, and the other infidel princes.'[1188]

As for the 'New Song', Augustine argues acerbically that God's praises are not to be found in the synagogues of the Jews, nor in the ways of pagans or the errors of heretics, nor in the applause of theatres. His praise is to be found in the churches of the saints: so as for the New Song, 'You are it!'.[1189] Augustine's commentary on verse 1 argues 'The Old Testament is an old song, the New Testament a new song. In the Old Testament are temporal and earthly promises. Whoso loveth earthly things singeth an old song: let him desire to sing a new song, live the things of eternity'.[1190] Jerome concurs: the new song is for the church, 'a new people that sings a new song'.[1191] *Cassiodorus expands and give a reason for this: the new song must be sung to Jesus Christ, for his having built the universal Jerusalem from out of the whole world (verse 2).[1192] *Bede and pseudo-Thomas take this further still: the psalm is the voice of Christ addressing the faithful about his resurrection and future judgement.[1193]

[1185] Metzger 1996: 98.
[1186] Neale and Littledale 1874–79: IV/436–7. See also Augustine trans. Uyl 2017: 695; and Cassiodorus trans. Walsh 1991b: 460.
[1187] Jerome trans Ewald 1963: Homily 59, pp.424–9, especially 427–8.
[1188] Selderhuis 2018: 396, citing Bellamine's *Commentary on the Psalms*, p. 376.
[1189] Wesselschmidt 2007: 428–29, citing Augustine's Sermon 34.6 in *WSA* 3 2:168.
[1190] Augustine trans. Uyl 2017: 693.
[1191] Jerome trans Ewald 1963: Homily 59, p. 424.
[1192] Cassiodorus trans. Walsh 1991b: 457–8.
[1193] Neale and Littledale 1874–79: IV/433.

In the light of this somewhat divisive commentary tradition on the sword and the song, it is somewhat of a relief to hear Orlando *di Lasso's sixteenth-century six-voice setting, *Cantate Domino*, and J. S. *Bach's three-part motet *Singet dem Herrn ein Neues Lied* (1726–7), which combines Pss. 149:1–3, 150:2 and 6 with a hymn by Johann Gramann.[1194] These, and other examples by, for example, William *Byrd, William Lawes, Heinrich *Schütz, Thomas Tomkins and Charles Villiers *Stanford breathe concord and spiritual meaning into this 'New Song'.[1195]

In the light of the Jewish readings about women resisting the violence in this psalm, it is ironic that some illuminated Psalters present women's presence in the psalm in a military light: the references to dancing and making melody with the tambourine (verses 3) are interpreted as about women's roles in celebrating victory in war (see for example Exod. 15:2 and 1 Sam. 18:6–7). But they are also given a Christian twist. So the *Utrecht Psalter* (fol. 83r) depicts *Christ-Logos to the upper right, with three women playing harps and drums and singing and dancing before him, with a group in front of a sanctuary looking on, and other saints (with a two-edged sword in their hands) praising God below the Christ figure. In the bottom register are all the nations Christ has rebuked: defenseless, handcuffed, or in stocks, they are the victims of the women's victory song.[1196] Some two hundred years later, the *Eadwine Psalter* (fol. 260v) has a very similar composition.[1197]

The *St. Albans Psalter* also represents the participation of women, but this is clearly more liturgical than military: God looks down to bless the church. Eight women stand in a building, probably a church, hands raised: they are singing the 'new song' in the congregation of the faithful (verse 1). But they also watch three soldiers with drawn swords (verse 6) facing two devils and ready to execute vengeance on the nations (verse 7). Here the women are the 'faithful ones': somewhat paradoxically, they observe the execution of justice not in violence but in song.[1198]

Despite its links with 148, Psalm 149 exhibits a very different mood. The call to the cosmos to give praise has been replaced by a call to the 'faithful' in Zion to offer praise, but not for the sake of creation but to defeat the powers of enemy nations. Psalm 149 has nothing like the aural, visual and poetic reception history of 148; one of its key elements in more recent reception is through a call to political action.

[1194] Dowling Long and Sawyer 2015: 221–22.
[1195] For a selection of other composers of this psalm see https://www2.cpdl.org/wiki/index.php/Psalm_149.
[1196] See https://psalter.library.uu.nl/page/173.
[1197] See https://bit.ly/33jG4Tc.
[1198] See https://www.albani-psalter.de/stalbanspsalter/english/commentary/page370.shtml.

Several scholars have compared the second-to-last psalm of the MT Psalter with Psalm 2, not least in their focus on the humiliation of kings (using different forms of *melakim* in 149:8 and 2:2,10) and of foreign nations (called both *goyim* and *'ummim* in 149:7 and 2:1), because of their refusal to bow the knee to Israel's God.[1199] In 149:8 God binds his enemies with 'chains of iron' (*bekable barzel*) whilst in 2:9 God breaks the nations with a 'rod of iron' (*beshebet barzel*). In Psalm 2:6–7 this victory is achieved through the Davidic King; in Psalm 149 the king is absent, and instead the victory is through God as King, but in each case the victory emanates from Zion (149:2; 2:6).[1200]

We have noted several times how Denis Tucker observes the way that the psalms, especially in Book Five, wrestle with the empires and enemies who remain a perpetual threat to the psalmists, and how this concern with a 'new order', starting from Zion, is maintained to the very end of the Psalter.[1201] Hence it is not surprising that through the ages Psalm 149 has been used politically. The German radical Reformer Thomas Müntzer used it to incite the Germans to rebellion in 1524–35. It was one of the psalms known as a 'Battle Hymn of the Lord'. It was sung by the Huguenots during the Wars of Religion from 1562 onwards. And, along with Psalm 2, it was used explicitly in condemnations of kings and secular powers by *Calvinist forces throughout the sixteenth century.[1202] The *Tate and Brady version of 149:7–8 has a clear political ring to it:[1203]

> Just vengeance to take for injuries past;
> To punish those lands for ruin design'd;
> With chains, as their captives, to tie their kings fast,
> With fetters of iron their nobles to bind...

The Cambridge edition of the Bible in 1629 offered contemporary titles to the psalms. Psalm 149 had an earlier title 'To praise the Lord for his victory and conquests that he giveth to his saints'. Its title is now 'The praises given to God for that power he hath given to the church to rule the consciences of men'. The power of the church in the political arena was retained as a focus for this psalm until 1743. It was frequently used in sermons opposing the monarchy during the civil war; the Puritan Hugh Peter used it in 1648 when he preached against the deposed and imprisoned Charles I. It was used by radical Puritans

---

[1199] See deClaissé-Walford 1997: 102; Wittman 2014: 57–61.
[1200] Gillingham 2013c: 11.
[1201] Tucker 2014a: 192–93.
[1202] Reid 1971: 36–54; Gillingham 2008: 156–57.
[1203] https://www2.cpdl.org/wiki/index.php/Psalm_149.

('The Fifth Monarchy Men') to validate their beliefs in their incitement for the quick establishment of God's Kingdom on earth. It was an ideal psalm for those who saw the European kings receiving their power not from God but from the Beast.[1204]

The American jazz pianist and composer David Brubeck's *The Gates of Justice* was first performed in 1969 at the Union of American Hebrew Congregations Convention in Miami, Florida. It is protest music, coming out of the Civil Rights demonstrations and anti-Vietnam war rallies of 1960s. It uses progressive jazz with a Jewish cantor; it also uses spirituals, blues, and a brass ensemble, assimilating the music of the Beatles and Simon and Garfunkel alongside Chopin, Mexican dances, and Russian folksongs. Psalm 149 is used at the very end: 'O Come Let us Sing a New Song' is used to consider the attributes of God not in praise but in practice, in working out justice in the world.[1205] This is a fitting final reflection on a psalm which has a somewhat different vision from its near neighbours.

Psalm 150: Praise in Music

Do the references to praising God in 'his sanctuary' and 'his mighty firmament' in verse 1 suggest that the psalm was sung in Temple liturgy, or that, as Zenger has argued, it is 'the linguistic and literary imagination of a cosmic liturgy'?[1206] Perhaps like Ezekiel's vision of the Jerusalem Temple in Ezek. 40–48, it has elements of both. The reference to the sanctuary (*qodesh*) is ambiguous but frequently refers to the Temple, and the firmament (*raqia'*) can imply the vault of heaven, as in Gen. 1:6. The *LXX* adds to this ambiguity by translating 'the assembly of the faithful' in the plural (*en tois hagiois autou*) which could refer either to the congregation, or to angelic beings in heaven. The abundant musical arrangements tend to interpret Psalm 150 as an actual liturgy, albeit pointing to a heavenly reality beyond. Artistic works similarly depict the interplay between both earthly and heavenly music.

When we examine the links with corresponding psalms, Psalm 150, like 148, moves from the praise of God in the heavens to praising God on earth. As we noted for Psalm 148, there are other links as well.[1207] In each case it would appear that the praise pertains to an actual and ordered liturgy: each psalm contains ten

---

[1204] A reference by *Milton in *Eikonoklastes, MCPW* III, p. 598, cited in Hill 1993: 351–3.
[1205] See Stern 2013: 177–85, especially p. 183 on Psalm 149.
[1206] Hossfeld and Zenger 2005: 657.
[1207] See p. 424 (Psalm 148).

imperative calls to praise God, with an Hallelujah at the beginning and another at the end to make twelve in all.[1208] Unlike 148, however, Psalm 150 only has one verse out of the six offering reasons for the praise (verse 3: God's 'mighty deeds' and 'surpassing greatness'): 150:4–6 are more concerned with the *sound* of the praise rather than, as was more prominent in Psalm 148, the *vision* of the whole created order joining in.[1209] Of all the psalms, 150 has the greatest auditory appeal. Ps. 149:3 has some specific examples of music and dance, but 150:3–4 has far more, and in each case it is likely that these refer to some actual liturgy, albeit without rubrics: the corresponding words are *maḥol* (dance), *toph* (tambourine) and *kinor* (translated by the NRSV as 'lyre' in 149:3 and 'harp' in 150:3).

Reception in the commentary tradition has focussed on different issues. One is a certain intrigue with numbers—first, with the calls to praise, and secondly, with the instruments used. We noted above that, like 148, there are ten imperative calls to praise. These are seen to represent the ten commandments, announced by the blowing of the **shofar* as in verse 3.[1210] They also remind us of the *sephirot*, or the ten attributes of God according to *Kabbalistic mysticism.[1211] According to Kimḥi, however, the ten calls refer to the ten heroes of faith, all referred to implicitly in the psalms (Adam, Melchizedek, Abraham, Moses, David, Solomon, Asaf, and the three sons of Korah).[1212] They also recall the ten pronouncements of God at creation in Genesis 1.[1213] Little is written about the importance of the number twelve, by adding on the two Hallelujahs: but references are made to the twelve tribes and the twelve gates of the Temple. The number thirteen is commented on by *Kimḥi (i.e. adding in not only the two Hallelujahs but also the eleventh use of the verb *h-l-l* in verse 6): this is a reminder of the Jewish belief in the Thirteen Attributes of God with which he governs the world.[1214] In all these (essentially Jewish) readings the psalm is given an allegorical meaning as well as a literal one, and less is made of the music itself.

The second interest in numbers concerns the instruments found in verses 3–5. Some argue that the number is seven (reading the 'cymbals' in verse 5 as of only one kind). Others, using verses 3–6, count the 'cymbals' twice and add the human voice ('everything that breathes') as well, thus creating the number nine. The latter better fits the Greek and Latin translations: the Greek refers to 'melodious cymbals' (*kumbalois euēchois*) as well as 'noisy cymbals' (*kumbalois*

[1208] See p. 424, especially note 1149 (Psalm 148). 150:6 uses the verb *h-l-l* in the jussive form, making the number thirteen.

[1209] See pp. 424, 426–27 (Psalm 148).

[1210] Translated as 'trumpet' in the NRSV. See for example R. Yosef in Feuer 2004: 1736–7.

[1211] Markus 2016: 305b.

[1212] Feuer 2004: 1736.

[1213] *Ros Has* 32a.

[1214] Cohen 1992: 479, citing *Kimḥi.

alalagmou), and the Latin follows this with *cymbalis bene sonantibus* and *cymbalis iubilationis*. Another emphasis is on the number three, by noting how the instruments fall into three comprehensive categories: wind ('trumpet' and 'pipe' in the NRSV), string ('lute' 'harp' and 'strings' in the NRSV) and percussion ('tambourine', 'clanging cymbals' and 'loud clashing cymbals' in the NRSV). The number five is reached if one adds to this human performance, evident in 'dance' and, presumably, song ('Let everything that breathes praise the Lord'). So we have three, five, seven and nine as key numbers. Of these, the number nine has received the most comment: this is seen as an allusion to the nine celestial bodies of the stars, planets and moon, following the tradition that as their forces are transmitted to earth, they each create a spiritual message akin to the sound of music. 'Thus, the musical accompaniment described in this psalm celebrates God's complete mastery over the affairs of earth through His celestial intermediaries'.[1215]

Christian commentators again note the importance of the number ten as an allusion to the Decalogue, but here read praise as the 'new law' for Christians.[1216] The number four is important in verses 1–2: the sanctuary, firmament, mighty deeds and surpassing greatness are now all symbols of the four Gospels.[1217] Eight musical instruments are identified (following the Greek and Latin use of two sort of cymbals in verse 5) and these are now a symbol of the eighth day after the resurrection, when Christ encouraged his church to reign with him.[1218]

Given Jewish reticence about singing to musical instruments in synagogues after the destruction of the Temple in 70 CE, the earlier commentary tradition on this psalm might explain its interest in the numerical values in the psalm rather than its contribution to music in liturgy, despite its use at *Pesukei de-Zimra*. There, however, it would have been recited, not sung to musical accompaniment. This would also have been the case at the end of marriage services and during *Rosh Hashanah*. It is only over the last three centuries that musical accompaniment in synagogue worship has been permitted in some traditions.

This does not exclude Jewish commentators reading the psalm in a way which is sensitive to music: the changes in the sounds, for example between the blast of the *shofar* and the soft tones of the harp and lyre, are seen to reflect a broad spectrum of emotions taken up in praise of God.[1219] Other commentators see the music as an analogy of the soul making its final ascent to God: God's place in his heavenly sanctuary in verse 1 becomes the place to which the soul

---

[1215] Feuer 2004: 1738, citing also *b.Yoma* 20b.
[1216] See p. 404 (on Psalm 144, where Augustine argues 'ten strings' stand for the ten commandments).
[1217] See Neale and Littledale 1874–79: IV/440.
[1218] For example, Neale and Littledale 1874–79: IV/464–66.
[1219] Feuer 2004: 1735.

also ascends in verse 6. The word *neshamah* (meaning both 'breath' and 'soul') is important in this respect, as the soul becomes absorbed into the musical harmony created by praise of God.[1220]

The early fathers also wrestled with singing and accompaniment to song in liturgy, although this was primarily because of pagan associations. So in the early monastic tradition Psalm 150 was chanted at *Lauds, but with no musical accompaniment; gradually, through the cathedral tradition, musical accompaniment became important and so echoed the spirit of the psalm itself. Early Christian commentary tradition, however, has little to say about the actual music, exploring more, like Jewish commentators, a moral and doctrinal reading of the psalm. *Origen, for example, is more interested in the *symbolic* significance of the musical instruments. The trumpet (verse 3) was to bring the mind into a state of contemplation whereby true teaching could be embraced. The lute and harp (verse 3) refer to the busy mind quickened by commands of Christ. The tambourine (verse 4) represents the death of fleshly desire, and dancing (verse 4) is about the unity of the church, denouncing divisions. The pipe (verse 4) similarly represents the unity of church brought about by reflective minds. The stringed instruments (verse 5) are to inspire our voices to achieve moral excellence. The melodious cymbal (verse 5) is the active mind affixed to a desire for Christ, and the joyous cymbal (verse 5) the mind purified by salvation in Christ.[1221]

*Clement of Alexandria is equally sceptical about musical performance: in his work on the right conduct at feasts, he uses Rom. 13:12–14 as the reason to avoid 'the licentious and mischievous art of music … Let the pipe be resigned to the shepherds, and the flute to the superstitious who are engrossed in idolatry…'[1222] So in Psalm 150, the trumpet is to remind us of the resurrection of the dead; the lyre is the mouth struck by the Spirit, as if by a plectrum, and so on. Listing the use of all the instruments in Psalm 150 by different *pagan* nations, Clement argues that the only instrument honouring God is the spoken word of God; if this is through song, given the associations of singing with drink, we encounter those 'liquid harmonies, which, through pernicious arts in the modulations of tones, train to effeminacy and scurrility'.[1223] *Chrysostom similarly interprets the possibility of using the psalm in song somewhat dismissively: the instruments denote our bodily parts, such as the eye, tongue, ear, hand, coordinated into worship of God.[1224] *Hilary of Poitiers, *Augustine and *Cassiodorus

---

[1220] Cohen 1992: 479.

[1221] Origen, *Commentary on the Psalms* 150:3–5, PG 12:1684, cited in Wesselschmidt 2007: 430.

[1222] Clement, in *Paedogogus*, Book Two Chapter 4, taken from ANCL 4, p. 216. I am grateful to Matthew Chalmers for this reference.

[1223] *Ibid.*

[1224] Chrysostom trans. Hill 1998: 381.

also emphasise that the psalm is about the mind, body and spirit in worship of God: exhortation to use music *per se* is avoided. Each is more interested in the use of numbers in the psalm, particularly with reference to the number 150.[1225]

One early Christian writer stands out in this respect. This is *Gregory of Nyssa.[1226] His other works on how each human represents the diverse musical harmony of the cosmos mean that he was already predisposed to seeing Psalm 150 as speaking of God as the 'conductor of the universe'. His writing on the soul's journey through the inscriptions of the Psalms mean that Gregory viewed Psalm 150 as the climax of the Psalter. This psalm brings to a finale the fifth and final stage of the ascent of the soul to God. It starts with the praise of humanity on earth (verses 2–4) and the clash of the cymbals in verse 5 marks a turn to 'the union of our nature with the angels', which is continued in verse 5 and 6.[1227] His commentary on the six verses emphasises how the soul is vitalised by the different instruments of music—from the trumpet silencing us to listen to the harmony of heaven, to the strings which take us upwards to enjoy the heavenly choirs, to the sound of the cymbals: although this is still a response to music in a non-literal way, it breathes a more positive spirit into the psalm compared with other commentators.[1228]

Many of the Reformers follow the Church Fathers in their commentaries on this psalm. The sixteenth-century French commentator, Wolfgang Musculus, for example, argues that '...the general and necessary things in the praise of God are not the expression, but the prayer: not the musical chords but the heart, not the song, but the love, joy, and exultation of the believing soul...'[1229] This can be achieved without the aid of music. *Luther, despite his love of music, used verse 6 as an injunction to 'Let Christ *Speak!*' in an argument about why liturgy should no longer be in Latin, but in the vernacular: hence he overlooks this last verse of the Psalter as the contribution of the human voice in accompanied song.[1230] *Calvin is quite different: in his discussion of the literal meaning of the musical instruments, he says nothing about their allegorical or tropological meaning. Indeed, he goes further still: in his understanding of the universality of praise found within the psalm, he concludes, as the last sentence in his entire commentary: '...We have been joined in the same symphony with the Jews, that

---

[1225] Hilary in Rigolot 2017: 183–87; Augustine trans. Uyl 2017: 697–99; Cassiodorus trans. Walsh 1991b: 461–69, especially 466. The division of the one hundred and fifty psalms into three groups, with fifty psalms in each, allowed for a 'one in three' Trinitarian reading of the Psalter as a whole.

[1226] For Gregory's contribution to our understanding of the reception of the psalms see Gillingham 2008: 30–31.

[1227] Heine 1995: 68–69, citing Inscriptions I. 117 and 122.

[1228] For the commentary on this psalm in English, see, Heine 1995: 120–21.

[1229] Musculus, *Psalms of David (Psalterium)* 1676, cited in Selderhuis 2018: 398.

[1230] Table Talk: Konrad Cordatus (1532) WA Tr 2:443, no. 2388b, using Ps 19:3; cited in Selderhuis 2018: 398.

we may worship God with constant sacrifices of praise, until being gathered into the kingdom of heaven, we sing with angels an eternal hallelujah.[1231]

Some of the restrained illustrations in early Psalters have been influenced by the writings of the Fathers. The *Theodore Psalter* (fol. 188r) has just one musician playing a tuba, with the hand of God coming out of heaven above him, an image found also in the *Barberini Psalter* (fol. 246v).[1232] *Biblioteca Vaticana gr. 752* (fol. 445v), following Chrysostom's commentary on verse 2, has no musicians at all, but focusses on the figure of Isaiah as an example of a vision of God's holiness in Isaiah 6.

Western Psalters, by contrast, are often quite bold. The *Utrecht Psalter* (fol. 83r) is perhaps the most interesting. In the centre of the image is a pipe 'organ', with huge bellows: four men work on these, whilst two others play it. Other groups of people praise God with trumpets, harps and cymbals on each side.[1233] The 'organ' is taken from the Latin *organo* (verse 4) which itself is a translation of the Greek *organon*, different from the Hebrew word *'ugab* which could be translated as 'flute' or 'pipe', as in Gen. 4:21. The *Stuttgart Psalter* (fol. 163v) offers another insight into ninth-century northern *Carolingian musical interpretation: in the bottom right a bellow organ, played by three men, is apparently producing dance music, as a naked figure to its left with a dancing band seems to indicate. In the top right is a woman percussionist, in the top left a man is playing a cornetto. In the centre is David, in Carolingian dress, strumming a lyre.[1234] The whole image, with its exuberant colours, is alive with music: it certainly flies in the face of the teaching of the Clement and Origen.

More contemporary images also use colour to evoke the sound of music—whereby 'colourscape' creates 'soundscape'. In the *Saint John's Bible*, Psalm 150 is the only psalm to be handwritten in gold: in a work which celebrates the music of the psalms through illumination, this illustrates the distinctive nature of this psalm. Golden neumes are thrown out of the text and others float at angles alongside it. This is a distinctive example of the use of art to create musical sound.[1235]

Perhaps the most notable is *Chagall's stained-glass window in Chichester Cathedral, with its title 'Let everything that hath breath praise the Lord'. People and animals join together in praise of God, using the instruments referred to in the psalm: this is a scene of sheer exuberance—the dominant red indicates the

[1231] Calvin trans. Beveridge and Calvin 1979: 321.

[1232] For *Theodore*, see http://www.bl.uk/manuscripts/Viewer.aspx?ref=add_ms_19352_f188r.

[1233] See https://psalter.library.uu.nl/page/173.

[1234] See https://bit.ly/338Pz7v.

[1235] Sink 2007: 44–45. See also https://saintjohnsbible.org/See/Explore_Book#book/429 and https://www.pinterest.co.uk/pin/202943526935615905/?nic_v2=1a3V5rre1.

triumphant and celebratory nature of the scene. Chagall's is a Jewish composition in a Christian Cathedral: the two figures in the centre hold the menorah, and David, astride a donkey, dominates the scene at the top, playing his harp.[1236] This image is found as PLATE 30.

A striking example bringing together both Jewish and Christian universal praise is by Debra *Band. For her illustrations of Psalm 150 in *I will Wake the Dawn*, the left page has an English version of the psalm, written in blue and red script, contained within a gold and blue tambourine, tied with a ribbon depicting a dawn landscape with rings of stars. The ribbons flow upwards and outwards: the music on them is the initial bars of *Mozart's *Concerto for the Flute and Harp* (K299), depicting 'wordless joy'. The Hebrew version is on the right facing page: the blue and red script is this time contained within a golden harp. But at the top of the harp, instead of strings, is an image of the dawn, encircled by interlocking rings and the word, in Hebrew, 'Hallelujah'. Both images speak of that earlier Jewish teaching about the way the celestial spheres come together to create 'crystalline music'. Again, the colourful vitality and rich symbolism make this a remarkable artistic-musical reception of the psalm.[1237]

Our last example in art dates much earlier. This is Luca della Robbia's *Cantoria* (1431–38), his first documented commission now in the Museo dell'Opera del Duomo, Florence. The 'singing gallery' was originally one of two marble organ pulpits (Donatello was later commissioned for the other) attached to the north-east and south-east crossing piers of Florence Cathedral, above the high altar, serving as raised platforms for singers and organists. The Cathedral was founded in 1296, so, almost one hundred and fifty years later, to use the text of Psalm 150 as a symbol of jubilant praise was appropriate in many ways. Robbia (?1399-1482), an already established sculptor born in Florence, modelled the upper part in the form of Roman sarcophagus, supported by consoles, and Psalm 150 was carved in Latin on the cornice, the base of the parapet and the base of the console. The ten reliefs are of groups of children and adolescents, some in Florentine dress, singing, dancing and playing instruments with genuine enthusiasm and delight. This reception of Psalm 150 in sculpture, here illustrating the simple praise of children, again enables us to hear the music inwardly through art.[1238]

Representations of Psalm 150 in poetry are less successful. Those which are set in rhyme have difficulties in representing the rich ethos of the psalm without over-simplifying it. One exception is a poem which develops the vision of the

---

[1236] Foster 2002: 17–21.

[1237] Band and Band 2007: 212–15 (illustrations and commentary).

[1238] See Paoletti and Radke 2005: 245. Also https://bit.ly/3mfyaB1.

psalm in a most original way. Again it is linked to the simple praise of children. Edward *Clarke's 'The Firmament' begins with the poet listening to the psalm sung by a girls' choir at the end of evensong. It is cold; they try to keep time, 'their little voice high/Inside the firmament'. The poet then considers his daughter:[1239]

> The weeks before last Christmas
> You sang throughout our house,
> In lines, half-lines, and odd words,
> A song you must have rehearsed
> Over and over again
> With friends at nursery:
> 'The angels are singing good news'.
> It was the first time that we
> Had ever heard you sing,
> And it took me several days
> To sit up and listen at last
> To your fine example of praise.

Psalm 150 is undoubtedly a musician's psalm of praise, and its actual musical reception is vast.[1240] Benjamin *Britten's *Psalm 150* (1960) deserves first mention for the way it, too, interprets the psalm through children's praise. Composed for the centenary celebrations of Britten's preparatory school in Aldeburgh, it lasts just five minutes, starting with a lively dance in F Major, initiated by 'the sound of the trumpet', moving into an animated round in A Major (let everything that hath breath…') and progressing into a percussive march in C major ('Praise the Lord!') and finishing with the *Gloria*. The children can both improvise and be guided in their selection of instruments, reflecting both the spontaneity and the form in the psalm itself.[1241]

A much earlier arrangement is Jan Pieterszoon *Sweelinck's sacred motet *Psaume 150. Or soit loué l'Eternel*, composed in 1614 for eight voices, for the Calvinist Oude Kirk in Amsterdam, where Sweelinck was organist for most of his life. As part of Sweelinck's ambitious project to set all the Psalter to music, this is a more predictable and unified composition, creating a sequence of waves of praise, joyful but also restrained.[1242]

By the nineteenth-century, hymnic versions of Psalm 150 were frequent. Catherine *Winkworth's translation of Joachim Neander's 'Lobe den Herren'

[1239] Clarke 2020: 155.
[1240] See for example https://www2.cpdl.org/wiki/index.php/Psalm_150.
[1241] See https://www.youtube.com/watch?v=d4Id5xgHVj8.
[1242] https://www.youtube.com/watch?v=tqI2HftcB3I.

(1665, taken from Luther's Bible) into 'Praise to the Lord, The Almighty' was published in *The Choral Book for England* in 1863. Its rhythmic contrast between long and short lines made it a popular hymn, drawing also from Psalm 103, and is still frequently used in Anglican worship today.[1243]

Another distinctive nineteenth-century example is the Austrian compooser Anton Bruckner's festive hymn, *Vermahnung zum Lobe Gottes*, also taken from Luther's Bible, and eventually performed in 1892 at the Musikverein Concert Hall in Vienna, with an orchestra representing the instruments of the psalm (wind, strings and percussion) and an *SATB chorus with solo soprano. Its strong opening, with repeated Hallelujahs, leading into a slower, more deliberate middle part celebrating the different instruments for praise, and its more contemplative ending indicate this composition was more for performance rather than liturgy, with parts of the melody reminiscent of Bruckner's earlier *Te Deum*.[1244]

An enduring example is Charles Villiers *Stanford's setting to 'O Praise God in his Holiness', using *Coverdale's version, composed as an Anglican chant in 1909. This is another majestic and measured version, and its appeal in the English Cathedral tradition continues to this day.[1245]

Perhaps one of the most original non-liturgical arrangements of Psalm 150 is Igor *Stravinsky's *Symphony of Psalms*, composed four years after his reaffirmation of his Russian Orthodox faith, and written to commemorate the anniversary of the Boston Symphony Orchestra in 1930. We have already discussed his composition of Ps. 39:12–13, and the connecting verses in Ps. 40:1–3.[1246] There we concluded that Stravinsky brought together the contradiction of faith and experience in Psalm 39, and the agony of waiting for God to act in Psalm 40, through an extraordinary interpretative use of rhythms, pitch, and orchestration, using melodic repetitions and unexpected echoes, adapting the Octatonic scale into alternate whole and half steps, with clashing keys and chords. These features also occur in Psalm 150 (which Stravinsky actually arranged first, but in anticipation of the other two psalms). His aim was to create a 'tryptich', as in a Byzantine altarpiece, where Psalm 150 is viewed as a 'prayer to the Russian image of the infant Christ with orb and sceptre'.[1247] The introductory 'Alleluias' are unexpectedly slow, almost whispered, 'aching … with tension and uncertainty'—very different from the confidence and verve of most arrangements of this psalm.[1248] (Figure 19). The tenor and bass then introduce a *laudate* figure who repeats the call to praise three times: it is hard to know if this threefold cry is of praise or of

---

[1243] See Watson 2002: 79–81.
[1244] See https://www.youtube.com/watch?v=1IkmI_Gx9yM.
[1245] See https://www.youtube.com/watch?v=EmMmN6G29AU.
[1246] See Gillingham 2018: 241 and 246–7.
[1247] Dowling Long and Sawyer 2015: 232; also Stern 2013: 159–67.
[1248] LeMon 2017: 39.

FIGURE 19   *The unexpected introduction to Psalm 150 by Ivor Stravinsky.*
Source: Public Domain/Creative Commons/Open Government (UK) Licence.

pain.[1249] The next section (verses 1b–2) is full of rhythmic and chromatic energy as the words 'his mighty firmament' and 'his mighty deeds' evoke for Stravinsky Elijah's chariot being taken up into the heavens. The following part (verse 3), opening with flutes and first trombone, introduces a sustained hymn (verses 4–6) but actually without tambourine and cymbals, piano or harp: this is fearful, vigorous, insistent praise, but it is certainly not jubilant.[1250] The extra finale returns to the whispered Alleluias and the earlier *laudate* figure, highlighting the nature of praise which lives as much with fear and pain as it does with sheer exuberance, and so fits well with the tenor of Psalms 39 and 40 before it.[1251]

Steve *Reich composed his *Tehillim* (1980) after the rekindling of his Jewish faith in the 1970s. The four psalms (19, 34, 18 and 150), each using Hebrew cantillation, all play imaginatively on the sound of Hebrew words.[1252] Psalm 150 focusses on the Hebrew word 'Hallelujah', using strings, wind, drums, percussion, keyboard and especially three soprano voices. Its imaginative use of percussion makes it distinctive: tambourines, hand-clapping, maracas, marimba, vibraphone, crotales all take the psalm beyond its Jewish roots. Its confident and celebrative tone could not be more different from Stravinsky's version.[1253]

This contrasts with John *Rutter's psalm setting, 'O Praise God in His Holiness', taken from Coverdale's version, was commissioned for the Golden Jubilee of Queen Elizabeth II in June 2002 and performed at St. Paul's Cathedral. The festive tenor and dancing rhythms are produced by the main choir, whilst three solo

[1249] LeMon 2017: 40.

[1250] LeMon 2017: 47.

[1251] See https://www.youtube.com/watch?v=VUSfrgPQjRM.

[1252] See the discussion of the three earlier psalms in Gillingham 2018: 121–22, 128, and 209 respectively.

[1253] Dowling Long and Sawyer 2015: 233–34. Also https://www.stevereich.com; and https://bit.ly/31T96s8.

sopranos (stationed in the dome for the first performance) add a more reflective and ethereal tone to a piece which is essentially one of majestic celebration.[1254]

Psalm 150 is also used in Karl *Jenkins' *Dewi Sant*. This thirty-minute piece was performed on Saint David's Day in 2018 by the BBC National Orchestra of Wales and its English premier was in Birmingham two months later. The performance starts with three reflections, in Welsh, on themes from Saint David's last sermon; three psalms, in Latin, follow: these are 22, 27 and 150. The finale is an English poem in honour of the saint. Despite its Welsh focus the rhythms of all three psalms have Afro-Caribbean affinities: so in Psalm 150 the instruments are brass, and percussion and strings, with the drums and tambourine playing the major part and voices working in syncopation. In stark contrast to Stravinsky, Psalm 150 starts with a massive shout from the choir, after which there are several repeated calls of 'Laudate', with the choir actually beating the copies of their scores.

The Messianic Jewish Band Miqedem, based in Tel Aviv, composed a version of the 'new song', based on Ps. 149:1–5, for their album in 2016. Psalm 150, entitled 'Halleluhu' was released on the same album. It was performed live in Tacoma WA in 2017 and makes a most striking contrast to the above examples.[1255]

I end with three composers who have each in different ways had associations with an ongoing project on the psalms based here at Oxford University, called the TORCH Oxford Psalms Network.[1256] The first composer is Howard *Goodall, who in 2019 gave a concert on his own psalms for this network and has supported it on several occasions.[1257] His arrangement of Psalm 150 comes from Scotland: 'The Rosslyn Psalm' was composed for the refurbishment of Rosslyn Chapel in Midlothian in 2012, and was performed by the National Youth Choir of Scotland. Using the text from *The Scottish Psalter* (1650) the arrangement is for SATB choir, organ and harp, and is full of exuberant syncopations.

Alexander Massey, composer of Jewish sacred music, instrumental music and arranger of Yiddish folksongs for Jewish communities worldwide has also performed for the Psalms Network.[1258] He has written two very different liturgical compositions of Psalm 150. One is a more contemplative solo performance with piano and wind accompaniment, in English, demonstrating quiet gratitude rather than exuberant praise, and playing on the ten-fold call to praise throughout the psalm. The other, in Hebrew, for four voices, is a 32-bar canon for singing, for example, at *Pesukei de-Zimra*. This piece also plays on the different calls to praise in the psalm—but in this case using the human voice to imitate the *shofar* and cymbals.[1259]

[1254] See https://www.youtube.com/watch?v=l-pxiduwAJE.

[1255] See https://www.youtube.com/watch?v=fvUgp6dwihg&list=RDfvUgp6dwihg&start_radio=1&t=21.

[1256] See https://www.torch.ox.ac.uk/the-oxford-psalms-network.

[1257] See https://www.torch.ox.ac.uk/event/pelicans-shepherds-0.

[1258] See https://www.torch.ox.ac.uk/event/god-is-in-the-detail.

[1259] See https://bit.ly/3s0YXVn; also https://bit.ly/3Il0JQQ.

Andy Mackay (of Roxy Music) has also offered ongoing support for Oxford's Psalms network. Psalms 150, 130 and 90 are used in his *3Psalms*, a post-rock oratorio begun in the mid–1990s; it is a synthesis of many musical influences, including the choral tradition, electronica and rock and roll. Psalm 150 is an energetic and exciting piece, having its premier at the Southbank Centre in 2018. The first call to praise uses the horn, followed by strings; the later calls, sung first in Latin and then in English (using Coverdale) rise repeatedly upwards to a final crescendo of praise: 'Amen, Amen'. All is still, and silent: but out of the unexpected stillness we then hear one single 'Amen', spoken by a child, illustrating the universal appeal of the psalm.[1260] *3Psalms* is a concert-hall performance for an audience unfamiliar with the psalms, illustrating yet again the way in which the praise can be performed both within and outside liturgy.

By ending on a note of silence, Andy Mackay also brought Psalm 150 closer to Psalm 1, with its emphasis on silent meditation (Ps. 1:2). The contrasting links between the six verses of both psalms suggest that the compilers intended two very different compositions to 'bookend' the Psalter. Psalm 1 introduces the Psalter with its themes of the 'two ways' and the importance of personal obedience to the Torah: the context is individual and the vision exclusivist. Psalm 150 concludes the Psalter with a vision of worship from the Temple outwards, so 'everything that breathes' praises God through music and song: the context is universal and the vision inclusivist. The two psalms seem to deliberately mirror one another: they suggest the complementary concerns of the compilers at the early stage of reception history.

The link between Psalms 1 and 150 is also brought out in the contemporary poet Malcolm Guite's *David's Crown*. This extraordinary collection of one hundred and fifty poems was composed during the lockdowns of Covid-19. Each poem on each psalm is fifteen lines long, set out in five *tercets of *terza rima*, imitating a 'miniature Psalter'. In imitation of John Donne, Guite has created a 'corona' or coronet of psalms, whereby the last line of one psalm is the same as the first line of the next. Sometimes the corona works as a 'garland of praise'; much of the collection, however, is more like a 'crown of thorns', as it mirrors the 'twists and turns of human experience' whilst living through the pandemic.[1261] Below is Guite's version of Psalm 150:

Psalm 150: CL *Laudate Dominum*

For buried seeds the time has come to flower,
To blossom into victory and praise.
So praise God in his firmament of power

[1260] See https://www.youtube.com/watch?v=2OcKIdL-RXc.
[1261] Guite 2021: xiii-xv. Psalm 150, following, is found on p. 150.

Whose only power is love: the power to raise
The dead to life, the power to restore
The lost, and turn our long lament to praise.

Oh praise him in his noble acts and for
His great redemption. Praise him with the sound
Of trumpets. Tune your music at the door

He is about to open. Beat the ground
With light and loosened feet, for all his ways
Are glory, and all places hallowed ground.

So come and bring him all your nights and days,
And come into his courts with joyful song,
Come to the place where every breath is praise.

Guite fashions the last line of Psalm 150 so that it is the same as the first line in Psalm 1. Anyone committed to reading the *Daily Office prays the Psalter in this sort of never-ending cycle, and Guite gives us refreshing insights as to how this connection between endings and beginnings might work out. So Psalm 1 (with a more explicit Christian focus) begins:[1262]

Psalm 1: *Beatus vir qui non abiit*

Come to the place where every breath is praise,
And God is breathing through each passing breeze.
Be planted by the waterside and raise

Your arms with Christ beneath these rooted trees…

And so we move from Psalm 150 to Psalm 1 and forward to Psalm 150 again— in a complete corona.

But *is* 150 the final psalm? This is not the case in several versions, including at least one scroll at *Qumran, 11QPs[a], where Psalm 150 is followed by the 'Hymn to the Creator' and then 2 Samuel 23, a biography of David, Psalms 140, 134 and 151.[1263] In the *Septuagint and the *Vulgate 'Psalm 151' is often placed next to Psalm 150, even though it is given the title 'supernumerary'. Hence commentators of the Greek and Latin versions are still interested in the number '150' and can still speak of the Psalters as comprising 'the Three Fifties', and illuminated Psalters often use illustrations at Psalms 51 and 101 (NRSV Psalms 52 and 102).

Because of its paradoxical relationship with the Psalter in later reception history we will look at Psalm 151 by way of it being a supernumerary psalm.

[1262] Guite 2021: 1.
[1263] In MasPs[b] at Masada, which is fragmentary, it does seem that Psalm 150 has nothing following it.

Psalm 151: Supernumerary: In Remembrance of David

The text of Psalm 151 is very difficult to analyse, as it is found in four differ-ent versions which are each different from the other. Many scholars believe the original psalm was in Hebrew, and that these four versions in different degrees derive from it.

The *Septuagint is probably the earliest version we have. Its threefold heading tells us that it is 'written by David's own hand' (*idiographos eis Dauid*), indicating the increasing importance of Davidic 'autobiography' by Hellenistic times; that it is 'outside enumeration' (*exōthen tou arithmou*), and that it concerns David's single-handed combat with Goliath.[1264] Only one of the other versions has this threefold title—the *Vulgate, because that is a translation of the Greek. David is the Shepherd Boy, who became, by God's choice, David the Musician (verses 1–5); but he is also David the Warrior who conquered the enemy 'the Philistine' (verses 6–7).[1265] The translation used in the NRSV is as follows:

> [1] I was small among my brothers,
> and the youngest in my father's house;
> I tended my father's sheep.
> [2] My hands made a harp;
> my fingers fashioned a lyre.
> [3] And who will tell my Lord?

[1264] The only psalm with a reference to Goliath is in the Septuagint's addition to the title of Psalm 143: see pp. 401–3.

[1265] *allofulos* usually means 'foreigner', but word is translated 'Philistine' in Ps. 55:1, in the context of the Gath, so it is appropriate to translate it the same way here, following 1 Sam. 17:40, even though there is no reference to Goliath.

Psalms Through the Centuries: A Reception History Commentary on Psalms 73–151, Volume Three, First Edition. Susan Gillingham.
© 2022 John Wiley & Sons Ltd. Published 2022 by John Wiley & Sons Ltd.

The Lord himself; it is he who hears.
⁴ It was he who sent his messenger (*angelos*)[1266]
and took me from my father's sheep,
and anointed me with his anointing oil.
⁵ My brothers were handsome and tall,
but the Lord was not pleased with them.

⁶ I went out to meet the Philistine,
and he cursed me by his idols.
⁷ But I drew his own sword;
I beheaded him,
and took away disgrace from the people of Israel.

It is unclear whether the Greek compilers tried to create links with previous psalms, because in many manuscripts Psalm 151 is detached from 150, being found near the end of the apocryphal collection. However, in the two important Greek manuscripts, *Codex Alexandrinus* and *Codex Sinaiticus*, Psalm 151 does follow Psalm 150. In both cases, it receives the title 'supernumerary'. Nevertheless, there are connections with 150: for example, in 151:3 the 'harp' (*organon*) and 'lyre' (*psaltērion*) which also occur in the Greek of Ps. 150:3 and 150:4 respectively. Furthermore, Greek Psalters such as *Theodore make a close connections between 150 and 151: in fol. 188r we see a boy blowing horn, as a hand emerges from heaven, illustrating Ps. 150:3; then fol. 188v is of David playing the lyre to the sheep; fol. 189v depicts David playing the pipe ('organ') to his flocks, but also of his being taken away from them by an angel (noting how his making music with the animals offers hints of the myth of Orpheus).[1267] Fol. 190r has an image of David's anointing by Samuel, and fol. 190v depicts David meeting Saul enthroned, whilst fol. 191r is of David's defeat of Goliath.[1268] The fact that there are five images for this one psalm, and only one for Psalm 150, suggests Psalm 151 was a well-known Byzantine psalm about David and closely connected with 150. *Benaki Vitr.* 34.3, a small handheld codex with one column per page and 162 illuminations, now preserved in the Benaki Museum, Athens, offers another such example: Psalm 150 (fol. 173v) is followed by Psalm 151 which has two superimposed images (fol. 174r, one of David fighting Goliath, the other of David as victor), divided by the last verse of the psalm.[1269]

[1266] 1 Sam. 16:16–23 records that God sent Saul: there is no reference to an angelic intervention.

[1267] See http://www.bl.uk/manuscripts/Viewer.aspx?ref=add_ms_19352_f189v; see the further reference to the Orpheus trope on p. 452.

[1268] See http://www.bl.uk/manuscripts/Viewer.aspx?ref=add_ms_19352_f191r.

[1269] See Cutler and Weyl Carr 1976: 283 and 289. See also https://bit.ly/3Gx1r1r.

There is a brief reference to Psalm 151 in *Athanasius' *Letter to Marcellinus*, where he speaks of singing Psalm 151 'which is especially a psalm of David' as a means of gaining comfort from a God who can gain victory over enemies like Goliath.[1270] But otherwise the Greek commentators make few references to this psalm.

There are translations of the *LXX* version in old Latin and of course in the *Vulgate*, where, following the Greek, Psalm 151 in several manuscripts follows 150.[1271] One difference in the *Psalterium Vetus* is the expansion of the ending of the psalm to speak of David slinging 'three stones' at Goliath in the middle of his forehead, thus laying him low by the might of the Lord (1 Sam. 17: 49–50 refers to only one stone). But in the *Psalterium Hebraicum*, for example, *Jerome did not incorporate Psalm 151 at all, presumably because the Hebrew did not have it. It appears in Jerome's *Psalterium *Gallicanum*, again because here Jerome was using the *LXX*, and because this version was incorporated into the *Vulgate*, Psalm 151 was included too.[1272] Most Latin commentators are, however, silent about the psalm: neither *Hilary, *Augustine, Jerome, nor *Cassiodorus have anything to say about it, stressing rather for Psalm 150 the idea of 'three fifties' which correspond with the three members of the Trinity.[1273]

A few Latin Psalters, some illuminated, give us some hint of the unique status of Psalm 151. *Cod Pal Lat 68*, which starts at Ps. 39:11 and ends at 151, is important because it also has a *Gloss on Psalm 151 in the form a *catena*, relating it to events in David's life from 1 Samuel: here it follows Psalm 150. By contrast, however, the *Psalter of Ouen* contains Psalm 151, but it has no heading, is written in a different hand, and comes after the *Canticles.[1274]

It is believed that there are some thirty-seven surviving Anglo-Saxon Psalters, some fragmentary, dating between the eighth and twelfth centuries, and of these eighteen Psalters contain Psalm 151.[1275] Here the ninth-century *Vespasian Psalter* is particularly significant, not only for its Old English Gloss on Psalm 151 (fol. 141r), but also for the way it translates the Latin to create a rhythmic psalm with a Mercian dialect, using poetic techniques such as lineation and alliteration. This is a very early poetic imitation of any psalm: it is on an inserted leaf, however, and was probably included by a later glossator, so did not originally follow Psalm 150 in this version.[1276]

[1270] https://bit.ly/3ILPLtZ.

[1271] On a full appraisal of Psalm 151 in the *LXX* and a look at the rewriting of Psalm 151 in different versions, see Segal 2002: 139–158.

[1272] See Gillingham 2008: 36–7.

[1273] See the references to Hilary, Augustine and Cassiodorus on pp. 438–9 and note 1225.

[1274] See McNamara 2000: 114.

[1275] See Hawk 2015: 805–21, cited in Atkin and Leneghan 2017, n. 26, p. 8.

[1276] See again Hawk 2015: 816–21. Hawk also offers a useful side-by-side comparison of the Middle English versions of Psalm 151 found in the *Vespasian Psalter* and in the *Eadwine Psalter*.

Other Psalters include the *Ramsey Psalter* (a late tenth-century illuminated Psalter possibly originally from Winchester) the *Utrecht Psalter*, and the *Eadwine Psalter*. Of these, the *Utrecht* has the earliest image, taken from the Latin, of Psalm 151 (fol. 91v). It offers four scenes from David's life, three (David as Shepherd, Musician and Warrior) being expressed in Psalm 151, and the fourth (David as King, enthroned with a sword in his right hand and a sceptre in his left) being the consequence of this story-in-poetry. David as Musician plays the same 'bellow organ', here with eight pipes, which we noted for Psalm 150.[1277] Here, however, Psalm 151 is placed not next to 150 but after the Canticles, following the Magnificat and the Athanasian Creed. Not surprisingly the related *Eadwine Psalter* also detaches Psalm 151 (fol. 281r, with image, and fol. 281v) from 150 (fol. 261v): Psalm 151 follows on from the Canticles, again indicating that this psalm does not have the same liturgical history. Furthermore, its gloss is also in a different *Carolingian miniscule, not the Anglo-Norman orthography as in the previous psalms.[1278] But it does depict David playing another splendid bellow organ with eight pipes.[1279]

Psalm 151 is also found in Syriac: it is unclear as to whether it is a translation from the Greek (its version is quite close to the *LXX), or whether it goes back to a Hebrew version, but its earliest date must be the beginning of the Christian era. 151 is found in two manuscripts at the end of the *Peshitta Psalter* along with Psalms 152–155, and these other four probably do derive from the Hebrew: Psalms 154 and 155 are actually found (in Hebrew) at *Qumran. Here the 'base text' is the twelfth-century *Baghdad MS 1113*, preserved in the Library of Chaldean Patriarchate, (fols. 118b–20b). The threefold title to 151, implying some knowledge of the Greek, reads 'This is its number. Of David. When he was alone (*'tktb*, probably better read as 'in combat with') with Goliath'. Verses 3–4 refer to David finding a lion and wolf and tearing them to pieces to protect his sheep: the same reference is found in Syriac Psalm 152, whose heading reads 'Said by David, when he was in combat with the lion and the wolf that took sheep from his flock.' The wolf is a puzzle: it may well be due to a misreading of the word of 'bear', for in 1 Sam. 17:34–37 David fights a lion and bear. Verse 7, difficult to translate in the Greek, also reads differently: 'Who will tell my Lord? The Lord Himself, He is my God'.[1280]

The Hebrew version of Psalm 151 is important because we are able to date it with a little more certainty, for it is found in 11QPs^a which most scholars

---

[1277] See https://psalter.library.uu.nl/page/190.
[1278] Faulkner 2017: 88–91 for Psalm 151.
[1279] See https://bit.ly/2QU5sJb.
[1280] Skehan 1976: 143–148; also Strugnell 1966: 257–81.

would date, on palaeographic grounds, to the first-century CE. Nothing was known about any Hebrew version of 'Psalm 151' until it was first discovered at Qumran in 1956. It has no reception history in Jewish commentary tradition, nor in liturgy, music or art. It is divided into two sections, 151A and 151B, and it is a therefore a longer version than in the Greek, although only two verses of 151B have survived.

The heading to 151A could be read as 'An Hallelujah of David the Son of Jesse'. There is nothing about it being supernumerary, as in the *LXX*, because of course its final place in 11QPs^a reveals it is not. Nor does the title have any reference to Goliath, because there is no reference to him in the Hebrew psalm. There is an interesting expansion in 151A:4–5, where although the mountains and hills cannot praise God, the trees and animals can give him praise. Although some scholars have seen this as 'non-biblical', Ps. 148:9–10, which calls 'wild animals and cattle' to praise God (verse 10) as well as 'mountains and all hills, fruit trees and all cedars' (verse 9) suggests that this is a variant of a biblical tradition. It is possible that there are some Hellenistic associations of David with the Orpheus myth, where trees and animals are charmed by music from the lyre.[1281]

The heading to 151B has a historical superscription which reads 'Beginning of the [mighty deeds] of David, after the prophet of God had anointed him'. The remaining verse begins with David encountering the 'Philistine' who 'utters insults'. The specific killing of Goliath is missing. Together both 151A and 151B are notable for their specifically Davidic 'autobiography': the use of the 'I' form is quite different from the *LXX* version.[1282] In some ways this Qumranic version would have been more appropriate (chronologically speaking) at the beginning of the Psalter, where the emphasis on David's early life is so much more extensive; but it is found at the very end of 11QPs^a and fits with the increasing emphasis on the complete life of David towards the end of that scroll: after the Hymn to the Creator we find 2 Sam. 23, then the list of David's Compositions, then Psalm 140 (a psalm 'of David'), then (somewhat curiously) 134, and finally 151A and 151B. The blank column after 151B indicates that this was indeed the finale to this scroll. As J. A. Sanders observes: '11QPs^a closes with psalms that deal with David's youth, his musicianship, his elevation to leadership of his people and his manifest ability to carry out, with piety and courage, the responsibilities of that office.'[1283]

So what do we make of this 'final' psalm with its four different modes of reception history?[1284] Its afterlife outside these traditions is minimal and also

---

[1281] See the earlier observation for the *Theodore Psalter*, p. 449. See also Sanders 1963: 82.

[1282] See Abeg *et al.* 1999: 585.

[1283] Sanders 1963: 85.

[1284] A useful account of the psalm is all these four languages is Dupont-Sommer 1964: 25–62.

quite specific. For example, it has a role in Ethiopian coronation rituals, and was recited by Emperor Haile Selassie at the beginning of his first address to the Council of State: this is about the 'lowly king' being promised great victory. It is used at *Matins in the Armenian church, but within a catena of canticles which also includes Psalms 52, 148–150, 113. It has not been adapted for regular liturgical use in either Protestant or Catholic liturgy; in most English translations 151 does not follow 150 but is on its own in an expanded version of the Apocrypha, following 3 and 4 Maccabees. Even though it is included in the (*Septuagint-based) Orthodox Psalter, and indeed follows on from 150, there is minimal evidence of its liturgical use. From this we can conclude that Psalm 151 is, overall, 'supernumerary'.

Its *Wikipedia* entry nevertheless notes a few contemporary uses. For example, in 1989 the Christian rock band called 'Jacob's Trouble' included, as Track 11 on their album *Door into Summer*, 'Psalm 151'; and in the TV Show *Touched by an Angel* (1998), one of the Episodes is entitled 'Psalm 151', on account of a song by Wynonna Judd called 'Testify to Love'; furthermore, in 2018 the rock artist Ezra Furman included a track 'Psalm 151' in his album *Transangelic Exodus*, although Judd confessed he had no idea that there really was a Psalm 151. In each case these artists probably chose their title to indicate some vague link with psalmody, but Psalm 151 was in fact their own 'extra psalm'. So perhaps this is what this psalm is about: an encouragement to anyone sufficiently creative in reception history to re-write their own '151'. In other words, when you want to compose an extra psalm, call it 'Psalm 151'; few people will know that another 'Psalm 151' already exists.

Psalms Numbering Table

NRSV	MT	LXX	VUL
Psalm 1.1	Psalm 1.1	Psalm 1.1	Psalm 1.1
Psalm 2.1	Psalm 2.1	Psalm 2.1	Psalm 2.1
Psalm 3.1	Psalm 3.1–2	Psalm 3.1–2	Psalm 3.1–2
Psalm 4.1	Psalm 4.1–2	Psalm 4.1–2	Psalm 4.1–2
Psalm 5.1	Psalm 5.1–2	Psalm 5.1–2	Psalm 5.1–2

Psalms Through the Centuries: A Reception History Commentary on Psalms 73–151, Volume Three,
First Edition. Susan Gillingham.
© 2022 John Wiley & Sons Ltd. Published 2022 by John Wiley & Sons Ltd.

NRSV	MT	LXX	VUL
Psalm 6.1	Psalm 6.1–2	Psalm 6.1–2	Psalm 6.1–2
Psalm 7.1	Psalm 7.1–2	Psalm 7.1–2	Psalm 7.1–2
Psalm 8.1	Psalm 8.1–2	Psalm 8.1–2	Psalm 8.1–2
Psalm 9.1	Psalm 9.1–2	Psalm 9.1–2	Psalm 9.1–2
Psalm 10.1	Psalm 10.1	Psalm 9.22	Psalm 9.22
Psalm 11.1	Psalm 11.1	Psalm 10.1	Psalm 10.1–2
Psalm 12.1	Psalm 12.1–2	Psalm 11.1–2	Psalm 11.1–2
Psalm 13.1	Psalm 13.1–2	Psalm 12.1–2	Psalm 12.1
Psalm 14.1	Psalm 14.1	Psalm 13.1	Psalm 13.1
Psalm 15.1	Psalm 15.1	Psalm 14.1	Psalm 14.1
Psalm 16.1	Psalm 16.1	Psalm 15.1	Psalm 15.1
Psalm 17.1	Psalm 17.1	Psalm 16.1	Psalm 16.1
Psalm 18.1	Psalm 18.1–2	Psalm 17.1–2	Psalm 17.1–2
Psalm 19.1	Psalm 19.1–2	Psalm 18.1–2	Psalm 18.1–2
Psalm 20.1	Psalm 20.1–2	Psalm 19.1–2	Psalm 19.1–2
Psalm 21.1	Psalm 21.1–2	Psalm 20.1–2	Psalm 20.1–2
Psalm 22.1	Psalm 22.1–2	Psalm 21.1–2	Psalm 21.1–2
Psalm 23.1	Psalm 23.1	Psalm 22.1	Psalm 22.1
Psalm 24.1	Psalm 24.1	Psalm 23.1	Psalm 23.1
Psalm 25.1	Psalm 25.1	Psalm 24.1	Psalm 24.1
Psalm 26.1	Psalm 26.1	Psalm 25.1	Psalm 25.1
Psalm 27.1	Psalm 27.1	Psalm 26.1	Psalm 26.1
Psalm 28.1	Psalm 28.1	Psalm 27.1	Psalm 27.1
Psalm 29.1	Psalm 29.1	Psalm 28.1	Psalm 28.1–2
Psalm 30.1	Psalm 30.1–2	Psalm 29.1–2	Psalm 29.1–2
Psalm 31.1	Psalm 31.1–2	Psalm 30.1–2	Psalm 30.1–2
Psalm 32.1	Psalm 32.1	Psalm 31.1	Psalm 31.1
Psalm 33.1	Psalm 33.1	Psalm 32.1	Psalm 32.1
Psalm 34.1	Psalm 34.1–2	Psalm 33.1–2	Psalm 33.1–2
Psalm 35.1	Psalm 35.1	Psalm 34.1	Psalm 34.1
Psalm 36.1	Psalm 36.1–2	Psalm 35.1–2	Psalm 35.1–2
Psalm 37.1	Psalm 37.1	Psalm 36.1	Psalm 36.1
Psalm 38.1	Psalm 38.1–2	Psalm 37.1–2	Psalm 37.1–2
Psalm 39.1	Psalm 39.1–2	Psalm 38.1–2	Psalm 38.1–2
Psalm 40.1	Psalm 40.1–2	Psalm 39.1–2	Psalm 39.1–2
Psalm 41.1	Psalm 41.1–2	Psalm 40.1–2	Psalm 40.1–2
Psalm 42.1	Psalm 42.1–2	Psalm 41.1–2	Psalm 41.1–2
Psalm 43.1	Psalm 43.1	Psalm 42.1	Psalm 42.1
Psalm 44.1	Psalm 44.1–2	Psalm 43.1–2	Psalm 43.1–2
Psalm 45.1	Psalm 45.1–2	Psalm 44.1–2	Psalm 44.1–2
Psalm 46.1	Psalm 46.1–2	Psalm 45.1–2	Psalm 45.1–2

(*Continued*)

NRSV	MT	LXX	VUL
Psalm 47.1	Psalm 47.1–2	Psalm 46.1–2	Psalm 46.1–2
Psalm 48.1	Psalm 48.1–2	Psalm 47.1–2	Psalm 47.1–2
Psalm 49.1	Psalm 49.1–2	Psalm 48.1–2	Psalm 48.1–2
Psalm 50.1	Psalm 50.1	Psalm 49.1	Psalm 49.1
Psalm 51.1	Psalm 51.1–3	Psalm 50.1–3	Psalm 50.1–3
Psalm 52.1	Psalm 52.1–3	Psalm 51.1–3	Psalm 51.1–4
Psalm 53.1	Psalm 53.1–2	Psalm 52.1–2	Psalm 52.1–2
Psalm 54.1	Psalm 54.1–3	Psalm 53.1–3	Psalm 53.1–3
Psalm 55.1	Psalm 55.1–2	Psalm 54.1–2	Psalm 54.1–2
Psalm 56.1	Psalm 56.1–2	Psalm 55.1–2	Psalm 55.1–2
Psalm 57.1	Psalm 57.1–2	Psalm 56.1–2	Psalm 56.1–2
Psalm 58.1	Psalm 58.1–2	Psalm 57.1–2	Psalm 57.1–2
Psalm 59.1	Psalm 59.1–2	Psalm 58.1–2	Psalm 58.1–2
Psalm 60.1	Psalm 60.1–3	Psalm 59.1–3	Psalm 59.1–3
Psalm 61.1	Psalm 61.1–2	Psalm 60.1–2	Psalm 60.1–2
Psalm 62.1	Psalm 62.1–2	Psalm 61.1–2	Psalm 61.1–2
Psalm 63.1	Psalm 63.1–2	Psalm 62.1–2	Psalm 62.1–3
Psalm 64.1	Psalm 64.1–2	Psalm 63.1–2	Psalm 63.1–2
Psalm 65.1	Psalm 65.1–2	Psalm 64.1–2	Psalm 64.1–2
Psalm 66.1	Psalm 66.1	Psalm 65.1	Psalm 65.1
Psalm 67.1	Psalm 67.1–2	Psalm 66.1–2	Psalm 66.1–2
Psalm 68.1	Psalm 68.1–2	Psalm 67.1–2	Psalm 67.1–2
Psalm 69.1	Psalm 69.1–2	Psalm 68.1–2	Psalm 68.1–2
Psalm 70.1	Psalm 70.1–2	Psalm 69.1–2	Psalm 69.1–2
Psalm 71.1	Psalm 71.1	Psalm 70.1	Psalm 70.1
Psalm 72.1	Psalm 72.1	Psalm 71.1	Psalm 71.1–2
Psalm 73.1	Psalm 73.1	Psalm 72.1	Psalm 72.1
Psalm 74.1	Psalm 74.1	Psalm 73.1	Psalm 73.1
Psalm 75.1	Psalm 75.1–2	Psalm 74.1–3	Psalm 74.1–2
Psalm 76.1	Psalm 76.1–2	Psalm 75.1–2	Psalm 75.1–2
Psalm 77.1	Psalm 77.1–2	Psalm 76.1–2	Psalm 76.1–2
Psalm 78.1	Psalm 78.1	Psalm 77.1	Psalm 77.1
Psalm 79.1	Psalm 79.1	Psalm 78.1	Psalm 78.1
Psalm 80.1	Psalm 80.1–2	Psalm 79.1–2	Psalm 79.1–2
Psalm 81.1	Psalm 81.1–2	Psalm 80.1–2	Psalm 80.1–2
Psalm 82.1	Psalm 82.1	Psalm 81.1	Psalm 81.1
Psalm 83.1	Psalm 83.1–2	Psalm 82.1–2	Psalm 82.1–2
Psalm 84.1	Psalm 84.1–2	Psalm 83.1–2	Psalm 83.1–2
Psalm 85.1	Psalm 85.1–2	Psalm 84.1–2	Psalm 84.1–2
Psalm 86.1	Psalm 86.1	Psalm 85.1	Psalm 85.1
Psalm 87.1	Psalm 87.1	Psalm 86.1	Psalm 86.1

NRSV	MT	LXX	VUL
Psalm 88.1	Psalm 88.1–2	Psalm 87.1–2	Psalm 87.1–2
Psalm 89.1	Psalm 89.1–2	Psalm 88.1–2	Psalm 88.1–2
Psalm 90.1	Psalm 90.1	Psalm 89.1	Psalm 89.1
Psalm 91.1	Psalm 91.1	Psalm 90.1	Psalm 90.1
Psalm 92.1	Psalm 92.1	Psalm 91.1–2	Psalm 91.1–2
Psalm 93.1	Psalm 93.1	Psalm 92.1	Psalm 92.1
Psalm 94.1	Psalm 94.1	Psalm 93.1	Psalm 93.1
Psalm 95.1	Psalm 95.1	Psalm 94.1	Psalm 94.1
Psalm 96.1	Psalm 96.1	Psalm 95.1	Psalm 95.1
Psalm 97.1	Psalm 97.1	Psalm 96.1	Psalm 96.1
Psalm 98.1	Psalm 98.1	Psalm 97.1	Psalm 97.1
Psalm 99.1	Psalm 91.1	Psalm 98.1	Psalm 98.1
Psalm 100.1	Psalm 100.1	Psalm 99.1	Psalm 99.1–2
Psalm 101.1	Psalm 101.1	Psalm 100.1–2	Psalm 100.1
Psalm 102.1	Psalm 102.1–2	Psalm 101.1–2	Psalm 101.1–2
Psalm 103.1	Psalm 103.1	Psalm 102.1	Psalm 102.1
Psalm 104.1	Psalm 104.1	Psalm 103.1	Psalm 103.1
Psalm 105.1	Psalm 105.1	Psalm 104.1	Psalm 104.1
Psalm 106.1	Psalm 106.1	Psalm 105.1	Psalm 105.1
Psalm 107.1	Psalm 107.1	Psalm 106.1	Psalm 106.1
Psalm 108.1	Psalm 108.1–2	Psalm 107.1–2	Psalm 107.1–2
Psalm 109.1	Psalm 109.1	Psalm 108.1	Psalm 108.1–2
Psalm 110.1	Psalm 110.1	Psalm 109.1	Psalm 109.1
Psalm 111.1	Psalm 111.1	Psalm 110.1	Psalm 110.1
Psalm 112.1	Psalm 112.1	Psalm 111.1	Psalm 111.1
Psalm 113.1	Psalm 113.1	Psalm 112.1	Psalm 112.1
Psalm 114.1	Psalm 114.1	Psalm 113.1	Psalm 113.1
Psalm 115.1	Psalm 115.1	Psalm 113.9	Psalm 113.9–10
Psalm 116.1	Psalm 116.1	Psalm 114.1	Psalm 114.1
Psalm 116.10	Psalm 116.10	Psalm 115.1	Psalm 115.1
Psalm 117.1	Psalm 117.1	Psalm 116.1	Psalm 116.1
Psalm 118.1	Psalm 118.1	Psalm 117.1	Psalm 117.1
Psalm 119.1	Psalm 119.1	Psalm 118.1	Psalm 118.1
Psalm 120.1	Psalm 120.1	Psalm 119.1	Psalm 119.1
Psalm 121.1	Psalm 121.1	Psalm 120.1	Psalm 120.1
Psalm 122.1	Psalm 122.1	Psalm 121.1	Psalm 121.1
Psalm 123.1	Psalm 123.1	Psalm 122.1	Psalm 122.1
Psalm 124.1	Psalm 124.1	Psalm 123.1	Psalm 123.1
Psalm 125.1	Psalm 125.1	Psalm 124.1	Psalm 124.1
Psalm 126.1	Psalm 126.1	Psalm 125.1	Psalm 125.1
Psalm 127.1	Psalm 127.1	Psalm 126.1	Psalm 126.1

(*Continued*)

NRSV	MT	LXX	VUL
Psalm 128.1	Psalm 128.1	Psalm 127.1	Psalm 127.1
Psalm 129.1	Psalm 129.1	Psalm 128.1	Psalm 128.1
Psalm 130.1	Psalm 130.1	Psalm 129.1	Psalm 129.1
Psalm 131.1	Psalm 131.1	Psalm 130.1	Psalm 130.1
Psalm 132.1	Psalm 132.1	Psalm 131.1	Psalm 131.1
Psalm 133.1	Psalm 133.1	Psalm 132.1	Psalm 132.1
Psalm 134.1	Psalm 134.1	Psalm 133.1–2	Psalm 133.1–2
Psalm 135.1	Psalm 135.1	Psalm 134.1	Psalm 134.1
Psalm 136.1	Psalm 136.1	Psalm 135.1	Psalm 135.1
Psalm 137.1	Psalm 137.1	Psalm 136.1	Psalm 136.1
Psalm 138.1	Psalm 138.1	Psalm 137.1	Psalm 137.1
Psalm 139.1	Psalm 139.1	Psalm 138.1	Psalm 138.1–2
Psalm 140.1	Psalm 140.1	Psalm 139.1–2	Psalm 139.1–2
Psalm 141.1	Psalm 141.1	Psalm 140.1	Psalm 140.1
Psalm 142.1	Psalm 142.1–2	Psalm 141.1–2	Psalm 141.1–2
Psalm 143.1	Psalm 143.1	Psalm 142.1	Psalm 142.1
Psalm 144.1	Psalm 144.1	Psalm 143.1	Psalm 143.1
Psalm 145.1	Psalm 145.1	Psalm 144.1	Psalm 144.1
Psalm 146.1	Psalm 146.1	Psalm 145.1	Psalm 145.1
Psalm 147.1	Psalm 147.1	Psalm 146.1	Psalm 146.1
Psalm 147.12	Psalm 147.12	Psalm 147.1	Psalm 147.1
Psalm 148.1	Psalm 148.1	Psalm 148.1	Psalm 148.1
Psalm 149.1	Psalm 149.1	Psalm 149.1	Psalm 149.1
Psalm 150.1	Psalm 150.1	Psalm 150.1	Psalm 150.1
[Psalm 151.1]	N/A	Psalm 151.1	Psalm 151.1

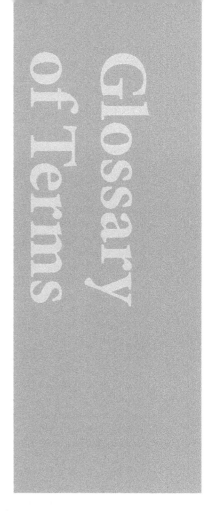

Glossary of Terms

A capella: singing without instrumental accompaniment.

Alcuin of York (c.735–804): Anglo-Saxon monk and scholar at court of Charlemagne. *De Psalmorum usu* (ALC 33) was a commentary on penitential psalms and psalms of ascents.

Ambrose of Milan (c.339–97): spiritual advisor of Augustine and opponent of Arianism; one of four fathers of the western church; his *Expositio Psalmi* combined pastoral and Christian allegorical readings of psalms.

Ambrosian chant: Milanese liturgical tradition associated with Ambrose of Milan, where psalms were chanted by choir and congregations (later known as *schola cantorum*).

'Amidah ('standing'): core prayer of the Jewish liturgy, recited standing three times daily; a.k.a. *Shemoneh Esrei* or 'Eighteen Benedictions'.

Antiphon: single psalm verse, often containing the central message of the psalm, sung by choir before and/or after singing whole psalm.

Psalms Through the Centuries: A Reception History Commentary on Psalms 73–151, Volume Three, First Edition. Susan Gillingham.
© 2022 John Wiley & Sons Ltd. Published 2022 by John Wiley & Sons Ltd.

Aquinas, Thomas (1225–74): Italian Dominican friar. *Postilla super Psalmos* (Psalms 1–54) was his unfinished commentary using a Scholastic approach to psalms.

Arianism: 4c. heresy that Jesus Christ was created and not fully divine; condemned at Councils of Nicaea (325), Constantinople (381) and Chalcedon (451).

Asaphite: guild of Levitical singers associated with music in Second Temple (see 1 Chronicles 15–16). Psalms 50 and 73–83 (mainly communal laments) are attributed to Asaph.

Ashkenazi: Jewish diaspora of Northern Europe; Yiddish culture, perpetuated partly through liturgy.

Athanasius (c. 296–373): Bishop of Alexandria (328–373) and chief defender of doctrine of Council of Nicaea (325); wrote an epistolary treatise on the psalms for Marcellinus.

Augustine of Hippo (354–430): One of four fathers of the western church; Bishop of Hippo from 396–430. His *Enarrationes in Psalmos* is first fully extant psalms commentary from this period with a notable Christological emphasis.

Bach, Johann Sebastian (1685–1750): German Lutheran composer; organist at Leipzig where his vast musical output of Biblical texts included some fifty on psalms.

Bacon, Francis (1561–1626): English peer, philosopher and poet who authored *Translation of Certain Psalms into English Verse*.

Baker, Henry Williams (1821–77): baronet and hymn writer. Helped produce *Hymns Ancient and Modern* (1861), including 'The King of Love My Shepherd Is' (Psalm 23).

Band, Debra: American commentator and illuminator of psalms in tradition of Hebrew manuscripts: see https://www.dbandart.com/.

Barberini Psalter (c.1050): Byzantine illustrated Psalter, kept at Biblioteca Apostolica Vaticana. (*Barb. gr. 372*)

Barnabas, Epistle of: Christian and allegorical polemical writing of from early second-century with many quotations from psalms.

Basil of Caesarea, a.k.a. Basil the Great (c.330–379): Cappadocian Father, brother of Gregory of Nyssa; reformer of monastic life and commentator on psalms.

Bay Psalm Book: *The Whole Booke of Psalmes Faithfully Translated into English* (1640) was printed in North America for congregationalist churches of New England.

BCP: '*Book of Common Prayer*' is name for number of related prayer books published in 1549, 1552, 1559, and especially in 1662 which continued to include Coverdale's version of the Psalms.

Bede (c.637–735): Benedictine monk at Jarrow. The *Abbreviated Psalter* attributed to him uses condensed readings of psalms to enable less literate monks to pray through Psalter. Several doubtful works attributed to 'Pseudo-Bede'.

Beethoven, Ludwig van (1770–1827): German composer based in Vienna, advancing the classical tradition of Mozart and Haydn: a few of his hymns adapted psalm texts.

Benedictine Rule: 'handbook' of Benedictine monks, with threefold emphasis on prayer, study and manual work. Psalms play a seminal part in the Rule and the Benedictine *Divine Office.

Benn (1905–89): known by his Christian name rather than his surname Rabinowicz; French Jewish artist originally from Poland, who produced evocative illustrations on the entire Psalter, many reflecting on his experience in a French concentration camp.

Berger, Moshe Tzvi Ha-Levi (1924–2015): Founder of *Museum of Psalms* (1995). His images of psalms reflect influence of Jewish mystical teaching in the Zohar.

Bernard of Cluny: 12c. Benedictine monk and author of satirical poem *De Contemptu Mundi* based on Psalms 48/87, translated by John Mason Neale as 'Jerusalem the Golden'.

Bernstein, Leonard (1918–90): American Jewish conductor. Composed *Chichester Psalms* (performed in 1965 at Chichester Cathedral).

Billings, William (1746–1800): American composer and choral master; published *The New England Psalm-Singer* (Boston, 1770).

Blake, William (1757–1827): English poet and painter, unorthodox in religion; created striking depictions of Biblical and mythical scenes, including several from Psalter.

Bonhoeffer, Dietrich (1906–45): German Lutheran pastor, theologian and anti-Nazi resistance activist. During imprisonment wrote works on praying the psalms.

Boyce, William (1711–79): English composer of choral music. Editor of *Cathedral Music* (first published 1760) which included many psalms.

Brahms, Johannes (1833–97): Viennese German composer whose religious pieces used psalm texts, for example in his 'German Requiem', composed after the death of his mother (1865).

Bristol Psalter: 11c. Byzantine Psalter containing Psalms and Biblical Odes; related to *Khludov Psalter* and *Theodore Psalter*. (*British Library Add. MS 41865*)

Britten, Benjamin (1913–76): English composer best known for opera. Performed several psalm settings, for example on Psalms 70 and 150.

Buber, Martin (1878–1965): Vienna-born Jewish philosopher. *I and Thou* (1923) often used psalms. *Right and Wrong* (1952) reflected on some psalms after the Holocaust.

Bucer, Martin (1491–1551): German Protestant reformer. Collection of metrical psalms (1524) influenced publication of French metrical psalmody by Calvin.

Bunyan, John (1628–88): critic of established church and author of *Grace Abounding to the Chief of Sinners* (1666) and *The Pilgrim's Progress* (1678) which include references to psalms.

Burns, Robert (1759–96): Scottish Romantic poet who occasionally adapted psalms (e.g. Psalm 1) to question religious orthodoxy of the Kirk (the Church of Scotland).

Buxtehude, Dietrich (c.1637–1707): German–Danish composer and organist. Vocal works frequently used psalms from Luther's Bible and *Vulgate*.

Byrd, William (c.1540–1623): composer, organist and colleague of Tallis at Chapel Royal. Composed English settings from Coverdale's Psalter as well as psalms for Latin Masses.

Calvin, John (1509–64): Protestant Reformer. Promoted metrical psalmody, in (French) vernacular; *Genevan Psalter* (1562) largely due to his influence.

Canticles: collection of 14 songs of praise from biblical texts outside Psalter.

Carolingian: 8/9c. dynasty and empire of Charlemagne and his successors: resultant revival of Roman Christian culture is called the 'Carolingian Renaissance'.

Cassian, John (c.360–435): monk and theologian. Author of monastic rule called *Institutes*: major influence on Benedictine Rule, prescribing certain psalms for the Divine Office.

Cassiodorus (c.485–585): Roman Senator then monk. His *Expositio Psalmorum* contributed to a later Gloss for the Psalter.

Catena: collection of diverse texts (also called *florilegia*) quoted as one text. Found at Qumran and used in the New Testament (especially in Romans and Hebrews).

Chagall, Marc (1887–1985): Russian born Jewish artist encouraging Jewish/Christian reconciliation through mosaics, tapestries, stained glass and sketches in books, including *Psaumes de David* (1979).

Chiasmus: rhetorical device where words, clauses or ideas are presented, then re-presented in reverse order, for example, A B C – C B A.

Christ-Logos: depiction of Christ as the eternal Word (*logos*) of God.

Chrysostom, John (c.344–407): Archbishop of Constantinople from 398. Vast corpus of homilies include some 60 on Psalms.

Clarke, Edward: contemporary poet, living in Oxford, who has published cycles of poems responding to the Psalter.

Clement of Alexandria (c.150–215): influenced by Neo-Platonist and Stoic philosophy and composed several homilies on psalms, using the allegorical method.

Clement of Rome (c.35–99): purported author of letter to Christians of Corinth at end of first-century attempting to reconcile different factions *(1 and 2 Clement)*; alludes to several psalms.

Commination Service: declaration of God's anger against all kinds of sin in order to encourage an experience of the mercy of God; prominent use of verses from Psalter, especially Psalm 51.

Common Worship: Prayer Book of the Church of England authorised in 2000.

Compline: night prayer of the Divine Office (usually around 9pm).

Cotter, Jim (1942–2014): Anglican priest, retreat leader, liturgist, poet; produced three-volume poems and prayers on Book of Psalms.

Coverdale, Miles (1488–1569): English Augustinian Friar turned Reformer; Bible translator and a contemporary of Tyndale; produced several versions of the Psalms including version in *BCP*.

Cyril of Jerusalem (c.315–386): Bishop of Jerusalem, best known for his catechetical lectures delivered to baptismal candidates (c.350); comments included many psalms.

Daily Office: text published by Joint Liturgical Group in 1968 with psalms/psalm verses appropriate for liturgy.

Dante, Alighieri (c. 1265–1321): Italian poet whose *Divine Comedy*, written in exile from Florence, drew upon the psalmists' depictions of heaven and hell and restoration after loss.

Davis, Irwin: American artist, influenced by Kabbalistic Judaism; produced simple but evocative images of the psalms for months of the year.

Dead Sea Scrolls: collection of over 900 texts (many fragmentary) found in the vicinity of Qumran from 1947 to 1956, written between 3c. BCE and 2c. CE; nearly forty scrolls are of psalm texts.

Denny, Thomas: contemporary painter and stained glass artist. See https://www.thomasdenny.co.uk/.

Divine Office: a.k.a. 'Daily Office' or 'Canonical Hours' or 'Cursus': refers to monastic hours of prayer.

Dominican Order: 13c. mendicant order founded to preach against (for example, the Albigensian) heresy; renewed liturgical use of psalms.

Dwight, Timothy (1752–1817): American congregationalist minister and hymn writer. Produced *The Psalms of David* (1817) to replace Isaac Watts's 18c. *Psalms and Hymns*.

Eadwine Psalter: 12c. illuminated, interlinear Psalter from Christ Church, Canterbury, showing influence of Utrecht Psalter. (Trinity College, Cambridge: *MS R. 17.1*)

Eighteen Benedictions: a.k.a. *Shemoneh Esrei* and the *'Amidah* prayer, now consisting of nineteen blessings, which are usually prayed three times a day.

Elgar, Sir Edward (1857–1934): English composer, arranged settings for several psalms.

Ephrem the Syrian (c.306–73): deacon at Nisibis, Syria, and composer of psalm-like hymns defending Christian orthodoxy in Syriac language.

Erasmus (1466–1536): Dutch Christian humanist from Rotterdam; wrote philological commentaries on psalms, applying them to contemporary theological and political concerns.

Eusebius of Caesarea (c.260–340): Bishop of Caesarea Maritima from 314 CE; biblical interpreter and author of *Ecclesiastical History* and *Commentaria in Psalmos*.

Evagrius of Pontus (c.345–399): deacon; student of Basil of Caesarea and Gregory of Nazianzus. Wrote psalms commentary and *scholia* (shorter comments predating the Gloss).

Evergood, Philip (1901–73): American artist and illustrator whose works often display a social and political critique.

Florilegium: collection of excerpts of texts. See also *catena*.

Franciscan Order: 13c. mendicant order founded by Saint Francis of Assisi, instructing life of poverty; psalms played a major part in their prayer and liturgy.

Gabrieli, Giovanni (c.1554–1612): composer and organist from San Marco, Venice, and nephew of Andrea Gabrieli; arranged many psalms and worked under Orlando di Lasso.

Gallican Psalter (386–87): a.k.a. *Psalterium Gallicanum*, translation into Latin based on Greek and old Latin versions, reputedly by Jerome in Caesarea and included in Vulgate.

Gehenna: valley outside Jerusalem, a synonym for death and fiery punishment.

Gelineau, Joseph (1920–2008): French Jesuit priest. Developed 'Gelineau' method of singing metrical psalms with responsorial antiphons between verses; popular at Taizé.

Genevan Psalter: 16c. metrical Psalter, also known as the *Huguenot Psalter*, associated with John Calvin and originally for the Reformed churches in Geneva.

Genizah: storage in synagogue or Jewish cemetery for old sacred texts which cannot be disposed of as is the case with profane literature.

Gibbons, Orlando (1583–1625): English composer, later senior organist of Chapel Royal; father of Christopher Gibbons who adapted psalm texts from Latin and English.

Gilbert of Poitiers (c.1080–1154): Bishop who worked with Anselm at Laon, where he wrote his Psalms Commentary which was expansion of a Gloss.

Gloss: the notes made in margins or between lines of a book, in which meaning of text is explained, by reference to other commentators, usually in Latin or Greek or the vernacular.

Glossa Ordinaria: compilation of comments from early church fathers, gradually brought together in Middle Ages; became standard point of reference in many psalm manuscripts.

Goodall, Howard: contemporary English composer of choral music, musicals, and film and television scores. Uses all-female choir with string accompaniment for his performances of psalms.

Goudimel, Claude (c.1515–1572): French composer who arranged metrical psalm settings for John Calvin's *Genevan Psalter: Psaumes de David* was produced c. 1564.

Gregorian Chant: associated with Gregory the Great; uses three inflections (beginning, middle and end of verse) rather than the two inflections of Ambrosian chant.

Gregory the Great (c.540–604): One of four fathers of the western church; Pope from 590. Commentaries on psalms were partly historical, partly allegorical, partly moral, fostering Benedictine use of psalmody.

Gregory of Nyssa (c.335–95): one of the Cappadocian fathers. Used psalms mainly allegorically: his *Inscriptiones Psalmorum* reads each psalm as progressive account of soul's ascent to God.

Gunkel, Hermann (1862–1932): categorised psalms according to their form, contextualising them within the history of ancient Israelite religion.

Haggadah: usually associated with stories told about the liberation from slavery in Egypt which are recited at Passover, often using psalms with Exodus themes.

Hamilton Psalter: 14c. bilingual Byzantine Greek and Latin psalter (with 12 canonical odes); suggests multiple scribal hands. (Berlin, Kupferstichkabinett; *MS 78 A 9*)

Handel, George Frideric (1685–1759): German/English composer; arranged psalms for his oratorios (e.g. *Messiah* [1741]); pioneer of performing psalms in concert halls.

Harbison, John: American composer whose acclaimed multi-vocal work *Four Psalms* (114, 126, 133 and 137) celebrated the fiftieth anniversary of the founding of the state of Israel.

Harley Psalter **(c.1020):** incomplete copy (up to Ps. 143) in style of *Utrecht Psalter*, also produced in Canterbury. (British Library, *Harley MS 603*)

Hasmonean: see Maccabean period.

Haydn, [Franz] Joseph (1732–1809): Austrian composer who influenced Mozart and Beethoven; his sacred choral music used psalms, including his metrical settings in *Six English Psalms*.

Herbert of Bosham (c.1120–90): influenced by Victorine School. His *Psalterium Hebraicum* included Gloss with comments from Jewish as well as Christian commentators.

Herbert, George (1593–1633): Church of England priest and poet, using many allusions to psalms, for example in his collected devotional poetry, published posthumously in 1633 as *The Temple*.

Hilary of Poitiers (c.310–67): opponent of Arianism. Used Origen's prosopological approach in his homilies on Psalms and in *Tractatus super Psalmum*.

Hill, Lauryn: American songwriter who alludes to several psalms.

Hiphil: a causative, active form of a Hebrew verb.

Hippolytus (c.170–235): Liturgist and Bishop, probably of Rome, who opposed heresies such as Montanism and whose psalms commentaries were read as prophecies about life, death and resurrection of Christ.

Hodayot **(c.50 BCE):** collection of thanksgiving hymns found at Qumran composed in style of psalms.

Hirsch, Samson Raphael (1808–88): Orthodox rabbi whose commentary on Psalms was much cited in twentieth-century Jewish commentaries.

Honegger, Arthur (1892–1955): Franco-Swiss composer; his *Le Roi David* (1921) used several psalms.

Hopkins, Gerard Manley (1844–89): English religious poet, whose many poems often allude to psalms. Initially a Tractarian, and influenced by Newman, he was later ordained a Jesuit priest.

Howells, Herbert (1892–1983): composer shaped by WW1 and death of his son in 1935; composed two sets of 'Psalm Preludes' (1915–16 and 1938–39).

Hugh of St. Victor (c.1096–1141): from Abbey of St. Victor, Paris; wrote seminal exegetical commentary on Psalms.

Ibn Ezra, Abraham (c.1089–1164): Hebrew grammarian who opposed a radical Jewish sect called the Karaites. His philological commentaries on Psalms were printed alongside Hebrew text in rabbinic Bibles.

Iconoclasticism: objection against the use of religious images, particularly of Christ and the saints, notably initially in the 8c. under Byzantine Emperor Leo III.

Inclusio: literary device whereby a repetition of similar words or phrases bracket a text.

Irenaeus (c.130–200): Bishop of Lyons whose polemical work *Against Heresies* uses many psalms as prophecies pointing to Christ.

Ives, Charles (1874–1954): American composer and organist. Used psalm settings as a form of experimentation with different musical styles.

Jenkins, Karl: Welsh oboist, saxophonist and composer. Uses psalms in interfaith context.

Jerome (c.347–402): One of four fathers of the western church; Psalms commentator (*Tractatus* and *Commentarioli* were works on select psalms). Prolific Bible translator who according to tradition produced three versions of Psalter; his *Gallican Psalter* was used in the *Vulgate*.

Jessing, Michael: contemporary Northumberland painter, with allegorical and ecological representations of psalms in several books: see https://goo.gl/Uggcah.

Justin Martyr (c.100–165): Christian Apologist based mainly in Rome; frequently used psalms in his argumentations against pagan and Jewish controversies.

Kabbalat Shabbat: the welcome of the arrival of the Sabbath, at which several psalms are sung.

Kabbalistic: an aspect of Jewish mysticism often expressed in esoteric symbolism.

Kaddish **(Aramaic for 'holy'):** a prayer of praise to God used in Jewish liturgy, used especially at funerals or memorial services.

Kedushah/Kedushah de-sidra: prayers recited in Jewish liturgy whose key components include Isa. 6:3, Eze. 3:12 and Ps 146:10.

Keble, John (1792–1866): Professor of Poetry at Oxford (1831–41); leader of Oxford Movement, co-founder of Tractarianism; produced *Psalter in English Verse* (1839).

Kethe, William (d. 1594): translator into English metrical psalmody of some of the *Genevan Psalter* for the *Anglo-Genevan Psalter*, and hence contributor to the *Scottish Psalter*.

Ketib/qere': places in which the text of the Hebrew Bible is written (*ketib*) in one way, but by tradition is recited (*qere'*) in another way.

Khludov Psalter: 9c. Byzantine Psalter using *Septuagint*; 80 miniatures illuminate a few verses of psalms in margins of text. (Moscow History Museum *MS D. 129*)

Kiddush: a blessing recited over wine at the start of a Jewish Sabbath or religious holiday.

Kimḥi, David (1160–1235): a.k.a. RADAK (Rabbi David Kimḥi), renowned for works of Hebrew grammar and philological (often anti-Christian) commentaries, including Psalms.

KJV: '*King James Version*' a.k.a. '*Authorised Version*' (*AV*); Bible translation authorised by King James in 1611 for preaching and teaching in Church of England.

Korahite: guild of Levites, singers and gatekeepers of Jerusalem Temple (see 1 Chronicles 15–16). Pss. 42/3, 44–49, and 84–85, 87–88 are attributed to the 'Sons of Korah'.

di Lasso (de Lassus), Orlando (c.1532–94): Franco-Flemish Roman Catholic composer of polyphonic sacred choral music; *Timor et Tremor* (1564) uses several psalms.

Lauds: in the Divine Office refers to dawn prayer (generally between 3 and 6am).

Lawes, Henry (1596–1662): English composer and songwriter for Chapel Royal; with brother William published *Choice Psalmes put into Musick* (1648).

lectio divina ('sacred reading'): use of scripture for meditative prayer, originally a monastic discipline especially using Psalms.

Lefèvre d'Étaples, Jacques (c.1455–1536): French Humanist; his *Quincuplex Psalter* placed other versions of psalms alongside the *Vulgate*. Influenced Luther's earlier use of Psalms.

Liturgy of Hours: see **Divine Office.**

Lollards: movement from 14c. following teachings of Oxford scholar John Wycliffe and advocating unique authority of Scripture above church tradition; condemned by secular and religious authorities.

Lombard, Peter (c.1100–60): scholastic theologian at Paris whose *Four Books of Sentences* was a formative textbook of mediaeval theology; wrote *Psalterium Scholasticorum* which contributed to the standardized Gloss on the Psalms.

Luther, Martin (1483–1546): Augustinian monk, priest, reformer, theologian, and composer; produced lectures, commentaries, sermons and hymns on psalms.

LXX: a.k.a. the *Septuagint*, a Greek translation of the Hebrew Bible purportedly completed in Alexandria by 72 rabbis in 72 days.

Lyra, Nicholas of: (c.1270–1349): Franciscan monk and Hebraist. *Postilla super Psalterium et Cantica Canticorum* is a glossed commentary on Psalms and Song of Songs.

Lyte, Henry Francis (1793–1847): Anglican minister, first of evangelical conversion and then of Oxford Movement; author of *The Spirit of the Psalms* (hymns based on the Psalter).

Maccabean period (167–63 BCE): a.k.a. Hasmonean, the period following the revolt of Judah (Judas) Maccabee and his four brothers which finally ended when Pompey conquered Jerusalem.

MacMillan, James: Scottish composer, using Celtic Roman Catholic traditions with world-wide eclectic influences; sacred music, including psalms, often performed in a secular context.

Mandorla: almond-shaped cloud of light used in Christian art to indicate a holy person.

Manichaeism: (from 3c. Iranian 'prophet' Mani); mix of Christian and traditional Persian religious beliefs and practices which influenced Augustine in his early life.

Marot, Clement (1496–1544): French poet and Protestant sympathiser; translator of many metrical psalms.

Masoretic Text (MT): text of Hebrew Bible standardised between 6c. and 9c. by addition of vowel symbols, cantillation marks and masoretic notes.

Matins: prayers of Divine Office of midnight and 2:30am, usually now combined into one.

Melisma: several different notes sung on a single syllable (as opposed to syllabic singing).

Mendelssohn, Felix (1809–47): son of Moses, a German Jewish convert. His music reflects his Jewish sympathies, e.g. in his oratorio *Elijah* which uses several psalms.

Menorah: seven-branched, golden lampstand decorated with cups shaped like buds and flowers (Exod. 25:31–40).

Merton, Thomas (1915–68): American Trappist monk, student of comparative religion; his poetry used psalms to evoke mystical focus on Roman Catholic faith.

Midrash Tehillim: 13c. commentary on the Psalms (*Tehillim*) relating Psalms to Jewish traditions of the Torah, compiled from 3c. onwards. Also known as *Midrash Shocher Tov*.

Milton, John (1608–74): schoolmaster, civil servant for Cromwell, poet and author of *Paradise Lost;* composed metrical psalms in style of the Sidneys and Sandys.

Mishnah ('repetition'): first main written collection of the orally memorised and 'repeated' rabbinic teachings dating from 3c. CE; contains six 'orders' concerned with ritual and legal aspects of Judaism, often showing how some psalms were used.

Montanism: 2c. Christian movement which emphasised contemporary prophecy and gifts of Holy Spirit.

de Monte, Philippe (c.1521–1603): Flemish composer at court of Hapsburg, collaborating with Di Lasso and Byrd; produced Italian madrigals and several motets using psalms.

Montgomery, James (1771–1854): hymn writer and poet, for whom psalms were a major source text; his 1825 hymnal was published as *The Christian Psalmist*.

Mozart, Wolfgang Amadeus (1756–91): prolific composer born in Salzburg; arrangements for the penitential psalms were amongst his many works.

Mycall, John (c.1750–1833): American printer; *The Psalms of David* used Watts's psalm translations, with references to Great Britain replaced with references to American Revolution.

Neale, John Mason (1818–66): Anglican priest and scholar; translated Greek and Latin ancient hymns and psalms for modern liturgical use; co-edited with J. F. Littledale 4-volume work on use of psalms, particularly in patristic and medieval periods.

Nestorianism: teaching that divine/human natures of Christ are distinct, not inseparable; advanced by Nestorius, condemned at Council of Ephesus (431) and Chalcedon (451).

Newman, John Henry (1801–90): Anglican priest, Tractarian, convert to Roman Catholicism (1845). Hymns and *Dream of Gerontius* include allusions to many psalms.

Newton, John: see **Olney Hymns**.

Nimb: in art, a nimbus or halo; so 'cross-nimbed', a halo containing within it the shape of a cross, typically seen in icons of Christ.

None: The hour of prayer, in the Divine Office, nine hours after dawn, i.e. at about 3.00pm.

Obbligato: a distinctive instrumental part which is essential to a piece of music.

Olney Hymns: evangelical hymns, paraphrasing metrical psalmody, collected by John Newton (1725–1807) and William Cowper (1731–1800).

Opus Dei ('work of God'): refers here either to seven offices of prayer of the Divine Office or to threefold monastic principle of prayer, study and manual work.

Origen of Alexandria (c.185–254): 3c. scholar, famed for *Hexapla* (first polyglot Bible) and for allegorical and prosopological approaches to psalms which influenced Augustine.

Ormesby Psalter: 14c. richly decorated Psalter of East Anglian origin. (Bodleian, Oxford: *MS. Douce 366*)

da Palestrina, Giovanni Pierluigi (c.1525–94): Italian composer of rich polyphonic liturgical music and madrigals for Catholic liturgy.

Pantokrator Psalter: 9c. Byzantine illustrated Psalter, kept at Pantokrator monastery, Mt. Athos. (*Pantokrator cod. 61*)

Paris Psalter: Old English *Metrical Psalms,* composed c. 950, comprising Psalms 51–150 (EV), were combined with an earlier prose version of Psalms 1–50 (EV) to create the 11c. *Paris Psalter,* a seminal text for study of early vernacular. (Bibliothèque nationale de France *MS lat. 8846*)

Paris Psalter: 11c. richly illustrated Byzantine manuscript, with fourteen additional full page illuminations. (Bibliothèque nationale de France *MS. gr. 139*)

Parker, Matthew (1504–75): Archbishop of Canterbury for Elizabeth I; produced an English Metrical Psalter with introductory notes and collect for each psalm. (See also Tallis.)

Parma Psalter: 13c. Hebrew Psalter, lavishly illustrating first word of each psalm; used Ibn Ezra's commentary. (Biblioteca Paletina *Ms. Parm. 1870*)

Parry, Hubert (1848–1918): English composer of many psalms; setting for Psalm 122 ('I was glad') used at many royal and state occasions.

Pärt, Arvo: controversial Estonian composer who converted from Lutheranism to Russian Orthodoxy; his *Miserere* (Psalm 51) shows eclectic musical influences from East and West.

Pelagianism: heresy of 4c. British monk Pelagius, arguing that humans are responsible for their own salvation; condemned at Councils of Carthage (418) and Ephesus (431). Opposed by Augustine.

Penitential Psalms: Pss. 6, 32, 38, 51, 102, 130 and 143, popularized by Augustine and Cassiodorus and used in medieval Books of Hours. Seven psalms used to make penitence for seven deadly sins (gluttony, lust, greed, pride, sorrow, anger, vainglory and sloth).

Pesukei de-Zimra ('verses of song'): Jewish prayers of morning praise, mostly drawn from the psalms, especially Psalms 145–150.

Pesher ('interpretation'): practice, for example at Qumran, of reading scriptures in light of contemporary events; this often combined psalm texts with other texts to create new meanings.

Peshitta: Syriac translation of Bible, used by Syriac/Aramaic speaking Christians, possibly from 2c. onwards.

Piers Plowman: Middle English poem (c.1380) on Christian discipleship, accredited to William Langland; includes the persona Will the Dreamer, a 'Psalter-clerk'.

Plainchant (a.k.a. plainsong): associated initially with Ambrose of Milan, later used in both monastic offices and cathedral liturgy. Monophonic, in that singers follow same melody.

Prime: early morning prayer of *Divine Office* recited during first hour of daylight.

Proper Psalm: specific psalm appointed for special occasions throughout church year.

Prosopological exegesis: interpretation used by Origen and Augustine to identify the two natures of Christ, human and divine, speaking in same psalm.

Purcell, Henry (1659–95): composer of many psalms; attached to the Chapel Royal for Charles II and James II.

Purim ('lots'): Jewish festival, usually held around February/March, to commemorate rescue of Jews from Haman's pogrom as narrated in Esther.

Qere': See *Ketib/ qere'*

Qumran: site of community centre of a second/first-century BCE Jewish sect, on shore of Dead Sea. Nearly a thousand biblical and religious texts hidden in jars in caves were discovered first in 1947–48.

Rashi (1045–1105): from **Ra**bbi **Sh**lomo **Yiṣḥaq** (Solomon Isaac); French exegete of Talmud and Bible; commentaries include anti-Christian polemic frequently using psalms.

Reich, Steve: American composer, pioneer of 'minimal music'; album *Tehillim* (1981) is based on the psalms.

Rosh Hashanah ('the head of the year'): Jewish New Year, usually around September.

Rossi, de' Salamone (c.1570–1630): Jewish Italian composer based in court of Mantua. His psalm settings were unaccompanied, polyphonic and melismatic, initially written for Jewish festal occasions.

Rutter, John: English composer in choral tradition of Howells and Vaughan Williams. His Christmas motets often use psalms, as seen in his *Psalmfest* (1993).

Saint John's Bible: first hand-illustrated Benedictine Bible since 15c., including the Psalter, commissioned by St. John's Benedictine Abbey and University of Collegeville and completed in 2011.

St Albans Psalter: 12c. Anglo-Norman Benedictine Psalter, with illustrations of first Latin letter of each psalm; now kept at St. Godehard's church (Hildesheim *MS1*)

Sandys, George (c.1577–1644): English poet whose *Paraphrase upon the Psalms of David* (1636) experimented with metrical psalms which were later set to hymn tunes.

SATB: Abbreviated version for soprano, alto, tenor and bass.

Schütz, Heinrich (1585–1672): German composer who applied Italian (Catholic) techniques to German (Lutheran) sacred music; works include *Psalmen Davids* (1619), which used Luther's Psalter, and *Becker Psalter* (1628) which were from Cornelius Becker's metrical psalms.

Selah: used 71 times in 39 psalms, usually in middle or at end of verse; unknown meaning, perhaps to mark an interlude or pause, as understood by *Septuagint* translation.

Septuagint: see *LXX*.

Sext: hour of prayer, in the Divine Office, about six hours after dawn: i.e. at noon.

Sforno, Obadiah Ben Jacob (c. 1455–1550): Italian rabbi and Biblical commentator.

Shekinah ('dwelling' or 'settling'): rabbinic term for divine presence, associated with Tabernacle or Temple, and later, with synagogue worship.

Shema (*shema*, 'Hear!'): Jewish confession of monotheism, taken from Deuteronomy 6:4, recited at morning and night prayer.

Shimmush Tehillim **('Magical Uses of the Psalms'):** Jewish text, dating from late antiquity.

Shofar: musical instrument made of a ram's horn, blown on *Rosh Hashanah* and *Yom Kippur*.

Siddur **('order'):** Jewish prayer book, for use at home and synagogue.

Sidney, Mary (1561–1621): Countess of Pembroke, sister of Philip; revised his work on Psalms 1–43 and added Psalms 44–150 to create *The Sidney Psalter*.

Simḥat Torah **('Joy of the Law'):** two-day thanksgiving for the Torah, celebrated as the culmination of *Sukkot* (usually in October).

Smart, Christopher (1722–71): influential poet known for his intense piety; several poems based on psalms.

Stanford, Sir Charles Villiers (1852–1924): composer of Anglican liturgical music including many psalm settings.

Stern, Max: American musical critic and composer of orchestral, chamber, choral and vocal works for synagogue and theatre, including some psalms.

Sternhold and Hopkins: their *Whole Book of Psalms*, published in England in 1562, became known by their names. This was the standard metrical Psalter of the reformed churches until the Psalter by Tate and Brady.

Stravinksy, Igor (1882–1971): Russian-born composer whose *Symphony of Psalms* produced an orchestral and choral performance of psalms for theatre as well as church or synagogue.

Stuttgart Psalter: : 9c. Carolingian Psalter with 316 colour images, many with Christian focus, using one or more illustrations for each psalm. (Württembergische Landesbibliothek, Stuttgart *Cod Bib Fol 23*)

Sukkot (**'booths' or 'tabernacles'**): one of three ancient Jewish (harvest) festivals. This one was in autumn, remembering how Israel made shelters in the desert after escaping from Egypt.

Sweelinck, Jan Pieterszoon (1562–1621): early Dutch organist who also composed polyphonic arrangements of psalms.

Tallis, Thomas (c.1510–85): English court composer attached to Chapel Royal from 1542; arranged psalms both as Latin motets and as metrical psalms (including eight for Archbishop Parker's 1567 Psalter).

Talmud: much expanded (Palestinian and Babylonian) version of *Mishnah*, produced between fourth and sixth centuries.

Tamid (**'always'**): perpetual morning and evening sacrifice; includes recital of Psalms 24, 48, 82, 94, 81, 93 and 92 as prescribed in *Mishnah* and, in part, by their *Septuagint* headings.

Targum: amplified translation/paraphrase of Hebrew Bible into Aramaic. *Targum Psalms (TgPss)* was translated between fourth and sixth centuries.

Tate and Brady: the authors of and name by which the *New Version of the Psalms of David* (1696) was also known. This metrical Psalter superseded 'Sternhold and Hopkins'.

Tavener, Sir John (1944–2013): British composer and Orthodox Christian; *Song for Athene*, sung at funeral of Diana, Princess of Wales (1997) used psalm texts from the Divine Liturgy.

Temmingh, Zorada: contemporary church organist in Stellenbosch. Integrates psalms with well-known melodies: https://goo.gl/BFpMjF.

Terce: hour of prayer, in the Divine Office, about three hours after dawn: i.e. at 9.00am.

Tertullian (c.160–240): convert from Carthage and author of polemical proof texts from psalms; joined Montanist sect which read psalms as prophecies being fulfilled in their own community.

Theodore of Mopsuestia (c.350–429): pupil of Diodore of Tarsus, central figure in development of Antiochene School; accused of Nestorianism after his death.

Theodore Psalter: 11c. Byzantine Psalter from Studious Monastery; 480 marginal and often Christological illustrations. (British Library *MS 19352*)

Theodoret of Cyrus (393–?458): Bishop of Cyrus and Antiochene psalms commentator, although also used Christological and typological readings.

Thomasius, Josephus Maria (1649–1713): Italian scholar and cardinal whose *Psalterium cum Canticis* (1697) represents thought of Thomas Aquinas. Cited frequently by Neale and Littledale.

Tissot, Jacques (James) (1836–1902): French Roman Catholic painter of biblical art.

Tractarianism: 19c. Anglo-Catholic Oxford movement; distributed ideas through series *Tracts for the Times* (see Newman and Keble). Psalms were central means of preaching for reform of church.

Tree of Jesse: image of tree often used in Christian art to depict lineage from Jesse of Bethlehem and David his son to Jesus Christ.

Turle, James (1802–1882): One-time organist and master of choristers at Westminster Abbey.

Tye, Christopher (c.1505–73): English composer of Latin psalm motets during reign of Mary, and of English metrical psalms during reigns of Edward VI and Elizabeth I.

Typika: service of Eastern Orthodox liturgy when no priest is present.

Utrecht Psalter: 9c. Carolingian Psalter from Hautvilliers, with 160 pen and ink drawings to create (often Christian) narratives of entire psalms. (Utrecht University *MSS 32*)

Vallotton, Annie (1915–2013): Swiss–French artist who illustrated the *Good News Bible* with iconic line-art drawings.

Vaticanus Graecus **752:** 11c. Byzantine Psalter with gilted colour images using liturgical and Christological concerns. (Vatican Library *VatGr* 752).

Vaughan Williams, Ralph (1872–1958): British Anglican composer who trained under Hubert Parry and Charles Stanford. Editor of *English Hymnal* (1906).

Venantius Fortunatus (c.540–605): Bishop and poet at court of Frankish kings; composed hymns using parts of psalms which are still sung today in translation.

'Verses of Song': see *Pesukei de-Zimra*

Vespers: the early evening prayer of the Divine Office.

de Victoria, Tomás Luis (c.1548–1611): Spanish composer, priest and organist who performed several polychoral psalm settings.

Vigils: midnight/middle of night prayer of the Divine Office, a.k.a. Nocturns or Matins.

Vivaldi, Antonio (1678–1741): Italian Baroque composer, also Roman Catholic priest, from Venice and later based in Vienna.

Vulgate **('common'):** the Latin translation of the Bible attributed to Jerome; this uses Jerome's *Gallican Psalter* which is a translation based primarily on the Greek and old Latin versions rather than the Hebrew.

Wagner, Roger: poet and artist, influenced by Albrecht Dürer in his use of various mediums including wood engravings, as in his *Book of Psalms* (https://goo.gl/fm95xD).

Walton, Sir William (1902–83): English composer, controversial for his modernist views. His *Belshazzar's Feast* (1931), a choral cantata, uses several psalms.

Watts, Isaac (1674–1748): English non-Conformist hymn writer who wrote a vast number of metrical psalms, many with Christian and political overtones.

Weelkes, Thomas (1576–1623): English composer and organist of Winchester College and Chichester Cathedral; his madrigals and choral music mainly used psalms taken from Coverdale's Psalter.

Wesley, Charles (1707–88): Co-founder with brother John of Methodist movement; prolific hymn writer whose *Collection of Psalms and Hymns* (1737) had a clear Christian overlay.

Wesley, John (1703–91): Anglican priest who with his brother Charles founded the Methodist movement. Psalms were central in their theology and hymn writing.

Wesley, Samuel Sebastian (1810–76): grandson of Charles Wesley; organist and composer of psalms.

Whittingham, William (c.1524–79): English minister at Geneva who helped produce 'Sternhold and Hopkins' Psalter.

Whittier, John Greenleaf (1807–92): American poet, Quaker and campaigner for abolition of slavery.

Wieder, Laurance: American poet, critic, and anthologist of poetic imitations of psalms by poets from 16c. onwards.

Winkworth, Catherine (1827–78): English translator of German hymns, many adapting psalms. *The Chorale Book for England* was published in 1860s.

Wisdom of Solomon: 1c. BCE text, probably from Alexandria, influenced both by Hebrew Bible and Hellenism; it incorporates allusions to several psalms.

Wragg, Arthur (1903–76): Christian Socialist and commercial illustrator of satirical black and white cartoon-like images, as in *The Psalms for Modern Life* (1934).

***Yom Kippur* (Day of Atonement):** a day of repentance, fasting and prayer before *Sukkot* (see Lev. 16:29), obligatory for all Jews, usually in September/October.

Psalms Through the Centuries, Volume Three: A Reception History Commentary on Psalms 73-150, First Edition. Susan Gillingham.

Abegg, M. Jr., P. W. Flint, and E. Ulrich. 1999. *The Dead Sea Scrolls Bible*. Edinburgh: T&T Clark.

Albertz, R. 1997. "Der jüdische Psalter – ein anti-imperiales Buch." Pages 95–108 in *Religion und Gesellschaft*. Edited by R. Albertz. AOAT 248. Münster: Ugarit-Verlag.

Aldridge, J. W. 1966. *The Hermeneutic of Erasmus*. Richmond, VA: John Knox Press.

Allen, L. C. 2002. *Psalms 101–150*. Revised Edition. WBC 21. Nashville, TN: Thomas Nelson Publishers.

Anderson, A. A. 1972. *The Book of Psalms Volume Two (73–150)*. NCB. Grand Rapids, MI: Eerdmans.

Anderson, F. R. 2016. *Singing God's Psalms – Metrical Psalms and Reflections for Each Sunday in the Church Year*. Grand Rapids, MI: Eerdmans.

Armstrong, R. M. 2012. "Psalms Dwelling Together in Unity: The Placement of Psalms 133 and 134 in Two Different Psalms Collections." *JBL* 131/3: 487–506.

Atkin, T. and F. Leneghan (eds.). 2017. *The Psalms and Medieval English Literature: From the Conversion to the Reformation*. Cambridge: Brewer.

Attridge, H. W. 2004. "The Psalms in Hebrews." Pages 197–212 in *The Psalms in the New Testament*. Edited by S. Moyise and M. J. J. Menken. London: T&T Clark International.

Attridge, H. W. 1987. *The Epistle to the Hebrews*. Philadelphia: Fortress Press.

Atwan, R. and L. Wieder (eds.). 1993. *Chapters into Verse. A Selection of Poetry in English inspired by the Bible from Genesis to Revelation*. Oxford: Oxford University Press.

Auffret, P. 1982. *La sagesse a bâti sa maison. Études de structures littéraires dans l'Ancien Testament et spécialement dans les Psaumes*. OBO 49. Göttingen: Vandenhoeck & Ruprecht.

Augustine, trans. Hegbin, E. T. S. and F. Corrigan. 1960. *St. Augustine: Expositions on the Psalms*. Vol 2. ACW 30. Westminster, MD: Newman Press.

Augustine, trans. E. Uyl. 2017. *Saint Augustine: Exposition on the Book of Psalms*. Woodstock, ON: Devoted Publishing.

Austern, L. P. 2011. "'For Musicke is the Handmaid of the Lord': Women, Psalms and Music-Making." Pages 77-114 in *Psalms in the Early Modern World*. Edited by L.P. Austern, K.B. McBride and D.L. Orvis. Farnham, Surrey: Ashgate Publishing.

Auwers, J. M. 2000. *La Composition Littéraire du Psautier: Un État de la Question*. Cahiers De La Revue Biblique. Paris: Gabalda.

Backhouse, J. 1993. *The Isabella Breviary*. London: British Library Board.

Baker, J. and E. W. Nicholson (trans. and eds.). 1973. *Commentary of Rabbi David Kimchi on Psalms 120–150*. UCOP 22. Cambridge: Cambridge University Press.

Balas, D. L. and D. J. Bingham. 1998. "Patristic Exegesis of the Books of the Bible." Pages 64–115 in *International Catholic Bible Commentary*. Edited by W. Farmer, *et al*. Collegeville, MN: Liturgical Press, 1998.

Baldwin, E. C. 1919. "Milton and the Psalms." *Modern Philology* 17: 457–63.

Ballhorn, E. 2004. *Zum Telos des Psalters: Der Textzusammenhang des Vierten und Fünften Psalmenbuches (Ps 90–150)*. BBB 138. Berlin: Philo & Philo.

Band, D. and A. J. Band. 2007. *I Will Wake the Dawn: Illuminated Psalms*. Philadelphia, PA: The Jewish Publication Society.

Bede, trans. G. M. Browne. 2002. *The Abbreviated Psalter of the Venerable Bede*. Grand Rapids, MI: Eerdmans.

Beit-Arie, M., E. Silver and T. Metzger (eds.). 1996. *The Parma Psalter: A Thirteenth-Century Illuminated Hebrew Book of Psalms with a Commentary by Abraham Ibn Ezra*. London: Facsimile Editions Limited.

Bellinger, W. H. 2019. "The Direction of the Psalter in Book V and the Question of Genre." Pages 69–81 *in Zur Theologie des Psalters und der Psalmen. Beiträge in memoriam Frank-Lothar Hossfeld*. Edited by U. Berges, J. Bremer and T. Magnus Steiner. BBB 189. Göttingen: Bonn University Press/ Vandenhoeck & Ruprecht.

Benn, R. B. 1970. *Les Psaumes*. Lyon: Musee des Beaux-Arts.

Berlin, A. 1987. "On the Interpretation of Psalm 133." Pages 141–47 in *Directions in Biblical Poetry*. Edited by F. R. Ellis. Sheffield: Sheffield Academic Press.

Berlin, A. 2005. "Psalms and the Literature of the Exile: Psalms 137, 44, 69, and 78." Pages 66–85 in *The Book of Psalms. Composition and Reception*. Edited by P. W. Flint and P. D. Miller. Leiden: Brill.

Bernstein, M. J. 1994. "Translation Technique in the Targum to Psalms. Two Test Cases: Psalms 2 and 137." Pages 326–45 in *SBL Annual Meeting 1994: 3 Seminar Papers*. Edited by E. H. Lovering Jr. Atlanta, GA: Scholars Press.

Bessette, L. 2005. *The Visualization of the Contents of the Psalms in the Early Middle Ages*. Ann Arbor, MI: University of Michigan.

Beyerlin, W. 1979. *Werden und Wesen des 107. Psalms*. BZAW 153, Berlin: de Gruyter.

Bilski, E. B. 2000. *Berlin Metropolis. Jews and the New Culture 1890–1918*. New York: Jewish Museum.

Bloch, C. 1992. *Spelling the Word: George Herbert and the Bible*. Oakland, CA: University of California Press.

Blumenthal, D. R. 1993. *Facing the Abusing God: A Theology of Protest*. Louisville, KY: Westminster John Knox.

Boeckler, A. M. 2014. "Moses' Prophecy or the Primordial Song of Humanity? Psalm 92 and the Liturgical Reading of Psalms in Judaism." Paper given at *Bibel Forum*, Haus Ohrbeck Georgsmarienhütte, August 2014

Böhm, C. 2017. *Die Rezeption der Psalmen in den Qumranschriften, bei Philo von Alexandrien und im Corpus Paulinium*. WUNT 2 Reihe 437. Tübingen: Mohr Siebeck

Bons, E. 2007. "Der Septuaginta Psalter. Übersetzung, Interpretation, Korrektur." Pages 450–70 in *Die Septuaginta. Texte – Kontexte – Lebenswelten*. Edited by M. Karrer and W. Kraus. WUNT 219. Tübingen: Mohr Siebeck.

Bons, E. 2008. "Translating and Annotating Ps. 72 LXX." Pages 133–46 in *Translating a Translation. The LXX and its Early Modern Translations in the Context of Early Judaism*. Edited by H. Ausloos, J. Cook *et al.* Leuven: Peeters.

Boulanger, F. 2010. "Le psaume dans la chanson populaire israélienne." Pages 209 – 10 in *Psaumes. Chants de Humanité*. Edited by D. M. Delmaire *et al.* Villeneuve d'Aseq: Presses Universitaires du Septentrion.

Boyce, W. 1790. *A Collection of Anthems and a Short Service in Score for 1, 2, 3, 4, 5 & 8 Voices*. London: Master of His Majesty's Band of Musicians.

Braude, W. G. (trans.). 1959. *The Midrash on Psalms*, Vols. 1 & 2. YJS XIII. New Haven, CT: Yale University Press.

Breed, B. 2014. "Reception of the Psalms: The Example of Psalm 91." Pages 297–310 in *The Oxford Handbook of the Psalms*. Edited by W. P. Brown. Oxford: Oxford University Press.

Brennan, J. P. 1976. "Some Hidden Harmonies in the Fifth Book of Psalms." Pages 126–58 in *The Sheaf. Bicentennial Issue. Essays in Honor of Joseph P. Brennan*. Edited by R. F. McNamara. Rochester, NY: St. Bernard's Seminary.

Brettler, M. Z. 1998. "Women and Psalms: Toward an Understanding of the Role of Women's Prayer in the Israelite Cult." Pages 25–56 in *Gender and Law in the*

Hebrew Bible and the Ancient Near East. Edited by B. M. Levenson. Sheffield: Sheffield Academic Press.

Brettler, M. Z. 2009. "A Jewish Approach to Psalm 111?" Pages 142–59 in *Jewish and Christian Approaches to Psalms.* Edited by M. Grohmann and Y. Zakovitch. Freiburg: Herder.

Brodersen, A. 2017. *The End of the Psalter. Psalms 146–150 in the Masoretic Text, the Dead Sea Scrolls, and the Septuagint.* BZAW 505. Berlin: de Gruyter.

Brook, J. 2001. *Arthur Wragg: Twentieth-century Prophet and Jester.* Bristol: Sansom & Co.

Brooke, G. J. 1996. "Shared Intertextual Interpretations in the Dead Sea Scrolls and the New Testament." Paper presented at the Orion Center for the Study of the Dead Sea Scrolls and Associated Literature, International Symposium on the Early Use and Interpretation of the Bible in Light of the Dead Sea Scrolls. http://orion.mscc.huji.ac.il/symposiums/1st/papers/Brooke96.html

Brueggemann, W. 1991. "Bounded by Obedience and Praise." *JSOT* 50: 63–92.

Brueggemann, W. and W. H. Bellinger 2014. *Psalms.* New Cambridge Bible Commentary. New York: Cambridge University Press.

Brunert, G. 1996. *Psalm 102 im Kontext des Vierten Psalmenbuches* SBB 30. Stuttgart: Katholisches Bibelwerk.

Brunson, A. C. 2003. *Psalm 118 in the Gospel of John: An Intertextual Study on the New Testament Exodus Pattern in the Theology of John.* Tübingen: Mohr Siebeck.

Buber, M. 1952. *At the Turning.* New York: Farrar, Straus and Young.

Buber, M. 1953. *Good and Evil: Two Interpretations.* New York: Schribner's.

Bullock, C. H. 2001. *Encountering the Book of Psalms,* Grand Rapids, MI: Baker Academic.

Calvin, J., trans. J. Anderson. 1849. *Commentary on the Book of Psalms. Volume Five (119–150).* Edinburgh: Calvin Translation Society.

Calvin, J., trans. H. Beveridge. 1979. *Commentary on the Book of Psalms. Volume Two.* Grand Rapids, MI: Baker Book House.

Cardenal, E. 1976. "I Cry in the Night from the Torture Chamber: Psalm 129." Pages 39–40 in *Mission Trends No.3: Third World Theologies.* Edited by G. H. Anderson and T. F. Stransky. New York: Paulist Press 1976.

Carleton Paget, J. N. B. 1996. "The Christian Exegesis of the Old Testament in the Alexandrian Tradition." Pages 478–542 in *Hebrew Bible/Old Testament. 1/1: From the Beginnings to the Middle Ages (Until 1300). Part 1: Antiquity.* Edited by M. Saebø. Göttingen: Vandenhoeck & Ruprecht.

Caruthers, M. 2001. "Memory, Imagination and the Interpretation of Scripture in the Middle Ages." Pages 216–18 in *The Oxford Handbook of Reception History.* Edited by M. Lieb, E. Mason and J. Roberts. Oxford: Oxford University Press.

Cassiodorus, trans. P. G. Walsh. 1991a. *Cassiodorus, Volume Two: Explanation of the Psalms 51–100.* ACW 52. Mahwah, NJ: Paulist Press.

Cassiodorus, trans. P. G. Walsh. 1991b. *Cassiodorus, Volume Three: Explanation of the Psalms 101–150.* ACW 53. Mahwah, NJ: Paulist Press.

Cathcart, K. 2011. "The Phoenician Inscriptions from Arslan Tash and some Old Testament Texts (Exodus 12; Micah 5: 4–5 [5–6]; Psalm 91)." Pages 87–100 in *On Stone and Scroll: Essays in Honour of Graham Ivor Davies*. Edited by J. A. Aitken, K. J. Dell, B. A. Martin. Berlin: de Gruyter.

Chrysostom, J., trans. R. C. Hill. 1998. *St. John Chrysostom: Commentary on the Psalms. Volumes One and Two*. Brookline, MA: Holy Cross Orthodox Press.

Church, J. R. 1990. *Hidden Prophecies in the Psalms*. Oklahoma: Prophecy Publications.

Chyutin, M. 1994. The Redaction of the Qumranic and the Traditional Book of Psalms on a Calendar. *RevQ* 16: 367–95.

Clarke, E. 2012. "Early Modern Women." Pages 169–83 in *The Blackwell Companion to the Bible in English Literature*. Edited by R. Lemon *et al*. Chichester: Wiley-Blackwell.

Clarke, E. 2018. *Eighteen Psalms*. Plymouth: Periplum Poetry.

Clarke, E. 2020. *A Book of Psalms*, Brewster, MA: Paraclete Press.

Coakley, S. 2011. "On the Fearfulness of Forgiveness: Psalm 130.4 and its Theological Implications." Pages 33–51 in *The Psalms in Early Christian Thought and Practice*. Edited by A. Andreopoulos, A. Casiday and C. Harrison. Turnhout: Brepols.

Cohen, A. 1992. *The Psalms. Soncino Books of the Bible*. London: Soncino Press. Second edition.

Cole, R. L. 2000. *The Shape and Message of Book III*. JSOTSup 307. Sheffield: Sheffield Academic Press.

Cook, E. M. 2002. "The Psalms Targum: Introduction to a New Translation with Sample Texts." Pages 185–201 in *Targum and Scripture: Studies in Aramaic Translations and Interpretation in Memory of Ernest G. Clarke*. Edited by P. V. M. Flesher. Leiden: Brill.

Corrigan, K. 1992. *Visual Polemics in the Ninth Century Byzantine Psalters*. Cambridge: Cambridge University Press.

Cotter, J. 1993. *Towards the City. A Version of Psalms 101–150*. Gwynedd: Cairns Publications.

Creach, J. F. D. 1996. "Between Text and Sermon." *Interpretation* 50: 47–51.

Creach, J. F. D. 1998. "The Shape of Book Four of the Psalter and the Shape of Second Isaiah." *JSOT* 80: 63–76.

Crostini, B, and G. Peers, (eds.). 2016. *A Book of Psalms from Eleventh-Century Constantinople. On the Complex of Texts and Images in Vat.gr.752*. STSA 504. Rome: Vatican Library Publications.

Crow, L. D. 1996. *The Songs of Ascents (Psalms 120–134). Their Place in Israelite History and Religion*. SBLDS 148. Atlanta, GA: SBL Press.

Cutler, A. and A. Weyl Carr. 1976. "The Psalter Benaki 34.3. An Unpublished Illustrated Manuscript from the Family 2400." *Revue de études byzantines* 34: 282–324.

Dahood, M. 1966. *Psalms III. Psalms 101–150, A New Translation with Introduction and Commentary*. ABC 17A. New Haven, CT: Yale University Press.

Daly-Denton, M. 2000. *David in the Fourth Gospel. The Johannine Reception of the Psalms*. Leiden: Brill.

Daly-Denton, M. 2004. "The Psalms in John's Gospel." Pages 119–38 in *The Psalms in the New Testament*. Edited by S. Moyise and M. J. J. Menken. London: T&T Clark.

Daly-Denton, M. 2010. *Psalm-Shaped Prayerfulness*. Dublin: Columba Press.

Davis, E. 1992. Psalms in Hebrew Medical Amulets. *VT* 42/2, 173–78.

Davison, L. 2001. "'My Soul is Like the Weaned Child that it is with me.' The Psalms and the Feminine Voice." *HBTh* 23: 155–67.

Day, J. 2013. "Ps. 104 and Akhenaten's Hymn to the Sun." Pages 211–28 in *Jewish and Christian Approaches to the Psalms: Conflict and Convergence.* Edited by S. E. Gillingham. Oxford: Oxford University Press.

deClaissé-Walford, N. L. 1997. *Reading from the Beginning: The Shaping of the Hebrew Psalter.* Macon, GA: Mercer University Press.

deClaissé-Walford, N. L. (ed.). 2014. *The Shape and Shaping of the Book of Psalms.* Ancient Israel and its Literature 20. Atlanta, GA: SBL Press.

deClaissé-Walford, N. L. 2017. "Feminine Imagery and Theology in the Psalter: Psalms 90, 91, and 92." Pages 15–25 in *The Psalter as Witness: Theology, Poetry, and Genre.* Edited by W. D. Tucker Jr. and W. H. Bellinger. Waco, TX: Baylor University Press.

deClaissé-Walford, N. L., Jacobson, R. A. and Tanner, B. L. (eds.). 2014. *The Book of Psalms.* NICOT. Grand Rapids, MI: Eerdmans.

Decleir, V. 2007. "Le Psaume 116 (117) dans la musique baroque et classique." *Études* 407/10: 399–401.

De Solms, E. 2001. *Bible Chrétienne V. Commentaires: Les Psaumes.* Quebec: Anne Signier.

Dion, P. E. 1991. "YHWH as Storm-god and Sun-god. The Double Legacy of Egypt and Canaan as Reflected in Psalm 104." *ZAW* 103: 43–71.

Doble, P. 2004. "The Psalms in Luke-Acts." Pages 83–118 in *The Psalms in the New Testament.* Edited by S. Moyise and M. J. J. Menken. London: T&T Clark International.

Dombkowski Hopkins, D. 2016. *Psalms Books 2–3.* Wisdom Commentary Vol. 21. Collegeville, MN: Liturgical Press.

Donin, H. H. 1980. *To Pray as A Jew: a Guide to the Prayer Book and the Synagogue Service.* New York: Basic Books.

Dowling Long, S. and J. F. A. Sawyer. 2015. *The Bible in Music: A Dictionary of Songs, Works, and More.* Lanham, MD: Rowman & Littlefield.

Dunn, J. 1988. *Romans 1–8.* Word Bible Commentary Vol. 38A. Nashville TN: Thomas Nelson.

Dupont, J. 1970. "Assis à la droite de Dieu. L'Interprétation du Ps.110 dans le Nouveau Testament." Pages 340–422 in *Resurrexit. Actes du Symposium International sur la Résurrection de Jésus.* Edited by E. Dhanis. Rome: Libreria Editrice Vaticana.

Dupont-Sommer, A. 1964. "Le Psaume CLI dans 11QPsª et le problème de son origine essénienne." *Semitica* 14: 25–62.

Dysinger, L. 2005. *Psalmody and Prayer in the Writings of Evagrius Ponticus.* Oxford: Oxford University Press.

Dysinger, L. 2015. "Evagrius Ponticus. The Psalters as a Handbook for the Christian Contemplative." Pages 97–125 in *The Harp of Prophecy. Early Christian Interpretation of the Psalms.* Edited by B. E. Daley and P. R. Kolbet. Christianity and Judaism in Antiquity 20. Notre Dame, IN: University of Notre Dame Press.

Eaton, J. 2003. *The Psalms: A Historical and Spiritual Commentary with and Introduction and New Translation.* London: T&T Clark International.

Edwards, T. 2007. *Exegesis in the Targum of Psalms. The Old, the New, and the Rewritten*. Gorgias Dissertations 28/Biblical Studies 1. Piscataway, NJ: Gorgias Press.

Elbogen, I., trans. R. P. Scheindlin. 1993. *Jewish Liturgy: A Comprehensive History*. Philadelphia, PA: Jewish Publication Society.

Enns, P. 1997. "The Interpretation of Psalm 96 in Hebrews 3.1—4.13." Pages 353–63 in *Early Christian Interpretation of the Scriptures of Israel*. Edited by C. E. Evans and J. A. Sanders. JSNTSup 148. Sheffield: Sheffield Academic Press.

Evans, C. E. 2011. "Jesus and Psalm 91 in Light of the Exorcism Scrolls." Pages 541–55 in *Celebrating the Dead Sea Scrolls. A Canadian Collection*. Edited by P. W. Flint, J. Duhaime and K. S. Back. EJL 30. Atlanta, GA: SBL Press.

Farmer, K. A. 1998. "Psalms." Pages 137–44 in *The Women's Bible Commentary*. Edited by C.A. Newsom and S.H. Ringe. London: SPCK.

Faulkner, M. 2017. "The Eadwine Psalter and Vernacular Literature." Pages 72–107 in *The Psalms and Medieval English Literature. From the Conversion to the Reformation*. Edited by T. Atkin and F. Leneghan. Cambridge: D. S. Brewer.

Feuer, A.C. (trans. and commentary). 1985, Nineteenth Impression 2004. *Tehillim: A New Translation with a Commentary Anthologized from Talmudic, Midrashic and Rabbinic Sources*. New York: Mesorah Publications.

Fiddes, P. 2009. "G.M. Hopkins." Pages 563-76 in *The Blackwell Companion to the Bible in English Literature*. Edited by R. Lemon *et al*. Chichester: Wiley-Blackwell.

Fischer, R. H. 1983. "Ecclesiastes." Pages 73–103 in *Seven-Headed Luther. Essays in Commemoration of a Quincentenary 1482-1982*. Edited by P. N. Brooks. Oxford: Oxford University Press.

Fisken, B. W. 1985. "Mary Sidney's *Psalmes*: Education and Wisdom." Pages 166–83 in *Silent but for the Word: Tudor Women as Patrons, Translators and Writers of Religious Works*. Edited by M. Patterson Hannay. Kent, OH: Kent State University Press.

Flint, P. W. 1997. *The Dead Sea Scrolls and the Book of Psalms*. STDJ 17. Leiden: Brill.

Flint, P. W. 2014. "The Contribution of Gerald Wilson toward Understanding the Book of Psalms in the Light of the Psalms Scrolls." Pages 209–30 in *The Shape and Shaping of the Book of Psalms. The Current State of Scholarship*. Edited by N. L. deClaissé-Walford. AIL 20. Atlanta, GA: SBL Press.

Foder, A. 1978. "The Use of Psalms in Jewish and Christian Arabic Magic." Pages 67–71 in *Jubilee Volume of the Oriental Collection 1951-1976: Papers presented on the Occasion of the 25ᵗʰ Anniversary of the Oriental Collection of the Library of the Hungarian Academy of Sciences*. Edited by E. Apor. Budapest: Magyar Tudonányos Akadémia.

Foster, P. (ed.). 2002. *Chagall Glass at Chichester and Tudely*. Otter Memorial Paper Number 14. Petworth: Bexley.

Frevel, C. 2010. "*Symeron* – Understanding Psalm 95 within, and without, Hebrews." Pages 165–93 in *Psalms and Hebrews: Studies in Reception*. Edited by D.J. Human and G.J. Steyn. LHBOTS 527. London: T&T Clark.

Geddes, J. 2005. *The St Albans Psalter. A Book for Christina of Markyate*. London: British Library.

Gelston, A. 2010. "Editorial Arrangement in Book IV of the Psalter. Pages 163–76 in *Genesis, Isaiah, and Psalms: A Festschrift to Honour Professor John Emerton for His*

Eightieth Birthday. Edited by J. A. Emerton, K. J. Dell, G. I. Davies, and Y. V. Koh. VTSup 135. Leiden: Brill.

German, B. T. 2017. *Psalms of the Faithful: Luther's Early Reading of the Psalter in Canonical Context.* Washington, DC: Lexham Press.

Gillingham, S. E. 1988. "The Poor in the Psalms." *ExpTim* 100/1: 15–19.

Gillingham, S. E. 2005. "The Zion Tradition and the Editing of the Hebrew Psalter." Pages 308–41 in *Temple and Worship. Proceedings of the Oxford Old Testament Seminar.* Edited by J. Day. Sheffield: Sheffield Academic Press.

Gillingham, S. E. 2008. *The Psalms Through the Centuries: Volume One.* Chichester: Blackwell.

Gillingham, S. E. 2010. "The Levitical Singers and the Editing of the Hebrew Psalter." Pages 91–123 in *The Composition of the Book of Psalms.* Edited by Erich Zenger. BETL 238. Leuven: Peeters.

Gillingham, S. E. 2012. "Entering and Leaving the Psalter: Psalms 1 and 150 and the Two Polarities of Faith." Pages 383–93 in *Let us Go up to Zion. Essays in Honour of H.G.M. Williamson on the Occasion of his Sixty-Fifth Birthday.* Edited by I. Provan and M. J. Boda. VTSup 153. Leiden: Brill.

Gillingham, S. E. (ed.). 2013a. *Jewish and Christian Approaches to the Psalms: Conflict and Convergence.* Oxford: Oxford University Press.

Gillingham, S. E. 2013b. "The Reception of Psalm 137 in Jewish and Christian Traditions." Pages 64–82 in *Jewish and Christian Approaches to the Psalms. Conflict and Convergence.* Edited by S. E. Gillingham Oxford: Oxford University Press.

Gillingham, S. E. 2013c. *A Journey of Two Psalms: The Reception of Psalms 1 and 2 in Jewish and Christian Tradition.* Oxford: Oxford University Press.

Gillingham, S. E. 2014. "The Levites and the Editorial Composition of the Psalms." Pages 201–13 in *The Oxford Handbook of the Psalms.* Edited by W. P. Brown. Oxford: Oxford University Press.

Gillingham, S. E. 2017. "The Levitical Singers and the Compilation of the Hebrew Psalter." Pages 35–59 in *Trägerkreise in den Psalmen.* Edited by F.L. Hossfeld, J. Bremer and T. Steiner. BBB 178. Göttingen: Bonn University Press/ Vandenhoeck & Ruprecht.

Gillingham, S. E. 2018. *Psalms Through the Centuries: A Reception History Commentary on Psalms 1–72. Volume Two.* Blackwell Bible Commentaries. Oxford: Wiley-Blackwell.

Gillingham, S. E. 2019. "Jewish and Christian Approaches to Suffering in the Reception of Psalm 137." *OTE* 32/2: 441-60.

Goldingay, J. 2007. *Psalms. Volume 2: Psalms 42–89.* Grand Rapids, MI: Baker Academic.

Goldingay, J. 2008. *Psalms. Volume 3: Psalms 90–150.* Grand Rapids, MI: Baker Academic.

Goodman, W. 2012. *Yearning for You: Psalms and the Song of Songs in Conversation with Rock and Worship Songs.* Sheffield: Sheffield Phoenix Press.

Gorali, M. 1993. *The Old Testament in Music.* Jerusalem: Maron.

Gould, W. H. and C. W. Quick (eds.). 1865. *The Works of John Owen.* Volume 6, Philadelphia, PA: Leighton Publications.

Goulder, M. D. 1975. "The Fourth Book of the Psalter." *JTS* 26: 269–89.

Goulder, M. D. 1997. "The Songs of Ascents and Nehemiah." *JSOT* 75: 43–58.

Goulder, M. D. 1998. *The Psalms of the Return (Book V, Psalms 107–150): Studies in the Psalter, IV.* JSOTSup 258. Sheffield: Sheffield Academic Press.

Grohmann, M. 2010. "The Imagery of the 'Weaned Child' in Psalm 131." Pages 513–22 in *The Composition of the Book of Psalms.* Edited by E. Zenger. BETL 228. Leuven: Peeters.

Grossberg, D. 1989. "Songs of Ascents." Pages in 15–54 in *Centrapetal and Centrifugal Structures in Biblical Poetry.* Edited by D. Grossberg. Atlanta, GA: Scholars Press.

Gross-Diaz, T. 1996. *The Psalms Commentary of Gilbert of Poitiers. From Lectio Divina to the Lecture Room.* Leiden: Brill.

Groves, B. 2007. "Shakespeare's Sonnets and Genevan marginalia." *Essays in Criticism* 58/2: 114–28.

Gruber, M. I. 2004. *Rashi's Commentary on Psalms.* Leiden: Brill.

Guite, M. 2021. *David's Crown. Sounding the Psalms.* Norwich: Canterbury Press.

Gunkel, H. 1929. *Die Psalmen.* HKAT. Göttingen: Vandenhoeck & Ruprecht.

Gwyn, R. 1997. *The Psalms in Haiku Form: A Simplified Psalter.* Leominster: Gracewing.

Hagen, K. 1997. "*Omnis homo mendax*: Luther on Psalm 116." Pages 85–102 in *Biblical Interpretation in the Era of the Reformation.* Edited by Muller, R. A. and J. L. Thompson. Grand Rapids MI: Eerdmans.

Haïk-Vantoura, S., D. Weber (trans.) and J. Wheeler (ed.). 1991. *The Music of the Bible Revealed.* Berkeley, CA: Bibal Press.

Hall, J. 1979. *Dictionary of Subjects and Symbols in Art.* Revised Edition. London: John Murray.

Haleem, M. A. S. Abdel. 2010. *The Qur'an. English Translation and Parallel Arabic Text* Oxford: Oxford University Press.

Hamlin, H. 2002. "Psalm Culture in the English Renaissance: Readings of Psalm 137 by Shakespeare, Spenser, Milton and Others." *Renaissance Quarterly* 55: 224–57.

Hamlin, H. 2004a. *Psalm Culture and Early Modern English Literature.* Cambridge: Cambridge University Press.

Hamlin, H. 2004b. "Psalm 137: singing the Lord's song in a strange land." Pages 218–252 in *Psalm Culture and Early Modern English Literature.* Edited by H. Hamlin. Cambridge: Cambridge University Press.

Hamlin, H., M. G. Brennan, M. P. Hannay, and N. J. Kinnamon (eds.). 2009. *The Sidney Psalter. The Psalms of Sir Philip and Mary Sidney.* Oxford World Classics. Oxford: Oxford University Press.

Harper, J. 1991. *The Forms and Orders of Western Liturgy from the Tenth to the Eighteenth Century.* Oxford: Clarendon Press

Hawk, B. W. 2015. "Psalm 151 in Anglo-Saxon England." *RES* 66: 805–21.

Hay, D. M. 1973. *Glory at the Right Hand. Psalm 110 in Early Christianity.* Nashville, TN: Abingdon.

Hays, R. B. 1980. "Psalm 143 and the Logic of Romans 3." *JBL* 99: 107–115.

Hays, R. B. 1989. *Echoes of Scripture in the Letters of Paul.* New Haven, CT: Yale University Press, 1989.

Hayward, R. 2011. "Saint Jerome, Jewish Learning, and the Symbolism of the Number Eight." Pages 141–59 in *Meditations of the Heart: The Psalms in Early Christian Thought and Practice. Essays in Honour of Andrew Louth*. Edited by A. Andreopoulos, A. Casiday and C. Harrison. Studia Traditionis Theologiae, 8. Turnhout: Brepols Publishers.

Hebron, S. (ed.). 2014. *Marks of Genius. Masterpieces from the Collections of the Bodleian Libraries*, Oxford: Bodleian.

Heine, R. E. 1995. *Gregory of Nyssa's Treatise on the Inscriptions of Psalms: Introduction, Translation and Notes*. OECS. Oxford: Clarendon Press.

Hendrix, S. 1974. *Ecclesia in Via*. Leiden: Brill.

Hensley, A. 2018. *Covenant Relationships and the Editing of the Psalter*. LHBOTS 666. London: Bloomsbury/T&T Clark.

Hertz, J. H. 1942. *The Authorised Daily Prayer Book. Hebrew Text, English Translation, with Commentary and Notes*. New York: Bloch Publishing Company.

Hill, E. 1973. *Prayer Praise and Politics. Reflections on 32 Psalms*. London: Sheed and Ward.

Hill, C. 1993. *The English Bible and the Seventeenth Century Revolution*. London: Penguin.

Ho, P. C. W. 2019. *The Design of the Psalter. A Macrostructural Analysis*. Eugene, OR: Wipf and Stock.

Hoenig, S. B. 1968. "The Dead Sea Psalms Scroll." *JQR* 58: 162–63.

Hoffman, L. A. 1997. *My People's Prayer Book: Traditional Prayers, Modern Commentaries*, Volume 3: *P'sukei d'Zimrah*. Woodstock, VT: Jewish Lights Publishing.

Hoffman, L. A. 2004. "Hallels, Midrash, Canon, and Loss: Psalms in Jewish Liturgy." Pages 33–60 in *Psalms in Community: Jewish and Christian Textual, Liturgical, and Artistic Traditions*. Edited by H. W. Attridge and M. E. Fassler. Leiden: Brill.

Holladay, W. L. 1993. *The Psalms through Three Thousand Years: A Prayerbook of a Cloud of Witnesses*. Minneapolis, MN: Augsburg.

Hossfeld, F.-L. and T. M. Steiner. 2013. "Problems and Prospects in Psalter Studies." Pages 240–58 in *Jewish and Christian Approaches to the Psalms: Conflict and Convergence*. Edited by S. E. Gillingham. Oxford: Oxford University Press.

Hossfeld, F.-L. and E. Zenger. 2000. *Psalmen 51–100, 2 Teilband*. Freiburg: Herder.

Hossfeld, F.-L. and E. Zenger, trans. L. M. Maloney. 2005. *Psalms 2: A Commentary on Psalms 51–100*. Minneapolis, MN: Fortress Press.

Hossfeld, F.-L. and E. Zenger. 2008. *Psalmen 101–150, 3 Teilband*. Freiburg: Herder.

Hossfeld, F.-L. and E. Zenger, trans. L. M. Maloney. 2011. *Psalms 3: A Commentary on Psalms 101–150*. Minneapolis, MN: Fortress Press.

Howard, D. M. 1993. "A Contextual Reading of Psalms 90–94." Pages 108–23 in *The Shape and Shaping of the Psalter*. Edited by J. Clinton McCann. JSOTSup 159. Sheffield: JSOT Press.

Howard, D. M. 1997. *The Structure of Psalms 93–100: Their Place in Israelite History*. Winona Lake, IN: Eisenbrauns.

Howell, J. C. 1987. "Jerome's Homilies on the Psalter in Bethlehem." Pages 180–97 in *The Listening Heart: Essays in Wisdom and the Psalms in Honor of Roland O. Murphy, O. Carm*. Edited by K. G. Hoglund, E. F. Huwiler, J. T. Glass, and R. W. Lee. JSOTSup 58. Sheffield: Continuum.

Human, D. J. 2010. "A Prophetic Voice for Africa from Psalm 95." Pages 147–64 in *Psalms and Hebrews: Studies in Reception*. Edited by D. J. Human and G. J. Steyn. LHBOTS 527. London: T&T Clark.

Human, D. J. 2011. "'Praise beyond Words.' Psalm 150 a *grand finale* of the Crescendo in the *Psalter.*" TS 67/1. Open Access https://hts.org.za/index.php/hts/article/view/917/1506.

Human, D. J. and G. J. Steyn (eds.). 2010. *Psalms and Hebrews: Studies in Reception.* LHBOTS 527. London: T&T Clark.

Hunter, A. G. 1999. *Psalms. Old Testament Readings.* London: Routledge.

Huxley, W. 1949. "The Psalms in Heraldry." *Evangelical Quarterly* 21: 297–305

Jackson, D. 2006. *Psalms. The Saint John's Bible.* Ireland: Veritas Ltd.

Jackson, G. 1997. *The Lincoln Psalter.* Manchester: Carcanet Press.

Janowski, B. 2010. "Ein Tempel aus Worten: Zur Theologischen Architektur des Psalters." Pages 279–306 in *The Composition of the Book of Psalms.* Edited by E. Zenger. BETL 238. Leuven: Peeters.

Jebb, J. 1846. *A literal translation of the Book of Psalms: intended to illustrate their poetical and moral structure: to which are added dissertations on the word selah, and on the authorship, order, titles, and poetical features of the Psalms.* 2 vols. London: Longman, Brown, Green and Longmans.

Jeffrey, D. L. (ed.). 2008. *A Dictionary of Biblical Tradition in English Literature.* Grand Rapids, MI: Eerdmans.

Jerome, trans. M. Ewald. 1963. *Jerome: Homilies Volume I (1–59 on the Psalms).* FC 48. Washington, DC: Catholic University of America Press.

Kaulbach, E. N. 2008a. "De Profundis." Pages 185–86 in *A Dictionary of Biblical Tradition in English Literature.* Edited by D. L. Jeffrey. Grand Rapids, MI: Eerdmans.

Kaulbach, E. N. 2008b. "Noonday Demon.'" Pages 553–54 in *A Dictionary of Biblical Tradition in English Literature.* Edited by D. L. Jeffrey. Grand Rapids, MI: Eerdmans.

Keet, C. C. 1969. *A Study of the Psalms of Ascents.* London: Mitre.

Kiley, M. 1986. "'Lord, Save My Life' (Ps 116:4) as Generative Text for Jesus' Gethsemane Prayer (Mark 14:36a)." *CBQ* 48: 655–59.

Kim, J. 2008. "The Strategic Arrangement of Royal Psalms in Books IV–V." *WTJ* 70: 143–58.

Kimmelmann, R. 1999. "Ashre. Psalm 145 and its Rhetorical Structure." Pages 31–39 in *P'Sukei D'Zimra (Morning Psalms).* Volume 3: My People's Prayer Book. Traditional Prayers, Modern Commentaries. Edited by L. A. Hoffmann. Woodstock, VT: Jewish Lights Publishing.

Kinnamon, N. 1981. "Notes on the Psalms in Herbert's *The Temple.*" *George Herbert Journal* 4/2: 10–29.

King'oo, C. C. 2012. *Miserere Mei: The Penitential Psalms in Late Medieval and Early Modern England.* Notre Dame, IN: University of Notre Dame Press.

Kirkpatrick, J. and Smith, G, (eds.). 1970. *Charles Ives: Psalm 90.* Bryn Mawr: Merion Music.

Kirschner, R. 1990. "Two Responses to Epochal Change: Augustine and the Rabbis on Psalm 137 (136)." *Vigiliae Christianae* 44/3: 242–62.

Kittel, R. 1916. *Das Alte Testament und unser Krieg* Leipzig: Dörffling und Franke.

Knowles, M. D. 2006. *Centrality Practiced. Jerusalem in the Religious Practice of Yehud and the Diaspora in the Persian Period.* Atlanta, GA: SBL Press.

Koch, K. 1994. "Der Psalter und seine Redaktionsgeschichte." Pages 242–77 in *Neue Wege der Psalmenforschung: für Walter Beyerlin*. Edited by K. S. Seybold and E. Zenger. Second Edition. Frieburg: Herder.

Kratz, R. G. 1995. Die Tora Davids: Psalm 1 und die doxologische Fünfteilung des Psalters. *ZThK* 93: 1–34.

Kratz, R. G. 2011. "Blessed be the Lord and Blessed be his Name forever": Psalm 145 in the Hebrew Bible and in the Psalms Scroll 11Q5." Pages 229–43 in *Prayer and Poetry in the Dead Sea Scrolls and Related Literature. Essays in Honor of Eileen Schuller on the Occasion of her 65*th *Birthday*. Edited by J. Penner. STDJ 98. Leiden: Brill.

Kraus, H.-J. trans. H. C. Oswald. 1989. *Psalms 60–150: A Commentary*. Minneapolis, MN: Augsburg.

Kruse, H. 1983. "Psalm CXXXII and the Royal Zion Festival." *VT* 33/3: 278–97.

Kselman, J. S. 1983. "Psalm 77 and the Book of Exodus." *JANES* 1: 51–58.

Kuczynski, M. P. 1995. *Prophetic Song: The Psalms as Moral Discourse in Late Medieval England*. Philadelphia, PA: University of Pennsylvania Press.

Kugel, J. 1990. "Psalm 137." Pages 173–213 in *Potiphar's House. The Interpretive Life of Biblical Times*. Edited by J. Kugel. Cambridge, MA: Harvard University Press.

Ladouceur, D. J. 2005. *The Latin Psalter. Introduction, Selected Text and Commentary*. London: Bristol Classical Press.

Lafran, A. 2018. "Le Psaume 108 et Judas." Pages 61–78 in *Les Psaumes de David*. Edited by J.-M. Vercruysse. Graphè 27. Arras Cedex: Artois Presses Université.

LaNeel Tanner, B. 1998. "Hearing the Cries Unspoken: an intertextual-feminist reading of Psalm 109." Pages 283–301 in *Wisdom and Psalms*. Edited by Brenner, A. and C. R. Fontaine. Sheffield: Sheffield Academic Press.

Laster, J. H. 2002. *Catalogue of Choral Music Arranged in Biblical Order. Supplement*. Folkestone: Scarecrow Press.

Law, F. C. E. 2017. *The Ormesby Psalter: Patrons and Artists in Medieval East Anglia*. Oxford: Bodleian Library.

LeMon, J. 2017. Symphonizing the Psalms: Igor Stravinsky's Musical Exegesis. *Interpretation* 71/1, 25–49.

Lemon, R. *et al* (ed.). 2009. *The Blackwell Companion to the Bible in English Literature*. Chichester: Wiley-Blackwell.

Leneghan, F. 2017. "Making the Psalter Sing." Pages 173–97 in *The Psalms and Medieval English Literature. From the Conversion to the Reformation*. Edited by T. Atkin and F. Leneghan. Cambridge: Brewer.

Levine, H. J. 1984. *Sing unto God a New Song: A Contemporary Reading of the Psalms*. Indianapolis, IN: Indiana University Press.

Leuenberger, M. 2004. *Konzeptionen des Königtums Gottes im Psalter: Untersuchungen zu Komposition und Redaktion der theokratischen Bücher IV-V im Psalter*. ATANT 83. Zürich: Theologischer Verlag Zürich.

Levenson, J. D. 1987. "The Sources of Torah: Psalm 119 and the Modes of Revelation in Second Temple Judaism." Pages 559–74 in *Ancient Israelite Religion. Essays in Honour of Frank Moore Cross*. Edited by P. D. Miller, P. D. Hanson, and S. D. McBride. Philadelphia, PA: Fortress Press.

Liebreich, L. J. 1955. "The Songs of Ascents and the Priestly Blessing." *JBL* 74: 33–36.

Limburg, J. 1999. "De Profundis." *CurTM* 26: 117–22.

Limburg, J. 2002. *Psalms for Sojourners*. Second Edition. Minneapolis, MN: Fortress Press.

Luther, M. trans. and ed. J. Pelikan. 1956. *Selected Psalms. Luther's Works*. Volume 12. St Louis, MO: Concordia Publishing House.

Luther, M. trans. and ed. H.T. Lehmann. 1960. *Luther's Works 34. Career of the Reformer IV*. St Louis: Concordia Publishing House.

Luther, M., trans. and ed. A. T. W. Steinhauser, F. C. Ahrens and A. R. Wentz. 1970. *On the Babylonian Captivity: Three Treatises*. Philadelphia, PA: University of Pennsylvania Press.

Magonet, J. 1994. *A Rabbi Reads the Psalms*. London: SCM Press.

Magonet, J. 1996. *Jewish Prayers for Shabbat and Weekdays*. Munich: Liberale Jüdische Gemeinde Beth Shalom.

Magonet, J. 1982. "Some Concentric Structures in Psalms." *HeyJ* 23/4, 365–76.

Maguire, E. D. (ed.). 1989. *Art and Holy Powers in the Early Christian House*. Illinois Byzantine Studies 2. Chicago, IL: University of Illinois.

Manley Hopkins, G., edited by W. H. Gardner and N. H. MacKenzie. 1967. *The Poems of Gerard Manley Hopkins*. Oxford: Oxford University Press.

Marks, R. and N. Morgan. 1981. *The Golden Age of English Manuscript Painting 1200–1500*. London: Chatto & Windus.

Markus, R. L. 2015. "Spiritual Longings and their Expression in the Biblical Art of Benn." Pages 271–85 in *The Bible Retold by Jewish Artists, Writers, Composers and Filmmakers*. Edited by H. Leneman and B. D. Wolfish. Sheffield: Sheffield Phoenix Press.

Markus, Y. (ed.). 2016. *Tehillim: Book of Psalms*. Brooklyn, NY: Kehot Publications Society.

Marshall, I. H. 1980. *The Acts of the Apostles*. TNTC. Leicester: Inter-Varsity Press.

Martínez, F. G. and E. J. C. Tigchelaar. 1995. *The Dead Sea Scrolls Study Edition*. Grand Rapids, MI: Eerdmans.

McCann, J. C. (ed.). 1993a. *The Shape and Shaping of the Psalter*. JSOTSup 159. Sheffield: JSOT Press.

McCann, J. C. 1993b. "Books I–III and the Editorial Purpose of the Hebrew Psalter." Pages 93–107 in *The Shape and Shaping of the Psalter*. Edited by J. C. McCann. JSOTSup 159. Sheffield: JSOT Press.

McCarthy, M. 2015. "An Ecclesiology of Groaning. Augustine, the Psalms and the Making of the Church." Pages 227–56 in *The Harp of Prophecy: Early Christian Interpretation of the Psalms*. Edited by B.E. Daley and P.R. Kolbet. Notre Dame, IN: University of Notre Dame.

McGuckin, J. A. 2011. "Origen's use of the Psalms." Pages 97–118 in *Meditations of the Heart: The Psalms in Early Christian Thought and Practice. Essays in Honour of Andrew Louth*. Edited by A. Andreopoulos, A. Casiday, C. Harrison. Studia Traditionis Theologiae 8. Turnhout: Brepols.

McKelvey, M.G. 2010. *Moses, David and the High Kingship of Yahweh*, Piscataway, NJ: Gorgias Press.

McLean, B. H. 1992. *Allusions and Citations to Jewish Scripture in Early Christian and Jewish Writings*. Lewiston, NY: Edwin Mellen Press.

McNamara, M. 2000. *The Psalms in the Early Irish Church*. JSOTSup 165. Sheffield: Sheffield Academic Press.

McPolin, J. 1989. "Psalms as Prayers of the Poor." Pages 79–103 in *Back to the Sources. Biblical and Ancient Near Eastern Studies*. Edited by K. J. Cathcart and J. F. Healey. Dublin: Glendale Publishing.

Mein, A. 2010. "Psalm 101 and the Ethics of Kingship." Pages 56–70 in *Ethical and Unethical in the Old Testament. Gods and Humans in Dialogue*. Edited by K. J. Dell. London: T&T Clark International.

Mein, A. 2019. "Psalms. Patriotism and Propaganda: A Favourite Book in Wartime Biblical Scholarship." Pages 163–85 in *The First World War and the Mobilization of Biblical Scholarship*. Edited by A. Mein, N. MacDonald and M. A. Collins. LHBOTS. London: T&T Clark, Bloomsbury Publishing.

Menken, M. J. J. 2004. "The Psalms in Matthew's Gospel." Pages 61–82 in *The Psalms in the New Testament*. Edited by S. Moyise and M. J. J. Menken. London: T&T Clark International.

Metzger, T. 1996. "A History and Analysis of the Manuscript." Pages 29–148 in *Companion Volume to the Facsimile Edition of the Parma Psalter*. London: Facsimile Editions Limited.

Meynet, R. 2017. *Le Psautier. Cinquième Livre (Ps 107–150)*. Rhetorica Biblica et Semitica 12. Leuven: Peeters.

Millard, M. 1994. *Die Komposition des Psalters: Ein formgeschichtlicher Ansatz*, FAT 9. Tübingen: Mohr Siebeck.

Miller, P. D. 1994. "Dietrich Bonhoeffer and the Psalms." *The Princeton Seminary Bulletin* 15/3: 274–82.

Miller, P. D. 1998. "The End of the Psalter: A Response to Erich Zenger." *JSOT* 80: 103–110.

Mitchell, D. C. 1997. *The Message of the Psalter: An Eschatological Programme in the Book of Psalms*. JSOTSup 252. Sheffield: Sheffield Academic Press.

Mitchell, D. C. 2012. Resinging the Temple Psalmody. *JSOT* 36.3: 355–78.

Mitchell, D. C. 2013. "How can we sing the Lord's Song? Deciphering the Masoretic Cantillation." Pages 117–33 in *Jewish and Christian Approaches to the Psalms. Conflict and Convergence*. Edited by S. E. Gillingham. Oxford: Oxford University Press.

Mitchell, D. C. 2015. *The Songs of Ascents: Psalms 120 to 134 in the Worship of Jerusalem's Temples*. Newton Mearns: Campbell.

Morin, G. E. A. (ed.). 1959. *Sancti Hieronymi Presbyteri Commentarioli in Psalmos*. CCL 72. Turnhout: Brepols.

Moritz, T. 1966. *A Profound Mystery: The Use of the Old Testament in Ephesians*. Leiden: Brill.

Moritz, T. 2004. "The Psalms in Ephesians and Colossians." Pages 181–196 in *The Psalms in the New Testament*. Edited by S. Moyise and M. J. J. Menken. London and New York: T&T Clark.

Moss, S. and D. Attenborough. 2016. *Planet Earth II. A New World Revealed*. BBC Books. London: Penguin Random House.

Mosser, C. 2005. "The Earliest Patristic Interpretations of Psalm 82, Jewish Anteced-ents and the Origin of Christian Deification." *JTS* 56/1: 30–74.

Moule, H. C. G. 1898. *Thy Keeper: Words Spoken from Simeon's Pulpit on Psalm CXXI.* Cambridge: A. P. Dixon.

Mournet, K. J. 2011. "Moses and the Psalms: The Significance of Psalms 90 and 106 within Book IV of the Masoretic Psalter." *Conversations with the Biblical World* 31: 66–79.

Murphy, M. 1992. "Four Daughters of God." Pages 290–91 in *A Dictionary of Biblical Tradition in English Literature.* Edited by In D. L. Jeffrey. Grand Rapids, MI: Eerdmans.

Neale, J.M. and R.F. Littledale (eds.). 1874–79. *A Commentary on the Psalms: From Primitive and Mediaeval Writers.* Second edition. 4 Volumes. London: Masters.

Neuwirth, A., N. Sinai and M. Marx (eds.). 2010. *The Qur'an in Context. Historical and Literary Investigations into the Qur'anic Mileu.* Leiden: Brill.

Neuwirth, A. 2009. "Quranic Readings of the Psalms." Pages 733-778 in *The Qur'ān in Context. Historical and Literary Investigations into the Qur'ānic Milieu.* Edited by A. Neuwirth, N. Sinai and Marx. Texts and Studies on the Qur'an Volume 6. Leiden: Brill.

Ngoda, S. S. 2014. "Revisiting the Theocratic Agenda of Book 4 of the Psalter for Interpretive Premise." Pages 147–59 in *The Shape and Shaping of the Book of Psalms. The Current State of Scholarship.* Edited by N. L. DeClaissé-Walford. Atlanta, GA: SBL Press.

Nitzan, B. 1994. *Qumran Prayers and Religious Poetry.* Leiden: Brill.

Nogalski, J. D. 2000. "From Psalm to Psalms to Psalter." Pages 37–54 in *An Introduction to Wisdom Literature and the Psalms: Festschrift Marvin E. Tate.* Edited by W. H. Ballard and D. W. Tucker. Macon, GA: Mercer University Press.

Ntreh, A. 2001. "The Survival of the Earth." Pages 98–108 in *The Earth Story in the Psalms and the Prophets.* Edited by N. Habel. Sheffield: Sheffield Academic Press.

Oeming, M. 2009. "Wisdom as a Hermeneutical Key to the Book of Psalms." Pages 154–62 in *Scribes, Sages, Seers: The Sage in the Eastern Mediterranean World.* Edited by L. G. Perdue. FRLANT 219. Göttingen: Vandenhoeck & Ruprecht.

Oeming, M. & Vette, J. 2016. *Das Buch der Psalmen: Psalm 90–151, Neuer Stuttgarter Kommentar Altes Testament.* Stuttgart: Katholisches Bibelwerk.

Oettinger, R. W. 2001. *Music as Propaganda in the German Reformation. St. Andrews Studies in Reformation History.* Abingdon, Oxon: Routledge 2001.

Osherow, J. 1999. *Dead Men's Praise.* New York, NY: Grove Atlantic.

Oswald, H. C. et al. (eds.). 1974. *Selected Commentaries on the Psalms. Luther's Works.* Volumes 10–14. St Louis, MO: Concordia.

Pak, G.S. 2010. *The Judaizing Calvin: Sixteenth-Century Debates over the Messianic Psalms.* Oxford: Oxford University Press.

Paoletti, J. T. and G. M. Radke. 2005. *Art in Renaissance Italy.* London: Laurence King.

Pavan, M. 2014. *"He remembered that they were but flesh, a breath that passes and does not return" (Ps 78:39). The Theme of Memory and Forgetting in the Third Book of the Psalter (Pss 73–89).* Österreichische Biblischen Studien, 44. Frankfurt am Main: Peter Lang.

Peterson, E. H. 1994. *The Message: Psalms*. Colorado Springs, CO: Navipress.

Pickett, B. 2002. *Songs for the Journey: The Psalms in Life and Liturgy*. London: Darton, Longman & Todd.

Pietersma, A. 2000. *The Psalms: A New English Translation of the Septuagint and Other Greek Translations Traditionally Included under That Title*. Oxford: Oxford University Press.

Pitkin, B. 1993. "Imitation of David: David as a Paradigm for Faith in Calvin's Exegesis of the Psalms." *Sixteenth Century Journal* 24: 843–64.

Plank, K. A. 2008. "By the Waters of a Death Camp: An intertextual Reading of Psalm 137." *Literature and Theology* 22/2: 180–194.

Poque, S. 1986. "Les Psaumes dans 'Les Confessions'." Pages 155–66 in *Saint Augustine et la Bible*. Edited by A.-M. Bonnardière. BTT 3. Paris: Beauchesne.

Preuss, J. S. 1967. "Luther: O.T. *Promissio.*" *HTR* 60:145–61.

Preuss, J. S. 1969. *From Shadow to Promise: Old Testament Interpretation from Augustine to the Young Luther*. Cambridge: Belknap Press.

Prescott, A. L. 2011. "Sibling Harps: The Sidneys and the Chérons Translate the Psalms." Pages 235–55 in *Psalms in the Early Modern World*. Edited by L. P. Austern, K. B. McBride and D. L. Orvis. Burlington VT and Farnham, Surrey: Ashgate.

Prothero, R. E. 1903. *The Psalms in Human Life*. London: John Murray.

Rabinowitz, L. 1936. "Does Midrash Tehillim reflect the Triennial Cycle of Psalms?" *JQR* 26: 349–68.

Rademaker, C. S. M. 1988. "Erasmus and the Psalms: His Commentary on Psalm 86 (85)." Pages 187–94 in *Erasmus of Rotterdam: The Man and the Scholar. Proceedings of the Symposium held at the Erasmus University, Rotterdam 9–11 November 1986.* Edited by J. S. Weiland and W. Frijhoff. Leiden: E. J. Brill.

Rathmell, J. C. A. (ed.). 1963. *The Psalms of Sir Philip Sidney and the Countess of Pembroke*. New York: New York University Press.

Reid, W. S. 1971. "The Battle Hymns of the Lord: Calvinist Psalmody of the Sixteenth Century." *Sixteenth Century Journal* 2/1: 36–54.

Reif, S. C. 1993. *Judaism and Hebrew Prayer. New Perspectives on Jewish Liturgical History*. Cambridge: Cambridge University Press.

Reif, S. C. 2010. "Psalm 93: An Historical and Comparative Survey of its Jewish Interpretations." Pages 193–204 in *Genesis, Isaiah and Psalms. A Festschrift for John Emerton for his Eightieth Birthday*. Edited by K. J. Dell. *et al.* VTSup 135. Leiden: Brill.

Rendtorff, R. 2005. "The Role of David: David in the Psalms." Pages 53–64 in *The Book of Psalms: Composition and Reception*. Edited by P. W. Flint and P. D. Miller. Leiden: Brill.

Renz, C. R. 1996. "Come, Let us Listen to the Voice of the Lord." *Worship* 70: 140–53.

Reynolds, K. A. 2010. *Torah as Teacher. The Exemplary Torah Student in Psalm 119*. Leiden: Brill.

Rienstra, M. V. 1992. *Swallow's Nest. A Feminine Reading of the Psalms*. Grand Rapids, MI: Eerdmans.

Rigolot, I. 2017. *Anthologie des Commentaires Patristiques des Psaumes*. Paris: Éditions du Cerf.

Robertson, D. 1977. "Literary Criticism of the Bible: Psalm 90 and Shelly's 'Hymn to Intellectual Beauty'." *Semeia* 8: 35–50.

Robertson, E. 2005. *Dietrich Bonhoeffer's Meditations on the Psalms.* Grand Rapids, MI: Zondervan.

Rondeau, M.-J. 1985. *Les Commentaires Patristiques du Psautier IIIe-Ve siècles.* Volume 2. OrChrAn 220. Rome: Pontificium Institutum Studiorum Orientalium.

Rose, A. 1983. "Quelques orientations de la tradition chrétienne dans la lecture du psaume 118." Pages 209–26 in *Liturgie und Dichtung.* Edited by H. Becker and R. Kaczynski. St Ottilien: Eos.

Rösel, C. 1999. *Die messianische Redaktion des Psalters. Studien zu Entstehung und Theologie der Sammlung Psalm 2–89.* Calwer Theologische Monographien, Reihe A; Bibelwissenschaft Band 19. Darmstadt: Weihert-Druck.

Rosen, A. 2013. "True Lights: Seeing the Psalms Through Chagall's Church Windows." Pages 105–18 in *Jewish and Christian Approaches to the Psalms: Conflict and Convergence.* Edited by S. E. Gillingham. Oxford: Oxford University Press.

Rosenberg, D. 1976. *Blues of the Sky interpreted from the Original Hebrew Book of Psalms.* New York: Harper and Row.

Russell, S. H. 1968. Calvin and the Messianic Interpretation of the Psalms. *SJT* 21: 37–47.

Russell, N. 2011. "The 'Gods' of Psalm 81 (82) in the Hesychast Debates." Pages 243–56 in *Meditations of the Heart: The Psalms in Early Christian Thought and Practice: Essays in Honour of Andrew Louth.* Edited by A. Andreopoulos, A. Casiday and C. Harrison. Turnhout: Brepols Publishers.

Sadler, R. S. 2014. "Singing a Subversive Song: Psalm 137 and 'Colored Pompey'." Pages 447–58 in *The Oxford Handbook of The Psalms.* Edited by W. P. Brown. Oxford: Oxford University Press.

Saebø, M. (ed.). 1996. *Hebrew Bible/Old Testament. 1/1: From the Beginnings to the Middle Ages (Until 1300). Part 1: Antiquity.* Göttingen: Vandenhoeck & Ruprecht.

Saleh, W. A. 2014. "The Psalms in the Qur'an and in the Islamic Religious Imagination." Pages 281-96 in *The Oxford Handbook of Psalms.* Edited by W. P. Brown. Oxford: Oxford University Press.

Sanders, J. A. 1963. "Ps. 151 in 11QPssᵃ." *ZAW* 75: 73–86.

Sanders, J. A. 1965. *The Psalms Scroll of Qumran Cave 11 (11 QPsᵃ).* DJD 4. Oxford: Clarendon Press.

Sarna, N. H. 1962. "Psalm for the Sabbath Day (Ps 92)." *JBL* 81: 155–68.

Sawyer, J. F. A. 1968. "An Analysis of the Context and Meaning of the Psalm Headings." *TGUOS* 22: 26–38.

Scaila, D. 2010. "The End of the Psalter." Pages 701–10 in *The Composition of the Book of Psalms.* Edited by E. Zenger. Leuven: Peeters. 701–710.

Schaper, J. 1995. *Eschatology in the Greek Psalter.* WUNT 2 Reihe 76. Tübingen:Mohr.

Schnocks, J. 2012. "Gott, es kamen Völker in dein Erbe. Ps 79 und seine Rezeption in 1 Makk." Pages 147–60 in *Juda und Jerusalem in der Seleukidenzeit: Herrschaft, Widerstand, Identität; Festschrift für Heinz-Josef Fabry.* Edited by U. Dahmen and J. Schnocks. Göttingen: Vandenhoeck & Ruprecht.

Schnocks, J. 2017. "Human Transience, Justice, and Mercy: Psalm 103." Pages 77–86 in *The Psalter as Witness: Theology, Poetry, and Genre*. Edited by W. D. Tucker and W. H. Bellinger. Waco, TX: Baylor University Press, 77–86.

Schonfield, J. 2017. "Psalms 113–118: Qualified Praise?" *European Judaism* 50/2: 145–57.

Segal, M. 2002. "The Literary Development of Psalm 151: A New Look at the Septuagint Version." *Textus* 21: 139–158.

Selderhuis, H. J. (ed.). 2018. *The Reformation Commentary on Scripture Old Testament VIII. Psalms 73–150*. Downers Grove, IL: IVP Academic.

Seybold, K. S. 1978. *Die Wallfahrtspsalmen: Studien zur Entstehungsgeschichte von Psalmen 120–134*. BThSt 3. Neukirchen-Vluyn: Neukirchener.

Seybold, K. S. 1979. "Die Redaktion der Wallfahrtspsalmen." *ZAW* 91: 247–68.

Shereshevsky, E. 1971. "Rashi and Christian Interpretations." *JQR* 61: 76–86.

Sink, S. 2007. *The Art of the Saint John's Bible. A Reader's Guide to Pentateuch, Psalms, Gospels and Acts*. Collegeville, MN: Liturgical Press.

Skarsaune, O. 1996. "The Development of Scriptural Interpretation in the Second and Third Centuries — except Clement and Origen." Pages 373–450 in *Hebrew Bible/ Old Testament. 1/1: From the Beginnings to the Middle Ages (Until 1300). Part 1: Antiquity*. Edited by M. Saebø. Göttingen: Vandenhoeck & Ruprecht.

Skehan, P. W. 1948. "Borrowing from the Psalms in the Book of Wisdom." *CBQ* 10: 384–97.

Skehan, P. W. 1976. "Again the Syriac Apocryphal Psalms." in *CBQ* 38: 143–148.

Slavitt, D. R. 1996. *Sixty-One Psalms of David*. Oxford: Oxford University Press.

Smith, J. A. 1990. "Which Psalms were Sung in the Temple?" *MusicLett* 71: 167–86.

Smith, M. S. 1992. "The Theology of the Redaction of the Psalter: Some Observations." *ZAW* 104/3: 408–12.

Snearly, M. K. 2016. *The Return of the King: Messianic Expectations in Book V of the Psalter*. LHBOTS 624. London: Bloomsbury T & T Clark.

Solopova, E. 2013a. "The Liturgical Psalter in Medieval Europe." Pages 89–104 in *Jewish and Christian Approaches to the Psalms. Conflict and Convergence*. Edited by S. E. Gillingham. Oxford: Oxford University Press.

Solopova, E. 2013b. *Latin Liturgical Psalters in the Bodleian Library: A Select Catalogue*. Oxford: Bodleian Library.

Speyer, H. 1961. *Die biblischen Erzählungen in Qoran*. Darmstadt: Wissenschaftliche Buchgesellschaft.

Spieckermann, H. 1989. *Heilsgegenwart: Eine Theologie der Psalmen*. FRLANT 148. Gottingen: Vandenhoeck & Ruprecht.

Spinks, B. D. 2004. "A Note on the Peshitta Psalms and their Use at Ramsa (Evening Prayer) in the East Syrian Tradition." Pages 207–2012 in *Psalms in Community: Jewish and Christian Textual, Liturgical, and Artistic Traditions*. Edited by H. W. Attridge and M. E. Fassler. Atlanta, GA: SBL.

Stackhouse, R. A. 1997. *The Language of the Psalms in Worship: American Revisions of Watts' Psalter*. Lanham, MD: Scarecrow Press.

Stec, D. M. 2004. *The Targum of Psalms, Translated, with a Critical Introduction, Apparatus, and Notes*. The Aramaic Bible Volume 16. Collegeville: Liturgical Press.

Steck, O. H. 1994. "Zur Rezeption des Psalters im apokryphen Baruchbuch." Pages 361–80 in *Neue Wege der Psalmenforschung*. Edited by K. S. Seybold and E. Zenger. Herder: Freiburg im Breisgau.

Stern, M. 2011. *Bible & Music: Influences of the Old Testament on Western Music*. Jersey City: KTAV Publishing House.

Stern, M. 2013. *Psalms & Music: Influences of the Psalms on Western Music*. Brooklyn, NY: KTAV Publishing House.

Stern, M. and H. Leneman. 2015. "Setting the Psalms to Music. Leonard Bernstein's *Chichester Psalms*." Pages 258–70 in *The Bible Retold by Jewish Artists, Writers, Composers & Filmmakers*. Edited by H. Leneman and B. D. Walfish. The Bible in the Modern World 71. Sheffield: Sheffield Phoenix Press.

Steyn, G. J. 2010. "The Reception of Psalm 95 (94):7–11 in Hebrews 3–4." Pages 194–228 in *Psalms and Hebrews: Studies in Reception*. Edited by D. J. Human and G. J. Steyn. LHBOTS 527. London: T&T Clark.

Stowe, D. W. 2016. *Song of Exile: The Enduring Mystery of Psalm 137*. New York: Oxford University Press.

Streett, A. 2014. *The Vine and the Son of Man: Eschatological Interpretation of Psalm 80 in Early Judaism*. Minneapolis, MN: Fortress Press.

Strugnell, J. 1966. "Notes on the Text and Transmission of the Apocryphal Psalms 151, 154 (=Syr.II) and 155 (=Syr III)." *HTR* 89: 257–81.

Sutherland, A. 2015. *English Psalms in the Middle Ages 1300–1450*. Oxford: Oxford University Press.

Taft, R. F. 1986. *The Liturgy of the Hours in East and West. The Origins of the Divine Office and its Meaning for Today*. Collegeville, MN: The Liturgical Press.

Tate, M. 1990. *Psalms 51–100*. WBC 20. Waco, TX: Word Books.

Terrien, S. 2003. *The Psalms: Strophic Structure and Theological Commentary*. Critical Eerdmans Commentary. Grand Rapids, MI: Eerdmans.

Thomas, R. S. (foreword), with L. Boadt and F.F. Bruce (eds.). 1997. *The Psalms: Ancient Poetry of the Spirit*. Oxford: Lion.

Thomson, R. W. 1997. "Uses of the Psalms in some early Armenian Authors." Pages 281–300 in *From Byzantium to Iran: Armenian studies in honour of Nina G. Garsoïan*. Edited by J.-P. Mahé and W. Thomson. Atlanta, GA: Scholars Press.

Toranova, N. and E. L. McGuire. 2003. *The Kiev Psalter of 1397: An Analysis*. published online 2003 at https://www.medievalists.net/2009/06/the-kiev-psalter-of-1397-an-analysis/.

Trudinger, P. L. 2004. *The Psalms of the Tamid Service. A Liturgical Text from the Second Temple*. Leiden: Brill.

Tucker, W. D. Jr. 2014a. *Constructing and Deconstructing Power in Psalms 107–150*. AIL 19. Atlanta, GA: SBL Press.

Tucker, W. D. Jr. 2014b. "The Role of the Foe in Book 5: Reflections on the Final Composition of the Psalter." Pages 179–191 in *The Shape and Shaping of the Book of Psalms. The Current State of Scholarship*. Edited by N. L. deClaissé-Walford. AIL 20. Atlanta, GA: SBL Press.

Tucker, W. D. Jr. & Bellinger, W. H. (eds.). 2017. *The Psalter as Witness: Theology, Poetry, and Genre*. Waco, TX: Baylor University Press.

Tur-Sinai, N. H. 1950. "The Literary Character of the Book of Psalms." *OtSt* 8: 263–81.

Vaillancourt, I. J. 2019. *The Multifaceted Saviour of Psalms 110 and 118. A Canonical Exegesis*. Hebrew Bible Monographs 86. Sheffield: Sheffield Phoenix Press.

Vaughan, R. R. 1702. *The Psalter of David with titles and collects according to the matter of each Psalm*. 12th edition. London: Meredith.

Van Grol, H. 2010. "David and His Chasidim: Place and Function of Psalms 138–145." Pages 309–38 in *Composition of the Book of Psalms*. Edited by E. Zenger. BETL 238 Leuven: Peeters.

Van der Horst, K., N. Noel, and W. C. M. Wüstefeld (eds.). 1996. *The Utrecht Psalter in Medieval Art. Picturing the Psalms of David*. London: Harvey Miller.

Vercruysee, J-M. (ed.) 2018. *Les Psaumes de David, Graphè 27*. Arras: Artois Presses Université.

Vermes, G. 1997. *The Complete Dead Sea Scrolls in English*. London: Penguin Books Ltd.

Vesco, J.-L. 1986. "La Lecture du Psautier selon L' Épître de Barnabé." *RB* 93: 5–37.

Vincent, M. A. 1999. "The Shape of the Psalter: An Eschatological Dimension?" Pages 61–82 in *New Heaven & New Earth. Prophecy & the Millennium: Essays in Honour of Anthony Gelston*. Edited by P. Harland and C. T. R. Hayward. VTSup 77. Leiden: Brill.

Viviers, H. 1994. "The Coherence of the ma'alôt Psalms (Pss 120–134)." *ZAW* 106/2: 275–89.

Wacholder, B. Z. 1988. "David's Eschatological Psalter: 11 Q Psalms." *HUCA* 59:23–72.

Wagner, J. R. 1997. "Psalm 118 in Luke-Acts: Tracing a Narrative Thread." Pages 154–78 in *Early Christian Interpretation of the Scriptures of Israel: Investigations and Proposals*. Edited by C. A. Evans and J. A. Sanders. JSNTSup 148. Sheffield: Sheffield Academic Press.

Wagner, R. 2013. *The Book of Praises: A Translation of the Psalms. Book Three*. Oxford: The Besalel Press.

Wagner, R. 2020. *The Book of Praises. Translations from the Psalms*. Norwich: Canterbury Press.

Walker-Jones, A. 2001. "Psalm 104: A Celebration of the Vanua." Pages 84–97 in *The Earth Story in the Psalms and the Prophets*. Edited by N. Habel. Sheffield: Sheffield Academic Press.

Wallace, R. A. 2007. *The Narrative Effect of Book IV of the Hebrew Psalter*. StBibLit 122. New York: Peter Lang.

Wallace, R. E. 2014. "Gerald Wilson and the Characterization of David in Book 5 of the Psalter." Pages 193–207 in *The Shape and Shaping of the Book of Psalms. The Current State of Scholarship*. Edited by N. L. deCliassé-Walford. AIL 20. Atlanta, GA: SBL Press.

Walter, C. 1986. Christological Themes in the Byzantine Marginal Psalters from the Ninth to the Eleventh Century. *Revue des Etudes Byzantines* 44: 269–87.

Waltke, B. K. and J. M. Houston. 2010. *The Psalms as Christian Worship: A Historical Commentary*. Grand Rapids, MI: Eerdmans.

Waltke, B. K., J. M. Houston and E. Moore. 2014. *The Psalms as Christian Lament: A Historical Commentary*. Grand Rapids, MI: Eerdmans.

Ward, B. 2002. *Bede and the Psalter.* Jarrow Lecture 1991. Oxford: SLG Press.

Watson, J. R. 2002. *An Annotated Anthology of Hymns.* Oxford: Oxford University Press.

Watts, R. 2004. "The Psalms in Mark's Gospel." Pages 25–46 in *The Psalms in the New Testament.* Edited by S. Moyise and M. J. J. Menken. London: T&T Clark International.

Wénin, A. 2018. "Le Psautier de David. Présentation du Livre." Pages 15–32 in *Les Psaumes de David, Graphè 27.* Arras Cedex: Artois Press Université.

Wesselschmidt, Q. F. (ed.). 2007. *Psalms 51–150.* ACCS VIII. Old Testament. Downers Grove, IL: InterVarsity Press.

Whybray, N. R. 1996. *Reading the Psalms as a Book.* JSOTSup 222. Sheffield: Sheffield Academic Press.

Wieder, L. (ed.). 1995. *The Poets' Book of Psalms. The Complete Psalter as Rendered by Twenty-Five Poets from the Sixteenth to the Twentieth Centuries.* Oxford: Oxford University Press.

Wilgren, D. 2016. *The Formation of the 'Book' of Psalms: Re-considering the Transmission and Canonisation of Psalmody in Light of Material Culture and the Poetics of Anthologies.* FAT 2 Reihe 88. Tübingen: Mohr Siebeck.

Willems, G. F. 1990. "Les psaumes dans la liturgie juive." *Bijdragen: tijdschrift voor filosofie en theologie* 51: 397–417.

Williams, H. H. D. 2004. "The Psalms in 1 and 2 Corinthians." Pages 163–80 in *The Psalms in the New Testament.* Edited by S. Moyise and M. J. J. Menken. London: T&T Clark International.

Willis, C. 1973. "The Song of Hannah and Psalm 113." *CBQ* 25.2: 139–154.

Wilson, G. H. 1985. *The Editing of the Hebrew Psalter.* Chico, CA: Scholars Press.

Wilson, G. H. 1993. "Understanding the Purposeful Arrangement of Psalms in the Psalter: Pitfalls and Promise." Pages 42–51 in *The Shape and Shaping of the Psalter.* Edited by J. C. McCann. JSOTSup 159. Sheffield: Sheffield Academic Press.

Wilson, G. H. 2005a. "King, Messiah, and the Reign of God: Revisiting the Royal Psalms and the Shape of the Psalter." Pages 391–406 in *The Book of Psalms: Composition and Reception.* Edited by P. W. Flint and P. D. Miller. Leiden: Brill.

Wilson, G. H. 2005b. "The Structure of the Psalter." Pages 229–46 in *Interpreting the Psalms: Issues and Approaches.* Edited by P. Johnston and D. G. Firth. Downers Grove, IL: InterVarsity Press.

Witherington, B. III. 2017. *Psalms Old and New: Exegesis, Intertextuality and Hermeneutics.* Minneapolis, MN: Fortress.

Wittman, D. E. 2014. "'Let us cast off their ropes from us:' The Editorial Significance of the Portrayal of Foreign Nations in Psalms 2 and 149." Pages 53–67 in *The Shape and Shaping of the Book of Psalms.* Edited by N. L. deClaissé-Walford. AIL 20. Atlanta, GA: SBL Press.

Witvliet, J. D. 1997. "The Spirituality of the Psalter: Metrical Psalms in Liturgy and Life in Calvin's Geneva." *CTJ* 32: 273–97.

Wragg, A. 1934. *The Psalms for Modern Life.* New York: Claude Kendall.

Zakovitch, Y. 2010. "The Interpretative Significance of the Sequence of Psalms 111–112.113–118.119." Pages 215–227 in *The Composition of the Book of Psalms*. Edited by E. Zenger. Leuven: Peeters.

Zenger, E. 1994. "Zur redaktionsgeschichlichen Bedeutung der Korahpsalmen." Pages 175–98 in *Neue Wege der Psalmenforschung*. Edited by K. S. Seybold and E. Zenger. Freiburg im Breisgau: Herder.

Zenger, E. 1997a. "'Daß alles Fleisch den Namen seiner Heiligung segne' (Ps 145, 21). Die Komposition Ps 145–150 als Anstoß zu einer christlich-jüdischen Psalmenhermeneutik." *BZ* 41: 1–27.

Zenger, E. 1997b. "Der jüdische Psalter – ein anti-imperiales Buch?" Pages 95–108 in *Religion und Gesellschaft*. Edited by R. Albertz. AOAT 248. Münster: Ugarit-Verglag.

Zenger, E. 1998. "The Composition and Theology of the Fifth Book of Psalms, Psalms 107 –145." *JSOT* 80: 77–102.

Zenger, E. 2003. "'Durch den Mond eines Weisen werde das Loblied geschprochen' (Sir.15:10). Weisheitstheolgie im Finale des Psalter 146–150." Pages 139-55 in *Auf den Spuren der Schriftgelehrten Weisen. Festschrift für Johannes Marboeck anlaesslich seiner Emeritierung*. Edited by I. Fischer. BZAW 331. Berlin: de Gruyter.

Zenger, E. 2004. "Der Zion als Ort der Gottesnähe. Beobtachtungen zum Weltbild des Wallfahrtpsalters Ps 120–134." Pages 84–114 in *Gottesnähe im Alten Testament*. Edited by G. Eberhardt and K. Liess. Stuttgarter Bibelstudien. Stuttgart: Verlag Katholosches Bibelwerk.

Zenger, E. (ed.) 2010. *The Formation of the Book of Psalms*. BETL 238. Leuven: Peeters.

Zim, R. 2011. *English Metrical Psalms: Poetry as Prose and Prayer 1535–1601*. Cambridge: Cambridge University Press.

Zvi, M. 2015. *The Revealed and Hidden Writings of Rabbi Nachman of Bratslav: His Worlds of Revelation and Rectification*. Berlin: de Gruyter.

Index of Names

Page numbers in *italics* refer to figures.

Psalms Through the Centuries: A Reception History Commentary on Psalms 73–151, Volume Three,
First Edition. Susan Gillingham.
© 2022 John Wiley & Sons Ltd. Published 2022 by John Wiley & Sons Ltd.

Psalms Index

Page spans in **bold** refer to main section for psalm. Page number in *italics* refer to figures.

Psalms Through the Centuries: A Reception History Commentary on Psalms 73–151, Volume Three,
First Edition. Susan Gillingham.
© 2022 John Wiley & Sons Ltd. Published 2022 by John Wiley & Sons Ltd.

Page numbers in *italics* refer to figures.

Psalms Through the Centuries: A Reception History Commentary on Psalms 73–151, Volume Three,
First Edition. Susan Gillingham.
© 2022 John Wiley & Sons Ltd. Published 2022 by John Wiley & Sons Ltd.